# The Oxford Book of

# Money

*Edited by*

## Kevin Jackson

Money is a kind of poetry.
Wallace Stevens
*Opus Posthumous*, 1957

Oxford   New York

OXFORD UNIVERSITY PRESS

1996

Oxford University Press, Walton Street, Oxford OX2 6DP

Oxford  New York
Athens  Auckland  Bangkok  Bombay
Calcutta  Cape Town  Dar es Salaam  Delhi
Florence  Hong Kong  Istanbul  Karachi
Kuala Lumpur  Madras  Madrid  Melbourne
Mexico City  Nairobi  Paris  Singapore
Taipei  Tokyo  Toronto

and associated companies in
Berlin  Ibadan

Oxford is a trade mark of Oxford University Press

First published 1995
First issued as an Oxford University Press
paperback 1996

British Library Cataloguing in Publication Data
Data available

Library of Congress Cataloging in Publication Data
The Oxford book of money / edited by Kevin Jackson.
p.  cm.
I. Jackson, Kevin.  II. Title: Book of money.
PN56.M54709  1995  808.8'0355—dc20  94–20563
ISBN 0–19–282510–0

1 3 5 7 9 10 8 6 4 2

Printed in Great Britain by
Biddles Ltd
Guildford and King's Lynn

# CONTENTS

'Papa! what's money?'

The abrupt question had such immediate reference to the subject of Mr Dombey's thoughts, that Mr Dombey was quite disconcerted.

'What is money, Paul?' he answered. 'Money?'

'Yes,' said the child, laying his hands upon the elbows of his little chair, and turning the old face up towards Mr Dombey's; 'what is money?'

Mr Dombey was in a difficulty. He would have liked to give him some explanation involving the terms circulating-medium, currency, depreciation of currency, paper, bullion, rates of exchange, value of precious metals in the market, and so forth; but looking down at the little chair, and seeing what a long way down it was, he answered: 'Gold, and silver, and copper. Guineas, shillings, half-pence. You know what they are?'

'Oh yes, I know what they are,' said Paul. 'I don't mean that, Papa. I mean what's money after all?'

CHARLES DICKENS, *Dombey and Son*, 1847–8

# INTRODUCTION

This is a book about money and the imagination. It tries to illustrate some of the main ways in which poets, novelists, dramatists, and wits have written about money, and to suggest some of the other ways in which money has been important for writers. Most of its entries have been culled from literature in English, with a leavening from the Greek and Latin classics and the Bible, as well as from other imaginative writers whose reputations enjoy currency in the Anglophone world: Flaubert, Tolstoy, Goethe, Borges, Levi, Paz. Its working definition of what may count as literature is, however, quite broad, and the anthology also includes some apposite published words of philosophers, statesmen, theologians and religious teachers, scientists, painters, film directors, visionaries, dadaists, and cranks.

The extracts have been arranged thematically rather than chronologically, since this is not intended to be a history of money; anyone seeking such a work had better invest in, say, J. K. Galbraith's *Money: Whence it Came, Where it Went* (1975) or Norman Angell's older but still useful *The Story of Money* (1930), both of them highly readable. Neither is it offered as a study of economics (though a few of the dismal science's more graceful and pungent prose stylists have earned their place beside the poets), of personal finance (except the personal finances of writers), Wall Street, the City, the Exchange Rate Mechanism, or schemes for monetary reform. It will certainly disappoint anyone who hopes to make a fortune by playing the markets.

On the other hand, the book does have a good deal to say about the fantasies, lunacies, and dreads which play their part in all those fields, and, since it takes the long view, affords at least a few historical perspectives on them. The monetary excitements of the 1980s, for example, may have been unprecedented in their complexity and scale, but speculation and sudden wealth are hardly new subjects for literature. Washington Irving and Heinrich Heine, Balzac and Dickens wrote about them well before Tom Wolfe. Avarice is an even older theme.

The ten sections which make up the book—it follows a decimal system—cannot pretend to be exhaustive. That ambition would be crazy, since the literature of money is unreadably vast: Cambridge University Library's database lists well over 500 new accessions with 'money' in their title in the last few years alone. Some monetary phenomena are simply too complex to have found their way out of the technical works and into the literary mainstream; others are too recent to have inspired sufficiently interesting subgenres of their own. Even so commonplace a tool as the credit card seems to have inspired relatively few memorable passages, though credit cards first appeared in fiction more than a century ago: see the extract from Edward Bellamy's *Looking Backward* (1888) on pp. 463–5.

I have also, with regrets, left out all but a very few of the passages in which money terms are used as metaphors but where the real focus of interest has not been pecuniary: Shakespeare's many word-plays on 'spending', 'tender', and the like, Donne's images of coins. The relative paucity of songs about cash in this anthology can be explained, if not fully excused, by reference to Morris Bishop's poem on pp. 59–60, though the principle explained there obviously applies not only to songwriters but to all other holders of copyrights. Despite these various omissions, however, I hope that the book's ten headings are capacious enough to indicate the extraordinary richness of the subject, from 'Opening Accounts' (definitions of money, myths about its origin) by way of the self-explanatory 'Getting and Spending' and 'Borrowing and Lending' to 'Hells and Heavens' (panics, crashes, and monetary Utopias).

Indeed, research for this book soon turned up an embarrassment of riches, since, after love and death, there have been few subjects of more general or commanding fascination for writers than money. Though there is no major genre devoted quite as steadily to money as tragedy is to death and comedy to love and marriage, the topic has inspired countless writers: Dante, Milton, Nietzsche, Baudelaire, Whitman, Beckett, Pope, Twain, Dostoevsky, Propertius, Rabelais, Joyce . . . It might almost be said that the theme of money is as old as literature, were it not that some accounts state that the composition of poetry in fact antedates the use of money—at least in the Western world, which inherits both institutions from Ancient Greece. Historians of the subject, following the authority of Herodotus (see p. 32) usually ascribe the invention of money, in the form of electrum coins, to the kings of Lydia some time in the eighth century BC. *The Iliad*, a product of the tenth century BC or thereabouts, seems to reckon values in terms of cattle.

But once money comes into circulation, writers seize on it eagerly. Aristophanes makes gibes about the depreciation of coinage; Sophocles laments the power of money to destroy cities and men; Xenophon muses on the true nature of wealth; Aristotle defines the nature and scope of the device, and unwittingly leaves a problematical legacy for the Middle Ages. Horace and Juvenal take up the old refrains, and portray the disruptive effect of rising mercantile fortunes. Virgil writes a verse about the corrupting lust for money which continues to be cited today even by those who have small Latin and less Greek: *auri sacra fames*: the accursed hunger for gold.

Later writers continue to build on these foundations, sometimes introducing new motifs in response to the changing fortunes of money itself, more often—consciously or otherwise—working variations on ancient themes and characters. The uglier *nouveaux riches* of Victorian fiction are reincarnations of Trimalchio in Petronius's *Satyricon*; its old rich may be as wealthy as Croesus of Lydia, or as far from redemption as the man who prompted Christ to his teaching about the camel and the needle's eye. Misers such as the unreformed Scrooge and Silas Marner are the nineteenth-century avatars of a figure who appears under different guises in the plays of Molière and Shakespeare, in the verses of Gay and Martial, in fairy-stories, and in coarse jokes about tight-fisted hoarders which Freud and his successors have helped to gloss (see pp. 42–4). The mutually destructive crooks and swindlers who populate modern detective fiction are descended from the three hooligans in Chaucer's *Pardoner's Tale* who go off in search of Death, and find him in a sack of coins. Chaucerian scholarship tells us that similar versions of this yarn are common throughout medieval Europe, and have been known in Asia since the time of the birth-tales of the Buddha.

There is plainly a common emphasis in these few examples: the avaricious are satirized, the arrogance of wealth is highlighted, the text of *radix malorum est cupiditas*—the love of money is the root of all evil—is expounded. Most readers, however they deal with their own finances, feel that it is right and proper that authors should take such a scathing attitude towards riches and their pursuit. A good deal can be said for this view, not least when one reflects on the more vehement writings of Carlyle, Ruskin, and kindred moralists: for further instances, consult the section headed 'Vice'. And yet many writers have taken notably less censorious perspectives on money. After all, to write of money is to write about the workings of a culture, and unless, like Timon of Athens in Shakespeare's most money-haunted play, one believes that culture to be rotten to the heart, there is little point in confining one's discourse to howls of outrage, disgust, and pain. Money is more than just an attractive subject for writers in the realist vein; it is almost mandatory.

Without its unembarrassed interest in money, the nineteenth-century novel—to take just one major literary form—would have been gravely impoverished, not to say a good deal shorter. No inheritances to be squabbled over, to rescue the hero from impending disaster or, as in *Great Expectations*, to test his moral fibre; no debts, bankruptcies, debtor's prisons, urban and rural poor; no strenuous, if subtly executed attempts to marry a gentleman or lady of fortune. The candour with which novelists treat the last of these can still appear mildly scandalous. W. H. Auden's poem *Letter to Lord Byron* wittily records his shock at seeing Jane Austen's fiction 'Reveal so frankly and with such sobriety | The economic basis of society'.

Moreover, without its concentration on money, the realist novel would be deprived not only of its misers and *nouveaux riches* but of its spendthrifts and gamblers and philanthropists, its embezzlers and blackmailers and swindlers, its banks and bankers and merchants and wage slaves, its financial manias and young provincial men on the make. In brief, the novel would have possessed none of its characteristic sharp attention to the ways in which the mechanisms of money draw up characters from all levels of society and ease or shove them towards their destinies.

Such an imaginative interest in the powers of money may actually have been essential to the early development of the novel—or, alternatively, the form may have been developed in response to the dramatic changes money was bringing about in the world, including the creation of a new class of potential readers. The American critic Lionel Trilling once speculated that 'the novel is born with the appearance of money as a social element—money, the great solvent of the solid fabric of the old society, the great generator of illusion'.

In the late twentieth century, no one—with the possible exception of a few as yet undiscovered tribespeople—is wholly exempt from the rule of money. It is the atmosphere we all breathe, and any writer who tries to suggest otherwise is guilty of falsifying accounts. And yet some readers have felt and continue to feel queasy, even indignant, at the suggestion that writers should treat money as anything other than the occasion for righteous indignation. (As Bob Dylan did when he sang that money doesn't talk, it swears.) Whether regarded as the heir to traditional religious doctrines, and thus as standing for the spirit as against the flesh and the devil, or—in more recent and secular terms—as championing humane values against the pitiless calculations of the market, literature has often been seen as the settled antagonist of the World's God.

This view has spawned quite a few myths about the literary life: the unworldly poet versus the wicked capitalist, the pure good of the book against the undiluted evil of the buck. Such fables can be true up to a point. As one commentator has pointed out, Ezra Pound spent fifty years writing a long poem—a long poem mostly about money and culture, *The Cantos*— which would barely have earned enough to support him for two of those years.

But the story becomes rather more complicated when one reflects that literature is a commodity as well as a calling, and that the business of a professional writer is to turn words into money. (Handy rule of thumb for distinguishing a gathering of amateur writers from a professional group: the former will talk about inspiration and the muse, the latter will talk about advances, royalties, and foreign rights.) Writers themselves may feel a little awkward or divided on such issues, though they generally have their economic insecurity to keep them clear-sighted. Idealistic readers may find the fact that authors expect to be paid for their work disillusioning—prophets should not care about profits—and suspect that literature is cheapened by its associations with money. James Boswell appears to have felt this way, at least when he was thinking about the man he regarded as a majestic teacher of moral wisdom, and his bafflement at the notion of a literary labourer being eager for his hire lends a humorous touch to a well-known passage in his great biography.

When I expressed an earnest wish for his remarks upon Italy, he said 'I do not see that I could make a book upon Italy; yet I should be glad to get two hundred pounds, or five hundred pounds, by such a work.' This showed both that a journal of his Tour upon the Continent was not wholly out of his contemplation, and that he uniformly adhered to that strange opinion, which his indolent disposition made him utter: 'No man but a blockhead ever wrote, except for money.' Numerous instances to refute this will occur to all who are versed in the history of literature.

(James Boswell, *The Life of Samuel Johnson*, 1791)

Boswell had a point, to be sure, and he need not have looked very far for his examples: the evidence lives, breathes, and fulminates in the pages of his own book. Far from sticking uniformly to this opinion, Johnson frequently wrote for charity (many letters of consolation and advice), for piety (prayers and meditations), and for both at once (he ghosted sermons for needy clerics). He wrote to attack injustice, to expose idiocy, and to anatomize the morbidity of his soul; and, like the Young Enthusiast in his poem *The Vanity of Human Wishes*, he also wrote for fame. In short, the *Life of Johnson* is an extensive if not exhaustive catalogue of all the causes other than strictly pecuniary which may prompt a writer to sit down to hard labour, and it is oddly short-sighted of Boswell not to point this out. There is more to this amusing set-piece than the comedy of myopia, however.

On Johnson's side, there is the fierce craving for financial independence— *mutatis mutandis*, the same craving which Virginia Woolf described in *A Room of One's Own*. Even though Johnson found writing an agonizing task, he knew that it was largely his ability to earn money from the book trade which freed him from the humiliation of waiting on the whims of patrons;

of Lord Chesterfield, for example. But that independence was fragile at best, and, whether or not he had particular men in mind, Johnson's 'block-heads' were more than vain or foppish, they were dangerous. A man who writes for nothing is helping to devalue the currency of letters: in an economy where writers can only thrive by making sure their words sell for an adequate price, a blockhead dumps surplus verbiage on the market. And—to pursue such worries to their extreme—in an economy where literary values are skewed or even set by the valuations of the market, the peculiar treachery of a blockhead is to demonstrate that words might be worth nothing.

On the other hand, Johnson seems to have been painfully aware of the darker implications of writing for money alone. Follow that principle too far and you will soon become a paid liar, a sycophant or, as Johnson disgustedly phrased it, a 'hireling':

> For Gold his Sword the Hireling Ruffian Draws,
> For Gold the hireling Judge distorts the laws . . .
> For growing names the weekly Scribbler lies,
> To growing Wealth the Dedicator flies. . . .

Hence Johnson's profound uneasiness on being offered a Crown Pension of £300, when it was well known throughout the land that he had defined 'pension' in his *Dictionary* as 'An allowance made to anyone without an equivalent. In England it is generally understood to mean pay given to a state hireling for treason to his country.' If a man's word is his bond, then selling one's words is perilously close to selling one's soul.

Johnson's mind was immensely complex, but his inconsistencies on the question of writing for money are not simply an index of that complexity. They echo some of the uncertain and often contradictory values his culture—like ours—could place on money. It is honourable to earn one's living; it is venal to make money the sole object of work. Artistic labour done without a view to money is an indulgence, a trifle; artistic labour done for money is hackwork, and so on. 'Inconsistencies', says the sage Imlac in Johnson's moral tale *Rasselas*, 'cannot both be right, but, imputed to man, they may both be true.'

At first sight, Boswell's side of the argument looks a good deal simpler, both because his mind was less brilliant and less troubled than Johnson's and because his attitudes—some version of them, anyway—are closer to the folklore, or cant, of our own times. Yet he was no fool, even if he sometimes played one, and his confident view that literature should have nothing to do with money also bears consideration. On the whole, we seem to feel that the literary conscience, like love and loyalty, ought to resist the seductions of money—that it is one of the things which cannot and should not be bought and sold. Many scholars have written searchingly on this point, notably Lewis Hyde in *The Gift* and Georg Simmel in *The Philosophy of Money*, but the argument which sets money in opposition to personal values is not hard to grasp. Woody Allen used to have a stand-up routine in which he would display his watch and tearfully explain to the audience that the timepiece had enormous sentimental value for him because it had belonged to his grandfather. When the old man was breathing his last, Allen continued, he summoned his grandson to his bedside, took off the watch and sold it to him. More recently, in Martin Amis's novel *Money*, the hero is understandably miffed when his father presents him with an itemized bill for the cost of his upbringing.

Literature is meant to take the side of paternal, grandpaternal, and many other types of financial altruism. Today, a poet who loudly maintained that he was only in it for the money would sound weirdly iconoclastic—as well as poorly advised by his accountant—because poets are assumed to write for love, which is to say, for nothing. (There are harsh names for the men and women who put their love on the market instead of giving it away.) Yet to write for nothing in this way has not commonly been held to render a poet's words worthless. On the contrary, it is seen as a guarantee of sincerity, if not of accomplishment, and can sometimes help establish them as priceless.

Though this belief may be expressed in foolish or sentimental ways, it is often well founded. Lewis Hyde, drawing on anthropological writings about the practice of potlatch, or ritual giving of gifts, has argued that works of art should be seen as belonging to the gift economy rather than the market economy. It may also be that there is a fundamental incompatibility between money and literature, or even money and language, though in many respects it is the similarities between the two that are immediately striking. Most obviously, money and literature are both conventional systems for representing things beyond themselves, of saying that X is Y. A poem asks us to believe that it represents a nightingale or a raven; a coin asks us to believe that it represents a bushel of wheat or a number of hours of labour. Neither money nor writing would have been possible without the human mind's capacity to grasp that one thing may be a substitute for another dissimilar thing, which is to say that both conventions are a product of our ability to make and grasp metaphors. My love is a rose petal; a loaf of bread is a groat.

These similarities between money and writing became all the more glaring after the invention of paper money. In physical terms, there is not a great deal of difference between the manuscript of a novel and a wad of banknotes: both are stacks of paper sheets which derive their value from the markings on them. The point was not lost on the satirists who helped fuel public outrage against paper money. Coins are nice and solid, and look as if they possess intrinsic worth; sheets of paper look not merely flimsy but, so to speak, _fictitious_, and no one but a blockhead would accept them as money. A schoolchild nowadays could see why this response was silly, though that does not mean that we are therefore all much clearer about the essentially imaginative nature of money. Yet analogies of function between writing and money had long antedated this accidental analogy of form— which is, anyway, becoming less potent for us as more and more of the world's money is stored and transferred by computers. (The critic Marc Shell has pointed out that money began its career as electrum and has ended as electrons.) Money is indeed, as Wallace Stevens wrote, a kind of poetry, and that is partly because money has always been a kind of language.

A few instances: the value of a given currency is not absolute, but the product of countless unseen negotiations; the meaning of a word is founded in social consensus and use, rather than in some natural correspondence with the world. By and large, neither coins nor words have any value outside the countries in which they circulate. Currencies may become inflated; language may be debased into cliché, or worse. Philosophers have argued the impossibility of private languages; the notion of a private money is equally empty. Given these and other family resemblances, it is not surprising that money should have exerted a theoretical as well as a practical fascination for many writers. But while money and literature may be offspring of the same parent, their sibling rivalries can be noisy.

Sir John Beaumont once paid Ben Jonson a handsome compliment:

> Since then, he made our language pure and good,
> And us to speak but what we understood,
> We owe this praise to him, that should we join
> To pay him, he were paid but with that coin
> Himself hath minted, which we know by this
> That no words pass for current now but his.

A clever compliment, too, since Beaumont was putting a neat spin on that widely recognized analogy between specie and vocabulary, 'to coin a phrase'. Not every poet is necessarily so keen on purifying the language as Jonson was, at least according to Beaumont's flattering account, but every self-respecting writer wants to coin phrases—to arrange words into new patterns, and emphasize the uniqueness of their arrangement—and be praised for his work. Governments, on the other hand, are in no doubt that those who decide to mint their own coins should be severely punished.

One reason for this rather dramatic distinction is that although money and literature both represent the world, they do so in extremely distinct ways: money is a fiction, but fiction is not money. Books tend to be specific, and to represent particular actions, characters, or thoughts. Banknotes are general, and represent any or all of the things that their face value can purchase. This attribute makes money protean. Through acts of exchange, it can transform itself into countless things, or be the agency through which countless things are transformed. Some writers have been charmed or even dazzled by the prospect. 'And who can deny its intrinsic appeal to the poet, for is not money literally the one true metaphor, the one commodity that can be translated into all else?', writes the poet Dana Gioia in his essay 'A Dilation of Money'. But this exhilarating power of money holds a curse. Implicit in money's function as a universal instrument of exchange is the worrying possibility that nothing can finally be immune from money's ability to work metamorphoses, that anything and anyone can ultimately be reduced to an equivalent in money. The young Marx wrote about this threat, but the fear can be found in symbolic form in earlier writers: in Ovid, for example, whose *Metamorphoses* give us our classic model for money terror in the story of Midas.

It might be pleasant simply to conclude that literature's insistence on the particular and the unique makes it a rebel against the tyranny of monetary exchange, were it not that the distinctive identity of a book or poem is one of the things which can help determine its market value. A writer who churned out *precisely* the same book every time, like a character in a Borges story, would soon go hungry, and my stubborn insistence on quoting from witty passages in copyright rather than comparable but less witty ones that are out of copyright will eventually cost me dear.

Only the most aggressively philistine of misers, however, could feel easy with the proposition that it is therefore appropriate or even possible to put a money price on literature. A given edition of Dante may retail for so many thousands of lire, but what is the *Commedia* itself worth? The calculation is impossible because there is nothing that could adequately replace the work, so that it cannot really be exchanged. Anyone who tried to buy the *Commedia* (whatever that might mean) would not merely be staggeringly vulgar, but caught in a confusion between monetary and other types of value.

Clearly, most of the work which goes under the heading of 'literature' is significantly less transcendent than Dante's epic. But just as poetry has been defined (contentiously) as that which is lost in translation or paraphrase, so literature in general might be defined as the kind of writing which, no matter how deeply it is enmeshed in the market economy, will always try to resist the process of substitution and exchange. That iconoclastic poet who brags that money is his sole motive for writing is working against the grain of his chosen medium.

It was his contemplation of these and related questions that set Ezra Pound to writing the *Cantos*, reading unorthodox economists, and making the radio broadcasts which eventually put him in a cage near Pisa and then into a mental institution. Pound's was a grimly instructive career, a warning to everyone who takes these matters seriously, and although it was reading the *Cantos* that first woke me up to the cultural interest of money, I am—like a great many of his other readers—variously baffled and appalled by where he was led and what he said.

Yet at least a few of the questions Pound asked were good ones: who pays for writing? Who owns it? How can serious writers live? And if he was an admirer of Mussolini, he was also an unlikely heir of Ruskin. In particular, the poet's earlier insights about the relationship of money to art continue to seem valuable seven or eight decades on. Despite this, there is only one extract from Pound in this collection, and though the reasons for such parsimony are primarily editorial, they are also monetary. Pound now costs too much.

I have too many debts to record in full, but particular credit for advice and encouragement should go to: John Alexander, the late Anthony Burgess, Emma Crichton-Miller, Charles Cuddon, Caroline Dawney, Roy Gibson, Mark Godowski, Thom Gunn, Glyn Johnson, Nick Lezard, Jeremy Maule, Adrian Poole, Claire Preston, Liz Rigbey, Peter Robinson, Martin Wallen, Clive Wilmer. Michael Kuczynski's knowledge of early and obscure economic tracts was invaluable, as was his wisdom on other matters. Without the firmness of my editor, Judith Luna, this book would have been in danger of becoming *The Oxford Book of Money in Dickens*; I'm also grateful for her tolerance and good humour, as well as for her sound judgement in helping to cut an unreadably large manuscript down to more humane proportions. Above all, I'm indebted to Kim Scott Walwyn for commissioning the anthology, and for trusting me to find the time to complete it. My thanks to all.

K. J.

*Easter Day 1994*

# Opening Accounts

*Gladstone once observed that not even love had made so many fools of men as pondering over the nature of money. This section collects a variety of definitions of money from those who have not minded the risk, from Aristotle to Andy Warhol. It then proceeds to speculations, myths, and anecdotes about the origins and subsequent history of the device, including some of its more eccentric embodiments and a final glimpse of money (or rather its notable absence) long ago, in galaxies far, far away.*

❧

Money is power: so said one.
Money is a cushion: so said another.
Money is the root of evil: so said still another.
Money means freedom: so runs an old saying.

And money is all of these—and more.
Money pays for whatever you want—if you have the money.
Money buys food, clothes, houses, land, guns, jewels, men, women,
    time to be lazy and listen to music.
Money buys everything except love, personality, freedom, immortality,
    silence, peace.

Therefore men fight for money.
Therefore men steal, kill, swindle, walk as hypocrites and whited
    sepulchers.
Therefore men speak softly carrying plans, poisons, weapons, each in
    the design: The words of his mouth were as butter but war was
    in his heart.

Therefore nations lay strangle holds on each other; bombardments
open, tanks advance, salients are seized, aviators walk on air;
truckloads of amputated arms and legs are hauled away.

Money is power, freedom, a cushion, the root of all evil, the sum of
blessings.

CARL SANDBURG, *The People, Yes*, s. 65, 1936

MONEY   Cause of all evil. *Auri sacra fames*. The god of the day—but not to
be confused with Apollo. Politicians call it emoluments; lawyers, retainers;
doctors, fees; employees, salary; workmen, pay; servants, wages. 'Money
is not happiness.'

GUSTAVE FLAUBERT, 'Dictionary of Received Ideas', *c.*1850–80, tr. A. J.
Krailsheimer, 1976

*Money* is human happiness in the abstract; and so the man who is no longer
capable of enjoying such happiness in the concrete, sets his whole heart on
money.

ARTHUR SCHOPENHAUER, *Parerga and Paralipomena*, 1851, tr. T. B. Saunders,
1890

Happiness is the deferred fulfilment of a prehistoric wish. That is why
wealth brings so little happiness; money is not an infantile wish.

SIGMUND FREUD to Wilhelm Fliess, 18 January 1898

By 'money' economists usually mean anything that is (1) passed from hand
to hand in payment for commodities and service, and (2) regularly taken
with the intention of offering it in payment to others, and (3) customarily
received without assay or other special test of quality or quantity, and (4)
received without reference to our reliance upon the personal credit of the
one who offers it.

The usual definition of the *functions* of money are that money is a medium of exchange, a measure of value, a standard of deferred payment and
a store of value.

SIR NORMAN ANGELL, *The Story of Money*, 1930

Money is the last enemy that shall never be subdued. While there is flesh there is money—or the want of money; but money is always on the brain so long as there is a brain in reasonable order.

SAMUEL BUTLER, *Notebooks*, 1912

Money is not, properly speaking, one of the subjects of commerce, but only the instrument which men have agreed upon to facilitate the exchange of one commodity for another. It is none of the wheels of trade: It is the oil which renders the motion of the wheels more smooth and easy.

DAVID HUME, 'Of Money', 1752

## MONEY

*Money is a kind of poetry.*

WALLACE STEVENS

Money, the long green,
cash, stash, rhino, jack
or just plain dough.

Chock it up, fork it over,
shell it out. Watch it
burn holes through pockets.

To be made of it! To have it
to burn! Greenbacks, double eagles,
megabucks and Ginnie Maes.

It greases the palm, feathers a nest,
holds heads above water,
makes both ends meet.

Money breeds money.
Gathering interest, compounding daily.
Always in circulation.

Money. You don't know where it's been,
but you put it where your mouth is.
And it talks.

DANA GIOIA, *The Lions of Winter*, 1991

'The fat man taught me', Victor explained, to those who wished to hear or read the complex moral of his anecdote, 'that money talks.' He did not know that such an insight was old hat and crassly simple. Or that his variations of this insight—such as 'Money is the peacemaker' and 'Money's muscle'—were simple complications of the truth. What the fat man had displayed was cynicism, if cynicism is the trick of seeming to engage with chance and danger but without taking any risks. Money has no moral tact. It's true, the rich have power to intervene, to heal and damage as they wish. Toss money in the ring and see the drama that it makes of other people's lives. But, more, they have the power, if they choose, to stay more silent and discrete than monks. The rich—and here was Victor's unacknowledged dream—can simply make a wall, a fortress shield of wealth, beyond which the dramas of the world can run their courses unobserved.

JIM CRACE, *Arcadia*, 1992

'Money talks' because money is a metaphor, a transfer, and a bridge. Like words and language, money is a storehouse of communally achieved work, skill, and experience. Money, however, is also a specialist technology like writing; and as writing intensifies the visual aspect of speech and order, and as the clock visually separates time from space, so money separates work from the other social functions. Even today money is a language for translating the work of the farmer into the work of the barber, doctor, engineer, or plumber. As a vast social metaphor, bridge, or translator, money—like writing—speeds up exchange and tightens the bonds of interdependence in any community. It gives great spatial extension and control to political organizations, just as writing does, or the calendar. It is action at a distance, both in space and in time. In a highly literate, fragmented society, 'Time is money,' and money is the store of other people's time and effort.

MARSHALL McLUHAN, *Understanding Media*, 1964

Remember, that *time* is money. He that can earn ten shillings a day by his labor, and goes abroad, or sits idle, one half of that day, though he spends but sixpence during his diversion or idleness, ought not to reckon *that* the only expense; he has really spent, or rather thrown away, five shillings besides.

Remember, that *credit* is money. If a man lets his money lie in my hands after it is due, he gives me the interest, or so much as I can make of it during that time. This amounts to a considerable sum where a man has good and large credit, and makes good use of it.

Remember, that money is of the prolific, generating nature. Money can beget money, and its offspring can beget more, and so on. Five shillings turned is six, turned again it is seven and three-pence, and so on till it becomes an hundred pounds. The more there is of it, the more it produces every turning, so that the profits rise quicker and quicker. He that kills a breeding sow, destroys all her offspring to the thousandth generation. He that murders a crown, destroys all that it might have produced, even scores of pounds.

BENJAMIN FRANKLIN, 'Advice to a Young Tradesman', 1748

Time is money—says the vulgarest saw known to any age or people. Turn it round about, and you get a precious truth—money is time. I think of it on these dark, mist-blinded mornings, as I come down to find a glorious fire crackling and leaping in my study. Suppose I were so poor that I could not afford that heartsome blaze, how different the whole day would be! Have I not lost many and many a day of my life for lack of the material comfort which was necessary to put my mind in tune? Money is time. With money I buy for cheerful use the hours which otherwise would not in any sense be mine; nay, which would make me their miserable bondsman. Money is time, and, heaven be thanked, there needs so little of it for this sort of purchase. He who has overmuch is wont to be as badly off in regard to the true use of money, as he who has not enough. What are we doing all our lives but purchasing, or trying to purchase, time? And most of us, having grasped it with one hand, throw it away with the other.

GEORGE GISSING, *The Private Papers of Henry Ryecroft*, 1903

It is very common to reproach those artists as useless, who produce only such superfluities as neither accommodate the body, nor improve the mind; and of which no other effect can be imagined, than that they are the occasions of spending money, and consuming time.

But this censure will be mitigated, when it is seriously considered, that money and time are the heaviest burdens of life, and that the unhappiest of all mortals are those who have more of either than they know how to use.

SAMUEL JOHNSON, *Idler*, 30, 11 November 1758

Beyond doubt: a secret connection exists between the measure of goods and the measure of life, which is to say, between money and time. The more trivial the content of a lifetime, the more fragmented, multifarious, and disparate are its moments, while the grand period characterizes a superior existence. Very aptly, Lichtenberg suggests that time whiled away should be seen as made smaller, rather than shorter, and he also observes: 'a few dozen million minutes make up a life of forty-five years, and something more.' When a currency is in use a few million units of which are insignificant, life will have to be counted in seconds, rather than years, if it is to appear a respectable sum. And it will be frittered away like a bundle of bank notes: Austria cannot break the habit of thinking in florins.

Money and rain belong together. The weather itself is an index of the state of this world. Bliss is cloudless, knows no weather. There also comes a cloudless realm of perfect goods, on which no money falls.

A descriptive analysis of bank notes is needed. The unlimited satirical force of such a book would be equalled only by its objectivity. For nowhere more naïvely than in these documents does capitalism display itself in solemn earnest. The innocent cupids frolicking about numbers, the goddesses holding tablets of the law, the stalwart heroes sheathing their swords before monetary units, are a world of their own: ornamenting the façade of hell. If Lichtenberg had found paper money in circulation, the plan of this work would not have escaped him.

WALTER BENJAMIN, *One-Way Street*, 1925–6, tr. E. F. N. Jephcott, 1978

An author's time, above all men's, is money. A manuscript once completed, he will as soon lock it in a box as a financier horde gold pieces in a vault.

ROBERT BYRON, *The Byzantine Achievement*, 1929

Mauss wrote of primitive society repaying itself with the false coin of magic. The metaphor of money admirably sums up what we want to assert of ritual. Money provides a fixed, external, recognisable sign for what would be confused, contradictable operations; ritual makes visible external signs of internal states. Money mediates transactions; ritual mediates experience, including social experience. Money provides a standard for measuring worth; ritual standardises situations, and so helps to evaluate them. Money makes a link between the present and the future, so does ritual. The more we reflect on the richness of the metaphor, the more it becomes clear that this is no metaphor. Money is only an extreme and specialised type of ritual.

In comparing magic with false currency Mauss was wrong. Money can only perform its role of intensifying economic interaction if the public has faith in it. If faith in it is shaken, the currency is useless. So too with ritual; its symbols can only have effect so long as they command confidence. In this sense all money, false or true, depends on a confidence trick. The test of money is whether it is acceptable or not. There is no false money except by contrast with another currency which has more total acceptability. So primitive ritual is like good money, not false money, so long as it commands assent.

MARY DOUGLAS, *Purity and Danger*, 1966

Money wants no followers.

GEORGE HERBERT, *Jacula prudentum*, 1640

When Lord Henry entered the room, the found his uncle sitting in a rough shooting coat, smoking a cheroot and grumbling over *The Times*. 'Well, Harry,' said the old gentleman, 'what brings you out so early? I thought you dandies never got up till two, and were not visible till five.'

'Pure family affection, I assure you, Uncle George. I want to get something out of you.'

'Money, I suppose,' said Lord Fermor, making a wry face. 'Well, sit down and tell me all about it. Young people, nowadays, imagine that money is everything.'

'Yes,' murmured Lord Henry, settling his button-hole in his coat; 'and when they grow older they know it. But I don't want money. It is only people who pay their bills who want that, Uncle George, and I never pay mine. Credit is the capital of a younger son, and one lives charmingly upon it.'

OSCAR WILDE, *The Picture of Dorian Gray*, 1891

Money is the Jugglers' cup and balls, whereby the unproductive part of society extracts the various proceeds of labour from its unthinking producers, or like the beads and feathers the Europeans have sometimes exchanged with the natives of savage countries for various kinds of food, etc. Just so have the useful classes been hitherto, and still are, tricked out of their real valuables by the money mongers of various kinds.

T. DAHLMANN, *A Refutation of Cobbett's Doctrine of Paper Money*, 1839

All money, properly so called, is an acknowledgment of debt; but as such, it may either be considered to represent the labour and property of the creditor, or the idleness and penury of the debtor. The intricacy of the question has been much increased by the (hitherto necessary) use of marketable commodities, such as gold, silver, salt, shells, etc., to give intrinsic value or security to currency; but the final and best definition of money is that it is a documentary promise ratified and guaranteed by the nation to give or find a certain quantity of labour on demand.

JOHN RUSKIN, *Unto This Last*, 1860

*Money* is the external, universal means and power (not derived from man as man nor from human society as society) to change *representation* into *reality* and *reality* into *mere representation*. It transforms *real human and natural faculties* into mere abstract representations, i.e. *imperfections* and tormenting chimeras; and on the other hand, it transforms *real imperfections and fancies*, faculties which are really impotent and which exist only in the individual's imagination, into *real faculties and powers*. In this respect, therefore, money is the general inversion of *individualities*, turning them into their opposites and associating contradictory qualities with their qualities.

Money, then, appears as a *disruptive* power for the individual and for the social bonds, which claim to be self-subsistent *entities*. It changes fidelity into infidelity, love into hate, hate into love, virtue into vice, vice into virtue, servant into master, stupidity into intelligence and intelligence into stupidity.

Since money, as the existing and active concept of value, confounds and exchanges everything, it is the universal *confusion and transposition* of all things, the inverted world, the confusion and transposition of all natural and human qualities.

KARL MARX, *Economical and Philosophical Manuscripts*, 1844, tr. T. B. Bottomore, 1963

'Tis true, w' have money, th' only pow'r
That all mankind falls down before;
Money, that, like the swords of kings,
Is the last reason of all things:
And therefore need not doubt our play
Has all advantages that way:

As long as men have faith to sell,
And meet with those that can pay well;
Whose half-starv'd pride and avarice,
One church and state will not suffice,
T' expose to sale, beside the wages
Of storing plagues to after-ages.
Nor is our money less our own,
Than 'twas before we laid it down:
For 'twill return, and turn t' account,
If we are brought in play upon't;
Or but by casting knaves, get in,
What pow'r can hinder us to win?

SAMUEL BUTLER, *Hudibras*, 1678, part iii

The true meaning of money yet remains to be popularly explained and comprehended. When each individual realises for himself that this thing primarily stands for and should only be accepted as a moral due—that it should be paid out as honestly stored energy, and not as a usurped privilege—many of our social, religious, and political troubles will have permanently passed. As for Carrie, her understanding of the moral significance of money was the popular understanding, nothing more. The old definition: 'Money: something everybody else has and I must get,' would have expressed her understanding of it thoroughly. Some of it she now held in her hand—two soft, green ten-dollar bills—and she felt that she was immensely better off for the having of them. It was something that was power in itself. One of her order of mind would have been content to be cast away upon a desert island with a bundle of money, and only the long strain of starvation would have taught her that in some cases it could have no value. Even then she would have had no conception of the relative value of the thing; her one thought would, undoubtedly, have concerned the pity of having so much power and the inability to use it.

THEODORE DREISER, *Sister Carrie*, 1900

The principle of living only to see and to hear some new thing, and the other principle of avoiding everything with which we are not perfectly familiar are equally old, equally universal, equally useful. They are the principles of conservation and accumulation on the one hand, and of adventure, speculation and progress on the other, each equally indispensable.

The money has been, and will probably always be more persistently in the hands of the first of these two groups. But, after all, is not money an art? Nay, is it not the most difficult on earth and the parent of all? And if life is short and art long, is not money still longer? And are not works of art, for the most part, more or less works of money also? In so far as a work of art is a work of money, it must not complain of being bound by the laws of money; in so far as it is a work of art, it has nothing to do with money and, again, cannot complain.

SAMUEL BUTLER, *Notebooks*, 1912

Money is not one particular type of wealth amongst others, but the universal form of all types so far as they are expressed in an external embodiment and so can be taken as 'things'. Only by being translated into terms of this extreme culmination of externality can services exacted by the state be fixed quantitatively and so justly and equitably.

G. W. F. HEGEL, *Philosophy of Right*, 1821, tr. T. M. Knox, 1952

There are two sorts of Money, Real and Imaginary. Real Money is a Piece of Metal coin'd by the Authority of the State, and is therefore a real Species, current at a certain Price, by vertue of the said Authority, and of its own intrinsick Value; such as a Guinea, a Crown, a Shilling, a Farthing, etc.

Imaginary Money is a denomination used to express a Sum of Money, of which there is no real Species: As a Pound in England, and a Livre in France, because there is no Species current, in this or that Kingdom, precisely of the Value of either of those Sums.

JOHN HEWITT, *A Treatise upon Money, Coins and Exchange*, 1740

Money is the MOMENT to me.

Money is my MOOD.

ANDY WARHOL, *From A to B and Back Again*, 1975

Money is the instrument by which men's wants are supplied, and many who possess it will part with it for that purpose, who would not gratify themselves at the expence of their visible property.

JAMES MADISON, *National Gazette*, 1791

Above all things, good policy is to be used that the treasure and monies in a state be not gathered into few hands. For otherwise a state may have a great stock, and yet starve. And money is like muck, not good except it be spread. This is done chiefly by suppressing, or at the least keeping a strait hand upon the devouring trades of usury, ingrossing, great pasturages, and the like.

FRANCIS BACON (1561–1626), 'Of Seditions and Troubles'

Mony is a Value made by a Law; And the Difference of its Value is known by the Stamp, and Size of the Piece.

One Use of MONY is, It is the Measure of Value, By which the Value of all other things are reckoned; as when the Value of any thing is expressed, its said, It's worth so many shillings, or so many Pounds: Another Use of Mony is; It is a Change or Pawn for the Value of all other Things: For this Reason, the Value of Mony must be made certain by Law, or else it could not be made a certain Measure, nor an Exchange for the Value of all things.

It is not absolutely necessary, Mony should be made of Gold or Silver; for having its sole Value from the Law, it is not Material upon what Metal the Stamp be set. Mony hath the same Value, and performs the same Uses, if it be made of Brass, Copper, Tin, or any thing else. The Brass Mony of *Spain*, the Copper Mony of *Sweeden*, and Tin Farthings of *England*, have the same Value in Exchange, according to the Rate they are set at and perform the same Uses, to Cast up the Value of things, as the Gold and Silver Mony does; Six Pence in Farthings will buy the same thing as Six Pence in Silver; and the Value of a thing is well understood by saying, It is worth Eight Farthings, as that it is worth Two Pence: Gold and Silver, as well as Brass, Copper and Tin Mony, change their Value in those Countries, where the Law has no Force, and yield no more than the Price of the Metal that bears the STAMP: Therefore, all Foreign Coins go by Weight, and are of no certain Value, but rise and fall with the Price of the Metal. Pieces of Eight, yield sometimes 4 *sh.* 6 *d.* 4 *sh.* 7 *d.* and 4 *sh.* 8 *d.* as the Value of Silver is higher or lower: And so doth Dollars, and all Forreign Coin, change their Value; and were it not for the Law that fixeth the Value, an *English* Crown Piece would now yield Five Shillings and Two Pence, for so much is the Value of it, if it were melted, or in a Foreign Country.

NICHOLAS BARBON, *A Discourse of Trade*, 1690

For Money is but the Fat of the Body-politick, whereof too much doth as often hinder its Agility, as too little makes it sick. 'Tis true, that as Fat lubricates the motion of the Muscles, feeds in want of Victuals, fills up uneven Cavities, and beautifies the Body, so doth Money in the State quicken its Action, feeds from abroad in the time of Dearth at Home; even accounts by reason of it's divisibility, and beautifies the whole, altho more especially the particular persons that have it in plenty.

SIR WILLIAM PETTY, *Verbum sapienti*, c.1665, pub. 1691

By concoction, I understand the reducing of all commodities, which are not presently consumed, but reserved for nourishment in time to come, to something of equal value, and withal so portable, as not to hinder the motion of men from place to place; to the end a man may have in what place soever, such nourishment as the place affordeth. And this is nothing else but gold, and silver, and money. For gold and silver, being, as it happens, almost in all countries of the world highly valued, is a commodious measure of the value of all things else between nations; and money, of what matter soever coined by the sovereign of a commonwealth, is a sufficient measure of the value of all things else, between the subjects of that commonwealth. By the means of which measures, all commodities, moveable and immoveable, are made to accompany a man to all places of his resort, within and without the place of his ordinary residence; and the same passeth from man to man, within the commonwealth; and goes round about, nourishing, as it passeth, every part thereof; in so much as this concoction, is as it were the sanguification of the commonwealth: for natural blood is in like manner made of the fruits of the earth; and circulating, nourisheth by the way every member of the body of man.

THOMAS HOBBES, *Leviathan; or, The Matter, Form, and Power of a Commonwealth, Ecclesiastical and Civil*, 1651

'Tis demonstrably true, if duly considered, that Money, or that which supplies it, is the Blood of the Body Politick, and circulates in Trade, as the Blood through all the Veins of the Natural Body, whereby every Man draws a competent Profit to himself.

EDWARD LEIGH, *An Essay upon Credit*, 1715

Money is a dangerous subject. Polite conversation avoids it. You may talk about economics, but not raw money. . . .

Money is so commonly the measure we usually apply to men that he who speaks of it critically will be quickly 'sized up'. The shrewd never tell of their own. 'Put money in thy purse', says Iago; and we take his advice, as secretly as possible. Income-tax communications are strictly private, and what a man is 'worth' is divulged only at his death. Rate money higher than wisdom, and in the world of men you will pass unreproved, for money is the token of civilized self-preservation, and fear insists upon the first law of nature. So money has a permanent place in all our thoughts. Our social roots are in money; no one can be allowed to live without it. We are tied to money. It is the shore to which every human craft is anchored, and will remain anchored until mankind has learnt the greatest lesson history can teach it—how to live by a more spiritual means of exchange. . . .

MAX PLOWMAN, 'Money and *The Merchant*', *Adelphi*, September 1931

Money is like fire, an element as little troubled by moralizing as earth, air and water. Men can employ it as a tool or they can dance around it as if it were the incarnation of a god. Money votes socialist or monarchist, finds a profit in pornography or translations from the Bible, commissions Rembrandt and underwrites the technology of Auschwitz. It acquires its meaning from the uses to which it is put.

LEWIS H. LAPHAM, *Money and Class in America*, 1988

It is very funny about money. The thing that differentiates man from animals is money. All animals have the same emotions and the same ways as men. Anybody who has lots of animals around knows that. But the thing no animal can do is count, and the thing no animal can know is money.

Men can count, and they do, and that is what makes them have money.

And so, as long as the earth turns around there will be men on it, and as long as there are men on it, they will count, and they will count money.

Everybody is always counting money.

The queen was in the parlor eating bread and honey the king was in his counting house counting out his money.

That is the way it is and the only trouble comes when they count money without counting it as money.

Counting is funny.

When you see a big store and see so many of each kind of anything that is in it, and on the counters, it is hard to believe that one more or less makes any difference to any one. When you see a cashier in a bank with drawers filled with money, it is hard to realize that one more or less makes any difference. But it does, if you buy it, or if you take it away, or if you sell it, or if you make a mistake in giving it out. Of course it does. But a government, well a government does just that, it does not really believe that when there is such a lot that one more or less does make any difference. It is funny, if you buy anything well it may cost four dollars and fifty-five cents or four hundred and eighty-nine dollars or any other sum, but when government votes money it is always even money. One or five or fifteen or thirty-six more or less does not make any difference. The minute it gets to be billions it does not make any difference, fifteen or twenty-five or thirty-six more or less. Well, everybody has to think about that, because when it is made up it has to be made up by all sorts of odd numbers, everybody who pays taxes knows that, and it does make a difference.

All these odd pieces of money have to go to make that even money that is voted, but does it. It is voted even but it is collected odd. Everybody has to think about that.

GERTRUDE STEIN, *Saturday Evening Post*, 22 August 1936

The functions of money in the act of exchange present a close analogy to the functions of language in relation to thought. As there may be a rude barter, so there may be a rude language of signs. But there is no true communication of thought except by articulate speech; and similarly there can be no real and effectual trade except by the use of a common measure.

Money, however, is only a means to an end—the machinery, namely, of trade.

JAMES E. THOROLD ROGERS, *A Mannual of Political Economy*, 1868

FOLLY *sings*.
Cast away care; he that loves sorrow
Lengthens not a day, nor can buy to-morrow:
Money is trash; and he that will spend it,
Let him drink merrily, Fortune will send it.

JOHN FORD and THOMAS DEKKER, *The Sun's Darling*, 1623–4

Money, after all, is extremely simple. It is a part of our transportation system. It is a simple and direct method of conveying goods from one person to another. Money is in itself most admirable. It is essential. It is not intrinsically evil. It is one of the most useful devices in social life. And when it does what it was intended to do, it is all help and no hindrance.

HENRY FORD, *My Life and Work*, 1922

'You have very little private means?' he asked at last.

'Very little,' answered Philip, with a sudden feeling of cold at his heart. 'Not enough to live on.'

'There is nothing so degrading as the constant anxiety about one's means of livelihood. I have nothing but contempt for the people who despise money. They are hypocrites or fools. Money is like a sixth sense without which you cannot make a complete use of the other five. Without an adequate income half the possibilities of life are shut off. The only thing to be careful about is that you do not pay more than a shilling for the shilling you earn. You will hear people say that poverty is the best spur to the artist. They have never felt the iron of it in their flesh. They do not know how mean it makes you. It exposes you to endless humiliation, it cuts your wings, it eats into your soul like a cancer. It is not wealth one asks for, but just enough to preserve one's dignity, to work unhampered, to be generous, frank, and independent. I pity with all my heart the artist, whether he writes or paints, who is entirely dependent for subsistence upon his art.'

W. SOMERSET MAUGHAM, *Of Human Bondage*, 1915

One of the reasons I had fought so hard, after all, was to wrest from the world fame and money and love. And here I was, at thirty-two, finding my notoriety hard to bear, since its principal effect was to make me more lonely; money, it turned out, was exactly like sex, you thought of nothing else if you didn't have it and thought of other things if you did; and love, as far as I could see, was over.

JAMES BALDWIN, 'The Black Boy Looks at the White Boy', 1961

Money is the jealous god of Israel, beside which no other god may exist. Money abases all the gods of mankind and changes them into commodities. Money is the universal and self-sufficient *value* of all things. It has, therefore, deprived the whole world, both the human world and nature, of their own proper value. Money is the alienated essence of man's work and existence; this essence dominates him and he worships it.

KARL MARX, 'On the Jewish Question', 1843, tr. T. B. Bottomore, 1963

Money, or that which supplies it, is the Sinews of Government both in War and Peace: where that is wanting, nothing can move regularly, the want of Money being the Root of all Political Evil.

EDWARD LEIGH, *An Essay upon Credit*, 1715

I have often been called a financial wizard. The French edition of my book of memoirs *76 Jahre meines Lebens* was published under the title *Mémoires d'un Magicien*. The American edition has the title *Confessions of the Old Wizard*. Yet the truth is that nothing in the world has so little to do with magic as dealing with money. Money must be handled with clear and cool calculation. Anyone who does not obey this maxim is in danger of tying himself up in all the many ways of earning and spending money. Money can no more be conjured into existence than the alchemists were able to make gold. But money has many different kinds of attributes, some of them very intricate, so that the majority of people frequently find themselves unable to understand certain financial transactions. For this reason the monetary system is enveloped in a cloak of mystery, secrecy and magic.

Money is not always synonymous with wealth. It is true that we call well-to-do people millionaires, and thus unwittingly link this term with the currency concept—Mark millionaire, Dollar millionaire. But wealth is not only money. It makes a great difference whether a millionaire possesses one million Deutschmarks in cash or in his bank account, or whether he owns property of the same value. The difference lies in the ways in which such wealth can be used. Money may at any time be converted into other goods, other properties, or other people's services, but the reverse is not true. The magic of money lies in its protean nature, which enables it to be used at all times, in all directions and for all purposes. This constitutes its wizardry, its secret, its mystery, its magic.

HJALMAR SCHACHT, *The Magic of Money*, tr. Paul Erskine, 1967

As one goes through life, it is extremely important to conserve funds, and one should never spend money on anything foolish, like pear nectar or a solid-gold hat. Money is not everything, but it is better than having one's health. After all, one cannot go into a butcher shop and tell the butcher, 'Look at my great suntan, and besides I never catch colds,' and expect him to hand over any merchandise. (Unless, of course, the butcher is an idiot.) Money is better than poverty, if only for financial reasons. Not that it can buy happiness. Take the case of the ant and the grasshopper: The grasshopper played all summer, while the ant worked and saved. When winter came, the grasshopper had nothing, but the ant complained of chest pains. Life is hard for insects. And don't think mice are having any fun, either. The point is, we all need a nest egg to fall back on, but not while wearing a good suit.

Finally, let us bear in mind that it is easier to spend two dollars than to save one. And for God's sake don't invest money with any brokerage firm in which one of the partners is named Frenchy.

WOODY ALLEN, *Without Feathers*, 1976

Whether money be not only so far useful, as it stirreth up industry, enabling men mutually to participate the fruits of each other's labour?

Whether any other means, equally conducing to excite and circulate the industry of mankind, may not be as useful as money?

Whether the real end and aim of men be not power? And whether he who could have everything else at his wish or will would value money?

Whether other things being given, as climate, soil, &c., the wealth be not proportioned to the industry, and this to the circulation of credit, be the credit circulated or transferred by what marks or tokens soever?

Whether, therefore, less money, swiftly circulating, be not, in effect, equivalent to more money slowly circulating? Or, whether, if the circulation be reciprocally as the quantity of coin, the nation can be a loser?

Whether money is to be considered as having an intrinsic value, or as being a commodity, a standard, a measure, or a pledge, as is variously suggested by writers? And whether the true idea of money, as such, be not altogether that of a ticket or counter? . . .

Whether arbitrary changing the denomination of coin be not a public cheat?

What makes a wealthy people? Whether mines of gold and silver are capable of doing this? And whether the negroes, amidst the gold sands of Afric, are not poor and destitute?

GEORGE BERKELEY, Bishop of Cloyne, *Querist*, 1735, rev. 1750

Money is not a real thing, but a mere means of exchanging real things; and any attitude towards it that involves recognising it as a real thing, and accepting the view that it can 'breed' is radically false. Against this deeply-seated prejudice—I use the word in its classical, and not in a bad, sense—all the economists' demonstrations of the nature and necessity of interest may break in vain.

G. D. H. Cole, *Principles of Economic Planning*, 1935

Money is a creature of Law, and if laws do not create enough money, then there will not be enough in circulation. If you want more wheat, you can go out and raise wheat; if you want more of any kind of manufactured goods, you can produce them; but if the people want more money, they cannot bring money into existence.

William Jennings Bryan, *The First Battle*, 1897

The value of money has been settled by general consent to express our wants and our property, as letters were invented to express our ideas; and both these institutions, by giving more active energy to the powers and passions of human nature, have contributed to multiply the objects they were designed to represent. The use of gold and silver is in a great measure factitious; but it would be impossible to enumerate the important and various services which agriculture, and all the arts, have received from iron, when tempered and fashioned by the operation of fire and the dexterous hand of man. Money, in a word, is the most universal incitement, iron the most powerful instrument, of human industry; and it is very difficult to conceive by what means a people, neither actuated by the one nor seconded by the other, could emerge from the grossest barbarism.

Edward Gibbon, *Decline and Fall of the Roman Empire*, 1776, book i

It is an error of all modern money-theories that they start from the value-token or even the material of the payment-medium instead of from the form of economic thought. In reality money, like number and law, is a *category of thought*. There is a monetary, just as there is a juristic and a mathematical and a technical, thinking of the world-around.

Oswald Spengler, *The Decline of the West*, 1918–22, tr. Charles Francis Atkinson

In a work of fiction I once wrote this sentence, which perhaps may be found, if considered, suggestive of some practical truths—'Money is character.'

In the humbler grades of life, certainly character is money. The man who gives me his labor in return for the wages which the labor is worth, pledges to me something more than his labor—he pledges to me certain qualities of his moral being, such as honesty, sobriety, and diligence. If, in these respects, he maintain his character, he will have my money as long as I want his labor; and, when I want his labor no longer, his character is money's worth to him from somebody else. If, in addition to the moral qualities I have named, he establish a character for other attributes which have their own price in the money market—if he exhibit a superior intelligence, skill, energy, zeal—his labor rises in value. Thus, in the humblest class of life, character is money; and according as the man earns or spends the money, money in turn becomes character.

As money is the most evident power in the world's uses, so the use that he makes of money is often all that the world knows about a man. Is our money gained justly and spent prudently? our character establishes a claim on respect. Is it gained nobly and spent beneficently? our character commands more than respect—it wins a place in that higher sphere of opinion which comprises admiration, gratitude, love. Is money, inherited without merit of ours, lavished recklessly away? our character disperses itself with the spray of the golden shower—it is not the money alone of which we are spendthrifts. Is money meanly acquired, selfishly hoarded? it is not the money alone of which we are misers; we are starving our own human hearts—depriving them of their natural aliment in the approval and affection of others. We invest the money which we fancy so safe out at compound interest, in the very worst possession a man can purchase—viz., an odious reputation. In fact, the more we look round, the more we shall come to acknowledge that there is no test of a man's character more generally adopted than the way in which his money is managed. Money is a terrible blab; she will betray the secrets of her owner whatever he do to gag her. His virtues will creep out in her whisper—his vices she will cry aloud at the top of her tongue.

Bulwer Lytton, 'On the Management of Money', *Caxtoniana*, 1864

Money is a scale by which wealth is estimated, and though it is not wealth, more than a barometer is weather, yet it is our only mode of computing it, and nothing, perhaps, is more natural than that the shadow should sometimes have been over-valued, or even taken for the substance.

THOMAS JOPLIN, *Outline of a System of Political Economy*, 1823


Money is representative, and follows the nature and fortunes of the owner. The coin is a delicate meter of civil, social, and moral changes. The farmer is covetous of his dollar, and with reason. It is no waif to him. He knows how many strokes of labor it represents. His bones ache with the days' work that earned it. He knows how much land it represents;—how much rain, frost, and sunshine. He knows that in the dollar he gives you so much discretion and patience, so much hoeing and threshing. Try to lift his dollar; you must lift all that weight. In the city, where money follows the skit of a pen or a lucky rise in exchange, it comes to be looked on as light. I wish the farmer held it dearer, and would spend it only for real bread; force for force.

RALPH WALDO EMERSON, 'Wealth', 1860


A feast is made for laughter, and wine maketh merry: but money answereth all things.

ECCLESIASTES 10: 19


In the end, the most disturbing thing about money is its abstractness. Like an ink blot, it allows one to see anything in it; like statistics, one can do anything with its numbers; like the deep blue sky, it has no limit. This is what makes it so wide open to the imaginative powers of want, and this is also what brings the inheritor around again from weakness to strength. For while the abstractness of money allows anyone to *imagine* whatever one likes in it, the same abstractness works similarly on the imagination of inheritors.

NELSON W. ALDRICH, Jr., *Old Money*, 1988


Heaven and Earth, how old his face was as he turned it up again towards his father's!

'What is money after all!' said Mr Dombey, backing his chair a little, that he might the better gaze in sheer amazement at the presumptuous atom that propounded such an inquiry.

'I mean, Papa, what can it do?' returned Paul, folding his arms (they were hardly long enough to fold), and looking at the fire, and up at him, and at the fire, and up at him again.

Mr Dombey drew his chair back to its former place, and patted him on the head. 'You'll know better by-and-by, my man,' he said, 'Money, Paul, can do anything.' He took hold of the little hand, and beat it softly against one of his own, as he said so.

But Paul got his hand free as soon as he could; and rubbing it gently to and fro on the elbow of his chair, as if his wit were in the palm, and he were sharpening it—and looking at the fire again, as though the fire had been his adviser and prompter—repeated, after a short pause:

'Anything, Papa?'

'Yes. Anything—almost,' said Mr Dombey.

'Anything means everything, don't it, Papa?' asked his son: not observing, or possibly not understanding, the qualification.

'It includes it: yes,' said Mr Dombey.

'Why didn't money save me my Mama?' returned the child. 'It isn't cruel, is it?'

'Cruel!' said Mr Dombey, settling his neckcloth, and seeming to resent the idea. 'No. A good thing can't be cruel.'

'If it's a good thing, and can do anything,' said the little fellow, thoughtfully, as he looked back at the fire, 'I wonder why it didn't save me my Mama.'

He didn't ask the question of his father this time. Perhaps he had seen, with a child's quickness, that it had already made his father uncomfortable. But he repeated the thought aloud, as if it were quite an old one to him, and had troubled him very much; and sat with his chin resting on his hand, still cogitating and looking for an explanation in the fire.

Mr Dombey having recovered from his surprise, not to say his alarm (for it was the very first occasion on which the child had ever broached the subject of his mother to him, though he had had him sitting by his side, in this same manner, evening after evening), expounded to him how that money, though a very potent spirit, never to be disparaged on any account whatever, could not keep people alive whose time was come to die; and how that we must all die, unfortunately, even in the City, though we were never so rich. But how that money caused us to be honoured, feared, respected, courted, and admired, and made us powerful and glorious in the eyes of all men; and how that it could, very often, even keep off death, for a long time together.

CHARLES DICKENS, *Dombey and Son*, 1847–8

The universal regard for money is the one hopeful fact in our civilization, the one sound spot in our social conscience. Money is the most important thing in the world. It represents health, strength, honor, generosity, and beauty as conspicuously and undeniably as the want of it represents illness, weakness, disgrace, meanness, and ugliness. Not the least of its virtues is that it destroys base people as certainly as it fortifies and dignifies noble people. It is only when it is cheapened to worthlessness for some and made impossibly dear to others, that it becomes a curse. In short, it is a curse only in such foolish social conditions that life itself is a curse. For the two things are inseparable: money is the counter that enables life to be distributed socially: it *is* life as truly as sovereigns and bank notes are money. The first duty of every citizen is to insist on having money on reasonable terms; and this demand is not complied with by giving four men three shillings each for ten or twelve hours' drudgery and one man a thousand pounds for nothing. The crying need of the nation is not for better morals, cheaper bread, temperance, liberty, culture, redemption of fallen sisters and erring brothers, nor the grace, love, and fellowship of the Trinity, but simply for enough money.

GEORGE BERNARD SHAW, Preface to *Major Barbara*, 1907

Money is coined liberty, and so it is ten times dearer to the man who is deprived of freedom. If money is jingling in his pocket, he is half consoled, even though he cannot spend it. But money can always and everywhere be spent, and, moreover, forbidden fruit is sweetest of all. Even vodka could be got in prison. Pipes were strictly forbidden, but every one smoked them. Money and tobacco saved them from scurvy and other diseases. Work saved them from crime; without work the convicts would have devoured one another like spiders in a glass jar. In spite of this, both work and money were forbidden.

FYODOR DOSTOEVSKY, *The House of the Dead*, 1862, tr. Constance Garnett, 1915

It is a foolish thing that without money one cannot either live as one pleases, or where and with whom one pleases. Swift somewhere says, that money is liberty; and I fear money is friendship too and society, and almost every external blessing. It is a great, though an ill-natured comfort, to see most of those who have it in plenty, without pleasure, without liberty, and without friends.

THOMAS GRAY to Dr Wharton, 11 December 1746

Money makes a man laugh. A blind fidler playing to a company, and playing scurvily, the company laugh'd at him; his boy that led him, perceiving it, cry'd, 'Father, let us be gone, they do nothing but laugh at you.' 'Hold thy peace, boy, said the fidler, we shall have their money presently, and then we will laugh at them.'

JOHN SELDEN, Table-Talk, collected c.1634–54; pub. 1689

WILLMORE. No, Child, Money speaks sense in a Language all Nations understand, 'tis Beauty, Wit, Courage, Honour, and undisputable Reason—see the virtue of a Wager, that new philosophical way lately found out of deciding all hard Questions—*Socrates*, without ready Money to lay down, must yield.

APHRA BEHN, The Rover, Part Two, 1681, III. iii

If Men considered how many Things there are that Riches cannot buy, they would not be so fond of them.

The Things to be bought with Money, are such as least deserve the giving a Price for them.

Wit and Money are so apt to be abused, that Men generally make a shift to be the worse for them.

Money in a Fool's Hand exposeth him worse than a pyed Coat.

Money hath too great a Preference given to it by States, as well as by particular Men.

Men are more the Sinews of War than Money.

The third part of an Army must be destroyed, before a good one can be made out of it.

They who are of opinion that Money will do every thing, may very well be suspected to do every thing for Money.

GEORGE SAVILE, First Marquess of Halifax (1633–95), Political, Moral and Miscellaneous Reflexions, 1750

INTERVIEWER. What, then, would you say is the source of most of your work?

PARKER. Need of money, dear. . . .

INTERVIEWER. Do you think economic security an advantage to the writer?

PARKER. Yes. Being in a garret doesn't do you any good unless you're some sort of a Keats. The people who lived and wrote well in the twenties were comfortable and easy-living. They were able to find stories and novels, and good ones, in conflicts that came out of two million dollars a year, not a garret. As for me, I'd like to have money. And I'd like to be a good writer. These two can come together, and I hope they will, but if that's too adorable, I'd rather have money. I hate almost all rich people, but I think I'd be darling at it. At the moment, however, I like to think of Maurice Baring's remark: 'If you would know what the Lord God thinks of money, you have only to look at those to whom He gives it.' I realize that's not much help when the wolf comes scratching at the door, but it's a comfort.

INTERVIEWER. What do you think about the artist being supported by the state?

PARKER. Naturally, when penniless, I think it's superb. I think that the art of the country so immeasurably adds to its prestige that if you want the country to have writers and artists—persons who live precariously in our country—the state must help. I do not think that any kind of artist thrives under charity, by which I mean one person or organization giving him money. Here and there, this and that—that's no good. The difference between the state giving and the individual patron is that one is charity and the other isn't. Charity is murder and you know it. But I do think that if the government supports its artists, they need have no feeling of gratitude—the meanest and most snivelling attribute in the world—or baskets being brought to them, or apple-polishing. Working for the state— for Christ's sake, are you grateful to your employers? Let the state see what its artists are trying to do— like France with the Académie Française. The artists are a part of their country and their country should recognize this, so both it and the artists can take pride in their efforts. Now I mean that, my dear.

INTERVIEWER. How about Hollywood as provider for the artist?

PARKER. Hollywood money isn't money. It's congealed snow, melts in your hand, and there you are.

DOROTHY PARKER, *Writers at Work: The Paris Review Interviews*, First Series, 1958

It is now nearly thirty years since the author became imbued with the conviction that the great writers on the civilization of Europe had left out of account one of the principal influences which has contributed to hasten or retard the progress of society. Race, climate, natural resources, religions, laws, customs, and other circumstances had been accorded their due weight.

Money only was slighted: Money which is essentially a social institution; Money, whose operation upon society one of these same writers likened to the circulation of blood in the human body; Money, without which another of them declared that organized society was inconceivable. Montesquieu, Hume, Alison, and Bastiat did indeed treat the subject; but neither of them accorded to it the importance it deserved.

ALEXANDER DEL MAR, *Money and Civilization*, 1886

Finally, of all enigmas was not that of money the most baffling?

For there, in fact, one found oneself face to face with a primordial law, a ruthless organic law decreed and enforced since the world began. Its regulations are formal and always precise. Money has its own power of self attraction, its own way of accumulating in the same hands, for choice in those of the scoundrel and the nonentity; nay! more, when, by an incalculable exception, it enriches a wealthy man whose soul is neither homicidal nor abject, then it remains barren, incapable of employment to any intelligible advantage, unfitted even with the charitable to achieve any elevated purpose. Thus one might say it revenges the wrong direction it has taken and condemns itself to an intentional paralysis when it belongs neither to the meanest of sharpers nor to the most despicable of noodles.

It is stranger still when, by an extraordinary accident, it strays into a poor man's house. Then instantly it befouls it if it is clean, makes the most chaste of paupers lecherous, works its wicked will alike on body and soul, presently teaches its possessor a base selfishness and an ignoble conceit, incites him to spend his money on himself and himself alone, turns the most unassuming into an insolent lickspittle, the most generous into a skinflint. In one word it transforms every habit, upsets every conviction, metamorphoses the most headstrong passions in the twinkling of an eye.

It affords the most nourishing diet for heinous sins and at the same time keeps vigilant account of their commission. If ever it suffers a rich man to forget himself and give alms or do a service to a poor neighbour instantly it stirs up the man's hatred against the benefactor; it replaces avarice by ingratitude, re-establishing so well the equilibrium that the account balances and not a sin the less is committed.

But where it becomes truly monstrous is when, hiding the lustre of its name under the obscuring veil of a new title, it dubs itself capital. Then its activity is no longer limited to individual suggestions of robbery and murder, but extends to humanity as a whole. With a word capital sets up monopolies, founds banks, forestalls commodities; it makes itself master of the means of life and at its pleasure condemns thousands of human beings to die of hunger!

Itself meanwhile is feeding, fattening, breeding all alone, inside a safe. The two worlds adore it on bended knees and die of longing before its altar as if it were a God.

Well then, either money, then the despot of men's souls, is of the devil, or it defies explanation.

J.-K. HUYSMANS, *Là-bas*, 1891, tr. anon. *c.*1920

## MONEY

Quarterly, is it, money reproaches me:
    'Why do you let me lie here wastefully?
I am all you never had of goods and sex.
    You could get them still by writing a few cheques.'

So I look at others, what they do with theirs:
    They certainly don't keep it upstairs.
By now they've a second house and car and wife:
    Clearly money has something to do with life

—In fact, they've a lot in common, if you enquire:
    You can't put off being young until you retire,
And however you bank your screw, the money you save
    Won't in the end buy you more than a shave.

I listen to money singing. It's like looking down
    From long french windows at a provincial town,
The slums, the canal, the churches ornate and mad
    In the evening sun. It is intensely sad.

PHILIP LARKIN, *High Windows*, 1974

On the level of values, money has two contrary meanings (it is an enantioseme): it is very harshly condemned, especially in the theater (many attacks on the *théâtre d'argent*, around 1954), then rehabilitated, following Fourier, in reaction to the three moralisms which are set in opposition to it: Marxist, Christian, and Freudian. However, of course, what is defended is not money saved, hoarded, blocked; it is money spent, wasted, swept away by the very movement of loss, made brilliant by the luxury of a production; thus money metaphorically becomes gold: the Gold of the Signifier.

ROLAND BARTHES, *Roland Barthes par Roland Barthes*, 1975, tr. Richard Howard, 1977

If you want to write a book about me then there is one thing you must put in: money. The cinema is all money but the money figures twice: first you spend all your time running to get the money to make the film but then in the film the money comes back again, in the image.

JEAN-LUC GODARD, in Colin MacCabe, *Godard: Images, Sounds, Politics*, 1980

In Western civilization the idea of money exercises a great fascination—it is the fascination of an actual thing which has attained a metaphysical ideality or of a metaphysical entity which has attained actual existence. Spirits and ghosts are beings in such a middling state of existence; and money is both real and not real, like a spook. We invented money and we use it, yet we cannot either understand its laws or control its actions. It has a life of its own which it properly should not have; Karl Marx speaks with a kind of horror of its indecent power to reproduce, as if, he says, love were working in its body. It is impious, being critical of existent social realities, and it has the effect of lessening their degree of reality. The social reality upon which it has its most devastating effect is of course that of class.

LIONEL TRILLING, 'Art and Fortune', 1948

Next to sexual matters there are none upon which there is such complete reserve between parents and children as on those connected with money. The father keeps his affairs as closely as he can to himself and is most jealous of letting his children into a knowledge of how he manages his money. His children are like monks in a monastery as regards money and he calls this training them up with the strictest regard to principle. Nevertheless he thinks himself ill-used if his son, on entering life, falls a victim to designing persons whose knowledge of how money is made and lost is greater than his own.

SAMUEL BUTLER, *Notebooks*, 1912

Is not money essentially secular—not only outside the domain of religion, but even its opposite?

Our common-sense feelings have been articulated by the sociologists, who in various ways contrast the sacred and the secular as polar opposites, always with money and rationality as syndromes in the Gestalt of the secular. In fact the notion of money as essentially secular is interconnected with our notion of its essential rationality. Hence, although sociology has used the antithesis of sacred and secular to probe irrational elements in society, and (e.g., Pareto, Durkheim) has even taken the position that society must always be a secular superstructure on a sacred base—i.e., that society can never get rid of irrational residues—yet sociology has not connected money with the irrational and the sacred. Money remains anchored in the domain of the secular. And since the essence of modern rationalism as a whole is simply autonomy from religion, money as secular is also rational.

But this static contrast of the sacred and the secular as mutually exclusive opposites is misleading, because it is undialectical. The secular is the negation of the sacred, and both Freud's and Hegel's negation affirms its own opposite. The psychological realities here are best grasped in terms of theology, and were already grasped by Luther. Modern secularism, and its companion Protestantism, do not usher in an era in which human consciousness is liberated from inhuman powers, or the natural world is liberated from supernatural manifestations; the essence of the Protestant (or capitalist) era is that the power over this world has passed from God to God's negation, God's ape, the Devil. And already Luther had seen in money the essence of the secular, and therefore of the demonic. The money complex is the demonic, and the demonic is God's ape; the money complex is therefore the heir to and substitute for the religious complex, an attempt to find God in things.

NORMAN O. BROWN, 'Filthy Lucre', *Life against Death*, 1959

On the cover of this book are grouped, in one design, the three emblems from which are derived the dollar symbol, $, and the pound-sterling symbol, £. The most prominent and interesting feature of the group is the two pillars, which were derived from the pillars of Hercules, one of the oldest symbols known to the human race. Their composition with the money symbols is due entirely to the emperor Charles the Fifth of Germany, who being also king of Spain adopted them as supporters on either side of his escutcheon, and also placed them in the device on the Spanish 'pillar dollar' of the value of fifty-four pence sterling, which became the unit of Federal money in America, and upon the basis of which the pound sterling was valued at $4.44.44. Charles derived the idea from the poetic conceit which gave the name of 'Pillars of Hercules' to the two mountains which stand on either side the Straits of Gibraltar, viz.: Calpe, or the Rock of Gibraltar, on the north, and Mount Abyla, in Africa, on the south. The scroll, which in the device on the dollar was twined about the pillars, has by long use been gradually modified, in making the symbol with the pen, so as to assume its present form in the dollar-mark. It is also presumed that in the pound-mark the £ was substituted for the scroll, thus still retaining the two pillars which had become what might be called the generic symbol of money in general, while the scroll and the £ referred to the two monetary units most widely known to the world—the £ being from *Libra*, a balance; or, in this connection, a standard of values. But before Charles adopted the pillars as supporters to his arms, they had been part of the metropolitan emblem of the city of Seville, and the scroll bore the device *Ne plus ultra*, referring to the ancient belief that westward of that coast of Spain there was nothing but sea and space. Charles elided the particle *ne*, and left the motto *Plus ultra*, in which form it appeared in the arms of the Empire and on the pillar dollar. Originally the pound-sterling symbol was made with two transverse bars. The custom of making it with only one horizontal bar, and the dollar-mark with only one upright bar, is an innovation of modern type makers.

W. L. FAWCETT, *Gold and Debt: An American Hand-Book of Finance*, 1877

Money is a sign which represents the value of all merchandise. Metal is taken for this sign, as being durable, because it consumes but little by use; and because, without being destroyed, it is capable of many divisions. A precious metal has been chosen as a sign, as being most portable. A metal is most proper for a common measure, because it can be easily reduced to the same standard. Every state fixes upon it a particular impression, to the end that the form may correspond with the standard and the weight, and that both may be known by inspection only.

The Athenians, not having the use of metals, made use of oxen, and the Romans of sheep; but one ox is not the same as another ox in the manner that one piece of metal may be the same as another.

As specie is the sign of the value of merchandise, paper is the sign of the value of specie; and when it is of the right sort, it represents this value in such a manner that as to the effects produced by it there is not the least difference.

In the same manner, as money is the sign and representative of a thing,

everything is a sign and representative of money; and the state is in a
prosperous condition when on the one hand money perfectly represents all
things, and on the other all things perfectly represent money, and are reciprocally the sign of each other; that is, when they have such a relative value
that we may have the one as soon as we have the other. This never happens in any other than a moderate government, nor does it always happen
there; for example, if the laws favour the dishonest debtor, his effects are
no longer a representative or sign of money. With regard to a despotic
government, it would be a prodigy did things there represent their sign.
Tyranny and distrust make every one bury their specie; things therefore are
not there the representative of money.

> M. DE SECONDAT, BARON DE MONTESQUIEU, *The Spirit of Laws,* 1748, book xxii,
> tr. Thomas Nugent, 1896

When the division of labour has been once thoroughly established, it is but
a very small part of a man's wants which the produce of his own labour can
supply. He supplies the far greater part of them by exchanging that surplus
part of the produce of his own labour, which is over and above his own
consumption, for such parts of the produce of other men's labour as he has
occasion for. Every man thus lives by exchanging, or becomes in some
measure a merchant, and the society itself grows to be what is properly a
commercial society.

But when the division of labour first began to take place, this power of
exchanging must frequently have been very much clogged and embarrassed
in its operations. One man, we shall suppose, has more of a certain commodity than he himself has occasion for, while another has less. The former
consequently would be glad to dispose of, and the latter to purchase, a part
of this superfluity. But if this latter should chance to have nothing that
the former stands in need of, no exchange can be made between them. The
butcher has more meat in his shop than he himself can consume, and the
brewer and the baker would each of them be willing to purchase a part of
it. But they have nothing to offer in exchange, except the different productions of their respective trades, and the butcher is already provided with all
the bread and beer which he has immediate occasion for. No exchange can,
in this case, be made between them. He cannot be their merchant, nor they
his customers; and they are all of them thus mutually less serviceable to
one another. In order to avoid the inconveniency of such situations, every
prudent man in every period of society, after the first establishment of the
division of labour, must naturally have endeavoured to manage his affairs

in such a manner, as to have at all times by him, besides the peculiar produce of his own industry, a certain quantity of some one commodity or other, such as he imagined few people would be likely to refuse in exchange for the produce of their industry.

Many different commodities, it is probable, were successively both thought of and employed for this purpose. In the rude ages of society, cattle are said to have been the common instrument of commerce; and, though they must have been a most inconvenient one, yet in old times we find things were frequently valued according to the number of cattle which had been given in exchange for them. The armour of Diomede, says Homer, cost only nine oxen; but that of Glaucus cost an hundred oxen. Salt is said to be the common instrument of commerce and exchanges in Abyssinia; a species of shells in some parts of the coast of India; dried cod at Newfoundland; tobacco in Virginia; sugar in some of our West India colonies; hides or dressed leather in some other countries; and there is at this day a village in Scotland where it is not uncommon, I am told, for a workman to carry nails instead of money to the baker's shop or the alehouse.

In all countries, however, men seem at last to have been determined by irresistible reasons to give the preference, for this employment, to metals above every other commodity. . . .

It is in this manner that money has become in all civilized nations the universal instrument of commerce, by the intervention of which goods of all kinds are bought and sold, or exchanged for one another.

ADAM SMITH, *The Wealth of Nations*, 1776

All things or services, then, which are to be exchanged must be in some way reducible to a common measure.

For this purpose money was invented, and serves as a medium of exchange; for by it we can measure everything, and so can measure the superiority and inferiority of different kinds of work—the number of shoes, for instance, that is equivalent to a house or to a certain quantity of food.

What is needed then is that so many shoes shall bear to a house (or a measure of corn) the same ratio that a builder [or a husbandman] bears to a shoemaker. For unless this adjustment be effected, no dealing or exchange of services can take place; and it cannot be effected unless the things to be exchanged can be in some way made equal.

We want, therefore, some one common measure of value, as we said before.

This measure is, in fact, the need for each other's services which holds the members of a society together; for if men had no needs, or no common needs, there would either be no exchange, or a different sort of exchange from that which we know.

But money has been introduced by convention as a kind of substitute for need or demand; and this is why we call it νόμισμα, because its value is derived, not from nature, but from law (νόμος), and can be altered or abolished at will.

ARISTOTLE (384–322 BC), *Nicomachean Ethics*, tr. F. H. Peters, 1891

The customs of the Lydians differ little from those of the Grecians, except that they prostitute their females. They are the first of all nations we know of that introduced the art of coining gold and silver; and they were the first retailers.

HERODOTUS (c.480–c.425 BC), *History*, tr. Cary, 1891

Among the many debts which civilization owes the Greeks, none is deeper than that due for the invention of the coinage; for whether money was first struck in Lydia or Aegina, the conception of a currency is Greek and not Asiatic. Indeed, the Asiatic races never accepted the coinage kindly, for the Asiatics have always been slow; and perhaps the introduction of a currency accelerated social movement more powerfully than any innovation during the historic period of antiquity. By a currency commercial transfers are made cheap and rapid, and international banking on a large scale becomes possible. To work well, however, the currency should be uniform, as the fluctuations of various standards entail loss in exchange. Under the archaic system each city struck its own money,—the disadvantage whereof the Greeks soon perceived; and one of the greatest triumphs of the Greek mind was the adoption of a common standard of value under Alexander; an achievement to be attributed to voluntary and intelligent cooperation, and not to physical force.

BROOKS ADAMS, *The New Empire*, 1902

So it is clear to us that a flute in the hands of a man who does not know how to use it, is not property to him, unless he sell it. So long as he keeps it, it is not property. And indeed, Socrates, we shall thus have reasoned consistently, since we before decided that a man's property must be something that benefits him. If the man does not sell the flute, it is not property, for it is of no use; but if he sell it, it becomes property.

To this Socrates answered, Yes, if he know how to sell it. But if he, again, were to sell it to a man who does not know how to use it, it would not be property even when sold, according to what you say.

Your words, Socrates, seem to imply that not even money would be property unless a man knew how to use it.

Well, you seem to agree with me that a man's property is only what benefits him. Suppose a man were to make this use of his money, to buy, say, a mistress, by whose influence his body would be worse, his soul worse, his household worse; how could we then say that his money was any benefit to him?

We could not,—unless, indeed, we are to count as property henbane, the herb that drives mad those who eat it.

We may, then, Critobulus, exclude money also from being counted as property, if it is in the hands of one who does not know how to use it.

XENOPHON (c.430–c.355 BC), *The Economist*, tr. Alexander Wedderburn and W. Gershom Collingwood, 1876

I will not speak of the innumerable adventures which have happened to money since it has been stamped, marked, valued, altered, increased, buried, and stolen, having through all its transformations constantly remained the idol of mankind. It is so much loved that among all Christian princes there still exists an old law which is not to allow gold and silver to go out of their kingdoms. This law implies one of two things—either that these princes reign over fools who lavish their money in a foreign country for their pleasure, or that we must not pay our debts to foreigners. It is, however, clear that no person is foolish enough to give his money without reason, and that, when we are in debt to a foreigner, we should pay him either in bills of exchange, commodities, or legitimate coin. Thus this law has not been executed since we began to open our eyes—which is not long ago.

VOLTAIRE (1694–1778), *Philosophical Dictionary*

Max Weber traces the origins of modern capitalism to certain Calvinists who, disregarding the parable of the camel and the eye of the needle, preached the doctrine of the just rewards of work. Yet the concept of shifting and increasing one's 'wealth on the hoof' has a history as old as herding itself. Domesticated animals are 'currency', 'things that run', from the French *courir*. In fact, almost all our monetary expressions—capital, stock, pecuniary, chattel, sterling—perhaps even the idea of 'growth' itself—have their origins in the pastoral world.

BRUCE CHATWIN, The Songlines, 1987

He also coined money, and stamped it with the image of an ox, either in memory of the Marathonian bull or of Taurus whom he vanquished, or else to put his people in mind to follow husbandry; and from this coin came the expression so frequent among the Greeks, of a thing being worth ten or a hundred oxen.

PLUTARCH (1st century AD), 'Theseus', Lives, the translation called Dryden's,<br>ed. A. H. Clough, 1859

It is the custom of the states to bestow by voluntary and individual contribution on the chiefs a present of cattle or of grain, which, while accepted as a compliment, supplies their wants. They are particularly delighted by gifts from neighbouring tribes, which are sent not only by individuals but also by the state, such as choice steeds, heavy armour, trappings, and neck-chains. We have now taught them to accept money also.

TACITUS (c.AD 55–117), Germany and its Tribes, tr. Church and Brodribb, 1877

It is a received opinion that in most ancient ages there was only bartery or change of wares and commodities amongst most nations. As in Homer, Glaucus' golden armour was valued at one hundred cows, and Diomedes' at ten. Afterward, in commutative Justice it was thought most necessary to have a common measure and valuation, as it were, of the equality and inequality of wares, which was invented first, as the Jews gather out of Josephus, in the time of Cain. Certainly, it was in use in the time of Abraham, as appeareth both by the 400 Sheckles he payed for a place of burial, Genes. 23, and the money which Joseph's brethren carried into Ægypt, Genes. 42.

The Greeks refer the invention of it to Hermodice, the wise wife of the foolish asse-eared Midas, as the Latines to Janus. This common measure or mean to reduce wares to an equality was called by the Greeks Nomisma, not from King Numa, but of Nomos, because it was ordained by law; by the Latines Pecunia, either for that all their wealth in elder times consisted in cattel, as now among the Irish, or that their first coyn (as Pliny will) was stamped with a Cow (although in a general signification Pecunia comprised all goods, moveable and immoveable). It was also by them called Moneta in a more restrict signification, à Monendo, (as Suidas saith) because when the Romans stood in need of money, Juno admonished them to use justice, and there should be no want of money: the effect whereof when they found, she was surnamed Juno Moneta, and money was coyned in her Temple. And albeit money had no temple erected to it at Rome for a long time, yet it was as much honoured as either Peace, Faith, Victory, Vertue; or according to that of Juvenal:

> 'Et si funesta pecunia templo
> Nondum habitat, nullas nummorum ereximus aras,
> Ut colitur Pax, atque Fides, Victoria, Virtus,' &c.

But afterward, when as all God's gifts were by Pagans made Gods and Goddesses, Money was also enshrined by the name of Dea Pecunia, in the figure of a woman holding a pair of ballances in one hand and Cornucopia in another: unto whom I doubt not but as many commit Idolatry now as then; when as the Greek proverb will be always verified, *Chremata, Chremata Aner*, Money, Money is the man, yea, and the fifth Element. And as he saith:

> 'Uxorem cum dote, fidemque, & amicos,
> Et genus & formam Regina Pecunia donat.'

From the Latin word Moneta came the old word among our English-Saxon Ancestours Munet, which we now call Money, as the Germans Muntz, the French Monoies, the Italians Moneta, and the Spaniards Moneda. Which, as Civilians note, must consist of matter, form, weight, and value: for the matter, copper, is thought to have been first coyned; afterward silver, for the cleanness, beauty, sweetness, and brightness; and lastly gold, as more clean, more beautiful, more sweet, more bright, more rare, more pliable and portable, aptest to receive form, and divisible without loss, never wasted by fire, but more purified, not lessened by occupying, rust or scurf; abiding fretting, and liquors of Salt and Vinegar without dammage; and may be drawn without wooll, as if it were wooll. So that these two metals have been chosen amongst all civil nations, as by the common consent, to be the instruments of exchange and measure of all things. Albeit other matter hath been used for money, as among the ancient Britains, besides brass, and iron rings, or, as some say, iron plates reduced to certain weight; and among the Lacedemonians iron lingets quenched with vineger, that they may serve to no other use; and now the Indians have their Cacoas in some parts, and shells in other, to serve for money. There also hath been stamped money of leather, as appeareth by Seneca, who mentioned that there was in ancient time *Corium forma publica percussum*: and also that Frederick the Second, when he besieged Millan, stamped leather for currant. And there is a tradition that in the confused state of the Barons' War, the like was used in England, yet I never saw any of them. But we have seen money made by the Hollanders of pastbord, *anno* 1574.

WILLIAM CAMDEN, *Remains Concerning Britain*, 1586

Provided we have a pledge of exchange for the necessary things of life, commerce will continually go on. It signifies not whether this pledge be of shells or paper. Gold and silver have prevailed everywhere, only because they have been the most rare.

It was in Asia that the first manufactures of money of these two metals commenced, because Asia was the cradle of all the arts.

There certainly was no money in the Trojan war. Gold and silver passed by weight; Agamemnon might have had a treasure, but certainly no money.

VOLTAIRE (1694–1778), *Philosophical Dictionary*

This emperor may dispend as much as he will without estimation; for he not dispendeth ne maketh no money but of leather imprinted or of paper. And of that money is some of greater price and some of less price, after the diversity of his statutes. And when that money hath run so long that it beginneth to waste, then men bear it to the emperor's treasury and then they take new money for the old. And that money goeth throughout all the country and throughout all his provinces, for there and beyond them they make no money neither of gold nor of silver; and therefore he may dispend enough, and outrageously.

SIR JOHN MANDEVILLE, *Travels*, mid-14th century

My master was yet wholly at a loss to understand what motives could incite this race of lawyers to perplex, disquiet, and weary themselves, and engage in a confederacy of injustice, merely for the sake of injuring their fellow-animals; neither could he comprehend what I meant in saying they did it for hire. Whereupon I was at much pains to describe to him the use of

---

*Corium . . . percussum*] leather struck with the official stamp

money, the materials it was made of, and the value of the metals; that when a *Yahoo* had got a great store of this precious substance, he was able to purchase whatever he had a mind to; the finest clothing, the noblest houses, great tracts of land, the most costly meats and drinks, and have his choice of the most beautiful females. Therefore since money alone was able to perform all these feats, our *Yahoos* thought they could never have enough of it to spend or to save, as they found themselves inclined from their natural bent either to profusion or avarice. That the rich man enjoyed the fruit of the poor man's labour, and the latter were a thousand to one in proportion to the former. That the bulk of our people were forced to live miserably, by labouring every day for small wages to make a few live plentifully.

JONATHAN SWIFT, *Gulliver's Travels*, 1726

Money aims at mobilizing *all* things. World-economy is the actualized economy of values that are completely detached in thought from the land, and made fluid. The Classical money-thinking, from Hannibal's day, transformed whole cities into coin and whole populations into slaves and thereby converted both into money that could be brought from everywhere to Rome, and used outwards from Rome as a power.

The Faustian money-thinking 'opens up' whole continents, the water-power of gigantic river-basins, the muscular power of the peoples of broad regions, the coal measures, the virgin forests, the laws of Nature, and transforms them all into financial energy, which is laid out in one way or in another—in the shape of press, or elections, or budgets, or armies—for the realization of masters' plans. Ever new values are abstracted from whatever world-stock is still, from the business point of view, unclaimed, 'the slumbering spirits of gold,' as John Gabriel Borkman says; and what the things themselves are, apart from this, is of no economic significance at all.

OSWALD SPENGLER, *The Decline of the West*, 1918–22, tr. Charles Francis Atkinson

When we bring money into the discussion we reach a higher level apparently outside the scope of this book. However a view of the whole picture from this vantage point enables us to understand monetary activity as a tool, a 'structure', a deep-seated regular feature of all slightly accelerated commercial life. Above all money is never an isolated reality; wherever it is, it influences all economic and social relationships. This makes it a wonderful indicator: a fairly reliable assessment can be made of all human activities down to the most humble level from the tempo of its circulation, or the way it becomes complicated or scarce. It is an important source of illumination for us.

Although it is an ancient fact of life, an ancient technique, money never ceases to surprise humanity. It seems to them mysterious and disturbing. First and foremost it is complicated in itself, for the monetary economy that goes with money was nowhere fully developed, even in a country like France in the sixteenth and seventeenth centuries, even in the eighteenth. It only made its way into certain regions and certain sectors. It continued to disturb the others. It was a novelty more because of what it brought with it than what it was itself. What did it actually bring? Sharp variations in prices of essential foodstuffs; incomprehensible relationships in which man no longer recognised either himself, his customs or his ancient values. His work became a commodity, himself a 'thing'. . . .

Actually every society that is based on an ancient structure and opens its doors to money sooner or later loses its acquired equilibria and liberates forces thenceforth inadequately controlled. The new form of interchange jumbles things up, favours a few rare individuals and rejects the others. Every society has to turn over a new leaf under the impact.

> FERNAND BRAUDEL, *Capitalism and Material Life 1400–1800*, 1967, tr. Miriam Kochan, 1973

That they buried a piece of money with them as a fee of the Elysian ferry-man, was a practice full of folly. But the ancient custom of placing coins in considerable urns, and the present practice of burying medals in the noble foundations of Europe, are laudable ways of historical discoveries, in actions, persons, chronologies; and posterity will applaud them.

> SIR THOMAS BROWNE, *Hydrotaphia*, 1658

When I was a Boy (before the Civil-warres) I heard 'em tell that in the old time they used to putt a Penny in dead persons mouth to give to St Peter: and I thinke that they did doe so in Wales and in the north countrey.

> JOHN AUBREY, *Remaines of Gentilisme and Judaisme*, 1686–7

The most *easy ratio* of multiplication and division, is that by ten. Everyone knows the facility of Decimal Arithmetic. Every one remembers, that when learning Money-Arithmetic, he used to be puzzled with adding the farthings, taking out the fours and carrying them on; adding the pence, taking out the twelves and carrying them on; adding the shillings, taking out the twenties and carrying them on; but when he came to the pounds, where he had only tens to carry forward, it was easy and free from error. The bulk of mankind are schoolboys through life. These little perplexities are always great to them. And even mathematical heads feel the relief of an easier, substituted for a more difficult process. Foreigners, too, who trade and travel among us, will find a great facility in understanding our coins and accounts from this ratio of subdivision. Those who have had occasion to convert the livres, sols and deniers of the French: the gilders, stivers and pfennigs of the Dutch; the pounds, shillings, pence, and farthings of these several States, into each other, can judge how much they would have been aided, had their several subdivisions been in a decimal ratio. Certainly, in all cases, where we are free to choose between easy and difficult modes of operation, it is most rational to choose the easy. The Financier [Robert Morris], therefore, in his report, well proposes that our coins should be in decimal proportion to one another.

THOMAS JEFFERSON, *Notes on a Money Unit*, 1784

How much the Upper Classes did actually, in any the most perfect Feudal time, return to the Under by way of recompense, in government, guidance, protection, we will not undertake to specify here. In Charity-Balls, Soup-Kitchens, in Quarter-Sessions, Prison-Discipline and Treadmills, we can well believe the old Feudal Aristocracy not to have surpassed the new. Yet we do say that the old Aristocracy were the governors of the Lower Classes, the guides of the Lower Classes; and even, at bottom, that they existed as an Aristocracy because they were found adequate for that. Not by Charity-Balls and Soup-Kitchens; not so; far otherwise! But it was their happiness that, in struggling for their own objects, they *had* to govern the Lower Classes, even in this sense of governing. For, in one word, *Cash Payment* had not then grown to be the universal sole nexus of man to man; it was something other than money that the high then expected from the low, and could not live without getting from the low. Not as buyer and seller alone, of land or what else it might be, but in many senses still as soldier and captain, as clansman and head, as loyal subject and guiding king, was the low related to the high. With the supreme triumph of Cash, a changed time has entered; there must a changed Aristocracy enter. We invite the British reader to meditate earnestly on these things.

THOMAS CARLYLE, *Chartism*, 1839

Aphra Behn proved that money could be made by writing at the sacrifice, perhaps, of certain agreeable qualities; and so by degrees writing became not merely a sign of folly and a distracted mind, but was of practical importance. A husband might die, or some disaster overtake the family. Hundreds of women began as the eighteenth century drew on to add to their pin money, or to come to the rescue of their families by making translations or writing the innumerable bad novels which have ceased to be recorded even in text-books, but are to be picked up in the fourpenny boxes in the Charing Cross Road. The extreme activity of mind which showed itself in the later eighteenth century among women—the talking, and the meeting, the writing of essays on Shakespeare, the translating of the classics—was founded on the solid fact that women could make money by writing. Money dignifies what is frivolous if unpaid for. It might still be well to sneer at 'blue stockings with an itch for scribbling', but it could not be denied that they could put money in their purses. Thus, towards the end of the eighteenth century a change came about which, if I were rewriting history, I should describe more fully and think of greater importance than the Crusades or the Wars of the Roses. The middle-class woman began to write.

VIRGINIA WOOLF, *A Room of One's Own*, 1929

Thus, in 1892, neither Hay, King, nor Adams knew whether they had attained success, or how to estimate it, or what to call it; and the American people seemed to have no clearer idea than they. Indeed, the American people had no idea at all; they were wandering in a wilderness much more sandy than the Hebrews had ever trodden about Sinai; they had neither serpents nor golden calves to worship. They had lost the sense of worship; for the idea that they worshipped money seemed a delusion. Worship of money was an old-world trait; a healthy appetite akin to worship of the Gods, or to worship of power in any concrete shape; but the American wasted money more recklessly than any one ever did before; he spent more to less purpose than any extravagant court aristocracy; he had no sense of relative values, and knew not what to do with his money when he got it, except use it to make more, or throw it away. Probably, since human society began, it had seen no such curious spectacle as the houses of the San Francisco millionaires on Nob Hill. Except for the railway system, the enormous wealth taken out of the ground since 1840, had disappeared. West of the Alleghenies, the whole country might have been swept clean, and could have been replaced in better form within one or two years. The American mind had less respect for money than the European or Asiatic mind, and bore its loss more easily; but it had been deflected by its pursuit till it could turn in no other direction. It shunned, distrusted, disliked, the dangerous attraction of ideals, and stood alone in history for its ignorance of the past.

HENRY ADAMS, *The Education of Henry Adams*, 1907

Political and technological developments are rapidly obliterating all cultural differences and it is possible that, in a not remote future, it will be impossible to distinguish human beings living on one area of the earth's surface from those living on any other, but our different pasts have not yet been completely erased and cultural differences are still perceptible. The most striking difference between an American and a European is the difference in their attitudes towards money. Every European knows, as a matter of historical fact, that, in Europe, wealth could only be acquired at the expense of other human beings, either by conquering them or by exploiting their labor in factories. Further, even after the Industrial Revolution began, the number of persons who could rise from poverty to wealth was small; the vast majority took it for granted that they would not be much richer nor poorer than their fathers. In consequence, no European associates wealth with personal merit or poverty with personal failure.

To a European, money means power, the freedom to do as he likes, which also means that, consciously or unconsciously, he says: 'I want to have as much money as possible myself and others to have as little money as possible.'

In the United States, wealth was also acquired by stealing, but the real exploited victim was not a human being but poor Mother Earth and her creatures who were ruthlessly plundered. It is true that the Indians were expropriated or exterminated, but this was not, as it had always been in Europe, a matter of the conqueror seizing the wealth of the conquered, for the Indian had never realized the potential riches of his country. It is also true that, in the Southern states, men lived on the labor of slaves, but slave labor did not make them fortunes; what made slavery in the South all the more inexcusable was that, in addition to being morally wicked, it didn't even pay off handsomely.

Thanks to the natural resources of the country, every American, until quite recently, could reasonably look forward to making more money than his father, so that, if he made less, the fault must be his; he was either lazy or inefficient. What an American values, therefore, is not the possession of money as such, but his power to make it as a proof of his manhood; once he has proved himself by making it, it has served its function and can be lost or given away. In no society in history have rich men given away so large a part of their fortunes. A poor American feels guilty at being poor, but less guilty than an American *rentier* who has inherited wealth but is doing nothing to increase it; what can the latter do but take to drink and psychoanalysis?

In the Fifth Circle on the Mount of Purgatory, I do not think that many Americans will be found among the Avaricious; but I suspect that the Prodigals may be almost an American colony. The great vice of Americans is not materialism but a lack of respect for matter.

W. H. AUDEN, The Dyer's Hand, 1963

A more deadly description by a foreigner is that by Henry James in *The Wings of the Dove*, which has also been much in my mind where the relations between Americans and English are concerned. Here the American disinterested idealism, indiscriminate amiability and carelessness about money, along with the aimlessness and petering-out of Americans who have made themselves rich and their helplessness outside of America, are contrasted with the desperate materialism that is implied by position in England. *We* find making money exhilarating, but we also find it exhilarating to spend it. Money for us is a medium, a condition of life, like air. But with the English it means always property. A dollar is something that you multiply—something that causes an expansion of your house and your mechanical equipment, something that accelerates like speed; and that may be also slowed up or deflated. It is a value that may be totally imaginary, yet can for a time provide half-realised dreams. But pounds, shillings and pence are tangible, solid, heavy; they are objects one gains and possesses. And every good in England is bound up with the things one can handle and hold.

EDMUND WILSON, Europe without Baedeker, 1947

The connections between the complexes of interest in money and of defaecation, which seem so dissimilar, appear to be the most extensive of all. Every doctor who has practised psycho-analysis knows that the most refractory and long-standing cases of what is described as habitual constipation in neurotics can be cured by that form of treatment. This is less surprising if we remember that that function has shown itself similarly amenable to hypnotic suggestion. But in psycho-analysis one only achieves this result if one deals with the patients' money complex and induces them to bring it into consciousness with all its connections. It might be supposed that the neurosis is here only following an indication of common usage in speech, which calls a person who keeps too careful a hold on his money 'dirty'or 'filthy'. But this explanation would be far too superficial. In reality, wherever archaic modes of thought have predominated or persist—in the ancient civilizations, in myths, fairy tales and superstitions, in unconscious thinking, in dreams and in neuroses—money is brought into the most intimate relationship with dirt. We know that the gold which the devil gives his paramours turns into excrement after his departure, and the devil is certainly nothing else than the personification of the repressed unconscious instinctual life. We also know about the superstition which connects the finding of treasure with defaecation, and everyone is familiar with the figure of the 'shitter of ducats [*Dukatenscheisser*]'. Indeed, even according to ancient Babylonian doctrine gold is 'the faeces of Hell' (Mammon = *ilu manman*). Thus in following the usage of language, neurosis, here as elsewhere, is taking words in their original, significant sense, and where it appears to be using a word figuratively it is usually simply restoring its old meaning.

It is possible that the contrast between the most precious substance known to men and the most worthless, which they reject as waste matter ('refuse'), has led to this specific identification of gold with faeces.

Yet another circumstance facilitates this equation in neurotic thought. The original erotic interest in defaecation is, as we know, destined to be extinguished in later years. In those years the interest in money makes its appearance as a new interest which had been absent in childhood. This makes it easier for the earlier impulsion, which is in process of losing its aim, to be carried over to the newly emerging aim.

SIGMUND FREUD, 'Character and Anal Erotism', 1908

It only needs one more step for the identification of faeces with gold to be complete. Soon even stones begin to wound the child's feeling of cleanliness—he longs for something purer—and this is offered to him in the shining pieces of money, the high appreciation of which is naturally also in part due to the respect in which they are held by adults, as well as to the seductive possibilities of obtaining through them everything that the child's heart can desire. Originally, however, it is not these purely practical considerations that are operative, enjoyment in the playful collecting, heaping up, and gazing at the shining metal pieces being the chief thing, so that they are treasured even less for their economic value than for their own sake as pleasure-giving objects. The eye takes pleasure at the sight of their lustre and colour, the ear at their metallic clink, the sense of touch at play with the round smooth discs, only the sense of smell comes away empty, and the sense of taste also has to be satisfied with the weak, but peculiar taste of the coins. With this the development of the money symbol is in its main outlines complete. Pleasure in the intestinal contents becomes enjoyment of money, which, however, after what has been said is seen to be nothing other than odourless, dehydrated filth that has been made to shine. *Pecunia non olet*.

In correspondence with the development of the organ of thought that in the meanwhile has been proceeding in the direction of logicality, the adult's symbolic interest in money gets extended not only to objects with similar physical attributes, but to all sorts of things that in any way signify value or possession (paper money, shares, bankbook, etc.). But whatever form may be assumed by money, the enjoyment at possessing it has its deepest and amplest source in coprophilia. Every sociologist and national economist who examines the facts without prejudice has to reckon with this irrational element. Social problems can be solved only by discovering the real psychology of human beings; speculations about economic conditions alone will never reach the goal.

> SANDOR FERENCZI, 'The Ontogenesis of the Interest in Money', 1914, tr.
> Ernest Jones, 1952; for *pecunia non olet* see Suetonius, p. 323 below.

From the earliest times of which we have record—back, say, to two thousand years before Christ—down to the beginning of the eighteenth century, there was no very great change in the standard of life of the average man living in the civilised centres of the earth. Ups and downs certainly. Visitations of plague, famine, and war. Golden intervals. But no progressive, violent change. Some periods perhaps 50 per cent better than others—at the utmost 100 per cent better—in the four thousand years which ended (say) in AD 1700.

This slow rate of progress, or lack of progress, was due to two reasons—to the remarkable absence of important technical improvements and to the failure of capital to accumulate.

The absence of important technical inventions between the prehistoric age and comparatively modern times is truly remarkable. Almost everything which really matters and which the world possessed at the commencement of the modern age was already known to man at the dawn of history. Language, fire, the same domestic animals which we have to-day, wheat, barley, the vine and the olive, the plough, the wheel, the oar, the sail, leather, linen and cloth, bricks and pots, gold and silver, copper, tin, and lead—and iron was added to the list before 1,000 B.C.—banking, statecraft, mathematics, astronomy, and religion. There is no record of when we first possessed these things.

At some epoch before the dawn of history—perhaps even in one of the comfortable intervals before the last ice age—there must have been an era of progress and invention comparable to that in which we live to-day. But through the greater part of recorded history there was nothing of the kind.

The modern age opened, I think, with the accumulation of capital which began in the sixteenth century. I believe—for reasons with which I must not encumber the present argument—that this was initially due to the rise of prices, and the profits to which that led, which resulted from the treasure of gold and silver which Spain brought from the New World into the Old. From that time until to-day the power of accumulation by compound interest, which seems to have been sleeping for many generations, was reborn and renewed its strength. And the power of compound interest over two hundred years is such as to stagger the imagination.

Let me give in illustration of this a sum which I have worked out. The value of Great Britain's foreign investments to-day is estimated at about £4,000,000,000. This yields us an income at the rate of about $6\frac{1}{2}$ per cent. Half of this we bring home and enjoy; the other half, namely, $3\frac{1}{4}$ per cent, we leave to accumulate abroad at compound interest. Something of this sort has now been going on for about 250 years.

For I trace the beginnings of British foreign investment to the treasure which Drake stole from Spain in 1580. In that year he returned to England bringing with him the prodigious spoils of the *Golden Hind*. Queen Elizabeth was a considerable shareholder in the syndicate which had financed the expedition. Out of her share she paid off the whole of England's foreign debt, balanced her Budget, and found herself with about £40,000 in hand. This she invested in the Levant Company—which prospered. Out of the profits of the Levant Company, the East India Company was founded; and the profits of this great enterprise were the foundation of England's subsequent foreign investment. Now it happens that £40,000 accumulating at $3\frac{1}{4}$ per cent compound interest approximately corresponds to the actual volume of England's foreign investments at various dates, and would actually amount to-day to the total of £4,000,000,000 which I have already quoted as being what our foreign investments now are. Thus, every £1 which Drake brought home in 1580 has now become £100,000. Such is the power of compound interest!

J. M. KEYNES, 'Economic Possibilities for our Grandchildren', 1930

## DE PECUNIA

Sir Abe Bailey with four relations, but only £3,000,000: dying under the impression that there must be something wrong with arithmetic.

Man like a scarecrow, at country auction bidding £50,000 for a property: deposit asked for: refused: one banknote given: referred to Bank of England: perfectly genuine: one of three in existence.

> *F. W. Winterbotham [once solicitor to the Madan family]*

Lord Cunliffe, giving evidence before a Royal Commission, at the special request of the Chancellor of the Exchequer, would only say that the Bank of England reserves were 'very, very considerable'. When pressed to give an even approximate figure, he replied that he would be 'very, very reluctant to add to what he had said'.

Harrison Hayter (1825–98), G.M.'s maternal grandfather, President of the Institute of Civil Engineers, holding nothing but Consols and Corporation Stocks: not seaside corporations, however, as light-minded people tend to go to the seaside, and also the South Coast might be attacked by the French.

O. T. Falk's father, if a share he had bought went up, writing to the transferor to offer a refund.

It depends on the rupee-value of the dollar in three months' time . . .

> *J. M. Keynes (quoted by Cyril Asquith)*

1. You don't make money by speculation. You make money by buying good shares, and keeping them.
2. Never be ashamed of going small.

> *Sir George Jessel*

Never hesitate to give top prices for what you want.

> *T. J. Wise*

Don't argue with the tape.
Don't buck the market.

> *American sayings*

Put all your eggs in one basket: and watch that basket.

> *Andrew Carnegie*

Morrison, of Fonthill; fortune made in three ways, crape, gloves, and standing instructions to his broker to buy and sell Consols within limits of 99R–S: afraid of dying poor: leaving nine million pounds.

GEOFFREY MADAN, *Notebooks*, 1981

Why does feudal life hold so great an attraction for writers of SF and fantasy? The answer in part is that the European Middle Ages need little research: one says 'feudal life' as easily as one says 'galactic empire' and, by long familiarity, a hazy picture is conjured up in the genre reader's mind. Similarly, galactic empires are often hazy reflections of the British Empire, where life was nasty, brutish, and in shorts.

Often galactic empires are revealed to have feudal bases—though how this politico-economic anomaly comes about is never explained. But perhaps the most compelling attraction of a feudal background is that money never has to change hands.

We are talking, after all, when we deal with this welter of fantasy, of the dreams of our society, our capitalist society. That society works by the circulation of money. What is the adolescent reader, the typical reader of these fantasies, most short of ? Money. And the power that money brings. The attractions of societies where no money changes hands are obvious. A young fantasy hero cast up on a strange planet can go straight into the nearest tavern and obtain a tankard of ale or *bexjquth*. When did a fantasy hero ever fish a ten dollar bill from his pocket? When did milady seek alimony? When were travellers' cheques needed in Atlantis or Cathay? When was the lead villain simply slung into prison for debt? When did the mortgage ever fall due on one of those labyrinthine castles?

BRIAN ALDISS and DAVID WINGROVE, *Trillion Year Spree*, 1986

# *Getting and Spending*

Wordsworth's phrase writes off our dealings with money as tiresome ob-
stacles to a more spiritual life. Other writers, though, have recognized the
poetry, as well as the pleasures and miseries, of earning wages or squandering them. This section surveys the everyday routines of making money,
and considers some of the other ways in which cash may be got or spent:
at the pawnbroker's, in marriage, over the counter of the bank, through
inheritances, by tipping, in taxes.

&

> The world is too much with us; late and soon,
> Getting and spending, we lay waste our powers . . .

WILLIAM WORDSWORTH, 1807

'My other piece of advice, Copperfield,' said Mr Micawber, 'you know.
Annual income twenty pounds, annual expenditure nineteen nineteen six,
result happiness. Annual income twenty pounds, annual expenditure twenty
pounds ought and six, result misery. The blossom is blighted, the leaf is
withered, the God of day goes down upon the dreary scene, and—and in
short you are for ever floored. As I am!'

CHARLES DICKENS, David Copperfield, 1849–50

'It struck me that she was getting moped, and beginning to settle down,
which wouldn't suit her a bit. The first symptom that I noticed was when
she began to complain that we were living beyond our income. All decent

people live beyond their incomes nowadays, and those who aren't respect-able live beyond other people's. A few gifted individuals manage to do both.'

SAKI (H. H. Munro), 'The Match-Maker', *The Chronicles of Clovis*, 1911

The earning of money should be a means to an end; for more than thirty years—I began to support myself at sixteen—I had to regard it as the end itself.

GEORGE GISSING, *The Private Papers of Henry Ryecroft*, 1903

Fair day's-wages for fair day's-work! exclaims a sarcastic man: alas, in what corner of this Planet, since Adam first awoke on it, was that ever realised? The day's-wages of John Milton's day's-work, named *Paradise Lost* and *Milton's Works*, were Ten Pounds paid by instalments, and a rather close escape from death on the gallows. Consider that: it is no rhetorical flourish; it is an authentic, altogether quiet fact,—emblematic, quietly documentary of a whole world of such, ever since human history began.

THOMAS CARLYLE, *Past and Present*, 1843

January 5. I can scarcely write the news. Mr Perkupp told me my salary would be raised £100! I stood gaping for a moment unable to realize it. I annually get £10 rise, and I thought it might be £15 or even £20; but £100 surpasses all belief. Carrie and I both rejoiced over our good fortune. Lupin came home in the evening in the utmost good spirits. I sent Sarah quietly round to the grocer's for a bottle of champagne, the same as we had before, 'Jackson Frères'. It was opened at supper, and I said to Lupin: 'This is to celebrate some good news I have received today.' Lupin replied: 'Hurray, Guv.! And I have some good news, also; a double event, eh?' I said: 'My boy, as a result of twenty-one years' industry and strict attention to the interests of my superiors in office, I have been rewarded with promotion and a rise in salary of £100.'

Lupin gave three cheers, and we rapped the table furiously, which brought in Sarah to see what the matter was. Lupin ordered us to 'fill up' again, and addressing us upstanding, said: 'Having been in the firm of Job Cleanands, stock and share-brokers, a few weeks, and *not* having paid particular atten-tion to the interests of my superiors in office, my Guv'nor, as a reward to me, allotted me £5 worth of shares in a really good thing. The result is, today I have made £200.' I said: 'Lupin, you are joking.' 'No, Guv., it's the good old truth; Job Cleanands *put me on to Chlorates.*'

GEORGE and WEEDON GROSSMITH, *The Diary of a Nobody*, 1892

IAGO. It is merely a lust of the blood, and a permission of the will. Come, be a man: Drown thyself? drown cats, and blind puppies. I have professed me thy friend, and I confess me knit to thy deserving with cables of perdurable toughness; I could never better stead thee than now. Put money in thy purse; follow these wars; defeat thy favour with an usurped beard; I say, put money in thy purse. It cannot be, that Desdemona should long continue her love to the Moor,—put money in thy purse;— nor he his to her: it was a violent commencement, and thou shalt see an answerable sequestration;—put but money in thy purse.—These Moors are changeable in their wills;—fill thy purse with money; the food that to him now is as luscious as locusts, shall be to him shortly as bitter as coloquintida. She must change for youth: when she is sated with his body, she will find the error of her choice.—She must have change, she must: therefore put money in thy purse.—If thou wilt needs damn thyself, do it a more delicate way than drowning. Make all the money thou canst: If sanctimony and a frail vow, betwixt an erring barbarian and a supersubtle Venetian, be not too hard for my wits, and all the tribe of hell, thou shalt enjoy her; therefore make money.

WILLIAM SHAKESPEARE, *Othello*, 1605

You talk about Govt. money. I take it every week, so that I haven't any scruples: but I'm worth more than 3/- a day only in politics & Middle East, & there I don't play: and a temporary job at a high salary would only cart me worse than ever at the end. It's hard enough, now, to go poor again: and every year of money would make it far worse.

T. E. LAWRENCE to D. G. Hogarth, 13 June 1923

Again, I always go to sea as a sailor, because they make a point of paying me for my trouble, whereas they never pay passengers a single penny that I ever heard of. On the contrary, passengers themselves must pay. And there is all the difference in the world between paying and being paid. The act of paying is perhaps the most uncomfortable infliction that the two orchard thieves entailed upon us. But *being paid*,—what will compare with it? The urbane activity with which a man receives money is really marvellous, considering that we so earnestly believe money to be the root of all earthly ills, and that on no account can a monied man enter heaven. Ah! how cheerfully we consign ourselves to perdition!

HERMAN MELVILLE, Moby-Dick, 1851

'Yes, what do you want?' the pawnbroker lifted her head up and asked with a huge voice. As Aina was looking on, I told the pawnbroker—'well, I come to pawn myself for money!'

'You little boy like this! But what are you going to do with the money?' the pawnbroker asked with wonder.

'I am going to spend the money for the funeral ceremony of my father who died recently!' I replied to the pawnbroker loudly.

'But I think you are still too young to do hard work,' the pawnbroker said with pride.

'Although I am still young but I am very strong enough to do hard work. You know, I was born and bred in poverty!' I explained without shame.

'All right, come nearer and let me test your body to know whether you are strong enough to do hard work!' the pawnbroker pressed every part of my body with both hands for about thirty minutes with doubtful mind.

'Ajaiyi is very strong to do hard work, madam!' Aina told the pawnbroker with a sharp voice.

'Well, of course, I shall give you only two pounds but you will be working for me from morning till two o'clock everyday and I am not going to feed you. Take the two pounds but you must come to start work as soon as you have finished the funeral ceremony of your father. But put it in your mind that you will be working for me until you will be able to refund my two pounds!' the pawnbroker reluctantly gave me only two pounds.

AMOS TUTUOLA, Ajaiyi and his Inherited Poverty, 1967

The preference for jobs offering greater 'security,' spurious as it may be, is also neurotic, since experience has shown that when security is most needed—during severe depressions, or political upheavals—such jobs do not usually offer more security than others. Selecting jobs for the pseudo independence that higher pay seems to offer, instead of for autonomous reasons—i.e., the job offering deepest satisfaction because it has intrinsic meaning for the person and adds to his self respect—is likewise due to neurotic tendencies, namely the unrecognized equation of money with true status. Here, too, the outer security (what money can buy) is accepted in lieu of inner security; the impersonal coin of exchange is given more relevance than the particular product of one's labor.

BRUNO BETTELHEIM, *The Informed Heart*, 1960

Working people are rarely, if ever, dilettanti. To be dilettante is to believe that one's activity is justified by the mere fact of one's wishing to engage upon it. This—which is a privilege not even of the middle class but rather of the aristocracy, or at any rate the very secure—constitutes a rejection of the success-motive before the question is even posed how success should be measured. At its worst, with which it is commonly identified, it leads to satisfaction with sloppy workmanship and to an unconcern with the position of one's work in society at large: a position which is, after all, integral to its meaning (including, if properly construed, its meaning to oneself). The worker is educated to lack such self-assurance. His—and I suspect it *is* more true of men than of women, imbued as we are with the 'bread-winner' ethos—his justification must be made manifest to him by society. But the only criterion which society allows—the only scale whereon worth may be measured—is money. Legitimate activity is that which pays.

DAI VAUGHAN, *Portrait of an Invisible Man*, 1982

In the matter of a career Murphy could not help feeling that his stars had been guilty of some redundance, and that once go-between had been ordained further specification was superfluous. For what was all working for a living but a procuring and a pimping for the money-bags, one's lecherous tyrants the money-bags, so that they might breed.

SAMUEL BECKETT, *Murphy*, 1938

Would that I had £300,000
    Invested in some strong security;
A Midland Country House with formal grounds,
    A Town House, and a House beside the sea,
And one in Spain, and one in Normandy,
    And Friends innumerable at my call

And youth serene—and underneath it all
　　One steadfast, passionate flame to nurture me.

Then would I chuck for good my stinking trade
　　Of writing tosh at 1s. 6d. a quire!
And soar like young Bellerophon arrayed
　　High to the filmy Heavens of my desire. . . .
　　　　　But that's all over. Here's the world again.
　　　　　Bring me the Blotter. Fill the fountain-pen.

HILAIRE BELLOC, Sonnets and Verse, 1938


Off and on I know Feet Samuels a matter of eight or ten years, up and down Broadway, and in and out, but I never have much truck with him because he is a guy I consider no dice. In fact, he does not mean a thing.

In the first place, Feet Samuels is generally broke, and there is no percentage in hanging around brokers. The way I look at it, you are not going to get anything off a guy who has not got anything. So while I am very sorry for brokers, and am always willing to hope that they get hold of something, I do not like to be around them. Long ago an old-timer who knows what he is talking about says to me:

'My boy,' he says, 'always try to rub up against money, for if you rub up against money long enough, some of it may rub off on you.'

DAMON RUNYON, 'A Very Honourable Guy', Furthermore, 1938


It is a fine world & I wish I knew how to make £200 a year in it without sucking James Milne's———.

EDWARD THOMAS to Gordon Bottomley, 16 June 1915; James Milne was the<br>editor of the Daily Chronicle, for which Thomas wrote reviews.


Stale smoky air hung in the study with the smell of drab abraded leather of its chairs. As on the first day he bargained with me here. As it was in the beginning, is now. On the sideboard the tray of Stuart coins, base treasure of a bog: and ever shall be. And snug in their spooncase of purple plush, faded, the twelve apostles having preached to all the gentiles: world without end.

A hasty step over the stone porch and in the corridor. Blowing out his rare moustache Mr Deasy halted at the table.

— First, our little financial settlement, he said.

He brought out of his coat a pocketbook bound by a leather thong. It slapped open and he took from it two notes, one of joined halves, and laid them carefully on the table strapping and

— Two, he said, strapping and stowing his pocketbook away.

And now his strongroom for the gold. Stephen's embarrassed hand moved over the shells heaped in the cold stone mortar: whelks and money cowries and leopard shells: and this, whorled as an emir's turban, and this, the scallop of Saint James. An old pilgrim's hoard, dead treasure, hollow shells.

A sovereign fell, bright and new, on the soft pile of the tablecloth.

— Three, Mr Deasy said, turning his little savingsbox about in his hand. These are handy things to have. See. This is for sovereigns. This is for shillings, sixpences, halfcrowns. And here crowns. See.

He shot from it two crowns and two shillings.

— Three twelve, he said. I think you'll find that's right.

— Thank you, sir, Stephen said, gathering the money together with shy haste and putting it all in a pocket of his trousers.

— No thanks at all, Mr Deasy said. You have earned it.

Stephen's hand, free again, went back to the hollow shells. Symbols too of beauty and of power. A lump in my pocket. Symbols soiled by greed and misery.

— Don't carry it like that, Mr Deasy said. You'll pull it out somewhere and lose it. You just buy one of these machines. You'll find them very handy.

Answer something.

— Mine would be often empty, Stephen said.

The same room and hour, the same wisdom: and I the same. Three times now. Three nooses round me here. Well. I can break them in this instant if I will.

— Because you don't save, Mr Deasy said, pointing his finger. You don't know yet what money is. Money is power, when you have lived as long as I have. I know, I know. If youth but knew. But what does Shakespeare say? *Put but money in thy purse.*

— Iago, Stephen murmured.

He lifted his gaze from the idle shells to the old man's stare.

— He knew what money was, Mr Deasy said. He made money. A poet but an Englishman too. Do you know what is the pride of the English? Do you know what is the proudest word you will ever hear from an Englishman's mouth?

The seas' ruler. His seacold eyes looked on the empty bay: history is to blame: on me and on my words, unhating.

— That on his empire, Stephen said, the sun never sets.

— Ba! Mr Deasy cried. That's not English. A French Celt said that. He tapped his savingsbox against his thumbnail.

— I will tell you, he said solemnly, what is his proudest boast. *I paid my way*.

Good man, good man.

— *I paid my way. I never borrowed a shilling in my life.* Can you feel that? *I owe nothing.* Can you?

Mulligan, nine pounds, three pairs of socks, one pair brogues, ties. Curran, ten guineas. McCann, one guinea. Fred Ryan, two shillings. Temple, two lunches. Russell, one guinea, Cousins, ten shillings, Bob Reynolds, half a guinea, Köhler, three guineas, Mrs McKernan, five weeks' board. The lump I have is useless.

— For the moment, no, Stephen answered.

Mr Deasy laughed with rich delight, putting back his savingsbox.

— I knew you couldn't, he said joyously. But one day you must feel it. We are a generous people but we must also be just.

— I fear those big words, Stephen said, which make us so unhappy.

JAMES JOYCE, *Ulysses*, 1922

Throw yourself on the world without any rational plan of support, beyond what the chance employ of booksellers would afford you!

Throw yourself rather, my dear sir, from the steep Tarpeian rock, slapdash headlong upon iron spikes. If you have but five consolatory minutes between the desk and the bed, make much of them, and live a century in them, rather than turn slave to the booksellers. They are Turks and Tartars when they have poor authors at their beck. Hitherto you have been at arm's length from them. Come not within their grasp. I have known many authors want for bread, some repining, others enjoying the blessed security of a spunging-house, all agreeing they had rather have been tailors, weavers—what not? rather than the things they were. I have known some starved, some to go mad, one dear friend literally dying in a workhouse. You know not what a rapacious set these booksellers are. Ask even Southey, who (a single case almost) has made a fortune by book-drudgery, what he has found them. O you know not, may you never know, the miseries of subsisting by authorship! 'Tis a pretty appendage to a situation like yours or mine; but a slavery, worse than all slavery, to be a bookseller's dependant, to drudge your brains for pots of ale, and breasts of mutton, *to change your* FREE THOUGHTS *and* VOLUNTARY NUMBERS *for ungracious* TASK-WORK. The booksellers hate us. The reason I take to be, that contrary to other trades, in which the master gets all the credit, (a jeweller or silversmith for instance,) and the journeyman, who really does the fine work, is in the back-ground: in *our* work the world gives all the credit to us, whom *they* consider as *their* journeymen, and therefore do they hate us, and cheat us, and oppress us, and would wring the blood of us out, to put another sixpence in their mechanic pouches! . . .

Keep to your bank, and the bank will keep you. Trust not to the public; you may hang, starve, drown yourself for any thing that worthy *personage* cares. I bless every star, that Providence, not seeing good to make me independent, has seen it next good to settle me upon the stable foundation of Leadenhall. Sit down, good B. B., in the banking-office; what! is there not from six to eleven, P.M. six days in the week, and is there not all Sunday? Fie, what a superfluity of man's time, if you could think so! Enough for relaxation, mirth, converse, poetry, good thoughts, quiet thoughts. O the corroding, torturing, tormenting thoughts, that disturb the brain of the unlucky wight, who must draw upon it for daily sustenance! Henceforth I retract all my fond complaints of mercantile employment; look upon them as lover's quarrels. I was but half in earnest. Welcome dead timber of the desk, that gives me life. A little grumbling is a wholesome medicine for the spleen, but in my inner heart do I approve and embrace this our close, but unharassing way of life. I am quite serious. If you can send me Fox, I will not keep it *six weeks*, and will return it, with warm thanks to yourself and friend, without blot or dog's-ear. You will much oblige me by this kindness.

Yours truly,

C. LAMB.

CHARLES LAMB to Bernard Barton, 9 January 1823, *Letters*, ed. Talfourd, 1837

He disuaded me from Poetrie, for that she had beggered him, when he might have been a rich lawer, Physitian or Marchant.

WILLIAM DRUMMOND of Hawthornden, *Notes of Conversations with Ben Jonson*, 1619

My dear Sirs—I am extremely indebted to you for your liberality in the shape of manufactured rag, value £20, and shall immediately proceed to destroy some of the minor heads of that hydra the dun; to conquer which the knight need have no Sword Shield Cuirass, Cuisses Herbadgeon Spear Casque Greaves Paldrons spurs Chevron or any other scaly commodity, but he need only take the Bank-note of Faith and Cash of Salvation, and set out against the monster, invoking the aid of no Archimago or Urganda, but finger me the paper, light as the Sibyl's leaves in Virgil, whereat the fiend skulks off with his tail between his legs. Touch him with this enchanted paper, and he whips you his head away as fast as a snail's horn—but then the horrid propensity he has to put it up again has discouraged many very valiant Knights. He is such a never-ending still-beginning sort of a body— like my landlady of the Bell. I should conjecture that the very spright that 'the green sour ringlets makes Whereof the ewe not bites' had manufac- tured it of the dew fallen on said sour ringlets. I think I could make a nice little allegorical poem, called 'The Dun,' where we would have the Castle of Carelessness, the drawbridge of credit, Sir Novelty Fashion's expedition against the City of Tailors, etc. etc.

JOHN KEATS to Messrs Taylor and Hessey, 16 May 1817

. . . I am very well—really so absurd a septuagenarian is seldom met with— and my stay at Whitby, where the weather grew to be almost weakly good- natured at last, did me good. A poem even got itself written there (which seems to me not altogether bad), and this intense activity of the brain has the same effect as exercise on my body, and somehow braces up the whole machine. My writing this was a lucky thing, for when I got back to London I found a letter from the New York *Ledger* enclosing a draft for 200l. for whatever I should choose to send. So I sent them what I had just written, pacifying my scruples with the thought that after all it was only my *name* they were paying for, and that they knew best what it was worth to them. The letter, by great good luck, had been overlooked and not forwarded to Whitby as it should have been. Had I got it before my poem got itself out of me, I should have been quite disabled and should have sent back the draft. . . .

JAMES RUSSELL LOWELL to Mrs Edward Burnett, 23 September 1889, *Letters*, 1894

Looked into the New Annual Register for 1795. The tone of politics in the History of Literature, and in the British and Foreign History, materially differ: but the wonder is, how so *much* consistency is preserved in works of this nature; and, instead of marvelling, with Johnson, how any thing but profit should incite men to literary labour, I am rather surprised that mere emolument should induce them to labour so well.

THOMAS GREEN, *Extracts from the Diary of a Lover of Literature*, 1810, entry for 14 September 1796

The following is a list of the books I have written, with the dates of publication and the sums I have received for them. The dates given are the years in which the works were published as a whole, most of them having appeared before in some serial form.

| Names of Works. | Date of Publication. | Total Sums Received. |
| --- | --- | --- |
| The Macdermots of Ballycloran, | 1847 | £48 6 9 |
| The Kellys and the O'Kellys, | 1848 | 123 19 5 |
| La Vendée, | 1850 | 20 0 0 |
| The Warden, | 1855 ⎫ | |
| Barchester Towers, | 1857 ⎭ | 727 11 3 |
| The Three Clerks, | 1858 | 250 0 0 |
| Doctor Thorne, | 1858 | 400 0 0 |
| The West Indies and the Spanish Main, | 1859 | 250 0 0 |
| The Bertrams, | 1859 | 400 0 0 |
| Castle Richmond, | 1860 | 600 0 0 |
| Framley Parsonage, | 1861 | 1000 0 0 |
| Tales of All Countries—1st Series, | 1861 ⎫ | |
|     "     "    —2d   " | 1863 ⎬ | 1830 0 0 |
|     "     "    —3d   " | 1870 ⎭ | |
| Orley Farm, | 1862 | 3135 0 0 |
| North America, | 1862 | 1250 0 0 |
| Rachel Ray, | 1863 | 1645 0 0 |
| The Small House at Allington, | 1864 | 3000 0 0 |
| Can You Forgive Her? | 1864 | 3525 0 0 |
| Miss Mackenzie, | 1865 | 1300 0 0 |
| The Belton Estate, | 1866 | 1757 0 0 |
| The Claverings, | 1867 | 2800 0 0 |
| The Last Chronicle of Barset, | 1867 | 3000 0 0 |
| Nina Balatka, | 1867 | 450 0 0 |
| Linda Tressel, | 1868 | 450 0 0 |
| Phineas Finn, | 1869 | 3200 0 0 |

| | | | |
|---|---|---|---|
| He Knew He Was Right, | 1869 | 3200 | 0 0 |
| Brown, Jones, and Robinson, | 1870 | 600 | 0 0 |
| The Vicar of Bullhampton, | 1870 | 2500 | 0 0 |
| An Editor's Tales, | 1870 | 378 | 0 0 |
| Cæsar (Ancient Classics), | 1870 | 0 | 0 0 |
| Sir Harry Hotspur of Humblethwaite, | 1871 | 750 | 0 0 |
| Ralph the Heir, | 1871 | 2500 | 0 0 |
| The Golden Lion of Granpère, | 1872 | 550 | 0 0 |
| The Eustace Diamonds, | 1873 | 2500 | 0 0 |
| Australia and New Zealand, | 1873 | 1300 | 0 0 |
| Phineas Redux, | 1874 | 2500 | 0 0 |
| Harry Heathcote of Gangoil, | 1874 | 450 | 0 0 |
| Lady Anna, | 1874 | 1200 | 0 0 |
| The Way We Live Now, | 1875 | 3000 | 0 0 |
| The Prime Minister, | 1876 | 2500 | 0 0 |
| The American Senator, | 1877 | 1800 | 0 0 |
| Is He Popenjoy? | 1878 | 1600 | 0 0 |
| South Africa, | 1878 | 850 | 0 0 |
| John Caldigate, | 1879 | 1800 | 0 0 |
| Sundries, | | 7800 | 0 0 |

£68,939 17 5

. . . . . . . . .

It may interest some if I state that during the last twenty years I have made by literature something near £70,000. As I have said before in these pages, I look upon the result as comfortable, but not splendid.

ANTHONY TROLLOPE, *An Autobiography*, 1883

### I HEAR AMERICA SINGING, CREDIT LINES[1]

The poets go hippety-hoppety
To the office to draw their pay;
'Proputty, proputty, proputty'—
That's what I 'ears 'em say.[2]


And there the office factotum
Watches o'er every phrase,

And if anyone wants to quote' em,
   By golly, he pays and pays.[3]

A fellow who writes or edits
   And includes a fragment of song
Had better give proper credits
   Or Ascap will do him wrong.[4]

When you read some novelist's hit, mark
   That no one sings or recites
A line unless Marks or Witmark
   Has ceded the copyrights.

Oh, I think it is frightfully funny
   That our words are restricted thus,
But put them all together they spell *money*,
   A name that means the world to us.[5]

---

[1] All rights reserved, including the right to reproduce anything or portions thereof, by the author and publisher.

[2] By permission of the heirs of Alfred, Lord Tennyson, Aldworth, Blackdown above Haslemere, Surrey, England.

[3] From *The Woman Who Pays*, by Will D. Cobb, music by Gus Edwards. By permission of the publishers, Edward B. Marks Music Corporation.

[4] From *Frankie and Johnny*, author unknown. A reserve fund has been established to pay eventual claims.

[5] From *Mother*, words by Howard Johnson and music by T. Morse. By permission of the publishers, Leo Feist Inc.

MORRIS BISHOP (1893–1973)

6005 Camino de la Costa
La Jolla, California
(February 1949)

. . . I have no idea what income I can count on. I am cutting my own throat by using up my time and energies doing things that have nothing to do with writing. But I can't make any stable arrangements until I know where and how I am going to live. I don't see how any writer except a writer of best-sellers, which I am not likely to be, can exist other than in the most modest way without either Hollywood money or a steady stream of serials in the big magazines. You can't depend on radio or selling motion picture rights. They are too chancy. If I write a book a year I can probably depend on an income of $25,000, but that wouldn't pay my way here. Gosh, when I think what that income would have bought when I was a schoolboy in England. A mansion standing in large grounds, three or four servants, a full time gardener and coachman, a couple of fine horses for the victoria and the brougham, and so on. High prices and heavy taxation will destroy a society just as effectively as war. Can you recall when amid howls of fury the English income tax reached a shilling in the pound?

RAYMOND CHANDLER to Carl Brandt, *Selected Letters*, ed. MacShane, 1981

PETRUCHIO. Signior Hortensio, 'twixt such friends as we,
   Few words suffice: and, therefore, if thou know
   One rich enough to be Petruchio's wife,
   (As wealth is burthen of my wooing dance,)
   Be she as foul as was Florentius' love,
   As old as Sybil, and as curst and shrewd
   As Socrates' Xantippe, or a worse,
   She moves me not, or not removes, at least,
   Affection's edge in me; were she as rough
   As are the swelling Adriatick seas:
   I come to wive it wealthily in Padua;
   If wealthily, then happily in Padua.
GRUMIO. Nay, look you, sir, he tells you flatly what his mind is: Why, give him gold enough and marry him to a puppet, or an aglet-baby; or an old trot with ne'er a tooth in her head, though she have as many diseases as two and fifty horses; why, nothing comes amiss, so money comes withal.

WILLIAM SHAKESPEARE, *The Taming of the Shrew*, 1593

'Is Mr Edward Ferrars,' said Elinor, with resolution, 'going to be married?'
   'It is not actually settled, but there is such a thing in agitation. He has a most excellent mother. Mrs Ferrars, with the utmost liberality, will come forward, and settle on him a thousand a year, if the match takes place. The lady is the Hon. Miss Morton, only daughter of the late Lord Morton, with thirty thousand pounds. A very desirable connection on both sides, and I have not a doubt of its taking place in time. A thousand a year is a great deal for a mother to give away, to make over for ever; but Mrs Ferrars has a noble spirit. To give you another instance of her liberality:—The other day, as soon as we came to town, aware that money could not be very plenty with us just now, she put bank-notes into Fanny's hands to the

amount of two hundred pounds. And extremely acceptable it is, for we must live at a great expense while we are here.'

He paused for her assent and compassion; and she forced herself to say—

'Your expenses both in town and country must certainly be considerable; but your income is a large one.'

'Not so large, I daresay, as many people suppose. I do not mean to complain, however; it is undoubtedly a comfortable one, and I hope will in time be better. The enclosure of Norland Common, now carrying on, is a most serious drain. And then I have made a little purchase within this half-year; East Kingham Farm, you must remember the place, where old Gibson used to live. The land was so very desirable for me in every respect, so immediately adjoining my own property, that I felt it my duty to buy it. I could not have answered it to my conscience to let it fall into any other hands. A man must pay for his convenience; and it *has* cost me a vast deal of money.'

'More than you think it really and intrinsically worth?'

'Why, I hope not that. I might have sold it again, the next day, for more than I gave: but, with regard to the purchase-money, I might have been very unfortunate indeed; for the stocks were, at that time, so low, that if I had not happened to have the necessary sum in my banker's hands, I must have sold out to very great loss.'

Elinor could only smile.

JANE AUSTEN, *Sense and Sensibility*, 1811

'I am going to marry Mlle. Eve Chardon.'

'Who may she be? What kind of victual does she eat?'

'She is the daughter of the late M. Chardon, the druggist in L'Houmeau.'

'You are going to marry a girl out of L'Houmeau! *you!* a burgess of Angoulême, and printer to His Majesty! This is what comes of book-learning! Send a boy to school forsooth! Oh! well, then she is very rich, is she, my boy?' and the old vinegrower came up closer with a cajoling manner; 'if you are marrying a girl out of L'Houmeau, it must be because she has lots of cash, eh? Good! you will pay me my rent now. There are two years and one-quarter owing, you know, my boy; that is two thousand seven hundred francs altogether; the money will come just in the nick of time to pay the cooper. If it was anybody else, I should have a right to ask for interest; for, after all, business is business, but I will let you off the interest. Well, how much has she?'

'Just as much as my mother had.'

The old vinegrower very nearly said, 'Then she has only ten thousand francs!' but he recollected just in time that he had declined to give an account of her fortune to her son, and exclaimed, 'She has nothing!'

HONORÉ DE BALZAC (1799–1850), *Lost Illusions*, tr. Ellen Marriage, 1897

'Our Maud's been waitin' for some money, to get a few things,' said the mother-in-law.

In silence, he put five-and-sixpence on the table.

'Take that up, Maud,' said the mother.

Maud did so.

'You'll want it for us board, shan't you?' she asked, furtively, of her mother.

'Might I ask if there's nothing you want to buy yourself, first?'

'No, there's nothink I want,' answered the daughter.

Mrs Marriott took the silver and counted it.

'And do you,' said the mother-in-law, towering upon the shrinking son, but speaking slowly and statelily, 'do you think I'm going to keep you and your wife for five-and-sixpence a week?'

'It's a' I've got,' he answered, sulkily.

'You've had a good jaunt, my sirs, if it's cost four-and-sixpence. You've started your game early, haven't you?'

He did not answer.

'It's a nice thing! Here's our Maud an' me been sitting since eleven o'clock this morning! Dinner waiting and cleared away, tea waiting and washed up; then in he comes crawling with five-and-sixpence. Five-and-sixpence for a man an' wife's board for a week, if you please!'

Still he did not say anything.

D. H. LAWRENCE (1885–1930), 'Strike-Pay'

Moreover, it is equally useless to ask what might have happened if Mrs Seton and her mother and her mother before her had amassed great wealth and laid it under the foundations of college and library, because, in the first place, to earn money was impossible for them, and in the second, had it been possible, the law denied them the right to possess what money they earned. It is only for the last forty-eight years that Mrs Seton has had a penny of her own. For all the centuries before that it would have been her husband's property—a thought which, perhaps, may have had its share in keeping Mrs Seton and her mothers off the Stock Exchange. Every penny

I earn, they may have said, will be taken from me and disposed of according to my husband's wisdom—perhaps to found a scholarship or to endow a fellowship in Balliol or Kings, so that to earn money, even if I could earn money, is not a matter that interests me very greatly. I had better leave it to my husband.

VIRGINIA WOOLF, A Room of One's Own, 1929

## EPITAPH ON AN ARMY OF MERCENARIES

These, in the day when heaven was falling,
    The hour when earth's foundations fled,
Followed their mercenary calling
    And took their wages and are dead.

Their shoulders held the sky suspended;
    They stood, and earth's foundations stay;
What God abandoned, these defended,
    And saved the sum of things for pay.

A. E. HOUSMAN, Last Poems, 1922

## ANOTHER EPITAPH ON AN ARMY OF MERCENARIES

It is a God-damned lie to say that these
Saved, or knew, anything worth any man's pride.
They were professional murderers and they took
Their blood money and impious risks and died.
In spite of all their kind some elements of worth
With difficulty persist here and there on earth.

HUGH MacDIARMID, Second Hymn to Lenin and Other Poems, 1935

'How sweet is mortal Sovranty!'—think some:
Others—'How blest the Paradise to come!'
    Ah, take the Cash in hand and waive the Rest;
Oh, the brave Music of a *distant* Drum!

1st edn., 1859

Some for the Glories of This World; and some
Sigh for the Prophet's Paradise to come;
Ah, take the Cash, and let the Credit go,
Nor heed the rumble of a distant Drum!

4th edn., 1879

EDWARD FITZGERALD (1809–93), *The Rubáiyát of Omar Khayyám*

The first of all English games is making money. That is an all-absorbing game; and we knock each other down oftener in playing at that, than at football, or any other roughest sport: and it is absolutely without purpose; no one who engages heartily in that game ever knows why. Ask a great money-maker what he wants to do with his money,—he never knows. He doesn't make it to do anything with it. He gets it only that he *may* get it. 'What will you make of what you have got?' you ask. 'Well, I'll get more,' he says. Just as, at cricket, you get more runs. There's no use in the runs, but to get more of them than other people is the game. And there's no use in the money, but to have more of it than other people is the game. So all that great foul city of London there,—rattling, growling, smoking, stinking,—a ghastly heap of fermenting brickwork, pouring out poison at every pore,—you fancy it is a city of work? Not a street of it! It is a great city of play; very nasty play, and very hard play, but still play. It is only Lord's cricket-ground without the turf:—a huge billiard-table without the cloth, and with pockets as deep as the bottomless pit; but mainly a billiard-table, after all.

JOHN RUSKIN, *The Crown of Wild Olive*, 1866

A man will be generally very old and feeble before he forgets how much money he has in the funds.

ANTHONY TROLLOPE, *An Autobiography*, 1883

I went into the city today, to put the £125 I got for the 'Book of Nonsense' into the funds. It is doubtless a very unusual thing for an artist to put by money, for the whole way from Temple Bar to the Bank was *crowded* with carriages and people,—so immense a sensation did this occurrence make. And all the way back it was the same, which was very gratifying.

EDWARD LEAR to Lady Waldegrave, 4 November 1862, *Letters of Edward Lear to Chichester Fortescue and Frances Countess Waldegrave*, ed. Lady Strachey, 1907

Entering the Bank in a composed manner, I drew a cheque and handed it to the cashier through the grating. Then I eyed him narrowly. Would not that astute official see that I was only posing as a Real Person? No; he calmly opened a little drawer, took out some real sovereigns, counted them carefully, and handed them to me in a brass shovel. I went away feeling I had perpetrated a delightful fraud. I had got some of the gold of the actual world!

Yet now and then, at the sight of my name on a visiting card, or of my face photographed in a group among other faces, or when I see a letter addressed in my hand, or catch the sound of my own voice, I grow shy in the presence of a mysterious Person who is myself, is known by my name, and who apparently does exist. Can it be possible that I am as real as any one else, and that all of us—the cashier and banker at the Bank, the King on his throne—all feel ourselves like ghosts and goblins in this authentic world?

LOGAN PEARSALL SMITH, *Trivia*, 1918

I shall have a little trouble in procuring the Money and a great ordeal to go through—no trouble indeed to any one else—or ordeal either. I mean I shall have to go to town some thrice, and stand in the Bank an hour or two—to me worse than anything in Dante.

JOHN KEATS to Benjamin Robert Haydon, 7–14 January 1819

I don't believe much of what my Lord Byron the poet says; but when he wrote, 'So, for a good old gentlemanly vice, I think I shall put up with avarice,' I think his lordship meant what he wrote, and if he practised what he preached, shall not quarrel with him. As an occupation in declining years, I declare I think saving is useful, amusing, and not unbecoming. It must be a perpetual amusement. It is a game that can be played by day, by night, at home and abroad, and at which you must win in the long run. I am tired and want a cab. The fare to my house, say, is two shillings. The cabman will naturally want half-a-crown. I pull out my book. I show him the distance is exactly three miles and fifteen hundred and ninety yards. I offer him my card—my winning card. As he retires with the two shillings, blaspheming inwardly, every curse is a compliment to my skill. I have played him and beat him; and a sixpence is my spoil and just reward. This is a game, by the way, which women play far more cleverly than we do. But what an interest it imparts to life! During the whole drive home I know

I shall have my game at the journey's end; am sure of my hand, and shall beat my adversary. Or I can play in another way. I won't have a cab at all, I will wait for the omnibus: I will be one of the damp fourteen in that steaming vehicle. I will wait about in the rain for an hour, and 'bus after 'bus shall pass, but I will not be beat. I *will* have a place, and get it at length, with my boots wet through, and an umbrella dripping between my legs. I have a rheumatism, a cold, a sore throat, a sulky evening,—a doctor's bill to-morrow perhaps? Yes, but I have won my game, and am gainer of a shilling on this rubber.

W. M. THACKERAY (1811–63), 'Autour de mon chapeau', *Roundabout Papers*

In the name of God, Amen. I William Shakspeare of Stratford-upon-Avon, in the county of Warwick, gent. in perfect health and memory (God be praised!) do make and ordain this my last will and testament in manner and form following; that is to say:

*First*, I commend my soul into the hands of God my Creator, hoping, and assuredly believing through the only merits of Jesus Christ my Saviour, to be made partaker of life everlasting; and my body to the earth whereof it is made.

*Item*, I give and bequeath unto my daughter Judith, one hundred and fifty pounds of lawful English money, to be paid unto her in manner and form following; that is to say, one hundred pounds in discharge of her marriage portion within one year after my decease, with consideration after the rate of two shillings in the pound for so long time as the same shall be unpaid unto her after my decease; and the fifty pounds residue thereof, upon her surrendering of, or giving of such sufficient security as the overseers of this my will shall like of, to surrender or grant, all her estate and right that shall descend or come unto her after my decease, or that she now hath, of, in, or to, one copyhold tenement, with the appurtenances, lying and being in Stratford-upon-Avon aforesaid, in the said county of Warwick, being parcel or holden of the manor of Rowington, unto my daughter Susanna Hall, and her heirs for ever. . . .

*Item*, I give unto my wife my second best bed, with the furniture.

WILLIAM SHAKESPEARE, *March* 1616

When Lord Erskine heard that somebody had died worth two hundred thousand pounds, he observed, 'Well, that's a very pretty sum to begin the next world with.'

SAMUEL ROGERS, *Table Talk*, 1856

'How much money do you expect for it?' Mrs Touchett asked of her companion, who had brought her to sit in the front parlour, which she had inspected without enthusiasm.

'I haven't the least idea,' said the girl.

'That's the second time you have said that to me,' her aunt rejoined. 'And yet you don't look at all stupid.'

'I'm not stupid; but I don't know anything about money.'

'Yes, that's the way you were brought up—as if you were to inherit a million. What have you in point of fact inherited?'

'I really can't tell you. You must ask Edmund and Lilian; they'll be back in half an hour.'

'In Florence we should call it a very bad house,' said Mrs Touchett; 'but here, I dare say, it will bring a high price. It ought to make a considerable sum for each of you. In addition to that you *must* have something else; it's most extraordinary your not knowing. The position's of value, and they'll probably pull it down and make a row of shops. I wonder you don't do that yourself; you might let the shops to great advantage.'

HENRY JAMES, *The Portrait of a Lady*, 1881

We have often lamented that so many worthy people should be at the expense and trouble of making last wills and testaments, and yet never enjoy what passes at the reading of them. On all the different occasions where we have been present at such affecting ceremonies, it was quite edifying to see how justly the sorrow was apportioned to the legacies; those enjoying the greatest being always the most profoundly distressed; their tears, by some sort of sympathy, flowing exactly in accordance with the amount of the sums of money, or the value of the chattels which they were appointed to receive.

JOHN GALT, *The Entail*, 1823

Mrs Daneeka had been widowed cruelly again, but this time her grief was mitigated somewhat by a notification from Washington that she was sole beneficiary of her husband's $10,000 GI insurance policy, which amount was obtainable by her on demand. The realization that she and the children were not faced immediately with starvation brought a brave smile to her face and marked the turning point in her distress. The Veterans Administration informed her by mail the very next day that she would be entitled to pension benefits for the rest of her natural life because of her husband's demise, and to a burial allowance for him of $250. A government check for $250 was enclosed. Gradually, inexorably, her prospects brightened. A letter arrived that same week from the Social Security Administration stating that, under the provisions of the Old Age and Survivors Insurance Act of 1935, she would receive monthly support for herself and her dependent children until they reached the age of eighteen, and a burial allowance of $250. With these government letters as proof of death, she applied for payment on three life insurance policies Doc Daneeka had carried, with a value of $50,000 each; her claim was honored and processed swiftly. Each day brought new unexpected treasures. A key to a safe-deposit box led to a fourth life insurance policy with a face value of $50,000, and to $18,000 in cash on which income tax had never been paid and need never be paid. A fraternal lodge to which he had belonged gave her a cemetery plot. A second fraternal organization of which he had been a member sent her a burial allowance of $250. His county medical association gave her a burial allowance of $250.

The husbands of her closest friends began to flirt with her. Mrs Daneeka was simply delighted with the way things were turning out and had her hair dyed. Her fantastic wealth just kept piling up, and she had to remind herself daily that all the hundreds of thousands of dollars she was acquiring were not worth a single penny without her husband to share this good fortune with her. It astonished her that so many separate organizations were willing to do so much to bury Doc Daneeka, who, back in Pianosa, was having a terrible time trying to keep his head above the ground and wondered with dismal apprehension why his wife did not answer the letter he had written.

JOSEPH HELLER, *Catch-22*, 1962

'I wonder why rich people always grow fat—I suppose it's because there's nothing to worry them. If I inherit, I shall have to be careful of my figure,' she mused, while the lawyer droned on through a labyrinth of legacies. The servants came first, then a few charitable institutions, then several remoter Melsons and Stepneys, who stirred consciously as their names rang out, and then subsided into a state of impassiveness befitting the solemnity of the occasion. Ned Van Alstyne, Jack Stepney, and a cousin or two followed, each coupled with the mention of a few thousands: Lily wondered that Grace Stepney was not among them. Then she heard her own name—'to my niece Lily Bart ten thousand dollars—' and after that the lawyer again lost himself in a coil of unintelligible periods, from which the concluding phrase flashed out with startling distinctness: 'and the residue of my estate to my dear cousin and name-sake, Grace Julia Stepney'.

There was a subdued gasp of surprise, a rapid turning of heads, and a surging of sable figures toward the corner in which Miss Stepney wailed out her sense of unworthiness through the crumpled ball of a black-edged handkerchief.

Lily stood apart from the general movement, feeling herself for the first time utterly alone. No one looked at her, no one seemed aware of her presence; she was probing the very depths of insignificance. And under her sense of the collective indifference came the acuter pang of hopes deceived. Disinherited—she had been disinherited—and for Grace Stepney! She met Gerty's lamentable eyes, fixed on her in a despairing effort at consolation, and the look brought her to herself. There was something to be done before she left the house: to be done with all the nobility she knew how to put into such gestures. She advanced to the group about Miss Stepney, and holding out her hand said simply: 'Dear Grace, I am so glad.'

EDITH WHARTON, *The House of Mirth*, 1905

SHARP. The will is very short—being all personal property. He was a man that always came to the point.

SIR JOHN. I wish there were more like him!— [*Groans and shakes his head*
                                          [*Chorus groan and shake their heads*

SHARP [*reading*]. 'I, Frederick James Mordaunt, of Calcutta, being at the present date of sound mind, though infirm body, do hereby give, will, and bequeath—Imprimis, To my second cousin, Benjamin Stout, Esq., of Pall Mall, London—

                                          [*Chorus exhibit lively emotion*

Being the value of the Parliamentary Debates with which he has been pleased to trouble me for some time past—deducting the carriage thereof, which he always forgot to pay—the sum of 14l. 2s. 4d.'

                                          [*Chorus breathe more freely*

STOUT. Eh, what?—14l.? Oh, hang the old miser!

SIR JOHN. Decency—decency! Proceed, sir.

SHARP. 'Item.—To Sir Frederick Blount, Baronet, my nearest male relative—'
                                          [*Chorus exhibit lively emotion*

BLOUNT. Poor old boy!

                                          [GEORGINA *puts her arm over* BLOUNT'S *chair*

SHARP. 'Being, as I am informed, the best-dressed young gentleman in

London, and in testimony to the only merit I ever heard he possessed, the sum of 500*l.* to buy a dressing-case.'

[*Chorus breathe more freely;* GEORGINA *catches her father's eye and removes her arm*

BLOUNT [*laughing confusedly*]. Ha! ha! ha! Vewy poor wit—low!—vewy—vewy—low!

SIR JOHN. Silence, now, will you?

SHARP. 'Item.—To Charles Lord Glossmore—who asserts that he is my relation—my collection of dried butterflies, and the pedigree of the Mordaunts from the reign of King John.'

[*Chorus as before*

GLOSSMORE. Butterflies!—Pedigree!—I disown the plebeian!

SIR JOHN [*angrily*]. Upon my word, this is too revolting! Decency! Go on.

SHARP. 'Item.—To Sir John Vesey, Baronet, Knight of the Guelph, F.R.S., F.S.A., &c.'

[*Chorus as before*

SIR JOHN. Hush! *Now* it is really interesting!

SHARP. 'Who married my sister, and who sends me every year the Cheltenham waters, which nearly gave me my death, I bequeath—the empty bottles.'

SIR JOHN. Why, the ungrateful, rascally, old—

CHORUS. Decency, Sir John—decency!

SHARP. 'Item.—To Henry Graves, Esq. of the Albany—'

[*Chorus as before*

GRAVES. Pooh, gentlemen—my usual luck—not even a ring, I dare swear!

SHARP. 'The sum of 5000*l.* in the Three per Cents.'

LADY FRANKLIN. I wish you joy!

GRAVES. Joy—pooh! Three per Cents!—Funds sure to go! Had it been *land*, now—though only an acre!—just like my luck.

SHARP. 'Item,—To my niece Georgina Vesey—'

[*Chorus as before*

SIR JOHN. Ah, now it comes!

SHARP. 'The sum of 10,000*l.* India stock, being, with her father's reputed savings, as much as a single woman ought to possess.'

SIR JOHN. And what the devil, then, does the old fool do with all his money?

CHORUS. Really, Sir John, this is too revolting. Decency! Hush!

SHARP. 'And, with the aforesaid legacies and exceptions, I do will and bequeath the whole of my fortune, in India Stock, Bonds, Exchequer Bills, Three per Cent Consols, and in the Bank of Calcutta (constituting him hereby sole residuary legatee and joint executor with the aforesaid Henry

Graves, Esq.), to Alfred Evelyn, now or formerly of Trinity College, Cambridge—

[*Universal excitement*

Being, I am told, an oddity like myself—the only one of my relations who never fawned on me; and who, having known privation, may the better employ wealth.'—And now, Sir, I have only to wish you joy, and give you this letter from the deceased—I believe it is important.

EVELYN [*crossing over to* CLARA]. Ah, Clara, if you had but loved me!

CLARA [*turning away*]. And his wealth, even more than poverty, separates us for ever!

EDWARD, FIRST BARON LYTTON, *Money*, 1840

Mr Bennet had very often wished before this period of his life that, instead of spending his whole income, he had laid by an annual sum for the better provision of his children, and of his wife, if she survived him. He now wished it more than ever. Had he done his duty in that respect, Lydia need not have been indebted to her uncle for whatever of honour or credit could now be purchased for her. The satisfaction of prevailing on one of the most worthless young men in Great Britain to be her husband might then have rested in its proper place.

JANE AUSTEN, *Pride and Prejudice*, 1813

If some persons were to bestow the one half of their fortune in learning how to spend the other half, it would be money extremely well laid out. He that spends two fortunes, and permitting himself to be twice ruined, dies at last a beggar, deserves no commiseration. He has gained neither experience from trial, nor repentance from reprieve. He has been all his life abusing fortune, without enjoying her, and purchasing wisdom, without possessing her.

REVD C. C. COLTON, *Lacon; or, Many Things in Few Words*, 1823

According to the interpretation of French sociologists, the fiesta is an excess, an expense. By means of this squandering the community protects itself against the envy of the gods or of men. Sacrifices and offerings placate or buy off the gods and the patron saints. Wasting money and expending energy affirms the community's wealth in both. This luxury is a proof of health, a show of abundance and power. Or a magic trap. For squandering is an effort to attract abundance by contagion. Money calls to money. When life is thrown away it increases; the orgy, which is sexual expenditure, is also a ceremony of regeneration; waste gives strength. New Year celebrations, in every culture, signify something beyond the mere observance of a date on the calendar. The day is a pause: time is stopped, is actually annihilated. The rites that celebrate its death are intended to provoke its rebirth, because they mark not only the end of an old year but also the beginning of a new. Everything attracts its opposite. The fiesta's function, then, is more utilitarian than we think: waste attracts or promotes wealth, and is an investment like any other, except that the returns on it cannot be measured or counted. What is sought is potency, life, health. In this sense the fiesta, like the gift and the offering, is one of the most ancient of economic forms.

OCTAVIO PAZ, *The Labyrinth of Solitude*, 1959

The decline of paganism led to a decline of the games and cults for which wealthy Romans were obliged to pay; thus it has been said that Christianity individualized property, giving its possessor total control over his products, and abrogating his social function. It abrogated at least the obligation of this expenditure, for Christianity replaced pagan expenditure prescribed by custom with voluntary alms, either in the form of distributions from the rich to the poor, or (and above all) in the form of extremely significant contributions to churches and later to monasteries. And these churches and monasteries precisely assumed, in the Middle Ages, the major part of the spectacular function.

Today, the great and free forms of unproductive social expenditure have disappeared. One must not conclude from this, however, that the very principle of expenditure is no longer the end of economic activity. A certain evolution of wealth, whose symptoms indicate sickness and exhaustion, leads to shame in oneself accompanied by petty hypocrisy. Everything that was generous, orgiastic, and excessive has disappeared; the themes of rivalry that continue to condition individual activity develop in obscurity, and are as shameful as belching. The representatives of the bourgeoisie have adopted an effaced manner: wealth is now displayed behind closed doors, in accordance with depressing and boring conventions. In addition, the middle class—employees and small shopkeepers—having attained mediocre or minute fortunes, have managed to debase ostentatious expenditure, which has been subdivided, and of which nothing remains but vain efforts accompanied by tiresome rancor.

GEORGES BATAILLE, 'The Notion of Expenditure', 1933, tr. Allan Stoekl, 1984

So then I met quite a delightful English lady who had a very, very beautiful diamond tiara in her hand bag because she said that she thought some Americans would be at the party and it was really a very, very great bargain. I mean I think a diamond tiara is delightful because it is a place where I really never thought of wearing diamonds before, and I thought I had almost one of everything until I saw a diamond tiara. The English lady who is called Mrs Weeks said it was in her family for years but the good thing about diamonds is they always look new. So I was really very intreeged and I asked her how much it cost in money and it seems it was $7,500.

So then I looked around the room and I noticed a gentleman who seemed to be quite well groomed. So I asked Major Falcon who he was and he said he was called Sir Francis Beekman and it seems he is very, very wealthy. So then I asked Major Falcon to give us an introduction to one another and we met one another and I asked Sir Francis Beekman if he would hold my hat while I could try on the diamond tiara because I could wear it backwards with a ribbon, on account of my hair being bobbed, and I told Sir Francis Beekman that I really thought it looked quite cute. So he thought it did to, but he seemed to have another engagement. So the Countess came up to me and she is really very unrefined because she said to me 'Do not waste your time on him' because she said that whenever Sir Francis Beekman spent a haypenny the statue of a gentleman called Mr Nelson took off his hat and bowed. I mean some people are so unrefined they seem to have unrefined thoughts about everything.

So I really have my heart set on the diamond tiara and I became quite worried because Mrs Weeks said she was going to a delightful party last night that would be full of delightful Americans and it would be snaped up. So I was so worried that I gave her 100 dollars and she is going to hold the diamond tiara for me. Because what is the use of traveling if you do not take advantadge of oportunities and it really is quite unusual to get a bargain from an English lady. So last night I cabled Mr Eisman and I told Mr Eisman that he does not seem to know how much it costs to get educated by traveling and I said I really would have to have $10,000 and I said I hoped I would not have to borrow the money from some strange English gentleman, even if he might be very very good looking. So I really could not sleep all night because of all of my worrying because if I do not get the money to buy the diamond tiara it may be a quite hard thing to get back $100 from an English lady.

ANITA LOOS, Gentlemen Prefer Blondes, 1925

MR STATE. And remember, gentlemen, that the middle-class woman of England, as of America . . . think of her in bulk . . . is potentially the greatest money-spending machine in the world.

MR HUXTABLE [*with a wag of his head; he is more at his ease now*]. Yes . . . her husband's money.

HARLEY GRANVILLE-BARKER, The Madras House, 1911

### THE HARDSHIP OF ACCOUNTING

Never ask of money spent
Where the spender thinks it went.
Nobody was ever meant
To remember or invent
What he did with every cent.

ROBERT FROST, as 'Money', Poetry, April 1936; in A Further Range, 1936

I never thought money so desirable as it is usually imagined. If you would enjoy, you must transform it; and the transformation is frequently attended with inconvenience: you must bargain, purchase, pay dear, be badly served, and often duped. If I want anything, I wish to have it good of its kind; for money I am given what is bad. I ask for an egg, am assured it is new-laid—I find it stale; fruit in perfection—'tis absolutely green; a damsel—she has some defect. I love good wine, but where shall I get it? Not at my wine-merchant's—he will poison me of a certainty. I wish to be well treated; how shall I compass my design? I would make friends, send messages, write letters, come, go, wait, and in the end must be frequently deceived. Money is the perpetual source of uneasiness; I fear it more than I love good wine.

A thousand times, both during and since my apprenticeship, have I gone forth to purchase some delicacy. I approach the pastry-cook's, perceive some women at the counter, and imagine they are laughing at the little epicure. I pass a fruit-shop, see some fine pears, their appearance tempts me; but then two or three young people are near, a man I am acquainted with is standing at the door, a girl is approaching—perhaps our own servant;

I take all that pass for persons I have some knowledge of, and my near sight contributes to deceive me: I am everywhere intimidated, restrained by some obstacle, my desire grows with my hesitancy; and at length, with money in my pocket, I return as I went, for want of resolution to purchase what I long for.

JEAN-JACQUES ROUSSEAU (1712–78) *Confessions*, tr. anon., 1924

## VENDING MACHINE

he puts four dimes into the slot
he gets himself some cigarettes

he gets cancer
he gets apartheid
he gets the king of greece
federal tax state tax sales tax and excise
he gets machine guns and surplus value
free enterprise and positivism
he gets a big lift big business big girls
the big stick the great society the big bang
the big puke
king size extra size super size

he gets more and more
for his four dimes
but for a moment all the things he is getting himself
disappear

even the cigarettes

he looks at the vending machine
but he doesn't see it
he sees himself
for a fleeting moment
and he almost looks like a man

then very soon he is gone again
with a little click
there are his cigarettes

he has disappeared
it was just a fleeting moment
some kind of sudden bliss

he has disappeared
he is gone
buried under all the stuff he has gotten
for his four dimes

HANS MAGNUS ENZENSBERGER, *Selected Poems*, tr. the author, 1968


## AN EPISODE FOR SARAH

Can you rest longer in the night with me than alone

but of course not, I'll stay, smoke rises from the
bedroom chair

so passive that money speaks, my being no more than
unemployed for the season, teaches me my shortcoming

my guarantee; I promise to pay the bearer on demand

those fields of evidence the government taps for us
of revenue, up to the hilt, we're the credit society

now, I mustn't breathe at the neither here nor there

it is neither
here nor there, my lungs disturb you by rule of, of

nature, of nature, the funny careful rhetoric that

burns a hole in my trouser pocket slung on the chair.

JOHN WILKINSON, *Useful Reforms*, 1975


Every one, even the richest and most munificent of men, pays much by
cheque more light-heartedly than he pays little in specie.

MAX BEERBOHM, 'Hosts and Guests', 1918

On Monday, April 19, he called on me with Mrs Williams, in Mr Strahan's coach, and carried me out to dine with Mr Elphinston, at his academy at Kensington. A printer having acquired a fortune sufficient to keep his coach, was a good topick for the credit of literature. Mrs Williams said, that another printer, Mr Hamilton, had not waited so long as Mr Strahan, but had kept his coach several years sooner. JOHNSON. 'He was in the right. Life is short. The sooner that a man begins to enjoy his wealth the better.'

JAMES BOSWELL, Life of Samuel Johnson, 1791, 19 April 1773

Riches are for spending, and spending for honour and good actions. Therefore extraordinary expense must be limited by the worth of the occasion; for voluntary undoing may be as well for a man's country as for the kingdom of heaven. But ordinary expense ought to be limited by a man's estate; and governed with such regard, as it be within his compass; and not subject to deceit and abuse of servants; and ordered to the best shew, that the bills may be less than the estimation abroad. Certainly, if a man will keep but of even hand, his ordinary expenses ought to be but to the half of his receipts; and if he think to wax rich, but to the third part. It is no baseness for the greatest to descend and look into their own estate. Some forbear it, not upon negligence alone, but doubting to bring themselves into melancholy, in respect they shall find it broken. But wounds cannot be cured without searching. He that cannot look into his own estate at all, had need both choose well those whom he employeth, and change them often; for new are more timorous and less subtle. He that can look into his estate but seldom, it behoveth him to turn all to certainties.

FRANCIS BACON (1561–1626), 'Of Expense'

PETO. Falstaff!—Fast asleep behind the arras, and snorting like a horse.
PRINCE. Hark, how hard he fetches breath. Search his pockets.
                              [*He searcheth his pockets, and findeth certain papers*]
    What hast thou found?
PETO. Nothing but papers, my lord.
PRINCE. Let's see what they be: read them.

| PETO [*reads*]. | Item, A capon, | 2s. 2d. |
| | Item, Sauce, | 4d. |
| | Item, Sack, two gallons, | 5s. 8d. |
| | Item, Anchovies and sack after supper, | 2s. 6d. |
| | Item, Bread, | ob. |

PRINCE. O monstrous! but one half-pennyworth of bread to this intolerable deal of sack! What there is else, keep close; we'll read it at more advantage: there let him sleep till day. I'll to the court in the morning. We must all to the wars, and thy place shall be honourable. I'll procure this fat rogue a charge of foot; and I know his death will be a march of twelve-score. The money shall be paid back again with advantage.

WILLIAM SHAKESPEARE, *1 Henry IV*, 1597

Compile the budget for 16 June 1904.

| Debit | £. | s. | D. | Credit | £. | s. | D. |
|---|---|---|---|---|---|---|---|
| 1 Pork kidney | 0. | 0. | 3 | Cash in hand | 0. | 4. | 9 |
| 1 Copy *Freeman's* | | | | Commission recd. *Freeman's* | 1. | 7. | 6 |
|   *Journal* | 0. | 0. | 1 |   *Journal* | | | |
| 1 Bath and gratification | 0. | 1. | 6 | Loan (Stephen Dedalus) | 1. | 7. | 0 |
| Tramfare | 0. | 0. | 1 | | | | |
| 1 In Memoriam Patrick | | | | | | | |
|   Dignam | 0. | 5. | 0 | | | | |
| 2 Banbury cakes | 0. | 0. | 1 | | | | |
| 1 Lunch | 0. | 0. | 7 | | | | |
| 1 Renewal fee for book | 0. | 1. | 0 | | | | |
| 1 Packet notepaper and | | | | | | | |
|   envelopes | 0. | 0. | 2 | | | | |
| 1 Dinner and | | | | | | | |
|   gratification | 0. | 2. | 0 | | | | |
| 1 Postal order and | | | | | | | |
|   stamp | 0. | 2. | 8 | | | | |
| Tramfare | 0. | 0. | 1 | | | | |
| 1 Pig's Foot | 0. | 0. | 4 | | | | |
| 1 Sheep's Trotter | 0. | 0. | 3 | | | | |
| 1 Cake Fry's plain | | | | | | | |
|   chocolate | 0. | 0. | 1 | | | | |
| 1 Square soda bread | 0. | 0. | 4 | | | | |
| 1 Coffee and bun | 0. | 0. | 4 | | | | |
| Loan (Stephen | | | | | | | |
|   Dedalus) refunded | 1. | 7. | 0 | | | | |
| BALANCE | 0. | 17. | 5 | | | | |
| | £. 2. | 19. | 3 | | £. 2. | 19. | 3 |

JAMES JOYCE, *Ulysses*, 1922

The English Ambassador to Naples gave a charming reception but had not spent a great deal of money on it. This was known, and the guests went away to denigrate the festivities, which had been a great success to start with. The ambassador avenged himself in a manner that was at once thoroughly English, and that of a man to whom guineas meant very little. He announced another reception. Everyone thought that he was planning to make up for the other one and that the entertainment would be magnificent. Everyone went. A huge assembly. Nothing for them. Finally an alcohol stove was brought in. The guests expected some miracle. 'Sirs,' said their host, 'it is the expenses and not the pleasure of an entertainment that matter to you. Watch. (He opened his coat and showed the lining.) This is a sacred painting worth five thousand guineas. And that is not all. You see these ten bank notes. They are worth a thousand guineas each, payable on demand at the Bank of Amsterdam.' He rolled them up and put them in the lighted alcohol stove. 'I have no doubt, sirs, that this entertainment met with your entire approval, and that you will leave with a good opinion of me. Good-night, sirs; the entertainment is over.'

CHAMFORT (?1740–94), *Products of the Perfected Civilization*, tr. W. S. Merwin, 1984

But on the desk in front of him—that's not a manuscript or even the beginnings of one . . . that's *last month's bank statement*, which just arrived in the mail. And those are his canceled checks in a pile on top of it. In that big ledger-style checkbook there (the old-fashioned kind, serious-looking, with no crazy Peter Max designs on the checks) are his check stubs. And those slips of paper in the promiscuous heap are all unpaid bills, and he's taking the nylon cover off his Texas Instruments desk calculator, and he is about to measure the flow, the tide, the mad sluice, the crazy current of the money that pours through his fingers every month and which is now running against him in the most catastrophic manner, like an undertow, a riptide, pulling him under—

—him and this apartment, which cost him $75,000 in 1972; $20,000 cash, which came out of the $25,000 he got as a paperback advance for his fourth book, *Under Uncle's Thumb*, and $536.36 a month in bank-loan payments (on the $55,000 he borrowed) ever since, plus another $390 a month in so-called maintenance, which has steadily increased until it is now $460 a month . . . and although he already knows the answer, the round number, he begins punching the figures into the calculator . . . 536.36 plus . . . 460 . . . times 12 . . . and the calculator keys go *chuck chuck chuck chuck* and the curious little orange numbers, broken up like stencil figures, go trucking across the black path of the display panel at the top of the machine, giving a little orange shudder every time he hits the *plus* button, until there it is, stretching out seven digits long—11956.32—$12,000 a year! One thousand dollars a month—this is what he spends on his apartment alone!—and by May he will have to come up with another $6,000 so he can rent the house on Martha's Vineyard again *chuck chuck chuck chuck* and by September another $6,750—$3,750 to send his daughter, Amy, to Dalton and $3,000 to send his son, Jonathan, to Collegiate (on those marvelous frog-and-cricket evenings up on the Vineyard he and Bill and Julie and Scott and Henry and Herman and Leon and Shelly and the rest, all Media & Lit. people from New York, have discussed why they send their children to private schools, and they have pretty well decided that it is the educational turmoil in the New York public schools that is the problem—the kids just wouldn't be educated!— plus some considerations of their children's personal safety—but—needless to say!—it has nothing to do with the matter of . . . well, *race*) and he punches that in . . . 6750 . . . *chuck chuck chuck chuck* . . . and hits the *plus* button . . . an orange shimmer . . . and beautiful! there's the figure—the three items, the apartment in town, the summer place, and the children's schooling— $24,706.32!—almost $25,000 a year in fixed costs, just for a starter! for lodging and schooling! nothing else included! A grim nut!

It's appalling, and he's drowning, and this is only the beginning of it, just the basic grim nut—and yet in his secret heart he loves these little sessions with the calculator and the checks and the stubs and the bills and the marching orange numbers that stretch on and on . . . into such magnificently huge figures. It's like an electric diagram of his infinitely expanding life, a scoreboard showing the big league he's now in. Far from throwing him into a panic, as they well might, these tote sessions are one of the most satisfying habits he has. A regular vice! Like barbiturates!

TOM WOLFE, *Mauve Gloves and Madmen, Clutter and Vine*, 1976

'I was leading a wild life then. Father said just now that I spent several thousand roubles in seducing young girls. That's a swinish invention, and there was nothing of the sort. And if there was, I didn't need money simply for *that*. With me money is an accessory, the overflow of my heart, the framework.'

FYODOR DOSTOEVSKY, *The Brothers Karamazov*, 1879–80, tr. Constance Garnett, 1912

Humboldt put his hands on Sewell's small yellow desk and thrust himself back in the chair so that the steel casters gave a wicked squeak. The ends of his hair were confused with cigarette smoke. His head was lowered. He was examining me as if he had just surfaced from many fathoms.

'Have you got a checking account, Charlie? Where do you keep your money?'

'What money?'

'Haven't you got a checking account?'

'At Chase Manhattan. I've got about twelve bucks.'

'My bank is the Corn Exchange,' he said. 'Now, where's your checkbook?'

'In my trench coat.'

'Let's see.'

I brought out the flapping green blanks, curling at the edges. 'I see my balance is only eight,' I said.

Then Humboldt reaching into his plaid jacket brought out his own checkbook and unclipped one of his many pens. He was bandoliered with fountain pens and ball-points.

'What are you doing, Humboldt?'

'I'm giving you *carte blanche* power to draw on my account. I'm signing a blank check in your name. And you make one out to me. No date, no amount, just "Pay to Von Humboldt Fleisher." Sit down, Charlie, and fill it out.'

'But what's it about? I don't like this. I have to understand what's going on.'

'With eight bucks in the bank, what do you care?'

'It's not the money. . . .'

He was very moved, and he said, 'Exactly. It isn't. That's the whole point. If you're ever up against it, fill in any amount you need and cash it. The same applies to me. We'll take an oath as friends and brothers never to abuse this. To hold it for the worst emergency. When I said mutual aid you didn't take me seriously. Well, now you see.' Then he leaned on the desk in all his heaviness and in a tiny script he filled in my name with trembling force.

My control wasn't much better than his. My own arm seemed full of nerves and it jerked as I was signing. Then Humboldt, big delicate and stained, heaved himself up from his revolving chair and gave me the Corn Exchange check. 'No, don't just stick it in your pocket,' he said. 'I want to see you put it away. It's dangerous. I mean it's valuable.'

We now shook hands—all four hands. Humboldt said, 'This makes us blood-brothers. We've entered into a covenant. This is a covenant.'

A year later I had a Broadway hit and he filled in my blank check and cashed it. He said that I had betrayed him, that I, his blood-brother, had broken a sacred covenant, that I was conspiring with Kathleen, that I had set the cops on him, and that I had cheated him. They had lashed him in a strait jacket and locked him in Bellevue, and that was my doing, too. For this I had to be punished. He imposed a fine. He drew six thousand seven hundred and sixty-three dollars and fifty-eight cents from my account at Chase Manhattan.

As for the check he had given me, I put it in a drawer under some shirts. In a few weeks it disappeared and was never seen again.

SAUL BELLOW, *Humboldt's Gift*, 1975

### LETTER FROM YOUNG MAN REFUSING TO PAY HIS TAILOR'S BILL

Mr Eustace Davenant has received the half-servile, half-insolent screed which Mr Yardley has addressed to him. Let Mr Yardley cease from crawling on his knees and shaking his fist. Neither this posture nor this gesture can wring one bent farthing from the pockets of Mr Davenant, who was a minor at the time when that series of ill-made suits was supplied to him and will hereafter, as in the past, shout (without prejudice) from the house-tops that of all the tailors in London Mr Yardley is at once the most grasping and the least competent.

MAX BEERBOHM. 'How Shall I Word It?', 1910

It is only our Western societies that quite recently turned man into an economic animal. But we are not yet all animals of the same species. In both lower and upper classes pure irrational expenditure is in current practice: it is still characteristic of some French noble houses. *Homo oeconomicus* is not behind us, but before, like the moral man, the man of duty, the scientific man and the reasonable man. For a long time man was something quite different; and it is not so long now since he became a machine—a calculating machine.

In other respects we are still far from frigid utilitarian calculation. Make a thorough statistical analysis, as Halbwachs did for the working classes, of the consumption and expenditure of our middle classes and how many needs are found satisfied? How many desires are fulfilled that have utility as their end? Does not the rich man's expenditure on luxury, art, servants

and extravagances recall the expenditure of the nobleman of former times
or the savage chiefs whose customs we have been describing?

Marcel Mauss, *Essai sur le don, forme archaïque de l'exchange*, 1925; tr. as
*The Gift* by Ian Cunnison, 1954

'I am sorry to perceive, sir,' said Mr Rugg, 'that you have been allowing
your own feelings to be worked upon. Now, pray don't, pray don't. These
losses are much to be deplored, sir, but we must look 'em in the face.'

'If the money I have sacrificed had been all my own, Mr Rugg,' sighed
Clennam, 'I should have cared far less.'

'Indeed, sir?' said Mr Rugg, rubbing his hands with a cheerful air. 'You
surprise me. That's singular, sir. I have generally found, in my experience,
that it's their own money people are most particular about. I have seen
people get rid of a good deal of other people's money, and bear it very well:
very well indeed.'

Charles Dickens, *Little Dorrit*, 1855–7


PLAIN MONEY

To my father nursing a drink near midnight
as he stares at the wall and beyond drawn curtains
—Dad, what's out there in the darkness
where the gasworks was? A by-pass
abandoning your parish in its hollow,
tail lights streaming elsewhere. Do you know:
is it worse to be corrupted by too little
or too much? Where does money go?

Entrusted with an errand—you remember—
greedy for distant places, I had spent
mum's change on foreign stamps: meshed grilles
with padlocks and a brisk ringing till
shut tightly. Lying to evade repayment,
I said I'd dropped her money in the street
where, doubtless unbelieving, she had sent me
back into the dusk to find it.

Whatever was thus lost, I'd not recover
there on Bootle's pavements, eyes cast down;

yet framing stories, wandered over
far as Johnson's Dyeworks once again.
Not to return without it, this was plain—
I'd have to go back home and make repentance,
but passing outside the Pacific Hotel—saw
a pool of someone's sick dried on the floor—

which marked how near he'd reached towards its door.

PETER ROBINSON, This Other Life, 1988

Hovering somewhere between charity and a bribe, the tip is one of our most polymorphous social transactions. At its most crude it can be a loutish expression of authority and disdain. At its purest it can approach a statement of love. At one end of the scale we had the foul decorum of those old lunch places where the men thought it their right to pat the waitresses on the backside. If a waitress objected to these caresses the tip would be thrown into the dirty plate. And at the other end we have the elevated *snobisme* of Marcel Proust, for whom the tip was a profound and complex form of social expression. 'When he left,' writes Proust's biographer George Painter of one meal in the Paris Ritz, 'his pockets were empty, and all but one of the staff had been fantastically tipped. "Would you be so kind as to lend me fifty francs," he asked the doorman, who produced a wallet of banknotes with alacrity. "No, please keep it—it was for you"; and Proust repaid the debt with interest the next evening.'

Hanns Sachs who grew up in Vienna at the same time as his 'master and friend' Sigmund Freud wrote a memoir of life in that city in the late nineteenth century in which he devoted some testy pages to the growing complexities of *trinkgeld*, complexities which he took to be evidence of the decadence of the Austro-Hungarian Empire. Everybody had their hand out for prescribed portions of *trinkgeld*—the coachman, the doorman, the hatcheck girl, the waiter, the wine waiter, the headwaiter, the maître d'hôtel:

Every door which you had to pass was opened for you by someone who demanded a tip; you could not get into the house you lived in after 10 p.m. nor seat yourself in the car in which you wanted to ride without giving a tip. Karl Kraus, Vienna's witty satirist, said the first thing a Viennese would see on the day of Resurrection would be the outstretched hand of the man who opened the door of his coffin.

Doctor Sachs' indignant portrait is clearly reminiscent of today's taxi driver, doorman, hatcheck lady, waiter, and so forth, all of whom, from

Manhattan to San Francisco and from Chicago to Corpus Christi expect and usually receive similar *trinkgeld*. Is America therefore in decline? Visitors to the young republic found to their surprise that coachmen and waiters refused their tips. An organization called the Anti-tipping Society of America, founded in 1905, attracted some hundred thousand members, most of them traveling salesmen. But anti-tipping laws were declared unconstitutional in the same year that Congress passed the Volstead Act, and Americans entered the twenties buying bootleg liquor and tipping big.

Tipping is even bigger money now, with some five billion dollars per annum being left on plates, scrawled on credit cards, squirmed through taxi partitions, and slapped into outstretched palms. This is not so much an art as an item in the federal budget serious enough to provoke certain provisions in the Tax Equity and Fiscal Responsibility Act of 1982, designed to insure that the US Treasury gets its tip too.

That's the trouble. Tipping is a paradox: formal yet informal, public yet private, commercial yet intimate, voluntary yet in reality so close to compulsory that most people, across the years, have little difficulty in remembering the times they felt compelled to leave no tip at all. If tipping becomes an entirely mechanical act, beneath government supervision, it loses its vitality.

A tip must, however fleetingly, be the acknowledgement of a personal relationship, which is why the process can instill such panic in people plunged into a ceremony where much is uncertain and where only a special familiarity will teach one the proper mode. Due contemplation of the appropriate tip, in size and allocation, discloses not only what sort of place you are in but what sort of person you are: the sort who self-righteously calculates fifteen percent of the pre-tax total and gives fifty cents to the hatcheck girl, or the sort who bangs down a big tip with the vulgar flourish that says, 'There! I've bought you!', or again someone like Proust, who saw the tip as a perverse gift. At the conclusion of an excellently cooked but badly served meal at Bœuf sur le Toit, Proust (in Painter's words) ignored the person who served him so badly and 'Summoned a distant waiter and rewarded him regally. "But he didn't do anything for us," protested [Paul] Brach and Proust replied, "Oh, but I saw such a sad look in his eyes when he thought he wasn't going to get anything."'

The tip can become a bond between tipper and tippee, leagued in a transaction against absentee ownership. We tip waiters, doormen, hat ladies, taxi drivers, and hairdressers. We don't tip airline hostesses. Bank clerks, no; croupiers, yes. The modalities are complicated, ever-expanding. The service economy, exploding decade by decade, will affect the tipping process. Seen more darkly, this could mean two increasingly divergent classes, one rich and one poor, with the latter increasingly dependent on tips, gratuities, presents, and other pretty expressions of the master–servant relationship to get by. Tipping in America may therefore become an ever more complex and fraught affair, approaching the status of necessary alms-giving as for the well-heeled traveler in India.

It would be better, some argue, to give up tipping altogether, as they have tried in Eastern Europe and China. Tipping is, after all, about the relationship between served and servant and should play no part in a free society of equals. It depends on what one thinks the origin of tipping is. It can be traced to the primitive gift exchange, the amiable and generous distribution of surplus goods and cash which, in its most abandoned expression takes the form of the potlatch, where the surplus was either disposed of by common consumption or heaved over the side of a cliff. In a perfectly equal society everyone would exchange equivalent gifts—portions of the surplus. Everyone would tip and everyone be tipped in universal rhythms of generosity and gratitude. But, of course, modern society is not equal and the surplus wealth is unequally controlled and allocated, so the distribution of surplus wealth must always be an expression of power and of domination.

All this was understood perfectly by P. G. Wodehouse who approached the intricacies of the served–servant relationship more boisterously than Proust, but who expressed it with equal realism as in the scenes at the end of so many of the Wooster–Jeeves sagas, in this case *The Inimitable Jeeves*.

'Jeeves!' I said.
'Sir?'
'How much money is there on the dressing table?'
'In addition to the ten-pound note which you instructed me to take, sir, there are two five pound notes, three one-pounds, a ten shillings, two half crowns, a florin, four shillings, a six pence and a half penny, sir.'
'Collar it all,' I said. 'You've earned it.'

ALEXANDER COCKBURN, 'Tipping in America', 1986

The hotel scored heavily by the fact that there are twenty-four hours in the day and Kipps had nothing to do in any of them. He was a little footsore from his previous day's pedestrianism, and he could make up his mind for no long excursions. He flitted in and out of the hotel several times, and it was the polite porter who touched his hat every time that first set Kipps tipping.

'What *e* wants is a tip,' said Kipps.

So at the next opportunity he gave the man an unexpected shilling, and, having once put his hand in his pocket, there was no reason why he should not go on. He bought a newspaper at the bookstall and tipped the boy the rest of the shilling, and then went up by the lift and tipped the man six-pence, leaving his newspaper inadvertently in the lift. He met his chamber-maid in the passage and gave her half a crown. He resolved to demonstrate his position to the entire establishment in this way. He didn't like the place; he disapproved of it politically, socially, morally; but he resolved no taint of meanness should disfigure his sojourn in its luxurious halls. He went down by the lift (tipping again), and, being accosted by a waiter with his gibus, tipped the finder half a crown. He had a vague sense that he was making a flank movement upon the hotel and buying over its staff. They would regard him as a 'character'; they would get to like him. He found his stock of small silver diminishing and replenished it at a desk in the hall. He tipped a man in bottle green, who looked like the man who had shown him his room the day before; and then he saw a visitor eyeing him, and doubted whether he was in this instance doing right. Finally he went out and took chance buses to their destinations, and wandered a little in remote wonder-ful suburbs, and returned. He lunched at a chop-house in Islington, and found himself back in the Royal Grand, now unmistakably footsore and London-weary, about three. He was attracted to the drawing-room by a neat placard about afternoon tea.

It occurred to him that the campaign of tipping upon which he had embarked was, perhaps after all, a mistake. He was confirmed in this by observing that the hotel officials were watching him, not respectfully, but with a sort of amused wonder, as if to see whom he would tip next. How-ever, if he backed out now, they would think him an awful fool. Every one wasn't so rich as he was. It was his way to tip. Still—

He grew more certain the hotel had scored again.

H. G. Wells, *Kipps*, 1905

I may mention as an old anecdote that Mr Ord of London, son of Chief Baron Ord, made an apology to my patron, John Mackenzie of Delvin[e], that he did not ask me to dine with him so often as he would have done, from his grudging to make me give the vails [tips] then always given by the guests to the servants of their entertainer. That vile custom was abolished by the resentment of gentlemen at a most insolent opposition made by the party-coloured tribe to Garrick's farce of *High Life below Stairs*; it had been almost extinct in Scotland some time before.

Lord Stair, who was extravagantly generous in everything, gave large vails when he dined from home. He frequently had his brother along with him on a joint invitation to both. His brother could not afford to give vails that could figure at all with those of the Earl; but he followed him close at leaving the house where they dined and tickled the hand of the servant held out to receive the money. Lord Stair observed the smile of the servant occasioned by this novel sort of reward, and asked his brother how he contrived to please the servant so much. The brother told him the secret, but said that it would only succeed once; therefore he practised it only at houses in which he was not likely to dine again.

HENRY MACKENZIE (1745–1831), *Anecdotes and Egotisms*

Then went the Pharisees, and took counsel how they might entangle him in his talk.

And they sent out unto him their disciples with the Herodians, saying, Master, we know that thou art true, and teachest the way of God in truth, neither carest thou for any man; for thou regardest not the person of men.

Tell us therefore, What thinkest thou? Is it lawful to give tribute unto Cæsar, or not?

But Jesus perceived their wickedness, and said, Why tempt ye me, ye hypocrites?

Shew me the tribute money. And they brought unto him a penny.

And he saith unto them, Whose is this image and superscription?

They say unto him, Cæsar's. Then saith he unto them, Render therefore unto Cæsar the things which are Cæsar's: and unto God the things that are God's.

When they had heard *these words*, they marvelled, and left him, and went their way.

Matthew 22: 15–22

A BALLAD ON THE TAXES

Good people, what will you of all be bereft—
Will you never learn wit while a penny is left?
You are all like the dog in the fable betray'd,
To let go the substance and snatch at the shade;
With specious pretences, and Foreign expenses,
    We war for Religion, and waste all our chink,

'Tis nipt, and 'tis clipt, 'tis lent, and 'tis spent,
   Till 'tis gone, 'tis gone to the Devil I think.

We pay for our new-born, we pay for our dead,
We pay if we're single, we pay if we're wed;
To show that our merciful senate don't fail,
They begin at the head and tax down to the tail.
We pay through the nose by subjecting foes,
   Yet for all our expenses get nothing but blows;
At home we are cheated, abroad we're defeated,
   But the end on't, the end on't—the Lord above knows!

We parted with all our old money, to shew
We foolishly hope for a plenty of new;
But might have remember'd, when we came to the push,
That a bird in the hand is worth two in the bush:
We now like poor wretches are kept under hatches,
   At rack and at manger like beasts in the ark,
Since our burgesses and knights make us pay for our lights—
   Why should we, why should we be kept in the dark?

EDWARD WARD, 1696

The following extracts from John Evelyn's Diary not only represent the inconveniences which the English public suffered at this period from a defective coinage, but more than confirm the justice of Edward Ward's complaint of oppressive taxation in this ballad. 'June 11, 1696.—Want of current money to carry on the smallest concerns, even for daily provisions in the markets. Guineas lowered to twenty-two shillings, and great sums transported to Holland, where it yields more, with other treasure sent to pay the armies, and nothing considerable coined of the new and now only current stamp, cause such a scarcity that tumults are every day feared, nobody paying or receiving money; so imprudent was the late Parliament to condemn the old, though clipt and corrupted, till they had provided supplies.

'July 26.—So little money in the nation that exchequer tallies, of which I had for 200*l.* on the best fund in England, the Post-office, nobody would take at 30 per cent discount.

'Aug. 3.—The Bank lending the 200,000*l.* to pay the army in Flanders, that had done nothing against the enemy, had so exhausted the treasure of the nation, that one could not have borrowed money under 14 or 15 per cent on bills, or on exchequer tallies under 30 per cent.'

JOHN EVELYN, cited in *Political Ballads of the Seventeenth and Eighteenth Centuries*, ed. W. Walker Wilkins, 1860

Churchwardens, constables, and overseers
Make up the round of commons and of peers;
With learning just enough to sign a name,
And skill sufficient parish rates to frame,
And cunning deep enough the poor to cheat,
This learned body for debatings meet;
Their secretary is the parish clerk,
Whom like a shepherd's dog they keep to bark,
And gather rates, and, when the next are due,
To cry them o'er at church-time from his pew.
He as their Jack of all trades steady shines
Thro' thick and thin to sanction their designs,
Who apes the part of king and magistrate
And acts Grand Signior of this Turkish state,
Who votes new laws to those already made
And acts by force when one is disobeyed;
Having no credit which he fears to lose,
He does whatever dirty jobs they choose,
Tasking the pauper labourer to stand,
Or clapping on his goods the parish brand,
Lest he should sell them for the want of bread,
On parish bounty rather pined than fed;
Or carrying the parish book from door to door,
Claiming fresh taxes from the needy poor.
And if one's hunger overcomes his hate
And buys a loaf with what should pay the rate,
He instant sets his tyrant laws to work,
In heart and deed the essence of a Turk,
Brings summons for an eighteen-penny rate
And gains the praises of the parish state,
Or seizes goods and from the burthened clown
Extorts for extra trouble half a crown,
Himself a beggar that may shortly take
A weekly pittance from the rates they make.

But the old proverb suits the subject well:
Mount such on horseback and they'll ride to hell.

JOHN CLARE, 'The Parish: A Satire', 1820–4

He fell next upon the management of our treasury; and said, he thought
my memory had failed me, because I computed our taxes at about five or
six millions a year, and when I came to mention the issues, he found they
sometimes amounted to more than double; for the notes he had taken were
very particular in this point, because he hoped, as he told me, that the
knowledge of our conduct might be useful to him, and he could not be
deceived in his calculations. But, if what I told him were true, he was still
at a loss how a kingdom could run out of its estate like a private person.
He asked me, who were our creditors; and where we should find money
to pay them.

JONATHAN SWIFT, *Gulliver's Travels*, 1726

HENDERSON [*now that order has been restored*]. According to our records, Mr
   Vanderhof, you have never paid an income tax.
GRANDPA. That's right.
HENDERSON. Why not?
GRANDPA. I don't believe in it.
HENDERSON. Well—you own property, don't you?
GRANDPA. Yes, sir.
HENDERSON. And you receive a yearly income from it?
GRANDPA. I do.
HENDERSON. Of—[*he consults his records*]—between three and four thousand
   dollars.
GRANDPA. About that.
HENDERSON. You've been receiving it for years.
GRANDPA. I have. 1901, if you want the exact date.
HENDERSON. Well, the Government is only concerned from 1914 on. That's
   when the income tax started.
GRANDPA. Well?
HENDERSON. Well—it seems, Mr Vanderhof, that you owe the Government
   twenty-two years' back income tax.
ED. Wait a minute! You can't go back that far—that's outlawed.
HENDERSON [*calmly regarding him*]. What's *your* name?
ED. What difference does that make?

HENDERSON. Ever file an income tax return?

ED. No, sir.

HENDERSON. What was your income last year?

ED. Ah—twenty-eight dollars and fifty cents, wasn't it, Essie?

[ESSIE *gives quick assent; the income tax man dismisses the whole matter with an impatient wave of the hand and returns to bigger game*]

HENDERSON. Now, Mr Vanderhof, you know there's quite a penalty for not filing an income tax return.

PENNY. Penalty?

GRANDPA. Look, Mr Henderson, let me ask you something.

HENDERSON. Well?

GRANDPA. Suppose I pay you this money—mind you, I don't say I'm going to do it—but just for the sake of argument—what's the Government going to do with it?

HENDERSON. How do you mean?

GRANDPA. Well, what do I get for my money? If I go into Macy's and buy something, there it *is*—I see it. What's the Government give me?

HENDERSON. Why, the Government gives you everything. It protects you.

GRANDPA. What from?

HENDERSON. Well—invasion. Foreigners that might come over here and take everything you've got.

GRANDPA. Oh, I don't think they're going to do that.

HENDERSON. If you didn't pay an income tax, they would. How do you think the Government keeps up the Army and Navy? All those battleships . . .

GRANDPA. Last time we used battleships was in the Spanish–American War, and what did we get out of it? Cuba—and we gave that back. I wouldn't mind paying if it were something sensible.

HENDERSON [*beginning to get annoyed*]. Well, what about Congress, and the Supreme Court, and the President? We've got to pay *them*, don't we?

GRANDPA [*ever so calmly*]. Not with my money—no, sir.

HENDERSON [*furious*]. Now wait a minute! I'm not here to argue with you. All I know is that you haven't paid an income tax and you've got to pay it!

GRANDPA. They've got to show me.

HENDERSON [*yelling*]. We *don't* have to show you! I just told you! All those buildings down in Washington, and Interstate Commerce, and the Constitution!

GRANDPA. The Constitution was paid for long ago. And Interstate Commerce—what *is* Interstate Commerce, anyhow?

HENDERSON [*with murderous calm*]. There are forty-eight states—see? And if there weren't Interstate Commerce, nothing could go from one state to another. See?

GRANDPA. Why not? They got fences?

HENDERSON. No, they haven't got fences! They've got *laws*! . . . My God, I never came across anything like this before!

GRANDPA. Well, I might pay about seventy-five dollars, but that's all it's worth.

HENDERSON. You'll pay every cent of it, like everybody else!

GEORGE S. KAUFMAN and MOSS HART, *You Can't Take It with You*, 1936

*November* 21.—*O me miseram!* not one wink of sleep the whole night through! so great the 'rale mental agony in my own inside' at the thought of that horrid appealing. It was with feeling like the ghost of a dead dog, that I rose and dressed and drank my coffee, and then started for Kensington. Mr C. said 'the voice of honour seemed to call on him to go himself.' But either it did not call loud enough, or he would not listen to that charmer. I went in a cab, to save all my breath for appealing. Set down at 30 Hornton Street, I found a dirty private-like house, only with Tax Office painted on the door. A dirty woman-servant opened the door, and told me the Commissioners would not be there for half-an-hour, but I might walk up. . . . 'First-come lady,' called the clerk, opening a small side-door, and I stept forward into a *grand peut-être*. There was an instant of darkness while the one door was shut behind and the other opened in front; and there I stood in a dim room where three men sat round a large table spread with papers. One held a pen ready over an open ledger; another was taking snuff, and had taken still worse in his time, to judge by his shaky, clayed appearance. The third, who was plainly the cock of that dungheap, was sitting for Rhadamanthus—a Rhadamanthus without the justice. 'Name,' said the horned-owl-looking individual holding the pen. 'Carlyle.' 'What?' 'Car-lyle.' Seeing he still looked dubious, I spelt it for him. 'Ha!' cried Rhadamanthus, a big, bloodless-faced, insolent-looking fellow. 'What is this? why is Mr Carlyle not come himself? Didn't he get a letter ordering him to appear? Mr Carlyle wrote some nonsense about being exempted from coming, and I desired an answer to be sent that he must come, must do as other people.' 'Then, sir,' I said, 'your desire has been neglected, it would seem, my husband having received no such letter; and I was told by one of your fellow Commissioners that Mr Carlyle's personal appearance was not indispensable.' 'Huffgh! Huffgh! what does Mr Carlyle mean by saying he has no income from his writings, when he himself fixed it in the beginning at a hundred and fifty?' 'It means, sir, that, in ceasing to write, one ceases to be paid for writing, and Mr Carlyle has published nothing for several years.' 'Huffgh! Huffgh! I understand nothing about that.' 'I do,' whispered the snuff-taking Commissioner at my ear. 'I can quite understand a literary man does not always make money. I would take it off, for my share, but (sinking his voice still lower) I am only one voice here, and not the most important.' 'There,' said I, handing to Rhadamanthus Chapman and Hall's account; 'that will prove Mr Carlyle's statement.' 'What am I to make of that? Huffgh! we should have Mr Carlyle here to swear to this before we believe it.' 'If a gentleman's word of honour written at the bottom of that paper is not enough, you can put me on my oath: I am ready to swear to it.' 'You! you, indeed! No, no! we can do nothing with your oath.' 'But, sir, I understand my husband's affairs fully, better than he does himself.' 'That I can well believe; but we can make nothing of this,' flinging my document contemptuously on the table. The horned owl picked it up, glanced over it while Rhadamanthus was tossing papers about, and grumbling about 'people that wouldn't conform to rules;' then handed it back to him, saying deprecatingly: 'But, sir, this is a very plain statement.' 'Then what has Mr Carlyle to live upon? You don't mean to tell me he lives on that?' pointing to the document. 'Heaven forbid, sir! but I am not here to explain what Mr Carlyle has to live on, only to declare his income from literature during the last three years.' 'True! true!' mumbled the not-most-important voice at my elbow. 'Mr Carlyle, I believe, has landed income.' 'Of which,' said I haughtily, for my spirit was up, 'I have fortun- ately no account to render in this kingdom and to this board.' 'Take off fifty pounds, say a hundred—take off a hundred pounds,' said Rhadamanthus to the horned owl. 'If we write Mr Carlyle down a hundred and fifty he has no reason to complain, I think. There, you may go. Mr Carlyle has no reason to complain.' Second-come woman was already introduced, and I was motioned to the door; but I could not depart without saying that 'at all events there was no use in complaining, since they had the power to enforce their decision.' On stepping out, my first thought was, what a mercy Carlyle didn't come himself! For the rest, though it might have gone better, I was thankful that it had not gone worse. When one has been threatened with a great injustice, one accepts a smaller as a favour.

JANE WELSH CARLYLE, in James Anthony Froude (ed.), *Letters and Memorials of Jane Welsh Carlyle*, 1883

A corrupt and improvident loan, like everything else corrupt or prodigal, cannot be too much condemned: but there is a short-sighted parsimony still more fatal than an unforeseeing expense. The value of money must be judged like everything else from its rate at market. To force that market, or any market, is of all things the most dangerous. For a small temporary benefit, the spring of all public credit might be relaxed for ever. The monied men have a right to look to advantage in the investment of their property. To advance their money, they risk it; and the risk is to be included in the price. If they were to incur a loss, that loss would amount to a tax on that peculiar species of property. In effect, it would be the most unjust and impolitic of all things—unequal taxation. It would throw upon one description of persons in the community, that burden which ought by fair and equitable distribution to rest upon the whole. None on account of their dignity should be exempt; none (preserving due proportion) on account of the scantiness of their means. The moment a man is exempted from the maintenance of the community, he is in a sort separated from it. He loses the place of a citizen.

EDMUND BURKE, 'Letters on a Regicide Peace', 1797

This failure on the part of the authorities to explain to the delinquent citizen what his rights are in such situations or what measures of reprisal are being taken against him is one of the intolerable features of the despotic IRS system. I was informed for the first time at this interview that the quarterly income from a family trust fund had already been seized by the government. When I complained that I had not been notified of this, I was told that I had been warned, on a printed slip which was sent me in demand of the sum assessed, that if I did not produce this assessed amount, I was liable to liens on my property. I was, in any case, now ordered to present to this bureau an itemized monthly accounting of every cent of income I received and every cent I spent for living expenses. When I came for a second interview, after two months of such accounting, I was reprimanded for spending too much money on liquor, for taking my Italian translator to the theatre, and for having bought a $6 mat for my dog. I was told that since I myself 'had no place to lay my head,' I had no business to buy my dog a cushion, the implication being that I myself was allowed a bed only by the grudging leniency of the Internal Revenue Service. In the meantime, without any notification, all my remaining sources of income were shut off by either levy or lien. The IRS agents had looked up all the publishers and editors that I had listed in my tax returns, including several from whom I had received only trifling amounts and those several years ago. In the case of the levy, a tax agent would go into the editor's or publisher's office and demand to receive on the spot any money that might be due me; in the case of the lien, the agent would tell the publisher that he could not pay me anything but must hold any money due me until the lien was lifted. This kept me strapped for nearly a year.

EDMUND WILSON, *The Cold War and the Income Tax: A Protest,* 1963

# Coins and Paper

*Coins inspire words, notes inspire pages, and the reasons are not far to seek. Many writers have felt the romance of old bits of specie, and melancholic contemplation of the journeys they have taken through time has provided lyric poetry with one of its minor refrains. However, nostalgia is not the only emotion coins may prompt. One poet, W. B. Yeats, helped to design a new coinage for his nation. Another, Wallace Stevens, could admire the head of his wife whenever he picked up a so-called Mercury dime—Mrs Stevens (née Kachel) had modelled for its face.*

*On the whole, writers have looked rather more harshly on notes, and this is true even of those who were not directly involved (as, say, Peacock and Cobbett were) in the political scuffles which attended the introduction of a paper currency. In Faust, Goethe represents paper money as the invention of the Devil. But the lines are not sharply drawn: just as some writers have derided certain coins (Swift on Wood's halfpence, Orwell's Gordon Comstock on the 'Joey'), others have spoken forcibly for the worth of certain notes (Scott on the Scottish paper issue) or, like Umberto Eco, looked with an interested eye at their intricate and notionally forger-proof designs.*

❧

Coins handsome as Nero's; of good substance and weight. *Offa Rex* resonant in silver, and the names of his moneyers. They struck with accountable tact. They could alter the king's face.

Exactness of design was to deter imitation; mutilation if that failed. Exemplary metal, ripe for commerce. Value from a sparse people, scrapers of salt-pans and byres.

Swathed bodies in the long ditch; one eye upstaring. It is safe to presume,
   here, the king's anger. He reigned forty years. Seasons touched and
   retouched the soil.

Heathland, new-made watermeadow. Charlock, marsh-marigold. Crepitant
   oak forest where the boar furrowed black mould, his snout intimate
   with worms and leaves.

GEOFFREY HILL, *Mercian Hymns*, 1971

Now this doubloon was of purest, virgin gold, raked somewhere out of the
heart of gorgeous hills, whence, east and west, over golden sands, the head-
waters of many a Pactolus flows. And though now nailed amidst all the
rustiness of iron bolts and the verdigris of copper spikes, yet, untouchable
and immaculate to any foulness, it still preserved its Quito glow. Nor,
though placed amongst a ruthless crew and every hour passed by ruthless
hands, and through the livelong nights shrouded with thick darkness which
might cover any pilfering approach, nevertheless every sunrise found the
doubloon where the sunset left it last. For it was set apart and sanctified to
one awe-striking end; and however wanton in their sailor ways, one and all,
the mariners revered it as the white whale's talisman. Sometimes they talked
it over in the weary watch by night, wondering whose it was to be at last,
and whether he would ever live to spend it.

   Now those noble golden coins of South America are as medals of the sun
and tropic token-pieces. Here palms, alpacas, and volcanoes; sun's disks and
stars; ecliptics, horns-of-plenty, and rich banners waving, are in luxuriant
profusion stamped; so that the precious gold seems almost to derive an
added preciousness and enhancing glories, by passing through those fancy
mints, so Spanishly poetic.

   It so chanced that the doubloon of the Pequod was a most wealthy
example of these things. On its round border it bore the letters, REPUBLICA
DEL ECUADOR: QUITO. So this bright coin came from a country planted in the
middle of the world, and beneath the great equator, and named after it; and
it had been cast midway up the Andes, in the unwaning clime that knows
no autumn. Zoned by those letters you saw the likeness of three Andes'
summits; from one a flame; a tower on another; on the third a crowing
cock; while arching over all was a segment of the partitioned zodiac, the
signs all marked with their usual cabalistics, and the keystone sun entering
the equinoctial point at Libra.

Before this equatorial coin, Ahab, not unobserved by others, was now pausing.

HERMAN MELVILLE, *Moby-Dick*, 1851

## THE COIN SPEAKS

Singers sing for coin: but I,
Struck in Rome's last agony,
Shut the lips of Melody.

Many years my thin white face
Peered in every market-place
At the Doomed Imperial Race.

Warmed against and worn between
Hearts uncleansed and hands unclean,—
What is there I have not seen?

Not an Empire dazed and old,—
Smitten blind and stricken cold,—
Bartering her sons for gold;

Not the Plebs her rulers please
From the public treasuries
With the bread and circuses;

Not the hard-won fields restored,
At the egregious Senate's word,
To the savage and the sword;

Not the People's Godlike voice
As it welcomes or destroys
Month-old idols of its choice;

Not the legions they disband,
Not the oarless ships unmanned,
Not the ruin of the land,
*These I know and understand.*

[Kipling wrote this poem on the fly-leaf of Sir Charles Oman's copy of *Puck of Pook's Hill*, and dated it 'June 1907'. Oman, the historian, was also a distinguished numismatist]

RUDYARD KIPLING, 1907

As the most famous and beautiful coins are the coins of the Greek Colonies, especially of those in Sicily, we decided to send photographs of some of these, and one coin of Carthage, to our selected artists, and to ask them, as far as possible, to take them as a model. But the Greek coins had two advantages that ours could not have, one side need not balance the other, and either could be stamped in high relief, whereas ours must pitch and spin to please the gambler, and pack into rolls to please the banker.

We asked advice as to symbols, and were recommended by the public: round towers, wolf hounds, shamrocks, single or in wreaths, and the Treaty Stone of Limerick; and advised by the Society of Antiquaries to avoid patriotic emblems altogether, for even the shamrock emblem was not a hundred years old. We would have avoided them in any case, for we had to choose such forms as permit an artist to display all his capacity for design and expression, and as Ireland is the first modern State to design an entire coinage, not one coin now and another years later, as old dies wear out or the public changes its taste, it seemed best to give the coins some relation to one another. The most beautiful Greek coins are those that represent some god or goddess, as a boy or girl, or those that represent animals or some simple object like a wheat-ear. Those beautiful forms, when they are re-named Hibernia or Liberty, would grow empty and academic, and the wheat-ear had been adopted by several modern nations. If we decided upon birds and beasts, the artist, the experience of centuries has shown, might achieve a masterpiece, and might, or so it seemed to us, please those that would look longer at each coin than anybody else, artists and children. Besides, what better symbols could we find for this horse-riding, salmon-fishing, cattle-raising country?

W. B. YEATS, 'What We Did or Tried to Do', *Coinage of Saorstat Eireann*, 1928

I asked for a brandy. They gave me the Zahir in my change. I stared at it for a moment and went out into the street, perhaps with the beginnings of a fever. I reflected that every coin in the world is a symbol of those famous coins which glitter in history and fable. I thought of Charon's obol; of the obol for which Belisarius begged; of Judas' thirty coins; of the drachmas of

Laïs, the famous courtesan; of the ancient coin which one of the Seven Sleepers proffered; of the shining coins of the wizard in the 1001 Nights, that turned out to be bits of paper; of the inexhaustible penny of Isaac Laquedem; of the sixty thousand pieces of silver, one for each line of an epic, which Firdusi sent back to a king because they were not of gold; of the doubloon which Ahab nailed to the mast; of Leopold Bloom's irreversible florin; of the louis whose pictured face betrayed the fugitive Louis XVI near Varennes. As if in a dream, the thought that every piece of money entails such illustrious connotations as these, seemed to me of huge, though inexplicable, importance. My speed increased as I passed through the empty squares and along the empty streets. At length, weariness deposited me at a corner. I saw a patient iron grating and, beyond, the black and white flagstones of the Concepción. I had wandered in a circle and was now a block away from the store where they had given me the Zahir.

I turned back. The dark window told me from a distance that the shop was now closed. In Belgrano Street I took a cab. Sleepless, obsessed, almost happy, I reflected that there is nothing less material than money, since any coin whatsoever (let us say a coin worth twenty centavos) is, strictly speaking, a repertory of possible futures. Money is abstract, I repeated; money is the future tense. It can be an evening in the suburbs, or music by Brahms; it can be maps, or chess, or coffee; it can be the words of Epictetus teaching us to despise gold; it is a Proteus more versatile than the one on the isle of Pharos. It is unforeseeable time, Bergsonian time, not the rigid time of Islam or the Porch. The determinists deny that there is such a thing in the world as a single possible act, *id est* an act that could or could not happen; a coin symbolizes man's free will. (I did not suspect that these 'thoughts' were an artifice opposed to the Zahir and an initial form of its demoniacal influence.) I fell asleep after much brooding, but I dreamed that I was the coins guarded by a griffon.

JORGE LUIS BORGES, 'The Zahir', tr. Dudley Fitts, 1950

The first Gold that King Edw. III. coined was in the year 1343, and the pieces were called Florences, because Florentines were the coiners. Shortly after he coined Nobles, of noble, fair and fine gold, the penny of gold; afterward the Rose-Noble then currant for six shillings eight-pence, and which our Alchymists do affirm (as an unwritten verity) was made by projection or multiplication Alchymical of Raymund Lully, in the Tower of London, who would prove it as Alchymically, beside the tradition of the Rabbies in that faculty by the inscription; for as upon the one side there is the King's

Image in a Ship, to notifie that he was Lord of the Seas, with his titles, so upon the reverse, a cross floury with Lioneux, inscribed, 'Jesus autem transiens per medium eorum ibat.' Which they profoundly expound, as Jesus passed invisible and in most secret manner by the middest of Pharisees, so that gold was made by invisible and secret art amidst the ignorant. But others say, that Text was the only Amulet used in that credulous warfaring age to escape dangers in battles.

WILLIAM CAMDEN, *Remains Concerning Britain*, 1586

To make use of the liberty you give us, says Eugenius, I must tell you what I believe surprises all beginners as well as myself. We are apt to think your medallists a little fantastical in the different prices they set upon their coins, without any regard to the ancient value or the metal of which they are composed. A silver medal, for example, shall be more esteemed than a gold one, and a piece of brass than either. To answer you, says Philander, in the language of a medallist, you are not to look upon a cabinet of medals as a treasure of money, but of knowledge; nor must you fancy any charms in gold, but in the figures and inscriptions that adorn it. The intrinsic value of an old coin does not consist in its metal, but its erudition. It is the device that has raised the species, so that at present an *as* or an *obolus* may carry a higher price than a *denarius* or a *drachma*; and a piece of money that was not worth a penny fifteen hundred years ago, may be now rated at fifty crowns, or perhaps a hundred guineas. I find, says Cynthio, that to have a relish for ancient coins, it is necessary to have a contempt of the modern. But I am afraid you will never be able, with all your medallic eloquence, to persuade Eugenius and myself that it is better to have a pocket full of *Othos* and *Gordians* than of *Jacobuses* or *Louis d'ors*. This, however, we shall be judges of, when you have let us know the several uses of old coins.

JOSEPH ADDISON, *Dialogues upon the Usefulness of Ancient Medals*, *c*.1699–1703

I was last night visited by a friend of mine, who has an inexhaustible fund of discourse, and never fails to entertain his company with a variety of thoughts and hints that are altogether new and uncommon. Whether it were in complaisance to my way of living, or his real opinion, he advanced the following paradox, 'That it required much greater talents to fill up and become a retired life, than a life of business.' Upon this occasion he rallied very agreeably the busy men of the age, who only valued themselves for being in motion, and passing through a series of trifling and insignificant actions. In the heat of his discourse, seeing a piece of money lying on my table, I defy (says he) any of these active persons to produce half the adventures that this twelvepenny piece has been engaged in, were it possible for him to give us an account of his life.'

My friend's talk made so odd an impression upon my mind, that soon after I was a-bed I fell insensibly into a most unaccountable reverie, that had neither moral nor design in it, and cannot be so properly called a dream as a delirium.

Methoughts the shilling that lay upon the table reared itself upon its edge, and turning the face towards me, opened its mouth, and in a soft silver sound, gave me the following account of his life and adventures:

'I was born (says he) on the side of a mountain, near a little village of Peru, and made a voyage to England in an ingot, under the convoy of Sir Francis Drake. I was, soon after my arrival, taken out of my Indian habit, refined, naturalized, and put into the British mode, with the face of Queen Elizabeth on one side, and the arms of the country on the other. Being thus equipped, I found in me a wonderful inclination to ramble, and visit all parts of the new world into which I was brought. The people very much favoured my natural disposition, and shifted me so fast from hand to hand, that before I was five years old, I had travelled into almost every corner of the nation. But in the beginning of my sixth year, to my unspeakable grief, I fell into the hands of a miserable old fellow, who clapped me into an iron chest, where I found five hundred more of my own quality who lay under the same confinement. The only relief we had, was to be taken out and counted over in the fresh air every morning and evening. After an imprisonment of several years, we heard somebody knocking at our chest, and breaking it open with a hammer. This we found was the old man's heir, who, as his father lay a dying, was so good as to come to our release: he separated us that very day. What was the fate of my companions I know not: as for myself, I was sent to the apothecary's shop for a pint of sack. The apothecary gave me to an herb-woman, the herb-woman to a butcher, the butcher to a brewer, and the brewer to his wife, who made a present of me to a nonconformist preacher. After this manner I made my way merrily through the world; for, as I told you before, we shillings love nothing so much as travelling. I sometimes fetched in a shoulder of mutton, sometimes a play-book, and often had the satisfaction to treat a Templar at a twelvepenny ordinary, or carry him, with three friends, to Westminster Hall.

In the midst of this pleasant progress which I made from place to place, I was arrested by a superstitious old woman, who shut me up in a greasy purse, in pursuance of a foolish saying, "That while she kept a Queen Elizabeth's shilling about her, she should never be without money." I continued here a close prisoner for many months, till at last I was exchanged for eight and forty farthings.

I thus rambled from pocket to pocket till the beginning of the civil wars, when, to my shame be it spoken, I was employed in raising soldiers against the king: for being of a very tempting breadth, a sergeant made use of me to inveigle country fellows, and list them in the service of the parliament.

As soon as he had made one man sure, his way was to oblige him to take a shilling of a more homely figure, and then practise the same trick upon another. Thus I continued doing great mischief to the crown, till my officer, chancing one morning to walk abroad earlier than ordinary, sacrificed me to his pleasures, and made use of me to seduce a milk-maid. This wench bent me, and gave me to her sweetheart, applying more properly than she intended the usual form of, "To my love and from my love." This ungenerous gallant marrying her within a few days after, pawned me for a dram of brandy, and drinking me out next day, I was beaten flat with a hammer, and again set a running.

After many adventures, which it would be tedious to relate, I was sent to a young spendthrift, in company with the will of his deceased father. The young fellow, who I found was very extravagant, gave great demonstrations of joy at the receiving of the will: but opening it, he found himself disinherited and cut off from the possession of a fair estate, by virtue of my being made a present to him. This put him into such a passion, that after having taken me in his hand, and cursed me, he squirred me away from him as far as he could fling me. I chanced to light in an unfrequented place under a dead wall, where I lay undiscovered and useless, during the usurpation of Oliver Cromwell.

About a year after the king's return, a poor cavalier that was walking there about dinner-time, fortunately cast his eye upon me, and, to the great joy of us both, carried me to a cook's shop, where he dined upon me, and drank the king's health. When I came again into the world, I found that I had been happier in my retirement than I thought, having probably, by that means, escaped wearing a monstrous pair of breeches.[1]

Being now of great credit and antiquity, I was rather looked upon as a medal than an ordinary coin; for which reason a gamester laid hold of me, and converted me to a counter, having got together some dozens of us for that use. We led a melancholy life in his possession, being busy at those hours wherein current coin is at rest, and partaking the fate of our master, being in a few moments valued at a crown, a pound, or a sixpence, according

*Coins and Paper*

to the situation in which the fortune of the cards placed us. I had at length the good luck to see my master break, by which means I was again sent abroad under my primitive denomination of a shilling.

I shall pass over many other accidents of less moment, and hasten to that fatal catastrophe, when I fell into the hands of an artist, who conveyed me under ground, and with an unmerciful pair of shears, cut off my titles, clipped my brims, retrenched my shape, rubbed me to my inmost ring, and, in short, so spoiled and pillaged me, that he did not leave me worth a groat. You may think what a confusion I was in, to see myself thus curtailed and disfigured. I should have been ashamed to have shown my head, had not all my old acquaintance been reduced to the same shameful figure, excepting some few that were punched through the belly. In the midst of this general calamity, when everybody thought our misfortune irretrievable, and our case desperate, we were thrown into the furnace together, and (as it often happens with cities rising out of a fire) appeared with greater beauty and lustre than we could ever boast of before. What has happened to me since this change of sex which you now see, I shall take some other opportunity to relate. In the mean time, I shall only repeat two adventures, as being very extraordinary, and neither of them having ever happened to me above once in my life. The first was, being in a poet's pocket, who was so taken with the brightness and novelty of my appearance, that it gave occasion to the finest burlesque poem in the British language, entitled from me, "The Splendid Shilling." The second adventure, which I must not omit, happened to me in the year 1703, when I was given away in charity to a blind man; but indeed this was by a mistake, the person who gave me having heedlessly thrown me into the hat among a pennyworth of farthings.'

---

[1] See the note to 'The State's New Coin', pp. 119–20 below.

JOSEPH ADDISON, *Tatler*, 249, 11 November 1710.

The right to vote, in itself by no means negligible, was mysteriously connected with another right of such immense value to the daughters of educated men that almost every word in the dictionary has been changed by it, including the word 'influence'. You will not think these words exaggerated if we explain that they refer to the right to earn one's living.

That, Sir, was the right that was conferred upon us less than twenty years ago, in the year 1919, by an Act which unbarred the professions. The door of the private house was thrown open. In every purse there was, or might be, one bright new sixpence in whose light every thought, every sight, every action looked different. Twenty years is not, as time goes, a long time; nor is a sixpenny bit a very important coin; nor can we yet draw upon biography to supply us with a picture of the lives and minds of the new-sixpenny owners. But in imagination perhaps we can see the educated man's daughter, as she issues from the shadow of the private house, and stands on the bridge which lies between the old world and the new, and asks, as she twirls the sacred coin in her hand, 'What shall I do with it? What do I see with it?' Through that light we may guess everything she saw looked different—men and women, cars and churches. The moon even, scarred as it is in fact with forgotten craters, seemed to her a white six- pence, a chaste sixpence, an altar upon which she vowed never to side with the servile, the signers-on, since it was hers to do what she liked with—the sacred sixpence that she had earned with her own hands herself. And if checking imagination with prosaic good sense, you object that to depend upon a profession is only another form of slavery, you will admit from your own experience that to depend upon a profession is a less odious form of slavery than to depend upon a father. Recall the joy with which you re- ceived your first guinea for your first brief, and the deep breath of freedom that you drew when you realized that your days of dependence upon Arthur's Education Fund were over. From that guinea, as from one of the magic pellets to which children set fire and a tree rises, all that you most value— wife, children, home—and above all that influence which now enables you to influence other men, have sprung. What would that influence be if you were still drawing £40 a year from the family purse, and for any addition to that income were dependent even upon the most benevolent of fathers?

VIRGINIA WOOLF, *Three Guineas*, 1938

## A COIN

I think of a coin I bought once
And gave away, not knowing how I valued it,
A greening copper relic of the Kushans;

Stamped on one side
The figure of a trousered king beside an altar;

On the other the God of the Wind
Leapt forward, bearded and naked, his cloak
Looped out in circles around him and behind—

The type of an energy
Which must run wild to bring itself to shape.

ROBERT WELLS, Selected Poems, 1986

### BYZANTINE COIN

How many hands, vicissitudes,
Have worn this gold to the thin ghost
That gleams in the shopkeeper's palm?
A millennium flickers, eludes
Us, is gone, as we bend engrossed
In blurred words and a surface charm.

DICK DAVIS, In the Distance, 1975

There are many things to be said on coined money; as on the unjust and
ridiculous augmentation of specie, which suddenly loses considerable sums
to a state on the melting down again; on the re-stamping, with an augmentation of ideal value, which augmentation invites all your neighbors and all
your enemies to re-coin your money and gain at your expense; in short, on
twenty other equally ruinous expedients.

VOLTAIRE (1694–1778), Philosophical Dictionary

It was a strange collection, like Billy Bones's hoard for the diversity of
coinage, but so much larger and so much more varied that I think I never
had more pleasure than in sorting them. English, French, Spanish, Portu-
guese, Georges, and Louises, doubloons and double guineas and moidores
and sequins, the pictures of all the kings of Europe for the last hundred
years, strange Oriental pieces stamped with what looked like wisps of string
or bits of spider's web, round pieces and square pieces, and pieces bored
through the middle, as if to wear them round your neck—nearly every
variety of money in the world must, I think, have found a place in that
collection; and for number, I am sure they were like autumn leaves, so that
my back ached with stooping and my fingers with sorting them out.

ROBERT LOUIS STEVENSON, Treasure Island, 1883

Money can become a crowd symbol, and, in certain circumstances, the
units of which it is composed may accumulate to form a crowd. But, in

contrast to the other crowd symbols I have discussed, the individuality of its units is always emphatically stressed. Each coin has a clear and firm edge and its own specific weight. It can be recognized at a glance and passes freely from hand to hand, continually changing its surroundings. Often it has the head of a ruler stamped on it, from whom, especially when it is a valuable coin, it will take its name; there have been Louis d'or and Maria Theresa thalers. People like imagining a coin as an individual. The hand closes round it, feeling its planes and edges as a whole. A tenderness for the coin which can do so much for them is universal amongst men, and part of its 'character'. In one respect the coin is superior to a living creature. Being made of metal, its hardness secures 'eternal' existence for it; except by fire, it can scarcely be destroyed at all. A coin does not attain its size through growth; it issues ready-made from the mint and should remain as it then is; it should never change.

Reliability is perhaps the most important attribute of coins. All the owner has to do is to guard them well from other people; they do not run away of their own accord like animals. They need not be watched; a use can always be found for them; and they have no moods to be considered. The status of each coin is further consolidated by its relation to other coins of different values. Their strict hierarchy makes them even more like people. One could speak of the social system of coins, the classes here being classes of value. A higher coin can always be exchanged for a lower, but never a lower for a higher.

Among most peoples a heap of coins has always been known as *treasure*, and treasure, as we saw, is a crowd symbol. It is felt to be a unit; one can come on it without knowing exactly how much it really contains; one can rummage in it and separate coin from coin; it is always expected to be larger than it is; and it is often hidden away, to come suddenly to light. But it is not only the man who cherishes life-long hopes of finding treasure who expects it to be greater than it is. The man who is in process of amassing it imagines it as continually growing and does everything in his power to promote this. It is certainly true that, with many men who live for their money alone, treasure takes the place of the human crowd. This is exemplified in the many stories of lonely misers. They are the successors of the mythical monsters who existed solely to guard, watch and cherish some treasure.

It may be objected that this connection between coins and treasure no longer holds for modern man; that paper money is in use everywhere; that the rich now keep their treasure in banks in an abstract and invisible form. But the importance of a gold reserve for a strong currency and the fact that there are still actual gold currencies to be found, prove that treasure has by no means entirely lost its old importance. The great majority of men, even in countries which are highly developed technically, are still paid for their work by the hour and, almost everywhere, the size of their wage still comes within the range imagined as covered by coins. Coins are still received as change for paper money, and the old feeling for them, the old attitude, is still familiar to everyone. Getting change is a daily part of the simplest and commonest processes of living, something which every child learns as early as possible.

ELIAS CANETTI, 'Inflation and the Crowd', *Crowds and Power*, 1960, tr. Carol Stewart, 1962

'Well, child,' said she, taking heart at sight of a personage so little formidable,—'well, my child, what did you wish for?'

'That Jim Crow there in the window,' answered the urchin, holding out a cent, and pointing to the gingerbread figure that had attracted his notice, as he loitered along to school; 'the one that has not a broken foot.'

So Hepzibah put forth her lank arm, and, taking the effigy from the shop-window, delivered it to her first customer.

'No matter for the money,' said she, giving him a little push towards the door; for her old gentility was contumaciously squeamish at sight of the copper coin, and, besides, it seemed such pitiful meanness to take the child's pocket-money in exchange for a bit of stale gingerbread. 'No matter for the cent. You are welcome to Jim Crow.'

The child, staring with round eyes at this instance of liberality, wholly unprecedented in his large experience of cent-shops, took the man of gingerbread, and quitted the premises. No sooner had he reached the sidewalk (little cannibal that he was!) than Jim Crow's head was in his mouth. As he had not been careful to shut the door, Hepzibah was at the pains of closing it after him, with a pettish ejaculation or two about the troublesomeness of young people, and particularly of small boys. She had just placed another representative of the renowned Jim Crow at the window, when again the shop-bell tinkled clamorously, and again the door being thrust open, with its characteristic jerk and jar, disclosed the same sturdy little urchin who, precisely two minutes ago, had made his exit. The crumbs and discoloration of the cannibal feast, as yet hardly consummated, were exceedingly visible about his mouth.

'What is it now, child?' asked the maiden lady rather impatiently; 'did you come back to shut the door?'

'No,' answered the urchin, pointing to the figure that had just been put up; 'I want that other Jim Crow.'

'Well, here it is for you,' said Hepzibah, reaching it down; but recognizing that this pertinacious customer would not quit her on any other terms, so long as she had a gingerbread figure in her shop, she partly drew back her extended hand, 'Where is the cent?'

The little boy had the cent ready, but, like a true-born Yankee, would have preferred the better bargain to the worse. Looking somewhat chagrined, he put the coin into Hepzibah's hand, and departed, sending the second Jim Crow in quest of the former one. The new shopkeeper dropped the first solid result of her commercial enterprise into the till. It was done! The sordid stain of that copper coin could never be washed away from her palm. The little school-boy, aided by the impish figure of the negro dancer, had wrought an irreparable ruin. The structure of ancient aristocracy had been demolished by him, even as if his childish gripe had torn down the seven-gabled mansion. Now let Hepzibah turn the old Pyncheon portraits with their faces to the wall, and take the map of her Eastern territory to kindle the kitchen fire, and blow up the flame with the empty breath of her ancestral traditions! What had she to do with ancestry? Nothing; no more than with posterity! No lady, now, but simply Hepzibah Pyncheon, a forlorn old maid, and keeper of a cent-shop!

NATHANIEL HAWTHORNE, The House of the Seven Gables, 1851

. . . . . . . . . . .

poor pile of coins, original reminders of the sadness, forgotten money of America—
nostalgia of the first touch of those coins, American change,
the memory in my aging hand, the same old silver reflective there,
the thin dime hidden between my thumb and forefinger
All the struggles for those coins, the sadness of their reappearance
my reappearance on those fabled shores
and the failure of that Dream, that Vision of Money reduced to this haunting recollection
of the gas lot in Paterson where I found half a dollar gleaming in the grass—

I have a $5 bill in my pocket—it's Lincoln's sour black head moled wrinkled, forelocked too, big eared, flags of announcement flying over the bill, stamps in green and spiderweb black,
long numbers in racetrack green, immense promise, a girl, a hotel, a

busride to Albany, a night of brilliant drunk in some faraway corner of Manhattan

a stick of several teas, or paper or cap of Heroin, or a $5 strange present to the blind.

Money money, reminder, I might as well write poems to you—dear American money—O statue of Liberty I ride enfolded in money in my mind to you—and last


Ahhh! Washington again, on the Dollar, same poetic black print, dark words, The United States of America, innumerable numbers

R956422481 One Dollar This Certificate is Legal Tender (tender!) for all debts public and private

My God My God why have you forsaken me

Ivy Baker Priest Series 1953 F

and over, the Eagle, wild wings outspread, halo of the Stars encircled by puffs of smoke & flame—

a circle the Masonic Pyramid, the sacred Swedenborgian Dollar America, bricked up to the top, & floating surreal above

the triangle of holy outstaring Eye sectioned out of the aire, shining

light emitted from the eyebrowless triangle—and a desert of cactus, scattered all around, clouds afar,

this being the Great Seal of our Passion, Annuit Coeptis, Novus Ordo Seclorum,

the whole surrounded by green spiderwebs designed by T-Men to prevent foul counterfeit—

ONE

*S.S. United States, July 1958*

ALLEN GINSBERG, from 'American Change', 1958


The King had no use for gold. Gold was the currency of his enemy, the King of Ashanti, whereas Dahomey used cowrie-shells that could neither be faked nor adulterated.

But the Cubans and Yankees who came to buy slaves in Ouidah always preferred to pay in gold: ingots, doubloons, louis d'or, napoleons, sovereigns and sometimes the coins of the Great Moghul. Dom Francisco kept his hoard in money barrels buried under the bedroom floor: it alarmed him terribly when the King commanded one of them to be taken up to Abomey.

The King peered at the coins, one after the other, and let them slide through his fingers. He learned the names of Louis Philippe, the Elector of

Brandenburg, Tsar Paul and the young Queen Victoria. Then he rolled his
eyes and threw the lot to the ground, snorting, 'I wouldn't let anyone walk
off with my head,' and never spoke of gold again.

BRUCE CHATWIN, *The Viceroy of Ouidah*, 1980


## MONEY

### *an introductory lecture*

This morning we shall spend a few minutes
Upon the study of symbolism, which is basic
To the nature of money. I show you this nickel.
Icons and cryptograms are written all over
The nickel: one side shows a hunchbacked bison
Bending his head and curling his tail to accommodate
The circular nature of money. Over him arches
UNITED STATES OF AMERICA, and, squinched in
Between that and his rump, E PLURIBUS UNUM,
A Roman reminiscence that appears to mean
An indeterminately large number of things
All of which are the same. Under the bison
A straight line giving him a ground to stand on
Reads FIVE CENTS. And on the other side of our nickel
There is the profile of a man with long hair
And a couple of feathers in the hair; we know
Somehow that he is an American Indian, and
He wears the number nineteen-thirty-six.
Right in front of his eyes the word LIBERTY, bent
To conform with the curve of the rim, appears
To be falling out of the sky Y first; the Indian
Keeps his eyes downcast and does not notice this;
To notice it, indeed, would be shortsighted of him.
So much for the iconography of one of our nickels,
Which is now becoming a rarity and something of
A collectors' item: for as a matter of fact
There is almost nothing you can buy with a nickel,
The representative American Indian was destroyed
A hundred years or so ago, and his descendants'
Relations with liberty are maintained with reservations,
Or primitive concentration camps; while the bison,

Except for a few examples kept in cages,
Is now extinct. Something like that, I think,
Is what Keats must have meant in his celebrated
Ode on a Grecian Urn.
                                    Notice, in conclusion,
A number of circumstances sometimes overlooked
Even by experts: (*a*) Indian and bison,
Confined to obverse and reverse of the coin,
Can never seen each other; (*b*) they are looking
In opposite directions, the bison past
The Indian's feathers, the Indian past
The bison's tail; (*c*) they are upside down
To one another; (*d*) the bison has a human face
Somewhat resembling that of Jupiter Ammon.
I hope that our studies today will have shown you
Something of the import of symbolism
With respect to the understanding of what is symbolized.

HOWARD NEMEROV, *The Blue Swallows*, 1967


## [From] GOLD HAIR

### *A Story of Pornic*

'Not my hair!' made the girl her moan—
    'All the rest is gone or to go;
But the last, last grace, my all, my own,
    Let it stay in the grave, that the ghosts may know!
Leave my poor gold hair alone!'

The passion thus vented, dead lay she;
    Her parents sobbed their worst on that;
All friends joined in, nor observed degree:
    For indeed the hair was to wonder at,
As it spread—not flowing free,

But curled around her brow, like a crown,
    And coiled beside her cheeks, like a cap,
And calmed about her neck—ay, down
    To her breast, pressed flat, without a gap
I' the gold, it reached her gown.

All kissed that face, like a silver wedge
   'Mid the yellow wealth, nor disturbed its hair:
E'en the priest allowed death's privilege,
   As he planted the crucifix with care
On her breast, 'twixt edge and edge.

And thus was she buried, inviolate
   Of body and soul, in the very space
By the altar; keeping saintly state
   In Pornic church, for her pride of race,
Pure life and piteous fate.

And in after-time would your fresh tear fall,
   Though your mouth might twitch with a dubious smile,
As they told you of gold, both robe and pall,
   How she prayed them leave it alone awhile,
So it never was touched at all.

Years flew; this legend grew at last
   The life of the lady; all she had done,
All been, in the memories fading fast
   Of lover and friend, was summed in one
Sentence survivors passed:

To wit, she was meant for heaven, not earth;
   Had turned an angel before the time:
Yet, since she was mortal, in such dearth
   Of frailty, all you could count a crime
Was—she knew her gold hair's worth.

At little pleasant Pornic church,
   It chanced, the pavement wanted repair,
Was taken to pieces: left in the lurch,
   A certain sacred space lay bare,
And the boys began research.

'T was the space where our sires would lay a saint,
   A benefactor,—a bishop, suppose,
A baron with armour-adornments quaint,
   Dame with chased ring and jewelled rose,
Things sanctity saves from taint;

So we come to find them in after-days
  When the corpse is presumed to have done with gauds
Of use to the living, in many ways:
  For the boys get pelf, and the town applauds,
And the church deserves the praise.

They grubbed with a will: and at length—*O cor*
    *Humanum, pectora cæca,* and the rest!—
They found—no gaud they were prying for,
  No ring, no rose, but—who would have guessed?—
A double Louis-d'or!

Here was a case for the priest: he heard,
  Marked, inwardly digested, laid
Finger on nose, smiled, 'There's a bird
  Chirps in my ear': then, 'Bring a spade,
Dig deeper!' —he gave the word.

And lo, when they came to the coffin-lid,
  Or rotten planks which composed it once,
Why, there lay the girl's skull wedged amid
  A mint of money, it served for the nonce
To hold in its hair-heaps hid!

Hid there? Why? Could the girl be wont
  (She the stainless soul) to treasure up
Money, earth's trash and heaven's affront?
  Had a spider found out the communion-cup,
Was a toad in the christening-font?

Truth is truth: too true it was.
  Gold! She hoarded and hugged it first,
Longed for it, leaned o'er it, loved it—alas—
  Till the humour grew to a head and burst,
And she cried, at the final pass,—

'Talk not of God, my heart is stone!
  Nor lover nor friend—be gold for both!

*O cor . . . cæca*] O human heart, blind breasts

Gold I lack; and, my all, my own,
   It shall hide in my hair. I scarce die loth
If they let my hair alone!'

Louis-d'or, some six times five,
   And duly double, every piece.
Now do you see? With the priest to shrive,
   With parents preventing her soul's release
By kisses that kept alive,—

With heaven's gold gates about to ope,
   With friends' praise, gold-like, lingering still,
An instinct had bidden the girl's hand grope
   For gold, the true sort—'Gold in heaven, if you will;
But I keep earth's too, I hope.'

Enough! The priest took the grave's grim yield:
   The parents, they eyed that price of sin
As if *thirty pieces* lay revealed
   On the place *to bury strangers in*,
The hideous Potter's Field.

But the priest bethought him: ' "Milk that's spilt"
   —You know the adage! Watch and pray!
Saints tumble to earth with so slight a tilt!
   It would build a new altar; that, we may!'
And the altar therewith was built.

ROBERT BROWNING, *Dramatis personae*, 1864

The money clinked in his trouser pocket as he got up. He knew the precise sum that was there. Fivepence halfpenny—twopence halfpenny and a Joey. He paused, took out the miserable little threepenny-bit, and looked at it. Beastly, useless thing! And bloody fool to have taken it! It had happened yesterday, when he was buying cigarettes. 'Don't mind a threepenny-bit, do you, sir?' the little bitch of a shop-girl had chirped. And of course he had let her give it him. 'Oh no, not at all!' he had said—fool, bloody fool!

His heart sickened to think that he had only fivepence halfpenny in the world, threepence of which couldn't even be spent. Because how can you buy anything with a threepenny-bit? It isn't a coin, it's the answer to a riddle. You look such a fool when you take it out of your pocket, unless it's in among a whole handful of other coins. 'How much?' you say. 'Threepence,' the shop-girl says. And then you feel all round your pocket and fish out that absurd little thing, all by itself, sticking on the end of your finger like a tiddley-wink. The shop-girl sniffs. She spots immediately that it's your last threepence in the world. You see her glance quickly at it—she's wondering whether there's a piece of Christmas pudding still sticking to it. And you stalk out with your nose in the air, and can't ever go to that shop again. No! We won't spend our Joey. Twopence halfpenny left—twopence halfpenny to last till Friday.

GEORGE ORWELL, Keep the Aspidistra Flying, 1936

As a rule, there is nothing that offends us more than a new kind of money. We felt humiliated in the early days of the war when we were no longer paid in heavy little discs of gold, and had to accept paper pounds and tenshillingses. We even sneered at the design. We always sneer at the design of new money or a new stamp. But we hated the paper even more than the design. We could not believe it had any value. We spent it as though it were paper. One would as soon have thought of collecting old newspapers as of playing the miser with it. That is probably the true-secret of the fall in the value of money. Economists explain it in other ways. But it seems likeliest that paper money lost its value because we did not value it. Shopkeepers took advantage of our foolish innocence, and the tailor demanded sums in paper that he would never have dared to ask in gold. I doubt if the habit of thrift will ever be restored till the gold currency comes back. Gold is the only metal for which human beings have any lasting respect. No one but a child would save up pennies. There is something in gold—the colour, perhaps, reminding us of the sun, the god of our ancestors—that puts us into the mood of worshippers. The children of Israel found it impossible not to worship the golden calf. They have gone on worshipping it ever since. Had the calf been of paper, they would, I feel confident, have remained good Christians.

The influence of hatred on the expenditure of money is seen in our attitude to threepenny bits. Nine out of ten people feel sincerely indignant when a threepenny bit is given to them in their change. The shopkeeper who gives you two threepenny bits instead of a sixpence knows this and, as he hands you the money, says apologetically: 'Do you mind?' You say: 'Not at all,' but you do. You know that they will be a constant misery to you till you get rid of them. You know that if you give one of them to a bus conductor, even if he is able to restrain himself, he will feel like throwing you off the top of the bus. When at length you spend one of them in a post office—one never has the same scruples about Government institutions—you hurry out with a guilty air, not having dared to look the lady at the counter in the eye. In the nineteenth century, when people went to church, they used to get rid of their threepenny bits at the collection. They at once relieved themselves of a nuisance, and enjoyed the luxury of flinging the gleam of silver on to the plate. Many a good Baptist has trusted to his threepenny bits being mistaken for a sixpence, by the neighbours, at least—perhaps even by Heaven. He has a notion that the widow's mite was a threepenny bit, and feels that his gift is in a great tradition.

ROBERT LYND, 'The Three-Halfpenny Bit', *The Pleasures of Ignorance*, 1930

Before the shameful liquidation of the British penny into a p, there had been an ancient and eminently rational coinage, with twelve pence to the shilling and twenty shillings to the pound. This meant divisibility of the major unit by all the even integers up to twelve. Time and money went together: only in Fritz Lang's *Metropolis* is there a ten-hour clock. Money could be divided according to time, and for the seven-day week it was necessary merely to add a shilling to a pound and create a guinea. A guinea was not only divisible by seven: it could be split ninefold and produce a Straits dollar. By brutal government fiat, at a time when computer engineers were protesting that the decimal system was out of date and that the octal principle was the only valid one for cybernetics, this beautiful and venerable monetary complex was abolished in favour of a demented abstraction that was a remnant of the French revolutionary nightmare. The first unit to go was the half-crown or tosheroon, the loveliest and most rational coin of all. It was a piece of eight, a genuine dollar though termed a half one (the dollar sign was originally an eight with a bar through it). It does not even survive as an American bit or an East Coast Malayan *kupang*. Britain's troubles began with this jettisoning of a traditional solidity, rendering Falstaff's tavern bill and 'Sing a song of sixpence' unintelligible. I have never been able to forgive this.

ANTHONY BURGESS, *You've Had your Time*, 1990

## THE STATE'S NEW COIN

[Shortly after the abrogation of the monarchy, the Parliament issued a new coinage. It consisted of pieces having on the obverse a shield with St George's cross, encircled by a laurel and palm branch, surrounding the simple inscription 'The Commonwealth of England.' On the reverse was the equally simple legend 'God with us,' and two shields bearing the arms of England and Ireland. The shields being conjoined at top were at once declared to resemble the breeches of the Rump; a declaration which continued to be a standing joke with the Cavaliers during the times of the Commonwealth, and with others long after the restoration of the monarchy. The other absurdities so ingeniously fitted to this innocent coinage will be best understood by a perusal of the ballad itself.]

> Saw you the State's money new come from the Mint?
>     Some people do say it is wonderous fine;
> And that you may read a great mystery in't,
>     Of mighty King Nol, the lord of the coin.
>
> They have quite omitted his politic head,
>     His worshipful face, and his excellent nose;
> But the better to show the life he had led,
>     They have fix'd upon it the print of his hose.
>
> For, if they had set up his picture there,
>     They needs must ha' crown'd him in Charles' stead;
> But 'twas cunningly done, that they did forbear,
>     And rather would set up aught else than his head.
>
> 'Tis monstrous strange, and yet it is true,
>     In this Reformation we should have such luck,
> That crosses were always disdain'd by you,
>     Who before pull'd them down, should now set them up.
>
> On this side they have circumscrib'd *God with us*,
>     And in this stamp and coin they confide;
> *Common-Wealth* on the other, by which we may guess,
>     That *God* and the *States* were not both of a side.
>
> On this side they have cross and harp,
>     And only a cross on the other set forth;
> By which we may learn, it falls to our part
>     Two crosses to have for one fit of mirth!

Anon. (*c.*1649), *Political Ballads of the Seventeenth and Eighteenth Centuries*, ed. W. Walker Wilkins, 1860

## SATYR ON THE ADULTERATE COYN INSCRIBED
## THE COMMON-WEALTH

That *Common-wealth* which was our *Common-woe*,
Did *Stamp* for *Currant*, *That*, which must not *Goe*:
Yet it was well to *Passe*, till *Heaven* thought meet
To shew both *This*, and *That* were *Counterfeit*.
Our *Crosses* were their *Coyn*! Their *God* our *Hell*!
Till *Saviour Charles* became *Emanuel*.
But now—The *Devill* take their *God*! Avaunt
Thou molten *Image* of the *Covenant*!
Thou lewd *Impostor*! *State's*, and *Traffique's* Sin!
A *Brazen Bulk*, fac'd with a *Silver Skin*!
Badge of Their *Saints-Pretences*, without doubt!
A *Wolfe within*, and *Innocence without*!
Like to Their *Masqu'd Designs*! *Rebellion*
Film'd with the Tinsell of Religion!
*Metall* on *Metall*, here, we may disclose;
Like *Sear-cloth* stript from *Cromwell's Copper Nose*.

Thou *Bastard Relique* of the *Trayterous Crew*!
A mere *Invent*, to Give the *Devill's Due*!
Or (as a Learned Modern *Author* sayth)
In their *Own Coyn*, to *Pay* the *Publique Faith*!
    *Heavens*! I thank you! that, in mine Extreme,
    I never lov'd Their *Mony More* than *Them*!

Curs'd be those *Wights*! whose *Godliness* was *Gain*,
Spoyling *Gods Image* in Their *Soveraign*!
They made *Our Angell's Evill*! and 'tis known,
Their *Crosse* and *Harp* were *Scandall* to the CROWN.
Had, 'mongst the *Jewes*, Their *Thirty Pence* been us'd
When *Judas* truckt for's *Lord*, 't had bin refus'd.
Worse than that *Coyn* which our *Boyes*, *Fibbs* do call!
A *Scottish Twenty-Pence* is *Worth* them *All*!

To their eternal *Shame*, be't brought to th'*Mint*!
Cast into *Medalls*; and Their *Names Stampt* in't!
That *Charon* (when they come for *Wastage* ore)
May dout *his Fare*, and make them wait on shore:

    For, if *Repentance ransome* any thence,
    Know!—*Charles* his *Coyn* must pay their *Peter-Pence*.

HENRY BOLD, 1661


EPIGRAM
ON THE NEW HALF-FARTHINGS

'Too small for any marketable shift,
What purpose can there be for coins like these?'
Hush, hush, good Sir!—Thus charitable Thrift
May give a *Mite* to him who wants a cheese!

THOMAS HOOD (1749–1845), Hood's Own: Second Series, 1861


'What is it, Harry?' she asks, her eyes widening.

   'Open it,' he tells her, and when she fumbles too long at the transparent
tape holding on the toilet-seat-shaped little lid he pries it off for her with his
big fingernails. He removes the wad of tissue paper and spills out upon the
quilted bedspread the fifteen Krugerrand. Their color is redder than gold in
his mind had been. 'Gold,' he whispers, holding up close to her face, paired
in his palm, two coins, showing the two sides, the profile of some old Boer
on one and a kind of antelope on the other. 'Each of these is worth about
three hundred sixty dollars,' he tells her. 'Don't tell your mother or Nelson
or anybody.'

   She does seem bewitched, taking one into her fingers. Her nails scratch
his palm as she lifts the coin off. Her brown eyes pick up flecks of yellow.
'Is it all right?' Janice asks. 'Where on earth did you get them?'

   'A new place on Weiser across from the peanut store that sells precious
metals, buys and sells. It was simple. All you got to do is produce a certified
check within twenty-four hours after they quote you a price. They guarantee to buy them back at the going rate any time, so all you lose is their six
per cent commission and the sales tax, which at the rate gold is going up
I'll have made back by next week. Here. I bought two stacks. Look.' He
takes the other thrillingly hefty cylinder from the drawer and undoes the lid
and spills those fifteen antelopes slippingly upon the bedspread, thus doub-
ling the riches displayed. The spread is a lightweight Pennsylvania Dutch
quilt, small rectangular patches sewed together by patient biddies, graded
from pale to dark to form a kind of dimensional effect, of four large boxes
having a lighter and darker side. He lies down upon its illusion and places

a Krugerrand each in the sockets of his eyes. Through the chill red pressure of the gold he hears Janice say, 'My God. I thought only the government could have gold. Don't you need a license or anything?'

'Just the bucks. Just the fucking bucks, Wonder Woman.' Blind, he feels amid the pure strangeness of the gold his prick firming up and stretching the fabric of his Jockey shorts.

'Harry. How much did you spend?'

He wills her to lift down the elastic of his underpants and suck, suck until she gags. When she fails to read his mind and do this, he removes the coins and gazes up at her, a dead man reborn and staring. No coffin dark greets his open eyes, just his wife's out-of-focus face, framed in dark hair damp and stringy from the shower and fringy across the forehead so that Mamie Eisenhower comes to mind. 'Eleven thousand five hundred more or less,' he answers. 'Honey, it was just sitting in the savings account drawing a lousy six per cent. At only six per cent these days you're losing money, inflation's running about twelve. The beauty of gold is, it loves bad news. As the dollar sinks, gold goes up. All the Arabs are turning their dollars into gold. Webb Murkett told me all about it, the day you wouldn't come to the club.'

She is still examining the coin, stroking its subtle relief, when he wants her attention to turn to him. He hasn't had a hard-on just blossom in his pants since he can't remember when. Lotty Bingaman days. 'It's pretty,' Janice admits. 'Should you be supporting the South Africans though?'

'Why not, they're making jobs for the blacks, mining the stuff. The advantage of the Krugerrand, the girl at this fiscal alternatives place explained, is it weights one troy ounce exactly and is easier to deal with. You can buy Mexican pesos if you want, or that little Canadian maple leaf, though there she said it's so fine the gold dust comes off on your hands. Also I liked the look of that deer on the back. Don't you?'

'I do. It's exciting,' Janice confesses, at last looking at him, where he lies tumescent amid scattered gold. 'Where are you going to keep them?' she asks. Her tongue sneaks forward in thought, and rests on her lower lip. He loves her when she tries to think.

'In your great big cunt,' he says, and pulls her down by the lapels of her rough robe. Out of deference to those around them in the house—Ma Springer just a wall's thickness away, her television a dim rumble, the Korean War turned into a joke—Janice tries to suppress her cries as he strips the terrycloth from her slippery body and the coins on the bedspread come in contact with her skin. The cords of her throat tighten; her face darkens as she strains in the grip of indignation and glee. His underwear off, the overhead light still on, his prick up like a jutting piece of pink wreckage, he calms her into lying motionless and places a Krugerrand on each nipple, one on her navel, and a number on her pussy, enough to mask the hair with a triangle of unsteady coins overlapping like snake scales. If she laughs and her belly moves the whole construction will collapse. Kneeling at her hips, Harry holds a Krugerrand by the edge as if to insert it in a slot. 'No!' Janice protests, loud enough to twitch Ma Springer awake through the wall, loud enough to jar loose the coins so some do spill between her legs. He hushes her mouth with his and then moves his mouth south, across the desert, oasis to oasis, until he comes to the ferny jungle, which his wife lays open to him with a humoring toss of her thighs. A kind of interest compounds as, seeing red, spilled gold pressing on his forehead, he hunts with his tongue for her clitoris. He finds what he thinks is the right rhythm but doesn't feel it take; he thinks the bright overhead light might be distracting her and risks losing his hard-on in hopping from the bed to switch it off over by the door. Turning then in the half-dark he sees she has turned also, gotten up onto her knees and elbows, a four-legged moonchild of his, her soft cleft ass held high to him in the gloom as her face peeks around one shoulder. He fucks her in this position gently, groaning in the effort of keeping his jism in, letting his thoughts fly far. The pennant race, the recent hike in the factory base price of Corollas. He fondles her underside's defenseless slack flesh, his own belly massive and bearing down. Her back looks so breakable and brave and narrow—the long dent of its spine, the cross-bar of pallor left by her bathing-suit bra. Behind him his bare feet release a faraway sad odor. Coins jingle, slithering in toward their knees, into the depressions their interlocked weights make in the mattress. He taps her ass and asks, 'Want to turn over?'

'Uh-huh.' As an afterthought: 'Want me to sit on you first?'

'Uh-huh.' As an afterthought: 'Don't make me come.'

Harry's skin is bitten as by ice when he lies on his back. The coins: worse than toast crumbs. So wet he feels almost nothing, Janice straddles him, vast and globular in the patchy light that filters from the streetlight through the big copper beech. She picks up a stray coin and places it glinting in her eye, as a monocle. Lording it over him, holding him captive, she grinds her wet halves around him; self to self, bivalve and tuber, this is what it comes to. 'Don't come,' she says, alarmed enough so that her mock-monocle drops to his tense abdomen with a thud. 'Better get underneath,' he grunts. Her body then seems thin and black, silhouetted by the scattered circles, reflecting according to their tilt. Gods bedded among stars, he gasps in her ear, then she in his.

After this payoff, regaining their breaths, they can count in the semi-dark only twenty-nine Krugerrands on the rumpled bedspread, its landscape of ridged green patches. He turns on the overhead light. It hurts their eyes. By its harshness their naked skins seem also rumpled. Panic encrusts Harry's drained body; he does not rest until, naked on his knees on the rug, a late strand of spunk looping from his reddened glans, he finds, caught in the crack between the mattress and the bed side-rail, the precious thirtieth.

JOHN UPDIKE, *Rabbit is Rich*, 1981

I must keep closer now to the contemplation of the stuff itself. Beautiful, terrifying sight and thought! I wish I could drop into poetry over it. Mind you, I mean the actual thing. If you like to be reasonable and common-place, you may say that the significance lies in what the thing can do, the peace of mind it may bring, the comfort, the sight of beautiful cities, ballets, pictures, the succouring of those we want to succour, or in what it saves us from: all very true, but there is such a crowd of these considerations that they all merge together, the mind does not separate them, and what you look at or think of, being a symbol of so much, ceases to be a symbol at all and is itself a strong, living entity, mystic, wonderful . Cash a cheque for ten pounds, if you can, reader, and hold the golden things in your hand and gaze at them. Are you not strangely moved? No? Then you have not been for days without a much-needed half-crown. But for me, at least, there is fear as well in the sight, a vague sense of danger as well as of strength and beauty, and that can hardly be rationally explained—unless one has stolen the money—and clearly shows the mystic nature of the thing. Why not? The use of this precious metal by humanity for so many thousands of years as power has begotten an intimate correspondence between our minds and it, and bank-notes or a balance at the bank (which are almost, though not quite, as frightening to me) stand immediately for it even to the least active imagination. We inherit certain feelings about it through innumerable generations (or if we don't the learned have given us much more unlikely things to believe), and we cannot analyse them all. But why fear? I protest I do not know, unless extreme unfamiliarity with money gives me such a sense of fear when I have any that some folk have when they visit a foreign country.

G. S. STREET, *On Money and Other Essays*, 1914

It has often struck our notice that the course our city runs
Is the same towards men and money.—She has true and worthy sons:

She has good and ancient silver, she has good and recent gold.
These are coins untouched with alloys; everywhere their fame is told;
Not all Hellas holds their equal, not all Barbary far and near,
Gold or silver, each well minted, tested each and ringing clear.
Yet, we never use them! Others always pass from hand to hand,
Sorry brass just struck last week and branded with a wretched brand.

ARISTOPHANES, *Frogs*, 405 BC, tr. Gilbert Murray, 1920


EPIGRAM
ON THE DEPRECIATED MONEY

They may talk of the plugging and sweating
    Of our coinage that's minted of gold,
But to me it produces no fretting
    Of its shortness of weight to be told:
All the sov'reigns I'm able to levy
    As to lightness can never be wrong,
But must surely be some of the heavy,
    *For I never can carry them long.*

THOMAS HOOD (1749–1845), *Hood's Own: Second Series*, 1861


Brethren, friends, countrymen and fellow-subjects,

What I intend now to say to you, is, next to your duty to God, and the
care of your salvation, of the greatest concern to yourselves, and your
children, your bread and clothing, and every common necessary of life
entirely depend upon it. Therefore I do most earnestly exhort you as men,
as Christians, as parents, and as lovers of your country, to read this paper
with the utmost attention, or get it read to you by others; which that you
may do at the less expense, I have ordered the printer to sell it at the lowest
rate. . . .

The fact is thus: It having been many years since COPPER HALFPENCE OR
FARTHINGS were last coined in this kingdom, they have been for some time
very scarce, and many counterfeits passed about under the name of *raps*,
several applications were made to England, that we might have liberty to
coin new ones, as in former times we did; but they did not succeed. At last
one Mr Wood, a mean ordinary man, a hardware dealer, procured a patent
under his Majesty's broad seal to coin fourscore and ten thousand pounds
in copper for this kingdom, which patent however did not oblige any one

here to take them, unless they pleased. Now you must know, that the halfpence and farthings in England pass for very little more than they are worth. And if you should beat them to pieces, and sell them to the brazier you would not lose above a penny in a shilling. But Mr Wood made his halfpence of such base metal, and so much smaller than the English ones, that the brazier would not give you above a penny of good money for a shilling of his; so that this sum of fourscore and ten thousand pounds in good gold and silver, must be given for trash that will not be worth above eight or nine thousand pounds real value. But this is not the worst, for Mr Wood when he pleases may by stealth send over another and another fourscore and ten thousand pounds, and buy all our goods for eleven parts in twelve, under the value. For example, if a hatter sells a dozen of hats for five shillings a-piece, which amounts to three pounds, and receives the payment in Mr Wood's coin, he really receives only the value of five shillings. . . .

For suppose you go to an alehouse with that base money, and the landlord gives you a quart for four of these halfpence, what must the victualler do? His brewer will not be paid in that coin, or if the brewer should be such a fool, the farmers will not take it from them for their bere, because they are bound by their leases to pay their rents in good and lawful money of England, which this is not, nor of Ireland neither, and the 'squire their landlord will never be so bewitched to take such trash for his land, so that it must certainly stop somewhere or other, and wherever it stops it is the same thing, and we are all undone.

> JONATHAN SWIFT, 'Letter to the Tradesmen, Shop-Keepers, Farmers, and
> Common-People in General of Ireland', 1724

The evils produced by this state of the currency were not such as have generally been thought worthy to occupy a prominent place in history. Yet it may well be doubted whether all the misery which had been inflicted on the English nation in a quarter of a century by bad Kings, bad Ministers, bad Parliaments, and bad Judges, was equal to the misery caused in a single year by bad crowns and bad shillings. Those events which furnish the best themes for pathetic and indignant eloquence are not always those which most affect the happiness of the great body of the people. The misgovernment of Charles and James, gross as it had been, had not prevented the common business of life from going steadily and prosperously on. While the honour and independence of the State were sold to a foreign power, while chartered rights were invaded, while fundamental laws were violated, hundreds of thousands of quiet, honest, and industrious families laboured and traded, ate their meals and lay down to rest, in comfort and security. Whether Whigs or Tories, Protestants or Jesuits were uppermost, the grazier drove his beasts to market: the grocer weighed out his currants: the draper measured out his broadcloth: the hum of buyers and sellers was as loud as ever in the towns: the harvest home was celebrated as joyously as ever in the hamlets: the cream overflowed the pails of Cheshire: the apple juice foamed in the presses of Herefordshire: the piles of crockery glowed in the furnaces of the Trent; and the barrows of coal rolled fast along the timber railways of the Tyne. But when the great instrument of exchange became thoroughly deranged, all trade, all industry, were smitten as with a palsy. The evil was felt daily and hourly in almost every place and by almost every class, in the dairy and on the threshing floor, by the anvil and by the loom, on the billows of the ocean and in the depths of the mine. Nothing could be purchased without a dispute. Over every counter there was wrangling from morning to night. The workman and his employer had a quarrel as regularly as the Saturday came round. On a fair day or a market day the clamours, the reproaches, the taunts, the curses, were incessant: and it was well if no booth was overturned and no head broken. No merchant would contract to deliver goods without making some stipulation about the quality of the coin in which he was to be paid. Even men of business were often bewildered by the confusion into which all pecuniary transactions were thrown. The simple and the careless were pillaged without mercy by extortioners whose demands grew even more rapidly than the money shrank. The price of the necessaries of life, of shoes, of ale, of oatmeal rose fast. The labourer found that the bit of metal, which, when he received it, was called a shilling, would hardly, when he wanted to purchase a pot of beer or a loaf of rye bread, go as far as sixpence. Where artisans of more than usual intelligence were collected in great numbers, as in the dockyard at Chatham, they were able to make their complaints heard and to obtain some redress. But the ignorant and helpless peasant was cruelly ground between one class which would give money only by tale and another which would take it only by weight. Yet his sufferings hardly exceeded those of the unfortunate race of authors. Of the way in which obscure writers were treated we may easily form a judgment from the letters, still extant, of Dryden to his bookseller Tonson. One day Tonson sends forty brass shillings, to say nothing of clipped money. Another day he pays a debt with pieces so bad that none of them will go. The great poet sends them all back, and demands in their place guineas at twenty-nine shillings each. 'I expect,' he says in one letter, 'good silver, not such as I have had formerly.' 'If you have any silver that will go,' he says in another letter, 'my wife will be glad of it. I lost thirty shillings or more by the last payment of fifty pounds.' These complaints and demands, which have been preserved from destruction only by the eminence of the writer, are doubtless merely a fair sample of the correspondence which filled all the mail bags of England during several months.

THOMAS MACAULAY, *History of England*, 1849–55

Before me lies a coin bearing the image and superscription of King George the Fourth, and of the nominal value of two-and-sixpence. But an official friend at a neighbouring turnpike says the piece is hopelessly bad; and a chemist tested it, returning a like unfavourable opinion. A cabman, who had brought me from a Club, left it with the Club porter, appealing to the gent who gave it a pore cabby, at ever so much o'clock of a rainy night, which he hoped he would give him another. I have taken that cabman at his word. He has been provided with a sound coin. The bad piece is on the table before me, and shall have a hole drilled through it, as soon as this essay is written, by a loyal subject who does not desire to deface the Sovereign's image, but to protest against the rascal who has taken his name in vain. *Fid. Def.* indeed! Is this what you call defending the faith? You dare to forge your Sovereign's name, and pass your scoundrel pewter as his silver? I wonder who you are, wretch and most consummate trickster? This forgery is so complete that even now I am deceived by it—I can't see the difference between the base and sterling metal. Perhaps this piece is a little lighter;— I don't know. A little softer:—is it? I have not bitten it, not being a connoisseur in the tasting of pewter or silver. I take the word of three honest men, though it goes against me; and though I have given two-and-sixpence worth of honest consideration for the counter, I shall not attempt to implicate anybody else in my misfortune, or transfer my ill-luck to a deluded neighbour.

W. M. THACKERAY (1811–63), 'On a Medal of George the Fourth', *Roundabout Papers*

In reality, Édouard had in the first place been thinking of certain of his fellow novelists when he began to think of *The Coiners*, and in particular of the Comte de Passavant. But this attribution had been considerably widened; according as the wind blew from Rome or from elsewhere, his heroes became in turn either priests or freemasons. If he allowed his mind to follow its bent, it soon tumbled headlong into abstractions, where it was as comfortable as a fish in water. Ideas of exchange, of depreciation, of inflation, etc., gradually invaded his book (like the theory of clothes in Carlyle's *Sartor Resartus*) and usurped the place of the characters. As it was impossible for Édouard to speak of this, he kept silent in the most awkward manner, and his silence, which seemed like an admission of penury, began to make the other three very uncomfortable.

'Has it ever happened to you to hold a counterfeit coin in your hands?' he asked at last.

'Yes,' said Bernard; but the two women's 'No' drowned his voice.

'Well, imagine a false ten-franc gold piece. In reality it's not worth two sous. But it will be worth ten francs as long as no one recognizes it to be false. So if I start from the idea that . . .'

'But why start from an idea?' interrupted Bernard impatiently. 'If you were to start from a fact and make a good exposition of it, the idea would come of its own accord to inhabit it. If I were writing *The Coiners* I should begin by showing the counterfeit coin—the little ten-franc piece you were speaking of just now.'

So saying, he pulled out of his pocket a small coin, which he flung on to the table.

'Just hear how true it rings. Almost the same sound as the real one. One would swear it was gold. I was taken in by it this morning, just as the grocer who passed it on to me had been taken in himself, he told me. It isn't quite the same weight, I think; but it has the brightness and the sound of a real piece; it is coated with gold, so that, all the same, it is worth a little more than two sous; but it's made of glass. It'll wear transparent. No; don't rub it; you'll spoil it. One can almost see through it, as it is.'

Édouard had seized it and was considering it with the utmost curiosity.

'But where did the grocer get it from?'

'He didn't know. He thinks he has had it in his drawer some days. He amused himself by passing it off on me to see whether I should be taken in. Upon my word, I was just going to accept it! But as he's an honest man, he undeceived me; then he let me have it for five francs. He wanted to keep it to show to what he calls "amateurs." I thought there couldn't be a better one than the author of *The Coiners*; and it was to show you that I took it. But now that you have examined it, give it back to me! I'm sorry that the reality doesn't interest you.'

'Yes, it does,' said Édouard, 'but it disturbs me too.'

'That's a pity,' rejoined Bernard.

ANDRÉ GIDE, *Les Faux-monnayeurs*, 1925, tr. as *The Coiners*, Dorothy Bussy, 1950

The coins of every country with which England carries on any intercourse, whether in Europe, Asia, or America, are counterfeited here and exported. An inexhaustible supply of halfpence was made for home consumption, till the new coinage put a stop to this manufactory: it was the common practice of the dealers in this article, to fry a pan-full every night after supper for the next day's delivery, thus darkening them, to make them look as if they had been in circulation.

Assignats were forged here during the late war; but this is less to be imputed to the Birmingham speculators, than to those wise politicians who devised so many wise means of ruining France.

ROBERT SOUTHEY, *Letters from England by Don Manuel Alvarez Espriella*, 1807

LEAR. No, they cannot touch me for coining; I am the king himself.

WILLIAM SHAKESPEARE, *King Lear*, 1605

Oh, no. What kind of mess has Boggs got himself (and the rest of us) into this time?

Readers will perhaps remember Mr Boggs from the Profile I did of him, which first appeared in these pages precisely five years ago this week: J. S. G. Boggs, to be exact, the young artist whose principal métier appeared to consist of drawing near-exact single-side renditions of various national currencies and then going out and 'spending' those drawings—that is, persuading merchants to accept them knowingly, at face value, in lieu of cash, as payment for a wide variety of goods and services, a trick that at the time of my original article he'd managed to pull off to the tune of more than thirty-five thousand dollars' worth of transactions in just two years. Although many collectors were eager to own Boggs's drawings, he made it a rule never to sell them; he only spent them. He would, however, occasionally sell collectors the receipt and the change from a given transaction (at a considerable markup), which would enable the collectors to track down the recently spent drawing and attempt to purchase it.

Boggs's was a comedy of compounding value, for such were the arcane realities of the art market that the entire concatenation of objects surrounding any given transaction—the drawing, the item purchased, the receipt, the change, the original 'model' of the bill on which the drawing was based—once documented and framed and offered up for auction, invariably and quite mysteriously sold for considerably more than the sum of the component parts. This comedy, however, generally failed to amuse the national

banks and treasury police of the various countries in which Boggs chose to
enact his elaborate performances, and he was regularly hauled in on a
variety of counterfeiting charges, all of which he righteously contested—
until now with an unbroken string of successes. In 1987, for example, a
British jury took only ten minutes to buck the presiding judge's express
instructions that Boggs be found guilty of 'reproducing' Bank of England
notes. Two years later, an Australian court not only found Boggs not guilty
of similar charges but ordered that he be awarded more than twenty thousand dollars as compensation for all his trouble. And in 1991 the United
States Attorney for the Wyoming District, who'd begun an investigation of
Boggs's transactions, ultimately decided not to participate in what he called
'the Boggs publicity game.' The Secret Service (our country's treasury police)
did, however, retain fifteen of Boggs's bills from that investigation.

Each of these run-ins with the law appears to have only further embold-
ened Boggs, provoking him to make ever more daring forays into the
borderland between artistic self-expression and legal constraint. Or so I
came to realize the other day, when he dropped by my office here in New
York to bring me up to date. (He was in town helping to prepare the way
for the première of 'Money Man,' Philip Haas's documentary film about
Boggs's activities and in particular his attempts to reclaim his Wyoming
bills from the Secret Service; the movie will begin a two-week run January
13th at Film Forum.) In many ways, these have been an immensely successful five years for Mr Boggs. To date he has 'spent' well over two hundred
and fifty thousand dollars of his bills; he has enjoyed major gallery shows
and a touring museum exhibition (entitled 'Smart Money'); and, perhaps
most improbable, for the past twenty months he has been comfortably
ensconced as the Fellow of Art and Ethics at the Center for the Advance-
ment of Applied Ethics of Pittsburgh's Carnegie Mellon University.

But these have also been years—at least, to hear him tell it—of endless
churning. 'Believe me, I've tried to kick this habit,' he says. 'I'll resolutely
start out on some new tangent—a series of abstract canvases, for example—but then somebody always comes along and asks me something like
"Well, what do you think that painting's worth?" and I find myself being
drawn right back in. Because what does anybody mean by "worth"? And
how's that different from "value"? And what, precisely, is it that one values
in value? What is good value? The questions lead me on, and before you
know it I'm right back in that hall of mirrors, with the mirrored door
clicking shut behind me.'

Short of escaping the hall altogether, he has endeavored to give each
new foray a clean, fresh edge—an edge that invariably seems to bring him

closer to The Edge. Thus, having begun by trading hand-drawn renditions of bills, he took to wondering, Why not attempt to traffic in multiples of various sorts, initially in lithographs (would people accept those?) and then in engravings (would those get him in trouble?) and, finally, in simple photocopies? People did keep accepting them—by no means everyone, but enough people to keep things interesting—and treasury police all over the world grew more and more nervous.

LAWRENCE WESCHLER, 'Money Changes Everything', *New Yorker*, 18 January 1993

As I have said it was easy for local people to discover the exchange rate of dollars and I was therefore surprised to be asked one day to advise on some dollar notes. My host pulled out a particularly fat roll wrapped in an old piece of newspaper and fastened with a length of thread. He unwrapped this carefully, explaining that these notes were in some ways unlike the dollars he had handled before, in other ways identical. What did I think? He peeled a note from the roll and passed it across.

The note was, as he had indicated, both like and unlike a dollar. I immediately saw the reason for this: it had been made by pasting together a photostat of the front and the back of a genuine dollar note. The quality of reproduction was good, almost perfect in fact, but whereas a genuine dollar bill has one surface printed in green and has a watermark, this one was uniformly black and white and had no watermark. I explained the matter to him. For a few seconds he was non-plussed; a trace of anger at the deception showed briefly behind his polite reception of my news. 'No matter', he said, after a little while, 'I will still use them.' I nodded and left it to him: he had not survived, even mildly prospered, in the city without great skills and cunning.

It was a few weeks before I felt I could mention the fake dollars. There had been no problem, he assured me, he had passed them through his network of associates and, when he had last heard of them, they were still being exchanged for other currencies somewhere in the countryside outside Accra. It was no great affair he assured me. After all, he pointed out, the possessors of black-market currency rarely if ever took it to a bank—that would be too dangerous. So long as the notes, fake or genuine, kept passing from hand to hand, and people were prepared to treat them as money, then they were money. And, while we were on the subject, he asked politely, did I know anyone with a photocopying machine?

MALCOLM MCLEOD, 'Paolozzi and Identity', in Eduardo Paolozzi, *Lost Magic Kingdoms*, 1985

In this city of Kanbalu is the mint of the grand khan, who may truly be said to possess the secret of the alchemists, as he has the art of producing money by the following process. He causes the bark to be stripped from those mulberry-trees the leaves of which are used for feeding silk-worms, and takes from it that thin inner rind which lies between the coarser bark and the wood of the tree. This being steeped, and afterwards pounded in a mortar, until reduced to a pulp, is made into paper, resembling (in substance) that which is manufactured from cotton, but quite black. When ready for use, he has it cut into pieces of money of different sizes, nearly square, but somewhat longer than they are wide. Of these, the smallest pass for a denier tournois; the next size for a Venetian silver groat; others for two, five, and ten groats; others for one, two, three, and as far as ten besants of gold. The coinage of this paper money is authenticated with as much form and ceremony as if it were actually of pure gold or silver; for to each note a number of officers, specially appointed, not only subscribe their names, but affix their signets also; and when this has been regularly done by the whole of them, the principal officer, deputed by his majesty, having dipped into vermilion the royal seal committed to his custody, stamps with it the piece of paper, so that the form of the seal tinged with the vermilion remains impressed upon it, by which it receives full authenticity as current money, and the act of counterfeiting it is punished as a capital offence. When thus coined in large quantities, this paper currency is circulated in every part of the grand khan's dominions; nor dares any person, at the peril of his life, refuse to accept it in payment. All his subjects receive it without hesitation, because, wherever their business may call them, they can dispose of it again in the purchase of merchandise they may have occasion for; such as pearls, jewels, gold, or silver. With it, in short, every article may be procured.

Several times in the course of the year, large caravans of merchants arrive with such articles as have just been mentioned, together with gold tissues, which they lay before the grand khan. He thereupon calls together twelve experienced and skilful persons, selected for this purpose, whom he commands to examine the articles with great care, and to fix the value at which they should be purchased. Upon the sum at which they have been thus conscientiously appraised he allows a reasonable profit, and immediately pays for them with this paper; to which the owners can have no objection, because, as has been observed, it answers the purpose of their own disbursements; and even though they should be inhabitants of a country where this kind of money is not current, they invest the amount in other articles of merchandise suited to their own markets. When any persons happen to be possessed of paper money which from long use has become damaged, they carry it to the mint, where, upon the payment of only three per cent, they may receive fresh notes in exchange. Should any be desirous of procuring gold or silver for the purposes of manufacture, such as of drinking-cups, girdles, or other articles wrought of these metals, they in like manner apply at the mint, and for their paper obtain the bullion they require. All his majesty's armies are paid with this currency, which is to them of the same value as if it were gold or silver. Upon these grounds, it may certainly be affirmed that the grand khan has a more extensive command of treasure than any other sovereign in the universe.

MARCO POLO (1254–1324), *Travels*

There was a run on the Bank of England, and Pitt was uncertain what measures to take in consequence of it. He passed the whole night (as Mrs —— told me) in walking up and down his drawing-room. Next morning he sent for certain bankers, and informed them that he had resolved on authorising the Bank to suspend cash-payments, and to stop the issue of gold.— I recollect a farmer coming to my father's bank, and receiving his money in five-pound notes. 'What can I do with these?' he exclaimed; 'how can I pay my men with them?'

SAMUEL ROGERS, *Table Talk*, 1856

The evils of this deluge of paper money are not to be removed, until our citizens are generally and radically instructed in their cause and consequences, and silence by their authority the interested clamors and sophistry of speculating, shaving, and banking institutions. Till then we must be content to return, *quoad hoc*, to the savage state, to recur to barter in the exchange of our property, for want of a stable, common measure of value, that now in use being less fixed than the beads and wampum of the Indian, and to deliver up our citizens, their property and their labor, passive victims to the swindling tricks of bankers and mountebankers.

THOMAS JEFFERSON to John Adams, 1819

FAUSTUS. The chancellor will please to state the case;
    It falls in with the duties of his place.
CHANCELLOR [*advancing slowly*]. Who could have ever dreamed such happiness

Would come the days of my old age to bless.
Listen! and look upon the heaven-sent leaf,
That into joy hath changed a people's grief.
[*Reads*]—'*To all whom it concerneth, and so forth:*—
This note of hand, that purports to be worth
A thousand crowns, subjects to such demand
The boundless treasure buried in the land.
*And furthermore*, said treasure underground,
To pay said sum is, whensoever found,
And wheresoever, firmly pledged and bound.'

KAISER. Audacity unheard of!—foul deceit!
Who signed the emperor's name to such vile cheat?
What punishment can for such crime atone?

TREASURER. Forget you, Sire, the writing is your own?
This last night you were in the character
Of PAN: we saw the Chancellor prefer
The suit. He said, 'A few strokes of your pen
Will bless the people over whom you reign.
Do make them happy on this festal night.'
And then you did take up the pen and write.
No time was lost. A thousand artists plied,
A thousand-fold the scroll was multiplied;
And that the good to every one might fall,
We stamped at once the series, one and all.
Tens—thirties—fifties—hundreds off we strike!
Never was anything that men so like:
Your city, mouldering and in despair,
Has caught new life, and joy is everywhere.
Long as your name was by the world held dear,
Never did it so brightly shine as here—
The alphabet! what is it to this sign?—
To this 'hoc signo vinces' note of thine?

KAISER. For good gold, then, in court and camp it passes,
And for good gold is taken by the masses?
I must permit it, tho' it does seem odd.

MARSHAL. The papers flying everywhere abroad—
Stop it—oh yes!—the lightning flashes stop—
At every banker's booth and money-shop,

---

*hoc signo vinces*] with this sign you shall conquer

For each leaf you can have (deducting still
Some discount) gold and silver, if you will.
Then off with you to butcher and to baker,
Vintner, and such like—tailor, sausage-maker.
Half the world passes—wealth is such a blessing—
Its days in feasting—the other half in dressing.
Flaunting in their new clothes—show their new riches—
The mercer cuts away—the stitcher stitches—
And 'long live Cæsar!' blurts out, 'mid the ringing
Of plates—of boiling, broiling, swearing, singing.

MEPHISTOPHELES. And he who walks alone the public ways,
And fixes on the fairest there his gaze,
And sees her move, with bland attractiveness,
In all the splendour of imposing dress;
The peacock's proud plume shades one eye, the while
She smirks, and simpers by with meaning smile—
Methinks she sees, and seems to understand
The import of this little note of hand.
Aye! and it wins from her, as by a spell,
The favours that my lady has to sell.
When words are weak, and wit all out of joint,
'Tis this that brings a woman to the point:
Close in the bosom, hidden there from view,
It lies so nicely in a billet-doux.
The priest—he now no purse or scrip need bear—
Devoutly folds it in his Book of Prayer.
The soldier moves more freely, at his loins
No longer carrying a weight of coins.
Pardon me, Sire; on such details to dwell,
No doubt seems trifling with the miracle.

FAUSTUS. The treasure that within the land lies deep,
Entranced, as 't were, in an enchanted sleep,
Frozen and fixed—useless, while unemployed—
This may be disemprisoned, be enjoyed.
Man, in imagination's boldest hour,
To reach such treasure's limit has no power.
The intellect strives ever, strives in vain,
Some dim anticipation to attain;
But Spirits grasp it—see beyond the sense—
Have in the Boundless boundless confidence.

MEPHISTOPHELES. An easy substitute for gold and pearls
  This paper is, and its convenience such,
  We know at once how little, and how much
  We have: no need of testing and of weighing;
  No chaffering, cheapening, proving, or assaying
  But to the vintner's, or the merry girl's,
  Off with us! Wish we specie—little danger
  Of waiting long to find a money-changer.
  At worst it is but digging—in a trice
  You shovel up cup and trinkets plenty; call
  An auction, for the bill make quick provision,
  To the discomfiture and shame of all
  Who looked upon our project with derision.
  Once used to them, men will have nothing but
  These leaves—so easy to receive and spend;
  And the realm circulates, from this hour out,
  Jewels, and gold, and paper to no end.

                    GOETHE, *Faust*, 1832, book ii, tr. John Anster, 1864


If, therefore, the proposed measure [to withdraw Scottish banknotes from circulation] shall take place, the banker's profession must suffer greatly, nay, in its present form, must cease to exist. We cannot, as a nation, afford to be deprived of such an honourable and profitable means of settling our sons in the world. We cannot afford to lose a resource which has proved to so many respectable and honourable families a means *ad re-ædificandum antiquam domum*, and which has held out to others a successful mode of elevating themselves, by liberal and useful industry, to the possession of wealth, at once to their own advantage and to that of Scotland. Thus it must needs be, if the proposed measure should pass; and when we come to count the gains we shall then have made, by change from a paper circulation to one in specie, I doubt it will form a notable example of the truth of the proverb, *'That gold may be bought too dear.'*

The Branches established by Banks in remote parts of Scotland must be given up. The parent Banks would vainly exhaust themselves in endeavouring to draw specie from London, and to force it, at whatever expense, into more fertile districts of Scotland, which, of course, would receive it in small quantity, and pay for it at a heavy charge. But as to the remote and sterile

---

*ad re-ædificandum antiquam domum*] for rebuilding the ancient house

regions, it must be with the Highlands and Isles of Scotland, as it is now in some remote districts of Ireland, where scarce any specie exists for the purpose of ordinary currency, and where, for want of that representative for value or paper money in its stead, men are driven back to the primitive mode of bartering for every thing—the peasant pays his rent in labour, and the fisher gets his wages in furnishings. Misery is universal—credit is banished—and with all the bounties of nature around them, ready to reward industry—the sinews of that industry are hewn asunder, and man starves where Nature has given abundance!

Sir Walter Scott, *Letters from Malachi Malagrowther, esq, on the Proposed Change of Currency*, letter ii, 28 February 1826

don't understand anything except GREEN BILLS. Not negotiable bonds, not personal checks, not Traveller's Checks.

And if you give anybody a hundred-dollar bill in the SUPERMARKET, they *call the manager*.

Money is SUSPICIOUS, because people think you're not supposed to have it, even if you do have it.

I'm PARANOID now when I go to D'Agostino's because I always have another SHOPPING BAG with me and they tell you that you have to check it, but I won't. A lady doesn't have to check her pocketbook, so I won't check my bag. It's principle. So then I'm paranoid they'll think I'm stealing, so I hold my head up high and LOOK RICH. Because I don't steal. I go right to the dairy counter with all my money and I'm so happy because I'm going to go down all the counters and buy things for my windowsill in my bedroom.

Rich people don't carry their money in wallets or Gucci this-es or Valentino thats. They carry their money in a business envelope. In a long business envelope. And the tens have a paper clip on them, so do the fives and twenties. And the money is usually new. It's sent over by special messenger from the bank offices—or their husbands' offices. They just sign for it. And it stays there until they have to dish out a twenty to their daughter.

The best way I like to carry money, actually, is messily. Crumpled wads. A paper bag is good.

One day I was having lunch with a princess and she had this little SCOTCH PURSE that was in the motif of a PLAID CAP with a POM-POM. We were at the

Women's Exchange on Madison Avenue. And she took this crisp money
out of her purse and she said, 'You see? I fold it in the Rothschild manner.
It lasts longer that way. I've been doing it all my life.' She folded each bill
separately, lengthwise, and then folded it again lengthwise. All new money.
All in a little stack. The theory is that it lasts longer. That's the Rothschild
way of folding money—that you can't see it.

That's *The Rothschild Story*.

I had a very good French wallet that I bought in Germany for a hundred
and fifty dollars. For the big money. The big-size foreign money. But then
in New York it ripped and I took it to the shoemaker and by mistake he
stitched up the part where you put the paper money, so I can only use it
now for change.

Cash. I just am not happy when I don't have it. The minute I have it I have
to spend it. And I just buy STUPID THINGS.

Checks aren't money.

ANDY WARHOL, *From A to B and Back Again*, 1975

As soon as I was out of sight of that house I opened my envelope, and saw
that it contained money! My opinion of those people changed, I can tell
you! I lost not a moment, but shoved note and money into my vest-pocket,
and broke for the nearest cheap eating-house. Well, how I did eat! When
at last I couldn't hold any more, I took out my money and unfolded it, took
one glimpse and nearly fainted. Five millions of dollars! Why, it made my
head swim.

I must have sat there stunned and blinking at the note as much as a
minute before I came rightly to myself again. The first thing I noticed, then,
was the landlord. His eye was on the note, and he was petrified. He was
worshipping, with all his body and soul, but he looked as if he couldn't stir
hand or foot. I took my cue in a moment, and did the only rational thing
there was to do. I reached the note towards him, and said carelessly:

'Give me the change, please.'

Then he was restored to his normal condition, and made a thousand
apologies for not being able to break the bill, and I couldn't get him to
touch it. He wanted to look at it, and keep on looking at it; he couldn't
seem to get enough of it to quench the thirst of his eye, but he shrank from

touching it as if it had been something too sacred for poor common clay to handle. I said:

'I am sorry if it is an inconvenience, but I must insist. Please change it; I haven't anything else.'

But he said that wasn't any matter; he was quite willing to let the trifle stand over till another time. I said I might not be in his neighbourhood again for a good while; but he said it was of no consequence, he could wait, and, moreover, I could have anything I wanted, any time I chose, and let the account run as long as I pleased. He said he hoped he wasn't afraid to trust as rich a gentleman as I was, merely because I was of a merry disposition, and chose to play larks on the public in the matter of dress. By this time another customer was entering, and the landlord hinted to me to put the monster out of sight; then he bowed me all the way to the door, and I started straight for that house and those brothers, to correct the mistake which had been made before the police should hunt me up, and help me do it.

MARK TWAIN, 'The £1,000,000 Bank-Note', 1893

In an era like ours, the era of cheque books and credit cards, bank drafts and standing orders, of the invisible circulation of money, the cinema is perhaps the only place in the world where it's still possible to see what a lot of the stuff *looks like*.

In film, to be sure, just as in life, money has been devalued by inflation over the years: these days, for example, nothing short of a billion dollars will any longer satisfy the criminals in a heist movie. Yet nothing, in the same heist movie, can ever devalue the *spectacle* of that money—nothing can ever diminish the thrill, when the gang returns to its hideout to divvy up the haul, of those wads and wads of crisp, tight new notes crammed like fresh linen inside a metal suitcase. It scarcely matters whether the movie is good or not, or that we know the money (its top layer excepted) to be necessarily false—a frisson is all but guaranteed.

The fact is that cash, paper money, the raw materiality of currency, tends to make the same, unvarying impact on the filmgoer whatever the filmmaker's own intentions might have been. It defies stylisation, it defies *direction*; put simply, it always looks the same. And in this, curiously, it may be said to resemble, not sex itself, which can after all be stylised, but the sexual organs, which cannot.

GILBERT ADAIR, 'The Last Detail', *Independent*, 21 August 1992

Bank of Italy, *Fifty Thousand Lire*, Italian National Mint, Rome, 1967

Bank of Italy, *One Hundred Thousand Lire*, Italian National Mint, Rome, 1967

The two works under examination could be described as *éditions numerotées* in folio. Printed on both recto and verso, they also reveal, against the light, a delicate watermarking, a product of the most skilled craftsmanship and a technology rarely achieved by other publishers (and then only with great effort and often at disastrous economic risk).

Still, while these works possess all the characteristics of a collector's edition, actually an immense number of copies has been printed. This publishing decision, however, has not resulted in an economic advantage to the collector, for the price is still beyond the reach of many fanciers' pocketbooks.

The paradox—editions that on the one hand flood the market and on the other can be valued only (forgive the expression) by their weight in gold—causes also the eccentricity of their circulation. Perhaps inspired by the example of municipal libraries, the amateur, to have the pleasure of possessing and admiring these editions, must be prepared to make serious sacrifices, but he will then quickly pass the works on to another reader, so that the edition keeps circulating, going from hand to hand. Inevitably the copies deteriorate through use, yet this wear and tear does not diminish their value. It might even be said that wear and tear makes these works more precious, so that those who wish to possess them redouble their efforts and energy, prepared to pay more than the list price.

These facts underline the ambitious nature of this publication, which has met with the widest approval, though the venture must be justified by the intrinsic value of the product.

And indeed, when the critic starts examining the actual stylistic merit of the works under review, some doubts about their validity begin to surface, even the suspicion that the reading public's enthusiasm is due to a misconception or else inspired by speculative aims. First of all, the narrative is in many respects incoherent. For example, in *Fifty Thousand Lire* the watermark appears on the recto, symmetrically opposite the head-and-shoulders portrait of Leonardo da Vinci, and this image can be interpreted as Leonardo's Saint Anne or Virgin of the Rocks; but in *One Hundred Thousand Lire* it is hard to conceive what relation, if any, exists between the apparently Hellenic woman in the watermark and the portrait of Alessandro Manzoni. Is the woman perhaps his Lucia interpreted in a neoclassical style, painted or engraved by an earlier artist like Appiani, who had somehow foreseen the creation of Manzoni's heroine? Or could she be—but here we sink to the most obvious and scholastic allegory—the image of an Italy that has some filial connection with the Lombard novelist? An exaggeration of the political activity of the author of *Carmagnola* or a typical avant-garde device reducing ideology to language (Manzoni father of the Italian language and hence father of the nation, etc., etc.—a dangerous syllogism in the style of Gruppo 63!). The narrative incoherence can only put the reader off, and in any case it will have a deleterious effect on the taste of the young, so we must hope that at least they and the less educated classes will be kept well away from these pages, in their own best interest.

But the incoherence goes deeper. In the context of such fastidiousness, whether neoclassical or bourgeois-realistic (the portraits of the two artists and the landscapes of the verso seem based on the canons of the cheapest sort of socialist realism: a concession to the policies of our center-left coalition?), it is hard to see any reason for the violent insertion of the exotic motive 'Payable to the Bearer,' which evokes the vision of an African safari and a line of blacks laden with bales of merchandise, forming a queue to obtain something in exchange for their extorted labor, a scene right out of Rider Haggard or Kipling and surely inappropriate to the subtext here.

But the incoherence found at the level of content appears also at the formal level. What is the purpose of the realistic tone of the portraits, when all the surrounding decoration is clearly inspired by psychedelic hallucinations, presented like the visual diary of a Henry Michaux journey into the realm of mescaline? With vortices, spirals, and undulant textures the work reveals its hallucinatory purpose, its determination to summon to the mind's eye a universe of fictive values, of perverse invention . . . The obsessive repetition of the mandala motif (every page includes at least four or five radiating symmetries of obvious Buddhist origin) betrays a metaphysics of the Void.

The work as pure sign of itself: this is the end result of contemporary literary theory, and these editions confirm it. Perhaps there are collectors who aspire to gather these pages in a volume, potentially infinite, as happened with Mallarmé's *Livre*. Vain effort, because the sign that refers to other signs is lost in its own vacuity, behind which, we suspect, no real value exists.

An extreme example of the cultural dissipation of our time. These works have been received by readers with an approbation that in our opinion bodes only ill: the taste for novelty conceals the aesthetic of obsolescence—of consumption, in other words. The numbered copy that we have before our eyes still seems to promise us, through the number that distinguishes

*Coins and Paper*

it, the possibilities of possession *ad personam*. Which is a fraud, because we know that the current aesthetic taste for conspicuous consumption will soon lead the reader to seek out more copies, other printings, as if to find in constant exchange the guarantee that the single copy cannot provide. A sign in a world of signs, each of these works becomes a way to distract us from things. Its realism is bogus, as its psychedelic *avant-gardisme* only hides deeper alienations. In any case, we are grateful to the publisher for having sent us these free copies for review.

UMBERTO ECO, *Misreadings*, 1967, tr. William Weaver, 1993

The Money Critic was wearing a floor-length djellaba of unparalleled richness, patterned with interlocking geometrical shapes and financial symbols. The robe was iridescent even in the muted light of the flat. As soon as he had opened the door he worked his way back to his high-backed Queen Anne armchair, where he picked up his bone-china cup and took a sip of a rarefied tisane. He didn't invite the trio to sit and indeed they couldn't have even if they had wanted to, for there were no other chairs.

Instead, the whole floor of the room which the front door opened into was covered with irregular piles and heaps of money. Money of all kinds: neat stocks of freshly printed bank notes as slick as stationery; plastic rolls of new coinage broken into elbows; used notes of all denominations and currencies, stacked in loose bundles; necklaces of cowrie shells; criss-crossed stacks of lead and iron plugs; notched bones; the filed teeth of narwhals; totemic spirit boards; myriads of different kinds of share-issue certificates, government bills, gilts, bonds (junk and otherwise) from all the two hundred and fifty-two countries of the world; dry-cleaning tokens; Indian State Railway chitties; Luncheon Vouchers; pemmican; piltjurri; balls of crude opium; pots of cocaine basta; gold (in HM Government ingots, also US issue from Fort Knox and Reichsbundesbank wartime loot still stamped with the Nazis' bonnet mascot eagle); other ingots of precious metals; diamonds, pearls, emeralds and dustbin bags full of semi-precious stones; and all kinds of plastic—there was a great slick drift, made up solely of service-till cards, which flooded into the kitchenette.

Here and there, there was an item of what might of been furniture, faintly visible beneath the riot of dosh, but overall the impression the Money Critic's room gave was of a relief map of currencies, in which the lumpings and moundings of diverse kinds indicated their relative liquidity and value.

The Money Critic's room was the room of a man who criticised money with a vengeance; for into these expensive spits and promontories of pelf there was written clear evidence of careful lapidary arrangement. There was nothing in the least vulgar about this, rather, the same mind that had conceived of the collection as an opportunity to demonstrate the raw mechanics of money—its great gearing, both into itself and into the subsidiary world of things—had also chosen to regard the things-that-were-money as aesthetic objects in their own right. A lacy bridal veil pinned with high-denomination drachma notes was draped over the lampshade; the sunlight from the window fell through—and was filtered by—a collection of abacuses that were ranged along the sill, each one like a miniature Venetian blind.

WILL SELF, *My Idea of Fun*, 1993

# Riches and Poverty

*The most obvious subjects for literary treatment, but also the themes which are hardest to write about in an objective spirit, since they are so surrounded by fantasies of envy, greed, pathos and despair. One recent wit has proposed the term 'plutography' to classify the type of modern subliterature which aims at arousing cupidity rather than concupiscence, though few literary accounts of riches are wholly free of a plutographic taint. The excessive nature of vast wealth can occasionally tempt writers to be spendthrift with their words, as in Sir Epicure Mammon's delirious speech.*

*Similarly, there may be something in the cramped and dreary condition of poverty which lures writers of fiction towards dullness or cliché—and this despite the number of authors who have themselves badly wanted money. There is still a measure of justice in Walter Bagehot's observation that 'nothing is so rare in fiction as a good delineation of the poor', though some of the writers cited here offer affecting exceptions to the rule.*

༝

We may see the small value God has for riches, by the people he gives them to.

ALEXANDER POPE, *Thoughts on Various Subjects*, 1727

Wealth is not without its advantages and the case to the contrary, although it has often been made, has never proved widely persuasive. But, beyond doubt, wealth is the relentless enemy of understanding. The poor man has always a precise view of his problem and its remedy: he hasn't enough and he needs more. The rich man can assume or imagine a much greater variety of ills and he will be correspondingly less certain of their remedy. Also, until he learns to live with his wealth, he will have a well-observed tendency to put it to the wrong purposes or otherwise to make himself foolish.

As with individuals so with nations. And the experience of nations with well-being is exceedingly brief. Nearly all throughout all history have been very poor. The exception, almost insignificant in the whole span of human existence, has been the last few generations in the comparatively small corner of the world populated by Europeans. Here, and especially in the United States, there has been great and quite unprecedented affluence.

The ideas by which the people of this favored part of the world interpret their existence, and in measure guide their behavior, were not forged in a world of wealth.

J. K. GALBRAITH, *The Affluent Society*, 1958

Wealth is the smallest thing on earth, the least gift that God has bestowed on mankind. What is it in comparison with God's Word—what, in comparison with corporal gifts, as beauty, health, &c.?—nay, what is it to the gifts of the mind, as understanding, wisdom, &c.? Yet are men so eager after it, that no labour, pains, or risk is regarded in the acquisition of riches. Wealth has in it neither material, formal, efficient, nor final cause, nor anything else that is good; therefore our Lord God commonly gives riches to those from whom he withholds spiritual good.

MARTIN LUTHER, *Table-Talk*, 1566, tr. William Hazlitt

SIR EPICURE MAMMON. I will have all my beds blown up, not stuffed:
Down is too hard; and then, mine oval room
Filled with such pictures as Tiberius took
From Elephantis, and dull Aretine
But coldly imitated. Then, my glasses
Cut in more subtle angles, to disperse
And multiply the figures, as I walk
Naked between my *succubae*. My mists
I'll have of perfume, vapoured 'bout the room,
To lose our selves in; and my baths, like pits
To fall into, from whence we will come forth,
And roll us dry in gossamer and roses.—
Is it arrived at ruby?—Where I spy

A wealthy citizen, or rich lawyer,
    Have a sublimed, pure wife, unto that fellow
    I'll send a thousand pound to be my cuckold.
FACE. And I shall carry it?
MAMMON.                         No, I'll ha' no bawds
    But fathers and mothers—they will do it best,
    Best of all others. And my flatterers
    Shall be the purest and gravest of divines
    That I can get for money. My mere fools
    Eloquent burgesses, and then my poets
    The same that writ so nobly of the fart,
    Whom I will entertain still for that subject.
    The few that would give themselves to be
    Court- and town-stallions and each-where bely
    Ladies who are known most innocent, for them,
    These will I beg, to make me eunuchs of,
    And they shall fan me with ten estrich tails
    Apiece, made in a plume to gather wind.
    We will be brave, Puff, now we ha' the med'cine.
    My meat shall all come in, in Indian shells,
    Dishes of agate set in gold, and studded
    With emeralds, sapphires, hyacinths, and rubies.
    The tongues of carps, dormice, and camels' heels,
    Boiled i' the spirit of Sol, and dissolved pearl
    (Apicius' diet, 'gainst the epilepsy);
    And I will eat these broths with spoons of amber,
    Headed with diamond and carbuncle.
    My foot-boy shall eat pheasants, calvered salmons,
    Knots, godwits, lampreys. I myself will have
    The beards of barbels served instead of salads;
    Oiled mushrooms; and the swelling unctuous paps
    Of a fat pregnant sow, newly cut off,
    Dressed with an exquisite and poignant sauce;
    For which, I'll say unto my cook, 'There's gold;
    Go forth, and be a knight!'

                                    BEN JONSON, *The Alchemist*, 1610.

'There are some things that money can't accomplish,' remarked young
Rockwall, rather gloomily.

'Now, don't say that,' said old Anthony, shocked. 'I bet my money on money every time. I've been through the encyclopædia down to Y looking for something you can't buy with it; and I expect to have to take up the appendix next week. I'm for money against the field. Tell me something money won't buy.'

'For one thing,' answered Richard, rankling a little, 'it won't buy one into the exclusive circles of society.'

'Oho! won't it?' thundered the champion of the root of evil. 'You tell me where your exclusive circles would be if the first Astor hadn't had the money to pay for his steerage passage over?'

Richard sighed.

> O. HENRY (William Sydney Porter, 1862–1910), 'Mammon and the Archer'


And a certain ruler asked him, saying, Good Master, what shall I do to inherit eternal life?

And Jesus said unto him, Why callest thou me good? None is good save one, that is, God.

Thou knowest the commandments, Do not commit adultery, Do not kill, Do not steal, Do not bear false witness, Honour thy father and thy mother.

And he said, All these have I kept from my youth up.

Now when Jesus heard these things, he said unto him, Yet lackest thou one thing: Sell all that thou hast, and distribute unto the poor, and thou shalt have treasure in heaven: and come, follow me.

And when he heard this, he was very sorrowful: for he was very rich.

And when Jesus saw that he was very sorrowful, he said, How hardly shall they that have riches enter into the kingdom of God!

For it is easier for a camel to go through a needle's eye, than for a rich man to enter into the kingdom of God!

> Luke 18: 18–25


[*Fitzgerald*:] The rich are different from us.
[*Ernest Hemingway*:] Yes, they have more money.

> F. SCOTT FITZGERALD, *The Crack-Up*, ed. Edmund Wilson, 1945


## THE RICH

I like the rich—the way
they say: 'I'm not made of money':

their favourite pastoral
is to think they're not rich at all—
poorer, perhaps, than you or me,
for they have the imagination of that fall
into the pinched decency
we take for granted. Of course,
they do want to be wanted
by all the skivvies and scrapers
who neither inherited nor rose.
But are they daft or deft,
when they proclaim themselves
men of the left, as if prepared
at the first premonitory flush
of the red dawn
to go rushing onto the street
and, share by share,
add to the common conflagration
their scorned advantage?
They know that it can't happen
in Worthing or Wantage:
with so many safety valves
between themselves and scalding,
all they have to fear
is wives, children, breath and balding.
And at worst
there is always some sunny
Aegean prospect. I like the rich—
they so resemble the rest
of us, except for their money.

Charles Tomlinson, The Way In, 1974

He had roll'd in money like pigs in mud,
Till it seem'd to have enter'd into his blood
   By some occult projection:
And his cheeks, instead of a healthy hue,
As yellow as any guinea grew,
Making the common phrase seem true
   About a rich complexion.

Thomas Hood, 'Miss Kilmansegg and her Precious Leg', 1841–3

Wealth, again, that end to which our prodigious works for material advantage are directed,—the commonest of commonplaces tells us how men are always apt to regard wealth as a precious end in itself; and certainly they have never been so apt thus to regard it as they are in England at the present time. Never did people believe anything more firmly, than nine Englishmen out of ten at the present day believe that our greatness and welfare are proved by our being so very rich. Now, the use of culture is that it helps us, by means of its spiritual standard of perfection, to regard wealth as but machinery, and not only to say as a matter of words that we regard wealth as but machinery, but really to perceive and feel that it is so. If it were not for this purging effect wrought upon our minds by culture, the whole world, the future as well as the present, would inevitably belong to the Philistines. The people who believe most that our greatness and welfare are proved by our being very rich, and who most give their lives and thoughts to becoming rich, are just the very people whom we call Philistines. Culture says: 'Consider these people, then, their way of life, their habits, their manners, the very tones of their voice; look at them attentively; observe the literature they read, the things which give them pleasure, the words which come forth out of their mouths, the thoughts which make the furniture of their minds; would any amount of wealth be worth having with the condition that one was to become just like these people by having it?' And thus culture begets a dissatisfaction which is of the highest possible value in stemming the common tide of men's thoughts in a wealthy and industrial community, and which saves the future, as one may hope, from being vulgarised, even if it cannot save the present.

MATTHEW ARNOLD, *Culture and Anarchy*, 1869

Mr Podsnap was well to do, and stood very high in Mr Podsnap's opinion. Beginning with a good inheritance, he had married a good inheritance, and had thriven exceedingly in the Marine Insurance way, and was quite satisfied. He never could make out why everybody was not quite satisfied, and he felt conscious that he set a brilliant social example in being particularly well satisfied with most things, and, above all other things, with himself.

CHARLES DICKENS, *Our Mutual Friend*, 1864–5

Money talks through the rich as alcohol swaggers in the drunken, calling softly to itself to unite into the lava flow which petrifies all it touches.

PALINURUS (Cyril Connolly), *The Unquiet Grave*, 1944

'She's got an indiscreet voice,' I remarked. 'It's full of—' I hesitated.

'Her voice is full of money,' he said suddenly.

That was it. I'd never understood before. It was full of money—that was the inexhaustible charm that rose and fell in it, the jingle of it, the cymbals' song of it. . . . High in a white palace the king's daughter, the golden girl. . . .

F. SCOTT FITZGERALD, The Great Gatsby, 1925

### THE TERRIBLE PEOPLE

People who have what they want are very fond of telling people who
      haven't what they want that they really don't want it,
And I wish I could afford to gather all such people into a gloomy
      castle on the Danube and hire half a dozen capable Draculas to
      haunt it.
I don't mind their having a lot of money, and I don't care how they
      employ it,
But I do think that they damn well ought to admit they enjoy it.
But no, they insist on being stealthy
About the pleasures of being wealthy,
And the possession of a handsome annuity
Makes them think that to say how hard it is to make both ends meet
      is their bounden duity.
You cannot conceive of an occasion
Which will find them without some suitable evasion.
Yes indeed, with arguments they are very fecund;
Their first point is that money isn't everything, and that they have no
      money anyhow is their second.
Some people's money is merited,
And other people's is inherited,
But wherever it comes from,
They talk about it as if it were something you got pink gums from.
This may well be,
But if so, why do they not relieve themselves of the burden by transferring
      it to the deserving poor or to me?
Perhaps indeed the possession of wealth is constantly distressing,
But I should be quite willing to assume every curse of wealth if I
      could at the same time assume every blessing.
The only incurable troubles of the rich are the troubles that money can't
      cure,

Which is a kind of trouble that is even more troublesome if you are
    poor.
Certainly there are lots of things in life that money won't buy, but it's very
    funny—
Have you ever tried to buy them without money?

Ogden Nash, Happy Days, 1933

They had all done so well for themselves, these Forsytes, that they were all
what is called 'of a certain position.' They had shares in all sorts of things,
not as yet—with the exception of Timothy—in consols, for they had no
dread in life like that of 3 per cent. for their money.

John Galsworthy, The Man of Property, 1906

He shewed me to-night his drawing-room, very genteelly fitted up; and
said, 'Mrs Thrale sneered when I talked of my having asked you and your
lady to live at my house. I was obliged to tell her, that you would be in as
respectable a situation in my house as in hers. Sir, the insolence of wealth
will creep out.'

James Boswell, Life of Samuel Johnson, 1791, 18 April 1778

Dr P. had a young patient whose father is a big employer and very wealthy.
The youth was suffering from tuberculosis in some form, and Dr P. suggested that a specialist should be consulted. 'The best,' said the father. A
consultation was arranged with the very eminent Dr Q. Dr P. was five
minutes late for the appointment, and found the patient, the father, and Dr
Q. already assembled. The father was telling Dr Q. wonderful tales about
Dr P. After some more general conversation the father suddenly said: 'Now,
gentlemen, let's get to business,' as though at a Directors' meeting. Dr Q.'s
verdict was sufficiently serious. At the end the father said: 'Now, doctor,
how much is your fee?' Dr Q. said five guineas. 'What?' cried the father. Dr
Q. repeated, five guineas. The father looked at Dr P. and said: 'I thought
you'd brought me to the best man in London?' 'So I have,' said Dr P.
'What?' cried the father again to Dr Q. 'You're the best man in London and
you only charge five guineas! You'll have to take more.' Dr Q. said that five
guineas was his charge, and he shouldn't take more. 'You'll have to,' said
the father, and pulled a roll of pound-notes out of his pocket two inches

thick, fastened with two indiarubber bands. He wet his thumb and began to count—up to ten. He then felt in his waistcoat pocket for a ten-shilling note, but couldn't find one. 'Never mind,' he said. 'Here's an extra ten shillings for luck, doctor,' and then added an eleventh pound-note, and offered the money to Dr Q., who protested. 'Either you'll take 'em or they'll go in the fire.' Dr Q. took the money. The father then proceeded: 'Now, doctor, this is an important day in my life, meeting the top man in London in his line. I don't mind telling you I had a bottle of Veuve Clikko at my London office before I came. Now you must come with me, and you too, Dr P., and we'll have another bottle. I've got my car waiting at the door. She was a damned clever old woman, was that widow.' It took the two doctors some time to make the father understand that they wouldn't and couldn't come. So he went off with his son, whose serious state did not seem to trouble him in the least.

ARNOLD BENNETT, *Things That Have Interested Me*, 1921

She was fond of dropping his sovereigns ostentatiously into the plate, and
    she liked to see them stand out rather conspicuously against the com-
    monplace half-crowns and shillings,
  So he took her to all the charity sermons, and if by any extraordinary
    chance there wasn't a charity sermon anywhere, he would drop a
    couple of sovereigns (one for him and one for her) into the poor-box
    at the door;
And as he always deducted the sums thus given in charity from the house-
    keeping money, and the money he allowed her for her bonnets and
    frillings,
  She soon began to find that even charity, if you allow it to interfere with
    your personal luxuries, becomes an intolerable bore.

W. S. GILBERT, 'Lost Mr Blake', *Fifty 'Bab' Ballads*, 1876

'Harrogate has millions in his safes, and I have—the hole in my pocket. But you daren't say—you can't say—that he's cleverer than I, or bolder than I, or even more energetic. He's not clever; he's got eyes like blue buttons; he's not energetic, he moves from chair to chair like a paralytic. He's a conscientious, kindly old blockhead; but he's got money simply because he collects money, as a boy collects stamps. You're too strong-minded for business, Ezza. You won't get on. To be clever enough to get all that money, one must be stupid enough to want it.'

G. K. Chesterton, 'The Paradise of Thieves', *The Wisdom of Father Brown*, 1914

## THE MILLIONAIRE

When you enquire of millionaires
   Their candid personal impressions
Of an existence such as theirs,
They emphasize the woes, the cares,
   Of those with great possessions;
They prove, with chapter and with verse,
That Money is a Perfect Curse.

But though with passion they maintain
   (And seem to have no doubt about it)
That lucre is but dross, and vain,
This truth does not appear so plain
   To those who are without it.
Wealth's a delusion, if you will,
But Poverty is trickier still!

With money, so they all profess—
   And I've no wish to beg the question—
One cannot purchase Happiness
Or Peace of Mind, or yet Success,
   Or a robust digestion;
But one *can* buy a good cigar
And plovers' eggs and caviare!

Harry Graham, *The World's Workers*, 1928

On the last day in Ascona, June 29, Paul and Mary Mellon each had an appointment with Jung. Mary reported later that her first words were: 'Dr Jung, we have too much money. What can we do with it?' In any event, Jung agreed to see them on a regular basis in Zurich beginning a year later.

William McGuire, *Bollingen: An Adventure in Collecting the Past*, 1982

'I've been with your father and mother for two days now, and I see no signs of anything going wrong. The only trouble with them is that they're too rich. That makes them fretful: it's like teething. Every time your father hears he's made another million it's like cutting a new tooth. They hurt to bite on when one has so many.'

EDITH WHARTON, *The Children*, 1928

*Enter* CHEATLY, SHAMWELL, *and* MRS TERMAGANT
*in her fine Lodgings.*

CHEAT. Madam, you must carry yourself somewhat stately, but courteously, to the bubble.

SHAM. Somewhat reservedly, and yet so as to give him hopes.

TERM. I warrant you, let me alone; and if I effect this business, you are best friends; such friends as I could never yet expect. 'Twill be an exquisite revenge.

CHEAT. He comes. Come, noble Squire.

*Enter* BELFOND SENIOR.

Madam, this is the gentleman whom I would recommend to your ladyship's favour, who is ambitious of kissing your hand.

BELF. SEN. Yes, madam, as Mr Cheatly says, I am ambitious of kissing your hand, and your lip too, madam; for I vow to Gad, madam, there is not a person in the world, madam, has a greater honour for your person. And, madam, I assure you I am a person—

TERM. My good friend, Mr Cheatly, with whom I intrust the management of my small fortune—

CHEAT. Small fortune! Nay, it is a large one.

TERM. Has told me of your family and character. To your name I am no stranger, nor to your estate, though this is the first time I have had the honour to see your person.

BELF. SEN. Hold, good madam, the honour lies on my side; she's a rare lady, ten times handsomer than my blowen, (and here's a lodging and furniture for a Queen!)—Madam, if your ladyship please to accept of my affection in an honourable way, you shall find I am no put, no country prigster, nor shall ever want the megs, the smelts, decusses and Georges, the ready and the rhino: I am rhinocerical.

*ready, rhino*] ready-money    *Megs*] guineas    *smelts*] half-guineas    *decus*] a crown-piece    *George*] a half-crown

THOMAS SHADWELL, *The Squire of Alsatia*, 1688

## ON LATE ACQUIRED WEALTH

Poor in my youth, and in life's later scenes
Rich to no end, I curse my natal hour,
Who naught enjoyed while young, denied the means;
And naught when old enjoyed, denied the power.

WILLIAM COWPER (1731–1800), *Poems*, 1803

## MONEY

I sit here eating milk-toast in my lap-robe—
They've got my nightshirt starchier than I told 'em . . . Huh! . . .
I'll tell 'em. . . .
                    Why, I wouldn't have given
A wooden nickel to a wooden Indian, when I began.
I never gave a soul a cent that I could help
That I remember: now I sit here hatching cheques
For any mortal cause that writes in asking,
And look or don't look—I've been used to 'em too long—
At seven Corots and the Gobelins
And my first Rembrandt I outbid Clay Frick for:
A dirty Rembrandt bought with dirty money—
But nowadays we've all been to the cleaners'.
(Harriet'd call Miss Tarbell Old Tarbaby—
It none of it will stick, she'd say when I got mad;
And she was right. She always was.)
I used to say I'd made my start in railroads
—'Stocks, that is,' I'd think and never say—
And made my finish in philanthropy:
To think that all along it'uz Service!
I could have kicked myself right in the face
To think I didn't think of that myself. . . .
'There isn't one of you that couldn't have done what I did—'
That was *my* line; and I'd think: 'if you'd been me.'
SEES U.S. LAND OF OPPORTUNITY,
A second-page two-column headline,
Was all I got, most years.

*They never knew a thing!*

Why, when I think of what I've done, I can't believe it!

. . . A Presbyterian'd say it's Providence.
In my time I've bought the whole Rhode Island Legislature
For—I disremember how much; what for too. . . .
Harriet'd have Nellie Melba in
To entertain our friends—it never entertained *me* none—
And I'd think: 'Birdie, I could buy you
The way you'd buy a piece of Melba toast.'

I had my troubles—nothing money wouldn't cure.
A percentage of the world resented me
There on my money bags in my silk hat.
(To hear Ward I'd still straw stuck in my fur.)
But in the end the money reconciled 'em all.
Don't someone call it the Great Reconciler?
When my boys dynamited thirteen trestles
On the New York Central, I went against my custom then
And told the papers: 'Money's a *responsibility*.'
I'd talk down money if I hadn't any. As it was,
The whole office force could hear me through two doors.
E. J. said they said: 'Listen to the Old Man go!'

Why, it was money
That got me shut of my poor trusting wife,
And bought my girl from her, and got me Harriet—
What else would Harriet've married *me* for? . . . She's gone now
And they're gone too, but it's not gone. . . .
You can take it with you anywhere I'm going.

. . . While I was looking up my second son-in-law
In Dun and Bradstreet, the social secretary
Came on him in the *Almanach de Gotha*.
It was like I figured, though: he didn't take.

You couldn't tell my grandson from a Frenchman.

And Senators! . . .
                              I never saw the man I couldn't buy.

When my Ma died I boarded with a farmer
In the next county; I used to think of her,
And I looked round me, as I could,
And I saw what it added up to: money.
Now I'm dying—I can't call this living—
I haven't any cause to change my mind.
They say that money isn't everything: it isn't;
Money don't help you none when you are sighing
For something else in this wide world to buy. . . .
The first time I couldn't think of anything
I didn't have, it shook me.

But giving does as well.

The hero of MONEY, an old man surviving into a different age, says the poem during the '20's, when businessmen used to say that they worked not for money but for Service. *Miss Tarbell* is Ida Tarbell, the famous muckraker; *Ward* is Ward MacAlister, equally famous as a 'social arbiter'. The city of Providence is the capital of Rhode Island. The old man's *But giving does as well* means that when you have bought everything there is to buy, you have only begun: you can still establish foundations, make bequests with conditions, and say *Go* and *Come* in many tax-exempt ways—money, in this 'etherealized' form, is as powerful as ever.

RANDALL JARRELL, *Selected Poems*, 1956

*Money* never made any man rich, but his mind. He that can order himselfe to the Law of nature, is not onely without the sense, but the feare of poverty. O! but to strike blind the people with our wealth, and pompe, is the thing! what a wretchednesse is this, to thrust all our riches outward, and be beggars within: to contemplate nothing, but the little, vile, and sordid things of the world; not the great, noble, and pretious? wee serve our avarice, and not content with the good of the Earth, that is offer'd us; wee search, and digge for the evill that is hidden. *God* offer'd us those things, and plac'd them at hand, and neere us, that hee knew were profitable for us; but the hurtfull hee laid deepe, and hid. Yet doe wee seeke onely the things, whereby wee may perish; and bring them forth, when *God* and nature hath buried them.

BEN JONSON, *Timber; or, Discoveries made upon Men and Matter*, 1641

Dressed up in white flannels I went over to his lawn a little after seven, and wandered around rather ill at ease among swirls and eddies of people I didn't know—though here and there was a face I had noticed on the commuting train. I was immediately struck by the number of young Englishmen dotted about; all well dressed, all looking a little hungry, and all talking in low, earnest voices to solid and prosperous Americans. I was sure that they were selling something: bonds or insurance or automobiles. They were at least agonizingly aware of the easy money in the vicinity and convinced that it was theirs for a few words in the right key.

F. SCOTT FITZGERALD, *The Great Gatsby*, 1925

Across the room, Putnam Blake, a thin, white-faced young man with a close collegiate haircut, an unsmiling expression, and a low, tense voice, was explaining what he called his 'Principle of Accumulated Guilt' to the naval officer.

'Mr Blake,' said Dottie with a twinkle, 'has a system for finding rich people to give money to Labour. He was telling about it earlier. It sounds terribly interesting,' she added warmly. Glancing at their watches, at Norine and the actor, and at the closed bedroom door, the two girls drew near to listen. Putnam ignored them, dividing his attention between his pipe and the naval officer. Using Gustavus Myers' *Great American Fortunes*, Poor's *Register of Directors*, and Mendel's Law, he was able to predict, he said, when a wealthy family was 'due'. As a rule, this occurred in the third generation. 'What I've done,' he said, 'is take the element of chance out of fund-raising and put it on a scientific basis. I'm simplifying, of course, but roughly speaking the money guilt has a tendency to skip a generation. Or if it crops out in the second generation, as with the Lamont family, you will find it in a younger son rather than in the first-born. And it may be transmitted to the females while remaining dormant in the males. This means that the guilt tends to separate from the chief property holdings, which are usually transmitted from first-born male to first-born male. Thus the guilt, being a recessive character, like blue eyes, may be bred out of a family without any profit to the Left.' A ghostly quiver, the phantom of a smile, passed across his lips; he appeared eager to take the naval officer into his confidence, like some crazy inventor, thought Helena, with a patent, and it was as if some bashful ectoplasmic joke hovered in the neighbourhood of his Principle. 'I'm working now,' he continued, 'on the relation between mental deficiency and money guilt in rich families. Your ideal contributor (the Communists have found this), scion of a fortune, has a mental age of twelve.' Without altering his expression, he gave a quick parenthetic little laugh.

Helena quirked her sandy eyebrows, thinking of the Rich Young Man in the Bible and idly imagining a series of camels with humps of accumulated guilt lining up to pass through the eye of a needle. The conversation at this party struck her as passing strange. 'Read the *Communist Manifesto*—for its style,' she had heard Harald telling Kay's supervisor (Wellesley '28). She grinned. 'Take *her*,' said Putnam suddenly to the naval officer, indicating Helena with a jab of his pipe. 'Her people live on the income of their income. Father is first vice-president of Oneida Steel. Self-made man—first generation. Bright girl, the daughter—only child. Does not respond to fund-raising appeals for labour victims. Charities confined, probably, to Red Cross and tuberculosis stamps. But if she has four children, you can expect that at least one of them will evince guilt characteristics. . . .'

Impressed despite herself, Helena lit a cigarette. She had met Mr Blake for the first time this afternoon and for a moment she felt he must have clairvoyance, like a mind reader in a movie house or, more accurately, a *fortune* teller.

MARY McCARTHY, *The Group*, 1954

Danger in Wealth.—Only a man of intellect should hold property: otherwise property is dangerous to the community. For the owner, not knowing how to make use of the leisure which his possessions might secure to him, will continue to strive after more property. This strife will be his occupation, his strategy in the war with ennui. So in the end real wealth is produced from the moderate property that would be enough for an intellectual man. Such wealth, then, is the glittering outcrop of intellectual dependence and poverty, but it looks quite different from what its humble origin might lead one to expect, because it can mask itself with culture and art—it can, in fact, purchase the mask. Hence it excites envy in the poor and uncultured—who at bottom always envy culture and see no mask in the mask—and gradually paves the way for a social revolution. For a gilded coarseness and a histrionic blowing of trumpets in the pretended enjoyment of culture inspires that class with the thought, 'It is only a matter of money,' whereas it is indeed to some extent a matter of money, but far more of intellect.

*

Being Ashamed of Wealth.—Our age endures only a single species of rich men—those who are ashamed of their wealth. If we hear it said of any one that he is very rich, we at once feel a similar sentiment to that experienced at the sight of a repulsively swollen invalid, one suffering from diabetes or dropsy. We must with an effort remember our humanity, in order to go about with this rich man in such a way that he does not notice our feeling of disgust. But as soon as he prides himself at all on his wealth, our feelings are mingled with an almost compassionate surprise at such a high degree of human unreason.

FRIEDRICH NIETZSCHE, Human, All-Too-Human, 1879, tr. Cohn, 1911

In democratic countries, however opulent a man is supposed to be, he is almost always discontented with his fortune, because he finds that he is less rich than his father was, and he fears that his sons will be less rich than himself. Most rich men in democracies are therefore constantly haunted by the desire of obtaining wealth, and they naturally turn their attention to trade and manufactures, which appear to offer the readiest and most powerful means of success. In this respect they share the instincts of the poor, without feeling the same necessities; say rather, they feel the most imperious of all necessities, that of not sinking in the world.

ALEXIS DE TOCQUEVILLE, Democracy in America, 1835–40

We have no aristocracy of blood, and having therefore as a natural, and indeed as an inevitable thing, fashioned for ourselves an aristocracy of dollars, the *display of wealth* has here to take the place and perform the office of the heraldic display in monarchical countries. By a transition readily understood, and which might have been as readily foreseen, we have been brought to merge in simple *show* our notions of taste itself.

EDGAR ALLAN POE, 'The Philosophy of Furniture', 1840

I cannot call Riches better than the baggage of virtue. The Roman word is better, *impedimenta*. For as the baggage is to an army, so is riches to virtue. It cannot be spared nor left behind, but it hindereth the march; yea and the care of it sometimes loseth or disturbeth the victory. Of great riches there is no real use, except it be in the distribution; the rest is but conceit. So saith Solomon, 'Where much is, there are many to consume it; and what hath the owner but the sight of it with his eyes?' The personal fruition in any man cannot reach to feel great riches: there is a custody of them; or a power of dole and donative of them; or a fame of them; but no solid use to the owner. Do you not see what feigned prices are set upon little stones and rarities? and what works of ostentation are undertaken, because there might seem to be some use of great riches? But then you will say, they may be of use to buy men out of dangers or troubles. As Solomon saith, 'Riches are as a strong hold, in the imagination of the rich man.' But this is excellently expressed, that it is in imagination, and not always in fact. For certainly great riches have sold more men than they have bought out. Seek not proud riches, but such as thou mayest get justly, use soberly, distribute cheerfully, and leave contentedly. Yet have no abstract nor friarly contempt of them. But distinguish, as Cicero saith well of Rabirius Posthumus, *In studio rei amplificandae apparebat, non avaritiae praedam, sed instrumentum bonitati quaeri.* Hearken also to Solomon, and beware of hasty gathering of riches; *Qui festinat ad divitias, non erit insons.*

The poets feign, that when Plutus (which is Riches) is sent from Jupiter, he limps and goes slowly; but when he is sent from Pluto, he runs and is swift of foot. Meaning that riches gotten by good means and just labour pace slowly; but when they come by the death of others (as by the course of inheritance, testaments, and the like), they come tumbling upon a man. But it mought be applied likewise to Pluto, taking him for the devil. For when riches come from the devil (as by fraud and oppression and unjust means), they come upon speed. The ways to enrich are many, and most of them foul. Parsimony is one of the best, and yet is not innocent; for it withholdeth men from works of liberality and charity. The improvement of the ground is the most natural obtaining of riches; for it is our great mother's blessing, the earth's; but it is slow. And yet where men of great wealth do stoop to husbandry, it multiplieth riches exceedingly. I knew a nobleman in England, that had the greatest audits of any man in my time; a great grazier, a great sheep-master, a great timber man, a great collier, a great corn-master, a great lead-man, and so of iron, and a number of the like points of husbandry. So as the earth seemed a sea to him, in respect of the perpetual importation. . . .

Believe not much them that seem to despise riches; for they despise them that despair of them; and none worse when they come to them. Be not penny-wise; riches have wings, and sometimes they fly away of themselves, sometimes they must be set flying to bring in more. Men leave their riches either to their kindred, or to the public; and moderate portions prosper best in both. A great state left to an heir, is as a lure to all the birds of prey round about to seize on him, if he be not the better stablished in years and judgment. Likewise glorious gifts and foundations are like sacrifices

---

*In studio . . . quaeri*] In his care for increasing his property, it was evident that what was being sought was not the prey for avarice but an instrument for benevolence.    *Qui festinat . . . insons*] He who hastens towards riches will not go unpunished (Proverbs 28: 20)

without salt; and but the painted sepulchres of alms, which soon will pu-
trefy and corrupt inwardly. Therefore measure not thine advancements by
quantity, but frame them by measure: and defer not charities till death; for,
certainly, if a man weigh it rightly, he that doth so is rather liberal of
another man's than of his own.

FRANCIS BACON (1561–1621), 'Of Riches'

P. Who shall decide, when doctors disagree,
And soundest casuists doubt, like you and me?
You hold the word, from Jove to Momus given,
That man was made the standing jest of Heaven;
And gold but sent to keep the fools in play,
For some to heap, and some to throw away.

But I, who think more highly of our kind,
(And surely Heaven and I are of a mind)
Opine, that Nature, as in duty bound
Deep hid the shining mischief underground:
But when by man's audacious labour won,
Flamed forth this rival to its sire, the sun,
Then careful Heaven supplied two sorts of men,
To squander these, and those to hide again.

Like doctors thus, when much dispute has passed,
We find our tenets just the same at last.
Both fairly owning, riches, in effect,
No grace of Heaven or token of the elect;
Given to the fool, the mad, the vain, the evil,
To Ward, to Waters, Chartres, and the Devil.

B. What Nature wants, commodious gold bestows,
'Tis thus we eat the bread another sows.

P. But how unequal it bestows, observe,
'Tis thus we riot, while, who sow it, starve:
What Nature wants (a phrase I much distrust)
Extends to luxury, extends to lust:
Useful, I grant, it serves what life requires,
But dreadful, too, the dark assassin hires.

B. Trade it may help, society extend:
P. But lures the pirate, and corrupts the friend.
B. It raises armies in a nation's aid:
P. But bribes a senate, and the land's betrayed.

In vain may heroes fight, and patriots rave;
If secret gold sap on from knave to knave.
Once, we confess, beneath the patriot's cloak,
From the cracked bag the dropping guinea spoke,
And jingling down the back-stairs, told the crew,
'Old Cato is as great a rogue as you.'
Blest paper-credit! last and best supply!
That lends Corruption lighter wings to fly!
Gold imp'd by thee, can compass hardest things,
Can pocket states, can fetch or carry kings;
A single leaf shall waft an army o'er,
Or ship off senates to some distant shore;
A leaf, like Sibyl's, scatter to and fro
Our fates and fortunes, as the wind shall blow:
Pregnant with thousands flits the scrap unseen,
And silent sells a king, or buys a queen.

ALEXANDER POPE, 'To Allen, Lord Bathurst, on the Use of Riches', 1732

With the greater part of rich people, the chief enjoyment of riches consists in the parade of riches, which in their eye is never so complete as when they appear to possess those decisive marks of opulence which nobody can possess but themselves.

ADAM SMITH, *The Wealth of Nations*, 1776

Their artistic taste is no longer satisfied with the simple rough hoes and axe-blades. And thus amongst the Bolongole lovers of display has been originated a fantastic kind of currency of greater exuberance than any that has probably yet been imagined by any Board of Trade. At the same time the origin itself of this remarkable species of money is characteristic of the people. At great dancing feasts the Bolongole natives are accustomed to make a display of their money, which on those occasions is set on shafts as spearheads might be. Then everybody delights in showing off his own, all striving to surpass each other with new forms. In this way the iron money with these natives has no longer the current value of strong axe-blades or serviceable spearheads, but only the merit of eccentricity.

LEO FROBENIUS, *The Childhood of Man*, tr. A. H. Keane, 1909

Gradually, as industrial activity further displaces predatory activity in the community's everyday life and in men's habits of thought, accumulated property more and more replaces trophies of predatory exploit as the conventional exponent of prepotence and success. With the growth of settled industry, therefore, the possession of wealth gains in relative importance and effectiveness as a customary basis of repute and esteem. Not that esteem ceases to be awarded on the basis of other, more direct evidence of prowess; not that successful predatory aggression or warlike exploit ceases to call out the approval and admiration of the crowd, or to stir the envy of the less successful competitors; but the opportunities for gaining distinction by means of this direct manifestation of superior force grow less available both in scope and frequency. At the same time opportunities for industrial aggression, and for the accumulation of property by the quasi-peaceable methods of nomadic industry, increase in scope and availability. And it is even more to the point that property now becomes the most easily recognised evidence of a reputable degree of success as distinguished from heroic or signal achievement. It therefore becomes the conventional basis of esteem. Its possession in some amount becomes necessary in order to attain any reputable standing in the community. It becomes indispensable to accumulate, to acquire property, in order to retain one's good name. When accumulated goods have in this way once become the accepted badge of efficiency, the possession of wealth presently assumes the character of an independent and definitive basis of esteem. The possession of goods, whether acquired aggressively by one's own exertion or passively by transmission through inheritance from others, becomes a conventional basis of reputability. The possession of wealth, which was at the outset valued simply as an evidence of efficiency, becomes, in popular apprehension, itself a meritorious act. Wealth is now itself intrinsically honourable and confers honour on its possessor. By a further refinement, wealth acquired passively by transmission from ancestors or other antecedents presently becomes even more honorific than wealth acquired by the possessor's own effort; but this distinction belongs at a later stage in the evolution of the pecuniary culture.

THORSTEIN VEBLEN, *The Theory of the Leisure Class*, 1899


After Claude was born, Pablo began to make a Freudian slip that was quite amusing: whenever he wanted to speak of the child, *l'enfant*, he would say *l'argent*, the money. At the Rue des Grands-Augustins Claude slept in the room next to ours. We went to bed about one or two in the morning, after Pablo had finished his work. One morning about three o'clock Pablo suddenly sat up in bed and said, 'The money is dead. I don't hear him breathing any more.' I had no idea what he was talking about. I saw he was awake, not dreaming, so I asked him what he meant.

'You know very well what I mean. I mean the child,' he said. I told him that was the most peculiar mix-up I'd ever heard.

'You don't know what you're talking about,' he said. 'That's the most natural thing in the world. Freud even says so. After all, the child is his mother's riches. Money is another form of riches. You just don't understand those things.' I told him I could hear breathing sounds very clearly from the next room.

'That's the wind,' he said. 'My money is dead. You go see.' I went in to look at Claude. He was sleeping peacefully. I returned to our bedroom and reported to Pablo that the child was not dead. That happened about twice a week. . . .

During the day his anxiety continued. Often when he got home he would say, 'Where's the money?' Sometimes I would say, 'In the trunk,' because Pablo always carried around with him an old red-leather trunk from Hermès in which he kept five or six million francs so that he'd always 'have the price of a package of cigarettes,' as he put it. But if I was assured he was referring to one of the children and said, 'In the garden,' then he would often say, 'No, I mean the money in the trunk. I want to count it.' There was never any real point in counting it because the trunk was always locked, Pablo had the only key and he kept it with him at all times. 'You're going to count it,' he'd say, 'and I'll help you.' He'd pull out all the money, pinned together at the bank in small sheaves of ten bills, and make little piles of it. He'd count one sheaf and it might turn out to be eleven. He'd pass it over to me and I'd count ten. So he'd try it again and this time come up with nine. This made him very suspicious, so each of us had to check again all the sheaves. He had much admired the way Chaplin had counted money in *Monsieur Verdoux* and he tried to do it fast like that. As a result, he made more and more mistakes and there were more and more recounts. Sometimes we spent as much as an hour on this ritual. Finally, when Pablo was tired of playing with the bills, he would give up and say he was satisfied, whether the books balanced or not.

FRANÇOISE GILOT and CARLTON LAKE, *Life with Picasso*, 1964

Riches, like insects, when concealed they lie,
Wait but for wings, and in their season fly.

Who sees pale Mammon pine amidst his store,
Sees but a backward steward for the poor;
This year a reservoir, to keep and spare;
The next, a fountain, spouting through his heir,
In lavish streams to quench a country's thirst,
And men and dogs shall drink him till they burst.

ALEXANDER POPE, 'To Allen, Lord Bathurst, on the Use of Riches', 1732

'The suddenly rich are on a level with any of us nowadays. Money buys position at once. I don't say that it isn't all right. The world generally knows what it's about, and knows how to drive a bargain. I dare say it makes the new rich pay too much. But there's no doubt but money is to the fore now. It is the romance, the poetry of our age. It's the thing that chiefly strikes the imagination. The Englishmen who come here are more curious about the great new millionaires than about any one else, and they respect them more. It's all very well. I don't complain of it.'

WILLIAM DEAN HOWELLS, *The Rise of Silas Lapham*, 1885

Every upstart of fortune, harnessed in the trappings of the mode, presents himself at Bath, as in the very focus of observation—Clerks and factors from the East Indies, loaded with the spoil of plundered provinces; planters, negro-drivers, and hucksters, from our American plantations, enriched they know not how; agents, commissaries, and contractors, who have fattened, in two successive wars, on the blood of the nation; usurers, brokers, and jobbers of every kind; men of low birth, and no breeding, have found themselves suddenly translated into a state of affluence, unknown to former ages; and no wonder that their brains should be intoxicated with pride, vanity, and presumption. Knowing no other criterion of greatness, but the ostentation of wealth, they discharge their affluence without taste or con-duct, through every channel of the most absurd extravagance; and all of them hurry to Bath, because here, without any further qualification, they can mingle with the princes and nobles of the land. Even the wives and daughters of low tradesmen, who, like shovel-nosed sharks, prey upon the blubber of those uncouth whales of fortune, are infected with the same rage of displaying their importance; and the slightest indisposition serves them for a pretext to insist upon being conveyed to Bath, where they may hobble country-dances and cotillons among lordlings, 'squires, counsellors, and clergy. These delicate creatures from Bedfordbury, Butcher-row, Crutched-Friers, and Botolph-lane, cannot breathe in the gross air of the

Lower Town, or conform to the vulgar rules of a common lodging-house; the husband, therefore, must provide an entire house, or elegant apartments in the new buildings. Such is the composition of what is called the fashionable company at Bath; where a very inconsiderable proportion of genteel people are lost in a mob of impudent plebeians, who have neither understanding nor judgment, nor the least idea of propriety and decorum; and seem to enjoy nothing so much as an opportunity of insulting their betters.

TOBIAS SMOLLETT, *The Expedition of Humphry Clinker*, 1771

'And how does it feel to have twelve hundred a year?' asked Masterman, holding his cigarette to his nose tip in a curious manner.

'It's rum,' confided Kipps, after a reflective interval. 'It feels juiced rum.'

'I've never felt it,' said Masterman.

'It takes a bit of getting into,' said Kipps. 'I can tell you that.'

Masterman smoked and regarded Kipps with curious eyes.

'I expect it does,' he said presently.

'And has it made you perfectly happy?' he asked abruptly.

'I couldn't 'ardly say *that*,' said Kipps.

Masterman smiled. 'No,' he said. 'Has it made you much happier?'

'It did at first.'

'Yes. But you got used to it. How long, for example, did the real delirious excitement last?'

'Oo, *that*! Perhaps a week,' said Kipps.

Masterman nodded his head. 'That's what discourages *me* from amassing wealth,' he said to Sid. 'You adjust yourself. It doesn't last. I've always had an inkling of that, and it's interesting to get it confirmed. I shall go on sponging for a bit longer on *you*, I think.'

'You don't,' said Sid. 'No fear.'

'Twenty-four thousand pounds,' said Masterman, and blew a cloud of smoke. 'Lord! Doesn't it worry you?'

'It is a bit worrying at times. . . . Things 'appen.'

'Going to marry?'

'Yes.'

'H'm. Lady, I guess, of a superior social position?'

'Rather,' said Kipps. 'Cousin to the Earl of Beauprés.'

Masterman readjusted his long body with an air of having accumulated all the facts he needed. He snuggled his shoulder-blades down into the chair and raised his angular knees. 'I doubt,' he said, flicking cigarette ash into the atmosphere, 'if any great gain or loss of money does—as things are at present—make more than the slightest difference in one's happiness. It ought to—if money was what it ought to be, the token given for service, one ought to get an increase in power and happiness for every pound one got. But the plain fact is, the times are out of joint, and money—money, like everything else—is a deception and a disappointment.'

H. G. WELLS, *Kipps*, 1905

It is more easy to write on money than to obtain it; and those who gain it, jest much at those who only know how to write about it.

VOLTAIRE (1694–1778), *Philosophical Dictionary*

### LETTERS TO THE WINNER

After the war, and just after marriage and fatherhood
ended in divorce, our neighbour won the special lottery,
an amount then equal to fifteen years of a manager's
salary at the bank, or fifty years' earnings by
a marginal farmer fermenting his clothes in the black
marinade of sweat, up in his mill-logging paddocks.

The district, used to one mailbag, now received two
every mailday. The fat one was for our neighbour.
After a dip or two, he let these bags accumulate
around the plank walls of the kitchen, over the chairs,
till on a rainy day, he fed the tail-switching calves,
let the bullocks out of the yard, and, pausing at the door
to wash his hands, came inside to read the letters.

Shaken out in a vast mound on the kitchen table
they slid down, slithered to his fingers. *I have 7 children
I am under the doctor if you could see your way clear
equal Pardners in the Venture God would bless you lovey
assured of our best service for a mere fifteen pounds down
remember you're only lucky I knew you from the paper straightaway*

Baksheesh, hissed the pages as he flattened them, baksheesh!
*mate if your interested in a fellow diggers problems*

*old mate a friend in need*—the Great Golden Letter
having come, now he was being punished for it.
*You sound like a lovely big boy we could have such times*
*her's my photoe Doll Im wearing my birthday swimsuit*
*with the right man I would share this infallible system.*

When he lifted the stove's iron disc and started feeding in
the pages he'd read, they clutched and streamed up the corrugated
black chimney shaft. And yet he went on reading,
holding each page by its points, feeling an obligation
to read each crude rehearsed lie, each come-on, flat truth, extremity:
*We might visit you the wise investor a loan a bush man like you*

*remember we met on Roma Street for your delight and mine*
*a lick of the sultana*—the white moraine kept slipping
its messages to him *you will be accursed* he husked them like cobs
*Mr Nouveau Jack old man my legs are all paralysed up.*
Black smuts swirled weightless in the room *some good kind person*
like the nausea of a novice free-falling in a deep mine's cage
*now I have lost his pension* and formed a sticky nimbus round him

but he read on, fascinated by a further human range
not even war had taught him, nor literature glossed for him
since he never read literature. Merely the great reject pile
which high style is there to snub and filter, for readers.
That his one day's reading had a strong taste of what he and war
had made of his marriage is likely; he was not without sympathy,

but his leap had hit a wire through which the human is policed.
His head throbbed as if busting with a soundless shout
of immemorial sobbed invective *God-forsaken, God-forsakin*
as he stopped reading, and sat blackened in his riches.

LES MURRAY, *The Daylight Moon*, 1987

When her mother went up to her dressing-room at night she followed her,
and made the important communication. Its effect was most extraordinary;
for, on first hearing it, Mrs Bennet sat quite still, and unable to utter a syllable. Nor was it under many, many minutes, that she could comprehend
what she heard, though not in general backward to credit what was for the

advantage of her family, or that came in the shape of a lover to any of them. She began at length to recover, to fidget about in her chair, get up, sit down again, wonder, and bless herself.

'Good gracious! Lord bless me! only think! dear me! Mr Darcy! Who would have thought it? And is it really true? Oh, my sweetest Lizzy! how rich and how great you will be! What pin-money, what jewels, what carriages you will have! Jane's is nothing to it—nothing at all. I am so pleased—so happy! Such a charming man!—so handsome! so tall!—Oh, my dear Lizzy! pray apologise for my having disliked him so much before. I hope he will overlook it. Dear, dear Lizzy! A house in town! Everything that is charming! Three daughters married! Ten thousand a year! Oh, Lord! what will become of me? I shall go distracted.'

This was enough to prove that her approbation need not be doubted; and Elizabeth, rejoicing that such an effusion was heard only by herself, soon went away. But before she had been three minutes in her own room, her mother followed her.

'My dearest child,' she cried, 'I can think of nothing else! Ten thousand a year, and very likely more! 'Tis as good as a lord! And a special license! You must and shall be married by a special license! But, my dearest love, tell me what dish Mr Darcy is particularly fond of, that I may have it to-morrow.'

JANE AUSTEN, Pride and Prejudice, 1813

In Old Money's imagination, wealth takes on many characteristics of real property, as many as it can bear in a capitalist system. Wealth is seen as an estate or a patrimony with a history and a posterity, literally or figuratively held in trust, and producing an income dedicated to specific social purposes: the support of a family and its cultural, social, and economic undertakings over as many generations as the family endures, or as the estate remains integrated and productive. Wealth in this view is a given, not something owned or possessed, which should be given on.

New Money conceives of wealth in the first instance as *money* (or credited money)—an abstract symbol as far removed from any referent in real property as the capitalist system can remove it, which is pretty far. There it becomes a measure and a tool of almost universal usefulness, and a reminder of almost infinite possibilities. New Money grasps this protean character of money more easily than the Old Rich grasp their inheritances. Its stance is insistently entrepreneurial. Everything is to be made; everything can be made. Nothing is given, not even the self. The entrepreneurial imagination thrives on possibility, opportunity, chances; and its preferred field of play is where these things, thanks to money and credit, seem most abundant—in the marketplace. The entrepreneur is a maker of markets: markets for the self, for the self's goods and services, for the self's ideas and notions, and for everyone else's as well, all the resources of nature and the cultures of man.

Markets and marketing provide the great preemptive metaphors of New Money's entrepreneurial vision. The entrepreneur is Market Man, a brilliant figure in that otherwise dismal composition known as Economic Man. And money, or credited money, is his medium: fluid, buoyant, and powerful, but otherwise as susceptible as water to whatever desire may dictate in shape, color, and taste. Wealth enters this view as a sort of sedimentary deposit of the flux and flow of market exchange. Mostly, though, it is just another form of money—stored possibility.

NELSON W. ALDRICH, Jr., Old Money, 1988

What was it but history, and of *their* kind very much, to have the assurance of the enjoyment of more money than the palace-builder himself could have dreamed of? This was the element that bore him up and into which Maggie scattered, on occasion, her exquisite colouring drops. They were of the colour—of what on earth? of what but the extraordinary American good faith?

HENRY JAMES, The Golden Bowl, 1904

May I ask, Cephalus, whether your fortune was for the most part inherited or acquired by you?

Acquired! Socrates; do you want to know how much I acquired? In the art of making money I have been midway between my father and grandfather: for my grandfather, whose name I bear, doubled and trebled the value of his patrimony, that which he inherited being much what I possess now; but my father Lysanias reduced the property below what it is at present: and I shall be satisfied if I leave to these my sons not less but a little more than I received.

That was why I asked you the question, I replied, because I see that you are indifferent about money, which is a characteristic rather of those who have inherited their fortunes than of those who have acquired them; the makers of fortunes have a second love of money as a creation of their own, resembling the affection of authors for their own poems, or of parents for their children, besides that natural love of it for the sake of use and profit which is common to them and all men. And hence they are very bad company, for they can talk about nothing but the praises of wealth.

PLATO (c.427–348 BC), *Republic*, book i, tr. B. Jowett, 1871

The use of money is all the advantage there is in having money.

For six pounds a year you may have the use of one hundred pounds, provided you are a man of known prudence and honesty.

He that spends a groat a day idly, spends idly above six pounds a year, which is the price for the use of one hundred pounds.

He that wastes idly a groat's worth of his time per day, one day with another, wastes the privilege of using one hundred pounds each day.

He that idly loses five shillings' worth of time, loses five shillings, and might as prudently throw five shillings into the sea.

He that loses five shillings, not only loses that sum, but all the advantage that might be made by turning it in dealing, which, by the time that a young man becomes old, will amount to a considerable sum of money.

BENJAMIN FRANKLIN, 'Necessary Hints to Those that would be Rich', 1736

To be truly rich, regardless of his fortune or lack of it, a man must live by his own values. If those values are not personally meaningful, then no amount of money gained can hide the emptiness of a life without them.

J. PAUL GETTY, *How to be Rich*, 1966

Lately in a wreck of a Californian ship, one of the passengers fastened a belt about him with two hundred pounds of gold in it, with which he was found afterwards at the bottom. Now, as he was sinking—had he the gold? or had the gold him?

JOHN RUSKIN, *Unto this Last*, 1860

Men will tell you sometimes that 'money's hard.' That shows it was not made to eat, I say. Only think of a man in this new world, in his log cabin, in the midst of a corn and potato patch, with a sheepfold on one side, talking about money being hard! So are flints hard; there is no alloy in them. What has that to do with his raising his food, cutting his wood (or breaking it), keeping in-doors when it rains, and, if need be, spinning and weaving his clothes? Some of those who sank with the steamer the other day found out that money was *heavy* too. Think of a man's priding himself on this kind of wealth, as if it greatly enriched him. As if one struggling in mid-ocean with a bag of gold on his back should gasp out, 'I am worth a hundred thousand dollars.' I see them struggling just as ineffectually on dry land, nay, even more hopelessly, for, in the former case, rather than sink, they will finally let the bag go; but in the latter they are pretty sure to hold and go down with it. I see them swimming about in their great-coats, collecting their rents, really *getting their dues*, drinking bitter draughts which only increase their thirst, becoming more and more water-logged, till finally they sink plumb down to the bottom. But enough of this.

HENRY DAVID THOREAU to Harrison Blake, 16 November 1857

. . . A Leg of Gold—solid gold throughout,

Nothing else, whether slim or stout,
 Should ever support her, God willing!
She must—she could—she would have her whim,
Her father, she turn'd a deaf ear to him—
 He might kill her—she didn't mind killing!
He was welcome to cut off her other limb—
 He might cut her all off with a shilling!

All other promised gifts were in vain,
Golden Girdle, or Golden Chain,
She writhed with impatience more than pain,
 And utter'd 'pshaws!' and 'pishes!'
But a Leg of Gold! as she lay in bed,
It danced before her—it ran in her head!
 It jump'd with her dearest wishes!

'Gold—gold—gold! Oh, let it be gold!'
Asleep or awake that tale she told,
 And when she grew delirious:
Till her parents resolved to grant her wish,
If they melted down plate, and goblet, and dish,
 The case was getting so serious.

So a Leg was made in a comely mould,
Of Gold, fine virgin glittering gold,
    As solid as man could make it—
Solid in foot, and calf, and shank,
A prodigious sum of money it sank;
In fact 'twas a Branch of the family Bank,
    And no easy matter to break it.

All sterling metal—not half-and-half,
The Goldsmith's mark was stamp'd on the calf—
    'Twas pure as from Mexican barter!
And to make it more costly, just over the knee,
Where another ligature used to be,
Was a circle of jewels, worth shillings to see,
    A new-fangled Badge of the Garter!

'Twas a splendid, brilliant, beautiful Leg,
Fit for the Court of Scander-Beg,
That Precious Leg of Miss Kilmansegg!
    For, thanks to parental bounty,
Secure from Mortification's touch,
She stood on a Member that cost as much
    As a Member for all the County!

THOMAS HOOD, 'Miss Kilmansegg and her Precious Leg', 1841–3

A sum of money is a leading character in this tale about people, just as a sum of honey might properly be a leading character in a tale about bees.

The sum was $87,472,033.61 on June 1, 1964, to pick a day. That was the day it caught the soft eyes of a boy shyster named Norman Mushari. The income the interesting sum produced was $3,500,000 a year, nearly $10,000 a day—Sundays, too.

The sum was made the core of a charitable and cultural foundation in 1947, when Norman Mushari was only six. Before that, it was the fourteenth largest family fortune in America, the Rosewater fortune. It was stashed into a foundation in order that tax-collectors and other predators not named Rosewater might be prevented from getting their hands on it. And the baroque masterpiece of legal folderol that was the charter of the Rosewater Foundation declared, in effect, that the presidency of the Foundation was to be inherited in the same manner as the British Crown. It was

to be handed down throughout all eternity to the closest and oldest heirs
of the Foundation's creator, Senator Lister Ames Rosewater of Indiana.

KURT VONNEGUT, *God Bless You, Mr Rosewater*, 1965

Money in sufficient quantity sustains the illusion of infinite possibility, and
the liquidity of gender, like the liquidity of cash, holds out the ceaselessly
renewable promise of buying into a better deal. In the world of the mirror
it is always permissible to seduce or betray almost anybody else in the
dream. Not at that particular moment, of course, not in front of the lady's
husband or the gentleman's wife, but on some convenient occasion when
a coincidence of schedules happens to place the concerned parties in the
same town or on the same beach at the same unencumbered moment out
of time.

The androgynous states of mind sustain the divorce rates and make it
possible to postpone the tiresome business of growing up. To the extent
that both sexes tailor their feeling to fit the measure of status and money,
the structures of gender, like the obligations to family or the loyalty to
principle, come to be seen as so much troublesome baggage impeding one's
movement into F. Scott Fitzgerald's 'orgiastic future.'

In the rarefied atmospheres of wealth and celebrity the liquidity of gender counts as an asset because it flows more freely into the molds of opulence. People find it easier to do the bidding of power, to make of themselves
a viscous substance that can be worked into the shape of a political slogan,
an expedient crime or a rock video routine. The idea of money becomes as
confused as the idea of sex. Understood not as a commodity, not as something that must be earned and has the value of the labor of getting it,
money becomes a magic wand, a mystery, a shower of fairy gold.

The more respectful the society's attitude toward money, the more predominant the androgynous sensibility in the company of the great as well
as in the temperament of the society's art and media.

LEWIS H. LAPHAM, *Money and Class in America*, 1988

I think this country is now suffering grievously under an excessive accumulation of capital, which, having no field for profitable operation, is in a state
of fierce civil war with itself.

SAMUEL TAYLOR COLERIDGE, *Table-Talk*, 1835, 4 May 1833

*Enter Barabas in his Counting-house, with heapes of gold before him.*

JEW. So that of thus much that returne was made:
  And of the third part of the *Persian* ships,
  There was the venture summ'd and satisfied.
  As for those *Samintes*, and the men of *Uzz*,
  That bought my *Spanish* Oyles, and Wines of *Greece*,
  Here have I purst their paltry silverlings.
  Fye; what a trouble tis to count this trash.
  Well fare the *Arabians*, who so richly pay
  The things they traffique for with wedge of gold,
  Whereof a man may easily in a day
  Tell that which may maintaine him all his life.
  The needy groome that never fingred groat,
  Would make a miracle of thus much coyne:
  But he whose steele-bard coffers are cramb'd full,
  And all his life time hath bin tired.
  Wearying his fingers ends with telling it,
  Would in his age be loath to labour so,
  And for a pound to sweat himselfe to death:
  Give me the Merchants of the *Indian* Mynes,
  That trade in mettall of the purest mould;
  The wealthy *Moore*, that in the *Easterne* rockes
  Without controule can picke his riches up,
  And in his house heape pearle like pibble-stones;
  Receive them free, and sell them by the weight,
  Bags of fiery *Opals*, *Saphires*, *Amatists*,
  *Iacints*, hard *Topas*, grasse-greene *Emeraulds*,
  Beauteous *Rubyes*, sparkling *Diamonds*,
  And seildsene costly stones of so great price,
  As one of them indifferently rated,
  And of a Carrect of this quantity,
  May serve in perill of calamity
  To ransome great Kings from captivity.
  This is the ware wherein consists my wealth:
  And thus me thinkes should men of judgement frame
  Their meanes of traffique from the vulgar trade,
  And as their wealth increaseth, so inclose
  Infinite riches in a little roome.

CHRISTOPHER MARLOWE, *The Jew of Malta*, c.1589–90

It was a common rumor that Montezuma still kept the treasures of his father, King Ayaxacatl, in this ancient palace. The Spaniards, acquainted with this fact, felt no scruple in gratifying their curiosity by removing the plaster. As was anticipated, it concealed a door. On forcing this, they found the rumor was no exaggeration. They beheld a large hall filled with rich and beautiful stuffs, articles of curious workmanship of various kinds, gold and silver in bars and in the ore, and many jewels of value. It was the private hoard of Montezuma, the contributions, it may be, of tributary cities, and once the property of his father. 'I was a young man,' says Diaz, who was one of those that obtained a sight of it, 'and it seemed to me as if all the riches of the world were in that room!'

W. H. PRESCOTT, *The History of the Conquest of Mexico*, 1843

There is something desirable as well as repellent about a quite barbarous excess of wealth. The purified and frigid senses of the ascetic, and the would-be ascetic, are easily stung, brutalized again. The saints who sought the solitudes of Egypt and Asia came face to face with the Tempter. He knew his business. Desire for worldly things became acute and sudden. Temptation found its source in the imperfectly subdued energies of the physical organism. Every excursion of the mind could be turned to evil account. The nearer they drew to God the more urgent became the efforts of the adversary. They prayed for sleeplessness that they might not be outwitted by dreams. St Hilarion, faint with fasting, was confronted with magnificent banquets. Before St Pelagia, who had once been an actress at Antioch, the Devil paraded rings and necklaces and bracelets to awaken the old desires. Again and again he performed the most fabulous conjuring tricks to undo them. We, the rank and file of sinners, are not so entertained.

The Harpagons and Sir Epicure Mammons and Eugénie Grandets are despised and condemned but it is easy to see what a delicious debauchery it must be to have bag upon bag of nuggets and ingots and bars, to have sack upon sack of gems, to have a room hung with crystal chandeliers and to have hundredweights of gold and silver poured out like cataracts upon ebony tables, to watch the light drenching the metal, quivering on sovereigns and nobles, crowns and Napoleons, to watch it lying in long deep lagoons on the black polished wood. What a base pleasure to bury one's arms to the elbows in hoards of jewels, to see them cascading from opening palms, to dally with pistoles and revel among doubloons.

It is not so difficult to understand why Caligula, according to Suetonius, developed such a passion for the feel of money that he liked to walk over heaps of gold pieces or else lie down and wallow in them. And it is no wonder that the most persuasive speech of all in the Council of Pandemonium was that of Mammon whose gaze, even in Heaven, was always cast down to admire the pavements of beaten gold.

J. A. CUDDON, *The Owl's Watchsong*, 1960

We can now compare our results with the fallacious views on Primitive Economic Man, sketched out at the beginning of this Division. We see that value and wealth exist, in spite of abundance of things, that indeed this abundance is valued for its own sake. Great quantities are produced beyond any possible utility they could possess, out of mere love of accumulation for its own sake; food is allowed to rot, and though they have all they could desire in necessities, yet the natives want always more, to serve in its character of wealth. Again, in manufactured objects . . . it is not rarity within utility which creates value, but a rarity sought out by human skill within the workable materials. In other words, not those things are valued, which being useful or even indispensable are hard to get, since all the necessities of life are within easy reach of the Trobriand Islander. But such an article is valued where the workman, having found specially fine or sportive material, has been induced to spend a disproportionate amount of labour on it. By doing so, he creates an object which is a kind of economic monstrosity, too good, too big, too frail, or too overcharged with ornament to be used, yet just because of that, highly valued.

BRONISLAW MALINOWSKI, *Argonauts of the Western Pacific*, 1922

Treasure, like all other heaps, is something which has been collected. But, in contrast to fruit and grain, it consists of units which are inedible and imperishable. What is essential is that each of these units should have a special value; it is only confidence in their retaining it which tempts men to amass treasure. A board of treasure is a heap which should be left to grow undisturbed. The man it belongs to may be powerful, but there are always others equally powerful to rob him. The prestige treasure gives its owner carries danger with it; fights and wars have arisen over treasure and many a man would have lived longer if his treasure had been smaller. Thus it is often of necessity kept secret. The peculiarity of treasure lies in the tension between the splendour it should radiate and the secrecy which is its protection. The lust of counting, of seeing numbers mount up, derives largely from treasure and is most comprehensible there. None of the other enumerations whose desired result is the highest possible figure—those of cattle, or of men, for example—share the same concentration of countable units. The image of the owner secretly counting his treasure is deeply engraved in the minds of men; and no less imperishable is their hope of discovering treasure for themselves, treasure which has been so well hidden that it lies forgotten in its hiding-place and no longer belongs to anyone. Disciplined armies have been corroded and overcome by their greed for treasure, and many victories turned to defeat. The transformation, even before battle, of an army into a band of treasure-seekers is described by Plutarch in his life of Pompey.

'As soon as Pompey landed his fleet near Carthage, 7,000 of the enemy deserted and came over to him. His own army consisted of six legions at full strength. Here, they say, a rather absurd thing happened to him. It seems that some of his soldiers came across some hidden treasure and got a considerable amount of money. The story of this got abroad and all the rest of the army fancied that the place must be full of money which had been buried by the Carthaginians at some time of calamity. And so, for many days, Pompey could do nothing at all with his soldiers who were all busy looking for treasure. He merely went about laughing at the sight of so many thousands of men together digging up the ground and turning it over, until in the end they got tired of it and asked him to lead them wherever he liked; they had already, they said, suffered enough for their foolishness.'

But apart from the heaps or hoards which are irresistible because they are hidden, there are others which are collected quite openly, as a kind of voluntary tax, and in the understanding that they will fall into the hands of one person, or of a few. To this group belong all kinds of lottery; they are quick accumulations of treasure. It is known that, immediately after the announcement of the result, they will be handed over to the fortunate winners. The smaller the number of these, the larger the treasure and the greater, therefore, its attraction.

The greed which unites people on such occasions presupposes an absolute confidence in the units composing the treasure. It is difficult to exaggerate the strength of this confidence. A man identifies himself with the unit of his money; doubt cast on it offends him and, if it is shattered, his self-confidence is shaken. He feels slighted and humiliated by the lowering of the value of his monetary unit and, if this process is accelerated and inflation occurs, it is *men* who are depreciated until they find themselves in formations which can only be equated with flight-crowds. The more people lose, the more united are they in their fate. What appears as panic in the few who are fortunate enough to be able to save something for themselves, turns into mass-flight for all those others who have become equals by being deprived of their money.

ELIAS CANETTI, *Crowds and Power*, 1960, tr. Carol Stewart, 1962

It is with industrious nations, who are advancing in the acquisition of riches, as with industrious individuals. A great stock, though with small profits, generally increases faster than a small stock with great profits. Money, says the proverb, makes money. When you have got a little, it is often easy to get more. The great difficulty is to get that little.

ADAM SMITH, *The Wealth of Nations*, 1776

Excessive wealth is perhaps harder to endure than poverty. I counsel every man who is in due need of money to go to M. de Rothschild, not to borrow (since I doubt whether in that case he would profit much), but to console himself by the sight of greater money-misery. The poor devil who has too little, and who cannot help himself, may there convince himself that there is a man who is far more tormented because he has too much money, because all the money in the world flows into his cosmopolite, giant pockets, and because he must drag such a burden about, while all around the great mob of starving men and thieves stretch forth to him their hands. And what terrible and dangerous hands! 'How do you do?' once asked a German poet of M. le Baron. 'I am driven mad,' was his reply. 'Until you throw money out of the windows, I cannot believe it,' said the poet. 'That is just my madness, that I often do not throw it out of the window.'

Ah! how unhappy the rich are in this world!—and yet after death they cannot enter the kingdom of heaven! 'It is easier for a camel to go through the eye of a needle than for a rich man to enter the kingdom of God.' This word of the Divine Communist is a terrible anathema, and shows his bitter hatred against the Bourse and *haute finance* of Jerusalem. The world swarms with philanthropists; there are societies for the protection of animals, yet withal very little is done for the poor, and for the rich, who are still more unfortunate, there is nothing done at all. Instead of prizes for questions as to silk culture, stall-feeding, and the Kantian philosophy, our learned societies should offer a reward for solving the problem 'How can a camel be threaded through the eye of a needle?' Until this great camel question is solved, and the rich see their way to getting into the kingdom of heaven, there will be no thorough benefit for the poor. The rich would be more benevolent if they were not obliged to seek all their happiness here on earth below, and not compelled to envy the poor, who up in heaven will enjoy, *in floribus*, eternal life. They say, 'Why should we here on earth do anything for the wretched rabble, who will one day be happier than we, and whom we shall never see again after death?' If the rich knew that they must live in common with us after death, they would give themselves some pains here on earth, and take care not to treat us too badly. Let us, therefore, before all things, try to solve the great question of the camel.

HEINRICH HEINE, *Lutetia*, 1854, tr. Charles Godfey Leland, 1906

THATCHER [*puts on his hat*]. I happened to see your Consolidated statement this morning, Charles. Don't you think it's rather unwise to continue this philanthropic enterprise—this 'Inquirer'—that's costing you one million dollars a year?

KANE. You're right. We did lose a million dollars last year. We expect to lose a million next year, too. You know, Mr Thatcher—at the rate of a million a year—we'll have to close this place—in sixty years.

[*Dissolve*

HERMAN J. MANKIEWICZ and ORSON WELLES, *Citizen Kane*, shooting script, dated 16 July 1940

In truth, poverty is an anomaly to rich people. It is very difficult to make out why people who want dinner do not ring the bell. One half of the world, according to the saying, do not know how the other half live. Accordingly, nothing is so rare in fiction as a good delineation of the poor.

WALTER BAGEHOT, 'The Waverley Novels', 1858

Now, wherever there is excessive wealth, there is also in the train of it excessive poverty; as, where the sun is brightest, the shade is deepest. Many republics have stood for ages while no citizen among them was in very great affluence, and while, on the contrary, most were very poor; but none hath stood long after many, or indeed a few, have grown inordinately wealthy. Riches cause poverty, then irritate, then corrupt it; so throughout their whole progress and action they are dangerous to the State.

WALTER SAVAGE LANDOR, 'Aristoteles and Callisthenes', *Imaginary Conversations*, 1824-9

'Well, society may be in its infancy,' said Egremont slightly smiling; 'but, say what you like, our Queen reigns over the greatest nation that ever existed.'

'Which nation?' asked the younger stranger, 'for she reigns over two.'

The stranger paused; Egremont was silent, but looked inquiringly.

'Yes,' resumed the younger stranger after a moment's interval. 'Two nations; between whom there is no intercourse and no sympathy; who are as ignorant of each other's habits, thoughts, and feelings, as if they were dwellers in different zones, or inhabitants of different planets; who are formed by a different breeding, are fed by a different food, are ordered by different manners, and are not governed by the same laws.'

'You speak of—' said Egremont, hesitatingly.

'THE RICH AND THE POOR.'

BENJAMIN DISRAELI, Sybil; or, The Two Nations, 1845

Rousseau's treatise on the inequality of mankind was at this time a fashionable topick. It gave rise to an observation by Mr Dempster, that the advantages of fortune and rank were nothing to a wise man, who ought to value only merit. JOHNSON. 'If man were a savage, living in the woods by himself, this might be true; but in civilized society we all depend upon each other, and our happiness is very much owing to the good opinion of mankind. Now, Sir, in civilized society, external advantages make us more respected. A man with a good coat upon his back meets with a better reception than he who has a bad one. Sir, you may analyse this, and say what is there in it? But that will avail you nothing, for it is a part of a general system. Pound St Paul's church into atoms, and consider any single atom; it is, to be sure, good for nothing: but, put all these atoms together, and you have St Paul's church. So it is with human felicity, which is made up of many ingredients, each of which may be shewn to be very insignificant. In civilized society, personal merit will not serve you so much as money will. Sir, you may make the experiment. Go into the street, and give one man a lecture on morality, and another a shilling, and see which will respect you most. If you wish only to support nature, Sir William Petty fixes your allowance at three pounds a year; but as times are much altered, let us call it six pounds. This sum will fill your belly, shelter you from the weather, and even get you a strong lasting coat, supposing it to be made of good bull's hide. Now, Sir, all beyond this is artificial, and is desired in order to obtain a greater degree of respect from our fellow-creatures. And, Sir, if six hundred pounds a year procure a man more consequence, and, of course, more happiness than six pounds a year, the same proportion will hold as to six thousand, and so on as far as opulence can be carried. Perhaps he who has a large fortune may not be so happy as he who has a small one; but that must proceed from other causes than from his having the large fortune; for, *cæteris paribus*, he who is rich in a civilized society, must be happier than he who is poor; as riches, if properly used, (and it is a man's own fault if they are not,) must be productive of the highest advantages. Money, to be sure, of itself is of no use; for its only use is to part with it. Rousseau, and all those who deal in paradoxes, are led away by a childish desire of novelty. When I was a boy, I used always to choose the wrong side of a debate, because most ingenious things, that is to say, most new things, could be said upon it. Sir, there is nothing for which you may not muster up more plausible arguments, than those which are urged against wealth and other external advantages. Why now, there is stealing; why should it be thought a crime? When we consider by what unjust methods property has been often acquired, and that what was unjustly got it must be unjust to keep, where is the harm in one man's taking the property of another from him? Besides, Sir, when we consider the bad use that many people make of their property, and how much better use the thief may make of it, it may be defended as a very allowable practice. Yet, Sir, the experience of mankind has discovered stealing to be so very bad a thing, that they make no scruple to hang a man for it. When I was running about this town a very poor fellow, I was a great arguer for the advantages of poverty; but I was, at the same time, very sorry to be poor. Sir, all the arguments which are brought to represent poverty as no evil, shew it to be evidently a great evil. You never find people labouring to convince you that you may live very happily upon a plentiful fortune.—'

JAMES BOSWELL, *Life of Samuel Johnson*, 1791, 20 July 1763

RICH AND POOR;

*or, Saint and Sinner*

The poor man's sins are glaring;
In the face of ghostly warning
  He is caught in the fact
  Of an overt act——
Buying greens on Sunday morning.

The rich man's sins are hidden
In the pomp of wealth and station;
   And escape the sight
   Of the children of light,
Who are wise in their generation.

The rich man has a kitchen,
And cooks to dress his dinner;
   The poor who would roast
   To the baker's must post,
And thus becomes a sinner.

The rich man has a cellar,
And a ready butler by him;
   The poor must steer
   For his pint of beer
Where the saint can't choose but spy him.

The rich man's painted windows
Hide the concerts of the quality;
   The poor can but share
   A crack'd fiddle in the air,
Which offends all sound morality.

The rich man is invisible
In the crowd of his gay society;
   But the poor man's delight
   Is a sore in the sight,
And a stench in the nose of piety.

The rich man has a carriage
Where no rude eye can flout him;
   The poor man's bane
   Is a third class train,
With the day-light all about him.

The rich man goes out yachting.
Where sanctity can't pursue him;
   The poor goes afloat
   In a fourpenny boat,
Where the bishop groans to view him.

THOMAS LOVE PEACOCK, 1831

The Master said, 'To be poor without murmuring is difficult. To be rich without being proud is easy.'

CONFUCIUS, *Analects*, tr. James Legge, 1870

'But how about money?' cried a voice within him. 'Where will you get it? You need money for everything.'

At this thought, the wealth that shone round Madame de Restaud glittered before his eyes. He had seen her lapped in luxury that was doubtless dear to a demoiselle Goriot; gilded and costly ornaments lay strewn about her *salons* with the unmeaning profusion that betrays the taste of a *parvenue* and her passion for squandering money. The fascinations of mere costliness had been effaced by the grandeur of the Hôtel Beauséant. His imagination now whirled him to the summits of Parisian life, and suggested thoughts which seared his heart, while they stimulated his intelligence and widened his perceptions. He saw the world in its true colors. He saw wealth triumphant over morality,—triumphant over law and order. He saw in riches the *ultima ratio mundi*. 'Vautrin is right,' he cried, 'luck makes the difference between vice and virtue.'

Having reached the Rue Neuve Sainte-Geneviève, he ran rapidly to his room and returned bringing ten francs for his coachman, and then entered the sickening dining-room where the eighteen guests sat eating their food like animals at a manger. The sight of their collective poverty and the dinginess of the place were horrible to him. The transition from the wealth and grace and beauty he had left was too abrupt, too complete, not to excite beyond all bounds his growing ambition. On the one hand fresh and lovely images of all that was elegant in social life, framed in marvels of art and luxury, and passionate with poetical emotion; on the other, a dark picture of degradation,—sinister faces where passions had blighted all but the sinews and the mere mechanism.

HONORÉ DE BALZAC (1799–1850), *Père Goriot*, English tr. 1886

Wealth flows into the country, but how does it circulate there? Not equally and healthfully through the whole system; it sprouts into wens and tumours, and collects in aneurisms which starve and palsy the extremities. The government indeed raises millions now as easily as it raised thousands in the days of Elizabeth: the metropolis is six times the size which it was a century ago; it has nearly doubled during the present reign; a thousand carriages drive about the streets of London, where, three generations ago, there were not an hundred; a thousand hackney coaches are licensed in the same city, where at the same distance of time there was not one; they whose grandfathers dined at noon from wooden trenchers, and upon the produce of their own farms, sit down by the light of waxen tapers to be served upon silver, and to partake of delicacies from the four quarters of the globe. But the number of the poor, and the sufferings of the poor, have continued to increase; the price of every thing which they consume has always been advancing, and the price of labour, the only commodity which they have to dispose of, remains the same. Work-houses are erected in one place, and infirmaries in another; the poor-rates increase in proportion to the taxes; and in times of dearth the rich even purchase food, and retail it to them at a reduced price, or supply them with it gratuitously: still every year adds to their number. Necessity is the mother of crimes; new prisons are built, new punishments enacted; but the poor become year after year more numerous, more miserable, and more depraved; and this is the inevitable tendency of the manufacturing system.

This system is the boast of England,—long may she continue to boast it before Spain shall rival her! Yet this is the system which we envy, and which we are so desirous to imitate. Happily our religion presents one obstacle; that incessant labour which is required in these task-houses can never be exacted in a Catholic country, where the Church has wisely provided so many days of leisure for the purposes of religion and enjoyment. Against the frequency of these holydays much has been said; but Heaven forbid that the clamour of philosophizing commercialists should prevail, and that the Spaniard should ever be brutalized by unremitting task-work, like the negroes in America and the labouring manufacturers in England!

ROBERT SOUTHEY, *Letters from England by Don Manuel Alvarez Espriella*, 1807

We could never imagine what a strange disproportion a few or a great many pieces of money make between men, if we did not see it every day with our own eyes.

JEAN DE LA BRUYÈRE, *Characters*, 1688–96

*You are farmers; I am a farmer myself.*
—FRANKLIN DELANO ROOSEVELT

Woods and Ricketts work for Michael and T. Hudson Margraves, two brothers, in partnership, who live in Cookstown. Gudger worked for the

Margraves for three years; he now (1936) works for Chester Boles, who lives two miles south of Cookstown.

On their business arrangements, and working histories, and on their money, I wrote a chapter too long for inclusion in this volume without sacrifice of too much else. I will put in its place here as extreme a précis as I can manage.

Gudger has no home, no land, no mule; none of the more important farming implements. He must get all these of his landlord. Boles, for his share of the corn and cotton, also advances him rations money during four months of the year, March through June, and his fertilizer.

Gudger pays him back with his labor and with the labor of his family.

At the end of the season he pays him back further: with half his corn; with half his cotton; with half his cottonseed. Out of his own half of these crops he also pays him back the rations money, plus interest, and his share of the fertilizer, plus interest, and such other debts, plus interest, as he may have incurred.

What is left, once doctors' bills and other debts have been deducted, is his year's earnings.

Gudger is a straight half-cropper, or sharecropper.

JAMES AGEE, *Let Us Now Praise Famous Men*, 1941


One dollar and eighty-seven cents. That was all. And sixty cents of it was in pennies. Pennies saved one and two at a time by bulldozing the grocer and the vegetable man and the butcher until one's cheeks burned with the silent imputation of parsimony that such close dealing implied. Three times Della counted it. One dollar and eighty-seven cents. And the next day would be Christmas.

O. HENRY (William Sydney Porter) (1862–1910), 'The Gift of the Magi'


## WORRY ABOUT MONEY

Wearing worry about money like a hair shirt
I lie down in my bed and wrestle with my angel.

My bank-manager could not sanction my continuance for another day
But life itself wakes me each morning, and love

Urges me to give although I have no money
In the bank at this moment, and ought properly

To cease to exist in a world where poverty
Is a shameful and ridiculous offence.

Having no one to advise me, I open the Bible
And shut my eyes and put my finger on a text

And read that the widow with the young son
Must give first to the prophetic genius
From the little there is in the bin of flour and the cruse of oil.

KATHLEEN RAINE, *The Pythoness and Other Poems*, 1949

### THIRTY BOB A WEEK

I couldn't touch a stop and turn a screw,
    And set the blooming world a-work for me,
Like such as cut their teeth—I hope, like you—
    On the handle of a skeleton gold key;
I cut mine on a leek, which I eat it every week:
    I'm a clerk at thirty bob as you can see.

But I don't allow it's luck and all a toss;
    There's no such thing as being starred and crossed;
It's just the power of some to be a boss,
    And the bally power of others to be bossed:
I face the music, sir; you bet I ain't a cur;
    Strike me lucky if I don't believe I'm lost!

For like a mole I journey in the dark,
    A-travelling along the underground
From my Pillar'd Halls and broad Suburban Park,
    To come the daily dull official round;
And home again at night with my pipe all alight,
    A-scheming how to count ten bob a pound.

And it's often very cold and very wet,
    And my missis stitches towels for a hunks;
And the Pillar'd Halls is half of it to let—
    Three rooms about the size of travelling trunks.
And we cough, my wife and I, to dislocate a sigh,
    When the noisy little kids are in their bunks.

But you never hear her do a growl or whine,
  For she's made of flint and roses, very odd;
And I've got to cut my meaning rather fine,
  Or I'd blubber, for I'm made of greens and sod:
So p'r'aps we are in Hell for all that I can tell,
  And lost and damn'd and served up hot to God.

I ain't blaspheming, Mr Silver-tongue;
  I'm saying things a bit beyond your art:
Of all the rummy starts you ever sprung,
  Thirty bob a week's the rummiest start!
With your science and your books and your the'ries about spooks,
  Did you ever hear of looking in your heart?

I didn't mean your pocket, Mr, no:
  I mean that having children and a wife,
With thirty bob on which to come and go,
  Isn't dancing to the tabor and the fife:
When it doesn't make you drink, by Heaven! it makes you think,
  And notice curious items about life.

I step into my heart and there I meet
  A god-almighty devil singing small,
Who would like to shout and whistle in the street,
  And squelch the passers flat against the wall;
If the whole world was a cake he had the power to take,
  He would take it, ask for more, and eat it all.

And I meet a sort of simpleton beside,
  The kind that life is always giving beans;
With thirty bob a week to keep a bride
  He fell in love and married in his teens:
At thirty bob he stuck; but he knows it isn't luck:
  He knows the seas are deeper than tureens.

And the god-almighty devil and the fool
  That meet me in the High Street on the strike,
When I walk about my heart a-gathering wool,
  Are my good and evil angels if you like.
And both of them together in every kind of weather
  Ride me like a double-seated bike.

That's rough a bit and needs its meaning curled.
  But I have a high old hot un in my mind—
A most engrugious notion of the world,
  That leaves your lightning 'rithmetic behind:
I give it at a glance when I say 'There ain't no chance,
  Nor nothing of the lucky-lottery kind.'

And it's this way that I make it out to be:
  No fathers, mothers, countries, climates—none;
Not Adam was responsible for me,
  Nor society, nor systems, nary one:
A little sleeping seed, I woke—I did, indeed—
  A million years before the blooming sun.

I woke because I thought the time had come;
  Beyond my will there was no other cause;
And everywhere I found myself at home,
  Because I chose to be the thing I was;
And in whatever shape of mollusc or of ape
  I always went according to the laws.

I was the love that chose my mother out;
  I joined two lives and from the union burst;
My weakness and my strength without a doubt
  Are mine alone for ever from the first:
It's just the very same with a difference in the name
  As 'Thy will be done.' You say it if you durst!

They say it daily up and down the land
  As easy as you take a drink, it's true;
But the difficultest go to understand,
  And the difficultest job a man can do,
Is to come it brave and meek with thirty bob a week,
  And feel that that's the proper thing for you.

It's a naked child against a hungry wolf;
  It's playing bowls upon a splitting wreck;
It's walking on a string across a gulf
  With millstones fore-and-aft about your neck;
But the thing is daily done by many and many a one;
  And we fall, face forward, fighting, on the deck.

John Davidson, Ballads and Songs, 1894

Some of you, we all know, are poor, find it hard to live, are sometimes, as it were, gasping for breath. I have no doubt that some of you who read this book are unable to pay for all the dinners which you have actually eaten, or for the coats and shoes which are fast wearing or are already worn out, and have come to this page to spend borrowed or stolen time, robbing your creditors of an hour. It is very evident what mean and sneaking lives many of you live, for my sight has been whetted by experience; always on the limits, trying to get into business and trying to get out of debt, a very ancient slough, called by the Latins *æs alienum*, another's brass, for some of their coins were made of brass; still living, and dying, and buried by this other's brass; always promising to pay, promising to pay, to-morrow, and dying to-day, insolvent; seeking to curry favor, to get custom, by how many modes, only not state-prison offences; lying, flattering, voting, contracting yourselves into a nutshell of civility, or dilating into an atmosphere of thin and vaporous generosity, that you may persuade your neighbor to let you make his shoes, or his hat, or his coat, or his carriage, or import his groceries for him; making yourselves sick, that you may lay up something against a sick day, something to be tucked away in an old chest, or in a stocking behind the plastering, or, more safely, in the brick bank; no matter where, no matter how much or how little.

Henry David Thoreau, *Walden*, 1859

The worst inconvenience of a small fortune is that it will not admit of inadvertency. Inadvertency, however, ought to be placed at the head of most men's yearly accounts, and a sum as regularly allotted to it as to any other article.

William Shenstone (1714–63), *Essays on Men and Manners*, 1764

A hand was laid on his arm and a young voice cried:
— Ah, gentleman, your own girl, sir! The first handsel today, gentleman. Buy that lovely bunch. Will you, gentleman?
The blue flowers which she lifted towards him and her young blue eyes seemed to him at that instant images of guilelessness; and he halted till the image had vanished and he saw only her ragged dress and damp coarse hair and hoydenish face.
— Do, gentleman! Don't forget your own girl, sir!
— I have no money, said Stephen.

— Buy them lovely ones, will you, sir? Only a penny.

— Did you hear what I said? asked Stephen, bending towards her. I told you I had no money. I tell you again now.

— Well, sure, you will some day, sir, please God, the girl answered after an instant.

— Possibly, said Stephen, but I don't think it likely.

JAMES JOYCE, A Portrait of the Artist as a Young Man, 1914–15

When Jesus talks about the poor he simply means personalities, just as when he talks about the rich he simply means people who have not developed their personalities. Jesus moved in a community that allowed the accumulation of private property just as ours does, and the gospel that he preached was, not that in such a community it is an advantage for a man to live on scanty, unwholesome food, to wear ragged, unwholesome clothes, to sleep in horrid, unwholesome dwellings, and a disadvantage for a man to live under healthy, pleasant, and decent conditions. Such a view would have been wrong there and then, and would, of course, be still more wrong now and in England; for as man moves northward the material necessities of life become of more vital importance, and our society is infinitely more complex, and displays far greater extremes of luxury and pauperism than any society of the antique world. What Jesus meant was this. He said to man, 'You have a wonderful personality. Develop it. Be yourself. Don't imagine that your perfection lies in accumulating or possessing external things. Your affection is inside of you. If only you could realize that, you would not want to be rich. Ordinary riches can be stolen from a man. Real riches cannot. In the treasury-house of your soul, there are infinitely precious things, that may not be taken from you. And so, try to so shape your life that external things will not harm you. And try also to get rid of personal property. It involves sordid preoccupation, endless industry, continual wrong. Personal property hinders Individualism at every step.' It is to be noted that Jesus never says that impoverished people are necessarily good, or wealthy people necessarily bad. That would not have been true. Wealthy people are, as a class, better than impoverished people, more moral, more intellectual, more well-behaved. There is only one class in the community that thinks more about money than the rich, and that is the poor. The poor can think of nothing else. That is the misery of being poor.

OSCAR WILDE, The Soul of Man under Socialism, 1891

## LETTER FROM POOR MAN TO OBTAIN MONEY
## FROM RICH ONE

[*The English law is particularly hard on what is called blackmail. It is therefore essential that the applicant should write nothing that might afterwards be twisted to incriminate him.*—ED.]

Dear Sir,

To-day, as I was turning out a drawer in my attic, I came across a letter which by a curious chance fell into my hands some years ago, and which, in the stress of grave pecuniary embarrassment, had escaped my memory. It is a letter written by yourself to a lady, and the date shows it to have been written shortly after your marriage. It is of a confidential nature, and might, I fear, if it fell into the wrong hands, be cruelly misconstrued. I would wish you to have the satisfaction of destroying it in person. At first I thought of sending it on to you by post. But I know how happy you are in your domestic life; and probably your wife and you, in your perfect mutual trust, are in the habit of opening each other's letters. Therefore, to avoid risk, I would prefer to hand the document to you personally. I will not ask you to come to my attic, where I could not offer you such hospitality as is due to a man of your wealth and position. You will be so good as to meet me at 3.0 A.M. (sharp) to-morrow (Thursday) beside the tenth lamp-post to the left on the Surrey side of Waterloo Bridge; at which hour and place we shall not be disturbed.

> I am, dear Sir,
> Yours respectfully,
> JAMES GRIDGE.

MAX BEERBOHM, 'How Shall I Word It?', 1910

Being poor is a mere trifle. It is being known to be poor that is the sting. It is not cold that makes a man without a greatcoat hurry along so quickly. It is not all shame at telling lies—which he knows will not be believed—that makes him turn so red when he informs you that he considers great-coats unhealthy, and never carries an umbrella on principle. It is easy enough to say that poverty is no crime. No; if it were men wouldn't be ashamed of it. It is a blunder though, and is punished as such. A poor man is despised the whole world over; despised as much by a Christian as by a lord, as much by a demagogue as by a footman, and not all the copy-book maxims ever set for ink-stained youth will make him respected. Appearances *are* everything, so far as human opinion goes, and the man who will walk down Piccadilly arm in arm with the most notorious scamp in London, provided he is a well-dressed one, will slink up a back street to say a couple of words to a seedy-looking gentleman. And the seedy-looking gentleman knows this—no one better—and will go a mile round to avoid meeting an acquaintance. Those that knew him in his prosperity need never trouble themselves to look the other way. He is a thousand times more anxious that they should not see him than they can be; and as to their assistance, there is nothing he dreads more than the offer of it. All he wants is to be forgotten; and in this respect he is generally fortunate enough to get what he wants.

JEROME K. JEROME, 'On Being Hard Up', *Idle Thoughts of an Idle Fellow*, 1886

Money does not mean the same thing to me it must mean to a rich man. I cannot, right now, think of one meaning to name. This is not so simple to understand. Even as a simple term of the English language, *money* does not possess the same meanings for the rich man as it does for me, a lower-middle-class American, albeit of laughably 'aristocratic' pretensions. What possibly can 'money' mean to a poor man? And I am not talking now about those courageous products of our permissive society who walk knowledge-ably into 'poverty' as they would into a public toilet. I mean, The Poor.

I look in my pocket; I have seventy cents. Possibly I can buy a beer. A quart of ale, specifically. Then I will have twenty cents with which to annoy and seduce my fingers when they wearily search for gainful employment. I have no idea at this moment what that seventy cents will mean to my neighbor around the corner, a poor Puerto Rican man I have seen hope-fully watching my plastic garbage can. But I am certain it cannot mean the same thing. Say to David Rockefeller, 'I have money,' and he will think you mean something entirely different. That is, if you also dress the part. He would not for a moment think, 'Seventy cents.' But then neither would many New York painters.

LEROI JONES, 'Expressive Language', 1963

Plautus turned a mill. Terence was a slave. Boethius died in a jail. Paulo Borghese, though he had fifteen different trades, yet starved with them all. Tasso was often distressed for five shillings. Servin (one of the *suite* of Maximilian, Duke of Sully, in his embassy to England during the reign of James the First, and one of the most learned and accomplished men of his age) died drunk in a common brothel. Bentivoglio was refused admittance into the very hospital which he erected. Edmund Alleyn, the celebrated actor and contemporary of Shakespeare, died in a similar institution of his own.

Corneille, the great French dramatic writer, was so poor that he has been seen in very old age standing at the entrance of a cobbler's stall with only one shoe on while the other was mending; and Racine left his family in such distress as to be supported by a pension which his friends solicited for them. Crichton (by way of distinction called *The admirable Crichton*), who was the most accomplished as well as the most learned and dissipated man of his time, lived on the supply of the day, and at length lost his life in a midnight brawl in the public street. Butler, though his talents were the delight of the age he lived in, and his immortal work the principal subject of the Court conversation, was never master of fifty pounds. Otway is said to have died of hunger; Camoens ended his days in an hospital; and Vauglas left his body to the surgeons to pay his debts.

> SAMUEL FOOTE (1720–77), *The Table-Talk and Bon-Mots of Samuel Foote*, ed. William Cooke. Cooke added further examples as follows.

Cervantes, the celebrated author of *Don Quixote*, after being imprisoned, and meeting many unaccountable slights and hardships, died for want. Churchill died a beggar; Lloyd, his friend and *brother* patriot, died in the Fleet, where he previously existed for some years by soliciting daily charity and subscriptions for works which he never meant to publish; Bickerstaff ran away as much for debt as for the crime imputed to him; Dr Goldsmith was nearly two thousand pounds in debt when he died; and Hugh Kelly, author of *False Delicacy*, &c., died in just the same condition.

Dr Paul Hiffernan, an author well known about the same period, contracted his last illness, which was a jaundice, from mere want, and was then supported by a friendly subscription.

Purdon, though bred at Trinity College, Dublin, and always considered as a good scholar and a man of taste, was so dissipated that, after subsisting for many years as a bookseller's hack, he ended his days in an hospital.

Jones, author of *The Earl of Essex*, &c., being run over by a night-cart in the street, was carried to an hospital (for want of any other lodging), and was supported there by the master of the Bedford coffee-house till he died.

Boyce, one of the earliest contemporaries of Dr Johnson, and originally a writer with him in the *Gentleman's Magazine*, expired in a miserable garret on Tower Hill.

Sterne, the celebrated author of *Tristram Shandy*, though his works sold uncommonly well, and his income as a clergyman, together with his reputation as a writer, might have commanded respect and independence, left a wife and daughter in great distress, dying seven hundred pounds in debt.

Mrs Manley, the author of the original *Atalantis*, and the *protégé* of Swift, Steele, Prior, &c., finally subsisted on the bounty of Alderman Barber; while Floyer Sydenham, the learned and elegant translator of Plato, was supported by one Nott, a publican near Temple Bar, who, having known him in better days, kindly remembered him in the time of sickness and misfortune.

To this melancholy catalogue we may add the subject of these Memoirs, who, though the heir and possessor of three successive fortunes, and the natural inheritor of as much wit and humour as perhaps ever fell to the lot of one man, yet was so thoughtless about pecuniary affairs that he was often at a loss for the supply of the day which was passing over him; and, except the income which he derived from the sale of his theatre, and which died with him, he did not leave as much behind him as discharged his funeral expenses.

WILLIAM COOKE, in *The Table-Talk and Bon-Mots of Samuel Foote*

MONEY

When I had money, money, O!
    I knew no joy till I went poor;
For many a false man as a friend
    Came knocking all day at my door.

Then felt I like a child that holds
    A trumpet that he must not blow
Because a man is dead; I dared
    Not speak to let this false world know.

Much have I thought of life, and seen
    How poor men's hearts are ever light;
And how their wives do hum like bees
    About their work from morn till night.

So, when I hear these poor ones laugh,
    And see the rich ones coldly frown—
Poor men, think I, need not go up
    So much as rich men should come down.

When I had money, money, O!
    My many friends proved all untrue;

But now I have no money, O!
My friends are real, though very few.

W. H. DAVIES, 1871–1940


## THE COMPLEINT OF CHAUCER TO HIS EMPTY PURSE

To you, my purse, and to non other wight
Compleyne I, for ye be my lady dere!
I am so sory, now that ye be light;
For certes, but ye make me hevy chere,    *unless you look gravely upon me*

Me were as leef be leyd up-on my bere;
For whiche un-to your mercy thus I crye:
Beth hevy ageyn, or elles mot I dye!

Now voucheth sauf this day, or hit be night,    *before it is night*
That I of you the blisful soun may here,
Or see your colour lyk the sonne bright,
That of yelownesse hadde never pere.
Ye be my lyf, ye be myn hertes stere,    *guide*
Quene of comfort and of good companye:
Beth hevy ageyn, or elles mot I dye!    *must*

Now purs, that be to me my lyves light,
And saveour, as doun in this worlde here,
Out of this toune help me through your might,
Sin that ye wole nat been my tresorere;    *since*
For I am shave as nye as any frere.    *as closely as any friar*

But yit I pray un-to your curtesye:
Beth hevy ageyn, or elles mot I dye!

GEOFFREY CHAUCER (*c.*1345–1400)


## THE EMPTY PURSE

*A sermon to our later prodigal son*

Thou, run to the dry on this wayside bank,
Too plainly of all the propellers bereft!
    Quenched youth, and is that thy purse?

Even such limp slough as the snake has left
Slack to the gale upon spikes of whin,
For cast-off coat of a life gone blank,
In its frame of a grin at the seeker, is thine;
    And thine to crave and to curse
    The sweet thing once within.

Accuse him: some devil committed the theft,
    Which leaves of the portly a skin,
    No more; of the weighty a whine.

                         GEORGE MEREDITH, 1892

We talked of the state of the poor in London.—JOHNSON. 'Saunders Welch, the Justice, who was once High-Constable of Holborn, and had the best opportunities of knowing the state of the poor, told me, that I under-rated the number, when I computed that twenty a week, that is, above a thousand a year, died of hunger; not absolutely of immediate hunger; but of the wasting and other diseases which are the consequences of hunger. This happens only in so large a place as London, where people are not known. What we are told about the great sums got by begging is not true: the trade is overstocked. And, you may depend upon it, there are many who cannot get work. A particular kind of manufacture fails: those who have been used to work at it, can, for some time, work at nothing else. You meet a man begging; you charge him with idleness: he says, "I am willing to labour. Will you give me work?"—"I cannot."—"Why, then you have no right to charge me with idleness."'

        JAMES BOSWELL, *Life of Samuel Johnson*, 1791, 10 October 1779

This mournful truth is ev'ry where confess'd,
'SLOW RISES WORTH, BY POVERTY DEPRESS D ;
But here more slow, where all are slaves to gold,
Where looks are merchandise, and smiles are sold;
Where won by bribes, by flatteries implor'd,
The groom retails the favours of his lord.

    SAMUEL JOHNSON, *London: An Imitation of the Third Satire of Juvenal*, 1738

Then Akaky Akakyevitch saw that there was no escape from a new overcoat and he was utterly depressed. How indeed, for what, with what money could he get it? Of course he could to some extent rely on the bonus for the coming holiday, but that money had long ago been appropriated and its use determined beforehand. It was needed for new trousers and to pay the cobbler an old debt for putting some new tops to some old boot-legs, and he had to order three shirts from a seamstress as well as two specimens of an undergarment which it is improper to mention in print; in short, all that money absolutely must be spent, and even if the director were to be so gracious as to assign him a gratuity of forty-five or even fifty, instead of forty roubles, there would still be left a mere trifle, which would be but as a drop in the ocean beside the fortune needed for an overcoat. Though, of course, he knew that Petrovitch had a strange craze for suddenly putting on the devil knows what enormous price, so that at times his own wife could not help crying out: 'Why, you are out of your wits, you idiot! Another time he'll undertake a job for nothing, and here the devil has bewitched him to ask more than he is worth himself.' Though, of course, he knew that Petrovitch would undertake to make it for eighty roubles, still where would he get those eighty roubles? He might manage half of that sum; half of it could be found, perhaps even a little more; but where could he get the other half? . . . But, first of all, the reader ought to know where that first half was to be found. Akaky Akakyevitch had the habit every time he spent a rouble of putting aside two kopecks in a little locked-up box with a slit in the lid for slipping the money in. At the end of every half-year he would inspect the pile of coppers there and change them for small silver. He had done this for a long time, and in the course of many years the sum had mounted up to forty roubles and so he had half the money in his hands, but where was he to get the other half, where was he to get another forty roubles?

NIKOLAI GOGOL, 'The Overcoat', 1842, tr. Constance Garnett, 1923

The last statement I took was that of a boy of thirteen. I can hardly say that he was clothed at all. He had no shirt, and no waistcoat; all his neck and a great part of his chest being bare. A ragged cloth jacket hung about him, and was tied, so as to keep it together, with bits of tape. What he had wrapped round for trousers did not cover one of his legs, while one of his thighs was bare. He wore two old shoes; one tied to his foot with an old ribbon, the other a woman's old boot. He had an old cloth cap. His features were distorted somewhat, through being swollen with the cold. 'I was born,' he said, 'at a place called Hadley, in Kent. My father died when I was three days old, I've heard my mother say. He was married to her, I believe, but I don't know what he was. She had only me. My mother went about begging, sometimes taking me with her; at other times she left me at the lodging-house in Hadley. She went in the country, round about Tunbridge and there, begging. Sometimes she had a day's work. We had plenty to eat then, but I haven't had much lately. My mother died at Hadley a year ago. I didn't know how she was buried. She was ill a long time, and I was out begging; for she sent me out to beg for myself a good while before that, and when I got back to the lodging-house they told me she was dead. I had sixpence in my pocket, but I couldn't help crying to think I'd lost my mother. I cry about it still. I didn't wait to see her buried, but I started on my own account. I met two navvies in Bromley, and they paid my first night's lodging; and there was a man passing, going to London with pota-toes, and the navvies gave the man a pot of beer to take me up to London in the van, and they went that way with me. I came to London to beg, thinking I could get more there than anywhere else, hearing that London was such a good place. I begged; but sometimes wouldn't get a farthing in a day; often walking about the streets all night. I have been begging about all the time till now. I am very weak—starving to death. I never stole anything: I always kept my hands to myself. A boy wanted me to go with him to pick a gentleman's pocket. We was mates for two days, and then he asked me to go picking pockets; but I wouldn't. I know it's wrong, though I can neither read nor write. The boy asked me to do it to get into prison, as that would be better than the streets. He picked pockets to get into prison. He was starving about the streets like me. I never slept in a bed since I've been in London: I am sure I haven't: I generally slept under the dry arches in Weststreet, where they're building houses—I mean the arches for the cellars. I begged chiefly from the Jews about Petticoat-lane, for they all give away bread that their children leave—pieces of crust, and such-like. I would do anything to be out of this misery.'

HENRY MAYHEW, *London Labour and the London Poor*, 1861

Poverty, though it no doubt discourages, does not always prevent mar-riage. It seems even to be favourable to generation. A half-starved Highland woman frequently bears more than twenty children, while a pampered fine lady is often incapable of bearing any, and is generally exhausted by two or three. Barrenness, so frequent among women of fashion, is very rare among those of inferior station. Luxury in the fair sex, while it inflames perhaps the passion for enjoyment, seems always to weaken, and frequently to destroy altogether, the powers of generation.

ADAM SMITH, *The Wealth of Nations*, 1776

You tell me that money cannot buy the things most precious. Your commonplace proves that you have never known the lack of it. When I think of all the sorrow and the barrenness that has been wrought in my life by want of a few more pounds per annum than I was able to earn, I stand aghast at money's significance. What kindly joys have I lost, those simple forms of happiness to which every heart has claim, because of poverty! Meetings with those I loved made impossible year after year; sadness, misunderstanding, nay, cruel alienation, arising from inability to do the things I wished, and which I might have done had a little money helped me; endless instances of homely pleasure and contentment curtailed or forbidden by narrow means. I have lost friends merely through the constraints of my position; friends I might have made have remained strangers to me; solitude of the bitter kind, the solitude which is enforced at times when mind or heart longs for companionship, often cursed my life solely because I was poor. I think it would scarce be an exaggeration to say that there is no moral good which has not to be paid for in coin of the realm.

GEORGE GISSING, *The Private Papers of Henry Ryecroft*, 1903

To London once, my stepps I bent,
Where trouth in no wyse should be faynt:
To Westmynster ward I forthwith went,
To a man of law to make complaynt.
I sayd, 'for Mary's love, that holy saynt!
Pity the poore that would proceede';
But for lack of mony I cold not spede.

And as I thrust the prese amonge,
By froward chaunce my hood was gone;
Yet for all that I stayd not longe,
Tyll to the Kyngs bench I was come.
Before the judge I kneled anon,
And prayd hym for God's sake to take heede;
But for lack of mony I myght not spede. . . .

Then I hyed me into Estchepe;
One cryes rybbs of befe, and many a pye;
Pewter potts they clattered on a heape,
There was harpe, pype, and mynstrelsye;
'Yea by cock!' 'nay by cock!' some began crye,
Some songe of Jenken and Julyan for there mede;
But for lack of mony I myght not spede.

Then into Cornhyll anon I yode,
Where was much stolen gere amonge;
I saw where honge myne owne hoode,
That I had lost amonge the thronge;
To by my own hood I thought it wronge,
I knew it well as I dyd my crede;
But for lack of mony I cold not spede.

The Taverner took me by the sleve;
'Sir,' sayth he, 'wyll you our wyne assay?'
I answered, that can not mutch me greve,
A peny can do no more than it may:
I dranke a pynt, and for it dyd pay;
Yet sore a hungerd from thence I yede,
And wantyng my mony I cold not spede.

Then hyed I me to Belynsgate;
And one cryed 'hoo, go we hence!'
I prayd a barge man for Gods sake,
That he wold spare me my expence.
'Thou scapst not here,' quod he, 'under two pence,
I lyst not yet bestow my almes dede':
Thus lacking mony I cold not spede.

Then I convayed me into Kent;
For of the law wold I meddle no more,
Because no man to me tooke entent,
I dyght me to do as I dyd before.
Now Jesus that in Bethlem was bore,
Save London, and send trew lawyers there mede,
For who so wants mony with them shall not spede.

ANON. (formerly attributed to John Lydgate), 'London Lickpenny', *c*.1450

Literally and truly, one cannot get on well in the world without money. To be in want of money, is to pass through life with little credit or pleasure; it is to live out of the world, or to be despised if you come into it; it is not to be sent for to court, or asked out to dinner, or noticed in the street; it is not to have your opinion consulted or else rejected with contempt, to have your acquirements carped at and doubted, your good things disparaged, and at last to lose the wit and the spirit to say them; it is to be scrutinized by strangers, and neglected by friends; it is to be a thrall to circumstances, an exile in a foreign land; to forego leisure, freedom, ease of body and mind, to be dependent on the good-will and caprice of others, or earn a precarious and irksome livelihood by some laborious employment: it is to be compelled to stand behind a counter, or to sit at a desk in some public office, or to marry your landlady, or not the person you would wish; or to go out to the East or West-Indies, or to get a situation as judge abroad, and return home with a liver-complaint; or to be a law-stationer, or a scrivener or scavenger, or newspaper reporter; or to read law and sit in court without a brief, or be deprived of the use of your fingers by transcribing Greek manuscripts, or to be a seal engraver and pore yourself blind; or to go upon the stage, or try some of the Fine Arts; with all your pains, anxiety, and hopes, most probably to fail, or, if you succeed, after the exertions of years, and undergoing constant distress of mind and fortune, to be assailed on every side with envy, back-biting, and falsehood, or to be a favourite with the public for awhile, and then thrown into the back-ground— or a jail, by the fickleness of taste and some new favourite; to be full of enthusiasm and extravagance in youth, of chagrin and disappointment in after-life; to be jostled by the rabble because you do not ride in your coach, or avoided by those who know your worth and shrink from it as a claim on their respect or their purse; to be a burden to your relations, or unable to do any thing for them; to be ashamed to venture into crowds; to have cold comfort at home; to lose by degrees your confidence and any talent you might possess; to grow crabbed, morose, and querulous, dissatisfied with every one, but most so with yourself; and plagued out of your life, to look about for a place to die in, and quit the world without any one's asking after your will. The *wiseacres* will possibly, however, crowd round your coffin, and raise a monument at a considerable expense, and after a lapse of time, to commemorate your genius and your misfortunes!

WILLIAM HAZLITT, 'On the Want of Money', 1827

The next day they talked much of this new project. As there was sunshine Amy accompanied her husband for his walk in the afternoon; it was long since they had been out together. An open carriage that passed, followed by two young girls on horseback, gave a familiar direction to Reardon's thoughts.

'If one were as rich as those people! They pass so close to us; they see us, and we see them; but the distance between is infinity. They don't belong to the same world as we poor wretches. They see everything in a different light; they have powers which would seem supernatural if we were suddenly endowed with them.'

'Of course,' assented his companion with a sigh.

'Just fancy, if one got up in the morning with the thought that no reasonable desire that occurred to one throughout the day need remain ungratified! And that it would be the same, any day and every day, to the end of one's life! Look at those houses; every detail, within and without, luxurious. To have such a home as that!'

'And they are empty creatures who live there.'

'They do *live*, Amy, at all events. Whatever may be their faculties, they all have free scope. I have often stood staring at houses like these until I couldn't believe that the people owning them were mere human beings like myself. The power of money is so hard to realise; one who has never had it marvels at the completeness with which it transforms every detail of life. Compare what we call our home with that of rich people; it moves one to scornful laughter. I have no sympathy with the stoical point of view; between wealth and poverty is just the difference between the whole man and the maimed. If my lower limbs are paralysed I may still be able to think, but then there is such a thing in life as walking. As a poor devil I may live nobly; but one happens to be made with faculties of enjoyment, and those have to fall into atrophy. To be sure, most rich people don't understand their happiness; if they did, they would move and talk like gods—which indeed they are.'

Amy's brow was shadowed. A wise man, in Reardon's position, would not have chosen this subject to dilate upon.

'The difference,' he went on, 'between the man with money and the man without is simply this: the one thinks, "How shall I use my life?" and the other, "How shall I keep myself alive?" A physiologist ought to be able to discover some curious distinction between the brain of a person who has never given a thought to the means of subsistence, and that of one who has never known a day free from such cares. There must be some special cerebral development representing the mental anguish kept up by poverty.'

'I should say,' put in Amy, 'that it affects every function of the brain. It isn't a special point of suffering, but a misery that colours every thought.'

'True. Can I think of a single subject in all the sphere of my experience without the consciousness that I see it through the medium of poverty? I have no enjoyment which isn't tainted by that thought, and I can suffer no pain which it doesn't increase. The curse of poverty is to the modern world just what that of slavery was to the ancient. Rich and destitute stand to each other as free man and bond. You remember the line of Homer I have often quoted about the demoralising effect of enslavement; poverty degrades in the same way.'

'It has had its effect upon me—I know that too well,' said Amy, with bitter frankness.

Reardon glanced at her, and wished to make some reply, but he could not say what was in his thoughts.

GEORGE GISSING, *New Grub Street*, 1891

O hateful harm! condicion of poverte!
With thurst, with cold, with hunger so confounded!
To asken help thee shameth in thyn herte;
If thou noon aske, with nede artow so wounded,
That verray nede unwrappeth al thy wounde hid!
Maugree thyn heed, thou most for indigence    *in spite of all you can do*
Or stele, or begge, or borwe thy despence!    *living expenses*

Thou blamest Crist, and seyst ful bitterly,
He misdeparteth richesse temporal;
Thy neighebour thou wytest sinfully,    *accuse*
And seyst thou hast to lyte, and he hath al.    *too little*
'Parfay,' seistow, 'somtyme he rekne shal,
Whan that his tayl shal brennen in the glede,    *burn in the glowing coals*
For he noght helpeth needfulle in hir nede.'

Herkne what is the sentence of the wyse:—
'Bet is to dyën than have indigence;'
Thy selve neighebour wol thee despyse;
If thou be povre, farwel thy reverence!    *the respect others show you*
Yet of the wyse man tak this sentence:—
'Alle the dayes of povre men ben wikke;'
Be war therfor, er thou come in that prikke!    *to that point*

If thou be povre, thy brother hateth thee,
And alle thy freendes fleen fro thee, alas!
O riche marchaunts, ful of wele ben ye,
O noble, o prudent folk, as in this cas!

GEOFFREY CHAUCER, Prologue to 'The Man of Lawe's Tale', *Canterbury Tales*, c.1387–94

'Don't you ever mind,' she asked suddenly, 'not being rich enough to buy all the books you want?'

He followed her glance about the room, with its worn furniture and shabby walls.

'Don't I just? Do you take me for a saint on a pillar?'

'And having to work—do you mind that?'

'Oh, the work itself is not so bad—I'm rather fond of the law.'

'No; but the being tied down: the routine—don't you ever want to get away, to see new places and people?'

'Horribly—especially when I see all my friends rushing to the steamer.'

She drew a sympathetic breath. 'But do you mind enough—to marry to get out of it?'

Selden broke into a laugh. 'God forbid!' he declared.

She rose with a sigh, tossing her cigarette into the grate.

'Ah, there's the difference—a girl must, a man may if he chooses.' She surveyed him critically. 'Your coat's a little shabby—but who cares? It doesn't keep people from asking you to dine. If I were shabby no one would have me: a woman is asked out as much for her clothes as for herself. The clothes are the background, the frame, if you like: they don't make success, but they are a part of it. Who wants a dingy woman? We are expected to be pretty and well-dressed till we drop—and if we can't keep it up alone, we have to go into partnership.'

Selden glanced at her with amusement: it was impossible, even with her lovely eyes imploring him, to take a sentimental view of her case.

'Ah, well, there must be plenty of capital on the look-out for such an investment. Perhaps you'll meet your fate to-night at the Trenors'.'

EDITH WHARTON, *The House of Mirth*, 1905

'But after all,' she continued with a smile, 'there's never any great risk as long as you have money.'

'Oh, shame! What a shocking speech!'

'Money pads the edges of things,' said Miss Schlegel. 'God help those who have none.'

'But this is something quite new!' said Mrs Munt, who collected new ideas as a squirrel collects nuts, and was especially attracted by those that are portable.

'New for me; sensible people have acknowledged it for years. You and I and the Wilcoxes stand upon money as upon islands. It is so firm beneath our feet that we forget its very existence. It's only when we see someone near us tottering that we realize all that an independent income means. Last night, when we were talking up here round the fire, I began to think that the very soul of the world is economic, and that the lowest abyss is not the absence of love, but the absence of coin.'

'I call that rather cynical.'

'So do I. But Helen and I, we ought to remember, when we are tempted to criticize others, that we are standing on these islands, and that most of the others are down below the surface of the sea. The poor cannot always reach those whom they want to love, and they can hardly ever escape from those whom they love no longer. We rich can. Imagine the tragedy last June, if Helen and Paul Wilcox had been poor people, and couldn't invoke railways and motor-cars to part them.'

'That's more like Socialism,' said Mrs Munt suspiciously.

'Call it what you like. I call it going through life with one's hand spread open on the table. I'm tired of these rich people who pretend to be poor, and think it shows a nice mind to ignore the piles of money that keep their feet above the waves. I stand each year upon six hundred pounds, and Helen upon the same, and Tibby will stand upon eight, and as fast as our pounds crumble away into the sea they are renewed—from the sea, yes, from the sea. And all our thoughts are the thoughts of six-hundred-pounders, and all our speeches; and because we don't want to steal umbrellas ourselves, we forget that below the sea people do want to steal them, and do steal them sometimes, and that what's a joke up here is down there reality—'

E. M. FORSTER, *Howard's End*, 1910

What I mean is this: that one can, with no romanticism, feel nostalgic for lost poverty. A certain number of years lived without money are enough to create a whole sensibility. In this particular case, the strange feeling which the son has for his mother constitutes *his whole sensibility*. The latent material memory which he has of his childhood (a glue that sticks to the soul) explains why this way of feeling shows itself in the most widely differing fields.

Whoever notices this in himself feels gratitude and therefore a guilty conscience. If he has moved into a different class, the comparison also gives him the feeling that he has lost great wealth. For rich people, the sky is just an extra, a gift of nature. The poor, on the other hand, can see it as it really is: an infinite grace.

ALBERT CAMUS, *Selected Essays and Notebooks*, May 1935

I desire, in closing the series of introductory papers, to leave this one great fact clearly stated. THERE IS NO WEALTH BUT LIFE. Life, including all its powers of love, of joy, and of admiration. That country is the richest which nourishes the greatest number of noble and happy human beings; that man is richest who, having perfected the functions of his own life to the utmost, has also the widest helpful influence, both personal, and by means of his possessions, over the lives of others.

JOHN RUSKIN, *Unto This Last*, 1860

# Borrowing and Lending

Debts and loans are plainly as much a part of everyday life as any of the transactions noted in 'Getting and Spending', but the literature of lending is so extensive as to demand a section of its own, particularly since the West (and not only the West) has so often been enraged by the practice of lending at interest, or, to use its older name, usury. When conducted on a sufficiently large scale, borrowing and lending may pass beyond the realm of personal ethics and become a political issue: this section also examines what both poets and politicians have had to say on the subject of national debts.

❧

Would you know what money is, go borrow some.

GEORGE HERBERT, *Jacula prudentum*, 1640

POLONIUS. Neither a borrower, nor a lender be:
  For loan oft loses both itself and friend;
  And borrowing dulls the edge of husbandry.

WILLIAM SHAKESPEARE, *Hamlet*, 1601

But, quoth Pantagruel, when will you be out of debt? At the next ensuing term of the Greek calends, answered Panurge, when all the world shall be content, and that it be your fate to become your own heir. The Lord forbid that I should be out of debt, as if, indeed, I could not be trusted. Who leaves not some leaven over night, will hardly have paste the next morning.

Be still indebted to somebody or other, that there may be somebody always to pray for you; that the giver of all good things may grant unto you a blessed, long, and prosperous life; fearing, if fortune should deal crossly with you, that it might be his chance to come short of being paid by you, he will always speak good of you in every company, ever and anon purchase new creditors unto you; to the end, that through their means you may make a shift by borrowing from Peter to pay Paul, and with other folk's earth fill up his ditch. When of old in the region of the Gauls, by the institution of the Druids, the servants, slaves, and bondsmen were burned quick at the funerals and obsequies of their lords and masters, had not they fear enough, think you, that their lords and masters should die? For, per force, they were to die with them for company. Did not they incessantly send up their supplications to their great God Mercury, as likewise unto Dis the Father of Wealth, to lengthen out their days, and preserve them long in health? Were not they very careful to entertain them well, punctually to look unto them, and to attend them faithfully and circumspectly? For, by those means, were they to live together at least until the hour of death. Believe me, your creditors, with a more fervent devotion, will beseech Almighty God to prolong your life, they being of nothing more afraid than that you should die; for that they are more concerned for the sleeve than the arm, and love silver better than their own lives. As it evidently appeareth by the usurers of Landerousse, who not long since hanged themselves, because the price of the corn and wines was fallen, by the return of a gracious season. To this Pantagruel answering nothing, Panurge went on in his discourse, saying, truly, and in good sooth, Sir, when I ponder my destiny aright, and think well upon it, you put me shrewdly to my plunges, and have me at a bay in twitting me with the reproach of my debts and creditors. And yet did I, in this only respect and consideration of being a debtor, esteem myself worshipful, reverend, and formidable. For against the opinion of most philosophers, that, of nothing ariseth nothing, yet, without having bottomed on so much as that which is called the First Matter, did I out of nothing become such a maker and creator, that I have created,—what?—a gay number of fair and jolly creditors. Nay, creditors, I will maintain it, even to the very fire itself exclusively, are fair and goodly creatures. Who lendeth nothing is an ugly and wicked creature, and an accursed imp of the infernal Old Nick. And there is made—what? Debts. A thing most precious and dainty, of great use and antiquity. Debts, I say, surmounting the number of syllables which may result from the combinations of all the consonants, with each of the vowels heretofore projected, reckoned and calculated by the noble Xenocrates. To judge of the perfection of debtors by the numerosity of their creditors is the readiest way for entering into the mysteries of practical arithmetic.

You can hardly imagine how glad I am, when every morning I perceive myself environed and surrounded with brigades of creditors, humble, fawning, and full of their reverences. And whilst I remark, that, as I look more favourably upon, and give a cheerfuller countenance to one than to another, the fellow thereupon buildeth a conceit that he shall be the first dispatched, and the foremost in the date of payment; and he valueth my smiles at the rate of ready money. It seemeth unto me, that I then act and personate the god of the passion of Saumure, accompanied with his angels and cherubims.

These are my flatterers, my soothers, my claw-backs, my smoothers, my parasites, my saluters, my givers of good morrows, and perpetual orators; which makes me verily think, that the supremest height of heroic virtue, described by Hesiod, consisteth in being a debtor, wherein I held the first degree in my commencement. Which dignity, though all humane creatures seem to aim at, and aspire thereto, few, nevertheless, because of the difficulties in the way, and incumbrances of hard passages, are able to reach it as is easily perceivable by the ardent desire and vehement longing harboured in the breast of every one, to be still creating more debts, and new creditors.

Yet doth it not lie in the power of every one to be a debtor. To acquire creditors is not at the disposure of each man's arbitrament. You nevertheless would deprive me of this sublime felicity. You ask me, when I will be out of debt. Well, to go yet further on, and possibly worse in your conceit, may Saint Bablin, the good saint, snatch me, if I have not all my life-time held debt to be as an union or conjunction of the heavens with the earth, and the whole cement whereby the race of mankind is kept together; yea, of such virtue and efficacy, that, I say, the whole progeny of Adam would very suddenly perish without it. Therefore, perhaps, I do not think amiss, when I repute it to be the great soul of the universe, which, according to the opinion of the Academics, vivifyeth all manner of things.

FRANÇOIS RABELAIS, *Gargantua and Pantagruel*, 1546, book iii, tr. Sir Thomas Urquhart, 1693

Ten pound thou begg'dst to borrow th' other day,
Which speedily thou promised to repay.
I had it not, as civil I did say.
But thou, by a friend's visit much surprised,

To borrow of me silver plate devised.
Art thou a fool? or me dost one suppose?
When ten I would not, fifty pound I'd lose?

MARTIAL (*c.* AD 40–140), *Epigrams*, IV. xv, 'To Caecilianus', tr. anon., 1695

The human species, according to the best theory I can form of it, is composed of two distinct races, *the men who borrow*, and *the men who lend*. To these two original diversities may be reduced all those impertinent classifications of Gothic and Celtic tribes, white men, black men, red men. All the dwellers upon earth, 'Parthians, and Medes, and Elamites,' flock hither, and do naturally fall in with one or other of these primary distinctions. The infinite superiority of the former, which I choose to designate as the *great race*, is discernible in their figure, port, and a certain instinctive sovereignty. The latter are born degraded. 'He shall serve his brethren.' There is something in the air of one of this cast, lean and suspicious; contrasting with the open, trusting, generous manners of the other.

Observe who have been the greatest borrowers of all ages—Alcibiades—Falstaff—Sir Richard Steele—our late incomparable Brinsley—what a family likeness in all four!

What a careless, even deportment hath your borrower! what rosy gills! what a beautiful reliance on Providence doth he manifest,—taking no more thought than lilies! What contempt for money,—accounting it (yours and mine especially) no better than dross! What a liberal confounding of those pedantic distinctions of *meum* and *tuum!* or rather, what a noble simplification of language (beyond Tooke), resolving these supposed opposites into one clear, intelligible pronoun adjective!—What near approaches doth he make to the primitive *community*,—to the extent of one half of the principle at least.

He is the true taxer who 'calleth all the world up to be taxed;' and the distance is as vast between him and *one of us*, as subsisted between the Augustan Majesty and the poorest obolary Jew that paid it tribute-pittance at Jerusalem!—His exactions, too, have such a cheerful, voluntary air! So far removed from your sour parochial or state-gatherers,—those ink-horn varlets, who carry their want of welcome in their faces! He cometh to you with a smile, and troubleth you with no receipt; confining himself to no set season. Every day is his Candlemas, or his Feast of Holy Michael. He applieth the *lene tormentum* of a pleasant look to your purse,—which to that gentle

*lene tormentum*] gentle torture

warmth expands her silken leaves, as naturally as the cloak of the traveller, for which sun and wind contended! He is the true Propontic which never ebbeth! The sea which taketh handsomely at each man's hand. In vain the victim, whom he delighteth to honour, struggles with destiny; he is in the net. Lend therefore cheerfully, O man ordained to lend—that thou lose not in the end, with thy worldly penny, the reversion promised. Combine not preposterously in thine own person the penalties of Lazarus and of Dives!— but, when thou seest the proper authority coming, meet it smilingly, as it were half-way. Come, a handsome sacrifice! See how light *he* makes of it! Strain not courtesies with a noble enemy.

CHARLES LAMB, *Essays of Elia*, 1823

On the first rule of the art of managing money all preceptors must be agreed. It is told in three words—'Horror of Debt.'

Nurse, cherish, never cavil away, the wholesome horror of DEBT. Personal liberty is the paramount essential to human dignity and human happiness. Man hazards the condition, and loses the virtues of freeman, in proportion as he accustoms his thoughts to view, without anguish and shame, his lapse into the bondage of debtor. Debt is to man what the serpent is to the bird; its eye fascinates, its breath poisons, its coil crushes sinew and bone, its jaw is the pitiless grave. If you mock my illustration, if you sneer at the truth it embodies, give yourself no farther trouble to learn how to manage your money. Consider yourself doomed; pass on your way with a jaunty step; the path is facile—paths to Avernus always are. But if, while I write, your heart, true to the instinct of manhood, responds to my words—if you say, 'Agreed; that which you call the first rule for the management of money, I hold yet more imperative as the necessity to freedom and the lifespring of probity'—then advance on your way, assured that wherever it wind it must ascend. You see but the temple of Honor; close behind it is the temple of Fortune. You will pass through the one to the other.

BULWER LYTTON, 'On the Management of Money', *Caxtoniana*, 1864

I have read Earl Bright's speech at Leeds, and I hope we shall now hear from John Derby. I trust that not only they, but Wm. E. Stanley and Lord Gladstone will cling inflexibly to those great fundamental principles, which they understand far better than I do, and I will add, that I do not understand anything about any of them whatever in the least—and let us all be happy, and live within our means, even if we have to borrer the money to do it with.—Very respectively yours,

Artemus Ward.

Artemus Ward (Charles Farrar Browne) (1834–67), *Artemus Ward in London*

Mrs Reilly took the sheet of paper and read the typed column of itemized figures beneath the contractor's letterhead.

'Lord! A thousand and twenty dollars. This is terrible. How I'm gonna pay that?' She dropped the estimate on the oilcloth. 'You sure that is right?'

'Yes, ma'm. He's got a lawyer working on it, too. It's all on the up and up.'

'Where I'm gonna get a thousand dollars, though? All me and Ignatius got is my poor husband's Social Security and a little two-bit pension, and that don't come to much.'

'Do I believe the total perversion that I am witnessing?' Ignatius screamed from the parlor. The music had a frantic, tribal rhythm; a chorus of falsettos sang insinuatingly about loving all night long.

'I'm sorry,' Patrolman Mancuso said, almost heartbroken over Mrs Reilly's financial quandary.

'Aw, it's not your fault, darling,' she said glumly. 'Maybe I can get a mortgage on the house. We can't do nothing about it, huh?'

'No, ma'm,' Patrolman Mancuso answered, listening to some sort of approaching stampede.

'The children on that program should all be gassed,' Ignatius said as he strode into the kitchen in his nightshirt. Then he noticed the guest and said coldly, 'Oh.'

'Ignatius, you know Mr Mancuso. Say "Hello." '

'I do believe that I've seen him about,' Ignatius said and looked out the back door.

Patrolman Mancuso was too startled by the monstrous flannel nightshirt to reply to Ignatius' pleasantry.

'Ignatius, honey, the man wants over a thousand dollars for what I did to his building.'

'A thousand dollars? He will not get a cent. We shall have him prosecuted immediately. Contact our attorneys, Mother.'

'Our attorneys? He's got a estimate from a contractor. Mr Mancuso here says they's nothing I can do.'

'Oh. Well, you shall have to pay him then.'

'I could take it to court if you think it's best.'

'Drunken driving,' Ignatius said calmly. 'You haven't a chance.'

Mrs Reilly looked depressed.

'But Ignatius, a thousand twenty dollars.'

'I am certain that you can procure some funds,' he told her. 'Is there any more coffee, or have you given the last to this carnival masker?'

'We can mortgage the house.'

'Mortgage the house? Of course we won't.'

'What else we gonna do, Ignatius?'

'There are means,' Ignatius said absently. 'I wish that you wouldn't bother me with this. That program always increases my anxiety anyway.' He smelled the milk before putting it into the pot. 'I would suggest that you telephone that dairy immediately. This milk is quite aged.'

'I can get a thousand dollars over by the Homestead,' Mrs Reilly told the silent patrolman quietly. 'The house is good security. I had me a real estate agent offered me seven thousand last year.'

'The ironic thing about that program,' Ignatius was saying over the stove, keeping one eye peeled so that he could seize the pot as soon as the milk began to boil, 'is that it is supposed to be an *exemplum* to the youth of our nation. I would like very much to know what the Founding Fathers would say if they could see these children being debauched to further the cause of Clearasil. However, I always suspected that democracy would come to this.' He painstakingly poured the milk into his Shirley Temple mug. 'A firm rule must be imposed upon our nation before it destroys itself. The United States needs some theology and geometry, some taste and decency. I suspect that we are teetering on the edge of the abyss.'

'Ignatius, I'm gonna have to go by the Homestead tomorrow.'

'We shall not deal with those usurers, Mother.' Ignatius was feeling around in the cookie jar. 'Something will turn up.'

JOHN KENNEDY TOOLE (1937–69), *A Confederacy of Dunces*


Mrs Sponge, laying aside that haughty look and voice, well known to such as had the misfortune to be in her debt, put on the hypocritical smile and soft canting tone which she always assumed when she meant to flatter her superiors, or take in her dependents. 'Betty,' said she, 'I am resolved to stand your friend. These are sad times to be sure. Money is money now. Yet I am resolved to put you into a handsome way of living. You shall have a barrow, and well furnished, too.' Betty could not have felt more joy or gratitude if she had been told that she should have a coach. 'O, madam!' said Betty, 'it is impossible. I have not a penny in the world towards helping me to set up.'—'I will take care of that,' said Mrs Sponge; 'only you must do as I bid you. You must pay me interest for my money; and you will of course be glad also to pay so much every night for a nice hot supper which I get ready, *quite out of kindness*, for a number of poor working people. This will be a great comfort for such a friendless girl as you, for my victuals and drink are the best, and my company the merriest of any house in all St Giles's.' Betty thought all this only so many more favours, and, courtesying to the ground, said, 'To be sure, ma'am, and thank you a thousand times into the bargain. I never could hope for such a rise in life.'

Mrs Sponge knew what she was about.

Hannah More, 'Betty Brown, the St Giles's Orange Girl', Works, 1830

*A Room in* SIR PETER TEAZLE's *House.*

SIR PETER TEAZLE, SIR OLIVER SURFACE, *and* ROWLEY.

ROW. Here comes the honest Israelite.

*Enter* MOSES.

—This is Sir Oliver.

SIR OLIV. Sir, I understand you have lately had great dealings with my nephew Charles.

MOS. Yes, Sir Oliver, I have done all I could for him; but he was ruined before he came to me for assistance.

SIR OLIV. That was unlucky, truly; for you have had no opportunity of showing your talents.

MOS. None at all; I hadn't the pleasure of knowing his distresses till he was some thousands worse than nothing.

SIR OLIV. Unfortunate, indeed! But I suppose you have done all in your power for him, honest Moses?

MOS. Yes, he knows that. This very evening I was to have brought him a gentleman from the city, who does not know him, and will, I believe, advance him some money.

SIR PET. What, one Charles has never had money from before?

MOS. Yes, Mr Premium, of Crutched Friars, formerly a broker.

SIR PET. Egad, Sir Oliver, a thought strikes me!—Charles, you say, does not know Mr Premium?

MOS. Not at all.

SIR PET. Now then, Sir Oliver, you may have a better opportunity of satisfying yourself than by an old romancing tale of a poor relation: go with my friend Moses, and represent Premium, and then, I'll answer for it, you'll see your nephew in all his glory.

SIR OLIV. Egad, I like this idea better than the other, and I may visit Joseph afterwards as old Stanley.

SIR PET. True—so you may.

ROW. Well, this is taking Charles rather at a disadvantage, to be sure. However, Moses, you understand Sir Peter, and will be faithful?

MOS. You may depend upon me.—[*Looks at his watch*] This is near the time I was to have gone.

SIR OLIV. I'll accompany you as soon as you please, Moses.—But hold! I have forgot one thing—how the plague shall I be able to pass for a Jew?

MOS. There's no need—the principal is Christian.

SIR OLIV. Is he? I'm very sorry to hear it. But, then again, ain't I rather too smartly dressed to look like a moneylender?

SIR PET. Not at all; 'twould not be out of character, if you went in your own carriage—would it, Moses?

MOS. Not in the least.

SIR OLIV. Well, but how must I talk? there's certainly some cant of usury and mode of treating that I ought to know.

SIR PET. Oh, there's not much to learn. The great point, as I take it, is to be exorbitant enough in your demands. Hey, Moses?

MOS. Yes, that's a very great point.

SIR OLIV. I'll answer for 't I'll not be wanting in that. I'll ask him eight or ten per cent. on the loan, at least.

MOS. If you ask him no more than that, you'll be discovered immediately.

SIR OLIV. Hey! what, the plague! how much then?

MOS. That depends upon the circumstances. If he appears not very anxious for the supply, you should require only forty or fifty per cent.; but if you find him in great distress, and want the moneys very bad, you may ask double.

SIR PET. A good honest trade you're learning, Sir Oliver!

SIR OLIV. Truly, I think so—and not unprofitable.

MOS. Then, you know, you haven't the moneys yourself, but are forced to borrow them for him of a friend.

SIR OLIV. Oh! I borrow it of a friend, do I?

MOS. And your friend is an unconscionable dog: but you can't help that.

SIR OLIV. My friend an unconscionable dog, is he?

MOS. Yes, and he himself has not the moneys by him, but is forced to sell stock at a great loss.

SIR OLIV. He is forced to sell stock at a great loss, is he? Well, that's very kind of him.

SIR PET. I 'faith, Sir Oliver—Mr Premium, I mean—you'll soon be master of the trade. But, Moses! would not you have him run out a little against the annuity bill? That would be in character, I should think.

MOS. Very much.

ROW. And lament that a young man now must be at years of discretion before he is suffered to ruin himself?

MOS. Ay, great pity!

SIR PET. And abuse the public for allowing merit to an act whose only object is to snatch misfortune and imprudence from the rapacious gripe of usury, and give the minor a chance of inheriting his estate without being undone by coming into possession.

SIR OLIV. So, so—Moses shall give me further instructions as we go together.

SIR PET. You will not have much time, for your nephew lives hard by.

SIR OLIV. Oh, never fear! my tutor appears so able, that though Charles lived in the next street, it must be my own fault if I am not a complete rogue before I turn the corner.                    [*Exit with* MOSES

RICHARD SHERIDAN, *The School for Scandal*, 1777

It was not often that Lord Hoddesdon visited his son and heir, but in some mysterious way there had floated into his lordship's mind as he left Lady Vera's flat the extraordinary idea that Biskerton might possibly have a little cash in hand and be willing to part with some of it to the author of his being.

'Er—Godfrey, my boy.'

'Hullo, guv'nor.'

Lord Hoddesdon coughed.

'Er—Godfrey,' he said, 'I wonder—it so happens that I am a little short at the moment—I suppose you could not possibly—'

'Guv'nor,' said the Biscuit, amusedly. 'This is To-day's Big Laugh. Don't tell me you've come to make a touch?'

'I thought—'

'What on earth led you to suppose I'd got a bean?'

'I fancied that possibly Mr Frisby might have made you some small present.'

'Why the dickens?'

'In celebration of the—er—happy event. After all, he is the uncle of your future bride. But, of course, if such is not the case—'

'Such,' the Biscuit assured him, 'is decidedly not. The old, moth-eaten fossil to whom you allude, guv'nor, is the one man in this great city who never makes small presents in celebration of any happy event. His family motto is *Nil desperandum*—Never give up.'

'Too bad,' sighed Lord Hoddesdon. 'I was hoping that you would be able to help me out. I am sorely in need of monetary assistance. Your aunt has asked me to take your *fiancée* to lunch at the Berkeley this afternoon, and her idea of expense-money is little short of Aberdonian. Twenty-five shillings!'

'Lavish,' said the Biscuit firmly. 'I wish somebody would give me twenty-five bob. I've just a quid to see me through to the end of the month.'

'As bad as that?'

'One pound, two and twopence, to be exact.'

'Still,' Lord Hoddesdon pointed out, 'you must remember that your prospects are now of the brightest. You have been wiser in your generation than I in mine, my boy.' He stroked his moustache and heaved another regretful sigh. 'As a young man,' he said, 'my great fault was impulsiveness. I should have married money, as you are sensibly doing. How clearly I see that now. And I had my opportunity—opportunity pressed down and running over. For months after I succeeded, wall-eyed heiresses were paraded before me in droves. But I was too romantic, too idealistic. Your poor mother was at that time a humble unit of the Gaiety Theatre company, and after I had been to see the piece in which she was performing sixteen times I suddenly noticed her. She was standing on the extreme O.P. side. Our eyes met—Not that I regret it for a moment, of course,' said Lord Hoddesdon. 'As fine a pal as a man ever had. On the other hand—Yes, you have shown yourself a wiser man than your old father, my boy.'

Several times during this address the Biscuit had given evidence of a desire to interrupt. He now spoke forcefully.

'I wish you wouldn't talk of Ann and wall-eyed heiresses without taking a long breath in between,' he said, justly annoyed. 'When you say I'm marrying money, it makes it sound as if the cash was all I cared about. Let me tell you, guv'nor, that this is love. The real thing. I'm crazy about Ann. In fact, when I think that a girl can be such a ripper and at the same time so dashed rich, it restores my faith in the Providence which looks after good men. She's the sweetest thing on earth, and if I had more than one pound, two and twopence I'd be taking her to lunch to-day myself.'

P. G. WODEHOUSE, *Big Money*, 1931

There are gentlemen of very good blood and fashion in this city who never have entered a lady's drawing-room; so that though Rawdon Crawley's

marriage might be talked about in his county, where, of course, Mrs Bute
had spread the news, in London it was doubted, or not heeded, or not
talked about at all. He lived comfortably on credit. He had a large capital
of debts, which, laid out judiciously, will carry a man along for many years,
and on which certain men about town contrive to live a hundred times
better than even men with ready money can do. Indeed who is there that
walks London streets, but can point out a half-dozen of men riding by him
splendidly, while he is on foot, courted by fashion, bowed into their carriages by tradesmen, denying themselves nothing, and living on who knows
what? We see Jack Thriftless prancing in the Park, or darting in his brougham
down Pall Mall: we eat his dinners served on his miraculous plate. 'How
did this begin,' we say, 'or where will it end?' 'My dear fellow,' I heard Jack
once say, 'I owe money in every capital in Europe.' The end must come
some day, but in the mean time Jack thrives as much as ever; people are
glad enough to shake him by the hand, ignore the little dark stories that are
whispered every now and then against him, and pronounce him a good-
natured, jovial, reckless fellow.

W. M. THACKERAY, *Vanity Fair*, 1847–8

*Enter* ANTONIO.

BASSANIO. This is signior Antonio.
SHYLOCK [*aside*]. How like a fawning publican he looks!
    I hate him for he is a Christian:
    But more, for that, in low simplicity,
    He lends out money gratis, and brings down
    The rate of usance here with us in Venice.
    If I can catch him once upon the hip,
    I will feed fat the ancient grudge I bear him.
    He hates our sacred nation; and he rails,
    Even there where merchants most do congregate,
    On me, my bargains, and my well-won thrift,
    Which he calls interest: Cursed be my tribe,
    If I forgive him!
BASS.                    Shylock, do you hear?
SHY. I am debating of my present store:
    And, by the near guess of my memory,
    I cannot instantly raise up the gross
    Of full three thousand ducats: What of that?

Tubal, a wealthy Hebrew of my tribe,
Will furnish me: But soft; How many months
Do you desire?—Rest you fair, good signior:

                                                                        [*To* ANTONIO

Your worship was the last man in our mouths.

ANT. Shylock, albeit I neither lend nor borrow,
By taking, nor by giving of excess,
Yet, to supply the ripe wants of my friend,
I'll break a custom:—Is he yet possess'd,
How much you would?

SHY.                   Ay, ay, three thousand ducats.

ANT. And for three months.

SHY. I had forgot,—three months, you told me so.
Well then, your bond; and, let me see,—But hear you;
Methought, you said, you neither lend, nor borrow,
Upon advantage.

ANT.               I do never use it.

SHY. When Jacob graz'd his uncle Laban's sheep,
This Jacob from our holy Abraham was
(As his wise mother wrought in his behalf,)
The third possessor; ay, he was the third.

ANT. And what of him? did he take interest?

SHY. No, not take interest; not, as you would say,
Directly interest: mark what Jacob did.
When Laban and himself were compromis'd,
That all the eanlings which were streak'd, and pied,
Should fall as Jacob's hire; the ewes, being rank,
In the end of autumn turned to the rams:
And when the work of generation was
Between these woolly breeders in the act,
The skilful shepherd peel'd me certain wands,
And, in the doing of the deed of kind,
He stuck them up before the fulsome ewes;
Who, then conceiving, did in eaning time
Fall party-colour'd lambs, and those were Jacob's.
This was a way to thrive, and he was blest;
And thrift is blessing, if men steal it not.

ANT. This was a venture, sir, that Jacob serv'd for;
A thing not in his power to bring to pass,
But sway'd, and fashion'd, by the hand of heaven.

Was this inserted to make interest good?

Or is your gold and silver, ewes and rams?

SHY. I cannot tell; I make it breed as fast:—

But note me, signior.

ANT.                         Mark you this, Bassanio,

The devil can cite scripture for his purpose.

An evil soul, producing holy witness,

Is like a villain with a smiling cheek;

A goodly apple rotten at the heart;

O, what a goodly outside falshood hath!

SHY. Three thousand ducats,—'tis a good round sum.

Three months from twelve, then let me see the rate.

ANT. Well, Shylock, shall we be beholden to you?

SHY. Signior Antonio, many a time and oft,

In the Rialto you have rated me

About my monies, and my usances:

Still have I borne it with a patient shrug;

For sufferance is the badge of all our tribe:

You call me—misbeliever, cut-throat dog,

And spit upon my Jewish gaberdine,

And all for use of that which is mine own.

Well then, it now appears, you need my help:

Go to then; you come to me, and you say,

*Shylock, we would have monies*; You say so;

You, that did void your rheum upon my beard,

And foot me, as you spurn a stranger cur

Over your threshold; monies is your suit.

What should I say to you? Should I not say,

*Hath a dog money? is it possible,*

*A cur can lend three thousand ducats?* or

Shall I bend low, and in a bondman's key,

With 'bated breath, and whispering humbleness,

Say this,—

*Fair sir, you spit on me on Wednesday last:*

*You spurn'd me such a day; another time*

*You call'd me—dog; and for these courtesies*

*I'll lend you thus much monies.*

ANT. I am as like to call thee so again,

To spit on thee again, to spurn thee too.

If thou wilt lend this money, lend it not

As to thy friends; (for when did friendship take
A breed for barren metal of his friend?)
But lend it rather to thine enemy;
Who if he break, thou may'st with better face
Exact the penalty.

SHY. Why, look you, how you storm!
I would be friends with you, and have your love,
Forget the shames that you have stain'd me with,
Supply your present wants, and take no doit
Of usance for my monies, and you'll not hear me:
This is kind I offer.

ANT. This were kindness.

SHY. This kindness will I show:—
Go with me to a notary, seal me there
Your single bond; and, in a merry sport,
If you repay me not on such a day,
In such a place, such sum, or sums, as are
Express'd in the condition, let the forfeit
Be nominated for an equal pound
Of your fair flesh, to be cut off and taken
In what part of your body pleaseth me.

ANT. Content, in faith; I'll seal to such a bond,
And say, there is much kindness in the Jew.

BASS. You shall not seal to such a bond for me,
I'll rather dwell in my necessity.

ANT. Why, fear not, man; I will not forfeit it;
Within these two months, that's a month before
This bond expires, I do expect return
Of thrice three times the value of this bond.

WILLIAM SHAKESPEARE, *The Merchant of Venice*, 1597

'I am obliged to tell you what will hurt you, Rosy. But there are things which husband and wife must think of together. I daresay it has occurred to you already that I am short of money.'

Lydgate paused; but Rosamond turned her neck and looked at a vase on the mantelpiece.

'I was not able to pay for all the things we had to get before we were married, and there have been expenses since which I have been obliged to meet. The consequence is, there is a large debt at Brassing—three hundred and eighty pounds—which has been pressing on me a good while, and in fact we are getting deeper every day, for people don't pay me the faster because others want the money. I took pains to keep it from you while you were not well; but now we must think together about it, and you must help me.'

'What can *I* do, Tertius?' said Rosamond, turning her eyes on him again. That little speech of four words, like so many others in all languages, is capable by varied vocal inflexions of expressing all states of mind from helpless dimness to exhaustive argumentative perception, from the completest self-devoting fellowship to the most neutral aloofness. Rosamond's thin utterance threw into the words 'What can *I* do!' as much neutrality as they could hold. They fell like a mortal chill on Lydgate's roused tenderness. He did not storm in indignation—he felt too sad a sinking of the heart. And when he spoke again it was more in the tone of a man who forces himself to fulfil a task.

'It is necessary for you to know, because I have to give security for a time, and a man must come to make an inventory of the furniture.'

Rosamond coloured deeply. 'Have you not asked papa for money?' she said, as soon as she could speak.

'No.'

'Then I must ask him!' she said, releasing her hands from Lydgate's, and rising to stand at two yards' distance from him.

'No, Rosy,' said Lydgate, decisively. 'It is too late to do that. The inventory will be begun to-morrow. Remember it is a mere security: it will make no difference: it is a temporary affair. I insist upon it that your father shall not know, unless I choose to tell him,' added Lydgate, with a more peremptory emphasis.

This certainly was unkind, but Rosamond had thrown him back on evil expectation as to what she would do in the way of quiet steady disobedience. The unkindness seemed unpardonable to her: she was not given to weeping and disliked it, but now her chin and lips began to tremble and the tears welled up. Perhaps it was not possible for Lydgate, under the double stress of outward material difficulty and of his own proud resistance to humiliating consequences, to imagine fully what this sudden trial was to a young creature who had known nothing but indulgence, and whose dreams had all been of new indulgence, more exactly to her taste. But he did wish to spare her as much as he could, and her tears cut him to the heart. He could not speak again immediately; but Rosamond did not go on sobbing: she tried to conquer her agitation and wiped away her tears, continuing to look before her at the mantelpiece.

'Try not to grieve, darling,' said Lydgate, turning his eyes up towards her. That she had chosen to move away from him in this moment of her trouble made everything harder to say, but he must absolutely go on. 'We must brace ourselves to do what is necessary. It is I who have been in fault: I ought to have seen that I could not afford to live in this way. But many things have told against me in my practice, and it really just now has ebbed to a low point. I may recover it, but in the mean time we must pull up— we must change our way of living. We shall weather it. When I have given this security I shall have time to look about me; and you are so clever that if you turn your mind to managing you will school me into carefulness. I have been a thoughtless rascal about squaring prices—but come, dear, sit down and forgive me.'

Lydgate was bowing his neck under the yoke like a creature who had talons, but who had Reason too, which often reduces us to meekness. When he had spoken the last words in an imploring tone, Rosamond re-turned to the chair by his side. His self-blame gave her some hope that he would attend to her opinion, and she said—

'Why can you not put off having the inventory made? You can send the men away to-morrow when they come.'

'I shall not send them away,' said Lydgate, the peremptoriness rising again. Was it of any use to explain?

'If we left Middlemarch, there would of course be a sale, and that would do as well.'

'But we are not going to leave Middlemarch.'

'I am sure, Tertius, it would be much better to do so. Why can we not go to London? Or near Durham, where your family is known?'

'We can go nowhere without money, Rosamond.'

'Your friends would not wish you to be without money. And surely these odious tradesmen might be made to understand that, and to wait, if you would make proper representations to them.'

'This is idle, Rosamond,' said Lydgate, angrily. 'You must learn to take my judgment on questions you don't understand. I have made necessary arrangements, and they must be carried out. As to friends, I have no expec-tations whatever from them, and shall not ask them for anything.'

Rosamond sat perfectly still. The thought in her mind was that if she had known how Lydgate would behave, she would never have married him.

'We have no time to waste now on unnecessary words, dear,' said Lydgate, trying to be gentle again. 'There are some details that I want to consider with you. Dover says he will take a good deal of the plate back again, and any of the jewellery we like. He really behaves very well.'

'Are we to go without spoons and forks then?' said Rosamond, whose very lips seemed to get thinner with the thinness of her utterance. She was determined to make no further resistance or suggestions.

'Oh no, dear!' said Lydgate. 'But look here,' he continued, drawing a paper from his pocket and opening it; 'here is Dover's account. See, I have marked a number of articles, which if we returned them would reduce the amount by thirty pounds and more. I have not marked any of the jewellery.' Lydgate had really felt this point of the jewellery very bitter to himself; but he had overcome the feeling by severe argument. He could not propose to Rosamond that she should return any particular present of his, but he had told himself that he was bound to put Dover's offer before her, and her inward prompting might make the affair easy.

'It is useless for me to look, Tertius,' said Rosamond, calmly; 'you will return what you please.' She would not turn her eyes on the paper, and Lydgate, flushing up to the roots of his hair, drew it back and let it fall on his knee. Meanwhile Rosamond quietly went out of the room, leaving Lydgate helpless and wondering. Was she not coming back? It seemed that she had no more identified herself with him than if they had been creatures of different species and opposing interests. He tossed his head and thrust his hands deep into his pockets with a sort of vengeance. There was still science—there were still good objects to work for. He must give a tug still—all the stronger because other satisfactions were going.

But the door opened and Rosamond re-entered. She carried the leather box containing the amethysts, and a tiny ornamental basket which contained other boxes, and laying them on the chair where she had been sitting, she said, with perfect propriety in her air—

'This is all the jewellery you ever gave me. You can return what you like of it, and of the plate also. You will not, of course, expect me to stay at home to-morrow. I shall go to papa's.'

To many women the look Lydgate cast at her would have been more terrible than one of anger: it had in it a despairing acceptance of the distance she was placing between them.

George Eliot, *Middlemarch*, 1871–2

After losing large sums at hazard, Fox would go home,—not to destroy himself, as his friends sometimes feared, but—to sit down quietly, and read Greek.

He once won about eight thousand pounds; and one of his bond-creditors, who soon heard of his good luck, presented himself, and asked for payment.

'Impossible, sir,' replied Fox; 'I must first discharge my debts of honour.' The bond-creditor remonstrated. 'Well, sir, give me your bond.' It was delivered to Fox, who tore it in pieces and threw them into the fire. 'Now, sir,' said Fox, 'my debt to you is a debt of honour;' and immediately paid him.

SAMUEL ROGERS, *Table Talk*, 1856

If they took people at the pawnshop I wonder how much I would get for myself. Debtors' prisons are really pawnshops in which money is lent not so much on goods as on the possessors of them.

GEORG CHRISTOPH LICHTENBERG, Notebook J (1789–93), tr. R. J. Hollingdale, 1990

There are two things that bestow consequence; great possessions, or great debts. Julius Cæsar consented to be millions of sesterces worse than nothing, in order to be every thing; he borrowed large sums of his officers, to quell seditions in his troops, who had mutinied for want of pay, and thus forced his partizans to anticipate their own success only through that of their commander.

REVD C. C. COLTON, *Lacon; or, Many Things in Few Words*, 1823

After a little while I missed, first Mr Skimpole, and afterwards Richard; and while I was thinking how could Richard stay away so long, and lose so much, the maid who had given me the keys looked in at the door, saying, 'If you please, miss, could you spare a minute?'

When I was shut out with her in the hall, she said, holding up her hands, 'Oh if you please, miss, Mr Carstone says would you come up-stairs to Mr Skimpole's room. He has been took, miss!'

'Took?' said I.

'Took, miss. Sudden,' said the maid.

I was apprehensive that his illness might be of a dangerous kind; but of course, I begged her to be quiet and not disturb any one; and collected myself, as I followed her quickly up-stairs, sufficiently to consider what were the best remedies to be applied if it should prove to be a fit. She threw open a door, and I went into a chamber; where, to my unspeakable surprise, instead of finding Mr Skimpole stretched upon the bed, or prostrate on the floor, I found him standing before the fire smiling at Richard, while Richard, with a face of great embarrassment, looked at a person on the sofa, in a white great-coat, with smooth hair upon his head and not much of it, which he was wiping smoother, and making less of, with a pocket-handkerchief.

'Miss Summerson,' said Richard, hurriedly, 'I am glad you are come. You will be able to advise us. Our friend, Mr Skimpole—don't be alarmed!—is arrested for debt.'

'And, really, my dear Miss Summerson,' said Mr Skimpole, with his agreeable candour, 'I never was in a situation, in which that excellent sense, and quiet habit of method and usefulness, which anybody must observe in you who has the happiness of being a quarter of an hour in your society, was more needed.'

The person on the sofa, who appeared to have a cold in his head, gave such a very loud snort, that he startled me.

'Are you arrested for much, sir?' I inquired of Mr Skimpole.

'My dear Miss Summerson,' said he, shaking his head pleasantly, 'I don't know. Some pounds, odd shillings, and halfpence, I think, were mentioned.'

'It's twenty-four pound, sixteen, and sevenpence ha'penny,' observed the stranger. 'That's wot it is.'

'And it sounds—somehow it sounds,' said Mr Skimpole, 'like a small sum?'

The strange man said nothing, but made another snort. It was such a powerful one, that it seemed quite to lift him out of his seat.

'Mr Skimpole,' said Richard to me, 'has a delicacy in applying to my cousin Jarndyce, because he has lately—I think, sir, I understood you that you had lately—'

'Oh, yes!' returned Mr Skimpole, smiling. 'Though I forgot how much it was, and when it was. Jarndyce would readily do it again; but I have the epicure-like feeling that I would prefer a novelty in help; that I would rather,' and he looked at Richard and me, 'develop generosity in a new soil, and in a new form of flower.'

'What do you think will be best, Miss Summerson?' said Richard, aside.

I ventured to inquire, generally, before replying, what would happen if the money were not produced.

'Jail,' said the strange man, coolly putting his handkerchief into his hat, which was on the floor at his feet. 'Or Coavinses.'

'May I ask, sir, what is—'

'Coavinses?' said the strange man. 'A 'ouse.'

Richard and I looked at one another again. It was a most singular thing that the arrest was our embarrassment, and not Mr Skimpole's. He observed us with a genial interest; but there seemed, if I may venture on such a contradiction, nothing selfish in it. He had entirely washed his hands of the difficulty, and it had become ours.

'I thought,' he suggested, as if good-naturedly to help us out, 'that, being parties in a Chancery suit concerning (as people say) a large amount of property, Mr Richard, or his beautiful cousin, or both, could sign something, or make over something, or give some sort of undertaking, or pledge, or bond? I don't know what the business name of it may be, but I suppose there is some instrument within their power that would settle this?'

'Not a bit on it,' said the strange man.

'Really?' returned Mr Skimpole. 'That seems odd, now, to one who is no judge of these things!'

'Odd or even,' said the stranger, gruffly, 'I tell you, not a bit on it!'

'Keep your temper, my good fellow, keep your temper!' Mr Skimpole gently reasoned with him, as he made a little drawing of his head on the fly-leaf of a book. 'Don't be ruffled by your occupation. We can separate you from your office; we can separate the individual from the pursuit. We are not so prejudiced as to suppose that in private life you are otherwise than a very estimable man, with a great deal of poetry in your nature, of which you may not be conscious.'

The stranger only answered with another violent snort; whether in acceptance of the poetry-tribute, or in disdainful rejection of it, he did not express to me.

'Now, my dear Miss Summerson, and my dear Mr Richard,' said Mr Skimpole, gaily, innocently, and confidingly, as he looked at his drawing with his head on one side; 'here you see me utterly incapable of helping myself, and entirely in your hands! I only ask to be free. The butterflies are free. Mankind will surely not deny to Harold Skimpole what it concedes to the butterflies!'

'My dear Miss Summerson,' said Richard, in a whisper, 'I have ten pounds that I received from Mr Kenge. I must try what that will do.'

I possessed fifteen pounds, odd shillings, which I had saved from my quarterly allowance during several years. I had always thought that some accident might happen which would throw me, suddenly, without any relation, or any property, on the world; and had always tried to keep some little money by me, that I might not be quite penniless. I told Richard of my having this little store, and having no present need of it; and I asked him delicately to inform Mr Skimpole, while I should be gone to fetch it, that we would have the pleasure of paying his debt.

When I came back, Mr Skimpole kissed my hand, and seemed quite touched. Not on his own account (I was again aware of that perplexing and extraordinary contradiction), but on ours; as if personal considerations were impossible with him, and the contemplation of our happiness alone affected him. Richard, begging me, for the greater grace of the transaction, as he said, to settle with Coavinses (as Mr Skimpole now jocularly called him), I counted out the money and received the necessary acknowledgment. This, too, delighted Mr Skimpole.

CHARLES DICKENS, *Bleak House*, 1852–3

When I walk the street and observe the hurry about me in this town,

> Where, with like haste, through diff'rent ways they run;
> Some to undo, and some to be undone!

I say, when I behold this vast variety of persons and humours, with the pains they both take for the accomplishment of the ends mentioned in the above verses of Denham, I cannot much wonder at the endeavour after gain, but am extremely astonished that men can be so insensible of the danger of running into debt. One would think it impossible a man who is given to contract debts should know, that his creditor has, from that moment in which he transgresses payment, so much as that demand comes to, in his debtor's honour, liberty, and fortune. One would think he did not know that his creditor can say the worst thing imaginable of him, to wit, 'That he is unjust,' without defamation; and can seize his person, without being guilty of an assault. Yet such is the loose and abandoned turn of some men's minds, that they can live under these constant apprehensions, and still go on to increase the cause of them. Can there be a more low and servile condition, than to be ashamed or afraid to see any one man breathing? Yet he that is much in debt, is in that condition with relation to twenty different people. There are indeed circumstances wherein men of honest natures may become liable to debts, by some unadvised behaviour in any great point of their life, or mortgaging a man's honesty as a security for that of another, and the like; but these instances are so particular and circumstantiated, that they cannot come within general considerations. For one such case as one of these, there are ten where a man, to keep up a farce of retinue and grandeur within his own house, shall shrink at the expectation of surly demands at his doors.

RICHARD STEELE, *Spectator*, 82, 4 June 1711

Thus, while my joyless minutes tedious flow,
With looks demure, and silent pace a *Dun*,
Horrible monster! hated by gods and men,
To my aërial citadel ascends,
With vocal heel thrice thund'ring at my gate,
With hideous accent thrice he calls; I know
The voice ill-boding, and the solemn sound.
What shou'd I do? or whither turn? amaz'd,
Confounded to the dark recess I fly
Of woodhole; strait my bristling hairs erect
Thro' sudden fear; a chilly sweat bedews
My shudd'ring limbs, and (wonderful to tell!)
My tongue forgets her faculty of speech;
So horrible he seems! his faded brow
Entrench'd with many a frown, and conic beard,
And spreading band, admir'd by modern saints.
Disastrous acts forebode; in his right hand
Long scrolls of paper solemnly he waves,
With characters, and figures dire inscrib'd,
Grievous to mortal eyes; (ye gods avert
Such plagues from righteous men;) behind him stalks
Another monster not unlike himself,
Sullen of aspect, by the vulgar call'd
A *Catchpole*, whose polluted hands the gods
With force incredible, and magic charms
First have endu'd, if he his ample palm
Should haply on ill-fated shoulder lay
Of debtor, strait his body, to the touch
Obsequious, (as whilom knights were wont)
To some inchanted castle is convey'd,
Where gates impregnable, and coercive chains
In durance strict detain him, till in form
Of money, PALLAS sets the captive free.

JOHN PHILLIPS, *The Splendid Shilling*, 1701

DEBT, *n.* An ingenious substitute for the chain and whip of the slavedriver.

> As, pent in an aquarium, the troutlet
> Swims round and round his tank to find an outlet,

Pressing his nose against the glass that holds him,
Nor ever sees the prison that enfolds him;
So the poor debtor, seeing naught around him,
Yet feels the limits pitiless that bound him;
Grieves at his debt and studies to evade it,
And finds at last he might as well have paid it.

                                    *Barlow S. Vode.*

AMBROSE BIERCE, *The Cynic's Word Book*, 1906


PIERRE. Then thou art ruin'd!
JAFFIER. That I long since knew;
   I and ill fortune have been long acquainted.
PIER. I past this very moment by thy doors,
   And found them guarded by a troop of villains;
   The sons of public rapine were destroying:
   They told me, by the sentence of the law
   They had commission to seize all thy fortune:
   Nay, more; Priuli's cruel hand had sign'd it.
   Here stood a ruffian, with a horrid face,
   Lording it o'er a pile of massy plate,
   Tumbled into a heap for public sale:
   There was another making villanous jests
   At thy undoing; he had ta'en possession
   Of all thy ancient most domestic ornaments,
   Rich hangings, intermix'd and wrought with gold;
   The very bed, which on thy wedding-night
   Receiv'd thee to the arms of Belvidera,
   The scene of all thy joys, was violated
   By the coarse hands of filthy dungeon-villains,
   And thrown amongst the common lumber.
JAFF. Now thank heav'n—
PIER. Thank heav'n! for what?
JAFF. That I'm not worth a ducat.

         THOMAS OTWAY, *Venice Preserv'd; or, A Plot Discovered*, 1682


'Well . . . I am ruined, Adolphe! You are going to lend me three thousand francs!'

   'But . . . but . . .' said he, rising gradually, while his face assumed a serious expression.

'You know,' she continued quickly, 'that my husband had deposited his whole fortune in the hands of a lawyer; he absconded. We borrowed; the clients did not pay. However, the realization is not completed; we shall get something later on. But to-day, for want of three thousand francs, we are going to be sold up; it is immediately, at this very moment; and, counting on your friendship, I am come.'

'Ah!' thought Rodolphe, who became suddenly very pale, 'that is why she has come!'

At last he said with a tranquil air:

'I have not got it, dear Madame.'

He was not lying. If he had had it, no doubt but that he would have given it, although it is generally disagreeable to perform such fine actions; a pecuniary demand, of all the tempests which overtake love, being the coldest and most uprooting.

For some minutes at first she continued to look at him.

'You have not got it!'

She repeated several times:

'You have not got it! . . . I might have spared myself this last humiliation. You never loved me! you are no better than the rest!'

She was betraying herself, she was losing her head.

Rodolphe interrupted her, affirming that he happened to be 'short of money' himself.

'Ah! I am sorry for you!' said Emma. 'Yes, considerably! . . .'

And, fixing her eyes upon a damascened rifle which gleamed in the panoply:

'But, when a man is so poor he does not put silver on the trigger of his gun! He does not buy a clock inlaid with tortoise-shell!' she continued, pointing at the buhl time-piece; 'nor plated whistles for his whips'—she touched them—'nor trinkets for his watch! Oh! he wants for nothing! even to a liqueur-stand in his bedroom; for you love yourself, you live well. You have a country-house, farms, woods; you ride to hounds, you take trips to Paris. . . . Eh! were it only that,' cried she, picking up his sleeve-links that lay on the mantel-piece, 'only the least of these trifles! they can be turned into money! . . . Oh! I do not want them! keep them!'

And she threw far from her the two links, of which the gold chain broke as it struck against the wall.

'But I—I would have given you everything, I would have sold every-thing, I would have worked with my hands, I would have begged on the roads, for a smile, for a look, to hear you say "Thank you!" And you sit there tranquilly in your easy chair, as if already you had not caused me enough suffering! Had it not been for you, do you not know, I might have lived happily! What drove you to interfere? Was it a wager? You loved me, nevertheless; you used to say so. . . . And just now again. . . . Ah! you had done better to turn me away! My hands are hot with your kisses, and there is the place, on the carpet, where you swore at my knees an eternity of love. You made me believe it; for two years you led me through the most magnificent and the sweetest of dreams! . . . Hey! our plans of travel, you remember? Oh! your letter, your letter! it broke my heart! . . . And then, when I come back to him, to him, who is rich, happy, free! to implore a succour which the first comer might give, supplicating and bringing to him again all my love, he repulses me, because it would cost him three thousand francs!'

'I have not got it!' answered Rodolphe with that perfect calm beneath which, as under a shield, a resigned anger takes refuge.

GUSTAVE FLAUBERT, Madame Bovary, 1857

Whenever you receive a letter from a creditor write fifty lines upon some extra-terrestrial subject, and you will be saved.

CHARLES BAUDELAIRE (1821–67), Intimate Journals, tr. Christopher Isherwood, 1930

It is easy no doubt for any friend to blame me for entering into connexion in commercial matters at all. But I wish to know what I could have done better in 1806 excluded from the bar by my being a clerk of Session and deprived of all emolument for six years by my colleagues prolonged life. Literature was not then what poor Constable has made it and with my little capital of £2000 or £2500 of principal I was too glad to make commercially the means of supporting my family. I got £600 for the Lay of the Last Minstrel and (a price which made mens hairs stand on end) £1000 for Marmion. I have been far from suffering by Ballantyne. I owe it to him to say that his difficulties are owing to me—to be sure so are his advantages which will greatly predominate.

I trusted too much to Constables assurances of his Correspondents and his own stability but yet I believe he was only sanguine but he got about £7000 from me under the idea that the support would carry them through—various things give me good security for that and other sums. Indeed the upshot is just on what H. & R. and Constable may be able to pay me. If 15/ in the pound I will not complain of my loss for I have gaind many thousands in my day. But while I live I shall regret the downfall of Constables house for never did there or can there exist so liberal so intelligent and so trustworthy an establishment. They went too far that is certain when money was plenty. Yet if every author in Britain had taxd himself half a years income he should have kept up the House which first broke in upon the monopoly of the London Trade and made letters what it now is.

I have had visits from all the monied people offering their purses and those who are creditors sending their managers and treasurers to assure me of joining in and adopting any measures. I am glad of this for their sake and my own for though I shall not desire to steer yet I am the only person that can conn as Lieut Hatchway says to any good purpose. A very odd anonymous offer I had of a loan for £30,000 which I rejected as I did every other. Unless I die I will beat up against this foul weather—a penny I will not borrow from any one since my creditors are content to be patient. I have the means perfectly and sufficient confidence to resort to them.

I would have given a good deal to have avoided the coup d'éclat but that having taken place I would not give sixpence for any other results. I fear you will think I am writing in heat of excited resistance to bad fortune but dear Lockhart I am as calm and temperate as you ever saw me and working at Woodstock like a very tiger. I am grieved for Lady S— and Anne who cannot conceive Adversity can have the better of them even for a moment: if it teaches a little of the frugality which I have never had the heart to enforce when money was plenty and it seemed cruel to interrupt the enjoyment of it in the way they liked best it will be well.

In consequence of Messrs Constable not taking up their bills and not repaying their loans to me the copy rights of two or three works return to me which must be worth much cash.

I hope you got my article. Yours dear Lockhart affectionately

WALTER SCOTT

Kindest Love to Sophia and tell her to study the song and keep her spirits up. Tyne heart Tyne all and it is making more of money than it is worth to grieve about it—Kiss Johnie for me.

SIR WALTER SCOTT to J. G. Lockhart, 20 January 1826

Your debts in the whole are not large, and of the whole but a small part is troublesome. Small debts are like small shot; they are rattling on every side, and can scarcely be escaped without a wound: great debts are like cannon; of loud noise, but little danger. You must, therefore, be enabled to discharge petty debts, that you may have leisure, with security, to struggle with the rest.

SAMUEL JOHNSON to Joseph Simpson, c.1766, in James Boswell, *Life of Samuel Johnson*, 1791

Men ought to take care of their means, ought to use them prudently and sparingly, and to keep their expenses always within the bounds of their income, be it what it may. One of the effectual means of doing this is to purchase with ready money. St Paul says, 'Owe no man anything,' and, of his numerous precepts, this is by no means the least worthy of our attention. Credit has been boasted of as a very fine thing; to decry credit seems to be setting oneself up against the opinions of the whole world; and I remember a paper in the *Freeholder* or the *Spectator*, published just after the funding system had begun, representing 'Public Credit' as a goddess, enthroned in a temple dedicated to her by her votaries, amongst whom she is dispensing blessings of every description. It must be more than forty years since I read this paper, which I read soon after the time when the late Mr Pitt uttered in Parliament an expression of his anxious hope, that his 'name would be inscribed on the monument which he should raise to public credit.' Time has taught me that public credit means the contracting of debts which a nation never can pay; and I have lived to see this goddess produce effects, in my country, which Satan himself never could have produced. It is a very bewitching goddess; and not less fatal in her influence in private than in public affairs. It has been carried in this latter respect to such a pitch, that scarcely any transaction, however low and inconsiderable in amount, takes place in any other way. There is a trade in London, called the 'tally trade,' by which household goods, coals, clothing, all sorts of things, are sold upon credit, the seller keeping a tally, and receiving payment for the goods little by little; so that the income and the earnings of the buyers are always anticipated; are always gone, in fact, before they come in or are earned; the sellers receiving, of course, a great deal more than the proper profit.

Without supposing you to descend to so low a grade as this, and even supposing you to be lawyer, doctor, parson, or merchant; it is still the same thing, if you purchase on credit, and not, perhaps, in a much less degree of disadvantage. Besides the higher price that you pay, there is the temptation to have what you really do not want. The cost seems a trifle, when you have not to pay the money until a future time. It has been observed, and very truly observed, that men used to lay out a one-pound note when they would not lay out a sovereign; a consciousness of the intrinsic value of the things produces a retentiveness in the latter case more than in the former: the sight and the touch assist the mind in forming its conclusions, and the one-pound note was parted with, when the sovereign would have been kept. Far greater is the difference between credit and ready money. Innumerable things are not bought at all with ready money, which would be bought in case of trust; it is so much easier to order a thing than to pay for it . A future day; a day of payment must come, to be sure, but that is little thought of at the time; but if the money were to be drawn out the moment the thing was received or offered, this question would arise, 'Can I do without it?' Is this thing indispensable; am I compelled to have it, or, suffer a loss or injury greater in amount than the cost of the thing? If this question were put every time we make a purchase, seldom should we hear of those suicides which are such a disgrace to this country.

WILLIAM COBBETT, 'Advice to a Young Man', Advice to Young Men, 1829


What evil results to this country, taken at large, from the National Debt? I never could get a plain and practical answer to that question. As to taxation to pay the interest, how can the country suffer by a process, under which the money is never one minute out of the pockets of the people? You may just as well say that a man is weakened by the circulation of his blood. There may, certainly, be particular local evils and grievances resulting from the mode of taxation or collection; but how can that debt be in any proper sense a burthen to the nation, which the nation owes to itself, and to no one but itself? It is a juggle to talk of the nation owing the capital or the interest to the stockholders; it owes to itself only. Suppose the interest to be owing to the Emperor of Russia, and then you would feel the difference of a debt in the proper sense. It is really and truly nothing more in effect than so much money, or money's worth, raised annually by the state for the purpose of quickening industry.

SAMUEL TAYLOR COLERIDGE, 31 March 1833, Table-Talk, 1835


The national debt has, in fact, made more men rich than have a right to be so, or, rather, any ultimate power, in case of a struggle, of actualizing their riches. It is, in effect, like an ordinary, where three hundred tickets have been distributed, but where there is, in truth, room only for one hundred. So long as you can amuse the company with any thing else, or make them come in successively, all is well, and the whole three hundred fancy themselves sure of a dinner; but if any suspicion of a hoax should arise, and they were all to rush into the room at once, there would be two hundred without a potatoe for their money; and the table would be occupied by the landholders, who live on the spot.

SAMUEL TAYLOR COLERIDGE, 27 April 1823, *Table-Talk*, 1835

It was Williamanmary who first discovered the National Debt and had the memorable idea of building the Bank of England to put it in. The National Debt is a very Good Thing and it would be dangerous to pay it off, for fear of Political Economy.

W. C. SELLAR and R. J. YEATMAN, *1066 and All That*, 1930

SIR,

You did me the favour, some time since, to insert in your valuable journal a petition of mine to the American Congress, for the repayment of a loan made by me, in common with many other unwise people, to the State of Pennsylvania. For that petition I have been abused in the grossest manner by many of the American papers. After some weeks' reflection, I see no reason to alter my opinions, or to retract my expressions. What I then said was not wild declamation, but measured truth. I repeat again, that no conduct was ever more profligate than that of the state of Pennsylvania. History cannot pattern it: and let no deluded being imagine that they will ever repay a single farthing—their people have tasted of the dangerous luxury of dishonesty, and they will never be brought back to the homely rule of right. The money transactions of the Americans are become a by-word among the nations of Europe. In every grammar school of the old world *ad Græcas Calendas* is translated—the American dividends.

I am no enemy to America. I loved and admired honest America when she respected the laws of pounds, shillings, and pence; and I thought the United States the most magnificent picture of human happiness: I meddle now in these matters because I hate fraud—because I pity the misery it has occasioned—because I mourn over the hatred it has excited against free institutions.

Among the discussions to which the moral lubricities of this insolvent people have given birth, they have arrogated to themselves the right of sitting in judgment upon the property of their creditors—of deciding who

*ad Græcas Calendas*] at the Greek calends, i.e. a time that never comes

among them is rich, and who poor, and who are proper objects of compassionate payment; but in the name of Mercury, the great god of thieves, did any man ever hear of debtors alleging the wealth of the lender as a reason for eluding the payment of the loan? Is the Stock Exchange a place for the tables of the money-lenders; or is it a school of moralists, who may amerce the rich, exalt the poor, and correct the inequalities of fortune? Is *Biddle* an instrument in the hand of Providence to exalt the humble, and send the rich empty away? Does American Providence work with such instruments as *Biddle*?

> SYDNEY SMITH to the Editor of the *Morning Chronicle*, 'Letters on the American Debts', 3 November 1843

It is incumbent on every generation to pay its own debts as it goes. A principle which, if acted on, would save one-half the wars of the world.

> THOMAS JEFFERSON to Destutt Tracy, 1820

The debt we may contract doth not deserve our regard if the work be but accomplished. No nation ought to be without a debt. A national debt is a national bond; and when it bears no interest, is in no case a grievance. Britain is oppressed with a debt of upwards of one hundred and forty millions sterling, for which she pays upwards of four millions interest. And as a compensation for her debt, she has a large navy; America is without a debt, and without a navy; yet for the twentieth part of the English national debt, could have a navy as large again. The navy of England is not worth at this time more than three millions and a half sterling.

> THOMAS PAINE, 'Common Sense', 1776

The national debt was chiefly contracted in two liberticide wars, undertaken by the privileged classes of the country—the first for the ineffectual purpose of tyrannizing over one portion of their subjects, the second, in order to extinguish the resolute spirit of obtaining their rights, in another. The labour which this money represents, and that which is represented by the money wrung for purposes of the same detestable character, out of the people since the commencement of the American war would, if properly employed, have covered our land with monuments of architecture exceeding the sumptuousness and the beauty of Egypt and Athens; it might have made every peasant's cottage, surrounded with its garden, a little paradise of comfort, with every convenience desirable in civilized life; neat tables and chairs, and good beds, and a nice collection of useful books; and our ships manned by sailors well-paid and well-clothed, might have kept watch round this glorious island against the less enlightened nations which assuredly would have envied, until they could have imitated, its prosperity. But the labour which is expressed by these sums has been diverted from these purposes of human happiness to the promotion of slavery, or the attempt at dominion, and a great portion of the sum in question is debt and must be paid. Is it to remain unpaid for ever, an eternal rent-charge upon the sacred soil from which the inhabitants of these islands draw their subsistence? This were to pronounce the perpetual institution of two orders of aristocracy, and men are in a temper to endure one with some reluctance. Is it to be paid now? If so what are the funds, or when and how is it to be paid? The fact is that the national debt is a debt not contracted by the whole nation towards a portion of it, but a debt contracted by the whole mass of the privileged classes towards one particular portion of those classes. If the principal were paid, the whole property of those who possess property must be valued and the public creditor, whose property would have been included in this estimate, satisfied out of the proceeds. It has been said that all the land in the nation is mortgaged for the amount of the national debt. This is a partial statement. Not only all the land in the nation, but all the property of whatever denomination, all the houses and the furniture and the goods and every article of merchandise, and the property which is represented by the very money lent by the fund-holder, who is bound to pay a certain portion as debtor whilst he is to receive another certain portion as creditor. The property of the rich is mortgaged: to use the language of the law, let the mortgagee foreclose.

P. B. SHELLEY, 'A Philosophical View of Reform', c.1819

A national debt if it is not excessive will be to us a national blessing; it will be powerfull cement of our union. It will also create a necessity for keeping up taxation to a degree which without being oppressive, will be a spur to industry; remote as we are from Europe and shall be from danger, it were otherwise to be feard our popular maxims would incline us to too great parsimony and indulgence. We labour less now than any civilized nation of Europe, and a habit of labour in the people is as essential to the health and vigor of their minds and bodies as it is conducive to the welfare of the State.

We ought not to Suffer our self-love to deceive us in a comparrison, upon these points.

ALEXANDER HAMILTON, 30 April 1781

For *the kingdom of heaven is* as a man travelling into a far country, who called his own servants, and delivered unto them his goods:

And unto one he gave five talents, to another two, and to another one; to every man according to his several ability, and straightway took his journey.

Then he that had received the five talents went and traded with the same, and made *them* other five talents.

And likewise he that had received two, he also gained other two.

But he that had received one went and digged in the earth, and hid his lord's money.

After a long time the lord of those servants cometh, and reckoneth with them.

And so he that had received five talents came and brought other five talents, saying, Lord, thou deliveredst unto me five talents: behold, I have gained beside them five talents more.

His lord said unto him, Well done, thou good and faithful servant: thou hast been faithful over a few things, I will make thee ruler over many things: enter thou into the joy of thy lord.

He also that had received two talents came and said, Lord, thou deliveredst unto me two talents: behold, I have gained two other talents beside them.

His lord said unto him, Well done, good and faithful servant; thou hast been faithful over a few things, I will make thee ruler over many things: enter thou into the joy of thy lord.

Then he which had received the one talent came and said, Lord, I knew thee that thou art an hard man, reaping where thou hast not sown, and gathering where thou hast not strawed:

And I was afraid, and went and hid thy talent in the earth: lo, there thou hast that is thine.

His lord answered and said unto him, Thou wicked and slothful servant, thou knewest that I reap where I sowed not, and gather where I have not strawed:

Thou oughtest therefore to have put my money to the exchangers, and then at my coming I should have received mine own with usury.

Take therefore the talent from him, and give it unto him which hath ten talents.

For unto every one that hath shall be given, and he shall have abundance: but from him that hath not shall be taken away, even that which he hath.

And cast ye the unprofitable servant into outer darkness: there shall be weeping and gnashing of teeth.

Matthew 25: 14–30

Of the two sorts of money-making one, as I have just said, is a part of household management, the other is retail trade: the former necessary and honourable, the latter a kind of exchange which is justly censured; for it is unnatural, and a mode by which men gain from one another. The most hated sort, and with the greatest reason, is usury, which makes a gain out of money itself, and not from the natural use of it. For money was intended to be used in exchange, but not to increase at interest. And this term usury [τόκος], which means the birth of money from money, is applied to the breeding of money because the offspring resembles the parent. Wherefore of all modes of making money this is the most unnatural.

Aristotle (384–322 BC), *Politics*, book i, tr. Benjamin Jowett, 1905

To take usury is contrary to Scripture; it is contrary to Aristotle; it is contrary to nature, for it is to live without labour; it is to sell time, which belongs to God, for the advantage of wicked men; it is to rob those who use the money lent, and to whom, since they make it profitable, the profits should belong; it is unjust in itself, for the benefit of the loan to the borrower cannot exceed the value of the principal sum lent him; it is in defiance of sound juristic principles, for when a loan of money is made, the property in the thing lent passes to the borrower, and why should the creditor demand payment from a man who is merely using what is now his own?

R. H. Tawney, *Religion and the Rise of Capitalism*, 1926

These two brothers had been brought up together in a school at Exeter, and being accustomed to go home once a week, had often heard, from their mother's lips, long accounts of their father's sufferings in his days of poverty, and of their deceased uncle's importance in his days of affluence, which recitals produced a very different impression on the two: for while the younger, who was of a timid and retiring disposition, gleaned from thence nothing but forewarnings to shun the great world and attach himself to the quiet routine of a country life; Ralph, the elder, deduced from the often-repeated tale the two great morals that riches are the only true source of happiness and power, and that it is lawful and just to compass their acquisition by all means short of felony. 'And,' reasoned Ralph with himself, 'if no good came of my uncle's money when he was alive, a great deal of good came of it after he was dead, inasmuch as my father has got it now, and is saving it up for me, which is a highly virtuous purpose; and, going back to the old gentleman, good *did* come of it to him too, for he had the pleasure of thinking of it all his life long, and of being envied and courted by all his family besides.' And Ralph always wound up these mental soliloquies by arriving at the conclusion, that there was nothing like money.

Not confining himself to theory, or permitting his faculties to rust even at that early age in mere abstract speculations, this promising lad commenced usurer on a limited scale at school, putting out at good interest a small capital of slate-pencil and marbles, and gradually extending his operations until they aspired to the copper coinage of this realm, in which he speculated to considerable advantage. Nor did he trouble his borrowers with abstract calculations of figures, or references to ready-reckoners; his simple rule of interest being all comprised in the one golden sentence, 'two pence for every half-penny,' which greatly simplified the accounts, and which, as a familiar precept, more easily acquired and retained in the memory than any known rule of arithmetic, cannot be too strongly recommended to the notice of capitalists, both large and small, and more especially of money-brokers and bill-discounters. Indeed, to do these gentlemen justice, many of them are to this day in the frequent habit of adopting it with eminent success.

CHARLES DICKENS, Nicholas Nickleby, 1838–9

I know of but two definitions that can possibly be given of usury. One is, the taking of a greater interest than the law allows of: this may be styled the *political* or *legal* definition. The other is, the taking of a greater interest than it is usual for men to give and take: this may be styled the *moral* one: and this, where the law has not interfered, is plainly enough the only one. It is plain, that in order for usury to be prohibited by law, a positive description must have been found for it by law, fixing, or rather superseding, the moral one. To say, then, that usury is a thing that ought to be prevented, is saying neither more nor less than that the utmost rate of interest which shall be taken ought to be fixed, and that fixation enforced by penalties, or such other means, if any, as may answer the purpose of preventing the breach of it. A law punishing usury supposes, therefore, a law fixing the allowed legal rate of interest: and the propriety of the penal law must depend upon the propriety of the simply-prohibitive, or, if you please, declaratory one.

One thing, then, is plain: that, antecedently to custom growing from convention, there can be no such thing as usury; for what rate of interest is there that can naturally be more proper than another? what natural fixed price can there be for the use of money, more than for the use of any other thing? Were it not, then, for custom, usury, considered in a moral view, would not so much as admit of a definition: so far from having existence, it would not so much as be conceivable; nor, therefore, could the law, in the definition it took upon itself to give of such offence, have so much as a guide to steer by. Custom, therefore, is the sole basis, which either the moralist in his rules and precepts, or the legislator in his injunctions, can have to build upon. But what basis can be more weak or unwarrantable, as a ground for coercive measures, than custom resulting from free choice? My neighbours, being at liberty, have happened to concur among themselves in dealing at a certain rate of interest. I, who have money to lend, and Titius, who wants to borrow it of me, would be glad, the one of us to accept, the other to give, an interest somewhat higher than theirs: why is the liberty they exercise to be made a pretence for depriving me and Titius of ours?

JEREMY BENTHAM, Defence of Usury, 1816

Many have made witty invectives against Usury. They say that it is a pity the devil should have God's part, which is the tithe. That the usurer is the greatest sabbath-breaker, because his plough goeth every Sunday. That the usurer is the drone that Virgil speaketh of;

Ignavum fucos pecus a praesepibus arcent.

That the usurer breaketh the first law that was made for mankind after the fall, which was, *in sudore vultus tui comedes panem tuum*; and *in sudore vultus alieni*. That usurers should have orange-tawny bonnets, because they do

---

*Ignavum . . . arcent*] They keep the drones, that idle herd, away from the hives        in *sudore . . . panem tuum*] in the sweat of your brow you shall eat bread        *in . . . alieni*] in the sweat of another's brow

judaize. That it is against nature for money to beget money; and the like. I say this only, that usury is a *concessum propter duritiem cordis*: for since there must be borrowing and lending, and men are so hard of heart as they will not lend freely, usury must be permitted. Some others have made suspicious and cunning propositions of banks, discovery of men's estates, and other inventions. But few have spoken of usury usefully. It is good to set before us the incommodities and commodities of usury, that the good may be either weighed out or culled out; and warily to provide, that while we make forth to that which is better, we meet not with that which is worse.

The discommodities of usury are, First, that it makes fewer merchants. For were it not for this lazy trade of usury, money would not lie still, but would in great part be employed upon merchandizing; which is the *vena porta* of wealth in a state. The second, that it makes poor merchants. For as a farmer cannot husband his ground so well if he sit at a great rent; so the merchant cannot drive his trade so well, if he sit at great usury. The third is incident to the other two; and that is the decay of customs of kings or states, which ebb or flow with merchandizing. The fourth, that it bringeth the treasure of a realm or state into a few hands. For the usurer being at certainties, and others at uncertainties, at the end of the game most of the money will be in the box; and ever a state flourisheth when wealth is most equally spread. The fifth, that it beats down the price of land; for the employment of money is chiefly either merchandizing or purchasing; and usury waylays both. The sixth, that it doth dull and damp all industries, improvements, and new inventions, wherein money would be stirring, if it were not for this slug. The last, that it is the canker and ruin of many men's estates; which in process of time breeds a public poverty.

On the other side, the commodities of usury are, first, that howsoever usury in some respect hindereth merchandizing, yet in some other it advanceth it; for it is certain that the greatest part of trade is driven by young merchants, upon borrowing at interest; so as if the usurer either call in or keep back his money, there will ensue presently a great stand of trade. The second is, that were it not for this easy borrowing upon interest, men's necessities would draw upon them a most sudden undoing; in that they would be forced to sell their means (be it lands or goods) far under foot; and so, whereas usury doth but gnaw upon them, bad markets would swallow them quite up. As for mortgaging or pawning, it will little mend

*concessum . . . cordis*] something granted out of the hardness of the heart     *vena porta*] anatomical term for a particular vein

the matter: for either men will not take pawns without use; or if they do, they will look precisely for the forfeiture. I remember a cruel monied man in the country, that would say, The devil take this usury, it keep us from forfeitures of mortgages and bonds. The third and last is, that it is a vanity to conceive that there would be ordinary borrowing without profit; and it is impossible to conceive the number of inconveniences that will ensue, if borrowing be cramped. Therefore to speak of the abolishing of usury is idle. All states have ever had it, in one kind or rate, or other. So as that opinion must be sent to Utopia.

FRANCIS BACON (1561–1621), 'Of Usury'

They who devour usury shall not arise *from the dead*, but as he ariseth whom Satan hath infected by a touch: this *shall happen to them* because they say, Truly selling is but as usury: and yet GOD hath permitted selling and forbidden usury. He therefore who when there cometh unto him an admonition from his Lord, abstaineth *from usury for the future*, shall have what is past *forgiven him*, and his affair belongeth unto GOD. But whoever returneth *to usury*, they shall be the companions of *hell* fire, they shall continue therein for ever. GOD shall take his blessing from usury, and shall increase alms: for GOD loveth no infidel, or ungodly person.

*The Koran*, tr. George Sale, 1734

Usury is a kind of lending of money, or corne, or oyle, or wine, or of any other thing, wherein, upon covenant and bargaine, we receive againe the whole principal which we delivered, and somewhat more, for the use and occupying of the same; as if I lend 100 pound, and for it covenant to receive 105 pound, or any other summe, greater then was the summe which I did lend: this is that which we call usury: such a kind of bargaining as no good man, or godly man ever used. Such a kind of bargaining as all men that ever feared God's judgements have alwaies abhorred and condemned. It is filthy gaines, and a worke of darkenesse, it is a monster in nature: the overthrow of mighty kingdoms, the destruction of flourishing States, the decay of wealthy cities, the plagues of the world, and the misery of the people: it is theft, it is the murthering of our brethren, its the curse of God, and the curse of the people. This is Usury. By these signes and tokens you may know it. For wheresoever it raigneth all those mischiefes ensue.

BISHOP JEWELL, cited by John Ruskin, Introduction to 'Usury and the English Bishops', 1885

## XLV

With *Usura*

With usura hath no man a house of good stone
each block cut smooth and well fitting
that design might cover their face,
with usura
hath no man a painted paradise on his church wall
*harpes et luz*
or where virgin receiveth message
and halo projects from incision,
with usura
seeth no man Gonzaga his heirs and his concubines
no picture is made to endure nor to live with
but it is made to sell and sell quickly
with usura, sin against nature,
is thy bread ever more of stale rags
is thy bread dry as paper,
with no mountain wheat, no strong flour
with usura the line grows thick
with usura is no clear demarcation
and no man can find site for his dwelling.
Stonecutter is kept from his stone
weaver is kept from his loom
WITH USURA
wool comes not to market
sheep bringeth no gain with usura
Usura is a murrain, usura
blunteth the needle in the maid's hand
and stoppeth the spinner's cunning. Pietro Lombardo
came not by usura
Duccio came not by usura
nor Pier della Francesca; Zuan Bellin' not by usura
nor was 'La Calunnia' painted.
Came not by usura Angelico; came not Ambrogio Praedis,
Came no church of cut stone signed: *Adamo me fecit*.
Not by usura St Trophime
Not by usura Saint Hilaire,
Usura rusteth the chisel

It rusteth the craft and the craftsman
It gnaweth the thread in the loom
None learneth to weave gold in her pattern;
Azure hath a canker by usura; cramoisi is unbroidered
Emerald findeth no Memling
Usura slayeth the child in the womb
It stayeth the young man's courting
It hath brought palsey to bed, lyeth
between the young bride and her bridegroom
                              CONTRA NATURAM
They have brought whores for Eleusis
Corpses are set to banquet
at behest of usura.

EZRA POUND, *The Fifth Decad of Cantos XLII–LI*, 1937

# Vice

'Money is the root of all evil' is a revealing misquotation from 1 Timothy 6, which in fact instructs us that *cupiditas*, the love of money rather than the thing itself, is the true source of vice. Moralists have been so horrified by the things men do in the pursuit or the enjoyment of money that they have sometimes mistaken a neutral instrument for the Devil himself. Perhaps, though, this is not such a mistaken line of thought after all. While money was invented by humanity, its behaviour has generally exceeded our control, and the results have proved catastrophic. Vice examines the wickedness done for and with money—everything from miserliness and Mammon-worship to bribery, forgery, theft—and assembles a chorus of lamentations by those who have believed that there really is something essentially filthy about lucre.

❧

For we brought nothing into this world, and it is certain we can carry nothing out.

And having food and raiment let us be therewith content.

But they that will be rich fall into temptation and a snare, and into many foolish and hurtful lusts, which drown men in destruction and perdition.

For the love of money is the root of all evil: which while some coveted after, they have erred from the faith, and pierced themselves through with many sorrows.

1 Timothy 6: 7–10

## OF MONEY AND GOLD

That shall come forth from hollow caves which shall cause all the nations of the world to toil and sweat with great agitation, anxiety and labour, in order to gain its aid.

LEONARDO DA VINCI (1452–1519), 'Prophecies', *Notebooks*, tr. Edward McCurdy, 1906


O sacred hunger of pernicious gold!
What bands of faith can impious lucre hold?

VIRGIL (70–19 BC), *Aeneid*, book iii, tr. John Dryden, 1697


That in some fields of his country, there are certain shining stones of several colours, whereof the *Yahoos* are violently fond, and when part of these stones is fixed in the earth, as it sometimes happeneth, they will dig with their claws for whole days to get them out, then carry them away, and hide them by heaps in their kennels; but still looking round with great caution, for fear their comrades should find out their treasure. My master said, he could never discover the reason of this unnatural appetite, or how these stones could be of any use to a *Yahoo*; but now he believed it might proceed from the same principle of avarice which I had ascribed to mankind: that he had once, by way of experiment, privately removed a heap of these stones from the place where one of his *Yahoos* had buried it: whereupon, the sordid animal missing his treasure, by his loud lamenting brought the whole herd to the place, there miserably howled, then fell to biting and tearing the rest, began to pine away, would neither eat, nor sleep, nor work, till he ordered a servant privately to convey the stones into the same hole, and hide them as before; which when his *Yahoo* had found, he presently recovered his spirits and good humour, but took good care to remove them to a better hiding place, and hath ever since been a very serviceable brute.

My master farther assured me, which I also observed myself, that in the fields where the shining stones abound, the fiercest and most frequent battles are fought, occasioned by perpetual inroads of the neighbouring *Yahoos*.

JONATHAN SWIFT, *Gulliver's Travels*, 1726

## AVARICE

Money, thou bane of bliss and source of woe,
   Whence comest thou, that thou art so fresh and fine?
   I know thy parentage is base and low:
Man found thee poor and dirty in a mine.

Surely thou didst so little contribute
   To this great kingdom, which thou now hast got,
   That he was fain, when thou wert destitute,
To dig thee out of thy dark cave and grot.

Then forcing thee, by fire he made thee bright:
   Nay, thou hast got the face of man; for we
   Have with our stamp and seal transferr'd our right:
Thou art the man, and man but dross to thee.

Man calleth thee his wealth, who made thee rich;
And while he digs out thee, falls in the ditch.

                        GEORGE HERBERT, *The Temple*, 1633

Division of labour and all that flows from it is thus based on a propensity that is, in the ethical terms laid down by the formal theology, evil. The foundations are laid on individual acquisitiveness, the love of money and pursuit of profit. Thus, good and evil are mixed in the roots of modern society.

Yet money, and all it symbolizes, is the root of all evil in a deeper sense than this. Viewed from outside the system, money can be seen to do something even more insidious. It subtly eliminates the very concept of evil. Or, rather, it makes it impossible to discriminate between good and evil, throwing people into that confusion that cast the angels from paradise and afflicted Shakespeare's central characters. 'Money', which is a shorthand way of saying capitalistic relations, market values, trade and exchange, ushers in a world of moral confusion. This effect of money has been most obvious where a capitalistic, monetary economy has clashed with another, opposed, system. Thus it is anthropologists, working in such areas of conflict, who have witnessed most dramatically the effect of the introduction of a monetized economy. They have noted how money disrupts the moral as well as the economic world. As Burridge, for example, writes of the effect of money in Melanesia: money complicates the moral order, turning what was formerly black and white into greyness. Money, he argues, 'reveals the vice in cultivated virtues, allows no vice without some virtue, concedes an element of right in wrong-doing, finds the sin of pride in an upright fellow . . . money invites a complex differentiation and multiplication of the parts and qualities of man'. More broadly, it is money, markets and market capitalism that eliminate absolute moralities. Not only is every moral system throughout the world equally valid, as Pascal noted, but, *within* every system, whatever is, is right.

Alan Macfarlane, *The Culture of Capitalism*, 1987

No thing in use by man, for power of ill,
Can equal money. This lays cities low,
This drives men forth from quiet dwelling-place,
This warps and changes minds of worthiest stamp,
To turn to deeds of baseness, teaching men
All shifts of cunning, and to know the guilt
Of every impious deed.

Sophocles (496–406 BC), *Antigone*, tr. E. H. Plumtree, 1880

MONEY-MADNESS

Money is our madness, our vast collective madness.

And of course, if the multitude is mad
the individual carries his own grain of insanity around with him.

I doubt if any man living hands out a pound note without a pang;
and a real tremor, if he hands out a ten-pound note.

We quail, money makes us quail.
It has got us down, we grovel before it in strange terror.
And no wonder, for money has a fearful cruel power among men.

But it is not money we are so terrified of,
it is the collective money-madness of mankind.
For mankind says with one voice: How much is he worth?
Has he no money? Then let him eat dirt, and go cold.—

And if I have no money, they will give me a little bread
so I do not die,
but they will make me eat dirt with it.
I shall have to eat dirt, I shall have to eat dirt
if I have no money.

It is that that I am frightened of.
And that fear can become a delirium.
It is fear of my money-mad fellow-men.

We must have some money
to save us from eating dirt.

And this is all wrong.

Bread should be free,
shelter should be free,
fire should be free
to all and anybody, all and anybody, all over the world.

We must regain our sanity about money
before we start killing one another about it.
It's one thing or the other.

D. H. LAWRENCE, *Pansies*, 1929


So then, vile money, 'tis to you
The troubles of our life are due!
Through you those dangerous paths we brave
That lead us to an early grave;
The cruel means 'tis you who find
That feed the vices of mankind:
Yours is the head from which there spring
The germs of every evil thing.
'Twas you, when Paetus hoisted sail
For Pharos, in that raging gale
Doomed him to perish in his prime:
You were his temptress, yours the crime.
And now his corpse is floating there,
Strange fishes' unaccustomed fare!

PROPERTIUS (*c*.50–*c*.16 BC), *Elegies*, III. vii, tr. Seymour G. Tremenheere, 1931

Mammon led them on—
Mammon, the least erected Spirit that fell
From Heaven; for even in Heaven his looks and thoughts
Were always downward bent, admiring more
The riches of Heaven's pavement, trodden gold,
Than aught divine or holy else enjoyed
In vision beatific. By him first
Men also, and by his suggestion taught,
Ransacked the Centre, and with impious hands
Rifled the bowels of their mother Earth
For treasures better hid. Soon had his crew
Opened into the hill a spacious wound,
And digged out ribs of gold. Let none admire
That riches grow in Hell; that soil may best
Deserve the precious bane.

JOHN MILTON, *Paradise Lost*, book i, 1667

I said in my last paper that nothing in history had ever been so disgraceful to human intellect as the acceptance among us of the common doctrines of political economy as a science. I have many grounds for saying this, but one of the chief may be given in few words. I know no previous instance in history of a nation's establishing a systematic disobedience to the first principles of its professed religion. The writings which we (verbally) esteem as divine, not only denounce the love of money as the source of all evil, and as an idolatry abhorred of the Deity, but declare mammon service to be the accurate and irreconcileable opposite of God's service: and, whenever they speak of riches absolute, and poverty absolute, declare woe to the rich, and blessing to the poor. Whereupon we forthwith investigate a science of becoming rich, as the shortest road to national prosperity.

'Tai Cristian dannerà l'Etiòpe,
Quando si partiranno i due collegi,
L'UNO IN ETERNO RICCO, E L'ALTRO INÒPE.'[1]

[1] [*Paradiso*, xix. 109. In Cary's translation:—

'Christians like these the Æthiop shall condemn,
When that the two assemblages shall part,
One rich eternally, the other poor.'

Dante's reference in the first line is to Matthew xii. 41: 'The men of Nineveh shall rise in judgment with this generation, and condemn it.']

JOHN RUSKIN, *Unto This Last*, 1860


Ill fares the land, to hastening ills a prey,
Where wealth accumulates, and men decay:
Princes and lords may flourish, or may fade;
A breath can make them, as a breath has made;
But a bold peasantry, their country's pride,
When once destroy'd, can never be supplied.


A time there was, ere England's griefs began,
When every rood of ground maintain'd its man;
For him light labour spread her wholesome store,
Just gave what life requir'd, but gave no more:
His best companions, innocence and health,
And his best riches, ignorance of wealth.


But times are alter'd; trade's unfeeling train
Usurp the land, and dispossess the swain:
Along the lawn where scatter'd hamlets rose,
Unwieldy wealth and cumbrous pomp repose;
And every want to opulence allied,
And every pang that folly pays to pride.
Those gentle hours that plenty bade to bloom,
Those calm desires that ask'd but little room,
Those healthful sports that grac'd the peaceful scene,
Liv'd in each look, and brighten'd all the green;
These, far departing, seek a kinder shore,
And rural mirth and manners are no more.

OLIVER GOLDSMITH, 'The Deserted Village', 1770


Mammon has two properties; it makes us secure, first, when it goes well with us, and then we live without fear of God at all; secondly, when it goes ill with us, then we tempt God, fly from him, and seek after another God.

MARTIN LUTHER, *Table-Talk*, 1566, tr. William Hazlitt

*Enter* MAMMON, *the Arch-Priest; and* PURGANAX, *Chief of the Council of Wizards.*

PURGANAX. The future looks as black as death, a cloud,
   Dark as the frown of Hell, hangs over it—
   The troops grow mutinous—the revenue fails—
   There's something rotten in us—for the level
   Of the State slopes, its very bases topple,
   The boldest turn their backs upon themselves!
MAMMON. Why what's the matter, my dear fellow, now?
   Do the troops mutiny?—decimate some regiments;
   Does money fail?—come to my mint—coin paper,
   Till gold be at a discount, and ashamed
   To show his bilious face, go purge himself,
   In emulation of her vestal whiteness.

                  P. B. SHELLEY, *Oedipus Tyrannus; or, Swellfoot the Tyrant,* 1820


       *Guyon findes Mammon in a delve,*
         *Sunning his threasure hore;*
      *Is by him tempted, and led downe*
         *To see his secret store.*


At last he came unto a gloomy glade,
   Cover'd with boughes and shrubs from heavens light,
Whereas he sitting found in secret shade
   An uncouth, salvage, and uncivile wight,
   Of griesly hew and fowle ill favour'd sight;
His face with smoke was tand, and eyes were bleard,
   His head and beard with sout were ill bedight,
His cole-blacke hands did seeme to have ben seard
In smithes fire-spitting forge, and nayles like clawes appeard.


His yron coate, all overgrowne with rust,
   Was underneath enveloped with gold,
Whose glistring glosse, darkned with filthy dust,
   Well yet appeared to have beene of old
   A worke of rich entayle and curious mould,
Woven with antickes and wild imagery:
   And in his lap a masse of coyne he told,

And turned upsidowne, to feede his eye
And covetous desire with his huge threasury.

And round about him lay on every side
Great heapes of gold, that never could be spent;
Of which some were rude owre, not purifide
Of Mulcibers devouring element;
Some others were new driven, and distent
Into great ingoes and to wedges square;
Some in round plates withouten moniment:
But most were stampt, and in their metal bare
The antique shapes of kings and kesars straunge and rare.

Soone as he Guyon saw, in great affright
And haste he rose, for to remove aside
Those pretious hils from straungers envious sight,
And downe them poured through an hole full wide
Into the hollow earth, them there to hide.
But Guyon, lightly to him leaping, stayd
His hand, that trembled as one terrifyde;
And though him selfe were at the sight dismayd,
Yet him perforce restraynd, and to him doubtfull sayd;

What art thou, man, (if man at all thou art,)
That here in desert hast thine habitaunce,
And these rich heapes of wealth doest hide apart
From the worldes eye, and from her right usaunce?
Thereat with staring eyes fixed askaunce,
In great disdaine, he answerd; Hardy Elfe,
That darest view my direful countenaunce,
I read thee rash, and heedlesse of thy selfe,
To trouble my still seate, and heapes of pretious pelfe.

God of the world and worldlings I me call,
Great Mammon, greatest god below the skye,
That of my plenty poure out unto all,
And unto none my graces do envye:
Riches, renowme, and principality,
Honour, estate, and all this worldes good,
For which men swinck and sweat incessantly,

Fro me do flow into an ample flood,
And in the hollow earth have their eternall brood.

Wherefore if me thou deigne to serve and sew,
At thy commaund lo all these mountaines bee:
Or if to thy great mind, or greedy vew,
All these may not suffise, there shall to thee
Ten times so much be nombred francke and free.
Mammon (said he) thy godheades vaunt is vaine,
And idle offers of thy golden fee;
To them that covet such eye-glutting gaine
Proffer thy giftes, and fitter servaunts entertaine.

EDMUND SPENSER, *The Faerie Queene*, II. vii, 1589

But anyway, how can you marry on two quid a week? Money, money, always money! The devil of it is, that outside marriage, no decent relationship with a woman is possible. His mind moved backwards, over his ten years of adult life. The faces of women flowed through his memory. Ten or a dozen of them there had been. Tarts, also. *Comme au long d'un cadavre un cadavre étendu.* And even when they were not tarts it had been squalid, always squalid. Always it had started in a sort of cold-blooded wilfulness and ended in some mean, callous desertion. That, too, was money. Without money, you can't be straightforward in your dealings with women. For without money, you can't pick and choose, you've got to take what women you can get; and then, necessarily, you've got to break free of them. Constancy, like all other virtues, has got to be paid for in money. And the mere fact that he had rebelled against the money code and wouldn't settle down in the prison of a 'good' job—a thing no woman will ever understand—had brought a quality of impermanence, of deception, into all his affairs with women. Abjuring money, he ought to have abjured women too. Serve the money-god, or do without women—those are the only alternatives. And both were equally impossible.

GEORGE ORWELL, *Keep the Aspidistra Flying*, 1936

Money is the possibility or the right to exploit the labours of others. Money is a new form of slavery, which differs from the old only in being impersonal, and in freeing people from all the human relations of the slave.

Money is money, a value which is always equal to itself, which is always considered absolutely regular and legal, and the use of which is not considered immoral, as the use of the right of slavery was considered to be.

In my youth it became fashionable in clubs to play lotto. Everybody rushed to play it, and, as they said, many persons were ruined, families were made unfortunate, other people's Crown money was gambled away, and men shot themselves, and the game was prohibited and is prohibited until this day.

I used to see, I remember, unsentimental old gamblers, who would tell me that this game was particularly agreeable in that a person did not see whom in particular he was beating, as is the case in other games; the lackey did not even bring money, but only chips, and each person lost but a small stake, and his grief could not be observed. The same is true of roulette, which is everywhere prohibited for good reasons.

The same is true of money. I have a magic never-failing rouble; I cut off the coupons and am removed from all the affairs of the world. Whom am I harming? I am a most innocuous and kindly man. But this is only playing lotto or roulette, where I do not see the man who shoots himself on account of his losses, while it furnishes me those little coupons which I regularly cut off at a right angle from the bonds.

I have done nothing and will do nothing but cut off those little coupons, and I believe firmly that money is a representative of labour. How strange! And they talk of insane persons! What madness can be more terrible than this? A clever and learned man, who in all other things is sensible, lives senselessly and eases his conscience by not enunciating the one word which it is necessary to say that there may be a meaning to his reflection, and considers himself righteous. The little coupons are representatives of labour! Of labour! Yes, but whose labour? Obviously not his who owns it, but his who works.

Money is the same as slavery; it has the same aims and the same consequences. Its aim is the liberation of self from the original law, as a profound writer from the masses has correctly said,—from the natural law of life, as we call it, from the law of personal labour for the gratification of one's wants. The consequences of money are the same as those of slavery were for the owner: the breeding and invention of new and endlessly new wants, which can never be satisfied, pampered wretchedness, debauch; and for the slaves: the oppression of man, his reduction to the level of an animal.

Money is a new and terrible form of slavery, and, like the old form of personal slavery, it corrupts both the slave and the slave-owner, but it is even much worse because it frees the slave and the slave-owner from personal human relations.

LEO TOLSTOY, *What Shall We Do Then?*, 1886, tr. Leo Weiner, 1904

Then, in full many a region, once like this
The assured domain of calm simplicity
And pensive quiet, an unnatural light
Prepared for never-resting Labour's eyes
Breaks from a many-windowed fabric huge;
And at the appointed hour a bell is heard—
Of harsher import than the curfew-knoll
That spake the Norman Conqueror's stern behest—
A local summons to unceasing toil!
Disgorged are now the ministers of day;
And, as they issue from the illumined pile,
A fresh band meets them, at the crowded door—
And in the courts—and where the rumbling stream,
That turns the multitude of dizzy wheels,
Glares, like a troubled spirit, in its bed
Among the rocks below. Men, maidens, youths,
Mother and little children, boys and girls,
Enter, and each the wonted task resumes
Within this temple, where is offered up
To Gain, the master idol of the realm,
Perpetual sacrifice.

WILLIAM WORDSWORTH, *The Excursion*, 1814


With her two brothers this fair lady dwelt,
    Enriched from ancestral merchandize,
And for them many a weary hand did swelt
    In torched mines and noisy factories,
And many once proud-quiver'd loins did melt
    In blood from stinging whip;—with hollow eyes
Many all day in dazzling river stood,
To take the rich-ored driftings of the flood.


For them the Ceylon diver held his breath,
    And went all naked to the hungry shark;
For them his ears gush'd blood; for them in death
    The seal on the cold ice with piteous bark
Lay full of darts; for them alone did seethe
    A thousand men in troubles wide and dark:

Half-ignorant, they turn'd an easy wheel,
That set sharp racks at work, to pinch and peel.

Why were they proud? Because their marble founts
   Gush'd with more pride than do a wretch's tears?—
Why were they proud? Because fair orange-mounts
   Were of more soft ascent than lazar stairs?—
Why were they proud? Because red-lined accounts
   Were richer than the songs of Grecian years?—
Why were they proud? again we ask aloud,
Why in the name of Glory were they proud?

Yet were these Florentines as self-retired
   In hungry pride and gainful cowardice,
As two close Hebrews in that land inspired,
   Paled in and vineyarded from beggar-spies;
The hawks of ship-mast forests—the untired
   And pannier'd mules for ducats and old lies—
Quick cat's-paws on the generous stray-away,—
Great wits in Spanish, Tuscan, and Malay,

How was it these same ledger-men could spy
   Fair Isabella in her downy nest?
How could they find out in Lorenzo's eye
   A straying from his toil? Hot Egypt's pest
Into their vision covetous and sly!
   How could these money-bags see east and west?—
Yes so they did—and every dealer fair
Must see behind, as doth the hunted hare.

JOHN KEATS, 'Isabella; or, The Pot of Basil', 1820

## MONEY

I was led into captivity by the bitch business
Not in love but in what seemed a physical necessity
And now I cannot even watch the spring
The itch for subsistence having become responsibility.

Money the she-devil comes to us under many veils
Tactful at first, calling herself beauty

Tear away this disguise, she proposes paternal solicitude
Assuming the dishonest face of duty.


Suddenly you are in bed with a screeching tear-sheet
This is money at last without her night-dress
Clutching you against her fallen udders and sharp bones
In an unscrupulous and deserved embrace.

C. H. SISSON, The London Zoo, 1961


## MONEY
### (*rant*)

.    .    .            .        .        .


Money meks a dream become reality
Money meks real life like a fantasy
Money has a habit of going to de head
I have some fe a rainy day underneath me bed,
Money problems mek it hard fe relax
Money meks it difficult fe get down to de facts
Money meks yu worship vanity an lies
Money is a drug wid legal eyes
Economists cum
Economists go
Yu try controlling yu cash flow
Food cost loads
House prices soar
An de Rich people try to dress like de Poor,
Nobody really understands de interest rate
When dere is interest den its all too late,
We cherish education
But how much do we pay?
Yu can't buy Race Relations or afford a holiday
Money can't mek yu happy, yu happiness is paper thin
When yu are lonely yu will invite yu poor friends in.
Now dem sey is money culture time
Is dis culture yours, cause it is not mine
Money culture who?
Money culture what?

Money culture thrives where luv is not,
Dem can buy an sell till dem gu to Hell
Dem can tax de wisher at de wishing well,
Now Frankenstein cum fe privatise
Empire fools, get penny wise.
Every government will tek what dem can get
Every government is quick to feget
Every government can mek money by killing
Every government luvs money, no kidding,
But money is paper an paper will burn
So tink about trees as yu earn,
It could do good but it does more bad
Money is fake    and
You've been had.

BENJAMIN ZEPHANIAH, City Psalms, 1992

What is that which I should turn to, lighting upon days like these?
Every door is barr'd with gold, and opens but to golden keys.

Every gate is throng'd with suitors, all the markets overflow.
I have but an angry fancy: what is that which I should do?

I had been content to perish, falling on the foeman's ground,
When the ranks are roll'd in vapour, and the winds are laid with sound.

But the jingling of the guinea helps the hurt that Honour feels,
And the nations do but murmur, snarling at each other's heels.

ALFRED, LORD TENNYSON, 'Locksley Hall', 1842

Money is so near you can almost touch it, but it is all on the other side—you can only press your face up against the glass. In my day, if you wanted, you could just drop out. You can't drop out any more. Money has seen to that. There's nowhere to go. You cannot hide out from money. You just cannot hide out from money any more. And so sometimes, when the nights are hot, they smash and grab.

Meanwhile, there are some pretty primitive creatures driving around with money in their Torpedoes and Boomerangs, or sitting down with money at the Mahatma or the Assisi, or just standing there with money,

in the shops, in the pubs, in the streets. They are all shapes and colours,
innocent beneficiaries of the global joke which money keeps cracking. They
don't do anything: it's their currencies that do things. Last year the pubs
were full of incredulously spendthrift Irishmen: they didn't have money in
their pockets any longer—they had Euromoney, which is much more powerful stuff. There's some bundle in the Middle East, and a new squad of fiscal
space invaders starts plundering the West. Every time the quid gets
gangbanged on the international exchange, all the Arab chicks get a new fur
coat. There are white moneymen, too, English, native. They *must* be criminals, with their wads, the crap they talk, their cruel, roasted faces. I am one.
I am one of them, white or at least sky-grey, with pub rug, and ashen arm
on the Fiasco doorjamb, unsmiling at the traffic light, fat-brained with
abuse—but holding money. I have money but I can't control it: Fielding
keeps supplying me with more. Money, I think, is uncontrollable. Even
those of us who have it, we can't control it. Life gets poor-mouthed all the
time, yet you seldom hear an unkind word about money. Money, now this
has to be some *good* shit.

Martin Amis, Money, a Suicide Note, 1984

What age so large a crop of vices bore,
Or when was avarice extended more?
When were the dice with more profusion thrown?
The well-filled fob not emptied now alone,
But gamesters for whole patrimonies play;
The steward brings the deeds which must convey
The lost estate: what more than madness reigns,
When one short sitting many hundreds drains,
And not enough is left him to supply
Board-wages, or a footman's livery?
   What age so many summer-seats did see?
Or which of our forefathers fared so well,
As on seven dishes at a private meal?
Clients of old were feasted; now, a poor
Divided dole is dealt at the outward door;
Which by the hungry rout is soon dispatched:
The paltry largess, too, severely watched,
Ere given; and every face observed with care,
That no intruding guest usurp a share.

Known, you receive; the crier calls aloud
Our old nobility of Trojan blood,
Who gape among the crowd for their precarious food.
The prætor's and the tribune's voice is heard;
The freedman jostles, and will be preferred;
'First come, first served,' he cries; 'and I, in spite
Of your great lordships, will maintain my right:
Though born a slave, though my torn ears are bored,
'Tis not the birth, 'tis money makes the lord.
The rents of five fair houses I receive;
What greater honours can the purple give?
The poor patrician is reduced to keep,
In melancholy walks, a grazier's sheep:
Not Pallas nor Licinius had my treasure;
Then let the sacred tribunes wait my leisure.
Once a poor rogue, 'tis true, I trod the street,
And trudged to Rome upon my naked feet:
Gold is the greatest God; though yet we see
No temples raised to money's majesty . . .'

JUVENAL (*c.* AD 60–*c.*136), First Satire, tr. John Dryden, 1693

Every building in the United States is an offense to invested capital. It occupies space which, as greed acknowledges no limits, can be better utilized. This depressing fact can be thought of as a kind of disease of the American city for which the only specific is law, and, to make a wild gesture toward common sense, aesthetics. One might as well say that multiple sclerosis can be cured with cough drops.

In Chicago six years ago they tore down Adler and Sullivan's Old Stock Exchange, a perfectly useful building. That it was bone and blood of Chicago history, that it was an architectural landmark, that its ornamentation was beautiful and irreplaceable were arguments that could not save it. Money has no ears, no eyes, no respect; it is all gut, mouth, and ass. The Heller International Building went up in its place, a glass cracker-box forty-three stories high. Its mortgage payments are $400,000 every first of the month: interest—*interest*, money which bankers earn by tightening their shoelaces, yawning, and testing teakwood surfaces for dust—on a $48,300,000 loan. The building cost $51,000,000, and is up for grabs, as the speculators can't hold onto it. This time nobody cares if, as they shall, they tear it down and put up something more 'economically viable,' as they say.

Heaps of New York are being torn down because what's left over after property taxes isn't quite what our greedy hearts would like to take to our investment broker. Between the banker and the tax-collector, life can be very hell. But then, they built the cities in the first place. One of the greatest of architects built snowmen for the Medici children (a use of Michelangelo we would have expected of J. Pierpont Morgan sooner than Lorenzo the Magnificent); all architects are now sculptors in ice.

GUY DAVENPORT, 'Making it Uglier to the Airport', *Every Force Evolves a Form*, 1987

True, it must be owned, we for the present, with our Mammon-Gospel, have come to strange conclusions. We call it a Society; and go about professing openly the totalest separation, isolation. Our life is not a mutual helpfulness; but rather, cloaked under due laws-of-war, named 'fair competition' and so forth, it is a mutual hostility. We have profoundly forgotten everywhere that *Cash-payment* is not the sole relation of human beings; we think, nothing doubting, that *it* absolves and liquidates all engagements of man. 'My starving workers?' answers the rich Mill-owner: 'Did not I hire them fairly in the market? Did I not pay them, to the last sixpence, the sum covenanted for? What have I to do with them more?'—Verily Mammon-worship is a melancholy creed.

THOMAS CARLYLE, *Past and Present*, 1843

But, scarce observ'd, the knowing and the bold
Fall in the gen'ral massacre of gold;
Wide wasting pest! that rages unconfin'd,
And crowds with crimes the records of mankind;
For gold his sword the hireling ruffian draws,
For gold the hireling judge distorts the laws;
Wealth heap'd on wealth, nor truth nor safety buys,
The dangers gather as the treasures rise.
    Let hist'ry tell where rival kings command,
And dubious title shakes the madded land,
When statutes glean the refuse of the sword,
How much more safe the vassal than the lord;
Low sculks the hind beneath the rage of power,
And leaves the wealthy traitor in the Tower,
Untouch'd his cottage, and his slumbers sound,
Though confiscation's vultures hover round.

The needy traveller, serene and gay,
Walks the wild heath, and sings his toil away.
Does envy seize thee? crush th' upbraiding joy;
Increase his riches, and his peace destroy;
Now fears, in dire vicissitude, invade,
The rustling brake alarms, and quiv'ring shade;
Nor light nor darkness bring his pain relief,
One shows the plunder, and one hides the thief.

SAMUEL JOHNSON, 'The Vanity of Human Wishes', 1749


## HOMAGE TO A GOVERNMENT

Next year we are to bring the soldiers home
For lack of money, and it is all right.
Places they guarded, or kept orderly,
Must guard themselves, and keep themselves orderly.
We want the money for ourselves at home
Instead of working. And this is all right.

It's hard to say who wanted it to happen,
But now it's been decided nobody minds.
The places are a long way off, not here,
Which is all right, and from what we hear
The soldiers there only made trouble happen.
Next year we shall be easier in our minds.

Next year we shall be living in a country
That brought its soldiers home for lack of money.
The statues will be standing in the same
Tree-muffled squares, and look nearly the same.
Our children will not know it's a different country.
All we can hope to leave them now is money.
1969

PHILIP LARKIN, *High Windows*, 1974


Mrs John Dashwood did not at all approve of what her husband intended to do for his sisters. To take three thousand pounds from the fortune of their dear little boy would be impoverishing him to the most dreadful degree. She begged him to think again on the subject. How could he answer it to himself to rob his child, and his only child too, of so large a sum? And what possible claim could the Miss Dashwoods, who were related to him only by half blood, which she considered as no relationship at all, have on his generosity to so large an amount? It was very well known that no affection was ever supposed to exist between the children of any man by different marriages; and why was he to ruin himself, and their poor little Harry, by giving away all his money to his half-sisters?

'It was my father's last request to me,' replied her husband, 'that I should assist his widow and daughters.'

'He did not know what he was talking of, I daresay; ten to one but he was light-headed at the time. Had he been in his right senses, he could not have thought of such a thing as begging you to give away half your fortune from your own child.'

'He did not stipulate for any particular sum, my dear Fanny; he only requested me, in general terms, to assist them, and make their situation more comfortable than it was in his power to do. Perhaps it would have been as well if he had left it wholly to myself. He could hardly suppose I should neglect them. But as he required the promise, I could not do less than give it: at least I thought so at the time. The promise, therefore, was given, and must be performed. Something must be done for them whenever they leave Norland and settle in a new home.'

'Well, then, *let* something be done for them; but *that* something need not be three thousand pounds. Consider,' she added, 'that when the money is once parted with, it never can return. Your sisters will marry, and it will be gone for ever. If, indeed, it could ever be restored to our poor little boy—'

'Why, to be sure,' said her husband, very gravely, 'that would make a great difference. The time may come when Harry will regret that so large a sum was parted with. If he should have a numerous family, for instance, it would be a very convenient addition.'

'To be sure it would.'

'Perhaps, then, it would be better for all parties if the sum were diminished one-half. Five hundred pounds would be a prodigious increase to their fortunes!'

'Oh! beyond anything great! What brother on earth would do half so much for his sisters, even if *really* his sisters! And as it is—only half blood! But you have such a generous spirit!'

'I would not wish to do anything mean,' he replied. 'One had rather, on such occasions, do too much than too little. No one, at least, can think I have not done enough for them: even themselves, they can hardly expect more.'

'There is no knowing what *they* may expect,' said the lady; 'but we are not to think of their expectations: the question is, what you can afford to do.'

'Certainly; and I think I may afford to give them five hundred pounds apiece. As it is, without any addition of mine, they will each have above three thousand pounds on their mother's death—a very comfortable fortune for any young woman.'

'To be sure it is; and, indeed, it strikes me that they can want no addition at all. They will have ten thousand pounds divided amongst them. If they marry, they will be sure of doing well, and if they do not, they may all live very comfortably together on the interest of ten thousand pounds.'

'That is very true, and therefore, I do not know whether, upon the whole, it would not be more advisable to do something for their mother while she lives, rather than for them—something of the annuity kind I mean. My sisters would feel the good effects of it as well as herself. A hundred a year would make them all perfectly comfortable.'

His wife hesitated a little, however, in giving her consent to this plan.

JANE AUSTEN, *Sense and Sensibility*, 1811

'I wish they would have loved me,' said Emmy, wistfully. 'They were always very cold to me.'

'My dear child, they would have loved you if you had had two hundred thousand pounds,' George replied. 'That is the way in which they have been brought up. Ours is a ready-money society. We live among bankers and city big-wigs, and be hanged to them, and every man, as he talks to you, is jingling his guineas in his pocket. There is that jackass Fred Bullock, is going to marry Maria—there's Goldmore, the East India Director, there's Dipley, in the tallow trade—*our* trade,' George said, with an uneasy laugh and a blush. 'Curse the whole pack of money-grubbing vulgarians!'

W. M. THACKERAY, *Vanity Fair*, 1847–8

## ON A MISER

They call thee rich—I deem thee poor,
Since, if thou darest not use thy store,
But savest it only for thine heirs,
The treasure is not thine, but theirs.

## ANOTHER

A miser, traversing his house,
Espied, unusual there, a mouse,
And thus his uninvited guest
Briskly inquisitive addressed:
'Tell me, my dear, to what cause is it
I owe this unexpected visit?'
The mouse her host obliquely eyed,
And, smiling, pleasantly replied:
'Fear not, good fellow, for your hoard!
I come to lodge, and not to board.'

WILLIAM COWPER (1731–1800), *Poems*, 1803

ÉLISE, CLÉANTE, HARPAGON

HARP. It is a terrible anxiety to have a large sum of money at one's house. Happy is the man who has all his money well invested and who retains only what will suffice for his current expenses. It is hard to find a safe hiding-place in any corner of the house. I should never think of trusting in strong boxes; they don't appeal to me; they are just a bait for thieves, the very first thing attacked. As it is, I don't know whether I did well to bury in my garden the ten thousand crowns sent me yesterday. Ten thousand crowns in gold, in one's house, is a large sum . . .

[*Here the brother and sister come in view, talking together, in a low voice.*]

O Heaven! I have betrayed myself; my anxiety has undone me. Surely I spoke aloud what was passing through my mind. What do you want?

CL. Nothing, father.

HARP. Have you been here long?

ÉL. We have only just come.

HARP. You heard . . .

CL. What, father?

HARP. You know perfectly well what I mean . . .

ÉL. What?

HARP. What I said just now.

CL. No.

HARP. Yes, you did; yes, you did.

ÉL. No, father.

HARP. I am quite sure you heard a few words. The fact is, I was talking to myself about how hard it is nowadays to find money, and I was saying how happy a man must be who has ten thousand crowns in his own house.

CL. We were hesitating to come near you, lest we should interrupt you.

HARP. I want to tell you this in order that you may not take things amiss and imagine I said I had ten thousand crowns.

CL. We were not thinking of your affairs.

HARP. Would to Heaven I had ten thousand crowns!

CL. I do not believe . . .

HARP. It would be a fortunate thing for me.

ÉL. These are things . . .

HARP. I am in great need of them.

CL. I think that . . .

HARP. It would suit me exactly.

ÉL. You are . . .

HARP. I should not then complain, as I do, that times are hard.

CL. Really, father, you have no cause to complain; every one knows you are comfortably off.

HARP. What? I am well off! People lie who say that. Nothing is further from the truth; they are villains who spread such reports abroad.

ÉL. Don't be angry.

HARP. It is miserable that my own children should betray me and become my enemies!

MOLIÈRE, L'Avare, 1668, tr. as The Miser, A. R. Waller, 1907

Harpagon, the miser, cared only for potentialities. The exercise of purchasing power left him cold. All that an ounce of gold might conceivably procure meant almost infinitely more to him than what it actually buys, and the prospect of pleasure thrilled him more than any activity which would exhaust that prospect. Also he relished the mystery of power in a material form. The miser is a visionary, whose inner life is everything to him.

PAUL VALÉRY, Bad Thoughts and Not so Bad, 1941, tr. Stuart Gilbert, 1970

So, Mister Moneybags, you're loaded? So?
You'll never take it with you when you go.

You've made your pile, but squandered time. Grown old
you can't gloat over age like hoarded gold.

TONY HARRISON, Palladas: Poems, 1975

*Le nouvel avare.*—There are two kinds of avarice. One, the archaic type, is the passion that spares oneself and others nothing; its physiognomic traits have been immortalized by Molière, and explained as the anal character by Freud. It is consummated in the miser, the beggar with secret millions, who is like the puritanical mask of the unrecognized caliph in the fairy-tale. He is related to the collector, the manic, finally to the great lover, as Gobseck is to Esther. He is still occasionally to be found as a curiosity in local columns of newspapers. The miser of our time is the man who considers nothing too expensive for himself, and everything for others. He thinks in equivalents, subjecting his whole private life to the law that one gives less than one receives in return, yet enough to ensure that one receives something. Every good deed is accompanied by an evident 'is it necessary?', 'do I have to?' This type are most surely revealed by the haste with which they 'avenge' kindness received, unwilling to tolerate, in the chain of exchange acts whereby expenses are recovered, a single missing link. Because with them everything is done in a rational above-board manner, they are, unlike Harpagon and Scrooge, neither to be convicted nor converted. They are as affable as they are implacable. If need be, they will place themselves irrefutably in the right and transform right into wrong, whereas the sordid mania of stinginess had the redeeming feature that the gold in the cash-box necessarily attracted thieves, indeed, that its passion was stilled only in sacrifice and loss, as is the erotic desire for possession in self-abandonment. The new misers, however, indulge their asceticism no longer as a vice but with prudence. They are insured.

THEODOR ADORNO, *Minima moralia*, 1951, tr. E. F. N. Jephcott, 1974

> The wind was high; the window shakes,
> With sudden start the Miser wakes,
> Along the silent room he stalks,
> Looks back and trembles as he walks,
> Each lock and ev'ry bolt he trys,
> In ev'ry creek and corner prys,
> Then opes the chest with treasure stor'd,
> And stands in rapture o'er his hoard.
> But now, with sudden qualms possest,
> He wrings his hands, he beats his breast,
> By conscience stung he wildly stares,
> And thus his guilty soul declares.
>
>   Had the deep earth her stores confin'd,
> This heart had known sweet peace of mind.

But virtue's sold. Good Gods, what price
Can recompense the pangs of vice!
O bane of good! seducing cheat!
Can man, weak man, thy power defeat?
Gold banish'd honour from the mind,
And only left the name behind;
Gold sow'd the world with ev'ry ill;
Gold taught the murd'rer's sword to kill;
'Twas gold instructed coward hearts
In treach'ry's more pernicious arts:
Who can recount the mischiefs o'er?
Virtue resides on earth no more!

   He spoke, and sigh'd. In angry mood
*Plutus*, his God, before him stood;
The Miser trembling lock'd his chest,
The Vision frown'd, and thus addrest.

   Whence is this vile ungrateful rant?
Each sordid rascal's daily cant:
Did I, base wretch, corrupt mankind?
The fault 's in thy rapacious mind.
Because my blessings are abus'd,
Must I be censur'd, curs't, accus'd?
Ev'n virtue's self by knaves is made
A cloak to carry on the trade,
And power (when lodg'd in their possession)
Grows tyranny, and rank oppression.
Thus when the villain crams his chest,
Gold is the canker of the breast;
'Tis av'rice, insolence, and pride,
And ev'ry shocking vice beside.
But when to virtuous hands 'tis given,
It blesses, like the dews of Heaven,
Like Heav'n, it hears the orphan's cries,
And wipes the tears from widows eyes.
Their crimes on gold shall misers lay,
Who pawn'd their sordid souls for pay?
Let bravos then (when blood is spilt)
Upbraid the passive sword with guilt.

JOHN GAY, 'The Miser and Plutus', *The Fables: First Series*, 1728

He was furious with the rich because they had plenty and spent and squandered it, but he passionately hated those who had nothing, that black, eternal poverty, that dragon with a million insatiable mouths. When people in the Residence wanted to annoy him, one of them would come up to him and in conversation, with an exaggeratedly sad expression and pitiful tone of voice, mention that someone deserved attention, 'because he was poor'. With the predictability of a machine, Baki would then jump up from his place, forgetting himself and shrieking in his high-pitched voice:

'What're you doing clinging to the poor? Let 'em go to the dogs, where they're heading. Am I God to make poor folk rich? Why, even *He* doesn't do that any more! He's got sick of it too.'

He would bow his head and lower his voice pathetically, caricaturing whoever had accosted him.

'"Because he's poor!" So what? Since when is it some kind of honour to be poor? Is it a title that gives a man rights? "He's poor!", as though you had said "he's a Hadji" or "he's a Pasha"!'

Then he would raise his voice and, foaming with rage, thrust his face right up to the other: 'Why does he keep on guzzling if he's poor? No one eats as much as the poor! Why doesn't he economize?'

IVO ANDRIĆ, *The Days of the Consuls*, 1945, tr. Celia Hawkesworth, 1992

This is the history of Silas Marner until the fifteenth year after he came to Raveloe. The livelong day he sat in his loom, his ear filled with its monotony, his eyes bent close down on the slow growth of sameness in the brownish web, his muscles moving with such even repetition that their pause seemed almost as much a constraint as the holding of his breath. But at night came his revelry: at night he closed his shutters, and made fast his doors, and drew out his gold. Long ago the heap of coins had become too large for the iron pot to hold them, and he had made for them two thick leather bags, which wasted no room in their resting-place, but lent themselves flexibly to every corner. How the guineas shone as they came pouring out of the dark leather mouths! The silver bore no large proportion in amount to the gold, because the long pieces of linen which formed his chief work were always partly paid for in gold, and out of the silver he supplied his own bodily wants, choosing always the shillings and sixpences to spend in this way. He loved the guineas best, but he would not change the silver—the crowns and half-crowns that were his own earnings, begotten by his labour; he loved them all. He spread them out in heaps and bathed his hands in them; then he counted them and set them up in regular piles, and felt their rounded outline between his thumb and fingers, and thought fondly of the guineas that were only half-earned by the work in his loom, as if they had been unborn children—thought of the guineas that were coming slowly through the coming years, through all his life, which spread far away before him, the end quite hidden by countless days of weaving. No wonder his thoughts were still with his loom and his money when he made his journeys through the fields and the lanes to fetch and carry home his work, so that his steps never wandered to the hedge-banks and the lane-side in search of the once familiar herbs: these too belonged to the past, from which his life had shrunk away, like a rivulet that has sunk far down from the grassy fringe of its old breadth into a little shivering thread, that cuts a groove for itself in the barren sand.

GEORGE ELIOT, *Silas Marner: The Weaver of Raveloe*, 1861

After the birth of his daughter, complaining of his poverty, and the burdens to which he was subjected, not only as an emperor, but a father, he made a general collection for her maintenance and fortune. He likewise gave public notice, that he would receive new-year's gifts on the calends of January following; and accordingly stood in the vestibule of his house, to clutch the presents which people of all ranks threw down before him by handfuls and lapfuls. At last, being seized with an invincible desire of feeling money, taking off his slippers, he repeatedly walked over great heaps of gold coin spread upon the spacious floor, and then laying himself down, rolled his whole body in gold over and over again.

SUETONIUS (*c.* AD 70–*c.*160), 'Caligula', *The Lives of the Twelve Caesars*, tr. Alexander Thompson, 1899

Cyril is lying in the bath brooding on Caligula who liked to pile all his gold coins into a heap and paddle in them with bare feet. We are on bad terms again. I hear him in his room murmuring at night, 'A million . . . Two million' or, simply, 'Just a million.'

BARBARA SKELTON, *Tears before Bedtime*, 1987

At times, when she knew that McTeague was far from home, she would lock her door, open her trunk, and pile all her little hoard on her table. By now it was four hundred and seven dollars and fifty cents. Trina would play with this money by the hour, piling it, and repiling it, or gathering it all into one heap, and drawing back to the farthest corner of the room to note the effect, her head on one side. She polished the gold pieces with a mixture of soap and ashes until they shone, wiping them carefully on her apron. Or, again, she would draw the heap lovingly toward her and bury her face in it, delighted at the smell of it and the feel of the smooth, cool metal on her cheeks. She even put the smaller gold pieces in her mouth, and jingled them there. She loved her money with an intensity that she could hardly express. She would plunge her small fingers into the pile with little murmurs of affection, her long, narrow eyes half closed and shining, her breath coming in long sighs.

'Ah, the dear money, the dear money,' she would whisper. 'I love you so! All mine, every penny of it. No one shall ever, ever get you. How I've worked for you! How I've slaved and saved for you! And I'm going to get more; I'm going to get more, more, more; a little every day.'

FRANK NORRIS, *McTeague: A Story of San Francisco*, 1899

The character of covetousness is what a man generally acquires more through some niggardliness, or ill grace, in little and inconsiderable things, than in expences of any consequence: a very few pounds a year would ease that man of the scandal of avarice.

ALEXANDER POPE, *Thoughts on Various Subjects*, 1727

It was a saying of his that some men were as stingy as if they expected to live for ever, and some as extravagant as if they expected to die immediately.

DIOGENES LAERTIUS (?2nd–3rd century AD), 'Aristotle', *The Lives and Opinions of Eminent Philosophers*, tr. C. D. Yonge, 1901

I knew once, a very covetous sordid fellow, who used frequently to say, 'Take care of the pence; for the pounds will take care of themselves'. This was a just and sensible reflection in a miser.

LORD CHESTERFIELD to his son, 6 November 1747

One great amusement of our houshold was
In a huge crystal magic globe to spy,

Still as you turn'd it, all things that do pass
Upon this ant-hill earth, where constantly
Of idly-busy men the restless fry
Run bustling to and fro with foolish haste,
In search of pleasures vain, that from them fly;
Or which, obtain'd, the caitiffs dare not taste:
When nothing is enjoy'd, can there be greater waste?

'Of vanity the mirrour,' this was call'd:
Here you a muckworm of the town might see
At his dull desk, amid his ledgers stall'd,
Eat up with carking care and penury,
Most like to carcase parch'd on gallow-tree.
'A penny saved is a penny got:'
Firm to this scoundrel maxim keepeth he,
Ne of its rigour will he bate a jot,
Till it has quench'd his fire, and banished his pot.

Straight from the filth of this low grub, behold!
Comes fluttering forth a gaudy spendthrift heir,
All glossy gay, enamell'd all with gold,
The silly tenant of the summer air,
In folly lost, of nothing takes he care;
Pimps, lawyers, stewards, harlots, flatterers vile,
And thieving tradesmen him among them share:
His father's ghost from limbo-lake, the while,
Sees this, which more damnation does upon him pile.

JAMES THOMSON, 'The Castle of Indolence', 1748

In our own times we have seen no Princes accomplish great results save
those who have been accounted miserly. All others have been ruined. Pope
Julius II, after availing himself of his reputation for liberality to obtain the
Popedom, made no effort to preserve that reputation when making war
on the King of France, but carried on all his numerous campaigns without
levying from his subjects a single extraordinary tax, providing for the increased expenditure out of his long-continued savings. Had the present
King of Spain been accounted liberal, he never could have engaged or
succeeded in so many enterprises.

A Prince, therefore, if he is enabled thereby to forbear from plundering his subjects, to defend himself, to escape poverty and contempt, and the necessity of becoming rapacious, ought to care little though he incur the reproach of miserliness, for this is one of those vices which enable him to reign.

NICCOLÒ MACHIAVELLI, *The Prince*, 1513

The sum of all is that which the Apostle says, *Covetousness is idolatry*; that is, it is an admiring money for itself, not for its use; it relies upon money, and loves it more than it loves God and religion. And *it is the root of all evil*; it teaches men to be cruel and crafty, industrious and evil, full of care and malice; it devours young heirs, and grinds the face of the poor, and undoes those who specially belong to God's protection, helpless, craftless, and innocent people; it inquires into our parents' age, and longs for the death of our friends; it makes friendship an art of rapine, and changes a partner into a vulture, and a companion into a thief: and after all this it is for no good to itself, for it dares not spend those heaps of treasure which it snatched: and men hate serpents and basilisks worse than lions and bears; for these kill because they need the prey, but they sting to death and eat not. And if they pretend all this care and heap for their heirs,—like the mice of Africa hiding the golden ore in their bowels and refusing to give back the indigested gold till their guts be out,—they may remember that what was unnecessary for themselves is as unnecessary for their sons; and why cannot they be without it as well as their fathers, who did not use it? And it often happens that to the sons it becomes an instrument to serve some lust or other; that as the gold was useless to their fathers, so may the sons be to the public, fools or prodigals, loads to their country, and the curse and punishment of their fathers' avarice: and yet all that wealth is short of one blessing; but it is a load coming with a curse, and descending from the family of a long-derived sin. However, the father transmits it to the son, or it may be the son to one more, till a tyrant, or an oppressor, or a war, or change of government, or the usurer, or folly, or an expensive vice makes a hole in the bottom of the bag, and the wealth runs out like water, and flies away like a bird from the hand of a child.

JEREMY TAYLOR, *The Rule and Exercises of Holy Living*, 1650–1

MIDAS. What say you *Mellacrites*?

MELLACRITES. Nothing, but that these two have said nothing. I would wish that everie thing I touched might turne to gold: this is the sinewes of

warre, and the sweetnesse of peace. Is it not gold that maketh the chast-
est to yeeld to lust, the honestest to lewdnes, the wisest to follie, the
faithfullest to deceit, and the most holy in heart, to be most hollow of
hart? In this word Gold are all the powers of the gods, the desires of men,
the woonders of the worlde, the miracles of nature, the losenes of fortune and triumphs of time. By gold may you shake the courts of other
Princes, and have your own setled; one spade of gold undermines faster
then an hundred mattocks of steele. Would one be thought religious &
devout? *Quantum quisque sua nummorum servat in arca, tantum habet &
fidei*: Religions ballance are golden bags. Desire you vertue? *quærenda
pecunia primum est, virtus post nummos*: the first staire of vertue is money.
Doeth anie thirst after gentrie, and wish to be esteemed beautiful? *&
genus & formam regina pecunia donat*: king Coin hath a mint to stamp
gentlemen, and art to make amiablenes. I denie not but love is sweet,
and the marrowe of a mans minde, that to conquere kings is the quin-
tessence of the thoughts of kings: why then follow both, *Aurea sunt verè
nunc sæcula, plurimus auro venit honos, auro conciliatur amor*: it is a world
for gold; honor and love are both taken up on interest. Doth *Midas*
determine to tempt the mindes of true Subjectes? to drawe them from
obedience to trecherie, from their allegiance and othes to treason and
perjurie? *quid non mortalia pectora cogit auri sacra fames?* what holes doth
not gold bore in mens hearts? Such vertue is there in golde, that being
bred in the barrennest ground, and troden under foote, it mounteth to
sit on Princes heads. Wish gold *Midas*, or wish not to be *Midas*.

JOHN LYLY, *Midas*, 1589

There are two sorts of *Avarice*, the one is but of a Bastard kind, and that is,
the rapacious Appetite of Gain; not for its own sake, but for the pleasure
of refunding it immediately through all the Channels of Pride and Luxury.
The other is the true kind, and properly so called; which is a restless and
unsatiable desire of Riches, not for any farther end or use, but onely to
hoard, and preserve, and perpetually encrease them. The Covetous Man, of
the first kind, is like a greedy *Ostrich*, which devours any Metall, but 'tis
with an intent to feed upon it, and in effect it makes a shift to digest and
excern it. The second is like the foolish Chough, which loves to steal Money
onely to hide it. The first does much harm to Mankind, and a little good
too to some few: The second does good to none; no, not to himself. The
first can make no excuse to God, or Angels, or Rational Men for his actions:
The second can give no Reason or colour, not to the Devil himself for what

he does; He is a slave to Mammon without wages. The first makes a shift
to be beloved; I, and envyed too by some People: The second is the universal Object of Hatred and Contempt. There is no Vice has been so pelted
with good Sentences, and especially by the Poets, who have pursued it with
Stories and Fables, and Allegories, and Allusions; and moved, as we say,
every Stone to fling at it: Among all which, I do not remember a more fine
and Gentleman-like Correction, then that which was given it by one Line
of *Ovids*.

> *Desunt Luxuriæ multa, Avaritiæ Omnia.*
> Much is wanting to Luxury, All to Avarice.

To which saying, I have a mind to add one Member, and render it thus,

> Poverty wants some, Luxury Many, Avarice All Things.

ABRAHAM COWLEY, *Several Discourses by Way of Essays, in Prose and Verse,*
1668


*Midas* from *Orpheus* had been taught his Lore,
And knew the Rites of *Bacchus* long before.
He, when he saw his venerable Guest,
In Honour of the God ordain'd a Feast.
Ten Days in Course, with each continu'd Night,
Were spent in genial Mirth, and brisk Delight:
Then on th' Eleventh, when with brighter Ray
*Phosphor* had chac'd the fading Stars away,
The King thro' *Lydia*'s Fields young *Bacchus* sought,
And to the God his Foster-Father brought.
Pleas'd with the welcome Sight, he bids him soon
But name his Wish, and swears to grant the Boon.
A glorious Offer! yet but ill bestow'd
On him whose Choice so little Judgment show'd.
Give me, says he, (nor thought he ask'd too much)
That with my Body whatsoe'er I touch,
Chang'd from the Nature which it held of old,
May be converted into yellow Gold.
He had his Wish; but yet the God repin'd,
To think the Fool no better Wish could find.
    But the brave King departed from the Place,
With Smiles of Gladness sparkling in his Face:

Nor could contain, but, as he took his Way,
Impatient longs to make the first Essay.
Down from a lowly Branch a Twig he drew,
The Twig strait glitter'd with a golden Hue:
He takes a Stone, the Stone was turn'd to Gold;
A Clod he touches, and the crumbling Mold
Acknowledg'd soon the great transforming Pow'r,
In Weight and Substance like a Mass of Ore.
He pluck'd the Corn, and strait his Grasp appears
Fill'd with a bending Tuft of Golden Ears.
An Apple next he takes, and seems to hold
The bright *Hesperian* vegetable Gold.
His Hand he careless on a Pillar lays,
With shining Gold the fluted Pillars blaze:
And while he washes, as the Servants pour,
His Touch converts the Stream to *Danae*'s Show'r.

   To see these Miracles so finely wrought,
Fires with transporting Joy his giddy Thought.
The ready Slaves prepare a sumptuous Board,
Spread with rich Dainties for their happy Lord;
Whose pow'rful Hands the Bread no sooner hold,
But its whole Substance is transform'd to Gold:
Up to his Mouth he lifts the sav'ry Meat,
Which turns to Gold as he attempts to eat:
His Patron's noble Juice of purple Hue,
Touch'd by his Lips, a gilded Cordial grew;
Unfit for Drink, and wondrous to behold,
It trickles from his Jaws a fluid Gold.

   The rich poor Fool, confounded with Surprize,
Starving in all his various Plenty lies:
Sick of his Wish, he now detests the Pow'r,
For which he ask'd so earnestly before;
Amidst his Gold with pinching Famine curst;
And justly tortur'd with an equal Thirst.
At last his shining Arms to Heav'n he rears,
And in Distress, for Refuge, flies to Pray'rs.
O Father *Bacchus*, I have sinn'd, he cry'd,
And foolishly thy gracious Gift apply'd;
Thy Pity now, repenting, I implore;
Oh! may I feel the golden Plague no more.

The hungry Wretch, his Folly thus confest,
Touch'd the kind Deity's good-natur'd Breast;
The gentle God annull'd his first Decree,
And from the cruel Compact set him free.
But then, to cleanse him quite from further Harm,
And to dilute the Relicks of the Charm,
He bids him seek the Stream that cuts the Land
Nigh where the Tow'rs of *Lydian Sardis* stand;
Then trace the River to the Fountain Head,
And meet it rising from its rocky Bed;
There, as the bubbling Tide pours forth amain,
To plunge his Body in, and wash away the Stain.
The King instructed to the Fount retires,
But with the golden Charm the Stream inspires:
For while this Quality the Man forsakes,
An equal Pow'r the limpid Water takes;
Informs with Veins of Gold the neighb'ring Land,
And glides along a Bed of golden Sand.
   Now loathing Wealth, th' Occasion of his Woes,
Far in the Woods he sought a calm Repose;
In Caves and Grottos, where the Nymphs resort,
And keep with Mountain *Pan* their Sylvan Court.
Ah! had he left his stupid Soul behind!
But his Condition alter'd not his Mind.

> OVID (43 BC–AD 18), *Metamorphoses*, book xi, 'translated by the Most
> Eminent Authors', 1773


SALANIO. I never heard a passion so confus'd,
So strange, outrageous, and so variable,
As the dog Jew did utter in the streets:
*My daughter!—O my ducats!—O my daughter!*
*Fled with a Christian?—O my christian ducats!—*
*Justice! the law! my ducats, and my daughter!*
*A sealed bag, two sealed bags of ducats,*
*Of double ducats, stol'n from me by my daughter!*
*And jewels; two stones, two rich and precious stones,*
*Stol'n by my daughter!—Justice! find the girl!*
*She hath the stones upon her, and the ducats!*

> WILLIAM SHAKESPEARE, *The Merchant of Venice*, 1597

There are some sordid minds, formed of slime and filth, to whom interest and gain are what glory and virtue are to superior souls; they feel no other pleasure but to acquire money and never to lose it; they are covetous and are always wanting their ten per cent.; they only occupy themselves with their creditors; always dread the lowering or calling in of certain monies; and are absorbed and immersed in contracts, deeds, and parchments. Such people are neither relatives, friends, citizens, Christians, nor perhaps men; they have money.

JEAN DE LA BRUYÈRE, *Characters*, 1688–96

However in every nation there are, and must always be, a certain number of these Fiend's servants, who have it principally for the object of their lives to make money. They are always, as I said, more or less stupid, and cannot conceive of anything else so nice as money. Stupidity is always the basis of the Judas bargain. We do great injustice to Iscariot, in thinking him wicked above all common wickedness. He was only a common money-lover, and, like all money-lovers, did not understand Christ;—could not make out the worth of Him, or meaning of Him. He never thought He would be killed. He was horror-struck when he found that Christ would be killed; threw his money away instantly, and hanged himself. How many of our present money-seekers, think you, would have the grace to hang themselves, whoever was killed?

JOHN RUSKIN, *The Crown of Wild Olive*, 1866

When the morning was come, all the chief priests and elders of the people took counsel against Jesus to put him to death:

And when they had bound him, they led him away, and delivered him to Pontius Pilate the governor.

Then Judas, which had betrayed him, when he saw that he was condemned, repented himself, and brought again the thirty pieces of silver to the chief priests and elders,

Saying, I have sinned, in that I have betrayed the innocent blood. And they said, What is that to us? see thou to that.

And he cast down the pieces of silver in the temple, and departed, and went and hanged himself.

And the chief priests took the silver pieces, and said, It is not lawful for to put them into the treasury, because it is the price of blood.

And they took counsel, and bought with them the potters field, to bury strangers in.

Wherefore that field was called, The field of blood, unto this day.

Matthew 27: 1–8

> Midas, they say, possessed the art of old
> Of turning whatsoe'er he touch'd to gold;
> This modern statesmen can reverse with ease—
> Touch *them* with gold, *they'll turn to what you please*.

JOHN WOLCOT (1738–1819)

There is another way of reasoning which seldom fails, though it be of a quite different nature to that I have last mentioned. I mean convincing a man by ready money, or, as it is ordinarily called, bribing a man to an opinion. This method has often proved successful when all the others have been made use of to no purpose. A man who is furnished with arguments from the Mint will convince his antagonist much sooner than one who draws them from reason and philosophy. Gold is a wonderful clearer of the understanding: it dissipates every doubt and scruple in an instant, accommodates itself to the meanest capacities, silences the loud and clamorous, and brings over the most obstinate and inflexible. Philip of Macedon was a man of most invincible reason this way. He refuted by it all the wisdom of Athens, confounded their statesmen, struck their orators dumb, and at length argued them out of all their liberties.

JOSEPH ADDISON, *Spectator*, 239, 4 December 1711

'Vholes? My dear Miss Clare, I had had that kind of acquaintance with him, which I have had with several gentlemen of his profession. He had done something or other, in a very agreeable, civil manner—taken proceedings, I think, is the expression—which ended in the proceeding of his taking *me*. Somebody was so good as to step in and pay the money—something and fourpence was the amount; I forget the pounds and shillings, but I know it ended with fourpence, because it struck me at the time as being so odd that I could owe anybody fourpence—and after that, I brought them together. Vholes asked me for the introduction, and I gave it. Now I come to think of it,' he looked inquiringly at us with his frankest smile as he made the discovery, 'Vholes bribed me, perhaps? He gave me something, and called it commission. Was it a five-pound note? Do you know, I think it *must* have been a five-pound note!'

CHARLES DICKENS, *Bleak House*, 1852–3

I had spent several days with the dirty money they sent me after the forced sale of the newspaper. For me now there neither was nor would be any Santa María rebuilt, nor *El Liberal*. Everything was dead, reduced to ashes, lost in the river, in nothingness. I ate with friends, got drunk with them, shut myself away for days on end in my flat. And always the filthy money in my pocket, without it ever getting less, without ever spending the least peseta of it. At times I was hungry, or too lazy to go and eat; at others I just watched the hours go by, from the senseless commotion of the dawns to nightfall, lying on my bed, saying my name over and over again syllable by syllable, staring at María José's photograph, which went automatically from pocket to night-table and back again every morning. Only in insomnia could I permit myself to realize that I was not happy and was missing everything. It was only twenty centimetres on my world map from Santa María to Madrid.

Occasionally I received *Presencia*, a news-sheet run off on a badly inked duplicator. It arrived from all the most absurd places in the world, and I used to imagine the unknown group of Sanmarianos taking turns to edit and distribute it. Always bad news. General Cot's tyranny was savage, and whoever was doing this work must have had the vocation of a martyr. And I felt obliged to spend the money from the expropriation on María José, entirely on her.

JUAN CARLOS ONETTI (1909–94), 'Presence', *Index on Censorship*, repr. 1989

## DANEGELD

### AD 1000

It is always a temptation to an armed and agile nation,
    To call upon a neighbour and to say:—
'We invaded you last night—we are quite prepared to fight,
    Unless you pay us cash to go away.'

And that is called asking for Dane-geld,
    And the people who ask it explain

That you've only to pay 'em the Dane-geld
And then you'll get rid of the Dane!

It is always a temptation to a rich and lazy nation,
To puff and look important and to say:—
'Though we know we should defeat you, we have
not the time to meet you,
We will therefore pay you cash to go away.'

And that is called paying the Dane-geld;
But we've proved it again and again,
That if once you have paid him the Dane-geld
You never get rid of the Dane.

It is wrong to put temptation in the path of any nation,
For fear they should succumb and go astray,
So when you are requested to pay up or be molested,
You will find it better policy to say:—

'We never pay any one Dane-geld,
No matter how trifling the cost,
For the end of that game is oppression and shame,
And the nation that plays it is lost!'

RUDYARD KIPLING, *A History of England*, 1911

LORD GORING. Robert, how could you have sold yourself for money?

SIR ROBERT CHILTERN [*excitedly*]. I did not sell myself for money. I bought success at a great price. That is all.

LORD GORING [*gravely*]. Yes; you certainly paid a great price for it. But what first made you think of doing such a thing?

SIR ROBERT CHILTERN. Baron Arnheim.

LORD GORING. Damned scoundrel!

SIR ROBERT CHILTERN. No; he was a man of a most subtle and refined intellect. A man of culture, charm, and distinction. One of the most intellectual men I ever met.

LORD GORING. Ah! I prefer a gentlemanly fool any day. There is more to be said for stupidity than people imagine. Personally I have a great admiration for stupidity. It is a sort of fellow-feeling, I suppose. But how did he do it? Tell me the whole thing.

SIR ROBERT CHILTERN [*throws himself into an arm-chair by the writing-table*]. One night after dinner at Lord Radley's the Baron began talking about success in modern life as something that one could reduce to an absolutely definite science. With that wonderfully fascinating quiet voice of his he expounded to us the most terrible of all philosophies, the philosophy of power, preached to us the most marvellous of all gospels, the gospel of gold. I think he saw the effect he had produced on me, for some days afterwards he wrote and asked me to come and see him. He was living then in Park Lane, in the house Lord Woolcomb has now. I remember so well how, with a strange smile on his pale, curved lips, he led me through his wonderful picture gallery, showed me his tapestries, his enamels, his jewels, his carved ivories, made me wonder at the strange loveliness of the luxury in which he lived; and then told me that luxury was nothing but a background, a painted scene in a play, and that power, power over other men, power over the world was the one thing worth having, the one supreme pleasure worth knowing, the one joy one never tired of, and that in our century only the rich possessed it.

LORD GORING [*with great deliberation*]. A thoroughly shallow creed.

SIR ROBERT CHILTERN [*rising*]. I didn't think so then. I don't think so now. Wealth has given me enormous power. It gave me at the very outset of my life freedom, and freedom is everything. You have never been poor, and never known what ambition is. You cannot understand what a wonderful chance the Baron gave me. Such a chance as few men get.

LORD GORING. Fortunately for them, if one is to judge by results. But tell me definitely, how did the Baron finally persuade you to—well, to do what you did?

SIR ROBERT CHILTERN. When I was going away he said to me that if I ever could give him any private information of real value he would make me a very rich man. I was dazed at the prospect he held out to me, and my ambition and my desire for power were at that time boundless. Six weeks later certain private documents passed through my hands.

LORD GORING [*keeping his eyes steadily fixed on the carpet*]. State documents?

SIR ROBERT CHILTERN. Yes.

LORD GORING *sighs, then passes his hand across his forehead and looks up.*

LORD GORING. I had no idea that you, of all men in the world, could have been so weak, Robert, as to yield to such a temptation as Baron Arnheim held out to you.

SIR ROBERT CHILTERN. Weak? Oh, I am sick of hearing that phrase. Sick of using it about others. Weak! Do you really think, Arthur, that it is weakness that yields to temptation? I tell you that there are terrible temptations that it requires strength, strength and courage, to yield to. To stake all one's life on a single moment, to risk everything on one throw, whether the stake be power or pleasure, I care not—there is no weakness in that. There is a horrible, a terrible courage. I had that courage. I sat down the same afternoon and wrote Baron Arnheim the letter this woman now holds. He made three-quarters of a million over the transaction.

LORD GORING. And you?

SIR ROBET CHILTERN. I received from the Baron £110,000.

LORD GORING. You were worth more, Robert.

SIR ROBERT CHILTERN. No; that money gave me exactly what I wanted, power over others. I went into the House immediately. The Baron advised me in finance from time to time. Before five years I had almost trebled my fortune. Since then everything that I have touched has turned out a success. In all things connected with money I have had a luck so extra-ordinary that sometimes it has made me almost afraid. I remember having read somewhere, in some strange book that when the gods wish to punish us they answer our prayers.

OSCAR WILDE, *An Ideal Husband*, 1895, ACT II


'I would not steal a penny, for my income's very fair—
I do not want a penny—I have pennies and to spare—
And if I stole a penny from a money-bag or till,
The sin would be enormous—the temptation being *nil*.

'But if I broke asunder all such pettifogging bounds,
And forged a party's Will for (say) Five Hundred Thousand Pounds,
With such an irresistible temptation to a haul,
Of course the sin must be infinitesimally small.

'There's fiilson who is dying—he has wealth from Stock and rent—
If I divert his riches from their natural descent,
I'm placed in a position to indulge each little whim.'
So he diverted them—and they, in turn, diverted him.

Unfortunately, though, by some unpardonable flaw,
Temptation isn't recognized by Britain's Common Law;
Men found him out by some peculiarity of touch,
And fiilliam got a 'lifer,' which annoyed him very much.

W. S. GILBERT, 'Mister William', *Fifty 'Bab' Ballads*, 1876

M. Favoral was leaning against the parlour-door, pale as death, and yet calm.

'Why attempt any explanations?' he said. 'The money is gone; and appearances are against me.'

His wife had drawn near to him, and taken his hand.

'The misfortune is immense,' she said, 'but not irreparable. We will sell everything we have.'

'Have you not friends? Are we not here,' insisted the others.

He pushed his wife aside, gently but coldly.

'All we had,' he said, 'would be as a grain of sand in an ocean. But we have no longer anything; we are ruined.'

'Ruined!' exclaimed M. Desormeaux—'ruined! And where are the forty-five thousand francs I placed into your hands?'

'And our hundred and twenty thousand francs?' groaned M. and Mme. Desclavettes.

'And my sixty thousand francs?' shouted M. Chapelain, with an oath.

The cashier shrugged his shoulders.

'Lost,' he said, 'irrevocably lost!'

Their rage exceeded all bounds. They forgot that this unfortunate man had been their friend for twenty years, that they were his guests.

'You should have told us that you speculated,' screamed M. Desclavettes.

On hearing these words, he straightened himself up.

'What!' he said, in a tone of crushing irony, 'it is this evening only, that you discover that I speculated? Where, then, and in whose pockets, did you suppose I was getting the enormous interests I have been paying you for years? Where have you ever seen honest money, the money of labour, yield twelve or fourteen per cent.? Why did you bring me your funds? Because you were fully satisfied that I knew how to handle the cards. I have lost: I am a thief. Well, so be it. But, then, you are all my accomplices. It is the avidity of the dupes which induces the trickery of the sharper.'

ÉMILE GABORIAU (1832–73), *Other People's Money*

SCENE I. *A Room in* VOLPONE'S *House.*
*Enter* VOLPONE *and* MOSCA.

VOLPONE. Good morning to the day; and next, my gold!—
　　Open the shrine, that I may see my saint.
　　[MOSCA *withdraws the curtain, and discovers piles of gold, plate, jewels, &c.*
　　Hail the world's soul, and mine! more glad than is
　　The teeming earth to see the long'd-for sun

Peep through the horns of the celestial Ram,
Am I, to view thy splendor darkening his;
That lying here, amongst my other hoards,
Shew'st like a flame by night, or like the day
Struck out of chaos, when all darkness fled
Unto the centre. O thou son of Sol,
But brighter than thy father, let me kiss,
With adoration, thee, and every relick
Of sacred treasure in this blessed room.
Well did wise poets, by thy glorious name,
Title that age which they would have the best;
Thou being the best of things, and far transcending
All style of joy, in children, parents, friends,
Or any other waking dream on earth:
Thy looks when they to Venus did ascribe,
They should have given her twenty thousand Cupids;
Such are thy beauties and our loves! Dear saint,
Riches, the dumb god, that giv'st all men tongues,
That can'st do nought, and yet mak'st men do all things;
The price of souls; even hell, with thee to boot,
Is made worth heaven. Thou art virtue, fame,
Honour and all things else. Who can get thee,
He shall be noble, valiant, honest, wise—
MOS. And what he will, sir. Riches are in fortune
A greater good than wisdom is in nature.
VOLP. True, my beloved Mosca. Yet I glory
More in the cunning purchase of my wealth,
Than in the glad possession, since I gain
No common way; I use no trade, no venture;
I wound no earth with plough-shares, fat no beasts,
To feed the shambles; have no mills for iron,
Oil, corn, or men, to grind them into powder:
I blow no subtle glass, expose no ships
To threat'nings of the furrow-faced sea;
I turn no monies in the public bank,
No usure private.

BEN JONSON, *Volpone*, 1606

A city clerk, but gently born and bred;
His wife, an unknown artist's orphan child—

One babe was theirs, a Margaret, three years old:
They, thinking that her clear germander eye
Droopt in the giant-factoried city-gloom,
Came, with a month's leave given them, to the sea:
For which his gains were dock'd, however small:
Small were his gains, and hard his work; besides,
Their slender household fortunes (for the man
Had risk'd his little) like the little thrift,
Trembled in perilous places o'er a deep:
And oft, when sitting all alone, his face
Would darken, as he cursed his credulousness,
And that one unctuous mouth which lured him, rogue,
To buy strange shares in some Peruvian mine.

ALFRED, LORD TENNYSON (1809–92), 'Sea Dreams'

Murphy pushed the tray away, tilted back his chair and considered his lunch with reverence and satisfaction. With reverence, because as an adherent (on and off) of the extreme theophanism of William of Champeaux he could not but feel humble before such sacrifices to his small but implacable appetite, nor omit the silent grace: On this part of himself that I am about to indigest may the Lord have mercy. With satisfaction, because the supreme moment in his degradations had come, the moment when, unaided and alone, he defrauded a vested interest. The sum involved was small, something between a penny and twopence (on the retail valuation). But then he had only fourpence worth of confidence to play with. His attitude simply was, that if a swindle of from twenty-five to fifty per cent of the outlay, and effected while you wait, was not a case of the large returns and quick turnover indicated by Suk, then there was a serious flaw somewhere in his theory of sharp practice. But no matter how the transaction were judged from the economic point of view, nothing could detract from its merit as a little triumph of tactics in the face of the most fearful odds. Only compare the belligerents. On the one hand a colossal league of plutomanic caterers, highly endowed with the ruthless cunning of the sane, having at their disposal all the most deadly weapons of the post-war recovery; on the other, a seedy solipsist and fourpence.

SAMUEL BECKETT, *Murphy*, 1938

But shortly myn entente I wol devyse;
I preche of no-thing but for coveityse.

Therfor my theme is yet, and ever was—
'*Radix malorum est cupiditas.*'
Thus can I preche agayn that same vyce
Which that I use, and that is avaryce.
But, though my-self be gilty in that sinne,
Yet can I maken other folk to twinne          *depart*
From avaryce, and sore to repente.
But that is nat my principal entente.
I preche no-thing but for coveityse;
Of this matere it oughte y-nogh suffyse.
  Than telle I hem ensamples many oon
Of olde stories, longe tyme agoon:
For lewed peple loven tales olde;            *uneducated*
Swich thinges can they wel reporte and holde.

GEOFFREY CHAUCER, Prologue to 'The Pardoner's Tale', *Canterbury Tales*
(*c.*1387–94)


'Now, sirs,' quod he, 'if that yow be so leef
To finde Deeth, turne up this croked wey,
For in that grove I lafte him, by my fey,
Under a tree, and ther he wol abyde;
Nat for your boost he wol him no-thing hyde.
See ye that ook? right ther ye shul him finde.
God save yow, that boghte agayn mankinde,
And yow amende!'—thus seyde this olde man.
And everich of thise ryotoures ran,
Til he cam to that tree, and ther they founde
Of florins fyne of golde y-coyned rounde
Wel ny an eighte busshels, as hem thoughte.
No lenger thanne after Deeth they soughte,
But ech of hem so glad was of that sighte,
For that the florins been so faire and brighte,
That doun they sette hem by this precious hord. . . .

[*The youngest conspirator leaves for town to bring back refreshments until
they can carry away the gold under cover of night.*]


'Now,' quod the firste, 'thou woost wel we be tweye,
And two of us shul strenger be than oon.

Look whan that he is set, and right anoon
Arys, as though thou woldest with him pleye;
And I shal ryve him thurgh the sydes tweye      *stab*
Whyl that thou strogelest with him as in game,
And with thy dagger look thou do the same;
And than shal al this gold departed be,      *divided*
My dere freend, bitwixen me and thee;
Than may we bothe our lustes al fulfille,
And pleye at dees right at our owene wille.'      *dice*
And thus acorded been thise shrewes tweye      *wretches*
To sleen the thridde, as ye han herd me seye.      *kill*
   This yongest, which that wente un-to the toun,
Ful ofte in herte he rolleth up and doun
The beautee of thise florins newe and brighte.
'O lord!' quod he, 'if so were that I mighte
Have al this tresor to my-self allone,
Ther is no man that liveth under the trone
Of god, that sholde live so mery as I!'
And atte laste the feend, our enemy,
Putte in his thought that he shold poyson beye,
With which he mighte sleen his felawes tweye;
For-why the feend fond him in swich lyvinge,      *living in such*

     *a way*
That he had leve him to sorwe bringe,      *permission*
For this was outrely his fulle entente      *utterly*
To sleen hem bothe, and never to repente.
And forth he gooth, no lenger wolde he tarie,
Into the toun, un-to a pothecarie,
And preyed him, that he him wolde selle
Som poyson, that he mighte his rattes quelle;
And eek ther was a polcat in his hawe,      *also; yard*
That, as he seyde, his capouns hadde y-slawe,
And fayn he wolde wreke him, if he mighte,
On vermin, that destroyed him by nighte.
   The pothecarie answerde, 'and thou shalt have
A thing that, al-so god my soule save,
In al this world ther nis no creature,
That ete or dronke hath of this confiture      *concoction*
Noght but the mountance of a corn of whete,      *size of a grain of*

     *wheat*

That he ne shal his lyf anon forlete;                        *lose*
Ye, sterve he shal, and that in lasse whyle                  *die*
Than thou wolt goon a paas nat but a myle;          *than it will take*
                                                      *you to walk a mile*

This poyson is so strong and violent.'
    This cursed man hath in his hond y-hent              *taken*
This poyson in a box, and sith he ran                    *then*
In-to the nexte strete, un-to a man,
And borwed [of] him large botels three;
And in the two his poyson poured he;
The thridde he kepte clene for his drinke.
For al the night he shoop him for to swinke      *planned to work*
In caryinge of the gold out of that place.
And whan this ryotour, with sory grace,
Had filled with wyn his grete botels three,
To his felawes agayn repaireth he.
    What nedeth it to sermone of it more?
For right as they had cast his deeth bifore,
Right so they han him slayn, and that anon.
And whan that this was doon, thus spak that oon,
'Now lat us sitte and drinke, and make us merie,
And afterward we wol his body berie.'
And with that word it happed him, par cas,          *by chance*
To take the botel ther the poyson was,
And drank, and yaf his felawe drinke also,              *gave*
For which anon they storven bothe two.                  *died*
    But, certes, I suppose that Avicen       *Avicenna (Arabic author of a*
                                                  *medical treatise)*
Wroot never in no canon, ne in no fen,       *set of rules; section*
Mo wonder signes of empoisoning
Than hadde thise wrecches two, er hir ending.          *before*
Thus ended been thise homicydes two,
And eek the false empoysoner also.

GEOFFREY CHAUCER, 'The Pardoner's Tale', *Canterbury Tales*, *c*.1387–94


Taking large slabs of money away from other people is, I am told, a simple action for anyone who is strong and brave and doesn't lose any sleep after hitting people on the head or breaking the law in other ways. Getting it into the fiscal system again in one's own favour is a different matter altogether. Take a few examples, starting from the bottom.

(A) Your simple villain whose only task in the caper was nicking a getaway car just before the event and wiping the fingerprints or 'dabs' off it afterwards. He gets perhaps £500 in used one-pound notes and, regardless of his superiors' warnings, splashes them about in his local pub, buying drinks for one and all. The boys in blue pick him up within 72 hours and kindly ask him to tell them the names of his superiors. He does not tell them, not out of honour-amongst-thieves but because his superiors have been too smart to let him know their names. This is unfortunate for the simple villain because the fuzz has to make quite sure that he does not know. He is often *tired* when he finally comes up before the magistrate.

(B) The slightly less simple villain with a sensible streak of cowardice who learns of the capture of villain (A) and, at dead of night, takes his £1,000 in used notes, dumps them in the nearest public lavatory, telephone-kiosk or other evil-smelling place and, in the morning, resumes his honest trade of scrap-metal merchant or whatever.

(C) The mealy-mouthed person who did nothing but 'finger' the caper slits open his Softa-Slumba mattress and tucks his £25,000 therein while his wife is getting her blue-rinse at the hairdressers. After eight or nine months, when he thinks all is safe, he buys a bungalow and pays the deposit in cash. Two nice gentlemen from the Inland Revenue call in for a chat; they go away quite satisfied. While he is heaving a sigh of relief, two other nice gentlemen in blue uniforms call in for a chat and suggest that he pack a toothbrush and a pair of pyjamas.

(D) Now we are among the Brass, the higher echelons of the piece of villainy under discussion. This villain, called (D), is old-fashioned; he believes that a numbered account in a Swiss bank is as safe as the Houses of Parliament. He hasn't heard about Guy Fawkes. He has heard about Interpol but he believes it is designed to protect chaps like him—chaps who have numbered accounts in Swiss banks. His trial is long, expensive and complicated. He gets a nice job in the prison library but *horrid* things happen to him in the showers.

(E) He thinks that he can run for it; he has two passports. His share is, perhaps, £150,000. His arithmetic is not good: that kind of money is very nice in, say, South Norwood, but it sort of dwindles as you scoot around the world at today's prices, especially if you feel bound to arrange for your ever-loving wife to meet you in Peru or places like that.

(F) Yes, well, (F) is nearly the smartest of the bunch. First he tucks away a handy little sum like £20,000 in a safe place in case he gets nicked. (£20,000 will get you out of any prison in the world, everyone knows that.) Then he takes the rest of his ill-gotten g's and, having bought a dinner-jacket far above his station in life, he joins one of those gaming-clubs where they sneer at you if you are seen with anything so plebeian as a £10 note. He buys a couple of hundred poundsworth of chips; plays at this table and that and, in the small hours of the morning, gives the lovely cashier-lady a handful of chips and bank-notes, say, £2,000, telling her to credit his account. He gives her a tenner for herself and she assumes that he has won. He does this discreetly for months, sometimes seeming to lose but usually winning. Every once in a while the lovely cashier-lady tells him that he has an awful lot of money in his account and he lets a big cheque which he can prove to be gambling-winnings slide into his account at the bank. You can legalize about a hundred thousand a year in this way if you are careful.

(G) He is the man who organized the whole thing. (G) is very rich already. There are no problems for him; his holding-companies can make his one-third of a million vanish like a snowflake on a frying-pan. I'm sure there's a moral there somewhere.

KYRIL BONFIGLIOLI, After You with the Pistol, 1979

But one painful, anxious matter remained, to occasionally worry the Roubauds. There was a particular part of the parquetry in the dining-room, whereon their eyes never chanced to rest, without an uncomfortable feeling again troubling them. This spot was to the left of the window. There they had taken up and put in place again, a piece of the pattern in the oak flooring, to hide beneath it the watch, and the 10,000 frcs. (£400) which they had taken from the body of Grandmorin, as well as a purse containing about 300 frcs. (£12) in gold. Roubaud had only drawn the watch and money from the pockets of the victim, to convey the impression that the motive of the crime was robbery.

He was not a thief. He would sooner die of hunger within arms' reach of the treasure, as he said, than profit by a centime, or sell the watch. The money of this old man, to whom he had dealt out justice—money, stained with infamy and blood? No! no! it was not clean enough for an honest man to finger. And he did not even give a thought to the house at La Croix-de-Maufras, which he had accepted as a present. The act of plundering the victim, of carrying off those notes in the abomination of murder, alone revolted him and aroused his conscience to the pitch of making him start back in fright at the idea of touching the ill-gotten gain.

Nevertheless, he had not had the courage to burn the notes; and then, one night, to go and cast watch and purse in the sea. If simple prudence urged him to act thus, inexorable instinct protested against the destruction. Unconsciously, he felt respect for such a large sum of money, and he could never have made up his mind to annihilate it. At the commencement, on the first night, he had thrust it under his pillow, considering no other place sufficiently secure. On the following days, he had exerted his ingenuity to discover hiding-places, changing them each morning, agitated at the least sound, in fear of the police arriving with a search-warrant. Never had he displayed so much imagination.

At last, at the end of artifices, weary of trembling, he one day had the coolness to take the money and watch, hidden the previous evening under the parquetry; and, now, for nothing in the world would he put his hand there. It was like a carnal house, a hole pregnant with terror and death, where spectres awaited him. He even avoided, when moving about the room, to place his feet on that part of the floor. The idea of doing so, caused him an unpleasant sensation, made him fancy he would receive a slight shock in the legs.

ÉMILE ZOLA (1840–1902), *La Bête humaine*, tr. Edward Vizetelly as *The Monomaniac*, 1901

## THAT ILL-GOTTEN GAIN NEVER PROSPERS

The weakest part of mankind have this saying commonest in their mouth. It is the trite consolation administered to the easy dupe, when he has been tricked out of his money or estate, that the acquisition of it will do the owner *no good*. But the rogues of this world—the prudenter part of them, at least—know better; and, if the observation had been as true as it is old, would not have failed by this time to have discovered it. They have pretty sharp distinctions of the fluctuating and the permanent. 'Lightly come, lightly go,' is a proverb, which they can very well afford to leave, when they leave little else, to the losers. They do not always find manors, got by rapine or chicanery, insensibly to melt away, as the poets will have it; or that all gold glides, like thawing snow, from the thief's hand that grasps it. Church land, alienated to lay uses, was formerly denounced to have this slippery quality. But some portions of it somehow always stuck so fast, that the denunciators have been fain to postpone the prophecy of refundment to a late posterity.

CHARLES LAMB, 'Popular Fallacies', *New Monthly Magazine*, 1826

'Since when was you no pardner of mine, Gaffer Hexam, Esquire?'

'Since you was accused of robbing a man. Accused of robbing a live man!' said Gaffer, with great indignation.

'And what if I had been accused of robbing a dead man, Gaffer?'

'You COULDN'T do it.'

'Couldn't you, Gaffer?'

'No. Has a dead man any use for money? Is it possible for a dead man to have money? What world does a dead man belong to? T'other world. What world does money belong to? This world. How can money be a corpse's? Can a corpse own it, want it, spend it, claim it, miss it? Don't try to be confounding the rights and wrongs of things in that way. But it's worthy of the sneaking spirit that robs a live man.'

CHARLES DICKENS, *Our Mutual Friend*, 1864–5

AIMWELL. The coast's clear, I see.—Now, my dear Archer, welcome to Lichfield.

ARCHER. I thank thee, my dear brother in iniquity.

AIM. Iniquity! prithee, leave canting; you need not change your style with your dress.

ARCH. Don't mistake me, Aimwell, for 'tis still my maxim, that there is no scandal like rags, nor any crime so shameful as poverty.

AIM. The world confesses it every day in its practice, though men won't own it for their opinion. Who did that worthy lord, my brother, single out of the side-box to sup with him t'other night?

ARCH. Jack Handycraft, a handsome, well-dressed, mannerly, sharping rogue, who keeps the best company in town.

AIM. Right! And, pray, who married my Lady Manslaughter t'other day, the great fortune?

ARCH. Why, Nick Marrabone, a professed pickpocket, and a good bowler; but he makes a handsome figure, and rides in his coach, that he formerly used to ride behind.

AIM. But did you observe poor Jack Generous in the Park last week?

ARCH. Yes, with his autumnal periwig, shading his melancholy face, his coat older than anything but its fashion, with one hand idle in his pocket, and with the other picking his useless teeth; and, though the Mall was crowded with company, yet was poor Jack as single and solitary as a lion in a desert.

AIM. And as much avoided, for no crime upon earth but the want of money.

ARCH. And that's enough. Men must not be poor; idleness is the root of all

evil; the world's wide enough, let 'em bustle. Fortune has taken the
weak under her protection, but men of sense are left to their industry.

AIM. Upon which topic we proceed, and I think luckily hitherto. Would not
any man swear, now, that I am a man of quality, and you my servant;
when if our intrinsic value were known—

ARCH. Come, come, we are the men of intrinsic value, who can strike our
fortunes out of ourselves, whose worth is independent of accidents in
life, or revolutions in government; we have heads to get money and
hearts to spend it.

GEORGE FARQUHAR, *The Beaux' Stratagem*, 1707

But that squandering of the public money cannot possibly be endured by
which he got rid of seven hundred millions of sesterces by forged entries
and deeds of gifts, so that it seems an absolute miracle that so vast a sum
of money belonging to the Roman people can have disappeared in so short
a time. What? are those enormous profits to be endured which the household of Marcus Antonius has swallowed up? He was continually selling
forged decrees; ordering the names of kingdoms and states, and grants of
exemptions to be engraved on brass, having received bribes for such orders.
And his statement always was, that he was doing these things in obedience
to the memoranda of Cæsar, of which he himself was the author. In the
interior of his house there was going on a brisk market of the whole republic. His wife, more fortunate for herself than for her husband, was holding
an auction of kingdoms and provinces: exiles were restored without any
law, as if by law: and unless all these acts are rescinded by the authority of
the senate, now that we have again arrived at a hope of recovering the
republic, there will be no likeness of a free city left to us.

Nor is it only by the sale of forged memoranda and autographs that a
countless sum of money was collected together in that house, while
Antonius, whatever he sold, said that he was acting in obedience to the
papers of Cæsar; but he even took bribes to make false entries of the resolutions of the senate; to seal forged contracts; and resolutions of the senate
that had never been passed were entered on the records of that treasury. Of
all this baseness even foreign nations were witnesses. In the meantime
treaties were made; kingdoms given away; nations and provinces released
from the burdens of the state; and false memorials of all these transactions
were fixed up all over the Capitol, amid the groans of the Roman people.
And by all these proceedings so vast a sum of money was collected in one

house, that if it were all made available, the Roman people would never want money again.

MARCUS TULLIUS CICERO (106–43 BC), *Fifth Philippic*, tr. C. D. Yonge, 1852

> *Within the Tent of* BRUTUS.
> LUCIUS *and* TITINIUS *at some distance from it.*
> *Enter* BRUTUS *and* CASSIUS.

CAS. That you have wrong'd me, doth appear in this:
  You have condemn'd and noted Lucius Pella,
  For taking bribes here of the Sardians;
  Wherein, my letters, praying on his side,
  Because I knew the man, were slighted off.
BRU. You wrong'd yourself, to write in such a case.
CAS. In such a time as this, it is not meet
  That every nice offence should bear his comment.
BRU. Let me tell you, Cassius, you yourself
  Are much condemn'd to have an itching palm;
  To sell and mart your offices for gold,
  To undeservers.
CAS.            I an itching palm?
  You know, that you are Brutus that speak this,
  Or, by the gods, this speech were else your last.
BRU. The name of Cassius honours this corruption,
  And chastisement doth therefore hide his head.
CAS. Chastisement!
BRU. Remember March, the ides of March remember!
  Did not great Julius bleed for justice' sake?
  What villain touch'd his body, that did stab,
  And not for justice? What, shall one of us,
  That struck the foremost man of all this world,
  But for supporting robbers; shall we now
  Contaminate our fingers with base bribes?
  And sell the mighty space of our large honours,
  For so much trash, as may be grasped thus?—
  I had rather be a dog, and bay the moon,
  Than such a Roman. . . .
CAS. Do not presume too much upon my love,
  I may do that I shall be sorry for.

BRU. You have done that you should be sorry for.
   There is no terror, Cassius, in your threats;
   For I am arm'd so strong in honesty,
   That they pass by me, as the idle wind,
   Which I respect not. I did send to you
   For certain sums of gold, which you deny'd me;—
   For I can raise no money by vile means:
   By heaven, I had rather coin my heart,
   And drop my blood for drachmas, than to wring
   From the hard hands of peasants their vile trash,
   By any indirection.

WILLIAM SHAKESPEARE, Julius Caesar, 1599

That the chance of gain is naturally over-valued, we may learn from the universal success of lotteries. The world neither ever saw, nor ever will see, a perfectly fair lottery; or one in which the whole gain compensated the whole loss; because the undertaker could make nothing by it. In the state lotteries the tickets are really not worth the price which is paid by the original subscribers, and yet commonly sell in the market for twenty, thirty, and sometimes forty per cent. advance. The vain hope of gaining some of the great prizes is the sole cause of this demand. The soberest people scarce look upon it as a folly to pay a small sum for the chance of gaining ten or twenty thousand pounds; though they know that even that small sum is perhaps twenty or thirty per cent. more than the chance is worth. In a lottery in which no prize exceeded twenty pounds, though in other respects it approached much nearer to a perfectly fair one than the common state lotteries, there would not be the same demand for tickets. In order to have a better chance for some of the great prizes, some people purchase several tickets, and others, small shares in a still greater number. There is not, however, a more certain proposition in mathematics, than that the more tickets you adventure upon, the more likely you are to be a loser. Adventure upon all the tickets in the lottery, and you lose for certain; and the greater the number of your tickets the nearer you approach to this certainty.

ADAM SMITH, The Wealth of Nations, 1776

I went on Saturday last to make a visit in the city; and as I passed through Cheapside, I saw crowds of people turning down towards the Bank, and struggling who should first get their money into the new-erected lottery. It gave me a great notion of the credit of our present government and administration, to find people press as eagerly to pay money as they would to receive it; and, at the same time, a due respect for that body of men who have found out so pleasing an expedient for carrying on the common cause, that they have turned a tax into a diversion. The cheerfulness of spirit, and the hopes of success, which this project has occasioned in this great city, lightens the burden of the war, and put me in mind of some games, which, they say, were invented by wise men, who were lovers of their country, to make their fellow-citizens undergo the tediousness and fatigues of a long siege. I think there is a kind of homage due to Fortune, if I may call it so; and that I should be wanting to myself, if I did not lay in my pretences to her favour, and pay my compliments to her by recommending a ticket to her disposal. For this reason, upon my return to my lodgings, I sold off a couple of globes and a telescope, which, with the cash I had by me, raised the sum that was requisite for that purpose. I find by my calculations, that it is but an hundred and fifty thousand to one against my being worth a thousand pounds per annum for thirty-two years; and if any plumb in the city will lay me an hundred and fifty thousand pounds to twenty shillings, which is an even bet, that I am not this fortunate man, I will take the wager, and shall look upon him as a man of singular courage and fair dealing; having given orders to Mr Morphew to subscribe such a policy in my behalf, if any person accepts of the offer. I must confess, I have had such private intimations from the twinkling of a certain star in some of my astronomical observations, that I should be unwilling to take fifty pounds a year for my chance, unless it were to oblige a particular friend. My chief business at present is to prepare my mind for this change of fortune: for as Seneca, who was a greater moralist, and a much richer man than I shall be with this addition to my present income, says—'*Munera ista Fortunæ putatis? Insidiæ sunt.*' 'What we look upon as gifts and presents of Fortune, are traps and snares which she lays for the unwary.' I am arming myself against her favours with all my philosophy; and that I may not lose myself in such a redundance of unnecessary and superfluous wealth, I have determined to settle an annual pension out of it upon a family of Palatines, and by that means give these unhappy strangers a taste of British property.

RICHARD STEELE, *Tatler*, 124, 24 January 1710

Speaking of profiteers reminds me that the existence of this genus—I have no wish to brand the whole genus with evil epithets—will probably do more than anything else to bring about the conscription of a certain amount of wealth when the post-war budgets come to be tackled. There are arguments for and against the conscription of wealth, but the sentimental argument in its favour will assuredly carry it. The war has divided the nation into two parts. The larger part has lived in safety, in comparative freedom, in comparative luxury; and a very considerable number of individuals in it will be monetarily richer at the end of the war than they were at the beginning. The smaller part—such portion of it as survives—has abandoned its civil position and prospects, has risked life and limb and health, has suffered terribly, has exchanged liberty for a harsh discipline, and has received at the best a miserably inadequate wage—a wage that scarcely anybody of corresponding status in the larger part would look at. Visitors to the front are well aware that this smaller part has exceedingly keen convictions as to the propriety of the conscription of wealth, together with a general desire for the blood of profiteers. Homicidal intentions may wither, but the intention to see that some wealth is conscripted will unquestionably not wither. And the philanthropic performances of wealth will not save wealth. In a new exhibition of war-pictures by Mr Nevinson (who is a wit as well as an artist) is a fanciful portrait of a repellent type, thus labelled: 'He made a fortune and gave a sum.'

ARNOLD BENNETT, *Things That Have Interested Me*, 1921

Then laid they their hands on them, and they received the Holy Ghost.

And when Simon saw that through laying on of the Apostles hands the Holy Ghost was given, he offered them money.

Saying, Give me also this power, that on whomsoever I lay hands, he may receive the Holy Ghost.

But Peter said unto him, Thy money perish with thee, because thou hast thought that the gift of God may be purchased with money.

Acts 8: 17–20

It is not the dealing in livings but the thinking they can buy the Holy Ghost for money which vulgar rich people indulge in when they dabble in literature, music and painting.

Nevertheless, on reflection it must be admitted that the Holy Ghost is very hard to come by without money. For the Holy Ghost is only another term for the Fear of the Lord, which is Wisdom. And though Wisdom cannot be gotten for gold, still less can it be gotten without it. Gold, or the value that is equivalent to gold, lies at the root of Wisdom, and enters so largely into the very essence of the Holy Ghost that 'No gold, no Holy Ghost' may pass as an axiom. This is perhaps why it is not easy to buy Wisdom by whatever name it be called—I mean, because it is almost impossible to sell it. It is a very unmarketable commodity, as those who have received it truly know to their own great bane and boon.

Samuel Butler, 'Modern Simony', Notebooks, 1912

The Creed of St Athanasius (my mother told me as a boy that my father had threatened the Vicar to walk out if it was read, but unfortunately happened to be asleep when the occasion arose) amounts to saying that the Father and the Son both are and are not identical, and that you will go to Hell unless you believe both. Christians have always been encouraged to recognize the negative half of this paradox by the insistent metaphors about money, which led them through their natural exasperation into persecution of the Jews. Terms such as 'redemption', deep into human experience though they undoubtedly plunge, are metaphors drawn from the slave-market. It is hard to call up the identity of Father and Son at such points, and envisage God as driving a hard money bargain with himself before he agrees to torture himself to death out of love for mankind. No wonder Milton found the clause 'By payment of the required price' enough reason for rejecting the Trinity altogether. And yet, as soon as we let slip the veil of identity enough to allow any sense to the money metaphors, the Christian God becomes nakedly bad.

William Empson, Milton's God, 1961, rev. 1965

I had a dream about a deadly new ailment that was transmitted by money. The first people to go down with it were usurers and croupiers and everyone said 'serves them right', PAY PLAGUE: GOD'S PUNISHMENT FOR AVARICE said the headlines; SERVE THE DIRTY BANKERS RIGHT said the graffiti. But they changed their tune, didn't they, when they found that any exchange of goods and services, even casual labour, might permit the spread of the dreaded Surplus Labour Value or SLV. Didn't the Government then lend its backing to a campaign against excessive monetarism, pointing out that while Safe Earning was some help (they encouraged the use of letters of credit, the so-called 'plastic johnnies'), real protection lay in abandoning the modern heresy of financial permissiveness and free growth, and a return to the mediaeval virtue of poverty? Closed down the Stock Exchange ('a cesspit of their own making'), denounced capitalist propaganda in the media and the loonies who taught business studies to the young, leafleted everybody saying that the real culprit was the profit motive, didn't they.

In my dream that is.

ERIC KORN, *Remainders*, 1989

*Virtue*

*After so many condemnations, a look at the other side of the coin. Money lives under so much suspicion that even when writers sing its praises they are not always in earnest. Even Shaw's insistence that money is the most important thing in the world is meant to raise eyebrows, though the arguments which demonstrate that money may be the source of moral as well as material good can be sound enough. This section also tries to balance the accounts a little further by examining different kinds of virtuous conduct towards money (incorruptibility, thrift) and with money, in acts of charity.*

❧

Money, which represents the prose of life, and which is hardly spoken of in parlors without an apology, is, in its effects and laws, as beautiful as roses.

RALPH WALDO EMERSON, 'Nominalist and Realist', Essays: Second Series, 1844

### FATIGUED

I'm tired of Love: I'm still more tired of Rhyme.
But Money gives me pleasure all the time.

HILAIRE BELLOC, Sonnets and Verse, 1923

### SPECTATOR AB EXTRA

As I sat at the Café I said to myself,
They may talk as they please about what they call pelf,

They may sneer as they like about eating and drinking,
But help it I cannot, I cannot help thinking
   How pleasant it is to have money, heigh-ho!
   How pleasant it is to have money.

I sit at my table *en grand seigneur*,
And when I have done, throw a crust to the poor;
Not only the pleasure itself of good living,
But also the pleasure of now and then giving:
   So pleasant it is to have money, heigh-ho!
   So pleasant it is to have money.

They may talk as they please about what they call pelf,
And how one ought never to think of one's self,
How pleasures of thought surpass eating and drinking,—
My pleasure of thought is the pleasure of thinking
   How pleasant it is to have money, heigh-ho!
   How pleasant it is to have money.

### Le Dîner

Come along, 'tis the time, ten or more minutes past,
And he who came first had to wait for the last;
The oysters ere this had been in and been out;
Whilst I have been sitting and thinking about
   How pleasant it is to have money, heigh-ho!
   How pleasant it is to have money.

A clear soup with eggs; *voilà tout*; of the fish
The *filets de sole* are a moderate dish
*A là Orly*, but you're for red mullet, you say:
By the gods of good fare, who can question to-day
   How pleasant it is to have money, heigh-ho!
   How pleasant it is to have money.

After oysters, sauterne; then sherry; champagne,
Ere one bottle goes, comes another again;
Fly up, thou bold cork, to the ceiling above,
And tell to our ears in the sound that they love
   How pleasant it is to have money, heigh-ho!
   How pleasant it is to have money.

I've the simplest of palates; absurd it may be,
But I almost could dine on a *poulet-au-riz*,
Fish and soup and omelette and that—but the deuce—
There were to be woodcocks, and not *Charlotte Russe*!
  So pleasant it is to have money, heigh-ho!
  So pleasant it is to have money.

Your chablis is acid, away with the hock,
Give me the pure juice of the purple médoc:
St Peray is exquisite; but, if you please,
Some burgundy just before tasting the cheese.
  So pleasant it is to have money, heigh-ho!
  So pleasant it is to have money.

As for that, pass the bottle, and d—n the expense,
I've seen it observed by a writer of sense,
That the labouring classes could scarce live a day,
If people like us didn't eat, drink, and pay.
  So useful it is to have money, heigh-ho!
  So useful it is to have money.

One ought to be grateful, I quite apprehend,
Having dinner and supper and plenty to spend,
And so suppose now, while the things go away,
By way of a grace we all stand up and say
  How pleasant it is to have money, heigh-ho!
  How pleasant it is to have money.

*Parvenant*

I cannot but ask, in the park and the streets
When I look at the number of persons one meets,
What e'er in the world the poor devils can do
Whose fathers and mothers can't give them a *sous*.
  So needful it is to have money, heigh-ho!
  So needful it is to have money.

I ride, and I drive, and I care not a d—n,
The people look up and they ask who I am;
And if I should chance to run over a cad,
I can pay for the damage, if ever so bad.

So useful it is to have money, heigh-ho!
So useful it is to have money.

It was but this winter I came up to town,
And already I'm gaining a sort of renown;
Find my way to good houses without much ado,
Am beginning to see the nobility too.
   So useful it is to have money, heigh-ho!
   So useful it is to have money.

O dear what a pity they ever should lose it,
Since they are the people that know how to use it;
So easy, so stately, such manners, such dinners,
And yet, after all, it is we are the winners.
   So needful it is to have money, heigh-ho!
   So needful it is to have money.

It's all very well to be handsome and tall,
Which certainly makes you look well at a ball;
It's all very well to be clever and witty,
But if you are poor, why it's only a pity.
   So needful it is to have money, heigh-ho!
   So needful it is to have money.

There's something undoubtedly in a fine air,
To know how to smile and be able to stare,
High breeding is something, but well-bred or not,
In the end the one question is, what have you got.
   So needful it is to have money, heigh-ho!
   So needful it is to have money.

And the angels in pink and the angels in blue,
In muslins and moirés so lovely and new,
What is it they want, and so wish you to guess,
But if you have money, the answer is Yes.
   So needful, they tell you, is money, heigh-ho!
   So needful it is to have money.

ARTHUR HUGH CLOUGH, Poems, 1862

People oppose money to culture, and imply that if a man has spent his time in making money he will not be cultivated—fallacy of fallacies! As though there could be a greater aid to culture than the having earned an honourable independence, and as though any amount of culture will do much for the man who is penniless, except make him feel his position more deeply. The young man who was told to sell all his goods and give to the poor, must have been an entirely exceptional person if the advice was given wisely, either for him or for the poor; how much more often does it happen that we perceive a man to have all sorts of good qualities except money, and feel that his real duty lies in getting every halfpenny that he can persuade others to pay him for his services, and becoming rich. It has been said that the love of money is the root of all evil. The want of money is so quite as truly.

SAMUEL BUTLER, Erewhon; or, Over the Range, 1872

[56 Wall Street]

My dear Mrs Brimmer

I just have a letter from Minna in which she speaks of the money you and Mr Brimmer sent her. It was very kind of you and I am ever so much obliged to you. The fine of all is money. It blesseth him that gives and him that takes, the rich man's peace, the poor man's comforter, tired nature's sweet restorer, the balm of life, the content that passeth all understanding—to be able to pay your bills. Why doesn't someone write a poem on money? Nobody does anything but abuse it. There's hardly a good word for money to be found in literature. The poets and writers have been needy devils and thought to brave out their beggary by pretending to despise it. This shows what liars poets and literary men are. The chief cry of their hearts has never found its way into their books during the last three thousand years. . . .

JOHN JAY CHAPMAN, 23 April, 1895, John Jay Chapman and his Letters, ed. Howe, 1937

Money is indeed the most important thing in the world; and all sound and successful personal and national morality should have this fact for its basis. Every teacher or twaddler who denies it or suppresses it, is an enemy of life. Money controls morality; and what makes the United Sates of America look so foolish even in foolish Europe is that they are always in a state of flurried concern and violent interference with morality, whereas they throw their money into the street to be scrambled for, and presently find that their cash reserves are not in their own hands, but in the pockets of a few millionaires who, bewildered by their luck, and unspeakably incapable of making any truly economic use of it, endeavor to 'do good' with it by letting themselves be fleeced by philanthropic committee men, building contractors, librarians and professors, in the name of education, science, art, and what not; so that sensible people exhale relievedly when the pious millionaire dies, and his heirs, demoralized by being brought up on his outrageous income, begin the socially beneficent work of scattering his fortune through the channels of the trades that flourish by riotous living.

GEORGE BERNARD SHAW, Preface to *The Irrational Knot*, 1905

O Gold! Why call we misers miserable?
   Theirs is the pleasure that can never pall;
Theirs is the best bower anchor, the chain cable
   Which holds fast other pleasures great and small.
Ye who but see the saving man at table,
   And scorn his temperate board, as none at all,
And wonder how the wealthy can be sparing,
Know not what visions spring from each cheese-paring.

Love or lust makes man sick, and wine much sicker;
   Ambition rends, and gaming gains a loss;
But making money, slowly first, then quicker,
   And adding still a little through each cross
(Which *will* come over things), beats love or liquor,
   The gamester's counter, or the statesman's *dross*.
O Gold! I still prefer thee unto paper,
Which makes bank credit like a bark of vapour.

Who hold the balance of the world? Who reign
   O'er congress, whether royalist or liberal?
Who rouse the shirtless patriots of Spain?
   (That make old Europe's journals squeak and gibber all.)
Who keep the world, both old and new, in pain
   Or pleasure? Who make politics run glibber all?
The shade of Buonaparte's noble daring?—
Jew Rothschild, and his fellow-Christian, Baring.

Those, and the truly liberal Lafitte,
    Are the true lords of Europe. Every loan
Is not a merely speculative hit,
    But seats a nation or upsets a throne.
Republics also get involved a bit;
    Columbia's stock hath holders not unknown
On 'Change; and even thy silver soil, Peru,
Must get itself discounted by a Jew.

Why call the miser miserable? as
    I said before: the frugal life is his,
Which in a saint or cynic ever was
    The theme of praise: a hermit would not miss
Canonization for the self-same cause,
    And wherefore blame gaunt wealth's austerities?
Because, you'll say, nought calls for such a trial;—
Then there's more merit in his self-denial.

He is your only poet;—passion, pure
    And sparkling on from heap to heap, displays,
*Possess'd*, the ore, of which *mere hopes* allure
    Nations athwart the deep: the golden rays
Flash up in ingots from the mine obscure;
    On him the diamond pours its brilliant blaze;
While the mild emerald's beam shades down the dies
Of other stones, to soothe the miser's eyes.

The lands on either side are his: the ship
    From Ceylon, Inde, or far Cathay, unloads
For him the fragrant produce of each trip;
    Beneath his cars of Ceres groan the roads,
And the vine blushes like Aurora's lip;
    His very cellars might be kings' abodes;
While he, despising every sensual call,
Commands—the intellectual lord of all.

Perhaps he hath great projects in his mind,
    To build a college, or to found a race,
A hospital, a church,—and leave behind
    Some dome surmounted by his meagre face:

Perhaps he fain would liberate mankind
 Even with the very ore which makes them base;
Perhaps he would be wealthiest of his nation,
Or revel in the joys of calculation.

But whether all, or each, or none of these
 May be the hoarder's principle of action,
The fool will call such mania a disease:—
 What is his *own?* Go—look at each transaction,
Wars, revels, loves—do these bring men more ease
 Than the mere plodding through each 'vulgar fraction'?
Or do they benefit mankind? Lean miser!
Let spendthrifts' heirs enquire of yours—who's wiser?

How beauteous are rouleaus! how charming chests
 Containing ingots, bags of dollars, coins
(Not of old victors, all whose heads and crests
 Weigh not the thin ore where their visage shines,
But) of fine unclipt gold, where dully rests
 Some likeness, which the glittering cirque confines,
Of modern, reigning, sterling, stupid stamp:—
Yes! ready money *is* Aladdin's lamp.

GEORGE GORDON, LORD BYRON, Don Juan, 1823, canto xii

If ever I complete that book which I began in the year 1898 called 'Advice to a Young Man' (I was twenty-eight years of age at the moment I undertook it) it will there be apparent by example, closely reasoned argument, and (what is more convincing than all) rhetoric, that money is the true source of every delight, satisfaction, and repose.

Do not imagine that, upon this account, I advise the young to seek money in amounts perpetually extending. Far from it! I advise the young (in this my uncompleted book) to regulate their thirst for money most severely.

'Great sums of money' (said I, and say I) 'are only to be obtained by risking ruin, and of a hundred men that run the risk ninety-nine get the ruin and only one the money.' But money as a solid object; money pursued, accumulated, possessed, enjoyed, bearing fruit: that is the captain good of human life.

When people say that money is only worth what it will purchase, and that it will purchase only certain things, they invariably make a category of certain material things which it will purchase, and imagine or hope that it will purchase no more. And these categories, remember, are drawn up always by unmoneyed men. For your moneyed man has no need to work and therefore no need to draw up categories, which is a very painful form of toil. They say money will purchase motor-cars and bathrooms—several bathrooms—and foods and drinks and the rest of it—and then its power is exhausted.

These fools leave out two enormous chapters—the biggest chapters of the lot. They leave out the services of other men, always purchasable. And they leave out the souls of other men, often purchasable. With money in a sufficient amount you can purchase any service, and with money you can purchase many individual souls.

Now, that is important.

HILAIRE BELLOC, 'A Few Kind Words to Mammon', *On*, 1923

LADY CLARINDA.—I am glad to see you can make yourself so happy with drawing old trees and mounds of grass.

CAPTAIN FITZCHROME.—Happy, Lady Clarinda! oh, no! How can I be happy when I see the idol of my heart about to be sacrificed on the shrine of Mammon?

LADY CLARINDA.—Do you know, though Mammon has a sort of ill name, I really think he is a very popular character; there must be at the bottom something amiable about him. He is certainly one of those pleasant creatures whom every body abuses, but without whom no evening party is endurable. I dare say, love in a cottage is very pleasant; but then it positively must be a cottage ornée: but would not the same love be a great deal safer in a castle, even if Mammon furnished the fortification?

CAPTAIN FITZCHROME.—Oh, Lady Clarinda! there is a heartlessness in that language that chills me to the soul.

LADY CLARINDA.—Heartlessness! No: my heart is on my lips. I speak just what I think. You used to like it, and say it was as delightful as it was rare.

CAPTAIN FITZCHROME.—True, but you did not then talk as you do now, of love in a castle.

LADY CLARINDA.—Well, but only consider: a dun is a horribly vulgar creature; it is a creature I cannot endure the thought of: and a cottage lets him in so easily. Now a castle keeps him at bay. You are a half-pay officer, and are at leisure to command the garrison: but where is the castle? and who is to furnish the commissariat?

CAPTAIN FITZCHROME.—Is it come to this, that you make a jest of my poverty? Yet is my poverty only comparative. Many decent families are maintained on smaller means.

LADY CLARINDA.—Decent families: aye, decent is the distinction from respectable. Respectable means rich, and decent means poor. I should die if I heard my family called decent. And then your decent family always lives in a snug little place: I hate a little place; I like large rooms and large looking-glasses, and large parties, and a fine large butler, with a tinge of smooth red in his face; an outward and visible sign that the family he serves is respectable; if not noble, highly respectable.

THOMAS LOVE PEACOCK, *Crotchet Castle*, 1831

People are often reproached for wishing for money above all things, and for loving it more than anything else; but it is natural and even inevitable for people to love that which, like an unwearied Proteus, is always ready to turn itself into whatever object their wandering wishes or manifold desires may for the moment fix upon. Everything else can satisfy only *one* wish, *one* need: food is good only if you are hungry; wine, if you are able to enjoy it; drugs, if you are sick; fur for the winter; love for youth, and so on. These are all only relatively good, ἀγαθὰ πρός τι. Money alone is absolutely good, because it is not only a concrete satisfaction of one need in particular; it is an abstract satisfaction of all.

ARTHUR SCHOPENHAUER, *Parerga and Paralipomena*, 1851, tr. T. B. Saunders, 1890

But now we arrive at the power of money well managed. You have got money—you have it; and, with it, the heart, and the sense, and the taste to extract from the metal its uses. Talk of the power of knowledge! What can knowledge invent that money can not purchase? Money, it is true, can not give you the brain of the philosopher, the eye of the painter, the ear of the musician, nor that inner sixth sense of beauty and truth by which the poet unites, in himself, philosopher, painter, musician; but money can refine and exalt your existence with all that philosopher, painter, musician, poet, accomplish. That which they are your wealth can not make you, but that which they do is at the command of your wealth. You may collect in your libraries all thoughts which all thinkers have confided to books; your galleries may teem with the treasures of art; the air that you breathe may be vocal with music; better than all, when you summon the Graces, they can come to your call in their sweet name of Charities. You can build up asylums for age and academies for youth. Pining Merit may spring to hope at your voice, and 'Poverty grow cheerful in your sight.' Money well managed deserves, indeed, the apotheosis to which she was raised by her Latin adorers; she is *Diva Moneta*—a goddess.

BULWER LYTTON, 'On the Management of Money', Caxtoniana, 1864

Almost everyone curses money, because almost everyone believes either that he does not have enough of it, or that some other person has too much. In the judgment of religion money represents the sacrifice of spiritual peace to wordly agitation; in the judgment of the enlightened moralist it represents the supreme triumph of means over ends, the 'instrumentalisation' of human purposes and the final self-alienation of man.

But money has survived these curses, and will always survive them. It bears the imprint of original sin—but only because it is all too human. Indeed, money is so integral a part of our social existence that we perceive it as a heraldic emblem of government. Caesar's head may be embossed upon his coinage, but not so deeply as his coinage is embossed upon his hand. Consider what man is without money. He must dispose of his surplus product by gift or barter. His transactions are limited, clumsy and time-consuming. He has no certain measure of the value of what is offered to him and will be reluctant to exchange his produce with those whom he does not know.

Money totally transforms his situation. It removes uncertainty, by providing a single scale of value. It permits transactions of the utmost flexibility with the widest circle of purchasers. By virtue of money, goods and services are rapidly dispersed to their natural destinations, and each man's surplus is poured at once into a common pool, from which it may be drawn off at some distant point imperceptible to the producer. Hence money focuses our economic impulses, while extending the sphere of their repercussions; under its influence, exchange multiplies quietly and peacefully to infinity.

And yet, apart from its function in exchange, money is worthless. It is a pure economic instrument: the means to almost everything, but the end of nothing. Money is the condensed residue of unspoken contracts, and its power lies in its ability to establish both the motive and the terms of ever new agreements, between ever new parties, concerning ever new matters of exchange. But there too lies its virtue. For money is 'crystallised agreement'—the sign and the consummation of social harmony.

ROGER SCRUTON, 'In Praise of Money', Untimely Tracts, 1987

What do you consider to be the greatest blessing which you have reaped from your wealth?

One, he said, of which I could not expect easily to convince others. For let me tell you, Socrates, that when a man thinks himself to be near death, fears and cares enter into his mind which he never had before; the tales of a world below and the punishment which is exacted there of deeds done here were once a laughing matter to him, but now he is tormented with the thought that they may be true: either from the weakness of age, or because he is now drawing nearer to that other place, he has a clearer view of these things; suspicions and alarms crowd thickly upon him, and he begins to reflect and consider what wrongs he has done to others. And when he finds that the sum of his transgressions is great he will many a time like a child start up in his sleep for fear, and he is filled with dark forebodings. But to him who is conscious of no sin, sweet hope, as Pindar charmingly says, is the kind nurse of his age:

'Hope,' he says, 'cherishes the soul of him who lives in justice and holiness, and is the nurse of his age and the companion of his journey;—hope which is mightiest to sway the restless soul of man.'

How admirable are his words! And the great blessing of riches, I do not say to every man, but to a good man, is, that he has had no occasion to deceive or to defraud others, either intentionally or unintentionally; and when he departs to the world below he is not in any apprehension about offerings due to the gods or debts which he owes to men. Now to this peace of mind the possession of wealth greatly contributes; and therefore I say, that, setting one thing against another, of the many advantages which wealth has to give, to a man of sense this is in my opinion the greatest.

PLATO (*c*.427–348 BC), *Republic*, book i, tr. B. Jowett, 1871

But now unto her Praise I will proceede,
Which is as ample, as the Worlde is wide:
What great Contentment doth her Pressence breede
In him, that can his wealth with Wysdome guide?
  She is the Soveraigne Queene, of all Delights:
    For her the Lawyer pleades; the Souldier fights.

For her, the Merchant venters on the Seas:
For her, the Scholler studdies at his Booke:
For her, the Usurer (with greater ease)

For sillie fishes, layes a silver hooke:
   For her, the Townsman leaves the Countrey Village:
   For her, the Plowman gives himselfe to Tillage.


For her, the Gentlemen doeth raise his rents:
For her, the Servingman attends his maister:
For her, the curious head new toyes invents:
For her, to Sores, the Surgeon layes his plaister.
   In fine for her, each man in his Vocation,
   Applies himselfe, in everie sev'rall Nation.


What can thy hart desire, but thou mayst have it,
If thou hast readie money to disburse?
Then thanke thy Fortune, that so freely gave it;
For of all friends, the surest is thy purse.
   Friends may prove false, and leave thee in thy need;
   But still thy Purse will bee thy friend indeed.


Admit thou come, into a place unknowne;
And no man knowes, of whence, or what thou art:
If once thy faire *Pecunia*, shee be showne,
Thou art esteem'd a man of great Desart:
   And placed at the Tables upper ende;
   Not for thine owne sake, but thy faithfull frende.

RICHARD BARNFIELD, *The Encomion of Lady Pecunia; or, The Praise of Money*,
1598


'What have wealth or grandeur to do with happiness?'

'Grandeur has but little,' said Elinor, 'but wealth has much to do with it.'

'Elinor, for shame!' said Marianne; 'money can only give happiness where there is nothing else to give it. Beyond a competence, it can afford no real satisfaction, as far as mere self is concerned.'

'Perhaps,' said Elinor, smiling, 'we may come to the same point. *Your* competence and *my* wealth are very much alike, I daresay; and without them, as the world goes now, we shall both agree that every kind of external comfort must be wanting. Your ideas are only more noble than mine. Come, what is your competence?'

'About eighteen hundred or two thousand a year; not more than *that*.'

Elinor laughed. '*Two* thousand a year! *One* is my wealth! I guessed how it would end.'

'And yet two thousand a year is a very moderate income,' said Marianne. 'A family cannot well be maintained on a smaller. I am sure I am not extravagant in my demands. A proper establishment of servants, a carriage, perhaps two, and hunters, cannot be supported on less.'

Elinor smiled again, to hear her sister describing so accurately their future expenses at Combe Magna.

'Hunters!' repeated Edward; 'but why must you have hunters? Everybody does not hunt.'

Marianne coloured as she replied, 'But most people do.'

'I wish,' said Margaret, striking out a novel thought, 'that somebody would give us all a large fortune apiece!'

'Oh that they would!' cried Marianne, her eyes sparkling with animation, and her cheeks glowing with the delight of such imaginary happiness.

'We are all unanimous in that wish, I suppose,' said Elinor, 'in spite of the insufficiency of wealth.'

'Oh dear!' cried Margaret, 'how happy I should be! I wonder what I should do with it.'

JANE AUSTEN, *Sense and Sensibility*, 1811

When little Alfred went to Harrow, you may be sure Colonel Newcome and Clive galloped over to see the little man and tipped him royally. What money is better bestowed than that of a schoolboy's tip? How the kindness is recalled by the recipient in after days? It blesses him that gives and him that takes. Remember how happy such benefactions made you in your own early time, and go off on the very first fine day and tip your nephew at school!

W. M. THACKERAY, *The Newcomes*, 1853–5

In the early nineteen-twenties, when I first settled in London, I did a great deal of reviewing. (There was much more space then for book reviews than there is now.) I was ready to review anything, and often did columns of short notes on new books. The books themselves were then sold—fiction for a third of the publisher's price, non-fiction for about a half—to a certain shop not far from the Strand, a shop that specialised in the purchase and re-sale of review copies, a traffic that had a faintly piratical air. At this shop, where human nature was understood, one was always paid at once and

paid in cash, generally in exquisite new pound notes. And of all the money
I have ever handled, this gave me most delight. Money for Jam, Money for
Old Rope, Money for nothing. When we receive our wages, salaries or fees,
we may be content, for this is what we have earned, but we are a long way
from delight. It is money that we have not earned, the windfall, the magical
bonus, that starts us capering. Many sociologists, who understand everything except their fellow creatures, are bewildered and saddened by the
ubiquitous passion among the mob for betting and gambling. But the more
we standardise wages, hours and prices, the more we insist upon social
security for everybody, the more we compel two and two to make four
everywhere, the more people will take to the greyhound tracks and the
football pools. For it is when two and two miraculously make five that the
heart leaps up at last. It is when money looks like manna that we truly
delight in it. Since those days when I used to sell my review copies I have
earned in one way and another very considerable sums of money indeed;
but they have all been lost in a dreary maze of bank accounts, stocks and
shares, tax certificates, cheques and bills and receipts. I have never felt rich
and careless, like a man returning from a lucky day at the races or a sailor
home from a long voyage. But when I used to hurry out of that shop with
five or six new pound notes singing in my pocket, for quarter of an hour
or so I felt like a tipsy millionaire or the man who broke the bank at Monte
Carlo. Money to Burn! And the only comparable moments I have known
since have been on certain very rare occasions when I happen to have been
fortunate in playing those fruit machines, which were so popular in the
American south-west when we were there. These machines are so rigged
that the odds are monstrously against the customer. Nickels and quarters
by the score could vanish as lemons tried to mate with plums. But the
jackpot, which must surely have been the invention of some poet, more
than compensated for all these losses. As the magic combination of symbols
showed itself, the machine would first hesitate, then shiver and noisily
gather its works together, and then, like an exasperated fairy godmother,
would splutteringly hurl whole handfuls of coin at you so that below your
waist it seemed to be raining nickels or quarters. This is acquisition lit with
wonder and glory. We could do with more of it.

J. B. PRIESTLEY, *Delight*, 1949

Fifteen hundred francs and all the clothes he needed! Our ardent son of the
south flung his hesitations to the wind, and went down to breakfast with
that indefinable air which a youth puts on when he is conscious of possessing

money. The moment that a student jingles coin in his pocket he feels that he is leaning on a pillar of strength. His step becomes assured; his lever has a fulcrum to work on; he looks ahead; he sees his way; his very movements grow alert. Yesterday, timid and despondent, he could hardly resent an injury; to-day he is ready to offer one to the chief of state. A curious transformation is at work within him. He wants all things, feels himself capable of all things; his desires rush forth at random; he is gay, generous, and open-hearted,—the fledgling has found his wings. As a penniless student he had been content to snatch a scrap of pleasure as a dog steals a bone, cracks it, sucks the marrow furtively, and runs away. But the young man who rattles money in his breeches pocket can afford to linger over his enjoyments; he can suck their juice at leisure; he floats in summer air; for him the harsh word *poverty* no longer has a meaning,—all Paris belongs to him. In youth how these things glitter! how they sparkle and flame!

HONORÉ DE BALZAC (1799–1850), *Père Goriot*, English tr. 1886

When his son Titus blamed him for even laying a tax upon urine, he applied to his nose a piece of the money he received in the first instalment, and asked him, 'if it stunk?' And he replying no, 'And yet,' said he, 'it is derived from urine.'

SUETONIUS (*c.* AD 70–*c.*160), 'Vespasian', *Lives of the Twelve Caesars*, tr. Alexander Thomson, 1845

I don't feel like I get germs when I hold money. Money has a certain kind of amnesty. I feel, when I'm holding money, that the dollar bill has no more germs on it than my hands do. When I pass my hand over money, it becomes perfectly clean to me. I don't know where it's been—who's touched it and with what—but that's all erased the moment I touch it.

ANDY WARHOL, *From A to B and Back Again*, 1975

## MONEY

It has such an inherent power to run itself clear of taint that human ingenuity cannot devise the means of making it work permanent mischief, any more than means can be found of torturing people beyond what they can bear. Even if a man founds a College of Technical Instruction, the chances are ten to one that no one will be taught anything and that it will have been practically left to a number of excellent professors who will know very well what to do with it.

SAMUEL BUTLER, *Notebooks*, 1912

I gave the waiter a ten-shilling note and he went to bring me change. There was another ten-shilling note in my purse; I noticed it, because it is a fact that still takes my breath away—the power of my purse to breed ten-shilling notes automatically. I open it and there they are. Society gives me chicken and coffee, bed and lodging, in return for a certain number of pieces of paper which were left me by an aunt, for no other reason than that I share her name.

My aunt, Mary Beton, I must tell you, died by a fall from her horse when she was riding out to take the air in Bombay. The news of my legacy reached me one night about the same time that the act was passed that gave votes to women. A solicitor's letter fell into the post-box and when I opened it I found that she had left me five hundred pounds a year for ever. Of the two—the vote and the money—the money, I own, seemed infinitely the more important. Before that I had made my living by cadging odd jobs from newspapers, by reporting a donkey show here or a wedding there; I had earned a few pounds by addressing envelopes, reading to old ladies, making artificial flowers, teaching the alphabet to small children in a kindergarten. Such were the chief occupations that were open to women before 1918. I need not, I am afraid, describe in any detail the hardness of the work, for you know perhaps women who have done it; nor the difficulty of living on the money when it was earned, for you may have tried. But what still remains with me as a worse infliction than either was the poison of fear and bitterness which those days bred in me. To begin with, always to be doing work that one did not wish to do, and to do it like a slave, flattering and fawning, not always necessarily perhaps, but it seemed necessary and the stakes were too great to run risks; and then the thought of that one gift which it was death to hide—a small one but dear to the possessor—perishing and with it my self, my soul—all this became like a rust eating away the bloom of the spring, destroying the tree at its heart. However, as I say, my aunt died; and whenever I change a ten-shilling note a little of that rust and corrosion is rubbed off; fear and bitterness go. Indeed, I thought, slipping the silver into my purse, it is remarkable, remembering the bitterness of those days, what a change of temper a fixed income will bring about. No force in the world can take from me my five hundred pounds. Food, house and clothing are mine for ever. Therefore not merely do effort and labour cease, but also hatred and bitterness. I need not hate any man; he cannot hurt me. I need not flatter any man; he has nothing to give me. So imperceptibly I found myself adopting a new attitude towards the other half of the human race.

VIRGINIA WOOLF, A Room of One's Own, 1929

As long as my purse contains money it secures my independence, and exempts me from the trouble of seeking other money, a trouble of which I have always had a perfect horror; and the dread of seeing the end of my independence makes me unwilling to part with my means. The money that we possess is the instrument of liberty, that which we lack and strive to obtain is the instrument of slavery. Thence it is that I hold fast to aught that I have, and yet covet nothing more.

JEAN-JACQUES ROUSSEAU (1712–78), Confessions, tr. anon. 1924

Money came pouring in upon him, and the faster it came the fonder he became of it, though, as he frequently said, he valued it not for its own sake, but only as a means of providing for his dear children.

Yet when a man is very fond of his money it is not easy for him at all times to be very fond of his children also. The two are like God and Mammon. Lord Macaulay has a passage in which he contrasts the pleasures which a man may derive from books with the inconveniences to which he may be put by his acquaintances. 'Plato,' he says, 'is never sullen. Cervantes is never petulant. Demosthenes never comes unseasonably. Dante never stays too long. No difference of political opinion can alienate Cicero. No heresy can excite the horror of Bossuet.' I dare say I might differ from Lord Macaulay in my estimate of some of the writers he has named, but there can be no disputing his main proposition, namely, that we need have no more trouble from any of them than we have a mind to, whereas our friends are not always so easily disposed of. George Pontifex felt this as regards his children and his money. His money was never naughty; his money never made noise or litter, and did not spill things on the tablecloth at meal times, or leave the door open when it went out. His dividends did not quarrel among themselves, nor was he under any uneasiness lest his mortgages should become extravagant on reaching manhood and run him up debts which sooner or later he should have to pay. There were tendencies in John which made him very uneasy, and Theobald, his second son, was idle and at times far from truthful. His children might, perhaps, have answered, had they known what was in their father's mind, that he did not knock his money about as he not infrequently knocked his children. He never dealt hastily or pettishly with his money, and that was perhaps why he and it got on so well together.

SAMUEL BUTLER, *The Way of All Flesh*, 1903

## MONEY

In order to be able to live
on the right side of the law.
To always use his own name
and phone number. To go bail
for a friend and not give
a damn if the friend skips town.
Hope, in fact, she does.
To give some money
to his mother. And to his
children and their mother.
Not save it. He wants
to use it up before it's gone.
Buy clothes with it.
Pay the rent and utilities.
Buy food, and then some.
Go out for dinner when he feels like it.
And it's okay
to order anything off the menu!
Buy drugs when he wants.
Buy a car. If it breaks
down, repair it. Or else
buy another. See that
boat? He might buy one
just like it. And sail it
around the Horn, looking
for company. He knows a girl
in Porto Alegre who'd love
to see him in
his own boat, sails full,
turn into the harbor for her.
A fellow who could afford

> to come all this way
> to see her. Just because
> he liked the sound
> of her laughter,
> and the way she swings her hair.

RAYMOND CARVER, *In a Marine Light: Selected Poems*, 1987

I received my £100, in advance, with profound delight. It was a positive and most welcome increase to my income, and might probably be regarded as a first real step on the road to substantial success. I am well aware that there are many who think that an author in his authorship should not regard money,—nor a painter, or sculptor, or composer in his art. I do not know that this unnatural self-sacrifice is supposed to extend itself further. A barrister, a clergyman, a doctor, an engineer, and even actors and architects, may without disgrace follow the bent of human nature, and endeavour to fill their bellies and clothe their backs, and also those of their wives and children, as comfortably as they can by the exercise of their abilities and their crafts. They may be as rationally realistic, as may the butchers and the bakers; but the artist and the author forget the high glories of their calling if they condescend to make a money return a first object. They who preach this doctrine will be much offended by my theory, and by this book of mine, if my theory and my book come beneath their notice. They require the practice of a so-called virtue which is contrary to nature, and which, in my eyes, would be no virtue if it were practised. They are like clergymen who preach sermons against the love of money, but who know that the love of money is so distinctive a characteristic of humanity that such sermons are mere platitudes called for by customary but unintelligent piety. All material progress has come from man's desire to do the best he can for himself and those about him, and civilisation and Christianity itself have been made possible by such progress. Though we do not all of us argue this matter out within our breasts, we do all feel it; and we know that the more a man earns the more useful he is to his fellow-men. The most useful lawyers, as a rule, have been those who have made the greatest incomes,—and it is the same with the doctors. It would be the same in the Church if they who have the choosing of bishops always chose the best man. And it has in truth been so too in art and authorship. Did Titian or Rubens disregard their pecuniary rewards? As far as we know, Shakespeare worked always for money, giving the best of his intellect to support his trade as an actor. In our own century what literary names stand higher than those of

Byron, Tennyson, Scott, Dickens, Macaulay, and Carlyle? And I think I may say that none of those great men neglected the pecuniary result of their labours. Now and then a man may arise among us who in any calling, whether it be in law, in physic, in religious teaching, in art, or literature, may in his professional enthusiasm utterly disregard money. All will honour his enthusiasm, and if he be wifeless and childless, his disregard of the great object of men's work will be blameless. But it is a mistake to suppose that a man is a better man because he despises money. Few do so, and those few in doing so suffer a defeat. Who does not desire to be hospitable to his friends, generous to the poor, liberal to all, munificent to his children, and to be himself free from the carking fear which poverty creates? The subject will not stand an argument;—and yet authors are told that they should disregard payment for their work, and be content to devote their unbought brains to the welfare of the public. Brains that are unbought will never serve the public much. Take away from English authors their copyrights, and you would very soon take away from England her authors.

ANTHONY TROLLOPE, *An Autobiography*, 1883

The idea that money, patronage and trade automatically corrupt the wells of imagination is a pious fiction, believed by some utopian lefties and a few people of genius such as Blake but flatly contradicted by history itself. The work of Titian and Bernini, Piero della Francesca and Poussin, Reisener and Chippendale would not exist unless someone paid for them, and paid well. Picasso was a millionaire at forty and that didn't harm him. On the other hand, some painters are millionaires at thirty and that can't help them. Against the art starlet one sees waddling about like a Strasbourg goose, his ego distended to gross proportion by the obsequies of the market, one has to weigh the many artists who have been stifled by indifference and the collapse of confidence it brings. On the whole, money does artists much more good than harm. The idea that one benefits from cold water, crusts and debt collectors is now almost extinct, like belief in the reformatory power of flogging.

ROBERT HUGHES, 'Art and Money', *Nothing if Not Critical*, 1990

Wealth, too,—what an endless repetition of the same foolish trivialities about it! Take the single fact of its alleged uncertain tenure and transitory character. In old times, when men were all the time fighting and robbing each other,—in those tropical countries where the Sabeans and the Chaldeans stole all a man's cattle and camels, and there were frightful tornadoes and rains of fire from heaven, it was true enough that riches took wings to themselves not unfrequently in a very unexpected way. But, with common prudence in investments, it is not so now. In fact, there is nothing earthly that lasts so well, on the whole, as money. A man's learning dies with him; even his virtues fade out of remembrance; but the dividends on the stocks he bequeathes to his children live and keep his memory green.

OLIVER WENDELL HOLMES, The Professor at the Breakfast-Table, 1859

A man who thinks he has got anything to say should always write for money. There is always some air of priggishness in one who 'gives his advice gratis.' Modesty is preserved by the money-motive. Besides, the subtlest truths are like the remoter stars: you cannot see them unless you look a little on one side of them. You are likely to say your say the better for having your direct gaze fixed upon the five, ten, or twenty pound note which your prophecy is to bring you.

COVENTRY PATMORE, letter c.1873–8, Memoirs and Correspondence, 1900

Mr Strahan talked of launching into the great ocean of London, in order to have a chance for rising into eminence; and, observing that many men were kept back from trying their fortunes there, because they were born to a competency, said, 'Small certainties are the bane of men of talents;' which Johnson confirmed. Mr Strahan put Johnson in mind of a remark which he had made to him; 'There are few ways in which a man can be more inno- cently employed than in getting money.' 'The more one thinks of this (said Strahan,) the juster it will appear.'

JAMES BOSWELL, Life of Samuel Johnson, 1791, 27 March 1775

Unsentimental, unheroic, some will say unchristian, as it may sound, our right or wrong use of money is the utmost test of character, as well as the root of happiness or misery, throughout our whole lives. And this secret lies not so much with men as with us women. Instead of striving to make ourselves their rivals, would it not be wiser to educate ourselves into being their helpmates? Not merely as wives, but as daughters, sisters,—every

relation in which a capable woman can help a man, and an incapable one
bring him to ruin? Especially on that particular point—money.

I know that I shall excite the wrath or contempt of the advocates of the
higher education of women, when I say that it is not necessary for every
woman to be an accomplished musician, an art-student, a thoroughly educated Girton girl; but it is necessary that she should be a woman of business. From the day when her baby fingers begin to handle pence and shillings,
and her infant mind is roused to laudable ambition by the possession of the
enormous income of threepence a week, she ought to be taught the true
value and wise expenditure of money; to keep accounts and balance them;
to repay the minutest debt, or, still better, to avoid incurring it; to observe
the just proportions of having and spending, and, above all, the golden rule
for every one of us, whether our income be sixpence a week or twenty
thousand a year—*waste nothing*.

Mrs D. M. Craik, About Money and Other Things, 1886

'It isn't difficult to be a country gentleman's wife,' Rebecca thought. 'I think
I could be a good woman if I had five thousand a year. I could dawdle
about in the nursery, and count the apricots on the wall. I could water
plants in a greenhouse, and pick off dead leaves from the geraniums. I could
ask old women about their rheumatisms, and order half a crown's worth
of soup for the poor. I shouldn't miss it much, out of five thousand a year.
I could even drive out ten miles to dine at a neighbour's, and dress in the
fashions of the year before last. I could go to church and keep awake in the
great family pew: or go to sleep behind the curtains, with my veil down,
if I only had practice. I could pay everybody, if I had but the money. This
is what the conjurers here pride themselves upon doing. They look down
with pity upon us miserable sinners who have none. They think themselves
generous if they give our children a five-pound note, and us contemptible
if we are without one.' And who knows but Rebecca was right in her
speculations—and that it was only a question of money and fortune which
made the difference between her and an honest woman? If you take temptations into account, who is to say that he is better than his neighbour? A
comfortable career of prosperity, if it does not make people honest, at least
keeps them so. An alderman coming from a turtle feast will not step out of
his carriage to steal a leg of mutton; but put him to starve, and see if he will
not purloin a loaf. Becky consoled herself by so balancing the chances and
equalizing the distribution of good and evil in the world.

W. M. Thackeray, Vanity Fair, 1847–8

But men are not to be judged by the consequences that may succeed their actions, but the facts themselves, and the motives which it shall appear they acted from. If an ill-natured miser, who is almost a plumb, and spends but fifty pounds a year, though he has no relation to inherit his wealth, should be robbed of five hundred or a thousand guineas, it is certain that as soon as this money should come to circulate, the nation would be the better for the robbery, and receive the same and as real a benefit from it, as if an archbishop had left the same sum to the public; yet justice and the peace of the society require that he or they who robbed the miser should be hanged, though there were half-a-dozen of them concerned.

Thieves and pick-pockets steal for a livelihood, and either what they can get honestly is not sufficient to keep them, or else they have an aversion to constant working: they want to gratify their senses, have victuals, strong drink, lewd women, and to be idle when they please. The victualler, who entertains them and takes their money, knowing which way they come at it, is very near as great a villain as his guests. But if he fleeces them well, minds his business and is a prudent man, he may get money and be punctual with them he deals with: the trusty out-clerk, whose chief aim is his master's profit, sends him in what beer he wants, and takes care not to lose his custom; whilst the man's money is good he thinks it no business of his to examine whom he gets it by. In the mean time the wealthy brewer, who leaves all the management to his servants, knows nothing of the matter, but keeps his coach, treats his friends and enjoys his pleasure with ease and a good conscience, he gets an estate, builds houses and educates his children in plenty, without ever thinking on the labour which wretches perform, the shifts fools make, and the tricks knaves play to come at the commodity by the vast sale of which he amasses his great riches.

BERNARD MANDEVILLE, *The Fable of the Bees; or, Private Vices, Public Benefits*, 1714

There must be some impulse besides public spirit, to put private interest into motion along with it. Monied men ought to be allowed to set a value on their money; if they did not, there could be no monied men. This desire of accumulation is a principle without which the means of their service to the state could not exist. The love of lucre, though sometimes carried to a ridiculous, sometimes to a vicious, excess, is the grand cause of prosperity to all states. In this natural, this reasonable, this powerful, this prolific principle, it is for the satirist to expose the ridiculous: it is for the moralist to censure the vicious; it is for the sympathetic heart to reprobate the hard and cruel; it is for the judge to animadvert on the fraud, the extortion, and the oppression; but it is for the statesman to employ it as he finds it, with all its concomitant excellencies, with all its imperfections on its head. It is his part, in this case, as it is in all other cases, where he is to make use of the general energies of nature, to take them as he finds them.

EDMUND BURKE, 'Letters on a Regicide Peace', 1797

The avaricious love of gain, which is so feelingly deplored, appears to us a principle which, in able hands, might be guided to the most salutary purposes. The object is to encourage the love of labour, which is best encouraged by the love of money.

SYDNEY SMITH, 'Benefits of Avarice', *Edinburgh Review*, 1803

The contempt of riches among the philosophers was a hidden desire to revenge their merit for the injustice of Fortune, by contempt of the very advantages of which she deprived them. It was a secret to secure themselves from the degradation of poverty: it was a byroad to arrive at that consideration which they could not obtain by riches.

FRANÇOIS, DUC DE LA ROCHEFOUCAULD (1613–80), *Moral Reflections, Sentences and Maxims*, 1665

We have already noted—in our account of Herodotus—that a first effect of money was to give freedom of movement and leisure to a number of people who could not otherwise have enjoyed these privileges. And that is the peculiar value of money to mankind. Instead of a worker or helper being paid in kind and in such a way that he is tied as much in his enjoyment as in his labour, money leaves him free to do as he pleases amidst a wide choice of purchasable aids, eases, and indulgences. He may eat his money or drink it or give it to a temple or spend it in learning something or save it against some foreseen occasion. That is the good of money, the freedom of its universal convertibility. But the freedom money gives the poor man is nothing to the freedom money has given the rich man. With money rich men ceased to be tied to lands, houses, stores, flocks and herds. They could change the nature and locality of their possessions with an unheard-of freedom.

H. G. WELLS, *The Outline of History*, 1920

## OF MONEY

Give money me; take friendship whoso list!
　For friends are gone, come once adversity;
When money yet remaineth safe in chest,
　That quickly can thee bring from misery.
Fair face show friends, when riches do abound;
　Come time of proof, farewell, they must away!
Believe me well, they are not to be found
　If God but send thee once a louring day.
　　Gold never starts aside; but, in distress,
　　Finds ways enough to ease thine heaviness.

BARNABE GOODGE, *Eclogues, Epitaphs and Sonnets*, 1563

Money enters in two different characters into the scheme of life. A certain amount, varying with the number and empire of our desires, is a true necessary to each one of us in the present order of society; but beyond that amount, money is a commodity to be bought or not to be bought, a luxury in which we may either indulge or stint ourselves, like any other. And there are many luxuries that we may legitimately prefer to it, such as a grateful conscience, a country life, or the woman of our inclination. Trite, flat, and obvious as this conclusion may appear, we have only to look round us in society to see how scantily it has been recognised; and perhaps even ourselves, after a little reflection, may decide to spend a trifle less for money, and indulge ourselves a trifle more in the article of freedom.

ROBERT LOUIS STEVENSON, Henry David Thoreau', *Familiar Studies of Men and Books*, 1882

HIGGINS. I suppose we must give him a fiver.
PICKERING. He'll make a bad use of it, I'm afraid.
DOOLITTLE. Not me, Governor, so help me I wont. Dont you be afraid that I'll save it and spare it and live idle on it. There wont be a penny of it left by Monday: I'll have to go to work same as if I'd never had it. It wont pauperize me, you bet. Just one good spree for myself and the missus, giving pleasure to ourselves and employment to others, and satisfaction to you to think it's not been throwed away. You couldnt spend it better.
HIGGINS [*taking out his pocket book and coming between Doolittle and the piano*]. This is irresistible. Lets give him ten. [*He offers two notes to the dustman*]

DOOLITTLE. No, Governor. She wouldnt have the heart to spend ten; and perhaps I shouldnt neither. Ten pounds is a lot of money: it makes a man feel prudent like; and then goodbye to happiness. You give me what I ask you, Governor: not a penny more, and not a penny less.

GEORGE BERNARD SHAW, Pygmalion, 1912

Lay not up for yourselves treasures upon earth, where moth and rust doth corrupt, and where thieves break through and steal:

But lay up for your selves treasures in heaven, where neither moth nor rust doth corrupt, and where thieves do not break through nor steal.

For where your treasure is, there will your heart be also.

Matthew 6: 19–21

Money never made any man rich. Contrariwise, there is not any man that hath gathered store of it together that is not become more covetous. Wouldst thou know the reason hereof? He that hath much beginneth to have a wish to have more. In sum, although thou set before me whom thou wilt, of those who are reputed as rich, as either Crœsus or Licinius, let him set down his revenues, and bring into the account both whatsoever he hath and whatsoever he hopeth to have; yet this man, if thou believest me, is poor, or, as thou thyself wilt admit, may become so. But he that hath composed himself to that which nature requireth of his hands, is not only without the sense, but also without the fear of poverty.

SENECA (d. AD. 65), Ad Lucilium epistulae morales, letter 119, tr. Thomas Lodge, 1614

The inhabitants, moreover, have none of that eagerness for gain, and rage for improvement, which keep our people continually on the move, and our country towns incessantly in a state of transition. There the magic phrases, 'town lots,' 'water privileges,' 'railroads,' and other comprehensive and soul-stirring words from the speculator's vocabulary, are never heard. The residents dwell in the houses built by their forefathers, without thinking of enlarging or modernizing them, or pulling them down and turning them into granite stores. The trees under which they have been born, and have played in infancy, flourish undisturbed; though, by cutting them down, they might open new streets, and put money in their pockets. In a word, the almighty dollar, that great object of universal devotion throughout our land, seems to have no genuine devotees in these peculiar villages; and unless some of its missionaries penetrate there, and erect banking-houses and other pious shrines, there is no knowing how long the inhabitants may remain in their present state of contented poverty.

WASHINGTON IRVING, 'The Creole Village', 1837

From him came the most notable of all the maxims which illustrate the disinterestedness of the chivalry of science. At the time he was absorbed in some minute investigations in a difficult department of zoölogy, he received a letter from the president of a lyceum at the West, offering him a large sum for a course of popular lectures on natural history. His answer was: 'I CANNOT AFFORD TO WASTE MY TIME IN MAKING MONEY.'

EDWIN PERCY WHIPPLE, 'Recollections of Agassiz', *Recollections of Eminent Men*, 1886

'I dislike money,' Magritte said, 'both for itself and for what it can buy, since I want nothing we know about.'

RENÉ MAGRITTE (1898–1967)

IAGO.  Good name, in man, and woman, dear my lord,
   Is the immediate jewel of their souls:
   Who steals my purse, steals trash; 'tis something, nothing;
   'Twas mine, 'tis his, and has been slave to thousands;
   But he, that filches from me my good name,
   Robs me of that, which not enriches him,
   And makes me poor indeed.

WILLIAM SHAKESPEARE, *Othello*, 1605

   The brazen tower, strong gates well barred,
      And wakeful dogs, had sure availed
   Imprisoned Danae to guard,
      And prowling ravishers had failed.

   But Jove and Venus saw, and mocked
      Acrisius jailor of the maid;

They knew the way could not be blocked,
    If Jove in gold would make the raid.

Gold, mightier than the lightning stroke,
    The guard can pierce, the rock can burst.
So the Greek augur's fortune broke,
    By force of bribe with ruin cursed.

King Philip clave by tools like these
    All city-gates, and sapped the throne
Of rivals. They that plough the seas,
    Though fierce, this fascination own.

But care with growing treasure grows,
    And thirst for more. With right I dread,
Maecenas, pride of knightly rows,
    Above the ranks to lift my head.

Deny thyself; the gods will give
    More freely. Bare, I march to find
The camp of them that sparely live,
    The camp of wealth I leave behind.

I shine more bright with modest means
    Than if within my barns I store
All that the Apulian tiller gleans,
    And, choked with treasures, were but poor.

A crop in sure possession held,
    A silver stream, a wood, if small;
Such happy share had far excelled
    All Afric's corn-lands held in thrall.

No honey from Calabrian bees,
    No Laestrygonian jars of wine
Grown ripe, no wools on Gaulish leas
    Rich-pastured; none of these are mine.

I suffer not the pinch of need,
    And thou wouldst not deny what lacks;

Better to curb unruly greed
   That so thy purse may rounder wax,

Than rule o'er wide Mygdonia's plains.
   Much they shall want, who much demand;
'Tis best, when Heaven for man ordains
   Enough, but with a thrifty hand.

HORACE, *Odes*, 23 BC, III. xvi; tr. W. E. Gladstone, 1895

Alyosha went to live in the house of two distant relations of Yefim Petrovitch, ladies whom he had never seen before. On what terms he lived with them he did not know himself. It was very characteristic of him, indeed, that he never cared at whose expense he was living. In that respect he was a striking contrast to his elder brother Ivan, who struggled with poverty for his first two years in the university, maintained himself by his own efforts, and had from childhood been bitterly conscious of living at the expense of his benefactor. But this strange trait in Alyosha's character must not, I think, be criticised too severely, for at the slightest acquaintance with him any one would have perceived that Alyosha was one of those youths, almost of the type of religious enthusiast, who, if they were suddenly to come into possession of a large fortune would not hesitate to give it away for the asking, either for good works or perhaps to a clever rogue. In general he seemed scarcely to know the value of money, not, of course, in a literal sense. When he was given pocket-money, which he never asked for, he was either terribly careless of it so that it was gone in a moment, or he kept it for weeks together, not knowing what to do with it.

FYODOR DOSTOEVSKY, *The Brothers Karamazov*, 1879–80, tr. Constance Garnett, 1912

Since all the riches of this world
May be gifts from the Devil and earthly kings,
I should suspect that I worshipp'd the Devil
If I thank'd my God for worldly things.

WILLIAM BLAKE, *Gnomic Verses*, c.1793–1810

As to money, I am not anxious—I am sure, if God give me health, to make all even before the End of this year—& I find that I can without any straining

gain 500 guineas a year, if I give up poetry—i.e. original Poetry—. If I had
the least love of money, I could make almost sure of 2000£ a year for
Stuart has offered me half shares in the two Papers, the M.P. & Courier, if
I would devote myself with him to them—but I told him, that I would not
give up the Country, & the lazy reading of Old Folios for two Thousand
Times two thousand Pound—in short, that beyond 250£ a year, I considered money as a real Evil—at which he stared; for such Ideas are
not animals indigenous in the Longitudes & Latitudes of a Scotchman's
Soul.

SAMUEL COLERIDGE to Thomas Poole, 21 March 1800, *Selected Letters, 1785–
1800*, ed. Earl Leslie Griggs, 1956

Only the importune Tempter still remained,
And with these words his temptation pursued:—
   'By hunger, that each other creature tames,
Thou art not to be harmed, therefore not moved;
Thy temperance, invincible besides,
For no allurement yields to appetite;
And all thy heart is set on high designs,
High actions. But wherewith to be achieved?
Great acts require great means of enterprise;
Thou art unknown, unfriended, low of birth,
A carpenter thy father known, thyself
Bred up in poverty and straits at home,
Lost in a desert here and hunger-bit.
Which way, or from what hope, dost thou aspire
To greatness? whence authority deriv'st?
What followers, what retinue canst thou gain,
Or at thy heels the dizzy multitude,
Longer than thou canst feed them on thy cost?
Money brings honour, friends, conquest, and realms.
What raised Antipater the Edomite,
And his son Herod placed on Judah's throne,
*Thy* throne, but gold, that got him puissant friends?
Therefore, if at great things thou wouldst arrive,
Get riches first, get wealth, and treasure heap—
Not difficult, if thou hearken to me.
Riches are mine, fortune is in my hand;
They whom I favour thrive in wealth amain,

While virtue, valour, wisdom, sit in want.'
    To whom thus Jesus patiently replied:—
'Yet wealth without these three is impotent
To gain dominion, or to keep it gained—
Witness those ancient empires of the earth,
In highth of all their flowing wealth dissolved;
But men endued with these have oft attained,
In lowest poverty, to highest deeds—
Gideon, and Jephtha, and the shepherd lad
Whose offspring on the throne of Judah sat
So many ages, and shall yet regain
That seat, and reign in Israel without end.
Among the Heathen (for throughout the world
To me is not unknown what hath been done
Worthy of memorial) canst thou not remember
Quintius, Fabricius, Curius, Regulus?—
For I esteem those names of men so poor,
Who could do mighty things, and could contemn
Riches, though offered from the hand of Kings.
And what in me seems wanting but that I
May also in this poverty as soon
Accomplish what they did, perhaps and more?
Extol not riches, then, the toil of fools,
The wise man's cumbrance, if not snare; more apt
To slacken virtue and abate her edge
Than prompt her to do aught may merit praise.'

JOHN MILTON, *Paradise Regained*, 1671, book ii


Money refused loseth its brightness.

GEORGE HERBERT, *Jacula prudentum*, 1640


Deployed as a tool and understood as a secular product (comparable to wheat, coal or intelligence), money ranks as one of the primary materials with which mankind builds the architecture of civilization. Large numbers of people, many of them Americans, continue to use money in this manner, and the success of the American economy testifies both to their energy and their clarity of mind. Although a constant motif in American history and metaphysics, the dream of money never provided the impetus from which the country drew its greatest strengths. George Washington was obliged to borrow money to pay his travel to his first inauguration. Abraham Lincoln had little use for riches, and Thomas Jefferson died bankrupt. A genuine indifference to the radiance of money has been characteristic not only of the nation's principal artists and scientists but also of the founders of its largest fortunes. Even the most humorless of the late nineteenth-century plutocrats seem to have taken money less seriously than their heirs and publicists. They understood that laissez-faire capitalism, like all economic systems, was amoral, a mechanism providing greater chances of liberty and prosperity to greater numbers of people than had been possible within the feudal or mercantile systems. But for money itself they often expressed a gambler's contempt. By and large they were interested in something else— in an idea, a contraption, a theory of combination or a geometry of markets. Money was something that followed with the luggage, a secondary proof of grace accumulating in the hall with the invitations to dinner and the requests for press interviews, with the flowers, the catering bills and the art collection. Neither John D. Rockefeller nor Henry Ford was impressed by the magical aspects of money. A similar indifference shows up in conversation with latter-day millionaires who have made their own fortunes; like highly paid athletes, the inventors of computer systems seem surprised that they should earn so much money for playing what they often describe as a game. Andrew Carnegie acknowledged the same primacy of mind over matter when he observed that the mere 'amassing of wealth is one of the worst species of idolatry.'

LEWIS H. LAPHAM, *Money and Class in America*, 1988

Last night I had a letter from Pinker enclosing for signature a most unsatisfactory contract for 'The Statue'. I flatter myself that this almost certain loss of money, at a time when I particularly want it, did not disturb me for more than a few minutes. Thanks partially to my diligence in daily absorbing Epictetus.

ARNOLD BENNETT, *Journals 1896–1910*, 1932, entry for 3 August 1907

The love of money and the love of learning rarely meet.

GEORGE HERBERT, *Jacula prudentum*, 1640

As we have seen, Blake's was no 'poetic poverty,' of a kind to excite the pensive interest of sentimental people without shocking their nerves; but real, prosaic poverty. Such 'appearances' as I have described tasked his whole income to maintain. And his was an honourable code: he was never, amid all his poverty, in debt. 'Money,' says Mr Palmer, 'he used with careful frugality, but never loved it; and believed that he should be always supplied with it as it was wanted: in which he was not disappointed. And he worked on with serenity when there was only a shilling in the house. Once (he told me) he spent part of one of these last shillings on a camel's hair brush. . . . He would have laughed very much at the word *status*, which has been naturalized into our language of late years.' Last shillings were, at all periods of Blake's life, a frequent incident of his household economy. For, while engrossed in designing, he had often an aversion to resuming his graver, or to being troubled about money matters. It put him out very much when Mrs Blake referred to the financial topic, or found herself constrained to announce, 'The money is going, Mr Blake.' 'Oh, d—— the money!' he would shout; 'it's always the money!' Her method of hinting at the odious subject became, in consequence, a very quiet and expressive one. She would set before him at dinner just what there was in the house, without any comment until, finally, the empty platter had to make its appearance: which hard fact effectually reminded him it was time to go to his engraving for awhile. At that, when fully embarked again, he was not unhappy; work being his natural element.

Alexander Gilchrist, Life of William Blake, 'Pictor Ignotus', 1863

I rose up at the dawn of day:
'Get thee away! get thee away!
Prayest thou for riches? away! away!
This is the throne of Mammon grey!'

Said I: 'This, sure, is very odd;
I took it to be the throne of God.
Everything besides I have:
It's only riches that I *can* crave.

I have mental joys and mental health,
Mental friends and mental wealth;
I've a wife that I love, and that loves me,
I've all but riches bodily.

Then if for riches I must not pray,
God knows, it's little prayers I need say.
I am in God's presence night and day;
He never turns His face away.

The accuser of sins by my side doth stand,
And he holds my money bag in his hand;
For my worldly things God makes him pay;
And he'd pay for more, if to him I would pray.

He says, if I worship not him for a god,
I shall eat coarser food, and go worse shod;
But as I don't value such things as these,
You must do, Mr Devil, just as God please.'

WILLIAM BLAKE, quoted in Alexander Gilchrist, *Life of William Blake*, 'Pictor
Ignotus', 1863


Remember this saying, *The good paymaster is lord of another man's purse*. He
that is known to pay punctually and exactly to the time he promises, may
at any time, and on any occasion, raise all the money his friends can spare.
This is sometimes of great use. After industry and frugality, nothing contributes more to the raising of a young man in the world than punctuality
and justice in all his dealings; therefore never keep borrowed money an
hour beyond the time you promised, lest a disappointment shut up your
friend's purse for ever.

The most trifling actions that affect a man's credit are to be regarded.
The sound of your hammer at five in the morning, or nine at night, heard
by a creditor, makes him easy six months longer; but, if he sees you at a
billiard-table, or hears your voice at a tavern, when you should be at work,
he sends for his money the next day; demands it, before he can receive it,
in a lump.

It shows, besides, that you are mindful of what you owe; it makes you
appear a careful as well as an honest man, and that still increases your
credit.

BENJAMIN FRANKLIN, 'Advice to a Young Tradesman', 1748


More important even than honesty is thrift, not to say outright tight-
fistedness. Money in the city is like money in Weimar Germany. You go to

the Citibank cash machine, get a wheelbarrowful of the stuff, and shovel it out whenever you're told. Then you cross your fingers and hope to die before the Visa Card people process your change of address. But Yankees are serious about spending money. And they give advice at length on the subject.

'Drive over to Portland, Maine,' they'll say, 'and you can get two cents off paper towels.' Or 'There's a special on five-gallon cans of margarine at the A&P. Limit, six to a customer.' And they're especially forthcoming with advice about what you should have paid for your house. 'You know that place sold for eight thousand in 1976.'

P. J. O'ROURKE, 'Moving to New Hampshire', *Republican Party Reptile*, 1987

## PROVIDE PROVIDE

The witch that came (the withered hag)
To wash the steps with pail and rag,
Was once the beauty Abishag,

The picture pride of Hollywood.
Too many fall from great and good
For you to doubt the likelihood.

Die early and avoid the fate.
Or if predestined to die late,
Make up your mind to die in state.

Make the whole stock exchange your own!
If need be occupy a throne,
Where nobody can call *you* crone.

Some have relied on what they knew;
Others on being simply true.
What worked for them might work for you.

No memory of having starred
Atones for later disregard,
Or keeps the end from being hard.

Better to go down dignified
With boughten friendship at your side
Than none at all. Provide, provide!

ROBERT FROST, *A Further Range*, 1936

*Attilius Regulus*, Generall of the Romans armie in *Affrike*, in the middest of his glorie and victorie against the Carthaginians, writ unto the common-wealth, that a hyne or plough-boy, whom he had left alone to oversee and husband his land (which in all was but seven acres of ground) was run away from his charge, and had stolne from him all his implements and tools, belonging to his husbandrie, craving leave to be discharged, and that he might come home to looke to his businesse, for feare his wife and children should therby be endomaged: the Senate tooke order for him, and appointed another man to looke to his land and businesse, and made that good unto him, which the other had stolne from him, and appointed his wife and children to be maintained at the common-wealths charge. *Cato* the elder returning Consul from *Spaine*, sold his horse of service, to save the monie he should have spent for his transport by sea into *Italy*: And being chiefe governor in *Sardinia*, went all his visitations a foot, having no other traine, but one officer of the common-welth, who carried his gowne, and a vessell to do sacrifice in, and for the most part carried his male himselfe. He boasted that he never woare gowne, that cost him more than ten crowns, nor sent more than one shilling sterling to the market for one whole daies provision, and had no Countrie house rough-cast or painted over. *Scipio Æmilianus*, after he had triumphed twice, and twice been Consull, went on a solemne Legation, accompanied and attended on only with seven servants. It is reported that *Homer* had never any more than one servant. *Plato* three, and *Zeno* chiefe of the Stoikes sect, none at all. *Tiberius Gracchus*, being then one of the principal men amongst the Romanes, and sent in commission about weightie matters of the common-wealth, was allotted but six-pence halfe-penie a day for his charges.

MICHEL DE MONTAIGNE, *Essais*, 1580, tr. John Florio, 1603

Just as people must have knives and pistols taken away from them when they are drunk, so under the same circumstances they ought to have their purses taken away from them, for fear they do too much good.

GEORG CHRISTOPH LICHTENBERG, Notebook K, 1793–6, tr. R. J. Hollingdale, 1990

There are people enough who despise money, but few who know how to bestow it.

FRANÇOIS, DUC DE LA ROCHEFOUCAULD, *Moral Reflections, Sentences and Maxims*, 1665

He is the only true reformer who is as careful and as anxious not to aid the unworthy as he is to aid the worthy, and, perhaps, even more so, for in almsgiving more injury is probably done by rewarding vice than by relieving virtue.

The rich man is thus almost restricted to following the examples of Peter Cooper, Enoch Pratt of Baltimore, Mr Pratt of Brooklyn, Senator Stanford, and others, who know that the best means of benefiting the community is to place within its reach the ladders upon which the aspiring can rise—free libraries, parks, and means of recreation, by which men are helped in body and mind; works of art, certain to give pleasure and improve the public taste; and public institutions of various kinds, which will improve the general condition of the people; in this manner returning their surplus wealth to the mass of their fellows in the forms best calculated to do them lasting good.

Thus is the problem of rich and poor to be solved. The laws of accumulation will be left free, the laws of distribution free. Individualism will continue, but the millionaire will be but a trustee for the poor, intrusted for a season with a great part of the increased wealth of the community, but administering it for the community far better than it could or would have done for itself. The best minds will thus have reached a stage in the development of the race in which it is clearly seen that there is no mode of disposing of surplus wealth creditable to thoughtful and earnest men into whose hands it flows, save by using it year by year for the general good. This day already dawns. Men may die without incurring the pity of their fellows, still sharers in great business enterprises from which their capital cannot be or has not been withdrawn, and which is left chiefly at death for public uses; yet the day is not far distant when the man who dies leaving behind him millions of available wealth, which was free for him to administer during life, will pass away 'unwept, unhonored, and unsung,' no matter to what uses he leaves the dross which he cannot take with him. Of such as these the public verdict will then be: 'The man who dies thus rich dies disgraced.'

Such, in my opinion, is the true gospel concerning wealth, obedience to which is destined some day to solve the problem of the rich and the poor, and to bring 'Peace on earth, among men good will.'

ANDREW CARNEGIE, The Gospel of Wealth and Other Timely Essays, 1900

This is the true philanthropy. He who makes a colossal fortune in the hosiery trade, and by his energy has succeeded in reducing the price of woollen goods by the thousandth part of a penny in the pound—this man is worth ten professional philanthropists. So strongly are the Erewhonians impressed with this, that if a man has made a fortune of over £20,000 a year they exempt him from all taxation, considering him as a work of art, and too precious to be meddled with; they say, 'How very much he must have done for society before society could have been prevailed upon to give him so much money;' so magnificent an organization overawes them; they regard it as a thing dropped from heaven.

'Money,' they say, 'is the symbol of duty, it is the sacrament of having done for mankind that which mankind wanted. Mankind may not be a very good judge, but there is no better.' This used to shock me at first, when I remembered that it had been said on high authority that they who have riches shall enter hardly into the kingdom of heaven; but the influence of Erewhon had made me begin to see things in a new light, and I could not help thinking that they who have not riches shall enter more hardly still.

SAMUEL BUTLER, Erewhon; or, Over the Range, 1872

I was not born unto riches, neither is it, I think, my star to be wealthy; or if it were, the freedom of my mind, and frankness of my disposition, were able to contradict and cross my fates: for to me avarice seems not so much a vice, as a deplorable piece of madness; to conceive ourselves urinals, or be persuaded that we are dead, is not so ridiculous, nor so many degrees beyond the power of hellebore, as this. The opinions of theory, and positions of men, are not so void of reason, as their practised conclusions. Some have held that snow is black, that the earth moves, that the soul is air, fire, water; but all this is philosophy: and there is no delirium, if we do but speculate the folly and indisputable dotage of avarice. To that subterraneous idol, and God of the earth, I do confess I am an atheist. I cannot persuade myself to honour that the world adores; whatsoever virtue its prepared substance may have within my body, it hath no influence nor operation without. I would not entertain a base design, or an action that should call me villain, for the Indies; and for this only do I love and honour my own soul, and have methinks two arms too few to embrace myself. Aristotle is too severe, that will not allow us to be truly liberal without wealth, and the bountiful hand of fortune; if this be true, I must confess I am charitable only in my liberal intentions, and bountiful well wishes. But if the example of the mite be not only an act of wonder, but an example of the noblest charity, surely poor men may also build hospitals, and the rich alone have not erected cathedrals. I have a private method which others observe not; I take the opportunity of myself to do good; I borrow occasion of charity from my own necessities, and supply the wants of others, when I am in most need myself: for it is an honest stratagem to take advantage of our-selves, and so to husband the acts of virtue, that, where they are defective in one circumstance, they may repay their want, and multiply their good-ness in another. I have not Peru in my desires, but a competence and ability to perform those good works to which [the Almighty] hath inclined my nature. He is rich who hath enough to be charitable; and it is hard to be so poor that a noble mind may not find a way to this piece of goodness. 'He that giveth to the poor lendeth to the Lord:' there is more rhetorick in that one sentence than in a library of sermons.

SIR THOMAS BROWNE, *Religio medici*, c.1633–5

Alms never make poor. Or thus,
Great alms-giving lessens no man's living.
Giving much to the poor, doth enrich a man's store.
It takes much from the account, to which his sin doth amount.

GEORGE HERBERT, *Jacula prudentum*, 1640

As a very large proportion of the wounded came up from the front without a cent of money in their pockets, I soon discover'd that it was about the best thing I could do to raise their spirits, and show them that somebody cared for them, and practically felt a fatherly or brotherly interest in them, to give them small sums in such cases, using tact and discretion about it. I am regularly supplied with funds for this purpose by good women and men in Boston, Salem, Providence, Brooklyn, and New York. I provide myself with a quantity of bright new ten-cent and five-cent bills, and, when I think it incumbent, I give 25 or 30 cents, or perhaps 50 cents, and occasion-ally a still larger sum to some particular case. As I have started this subject,

I take opportunity to ventilate the financial question. My supplies, altogether voluntary, mostly confidential, often seeming quite Providential, were numerous and varied. For instance, there were two distant and wealthy ladies, sisters, who sent regularly, for two years, quite heavy sums, enjoining that their names should be kept secret. The same delicacy was indeed a frequent condition. From several I had *carte blanche*. Many were entire strangers. From these sources, during from two to three years, in the manner described, in the hospitals, I bestowed, as almoner for others, many, many thousands of dollars. I learn'd one thing conclusively—that beneath all the ostensible greed and heartlessness of our times there is no end to the generous benevolence of men and women in the United States, when once sure of their object. Another thing became clear to me—while *cash* is not amiss to bring up the rear, tact and magnetic sympathy and unction are, and ever will be, sovereign still.

WALT WHITMAN, *Specimen Days*, 1882

I have, in truth, observed, and shall never have a better opportunity than at present to communicate my observation, that the world are in general divided into two opinions concerning charity, which are the very reverse of each other. One party seems to hold, that all acts of this kind are to be esteemed as voluntary gifts, and, however little you give (if indeed no more than your good wishes), you acquire a great degree of merit in so doing. Others, on the contrary, appear to be as firmly persuaded, that beneficence is a positive duty, and that whenever the rich fall greatly short of their ability in relieving the distresses of the poor, their pitiful largesses are so far from being meritorious, that they have only performed their duty by halves, and are in some sense more contemptible than those who have entirely neglected it.

To reconcile these different opinions is not in my power. I shall only add, that the givers are generally of the former sentiment, and the receivers are almost universally inclined to the latter.

HENRY FIELDING, *Tom Jones*, 1749

For the first eight days, everything went smoothly. We both agreed that there should be a hierarchy of worthiness, and that gave me a free hand to act as I saw fit. The idea wasn't to hand out money to anyone who happened to pass by, but to look conscientiously for the most deserving people, to zero in on those whose want was greatest. The poor automatically deserved consideration over the rich, the handicapped were to be favored over the well, the mad were to take precedence over the sane. We established those rules at the outset, and given the nature of New York's streets, it was not very difficult to follow them.

Some people broke down and cried when I gave them the money; others burst out laughing; still others said nothing at all. It was impossible to predict their responses, and I soon learned to stop expecting people to do what I thought they would do. There were the suspicious ones who felt we were trying to trick them—one man even went so far as to tear up the money, and several others accused us of being counterfeiters; there were the greedy ones who didn't think fifty dollars was enough; there were the friendless ones who latched on to us and wouldn't let go; there were the jolly ones who wanted to buy us a drink, the sad ones who wanted to tell us their life stories, the artistic ones who danced and sang songs to show their gratitude. To my astonishment, not one of them tried to rob us. That was probably due to simple good luck, although it must also be said that we moved quickly, never lingering in one spot for very long. Most of the time, I handed out the money in the streets, but there were several forays into low-life bars and coffee shops—Blarney Stones, Bickfords, Chock Full o' Nuts—where I slapped down a fifty-dollar bill in front of each person sitting at the counter. 'Spread a little sunshine!' I would shout, peeling off the money as fast as I could, and before the dazed customers could absorb what was happening to them, I would be racing back out to the street. I gave money to bag ladies and hookers, to winos and bums, to hippies and runaway children, to beggars and cripples—all the riffraff who clutter the boulevards after sundown. There were forty gifts to be given every night, and it never took us more than an hour and a half to finish the job.

PAUL AUSTER, *Moon Palace*, 1989

And Jesus sat over against the treasury, and beheld how the people cast money into the treasury: and many that were rich cast in much.

And there came a certain poor widow, and she threw in two mites, which make a farthing.

And he called unto him his disciples, and saith unto them, Verily I say unto you, That this poor widow hath cast more in, than all they which have cast into the treasury:

For all they did cast in of their abundance: but she of her want did cast in all that she had, *even* all her living.

Mark 12: 41–4

So merciless is the tyranny of economic appetites, so prone to self-aggrandisement the empire of economic interests, that a doctrine which confines them to their proper sphere, as the servant, not the master, of civilization, may reasonably be regarded as among the pregnant truisms which are a permanent element in any sane philosophy. Nor is it, perhaps, as clear today as it seemed a century ago, that it has been an unmixed gain to substitute the criterion of economic expediency, so easily interpreted in terms of quantity and mass, for the conception of a rule of life superior to individual desires and temporary exigencies, which was what the mediæval theorist meant by 'natural law.'

When all is said, the fact remains that, on the small scale involved, the problem of moralizing economic life was faced and not abandoned. The experiment may have been impracticable, and almost from the first it was discredited by the notorious corruption of ecclesiastical authorities, who preached renunciation and gave a lesson in greed. But it had in it something of the heroic, and to ignore the nobility of the conception is not less absurd than to idealize its practical results. The best proof of the appeal which the attempt to subordinate economic interests to religion had made is the persistence of the same attempt among reformers, to whom the Pope was anti-Christ and the canon law an abomination, and the horror of decent men when, in the sixteenth century, its breakdown became too obvious to be contested.

R. H. Tawney, *Religion and the Rise of Capitalism*, 1926

I mentioned to Johnson a respectable person of a very strong mind, who had little of that tenderness which is common to human nature; as an instance of which, when I suggested to him that he should invite his son, who had been settled ten years in foreign parts, to come home and pay him a visit, his answer was, 'No, no, let him mind his business.' Johnson. 'I do not agree with him, Sir, in this. Getting money is not all a man's business: to cultivate kindness is a valuable part of the business of life.'

James Boswell, *Life of Samuel Johnson*, 1791, 21 September 1777

It is physically impossible for a well-educated, intellectual, or brave man to make money the chief object of his thoughts; just as it is for him to make his dinner the principal object of them. All healthy people like their dinners, but their dinner is not the main object of their lives. So all healthily-minded people like making money—ought to like it, and to enjoy the sensation of winning it: but the main object of their life is not money; it is something better than money.

JOHN RUSKIN, *The Crown of Wild Olive*, 1866

# Exchange and Mart

The classical scholar George Thomson suggests that writing was first invented to facilitate trade; 'Exchange and Mart' shows some of the ways in which trade has subsequently become a subject of writing, and reviews how writers have imagined the place of money in commerce, in banking and in finance. If the picture of trade which results is not always flattering, it may be for some of the reasons suggested in the general Introduction, or more simply because writers, like aristocrats, are conventionally meant to be snooty about the merchant classes. Harder-headed members of the literati follow Dr Johnson's wisdom, and recognize that literature itself is also partly a trade.

⁓

Where wealth and freedom reign, contentment fails,
And honour sinks where commerce long prevails.

OLIVER GOLDSMITH, 'The Traveller', 1764

COMMERCE, *n*. A kind of transaction in which A plunders from B the goods of C, and for compensation B picks the pocket of D of money belonging to E.

AMBROSE BIERCE, *The Cynic's Word Book*, 1906

Commerce is, in its very essence, *satanic*. Commerce is return of the loan, a loan in which there is the understanding: *give me more than I give you.*
The spirit of every business-man is completely depraved.

Commerce is *natural*, therefore *shameful*.

The least vile of all merchants is he who says: 'Let us be virtuous, since, thus, we shall gain much more money than the fools who are dishonest'.

For the merchant, even honesty is a financial speculation.

Commerce is satanic, because it is the basest and vilest form of egoism.

CHARLES BAUDELAIRE (1821–67), *Intimate Journals*, tr. Christopher Isherwood, 1930

If we imagine an ancient road at dusk, a road passing through no-man's-land and connecting two towns but itself neither here nor there, we will begin to imagine the ancient Hermes, for he is the God of the Roads, identified not with any home or hearth or mountain but with the traveler on the highway. His name means 'he of the stone heap': a traveler seeking the protection of Hermes would pile rocks into a cairn by the road or erect a herma, a stone pillar with a head on top.

At these roadside altars Hermes assumed his other ancient forms, the God of Commerce and the Protector of Thieves. He wants everything to be on the road: travelers, money, and merchandise. And as his patronage of *both* merchants and thieves shows, the moral tone of an exchange does not concern him. Hermes is an amoral connecting deity. When he's the messenger of the gods he's like the post office: he'll carry love letters, hate letters, stupid letters or smart letters. His concern is the delivery, not what's in the envelope. He wants money to change hands, but he does not distinguish between the just price and a picked pocket. Hermes still appears at a country auction whenever the auctioneer awakens our daydreams of 'making a steal,' that Hermetic mixture of commerce and larceny that cannot fail to loosen the cash. When we come to our senses later, wondering why we bought a cardboard carton full of pan lids, we know that Hermes was the auctioneer.

Hermes is not greedy, however. He likes the clink of coin but he has no hidden pile. Pictures of Hermes usually show him with a little bag of change, just enough to get the trading started. He's no miser asleep on heaps of gold. He loves the fluidity of money, not the weight.

LEWIS HYDE, *The Gift: Imagination and the Erotic Life of Property*, 1979

Foul cankering rust the hidden treasure frets,
But gold that's put to use more gold begets.

WILLIAM SHAKESPEARE, *Venus and Adonis*, 1593

This division of labour, from which so many advantages are derived, is not originally the effect of any human wisdom, which foresees and intends that general opulence to which it gives occasion. It is the necessary, though very slow and gradual consequence of a certain propensity in human nature which has in view no such extensive utility; the propensity to truck, barter, and exchange one thing for another.

Whether this propensity be one of those original principles in human nature, of which no further account can be given; or whether, as seems more probable, it be the necessary consequence of the faculties of reason and speech, it belongs not to our present subject to inquire. It is common to all men, and to be found in no other race of animals, which seem to know neither this nor any other species of contracts. Two greyhounds, in running down the same hare, have sometimes the appearance of acting in some sort of concert. Each turns her towards his companion, or endeavours to intercept her when his companion turns her towards himself. This, however, is not the effect of any contract, but of the accidental concurrence of their passions in the same object at that particular time. Nobody ever saw a dog make a fair and deliberate exchange of one bone for another with another dog. Nobody ever saw one animal by its gestures and natural cries signify to another, this is mine, that yours; I am willing to give this for that.

ADAM SMITH, *The Wealth of Nations*, 1776

'Will anybody buy her?' said the man.

'I wish somebody would,' said she firmly. 'Her present owner is not at all to her liking!'

'Nor you to mine,' said he. 'So we are agreed about that. Gentlemen, you hear? It's an agreement to part. She shall take the girl if she wants to, and go her ways. I'll take my tools, and go my ways. 'Tis simple as Scripture history. Now then, stand up, Susan, and show yourself.'

'Don't, my chiel,' whispered a buxom staylace dealer in voluminous petticoats, who sat near the woman; 'yer good man don't know what he's saying.'

The woman, however, did stand up. 'Now, who's auctioneer?' cried the hay-trusser.

'I be,' promptly answered a short man, with a nose resembling a copper knob, a damp voice, and eyes like button-holes. 'Who'll make an offer for this lady?'

The woman looked on the ground, as if she maintained her position by a supreme effort of will.

'Five shillings,' said some one, at which there was a laugh.

'No insults,' said the husband. 'Who'll say a guinea?'

Nobody answered; and the female dealer in staylaces interposed.

'Behave yerself moral, good man, for Heaven's love! Ah, what a cruelty is the poor soul married to! Bed and board is dear at some figures, 'pon my 'vation 'tis!'

'Set it higher, auctioneer,' said the trusser.

'Two guineas!' said the auctioneer; and no one replied.

'If they don't take her for that, in ten seconds they'll have to give more,' said the husband. 'Very well. Now, auctioneer, add another.'

'Three guineas—going for three guineas!' said the rheumy man.

'No bid?' said the husband. 'Good Lord, why she's cost me fifty times the money, if a penny. Go on.'

'Four guineas!' cried the auctioneer.

'I'll tell ye what—I won't sell her for less than five,' said the husband, bringing down his fist so that the basins danced. 'I'll sell her for five guineas to any man that will pay me the money, and treat her well; and he shall have her for ever, and never hear aught o' me. But she shan't go for less. Now then—five guineas—and she's yours. Susan, you agree?'

She bowed her head with absolute indifference.

'Five guineas,' said the auctioneer, 'or she'll be withdrawn. Do anybody give it? The last time. Yes or no?'

'Yes,' said a loud voice from the doorway.

All eyes were turned. Standing in the triangular opening which formed the door of the tent was a sailor, who, unobserved by the rest, had arrived there within the last two or three minutes. A dead silence followed his affirmation.

'You say you do?' asked the husband, staring at him.

'I say so,' replied the sailor.

'Saying is one thing, and paying is another. Where's the money?'

The sailor hesitated a moment, looked anew at the woman, came in, unfolded five crisp pieces of paper, and threw them down upon the table-cloth. They were Bank-of-England notes for five pounds. Upon the face of this he chinked down the shillings severally—one, two, three, four, five.

The sight of real money in full amount, in answer to a challenge for the same till then deemed slightly hypothetical, had a great effect upon the spectators. Their eyes became riveted upon the faces of the chief actors, and then upon the notes as they lay, weighted by the shillings, on the table.

Up to this moment it could not positively have been asserted that the man, in spite of his tantalizing declaration, was really in earnest. The spectators had indeed taken the proceedings throughout as a piece of mirthful irony carried to extremes; and had assumed that, being out of work, he was, as a consequence, out of temper with the world, and society, and his nearest kin. But with the demand and response of real cash the jovial frivolity of the scene departed. A lurid colour seemed to fill the tent, and change the aspect of all therein. The mirth-wrinkles left the listeners' faces, and they waited with parting lips.

'Now,' said the woman, breaking the silence, so that her low dry voice sounded quite loud, 'before you go further, Michael, listen to me. If you touch that money, I and this girl go with the man. Mind, it is a joke no longer.'

'A joke? Of course it is not a joke!' shouted her husband, his resentment rising at her suggestion. 'I take the money: the sailor takes you. That's plain enough. It has been done elsewhere—and why not here?'

'"Tis quite on the understanding that the young woman is willing,' said the sailor blandly. 'I wouldn't hurt her feelings for the world.'

'Faith, nor I,' said her husband. 'But she is willing, provided she can have the child. She said so only the other day when I talked o't!'

'That you swear?' said the sailor to her.

'I do,' said she, after glancing at her husband's face and seeing no repentance there.

'Very well, she shall have the child, and the bargain's complete,' said the trusser. He took the sailor's notes and deliberately folded them, and put them with the shillings in a high remote pocket, with an air of finality.

The sailor looked at the woman and smiled. 'Come along!' he said kindly. 'The little one too—the more the merrier!' She paused for an instant, with a close glance at him. Then dropping her eyes again, and saying nothing, she took up the child and followed him as he made towards the door. On reaching it, she turned, and pulling off her wedding-ring, flung it across the booth in the hay-trusser's face.

THOMAS HARDY, *The Mayor of Casterbridge*, 1886

As the currency conveys right of choice out of many things in exchange for one, so Commerce is the agency by which the power of choice is obtained; so that countries producing only timber can obtain for their timber silk and gold; or, naturally producing only jewels and frankincense, can obtain for them cattle and corn. In this function, commerce is of more importance to a country in proportion to the limitations of its products, and the restlessness of its fancy;—generally of greater importance towards Northern latitudes.

JOHN RUSKIN, *Munera pulveris*, 1862

Trade in general is built upon, and supported by two essential and principal foundations, viz., Money and Credit. These two essentials maintain and preserve our trade; they are the life and soul of trade, and they are the support of one another too. Money raises Credit, and Credit in its turn is an equivalent to Money.

From hence it follows, that trade always bears a proportion to Money and Credit; and consequently, they who by any methods diminish the stock of cash or Credit, equally injure our trade.

Though it would seem needless to go back to particular cases for the proof of this assertion, yet it may not be amiss to see a little from whence it comes to pass, that our trade is less now the war is over, than it was before it began.

The calling in our coin visibly put a stop to trade, because the stream which drove the mill, the oil that moved the wheel, was ceased. The prodigious Paper-Credit which past in Lombard-Street, and which supply'd more than twice the quantity of the coin, equally supported trade with the Money, and sunk at once with the coin.

DANIEL DEFOE, *The Villainy of Stock-Jobbers Detected*, 1710

Writing was invented to serve the needs of trade. Trade presupposes the exchange of goods between persons engaged in different kinds of labour. These divisions of labour led to others—between mental and manual labour, town and country, rich and poor. All these relations were mediated by money. Without money there could have been no markets or fairs, no accumulation of wealth or leisure, no flowering of the arts and sciences, such as was seen in ancient Greece and again later in Western Europe—in a word, none of the cultural achievements of modern civilisation.

Money began to circulate in Greece as far back as the seventh century BC and came into general use throughout the Roman Empire, but after the collapse of the Empire there was a setback. Long-distance trade was at a standstill. The revival that followed marked the beginning of the capitalist era in Western Europe. There were, however, many outlying or secluded communities whose economic relations remained for a long time confined to the local market. The Blasket was one of these.

Thus, when we describe the Blasket culture as medieval, we mean that it was relatively untouched by the advance of modern industrial society. But, like everything else, civilisation has a double aspect. If the Blasket people were unaffected by its positive aspect, they had no part in its negative aspect either. What is the negative aspect of civilisation?

The circulation of money dissolved the old village communities, based on co-operation and mutual aid, and merged them into larger units in which people confronted one another as buyer and seller, with money as the only bond between them. In the words of an ancient Greek poet, 'man is money'; that is to say, a man is worth the money in his pocket. There was nothing that could not be bought or sold. 'Gold,' wrote Columbus, 'constitutes treasure, and he who possesses it has all the needs in this world as well as the means to rescue souls from purgatory and restore them to the enjoyment of paradise.' Peig Sayers had a quatrain expressing the same idea from the opposite point of view:

> The man without riches is not recognised at the wedding;
> The man without riches speaks and his voice is ignored;
> The man without riches is unable to order or spend;
> The man without riches is a prey to the woes of the world.

*Machnamh Seanmhná*

GEORGE THOMSON, *Island Home*, 1987

There were no shops in Mexico, but the various manufactures and agricultural products were brought together for sale in the great market-places of the principal cities. Fairs were held there every fifth day, and were thronged by a numerous concourse of persons, who came to buy or sell from all the neighbouring country. A particular quarter was allotted to each kind of article. The numerous transactions were conducted without confusion, and with entire regard to justice, under the inspection of magistrates appointed for the purpose. The traffic was carried on partly by barter, and partly by means of a regulated currency, of different values. This consisted of transparent quills of gold dust; of bits of tin, cut in the form of a $\top$; and of bags of cacao, containing a specified number of grains. 'Blessed money,' exclaims Peter Martyr, 'which exempts its possessors from avarice, since it cannot be long hoarded, nor hidden under ground!'

W. H. PRESCOTT, *The History of the Conquest of Mexico*, 1843

They never refuse to give any thing away which is demanded of them, and will even themselves entreat an acceptance of their property. They exhibit a great friendship towards every one, and will give whatever they have for a trifle or nothing at all. I forbade my men to purchase any thing of them with such worthless articles as bits of earthenware, fragments of platters, broken glass, nails, and thongs of leather, although when they got possession of any such thing they valued it as highly as the most precious jewel in the world. In this manner of bartering, a sailor has acquired for a leather strap or piece of rope, gold to the amount of three *sueldos*. Others have obtained as much for a matter of still lower value. For new Spanish coins they would give any thing asked of them, as an ounce and a half or two ounces of gold, or thirty or forty pounds of cotton. Thus they would trade away their cotton and gold like idiots, for broken hoops, platters and glass. I prohibited their traffic on account of its injustice, and made them many presents of useful things which I had carried with me, for the purpose of gaining their affection, in order that they may receive the faith of Jesus Christ, be well disposed towards us, and inclined to submit to the King and Queen our Princes, and all the Spaniards, and furthermore that they may furnish us with the commodities which abound among them and we are in want of.

CHRISTOPHER COLUMBUS to Rafael Sanchez, 14 March 1493

Attention to money is commonplace enough, even in the remotest communities of rural Ireland, but single-minded preoccupation with profit is rare indeed. All farmers must today give some thought to the viability of an undertaking, all are in some degree mastering the ways and wiles of the marketplace, but the large majority assume within their marketing activities a need for community. In the last resort this need is met by a show of goodwill to the man with whom the deal is being effected, a drink in the bar to clinch it, the ancient tradition of giving a penny with every bargain, the very lack of haste—these things are aimed at the obviation of hostility. Behind them lies a concealed assumption that dealing is inimical to friendliness, and therefore to community. The more developed and widespread such practices are, the less ascendant the pure motive of profit; again they are clues to a traditional mentality.

HUGH BRODY, *Inishkillane*, 1973

All the world is becoming commercial. Were it practicable to keep our new empire separated from them, we might indulge ourselves in speculating whether commerce contributes to the happiness of mankind. But we cannot separate ourselves from them. Our citizens have had too full a taste of the comforts furnished by the arts and manufactures to be debarred the use of them. We must, then, in our defence endeavor to share as large a portion as we can of this modern source of wealth and power.

THOMAS JEFFERSON to General Washington, 1784

In fact, the *summum bonum* of this ethic, the earning of more and more money, combined with the strict avoidance of all spontaneous enjoyment of life, is above all completely devoid of any eudæmonistic, not to say hedonistic, admixture. It is thought of so purely as an end in itself, that from the point of view of the happiness of, or utility to, the single individual, it appears entirely transcendental and absolutely irrational. Man is dominated by the making of money, by acquisition as the ultimate purpose of his life. Economic acquisition is no longer subordinated to man as the means for the satisfaction of his material needs. This reversal of what we should call the natural relationship, so irrational from a naïve point of view, is evidently as definitely a leading principle of capitalism as it is foreign to all peoples not under capitalistic influence. At the same time it expresses a type of feeling which is closely connected with certain religious ideas. If we thus ask, *why* should 'money be made out of men', Benjamin Franklin himself, although he was a colourless deist, answers in his autobiography with a quotation from the Bible, which his strict Calvinistic father drummed into him again and again in his youth: 'Seest thou a man diligent in his business? He shall stand before kings' (Prov. xxii. 29). The earning of money within the modern economic order is, so long as it is done legally, the result and the expression of virtue and proficiency in a calling; and this virtue and proficiency are, as it is now not difficult to see, the real Alpha and Omega of Franklin's ethic, as expressed in the passages we have quoted, as well as in all his works without exception.

And in truth this peculiar idea, so familiar to us to-day, but in reality so little a matter of course, of one's duty in a calling, is what is most characteristic of the social ethic of capitalistic culture, and is in a sense the fundamental basis of it.

MAX WEBER, The Protestant Ethic and the Spirit of Capitalism, 1904–5, tr.<br>Talcott Parsons, 1930

Hence commerce springs, the venal interchange
Of all that human art or nature yield;

Which wealth should purchase not, but want demand,
And natural kindness hasten to supply
From the full fountain of its boundless love,
For ever stifled, drained, and tainted now.
Commerce! beneath whose poison-breathing shade
No solitary virtue dares to spring,
But Poverty and Wealth with equal hand
Scatter their withering curses, and unfold
The doors of premature and violent death,
To pining famine and full-fed disease,
To all that shares the lot of human life,
Which poisoned, body and soul, scarce drags the chain,
That lengthens as it goes and clanks behind.

Commerce has set the mark of selfishness,
The signet of its all-enslaving power
Upon a shining ore, and called it gold:
Before whose image bow the vulgar great,
The vainly rich, the miserable proud,
The mob of peasants, nobles, priests, and kings,
And with blind feelings reverence the power
That grinds them to the dust of misery.
But in the temple of their hireling hearts
Gold is a living god, and rules in scorn
All earthly things but virtue.

Since tyrants, by the sale of human life,
Heap luxuries to their sensualism, and fame
To their wide-wasting and insatiate pride,
Success has sanctioned to a credulous world
The ruin, the disgrace, the woe of war.
His hosts of blind and unresisting dupes
The despot numbers; from his cabinet
These puppets of his schemes he moves at will,
Even as the slaves by force or famine driven,
Beneath a vulgar master, to perform
A task of cold and brutal drudgery;—
Hardened to hope, insensible to fear,
Scarce living pulleys of a dead machine,

Mere wheels of work and articles of trade,
That grace the proud and noisy pomp of wealth!

P. B. Shelley, *Queen Mab*, c.1812

There is a shrub in some of the East Indian islands which the French call *veloutier*; it exhales an odour that is agreeable at a distance, becomes less so as you draw nearer, and, when you are quite close to it, is insupportably loathsome. Alciatus himself could not have imagined an emblem more appropriate to the commercial prosperity of England.

Mr —— remarked that nothing could be so beneficial to a country as manufactures. 'You see these children, sir,' said he. 'In most parts of England poor children are a burthen to their parents and to the parish; here the parish, which would else have to support them, is rid of all expense; they get their bread almost as soon as they can run about, and by the time they are seven or eight years old bring in money. There is no idleness among us:—they come at five in the morning; we allow them half an hour for breakfast, and an hour for dinner; they leave work at six, and another set relieves them for the night; the wheels never stand still.' I was looking, while he spoke, at the unnatural dexterity with which the fingers of these little creatures were playing in the machinery, half giddy myself with the noise and the endless motion: and when he told me there was no rest in these walls, day nor night, I thought that if Dante had peopled one of his hells with children, here was a scene worthy to have supplied him with new images of torment.

. . . Mr —— was a man of humane and kindly nature, who would not himself use any thing cruelly, and judged of others by his own feelings. I thought of the cities in Arabian romance, where all the inhabitants were enchanted: here Commerce is the queen witch, and I had no talisman strong enough to disenchant those who were daily drinking of the golden cup of her charms.

Robert Southey, *Letters from England by Don Manuel Alvarez Espriella*, 1807

'But about England and Carthage,' said Tom, shirking the subject of his own peculiarities; 'you don't really think us like them? It gave me a turn to hear you translating "Punica fides" into Brummagem wares just now.'

'I think that successful trade is our rock ahead. The devil who holds new markets and twenty per cent profits in his gift is the devil that England has most to fear from. "Because of unrighteous dealings, and riches gotten by deceit, the kingdom is translated from one people to another," said the wise man. Think of that opium war the other day: I don't believe we can get over many more such businesses as that. Grey falls back on the Church, you see, to save the nation; but the Church he dreams of will never do it. Is there any that can? There *must* be surely, or we have believed a lie. But this work of making trade righteous, of Christianizing trade, looks like the very hardest the Gospel has ever had to take in hand—in England at any rate.'

Hardy spoke slowly and doubtfully, and paused as if asking for Tom's opinion.

'I never heard it put in that way. I know very little of politics or the state of England. But come, now; the putting down the slave-trade and compensating our planters, *that* shows that we are not sold to the trade devil yet, surely.'

'I don't think we are. No, thank God, there are plenty of signs that we are likely to make a good fight of it yet.'

THOMAS HUGHES, *Tom Brown at Oxford*, 1861

|                                                      |                        |
| ---------------------------------------------------- | ---------------------- |
| A Marchant was ther with a forked berd,              |                        |
| In mottelee, and hye on horse he sat,                | *parti-coloured cloth* |
| Up-on his heed a Flaundrish bever hat;               |                        |
| His botes clasped faire and fetisly.                 | *elegantly*            |
| His resons he spak ful solempnely,                   |                        |
| Souninge alway thencrees of his winning.             | *concerned with*       |
| He wolde the see were kept for any thing             | *protected at all costs* |
| Bitwixe Middelburgh and Orewelle.                    |                        |
| Wel coude he in eschaunge sheeldes selle.            |                        |
| This worthy man ful wel his wit bisette;             |                        |
| Ther wiste no wight that he was in dette,            |                        |
| So estatly was he of his governaunce,                |                        |
| With his bargaynes, and with his chevisaunce.        | *financial dealings*   |

GEOFFREY CHAUCER, General Prologue to the *Canterbury Tales*, c.1387–94

Yossarian's mission on the trip was to distract Orr from observing where Milo bought his eggs, even though Orr was a member of Milo's syndicate and, like every other member of Milo's syndicate, owned a share. His mission was silly, Yossarian felt, since it was common knowledge that Milo bought his eggs in Malta for seven cents apiece and sold them to the mess halls in his syndicate for five cents apiece.

'I just don't trust him,' Milo brooded in the plane, with a backward nod toward Orr, who was curled up like a tangled rope on the low bushels of chick-peas, trying torturedly to sleep. 'And I'd just as soon buy my eggs when he's not around to learn my business secrets. What else don't you understand?'

Yossarian was riding beside him in the co-pilot's seat. 'I don't understand why you buy eggs for seven cents apiece in Malta and sell them for five cents.'

'I do it to make a profit.'

'But how can you make a profit? You lose two cents an egg.'

'But I make a profit of three and a quarter cents an egg by selling them for four and a quarter cents an egg to the people in Malta I buy them from for seven cents an egg. Of course, *I* don't make the profit. The syndicate makes the profit. And everybody has a share.'

Yossarian felt he was beginning to understand. 'And the people you sell the eggs to at four and a quarter cents apiece make a profit of two and three quarter cents apiece when they sell them back to you at seven cents apiece. Is that right? Why don't you sell the eggs directly to you and eliminate the people you buy them from?'

'Because I'm the people I buy them from,' Milo explained. 'I make a profit of three and a quarter cents apiece when I sell them to me and a profit of two and three quarter cents apiece when I buy them back from me. That's a total profit of six cents an egg. I lose only two cents an egg when I sell them to the mess halls at five cents apiece, and that's how I can make a profit buying eggs for seven cents apiece and selling them for five cents apiece. I pay only one cent apiece at the hen when I buy them in Sicily.'

'In Malta,' Yossarian corrected. 'You buy your eggs in Malta, not Sicily.'

Milo chortled proudly. 'I don't buy eggs in Malta,' he confessed, with an air of slight and clandestine amusement that was the only departure from industrious sobriety Yossarian had ever seen him make. 'I buy them in Sicily for one cent apiece and transfer them to Malta secretly at four and a half cents apiece in order to get the price of eggs up to seven cents apiece when people come to Malta looking for them.'

'Why do people come to Malta for eggs when they're so expensive there?'

'Because they've always done it that way.'

'Why don't they look for eggs in Sicily?'

'Because they've never done it that way.'

'Now I really don't understand. Why don't you sell your mess halls the eggs for seven cents apiece instead of for five cents apiece?'

'Because my mess halls would have no need for me then. Anyone can buy seven-cents-apiece eggs for seven cents apiece.'

'Why don't they bypass you and buy the eggs directly from you in Malta at four and a quarter cents apiece?'

'Because I wouldn't sell it to them.'

'Why wouldn't you sell it to them?'

'Because then there wouldn't be as much room for a profit. At least this way I can make a bit for myself as a middleman.'

'Then you do make a profit for yourself,' Yossarian declared.

'Of course I do. But it all goes to the syndicate. And everybody has a share. Don't you understand? It's exactly what happens with those plum tomatoes I sell to Colonel Cathcart.'

'*Buy*,' Yossarian corrected him. 'You don't *sell* plum tomatoes to Colonel Cathcart and Colonel Korn. You *buy* plum tomatoes from them.'

'No, *sell*,' Milo corrected Yossarian. 'I distribute my plum tomatoes in markets all over Pianosa under an assumed name so that Colonel Cathcart and Colonel Korn can buy them up from me under their assumed names at four cents apiece and sell them back to me the next day for the syndicate at five cents apiece. They make a profit of one cent apiece, I make a profit of three and a half cents apiece, and everybody comes out ahead.'

'Everybody but the syndicate,' said Yossarian with a snort. 'The syndicate is paying five cents apiece for plum tomatoes that cost you only half a cent apiece. How does the syndicate benefit?'

'The syndicate benefits when I benefit,' Milo explained, 'because everybody has a share. And the syndicate gets Colonel Cathcart's and Colonel Korn's support so that they'll let me go out on trips like this one. You'll see how much profit that can mean in about fifteen minutes when we land in Palermo.'

'Malta,' Yossarian corrected him. 'We're flying to Malta now, not Palermo.'

'No, we're flying to Palermo,' Milo answered. 'There's an endive exporter in Palermo I have to see for a minute about a shipment of mushrooms to Bern that were damaged by mold.'

'Milo, how do you do it?' Yossarian inquired with laughing amazement and admiration. 'You fill out a flight plan for one place and then you go to another. Don't the people in the control towers ever raise hell?'

'They all belong to the syndicate,' Milo said. 'And they know that what's good for the syndicate is good for the country, because that's what makes

Sammy run. The men in the control towers have a share, too, and that's why they always have to do whatever they can to help the syndicate.'

'Do I have a share?'

'Everybody has a share.'

'Does Orr have a share?'

'Everybody has a share.'

'And Hungry Joe? He has a share, too?'

'Everybody has a share.'

'Well, I'll be damned,' mused Yossarian, deeply impressed with the idea of a share for the very first time.

Joseph Heller, Catch-22, 1962

corporation, *n.* An ingenious device for securing individual profit without individual responsibility.

Ambrose Bierce, The Cynic's Word Book, 1906

'In grasping at money and in driving hard bargains—I have begun, and I must speak of such things now, mother—some one may have been grievously deceived, injured, ruined. You were the moving power of all this machinery before my birth; your stronger spirit has been infused into all my father's dealings, for more than two score years. You can set these doubts at rest, I think, if you will really help me to discover the truth. Will you, mother?'

He stopped in the hope that she would speak. But her grey hair was not more immovable in its two folds, than were her firm lips.

'If reparation can be made to any one, if restitution can be made to any one, let us know it and make it. Nay, mother, if within my means, let *me* make it. I have seen so little happiness come of money; it has brought within my knowledge so little peace to this house, or to any one belonging to it; that it is worth less to me than to another. It can buy me nothing that will not be a reproach and misery to me, if I am haunted by a suspicion that it darkened my father's last hours with remorse, and that it is not honestly and justly mine.'

Charles Dickens, Little Dorrit, 1855–7

My good Yorkshire friends, you asked me down here among your hills that I might talk to you about this Exchange you are going to build: but, earnestly and seriously asking you to pardon me, I am going to do nothing of the kind. I cannot talk, or at least can say very little, about this same Exchange. I must talk of quite other things, though not willingly;—I could not deserve your pardon, if, when you invited me to speak on one subject, I *wilfully* spoke on another. But I cannot speak, to purpose, of anything about which I do not care; and most simply and sorrowfully I have to tell you, in the outset, that I do *not* care about this Exchange of yours. . . .

If you chose to take the matter up on any such soldierly principle; to do your commerce, and your feeding of nations, for fixed salaries; and to be as particular about giving people the best food, and the best cloth, as soldiers are about giving them the best gunpowder, I could carve something for you on your exchange worth looking at. But I can only at present suggest decorating its frieze with pendant purses; and making its pillars broad at the base, for the sticking of bills. And in the innermost chambers of it there might be a statue of Britannia of the Market, who may have, perhaps advisably, a partridge for her crest, typical at once of her courage in fighting for noble ideas, and of her interest in game; and round its neck, the inscription in golden letters, 'Perdix fovit quæ non peperit.'* Then, for her spear, she might have a weaver's beam; and on her shield, instead of St George's Cross, the Milanese boar, semi-fleeced, with the town of Gennesaret proper, in the field; and the legend, 'In the best market,' and her corslet, of leather, folded over her heart in the shape of a purse, with thirty slits in it, for a piece of money to go in at, on each day of the month. And I doubt not but that people would come to see your exchange, and its goddess, with applause.

* Jerem. xvii. 11, (best in Septuagint and Vulgate). 'As the partridge, fostering what she brought not forth, so he that getteth riches, not by right, shall leave them in the midst of his days, and at his end shall be a fool.'

JOHN RUSKIN, 'Traffic', a lecture given in Bradford, *The Crown of Wild Olive*, 1866

Publication is the auction
Of the mind of man,
Poverty be justifying
For so foul a thing.

Possibly,—but we would rather
From our garret go
White unto the White Creator,
Than invest our snow.

Thought belongs to Him who gave it—
Then to him who bear
Its corporeal illustration.
Sell the Royal air
In the parcel,—be the merchant
Of the Heavenly Grace,
But reduce no human spirit
To disgrace of price!

EMILY DICKINSON (1830–86)

Literature is a thriving trade. Moxon has just brought me the account of my fifth (popular) edition of 'Faust,' of which he has sold 1,500 copies. I find myself £6. 2s. 7d. out of pocket. He proposes a sixth on the same terms. Best regards to Lady Theresa, and believe me,

Ever most truly yours,
A. HAYWARD.

ABRAHAM HAYWARD to Sir G. C. Lewis, 8 February 1855

People of the same trade seldom meet together, even for merriment and diversion, but the conversation ends in a conspiracy against the public, or in some contrivance to raise prices.

ADAM SMITH, *The Wealth of Nations*, 1776

*The character qualities of merchants are
inferior to those of noblemen and rulers.*

This is because merchants are mostly occupied with buying and selling. This necessarily requires cunning. If a merchant always practices cunning, it becomes his dominant character quality. The quality of cunning is remote from that of manliness which is the characteristic quality of rulers and noblemen.

If the character of (the merchant) then adopts the bad qualities that follow from (cunning) in low-class merchants, such as quarrelsomeness, cheating, defrauding, as well as (the inclination to) commit perjury in rejecting and accepting statements concerning prices, his character can be expected to be one of the lowest sort, for well-known reasons. It is because of the character that one acquires through the practice of commerce that political leaders avoid engaging in it. There are some merchants who are not affected by those character qualities and who are able to avoid them, because they have noble souls and are magnanimous, but they are very rare in this world.

Ibn Khaldūn (*c*.1332–1406) *The Muqaddimah*, tr. Rosenthal, 1958

'I must not hope to be ever situated as you are, in the midst of every dearest connection, and therefore I cannot expect that simply growing older should make me indifferent about letters.'

'Indifferent! Oh no—I never conceived you could become indifferent. Letters are no matter of indifference; they are generally a very positive curse.'

'You are speaking of letters of business; mine are letters of friendship.'

'I have often thought them the worse of the two,' replied he coolly. 'Business, you know, may bring money, but friendship hardly ever does.'

Jane Austen, *Emma*, 1816

It is difficult but not impossible to conduct strictly honest business. The fact is that the honester a business the more successful it is. Hence the proverb coined by businessmen 'Honesty is the best policy'. . . . What is true is that honesty is incompatible with the amassing of a large fortune. 'Verily, verily, it is easier for a camel to go through the eye of a needle than for a rich man to enter into the Kingdom of God.'

M. K. Gandhi, *Non-violence in Peace and War*, ii, 1949

And they come to Jerusalem: and Jesus went into the temple, and began to cast out them that sold and bought in the temple, and overthrew the tables of the moneychangers, and the seats of them that sold doves.

And would not suffer that any man should carry any vessel through the temple.

And he taught, saying unto them, Is it not written, My house shall be called of all nations the house of prayer? but ye have made it a den of thieves.

And the scribes and chief priests heard *it*, and sought how they might destroy him: for they feared him, because all the people was astonished at his doctrine.

Mark 11: 15–18

A man of business may talk of philosophy; a man who has none may practise it.

ALEXANDER POPE, *Thoughts on Various Subjects*, 1727


Philosophers, not all of course, but many, from Aristotle to Carlyle, have decried those engaged in trade and commerce; or rather perhaps I should say Trade and Commerce themselves, as mean and almost degrading. Plato excluded all traders from citizenship in his Republic. Such a degrading occupation was to be left to foreigners, if any chose to engage in it. Trade and Commerce, however, being necessarily the occupations of many, it would indeed be grievous if their influence on the character was necessarily injurious and incompatible with intellectual culture. But happily it is not so. Of course business men can only give their spare time to other pursuits, but, taking illustrations from Science and Literature only, I might mention Nasmyth, the astronomer and manufacturer; Grote, banker and historian; Sir J. Evans, papermaker and President of the Society of Antiquaries, as well as Treasurer of the Royal Society; Prestwich, merchant, and afterwards Professor of Geology at Oxford; Rogers, banker and poet; Praed, banker and poet; may I say my own father, banker and mathematician, for many years Treasurer and Vice-President of the Royal Society; and many others.

SIR JOHN LUBBOCK, 'On Money Matters', *The Use of Life*, 1895


When a nation is running to decay and ruine, the merchant and monied man, do what you can, will be sure to starve last.

JOHN LOCKE, *Some Considerations of the Consequences of the Lowering of Interests and Raising the Value of Money*, 1692


There is observable among the many a false and bastard sensibility that prompts them to remove those evils and those evils alone, which by hideous spectacle or clamorous outcry are present to their senses, and disturb their selfish enjoyments. Other miseries, though equally certain and far more horrible, they not only do not endeavour to remedy—they support, they fatten on them. Provided the dunghill be not before their parlour window, they are well content to know that it exists, and that it is the hotbed of their pestilent luxuries.—To this grievous failing we must attribute the frequency of wars, and the continuance of the Slave-trade. The merchant finds no argument against it in his ledger: the citizen at the crowded feast is not nauseated by the stench and filth of the slave-vessel—the fine lady's nerves are not shattered by the shrieks! She sips a beverage sweetened with human blood, even while she is weeping over the refined sorrows of Werter or of Clementina.

S. T. COLERIDGE, 'On the Slave Trade', 25 March 1796

And there was no bread in all the land; for the famine was very sore, so that the land of Egypt and all the land of Canaan fainted by reason of the famine.

And Joseph gathered up all the money that was found in the land of Egypt, and in the land of Canaan, for the corn which they bought: and Joseph brought the money into Pharaoh's house.

And when money failed in the land of Egypt, and in the land of Canaan, all the Egyptians came unto Joseph, and said, Give us bread: for why should we die in thy presence? for the money faileth.

And Joseph said, Give your cattle: and I will give you for your cattle, if money fail.

And they brought their cattle unto Joseph: and Joseph gave them bread *in exchange* for horses, and for the flocks, and for the cattle of the herds, and for the asses, and he fed them with bread for all their cattle for that year.

When that year was ended, they came unto him the second year, and said unto him, We will not hide it from my lord, how that our money is spent, my lord also hath our herds of cattle: there is not ought left in the sight of my lord, but our bodies, and our lands.

Wherefore shall we die before thine eyes, both we and our land? buy us and our land for bread, and we and our land will be servants unto Pharaoh: and give *us* seed that we may live and not die, that the land be not desolate.

And Joseph bought all the land of Egypt for Pharaoh: for the Egyptians sold every man his field, because the famine prevailed over them: so the land became Pharaoh's.

Genesis 47: 13–20

Father Purdon knelt down, turned towards the red speck of light and, covering his face with his hands, prayed. After an interval, he uncovered his face and rose. The congregation rose also and settled again on its benches.

Mr Kernan restored his hat to its original position on his knee and presented an attentive face to the preacher. The preacher turned back each wide sleeve of his surplice with an elaborate large gesture and slowly surveyed the array of faces. Then he said:

'For the children of this world are wiser in their generation than the children of light. Wherefore make unto yourselves friends out of the mammon of iniquity so that when you die they may receive you into everlasting dwellings.'

Father Purdon developed the text with resonant assurance. It was one of the most difficult texts in all the Scriptures, he said, to interpret properly. It was a text which might seem to the casual observer at variance with the lofty morality elsewhere preached by Jesus Christ. But, he told his hearers, the text had seemed to him specially adapted for the guidance of those whose lot it was to lead the life of the world and who yet wished to lead that life not in the manner of worldlings. It was a text for business men and professional men. Jesus Christ, with His divine understanding of every cranny of our human nature, understood that all men were not called to the religious life, that by far the vast majority were forced to live in the world, and, to a certain extent, for the world: and in this sentence He designed to give them a word of counsel, setting before them as exemplars in the religious life those very worshippers of Mammon who were of all men the least solicitous in matters religious.

JAMES JOYCE, 'Grace', *Dubliners*, 1914

The only absolutely and unapproachably heroic element in the soldier's work seems to be—that he is paid little for it—and regularly: while you traffickers, and exchangers, and others occupied in presumably benevolent business, like to be paid much for it—and by chance. I never can make out how it is that a *knight*-errant does not expect to be paid for his trouble, but a *pedlar*-errant always does;—that people are willing to take hard knocks for nothing, but never to sell ribands cheap; that they are ready to go on fervent crusades, to recover the tomb of a buried God, but never on any travels to fulfil the orders of a living one;—that they will go anywhere barefoot to preach their faith, but must be well bribed to practise it, and are perfectly ready to give the Gospel gratis, but never the loaves and fishes.

JOHN RUSKIN, *The Crown of Wild Olive*, 1866

You may imagine that I am anxious to have the Peace, and to see Mr Conway safe in England. I wish it privately and publicly—I pray for an end to the woes of mankind; in one word, I have no public spirit, and don't care a farthing for the interests of the merchants. Soldiers and sailors who are knocked on the head, and peasants plundered or butchered, are to my eyes as valuable as a lazy luxurious set of men, who hire others to acquire riches for them; who would embroil all the earth, that they may heap or squander; and I *dare* to say this, for I am no minister. Beckford is a patriot, because he will clamour if Guadaloupe or Martinico is given up, and the price of sugars falls. I am a bad Englishman, because I think the advantages of commerce are dearly bought for some by the lives of many more. This wise age counts its merchants, and reckons its armies ciphers. But why do I talk of this age?—every age has some ostentatious system to excuse the havoc it commits. Conquest, honour, chivalry, religion, balance of power, commerce, no matter what, mankind must bleed, and take a term for a reason. 'Tis shocking! Good night.

HORACE WALPOLE to Sir Horace Mann, 26 May 1762, *Letters*

Before inflation, they used to say of Hollywood, 'There's nothing as scared as a million dollars.' After all, movie-making is the process of turning money into light. All they have at the end of the day is images flickering on a wall.

JOHN BOORMAN, *Money into Light*, 1985

National Power and Wealth consists in numbers of People, and Magazines of Home and Forreign Goods. These depend on Trade, and Trade depends on Money. So to be Powerful and Wealthy in proportion to other Nations, we should have Money in proportion with them; for the best Laws without Money cannot employ the People, Improve the Product, or advance Manufacture and Trade.

JOHN LAW, *Money and Trade Considered*, 1705

Christie Malry was a simple person.

It did not take him long to realise that he had not been born into money; that he would therefore have to acquire it as best he could; that there were unpleasant (and to him unacceptable) penalties for acquiring it by those methods considered to be criminal by society; that there were other methods not (somewhat arbitrarily) considered criminal by society; and that the course most likely to benefit him would be to place himself next to the money, or at least next to those who were making it. He therefore decided that he should become a bank employee.

I did tell you Christie was a simple person.

                                                      B. S. JOHNSON, *Christie Malry's Own Double-Entry*, 1973

## BANKERS ARE JUST LIKE ANYBODY ELSE,
## EXCEPT RICHER

This is a song to celebrate banks,

Because they are full of money and you go into them and all you
    hear is clinks and clanks,

Or maybe a sound like the wind in the trees on the hills,

Which is the rustling of the thousand-dollar bills.

Most bankers dwell in marble halls,

Which they get to dwell in because they encourage deposits and dis-
    courage withdralls,

And particularly because they all observe one rule which woe betide
    the banker who fails to heed it,

Which is you must never lend any money to anybody unless they
    don't need it.

O you cautious conservative banks, what I know about you!

If people are worried about their rent it is your duty to deny them
    the loan of one Confederate sou;

But suppose people come in and they have a million and they want
    another million to pile on top of it,

Why, you brim with the milk of human kindness and you urge them
    to accept every drop of it,

And you lend them the million so then they have two million and
    this gives them the idea that they would be better off with four.

So they already have two million as security so you have no hesita-
    tion in lending them two more,

And all the vice-presidents nod their heads in rhythm,

And the only question asked is Do the borrowers want the money
    sent or do they want to take it withm?

But please do not think that I am not fond of banks,

Because I think they deserve our appreciation and thanks,

Because they perform a valuable public service in eliminating the jack-

asses who go around saying that health and happiness are everything and money isn't essential.
Because as soon as they have to borrow some unimportant money to
maintain their health and happiness they starve to death so they
can't go around any more sneering at good old money, which is
nothing short of providential.

OGDEN NASH, *The Face is Familiar*, 1954

Of all institutions in the world the Bank of England is now probably the
most remote from party politics and from 'financing.' But in its origin it
was not only a finance company, but a Whig finance company. It was
founded by a Whig Government because it was in desperate want of money,
and supported by the 'City' because the 'City' was Whig. Very briefly, the
story was this. The Government of Charles II. (under the Cabal Ministry)
had brought the credit of the English State to the lowest possible point. It
had perpetrated one of those monstrous frauds which are likewise gross
blunders. The goldsmiths, who then carried on upon a trifling scale what
we should now call banking, used to deposit their reserve of treasure in the
'Exchequer,' with the sanction and under the care of the Government. In
many European countries the credit of the State had been so much better
than any other credit, that it had been used to strengthen the beginnings of
banking. The credit of the State had been so used in England: though there
had lately been a civil war and several revolutions, the honesty of the
English Government was trusted implicitly. But Charles II. showed that it
was trusted undeservedly. He shut up the 'Exchequer,' would pay no one,
and so the 'goldsmiths' were ruined.

The credit of the Stuart Government never recovered from this monstrous robbery, and the Government created by the Revolution of 1688
could hardly expect to be more trusted with money than its predecessor. A
Government created by a revolution hardly ever is. There is a taint of
violence which capitalists dread instinctively, and there is always a rational
apprehension that the Government which one revolution thought fit to set
up another revolution may think fit to pull down. In 1694, the credit of
William III.'s Government was so low in London that it was impossible for
it to borrow any large sum; and the evil was the greater, because in consequence of the French war the financial straits of the Government were
extreme. At last a scheme was hit upon which would relieve their necessities. 'The plan,' says Macaulay, 'was that twelve hundred thousand pounds
should be raised at what was then considered as the moderate rate of 8 per

cent.' In order to induce the subscribers to advance the money promptly on terms so unfavourable to the public, the subscribers were to be incorporated by the name of the Governor and Company of the Bank of England. They were so incorporated, and the 1,200,000*l.* was obtained.

On many succeeding occasions, their credit was of essential use to the Government. Without their aid, our National Debt could not have been borrowed; and if we had not been able to raise that money we should have been conquered by France and compelled to take back James II. And for many years afterwards the existence of that debt was a main reason why the industrial classes never would think of recalling the Pretender, or of upsetting the revolution settlement. The 'fund-holder' is always considered in the books of that time as opposed to his 'legitimate' sovereign, because it was to be feared that this sovereign would repudiate the debt which was raised by those who dethroned him, and which was spent in resisting him and his allies. For a long time the Bank of England was the focus of London Liberalism, and in that capacity rendered to the State inestimable services.

WALTER BAGEHOT, *Lombard Street: A Description of the Money Market*, 1873

The Myles na gCopaleen Banking Corporation is experimenting with a new kind of cheque book. The whole thing would be laughable were it not so tragic. Each cheque looks perfectly ordinary, but when it is drawn, cashed and returned to the Bank, strange things happen behind closed doors. The Bank's officials get to work on it, and if you could only see them at it, you would observe that each cheque is in reality two cheques cleverly stuck together and separated by a sheet of fine carbon. Thus, when you draw a cheque in favour of 'Self' for ten pounds, you get that much money, but the Bank gets *two* cheques for ten pounds. Furthermore, since the genuine endorsement is on the back of the second cheque and the drawer's genuine hand-writing on the face of the first, both can readily be established, in a court of law or elsewhere, to be genuine documents, notwithstanding any minor pretexts for suspicion; it is a simple matter to forge a colourable endorsement on the back of the 'genuine' top cheque.

All this means, of course, that our clients are unwittingly spending their substance twice as fast as they think they are and qualifying speedily for a permanent abode in that populous thoroughfare, Queer St. And the Bank gets more and more dough.

I will tell you a good one. It was tried on us recently at the Myles na gCopaleen Central Banking Corporation (all stand and uncover, please), and we were not the slowest to learn our lesson and take the recipe for our very own. It is a new dodge and one that will save you hundreds of pounds a year if it is used intelligently. Cross that out and say thousands. It is a secret weapon that will close the doors of our fancy competitors in College Green if you see fit to use it against them. (And why shouldn't you, pray, what about the £31 10. 0, is that forgotten already?)

It is a new sort of ink. It looks no different from the sort you use every day. It is blue-black, bright, thin, clean, and runs like sweet fancy through your fountain pen. It has this great virtue, though. *Six hours after you write something with it, the writing has completely disappeared.* The paper is again restored to its virgin white. Not a speck of 'ink' remains. Just think about that for a minute.

FLANN O'BRIEN (Myles na Gopaleen 1911–66), *The Best of Myles*, 1968

## THE RUN UPON THE BANKERS

The bold encroachers on the deep
   Gain by degrees huge tracts of land,
Till Neptune, with one general sweep,
   Turns all again to barren strand.

The multitude's capricious pranks
   Are said to represent the seas,
Breaking the bankers and the banks,
   Resume their own whene'er they please.

Money, the life-blood of the nation,
   Corrupts and stagnates in the veins,
Unless a proper circulation
   Its motion and its heat maintains.

Because 'tis lordly not to pay,
   Quakers and aldermen in state,
Like peers, have levees every day
   Of duns attending at their gate.

We want our money on the nail;
   The banker 's ruin'd if he pays:
They seem to act an ancient tale;
   The birds are met to strip the jays.

'Riches,' the wisest monarch sings,
   'Make pinions for themselves to fly;'
They fly like bats on parchment wings,
   And geese their silver plumes supply.

No money left for squandering heirs!
   Bills turn the lenders into debtors:
The wish of Nero now is theirs,
   'That they had never known their letters.'

Conceive the works of midnight hags,
   Tormenting fools behind their backs:
Thus bankers, o'er their bills and bags,
   Sit squeezing images of wax.

Conceive the whole enchantment broke;
   The witches left in open air,
With power no more than other folk,
   Exposed with all their magic ware.

So powerful are a banker's bills,
   Where creditors demand their due;
They break up counters, doors, and tills,
   And leave the empty chests in view.

Thus when an earthquake lets in light
   Upon the god of gold and hell,
Unable to endure the sight,
   He hides within his darkest cell.

As when a conjurer takes a lease
   From Satan for a term of years,
The tenant 's in a dismal case,
   Whene'er the bloody bond appears.

A baited banker thus desponds,
   From his own hand foresees his fall,
They have his soul, who have his bonds;
   'Tis like the writing on the wall.

How will the caitiff wretch be scared,
   When first he finds himself awake
At the last trumpet, unprepared,
   And all his grand account to make!

For in that universal call,
   Few bankers will to heaven be mounters;
They'll cry, 'Ye shops, upon us fall!
   Conceal and cover us, ye counters!'

When other hands the scales shall hold,
   And they, in men's and angels' sight
Produced with all their bills and gold,
   'Weigh'd in the balance and found light!'

JONATHAN SWIFT, 1720; Poems, 1735

INT. OUTER OFFICE BUILDING AND LOAN—NIGHT

CLOSE SHOT—GEORGE, UNCLE BILLY *and* COUSIN TILLY *are behind the counter,
watching the minute hand of a clock on the wall as* GEORGE *counts off the
seconds.* COUSIN EUSTACE *is ready to close the door.*

UNCLE BILLY [*excitedly*]. We're going to make it, George. They'll never close
us up today!

GEORGE [*counting*]. Six . . . five . . . four . . . three . . . two . . . one . . . Bingo!

COUSIN EUSTACE *slams and locks the door, and scurries around the counter to
join the others.*

GEORGE [*cont'd*]. We made it! Look . . . [*holds up bills*] . . . look, we're still in
business! We've still got two bucks left!

[UNCLE BILLY *is taking a drink out of his bottle.*]

GEORGE [*cont'd*]. Well, let's have some of that. Get some glasses, Cousin
Tilly. [*to* UNCLE BILLY] We're a couple of financial wizards.

UNCLE BILLY. Those Rockefellers!

GEORGE. Get a tray for these great big important simoleons.

UNCLE BILLY. We'll save them for seed. A toast!

[*They raise their glasses*]

GEORGE. A toast! A toast to Papa Dollar and to Mama Dollar, and if you
want the old Building and Loan to stay in business, you better have a
family real quick.

COUSIN TILLY. I wish they were rabbits.

GEORGE. I wish they were too. Okay, let's put them in the safe and see what happens.

*The four of them parade through the office;* GEORGE *puts the two dollars in the safe.*

ALBERT HACKETT, FRANCES GOODRICH, and FRANK CAPRA, *It's a Wonderful Life,* final script as shot: 4 March 1947

## WEATHERING

Gorging on the pointed brick
—Spaces fattening plenteous time—
Seasons picnic stretched full length.
Rains are spreading capes.

The years are crumbling vivid stone
Revetment with their feet.
Why roseate? The Bank dome hoards
All poaching thrusting fingers.

The figures of the balance show
Rich deposits, swollen greed;
While the hours are nosing paint
Silently as fungi feed.

ADRIAN STOKES, *With All the Views: Collected Poems,* 1981

Business was by no means Leigh Hunt's strong point. In this respect, but not otherwise, he may have suggested Skimpole to Charles Dickens. On one of my visits I found him trying to puzzle out the abstruse question of how he should deduct some such sum as thirteen shillings and ninepence from a sovereign. On another occasion I had to pay him a sum of money, 100*l*. or 200*l*., and I wrote him a cheque for the amount. 'Well,' he said, 'what am I to do with this little bit of paper?' I told him that if he presented it at the bank they would pay him cash for it, but I added, 'I will save you that trouble.' I sent to the bank and cashed the cheque for him. He took the notes away carefully enclosed in an envelope. Two days afterwards Leigh Hunt came in a state of great agitation to tell me that his wife had burned them. He had thrown the envelope with the bank-notes inside carelessly down and his wife had flung it into the fire. Leigh Hunt's agitation while on his way to bring this news had not prevented him from purchasing on the road a little statuette of Psyche which he carried, without any paper round it, in his hand. I told him I thought something might be done in the matter; I sent to the bankers and got the numbers of the notes, and then in company with Leigh Hunt went off to the Bank of England. I explained our business and we were shown into a room where three old gentlemen were sitting at tables. They kept us waiting some time, and Leigh Hunt, who had meantime been staring all round the room, at last got up, walked up to one of the staid officials, and addressing him said in wondering tones, 'And this is the Bank of England! And do you sit here all day, and never see the green woods and the trees and flowers and the charming country?' Then in tones of remonstrance he demanded, 'Are you contented with such a life?' All this time he was holding the little naked Psyche in one hand, and with his long hair and flashing eyes made a surprising figure. I fancy I can still see the astonished faces of the three officials; they would have made a most delightful picture. I said, 'Come away, Mr Hunt, these gentlemen are very busy.' I succeeded in carrying Leigh Hunt off, and after entering into certain formalities, we were told that the value of the notes would be paid in twelve months. I gave Leigh Hunt the money at once, and he went away rejoicing.

GEORGE M. SMITH, 'In the Early Forties', *Cornhill Magazine*, November 1900

Now I had already collected that the mercantile affairs of the Erewhonians were conducted on a totally different system from our own; I had, however, gathered little hitherto, except that they had two distinct commercial systems, of which the one appealed more strongly to the imagination than anything to which we are accustomed in Europe, inasmuch as the banks that were conducted upon this system were decorated in the most profuse fashion, and all mercantile transactions were accompanied with music, so that they were called Musical Banks, though the music was hideous to a European ear.

As for the system itself I never understood it, neither can I do so now: they have a code in connection with it, which I have not the slightest doubt that they understand, but no foreigner can hope to do so. One rule runs into, and against, another as in a most complicated grammar, or as in Chinese pronunciation, wherein I am told that the slightest change in accentuation or tone of voice alters the meaning of a whole sentence. Whatever is incoherent in my description must be referred to the fact of my never having attained to a full comprehension of the subject.

So far, however, as I could collect anything certain, I gathered that they have two distinct currencies, each under the control of its own banks and mercantile codes. One of these (the one with the Musical Banks) was supposed to be *the* system, and to give out the currency in which all monetary transactions should be carried on; and as far as I could see, all who wished to be considered respectable kept a larger or smaller balance at these banks. On the other hand, if there is one thing of which I am more sure than another, it is that the amount so kept had no direct commercial value in the outside world; I am sure that the managers and cashiers of the Musical Banks were not paid in their own currency. Mr Nosnibor used to go to these banks, or rather, to the great mother bank of the city, sometimes, but not very often. He was a pillar of one of the other kind of banks, though he appeared to hold some minor office also in the musical ones. The ladies generally went alone; as indeed was the case in most families, except on state occasions.

SAMUEL BUTLER, Erewhon; or, Over the Range, 1872

'Well, are you rich?'

'No, but I been rich wunst, and gwyne to be rich agin. Wunst I had foteen dollars, but I tuck to speculat'n', en got busted out.'

'What did you speculate in, Jim?'

'Well, fust I tackled stock.'

'What kind of stock?'

'Why, live stock. Cattle, you know. I put ten dollars in a cow. But I ain' gwyne to resk no mo' money in stock. De cow up 'n' died on my han's.'

'So you lost the ten dollars.'

'No, I didn' lose it all. I on'y los' 'bout nine of it. I sole de hide en taller for a dollar en ten cents.'

'You had five dollars and ten cents left. Did you speculate any more?'

'Yes. You know dat one-laigged nigger dat b'longs to old Misto Bradish? Well, he sot up a bank, en say anybody dat put in a dollar would git fo' dollars mo' at de en' er de year. Well, all de niggers went in, but dey didn' have much. I wuz de on'y one dat had much. So I stuck out for mo' dan fo' dollars, en I said 'f I didn' git it I'd start a bank mysef. Well, o' course dat nigger want' to keep me out er de business, bekase he say dey warn't business 'nough for two banks, so he say I could put in my five dollars en he pay me thirty-five at de en' er de year.

'So I done it. Den I reck'n'd I'd inves' de thirty-five dollars right off en keep things a-movin'. Dey wuz a nigger name' Bob, dat had ketched a

wood-flat, en his marster didn' know it; en I bought it off'n him en told him
to take de thirty-five dollars when de en' er de year come; but somebody
stole de wood-flat dat night, en nex' day de one-laigged nigger say de bank's
busted. So dey didn' none uv us git no money.'

'What did you do with the ten cents, Jim?'

'Well, I wuz gwyne to spen' it, but I had a dream, en de dream tole me
to give it to a nigger name' Balum—Balum's Ass dey call him for short, he's
one er dem chuckle-heads, you know. But he's lucky, dey say, en I see I
warn't lucky. De dream say let Balum inves' de ten cents en he'd make a
raise for me. Well, Balum he tuck de money, en when he wuz in church
he hear de preacher say dat whoever give to de po' len' to de Lord, en
boun' to git his money back a hund'd times. So Balum he tuck en give de
ten cents to de po', en laid low to see what wuz gwyne to come of it.'

'Well, what did come of it, Jim?'

'Nuffn' never come of it. I couldn' manage to k'leck dat money no way;
en Balum he couldn'. I ain't gwyne to len' no mo' money 'dout I see de
security. Boun' to git yo' money back a hund'd times, de preacher says!
Ef I could git de ten *cents* back, I'd call it squah, en be glad er de chanst.'

'Well, it's all right, anyway, Jim, long as you're going to be rich again
some time or other.'

'Yes—en I's rich now, come to look at it. I owns myself, en I's wuth
eight hund'd dollars. I wisht I had de money, I wouldn' want no mo'.'

MARK TWAIN, *The Adventures of Huckleberry Finn*, 1884


'As I've told you before, he was a clerk in a bank, like thousands of others.
He got that berth as a second start in life and there he stuck again, giving
perfect satisfaction. Then one day as though a supernatural voice had
whispered into his ear or some invisible fly had stung him, he put on his
hat, went out into the street and began advertising. That's absolutely all
that there was to it. He caught in the street the word of the time and
harnessed it to his preposterous chariot.

One remembers his first modest advertisements headed with the magic
word Thrift, Thrift, Thrift, thrice repeated; promising ten per cent. on all
deposits and giving the address of the Thrift and Independence Aid Association in Vauxhall Bridge Road. Apparently nothing more was necessary.
He didn't even explain what he meant to do with the money he asked the
public to pour into his lap. Of course he meant to lend it out at high rates
of interest. He did so—but he did it without system, plan, foresight or
judgment. And as he frittered away the sums that flowed in, he advertised

for more—and got it. During a period of general business prosperity he set up The Orb Bank and The Sceptre Trust, simply, it seems for advertising purposes. They were mere names. He was totally unable to organize anything, to promote any sort of enterprise if it were only for the purpose of juggling with the shares. At that time he could have had for the asking any number of Dukes, retired Generals, active M.P.'s, ex-ambassadors and so on as Directors to sit at the wildest boards of his invention. But he never tried. He had no real imagination. All he could do was to publish more advertisements and open more branch offices of the Thrift and Independence, of The Orb, of The Sceptre, for the receipt of deposits; first in this town, then in that town, north and south—everywhere where he could find suitable premises at a moderate rent. For this was the great characteristic of the management. Modesty, moderation, simplicity. Neither The Orb nor The Sceptre nor yet their parent the Thrift and Independence had built for themselves the usual palaces. For this abstention they were praised in silly public prints as illustrating in their management the principle of Thrift for which they were founded. The fact is that de Barral simply didn't think of it. Of course he had soon moved from Vauxhall Bridge Road. He knew enough for that. What he got hold of next was an old, enormous, rat-infested brick house in a small street off the Strand. Strangers were taken in front of the meanest possible, begrimed, yellowy, flat brick wall, with two rows of unadorned window-holes one above the other, and were exhorted with bated breath to behold and admire the simplicity of the head-quarters of the great financial force of the day. The word THRIFT perched right up on the roof in giant gilt letters, and two enormous shield-like brass-plates curved round the corners on each side of the doorway were the only shining spots in de Barral's business outfit. Nobody knew what operations were carried on inside except this—that if you walked in and tendered your money over the counter it would be calmly taken from you by somebody who would give you a printed receipt. That and no more. It appears that such knowledge is irresistible. People went in and tendered; and once it was taken from their hands their money was more irretrievably gone from them than if they had thrown it into the sea. This then, and nothing else was being carried on in there . . .'

'Come, Marlow,' I said, 'you exaggerate surely—if only by your way of putting things. It's too startling.'

'I exaggerate!' he defended himself. 'My way of putting things! My dear fellow I have merely stripped the rags of business verbiage and financial jargon off my statements. And you are startled! I am giving you the naked truth. It's true too that nothing lays itself open to the charge of exaggeration more than the language of naked truth. What comes with a shock is admitted with difficulty. But what will you say to the end of his career?'

JOSEPH CONRAD, *Chance*, 1914

Mr Merdle was immensely rich; a man of prodigious enterprise; a Midas without the ears, who turned all he touched to gold. He was in everything good, from banking to building. He was in Parliament, of course. He was in the City, necessarily. He was Chairman of this, Trustee of that, President of the other. The weightiest of men had said to projectors, 'Now, what name have you got? Have you got Merdle?' And, the reply being in the negative, had said 'Then I won't look at you.'

This great and fortunate man had provided that extensive bosom, which required so much room to be unfeeling enough in, with a nest of crimson and gold some fifteen years before. It was not a bosom to repose upon, but it was a capital bosom to hang jewels upon. Mr Merdle wanted something to hang jewels upon, and he bought it for the purpose. Storr and Mortimer might have married on the same speculation.

Like all his other speculations, it was sound and successful. The jewels showed to the richest advantage. The bosom moving in Society with the jewels displayed upon it, attracted general admiration. Society approving, Mr Merdle was satisfied. He was the most disinterested of men,—did everything for Society, and got as little for himself out of all his gain and care, as a man might.

That is to say, it may be supposed that he got all he wanted, otherwise with unlimited wealth he would have got it. But his desire was to the utmost to satisfy Society (whatever that was), and take up all its drafts upon him for tribute. He did not shine in company; he had not very much to say for himself; he was a reserved man, with a broad, overhanging, watchful head, that particular kind of dull red colour in his cheeks which is rather stale than fresh, and a somewhat uneasy expression about his coat-cuffs, as if they were in his confidence, and had reasons for being anxious to hide his hands. In the little he said, he was a pleasant man enough; plain, emphatic about public and private confidence, and tenacious of the utmost deference being shown by every one, in all things, to Society. In this same Society (if that were it which came to his dinners, and to Mrs Merdle's receptions and concerts), he hardly seemed to enjoy himself much, and was mostly to be found against walls and behind doors. Also when he went out to it, instead of its coming home to him, he seemed a little fatigued, and upon the whole rather more disposed for bed; but he was always cultivating it nevertheless, and always moving in it, and always laying out money on it with the greatest liberality.

CHARLES DICKENS, *Little Dorrit*, 1855–7

The shopping center where the Penn Square Bank lived and died is about twenty minutes northwest of downtown and it sits a literal stone's throw from Route 66, very centrally located on the North American continent. It opened in 1960, the first satellite shopping center of its kind in Oklahoma City. Twenty-one years later, after a major renovation, it became an enclosed air-conditioned mall. When you cruise through one of those places you can easily fancy that you are comfortably outdoors, although climate-controlled shopping malls are not mentioned in the Bible and therefore, in the eyes of God, you are perhaps nowhere at all—just like downtown. This, for the sake of history, happens to matter. The Penn Square Bank did not vanish without a trace. Its fall resonated, with grotesque consequences. The largest bank in the Pacific Northwest, Seattle-First National Bank, turned to ash, courtesy of Penn Square. Then the Continental Illinois National Bank & Trust Company, of Chicago—an institution that had lent more money to American business and industry than any other bank in the country— found itself so deep in the turbid backwash of Penn Square that only a multibillion-dollar government-sponsored rescue was able to prevent its failure. Defending this extreme intervention, federal banking regulators argued that neglecting to save Continental Illinois would lead to the demise of dozens and perhaps hundreds of other banks.

Not since the Depression had there occurred a banking event so bizarre or so unsettling. Bad fantasies loomed within easy traveling distance. What if first the Penn Square Bank folded, followed closely by the largest banks in the Pacific Northwest and the Midwest, and what if those failures were followed by the failures of the industrial economies of, say, Mexico and Argentina? What if Western capitalism took a dive? What if a global economic apocalypse started in an enclosed air-conditioned mall in Oklahoma City—out there in the company of the Stout Shoppe and the Peanut Shack and the video arcade and the gift store where for $12.95 you got a room freshener disguised as a porcelain duck? Exercising your imagination with that bad fantasy, you could be excused for thinking that the Penn Square Bank seemed like a peculiar first domino.

MARK SINGER, *Funny Money*, 1985

## THE SPECULATORS

The night was stormy and dark,   The town was shut up in sleep:   Only those were abroad who were out on a lark,   Or those who'd no beds to keep.

I pass'd through the lonely street,   The wind did sing and blow;   I could hear the policeman's feet   Clapping to and fro.

There stood a potato-man   In the midst of all the wet;   He stood with his 'tato-can   In the lonely Haymarket.

Two gents of dismal mien,   And dank and greasy rags,   Came out of a shop for gin,   Swaggering over the flags:

Swaggering over the stones,   These shabby bucks did walk;   And I went and followed those seedy ones,   And listened to their talk.

Was I sober or awake?   Could I believe my ears?   Those dismal beggars spake   Of nothing but railroad shares.

I wondered more and more:   Says one—'Good friend of mine,   How many shares have you wrote for?   In the Diddlesex Junction line?'

'I wrote for twenty,' says Jim,   'But they wouldn't give me one;'   His comrade straight rebuked him   For the folly he had done:

'O Jim, you are unawares   Of the ways of this bad town;   *I* always write for five hundred shares,   And *then* they put me down.'

'And yet you got no shares,'   Says Jim, 'for all your boast;'   'I *would* have wrote,' says Jack, 'but where   Was the penny to pay the post?'

'I lost, for I couldn't pay   That first instalment up;   But here's taters smoking hot—I say   Let's stop my boy and sup.'

And at this simple feast   The while they did regale,   I drew each ragged capitalist   Down on my left thumb-nail.

Their talk did me perplex,   All night I tumbled and tost,   And thought of railroad specs.,   And how money was won and lost.

'Bless railroads everywhere,'   I said, 'and the world's advance;   Bless
every railroad share   In Italy, Ireland, France;   For never a beggar need
now despair,   And every rogue has a chance.'

W. M. THACKERAY, *Miscellanies; Prose and Verse*, 1855


Dear Monsieur Léon,
   . . . I've sold my Rios below the high prices they had reached, but I feel
it's a healthy thing not always to sell 'at the top' for then one risks
waiting . . . for the bottom!
   I've been told about a bank with splendid prospects which has just been
founded by an Englishman, very well known it seems, called Cassel. The
name of the bank begins with something I can't remember and ends I think
with Egyptian Bank. The remote possibility of procuring me some shares
in it was held out to me as a chance I ought to bless. But I'm not at all sure
about it and I don't know whether I ought to want it to happen.
   When I heard that the New York City Bonds were at $102\frac{1}{8}$ I hesitated to
buy them. But I didn't dare write to you again and I bought them since it's
a good investment and after all fairly remunerative.
   As I was telling you about the frivolities (*confidentially!*) of the Maison
Guastalla I couldn't help laughing rather sadly: my poor parents were convinced that I would always be incapable of reading a business letter or
taking the slightest interest in money matters. I know it was a real source
of anxiety to them. And I think with sadness of the pleasure it would have
given them to see what a good accountant I am.
   Please accept, dear Monsieur Léon, my affectionate and grateful respects.
                                                            Marcel Proust

MARCEL PROUST to Léon Neuburger, November 1908, *Selected Letters*, ii:
*1904–1909*, tr. Kilmartin, 1989


—Put not your trust in money, but put your money in trust.

OLIVER WENDELL HOLMES, *The Autocrat of the Breakfast-Table*, 1857


No man is safe from losing every penny he has in the world, unless he has
had his facer. How often do I not hear middle-aged women and quiet
family men say that they have no speculative tendency: *they* never had
touched, and never would touch, any but the very soundest, best reputed

investments, and as for unlimited liability, oh dear! dear! and they throw up their hands and eyes.

Whenever a person is heard to talk thus he may be recognised as the easy prey of the first adventurer who comes across him; he will commonly, indeed, wind up his discourse by saying that in spite of all his natural caution, and his well knowing how foolish speculation is, yet there are some investments which are called speculative but in reality are not so, and he will pull out of his pocket the prospectus of a Cornish gold mine. It is only on having actually lost money that one realises what an awful thing the loss of it is, and finds out how easily it is lost by those who venture out of the middle of the most beaten path. Ernest had had his facer, as he had had his attack of poverty, young, and sufficiently badly for a sensible man to be little likely to forget it. I can fancy few pieces of good fortune greater than this as happening to any man, provided, of course, that he is not damaged irretrievably.

So strongly do I feel on this subject that if I had my way I would have a speculation master attached to every school. The boys would be encouraged to read the *Money Market Review*, the *Railway News*, and all the best financial papers, and should establish a stock exchange amongst themselves in which pence should stand as pounds. Then let them see how this making haste to get rich moneys out in actual practice. There might be a prize awarded by the head-master to the most prudent dealer, and the boys who lost their money time after time should be dismissed. Of course if any boy proved to have a genius for speculation and made money—well and good, let him speculate by all means.

If Universities were not the worst teachers in the world I should like to see professorships of speculation established at Oxford and Cambridge. When I reflect, however, that the only things worth doing which Oxford and Cambridge can do well are cooking, cricket, rowing and games, of which there is no professorship, I fear that the establishment of a professorial chair would end in teaching young men neither how to speculate, nor how not to speculate, but would simply turn them out as bad speculators.

SAMUEL BUTLER, *The Way of All Flesh*, 1903

As for Nicholas, he lived a single man on the patrimonial estate until he grew tired of living alone, and then he took to wife the daughter of a neighbouring gentleman with a dower of one thousand pounds. This good lady bore him two children, a son and a daughter, and when the son was about nineteen, and the daughter fourteen, as near as we can guess—

impartial records of young ladies' ages being, before the passing of the new act, nowhere preserved in the registries of this country—Mr Nickleby looked about him for the means of repairing his capital, now sadly reduced by this increase in his family and the expenses of their education.

'Speculate with it,' said Mrs Nickleby.

'Spec—u—late, my dear?' said Mr Nickleby, as though in doubt.

'Why not?' asked Mrs Nickleby.

'Because, my dear, if we *should* lose it,' rejoined Mr Nickleby, who was a slow and time-taking speaker, 'if we *should* lose it, we shall no longer be able to live, my dear.'

'Fiddle,' said Mrs Nickleby.

'I am not altogether sure of that, my dear,' said Mr Nickleby.

'There's Nicholas,' pursued the lady, 'quite a young man—it's time he was in the way of doing something for himself; and Kate too, poor girl, without a penny in the world. Think of your brother; would he be what he is, if he hadn't speculated?'

'That's true,' replied Mr Nickleby. 'Very good, my dear. Yes. I *will* speculate, my dear.'

Speculation is a round game; the players see little or nothing of their cards at first starting; gains *may* be great—and so may losses. The run of luck went against Mr Nickleby; a mania prevailed, a bubble burst, four stockbrokers took villa residences at Florence, four hundred nobodies were ruined, and among them Mr Nickleby.

CHARLES DICKENS, *Nicholas Nickleby*, 1838–9

Herr von Rothschild is, in fact, the best political thermometer; I will not say weather-frog, because the word is not sufficiently respectful. And certes! one must have respect for this man, be it only for the respect which he inspires in others. I like best to visit him in his banking-house, where I can as a philosopher observe how people, and not only God's chosen, but all other kinds, bow and duck before him. There you may behold such a twisting and bending of back-bones as the best acrobat could hardly equal. I have seen people who, when they drew near the great Baron, shrunk up as if they had touched an electric battery. Even while approaching the door of his cabinet many experience a thrill of awe such as Moses felt on Mount Horeb when he saw that he stood on holy ground, and even as Moses took off his shoes, so more than one courtier or broker would fain remove his boots before entering the private cabinet of M. de Rothschild. That private cabinet is indeed a remarkable place, which inspires sublime thoughts and feelings, as does the sight of the sea or of the starry heavens. We see here how small man is and how great is God! For gold is the God of our time and Rothschild is his prophet.

Some years ago, when I was about to call on Herr von Rothschild, a servant in livery crossed the corridor carrying the chamber-pot of the latter, while a speculator on the Bourse who was passing at the instant most respectfully took off his hat before the mighty pot.

HEINRICH HEINE, *Lutetia*, 1854, tr. Charles Godfrey Leland, 1906

FINANCE, *n.* The art or science of managing revenues and resources for the best advantage of the manager. The pronunciation of this word with the i long and the accent on the first syllable is one of America's most precious discoveries and possessions.

AMBROSE BIERCE, *The Cynic's Word Book*, 1906

In 1833, M. Thiers made a ten-days' journey in England, and pledged himself to Louis Philippe to learn in that time all that was worth knowing of the politics, commerce, revenues, religion, arts, sciences, and social economy of this nation. While here he wrote to a gentleman connected with the Treasury the following note: 'My dear Sir,—Would you give me a short quarter of an hour, to explain to me the financial system of your country? Always yours, T.'

JOHN TIMBS, *A Century of Anecdote*, 1864

People who understand high finance are of two kinds; those who have vast fortunes of their own and those who have nothing at all. To the actual millionaire a million pounds is something real and comprehensible. To the applied mathematician and the lecturer in economics (assuming both to be practically starving) a million pounds is at least as real as a thousand, they having never possessed either sum. But the world is full of people who fall between these two categories, knowing nothing of millions but well accustomed to think in thousands, and it is of these that finance committees are mostly comprised. The result is a phenomenon that has often been observed but never yet investigated. It might be termed the Law of Triviality. Briefly stated, it means that the time spent on any item of the agenda will be in inverse proportion to the sum involved.

C. NORTHCOTE PARKINSON, *Parkinson's Law*, 1958

'Well, sir,' said Mr Dooley, 'I see th' Titans iv Finance has clutched each other be th' throat an' engaged in a death sthruggle. Glory be, whin business gets above sellin' tinpinny nails in a brown paper cornucopy, 'tis hard to tell it fr'm murther.'

'What's a Titan iv Fi-nance?' asked Mr Hennessy.

'A Ti-tan iv Fi-nance,' said Mr Dooley, 'is a man that's got more money thin he can carry without bein' disordherly. They'se no intoxicant in th' wurruld, Hinnissy, like money. It goes to th' head quicker thin th' whiskey th' dhruggist makes in his back room. A little money taken fr'm frinds in a social way or f'r th' stomach's sake is not so bad. A man can make money slowly an' go on increasin' his capacity till he can carry his load without staggerin' an' do nawthin' vilent with a millyon or two aboord. But some iv these la-ads has been thryin' to consume th' intire output, an' it looks to me as though 't was about time to call in th' polis.'

F. P. Dunne, *Mr Dooley's Opinions*, 1902

The Human Piranha came to tell us about government bonds, though he was so knowledgeable about the handling of money that he could have spoken about whatever he wished. He was the only bond salesman who made traders nervous, because he generally knew their job better than they did, and if they screwed up by giving him a wrong price, he usually made a point of humiliating them on the hoot and holler. It gave other salespeople great satisfaction to watch him do this.

The Human Piranha was short and square, like the hooker on a rugby team. The most unusual thing about him was the frozen expression on his face. His dark eyes, black holes really, rarely moved. And when they did, they moved very slowly, like a periscope. His mouth never seemed to alter in shape; rather it expanded and contracted proportionally when he spoke. And out of that mouth came a steady stream of bottom-line analysis and profanity.

The Piranha, that day, began by devouring the government of France. The French government had issued a bond known as the Giscard (yes, the one described by Tom Wolfe in *Bonfire of the Vanities*. Wolfe learned of the Giscard from a Salomon trader; in fact, to research his fictional bond salesman, Wolfe had come to 41 and sat spitting distance from the Human Piranha). The Piranha was troubled by the Giscard, so dubbed because it had been the brainchild of the governent of Valéry Giscard d'Estaing. The French had raised about a billion dollars in 1978 with the bond. That wasn't the problem. The problem was that the bond was, under certain conditions, exchangeable into gold at thirty-two dollars an ounce—i.e., the holder of, say, thirty-two million dollars of the bonds, rather than accept cash, could demand one million ounces of gold.

'The fuckin' frogs are getting their faces ripped off,' said the Piranha, meaning that the French were losing a lot of money on the bond issue now that the bond had indeed become convertible and the price of gold was five hundred dollars an ounce. The stupidity of the fuckin' frogs disgusted the Piranha. He associated it with their habit of quitting work at five p.m. The European work ethic was his *bête noire*, though he put it differently. He had once derided a simpering group of Salomon's Englishmen and Continental Europeans who had complained of being overworked by calling them 'Eurofaggots'.

Once he'd finished with France, he whipped out charts to show the way a government bond arbitrage trade worked. As he spoke, the people in the front row grew nervous, and the people in the back row began to giggle, and the people in the front row grew more nervous still, fearing that the people in the back row would cause the Piranha to feed on us all. *The Piranha didn't talk like a person.* He said things like 'If you fuckin' buy this bond in a fuckin' trade, you're fuckin' fucked.' And 'If you don't pay fuckin' attention to the fuckin' two-year, you get your fuckin' face ripped off.' Noun, verb, adjective: fucker, fuck, fucking. No part of speech was spared. His world was filled with copulating inanimate objects and people getting their faces ripped off. We had never before heard of people getting their faces ripped off. And he said it so often, like a nervous tic, that each time he said it again, the back row giggled. The Human Piranha, a Harvard graduate, thought nothing of it. He was always like this.

MICHAEL LEWIS, *Liar's Poker*, 1989

How these sons of the great universities, these legatees of Jefferson, Emerson, Thoreau, William James, Frederick Jackson Turner, William Lyons Phelps, Samuel Flagg Bemis, and the other three-name giants of American scholarship—how these inheritors of the *lux* and the *veritas* now flocked to Wall Street and to the bond trading room of Pierce & Pierce! How the stories circulated on every campus! If you weren't making $250,000 a year within five years, then you were either grossly stupid or grossly lazy. That was the word. By age thirty, $500,000—and that sum had the taint of the mediocre. By age forty you were either making a million a year or you were timid and incompetent. *Make it now!* That motto burned in every heart, like myocarditis. Boys on Wall Street, mere boys, with smooth jawlines and clean arteries, boys still able to blush, were buying three-million-dollar apartments on Park and Fifth. (Why wait?) They were buying thirty-room, four-acre summer places in Southampton, places built in the 1920s and written off in the 1950s as white elephants, places with decaying servants' wings, and they were doing over the servants' wings, too, and even adding on. (Why not? We've got the servants.) They had carnival rides trucked in and installed on the great green lawns for their children's birthday parties, complete with teams of carnival workers to operate them. (A thriving little industry.)

And where did all of this astonishing new money come from? Sherman had heard Gene Lopwitz discourse on that subject. In the Lopwitz analysis, they had Lyndon Johnson to thank. Ever so quietly, the U.S. had started printing money by the billions to finance the war in Vietnam. Before anyone, even Johnson, knew what was happening, a worldwide inflation had begun. Everyone woke up to it when the Arabs suddenly jacked up oil prices in the early 1970s. In no time, markets of all sorts became heaving crap-shoots: gold, silver, copper, currencies, bank certificates, corporate notes—even bonds. For decades the bond business had been the bedridden giant of Wall Street. At firms such as Salomon Brothers, Morgan Stanley, Goldman Sachs, and Pierce & Pierce, twice as much money had always changed hands on the bond market as on the stock market. But prices had budged by only pennies at a time, and mostly they went down. As Lopwitz put it, 'The bond market has been going down ever since the Battle of Midway.' The Battle of Midway (Sherman had to look it up) was in the Second World War. The Pierce & Pierce bond department had consisted of only twenty souls, twenty rather dull souls known as the Bond Bores. The less promising members of the firm were steered into bonds, where they could do no harm.

Tom Wolfe, The Bonfire of the Vanities, 1987

At first Robyn thought that Debbie's Cockney accent was some sort of joke, but soon realised that it was authentic. In spite of her Sloaney clothes and hair-do, Debbie was decidedly lower-class. When Basil mentioned that she worked in the same bank as himself, Robyn assumed that she was a secretary or typist, but was quickly corrected by her brother when he followed her out to the kitchen where she was making tea.

'Good Lord, no,' he said. 'She's a foreign-exchange dealer. Very smart, earns more than I do.'

'And how much is that?' Robyn asked.

'Thirty thousand, excluding bonuses,' said Basil, his arms folded smugly across his chest.

Robyn stared. 'Daddy said you were getting disgustingly rich, but I didn't realise just how disgusting. What do you do to earn that sort of money?'

'I'm in capital markets. I arrange swaps.'

'Swaps?' The word reminded her of Basil when he was her kid brother, a gangling boy in scuffed shoes and a stained blazer, sorting conkers or gloating over his stamp collection.

'Yes. Suppose a corporate has borrowed $x$ thousands at a fixed rate of interest. If they think that interest rates are going to fall, they could execute a swap transaction whereby we pay them a fixed rate and they pay us LIBOR, that's the London Interbank Offered Rate, which is variable . . .'

While Basil told Robyn much more than she wanted to know, or could understand, about swaps, she busied herself with the teacups and tried to conceal her boredom. He was anxious to assure her that he was only earning less than Debbie because he had started later. 'She didn't go to University, you see.'

'No, I thought she probably didn't.'

'Not many spot dealers are graduates, actually. They've usually left school at sixteen and gone straight into the bank. Then somebody sees that they've got what it takes and gives them a chance.'

Robyn asked what it took.

'The barrow-boy mentality, they call it. Quick wits and an appetite for non-stop dealing. Bonds are different, you have to be patient, spend a long time preparing a package. There are lulls. I couldn't last for half-an-hour in Debbie's dealing room—fifty people with about six telephones in each hand shouting across the room things like *'Six hundred million yen 9th of January!'* All day. It's a madhouse, but Debbie thrives on it. She comes from a family of bookies in Whitechapel.'

DAVID LODGE, *Nice Work*, 1988

SCILLA. I work on the floor of LIFFE, the London International Financial Futures Exchange.

Trading options and futures looks tricky if you don't understand it.
But if you're good at market timing you can make out like a bandit.
    (It's the most fun I've had since playing cops and robbers with Jake when we were children.)
A simple way of looking at futures is take a commodity,

Coffee, cocoa, sugar, zinc, pork bellies, copper, aluminium, oil—
 I always think pork bellies is an oddity.
 (They could just as well have a future in chicken wings.)
Suppose you're a coffee trader and there's a drought in Brazil like last year
  or suppose there's a good harvest, either way you might lose out,
So you can buy a futures contract that works in the opposite direction
  so you're covered against loss, and that's what futures are basically
  about.
But of course you don't have to take delivery of anything at all.
You can buy and sell futures contracts without any danger of ending up
  with ten tons of pork bellies in the hall.

On the floor of LIFFE the commodity is money.
You can buy and sell money, you can buy and sell absence of money, debt,
  which used to strike me as funny.

For some it's hedging, for most it's speculation.
In New York they've just introduced a futures contract in inflation.
 (Pity it's not Bolivian inflation, which hit forty thousand per cent.)

I was terrified when I started because there aren't many girls and they line
  up to watch you walk,
And every time I opened my mouth I felt self-conscious because of the way
  I talk.
I found O levels weren't much use, the best qualified people are street
  traders.
But I love it because it's like playing a cross between roulette and space
  invaders.

                                        CARYL CHURCHILL, *Serious Money*, 1987

At forty-five seconds before the auction deadline of 1:00 p.m., George
Connor, at a telephone in the middle of the bond trading room, read off his
final scaled-in bids to a Pierce & Pierce functionary sitting at a telephone at
the Federal Building, which was the physical site of the auction. The bids
averaged $99.62643 per $100 worth of bonds. Within a few seconds after
1:00 p.m., Pierce & Pierce now owned, as planned, $6 billion worth of the
twenty-year bond. The bond department had four hours in which to create
a favorable market. Vic Scaasi led the charge on the bond trading desk,
reselling the bonds mainly to the brokerage houses—by telephone. Sherman

and Rawlie led the bond salesmen, reselling the bonds mainly to insurance companies and trust banks—by telephone. By 2:00 p.m., the roar in the bond trading room, fueled more by fear than greed, was unearthly. They all shouted and sweated and swore and devoured their electric doughnuts.

By 5:00 p.m. they had sold 40 percent—$2.4 billion—of the $6 billion at an average price of $99.75062 per $100 worth of bonds, for a profit of not two but four ticks! *Four ticks!* That was a profit of twelve and a half cents per one hundred dollars. *Four ticks!* To the eventual retail buyer of these bonds, whether an individual, a corporation or an institution, this spread was invisible. But—*four ticks!* To Pierce & Pierce it meant a profit of almost $3 million for an afternoon's work. And it wouldn't stop there. The market was holding firm and edging up. Within the next week they might easily make an additional $5 to $10 million on the 3.6 billion bonds remaining. *Four ticks!*

Tom Wolfe, The Bonfire of the Vanities, 1987

Every now and then the world is visited by one of these delusive seasons, when 'the credit system,' as it is called, expands to full luxuriance: everybody trusts everybody; a bad debt is a thing unheard of; the broad way to certain and sudden wealth lies plain and open; and men are tempted to dash forward boldly, from the facility of borrowing.

Promissory notes, interchanged between scheming individuals, are liberally discounted at the banks, which become so many mints to coin words into cash; and as the supply of words is inexhaustible, it may readily be supposed what a vast amount of promissory capital is soon in circulation. Every one now talks in thousands; nothing is heard but gigantic operations in trade; great purchases and sales of real property, and immense sums made at every transfer. All, to be sure, as yet exists in promise; but the believer in promises calculates the aggregate as solid capital, and falls back in amazement at the amount of public wealth, the 'unexampled state of public prosperity!'

Now is the time for speculative and dreaming or designing men. They relate their dreams and projects to the ignorant and credulous, dazzle them with golden visions, and set them maddening after shadows. The example of one stimulates another; speculation rises on speculation; bubble rises on bubble; every one helps with his breath to swell the windy superstructure, and admires and wonders at the magnitude of the inflation he has contributed to produce.

Speculation is the romance of trade, and casts contempt upon all its sober realities. It renders the stock-jobber a magician, and the Exchange a region of enchantment. It elevates the merchant into a kind of knight-errant, or rather a commercial Quixote. The slow but sure gains of snug percentage become despicable in his eyes: no 'operation' is thought worthy of attention, that does not double or treble the investment. No business is worth following, that does not promise an immediate fortune. As he sits musing over his ledger, with pen behind his ear, he is like La Mancha's hero in his study, dreaming over his books of chivalry. His dusty counting-house fades before his eyes, or changes into a Spanish mine; he gropes after diamonds, or dives after pearls. The subterranean garden of Aladdin is nothing to the realms of wealth that break upon his imagination.

Could this delusion always last, the life of a merchant would indeed be a golden dream; but it is as short as it is brilliant.

WASHINGTON IRVING (1783–1859), 'A Time of Unexampled Prosperity'

# Prices and Values

Lady Windermere's Fan *offers a particularly neat formulation of the thorny relationship between monetary and other kinds of value. Neat, but not final, since prices may be just, and values—particularly literary ones—grotesquely distorted. Moreover, the precise value of money may be a question every bit as elusive as the value of a poem or novel. This section collects observations on and anxieties about the business of pricing and valuing, including notes on inflation, devaluation, and the Gold and Silver Standards.*

ɞ

LORD DARLINGTON. What cynics you fellows are!

CECIL GRAHAM. What is a cynic? [*Sitting on the back of the sofa*]

LORD DARLINGTON. A man who knows the price of everything and the value of nothing.

CECIL GRAHAM. And a sentimentalist, my dear Darlington, is a man who sees an absurd value in everything, and doesn't know the market price of any single thing.

OSCAR WILDE, *Lady Windermere's Fan*, 1892, Act III

For Mr Whistler's own sake, no less than for the protection of the purchaser, Sir Coutts Lindsay ought not to have admitted works into the gallery in which the ill-educated conceit of the artist so nearly approached the aspect of wilful imposture. I have seen, and heard, much of cockney impudence before now; but never expected to hear a coxcomb ask two hundred guineas for flinging a pot of paint in the public's face.

JOHN RUSKIN, *Fors clavigera*, 2 July 1877

In the Court of Exchequer Division on Monday, before Baron Huddleston and a special jury, the case of Whistler *v.* Ruskin came on for hearing. In this action the plaintiff claimed £1,000 damages.

Mr Serjeant Parry and Mr Petheram appeared for the plaintiff; and the Attorney-General and Mr Bowen represented the defendant. . . .

Mr WHISTLER, cross-examined by the ATTORNEY-GENERAL, said: 'I have sent pictures to the Academy which have not been received. I believe that is the experience of all artists. . . . The nocturne in black and gold is a night piece, and represents the fireworks at Cremorne.'

'Not a view of Cremorne?'

'If it were called a view of Cremorne, it would certainly bring about nothing but disappointment on the part of the beholders. (*Laughter.*) It is an artistic arrangement. It was marked two hundred guineas.'

'Is not that what we, who are not artists, would call a stiffish price?'

'I think it very likely that that may be so.'

'But artists always give good value for their money, don't they?'

'I am glad to hear that so well established. (*A laugh.*) I do not know Mr Ruskin, or that he holds the view that a picture should only be exhibited when it is finished, when nothing can be done to improve it, but that is a correct view; the arrangement in black and gold was a finished picture, I did not intend to do anything more to it.'

'Now, Mr Whistler. Can you tell me how long it took you to knock off that nocturne?'

. . . 'I beg your pardon?' (*Laughter.*)

'Oh! I am afraid that I am using a term that applies rather perhaps to my own work. I should have said, "How long did you take to paint that picture?"'

'Oh, no! permit me, I am too greatly flattered to think that you apply, to work of mine, any term that you are in the habit of using with reference to your own. Let us say then how long did I take to—"knock off," I think that is it—to knock off that nocturne; well, as well as I remember, about a day.'

'Only a day?'

'Well, I won't be quite positive; I may have still put a few more touches to it the next day if the painting were not dry. I had better say then, that I was two days at work on it.'

'Oh, two days! The labour of two days, then, is that for which you ask two hundred guineas!'

'No;—I ask it for the knowledge of a lifetime.' (*Applause.*) . . .

Verdict for plaintiff.      Damages one farthing.

J. A. M. WHISTLER, *The Gentle Art of Making Enemies*, 1890

A millionaire—one who was getting up an art-gallery—went to Whistler's studio and glanced casually at the pictures.

'How much for the lot?' he asked, with the confidence of one who owns gold mines.

'Your millions,' said Whistler.

'What!'

'My posthumous prices.' And the painter added, 'Good-morning.'

ARTHUR JEROME EDDY, *Recollections and Impressions of James A. MacNeill Whistler*, 1903

The flight of speculative capital to the art market has done more to alter and distort the way we experience painting and sculpture in the last twenty years than any style, movement or polemic. It has shifted the ground rules of museumgoing: what was once a tomb becomes a bank vault, as every kind of art object is converted into actual or potential bullion. (Strangely enough, this phenomenon has not yet found its Walter Benjamin, although the subversion of aesthetic experience by monetary value is by now as pervasive and visible as the alteration of unique objects by mass reproduction.) Colossal sums of money are exchanged, every day, on the art market. But the market remains wholly unregulated, and almost uninspected. It is the last refuge of nineteenth-century laissez-faire capitalism, in all its self-sufficiency and arrogance. If the units of value traded in the world's galleries were debentures or commodity futures, the Securities and Exchange Commission would be watching; but there is no regulation of the American art market, nor is there likely to be. One of the reasons dealers are so resistant to the idea of outside inspection lies in the inherent irrationality of art prices. No work of art has an intrinsic value, as does a brick or a car. Its price cannot, of course, be discussed in terms of the labor theory of value. The price of a work of art is an index of pure, irrational desire; and nothing is more manipulable than desire. It is no accident that the immense fetishism that sustains the art market should have reached its present level—a delirium whose only historical parallel was the Dutch tulip mania of the seventeenth century—just at the time when the old purposes of art, the manifestation of myth and the articulation of social meaning, have largely been taken away from painting and sculpture by film, television and photography. Only when an object is truly useless, it seems, can capitalism see it as truly priceless. The desire for all commodities and hence their price are affected in greater or lesser degrees by manipulation—apart from diamonds, art is the only commodity whose price is purely and intrinsically manipulative and has no objective relationship to any social machinery except that of 'rarity' and promotion.

ROBERT HUGHES, 'Mark Rothko in Babylon', *Nothing if Not Critical*, 1990

## PRICES CURRENT

In all ordinary lines Prices were well maintained and rising at the outbreak of the Spanish-American War. They rose sharply thenceforward till the second week of the war in South Africa, since which date they have been sagging, touching bed rock in the spring of this year (March, 1903). There has been a slight reaction since the beginning of the season, but it is not supported, and the market is still extremely dull. Patriotic Poems have fallen out of sight, and Criticism is going begging: in some offices books are no longer given to their reviewers: sub-editors have latterly been asked to bring their own suppers. The pinch is being felt everywhere. Police reports are on piece-work and the Religious Column is shut down to half shifts. Leader writers have broken from 1,100 a year to 300. Editors have suffered an all-round cut in wages of 25 per cent. Publishers' carrying-over days are more anxious than ever. Several first-class houses were hammered on the last contango, and the Banks are calling in loans. Private capital can hardly be obtained save for day-to-day transactions, and even so at very high rates of interest. The only lines that are well maintained are City Articles and Special Prose. Snippets are steady.

The following list is taken from Hunter's Handbook, and represents Prices at the close of May:

### PROSE

*(Prices in shillings per thousand words.)*

|  |  |  |  | Rise or Fall. |
|---|---|---:|---:|---|
| Special Prose | ... ... | 30/- | 35/- | Unchanged. |
| Street Accidents | ... ... | 10/- | 12/- | − 5/- |
| Reviews | ... ... ... | 7/6 | 10/- | −20/- |
| Police Court Notices | ... | 15/- | 18/- | − 5/- |
| Guaranteed Libels | ... | 25/- | 30/- | − 3/- |
| Unguaranteed ditto | ... | 5/- | 7/- | + 2/- |
| Deferred ditto | ... ... | 14/- | 16/- | + 4/- |
| Pompous Leaders | ... | 8/- | 10/- | −25/-! |
| Smart Leaders | ... ... | 9/- | 11/6 | + 3/- |

| | | | |
|---|---|---|---|
| Ten-line Leaderettes ... | 10/- | 12/- | Unchanged. |
| Political Appeals ... ... | 15/- | 17/- | – 30/- |
| Attacks on Foreign Nations | 3/- | 3/6 | – 48/-!! |
| Dramatic Criticism ... | 20/- | 25/- | Unchanged. |
| Historical Work ... ... | — | 6d.? | (Practically no demand). |
| Religious Notes ... ... | 12/- | 18/- | – 8/- |
| Attacks upon Christianity | 4/- | 4/6 | – 5/- (A very heavy fall for this kind of matter). |

## VERSE

*(Prices in pence per line.)*

Bad Verse ... No price can be given—very variable.
Good minor Verse 3d. (much the same as last year).
Special Verse ... 1/- (a heavy fall).

HILAIRE BELLOC, *The Aftermath*, 1920

A history of the prices that have been paid for literary labour, from the invention of printing, to the present time, would form a highly interesting subject. It would be curious to observe how, on the one hand, works that have rendered their authors immortal, were sold for the most contemptible sums; while the ephemeral popularity of an author, or a subject, has ensured the most extravagant sums for productions the most worthless. Shakespeare is said to have received no more than £5 for his tragedy of Hamlet; a sum not equal to the twentieth part of what a single copy of his works has since produced. While the bard, who was 'not for an age, but for all time,' was niggardly rewarded for his immortal works, his commentators have been enriched by the editions of them which they have respectively superintended; as appears by the following list of prices paid to his different editors:

| | £. | s. | d. |
|---|---|---|---|
| Mr Rowe was paid | 36 | 10 | 0 |
| Mr Hughes | 28 | 7 | 0 |
| Mr Pope | 217 | 12 | 0 |
| Mr Fenton | 30 | 14 | 0 |
| Mr Gay | 35 | 17 | 6 |
| Mr Whalley | 12 | 0 | 0 |
| Mr Theobald | 652 | 10 | 0 |

| Mr Warburton | · | · | · | · | · | · | · | 500 | 0 | 0 |
| Mr Chapel | · | · | · | · | · | · | · | 300 | 0 | 0 |
| Dr Johnson, for first edition | · | · | · | · | · | · | 375 | 0 | 0 |
| —————————— second edition | · | · | · | · | · | 100 | 0 | 0 |

|  | Total |  | £2288 | 10 | 6 |

The editors of Milton, like the commentators of Shakespeare, have also been much better paid than the original author.

Otway sold his Venice Preserved, to Jacob Tonson, for £15; while, in latter times, Sheridan, for translating Pizarro, received the sum of £1500; and George Colman had a thousand guineas for his romance of Blue Beard. . . .

To come to later times, Goldsmith sold his Vicar of Wakefield to Dodsley, for £10, with an eventual condition on its future sale. Johnson got three hundred guineas for his Lives of the Poets, and one hundred guineas for a new edition. Dr Darwin had £600 for his Botanic Garden; and Gibbon £600 for his History. The sums paid at the present day, to a few favourite authors, are said to exceed any thing ever before known, and to have rendered this the Golden Age of Literature.

Sholto and Reuben Percy, The Percy Anecdotes, 1823

May 7. Dined with Sidney Colvin. He told me he once heard Tennyson read *The Revenge* in his deep chant—a sort of intoning with little variety of manner or expression, and he ended 'To be lost evermore in the main!' adding immediately in exactly the same voice and attitude without any pause 'And the scoundrels only gave me £300 for that! It was worth £500!' I don't like the story, but record it as first-hand and oddly characteristic of one side of Tennyson. If he had said it was worth £3,000 it would have been less absurd.

John Bailey, Letters and Diaries, 1935, entry for 7 May 1925

I find, by several letters which I receive daily, that many of my readers would be better pleased to pay three-halfpence for my paper, than two-pence. The ingenious T. W. tells me, that I have deprived him of the best part of his breakfast, for that, since the rise of my paper, he is forced every morning to drink his dish of coffee by itself without the addition of the Spectator, that used to be better than lace to it. Eugenius informs me very obligingly, that he never thought he should have disliked any passage in my paper, but that of late there have been two words in every one of them, which he could heartily wish left out, viz. 'Price Two-pence.' I have a letter from a soap-boiler who condoles with me very affectionately, upon the necessity we both lie under of setting an higher price on our commodities since the late tax has been laid upon them, and desiring me, when I write next on that subject, to speak a word or two upon the present duties on Castle-soap. But there is none of these my correspondents, who writes with a greater turn of good sense and elegance of expression, than the generous Philomedes, who advises me to value every Spectator at six-pence, and promises that he himself will engage for above a hundred of his acquaintance, who shall take it in at that price.

JOSEPH ADDISON, *Spectator*, 488, 19 September, 1712

I have sometimes thought that in putting down very large sums, such as occur in statements of finance, it were better, instead of making the denominations by tens, hundreds, and thousands of millions, to call the next decimal on the left hand, after passing a million, a *billion*, the next a *trillion* and so on, as I have found the great number and length of ciphers delay and sometimes mislead the reader.

I think another change (of which, however, I am aware of the difficulty, perhaps the impracticability) might be made, if the nations civilized and advanced in political economy would agree to it to establish one common measure of value to save the puzzle of different values and different coins, such as *pounds, livres, dollars, zequins, and rupees*. Of all these, I think, the French *livre* is the worst, not only as too small for large concerns, but as being fractional. Were any denomination of value easily divisible into decimal parts to be agreed on by commercial men, it would save a good deal of troublesome reduction.

Denominations of value are to nations what weights and measures are to individual countries. Long habit and usage indeed have made such a reform exceedingly difficult. The absolute power of Buonaparte introduced it into France; but I understand that now (1826) it is scarcely ever put in practice.

HENRY MACKENZIE (1745–1831), *Anecdotes and Egotisms*

At the end of the Great Struggle with Napoleon, when the power of France was crushed, and the Allies occupied Paris, we agreed to terms which left

France her territories and colonies intact (on the sole condition, as regards the latter, that she would agree to surrender the slave trade), and free from debt, while we ourselves had incurred one, mainly arising from the war, of over £900,000,000! When we look back on the terms, our statesmen behaved with a generosity which was perhaps hardly wise; and we can scarcely wonder that some Frenchmen claim Waterloo as a French victory. At any rate the terms of peace were far more favourable to her than to us.

I have mentioned the restoration of the French Colonies—a small part of the exertions and sacrifices made to put down this abominable traffic. We paid Portugal £300,000 and Spain £400,000 to induce those countries to give up the traffic. For more than half a century, at a time when we had a crushing debt, and were far less prosperous or powerful than we are now, we kept a squadron on the West Coast of Africa, at an annual cost estimated by Mr Gladstone when Chancellor of the Exchequer at £700,000 a year, and at a great sacrifice of valuable lives. We paid the West Indies and Mauritius £20,000,000 to free their slaves. Altogether the noble efforts to put down this abominable traffic must have cost the country something between £50,000,000 and £100,000,000 sterling.

SIR JOHN LUBBOCK, 'Patriotism', The Use of Life, 1895

We all know how the size of sums of money appears to vary in a remarkable way according as they are being paid in or paid out.

JULIAN HUXLEY, Essays of a Biologist, 1923

'The cost of a thing,' says he, 'is *the amount of what I will call life* which is required to be exchanged for it, immediately or in the long run.' I have been accustomed to put it to myself, perhaps more clearly, that the price we have to pay for money is paid in liberty. Between these two ways of it, at least, the reader will probably not fail to find a third definition of his own; and it follows, on one or other, that a man may pay too dearly for his livelihood, by giving, in Thoreau's terms, his whole life for it, or, in mine, bartering for it the whole of his available liberty, and becoming a slave till death. There are two questions to be considered—the quality of what we buy, and the price we have to pay for it. Do you want a thousand a year, a two thousand a year, or a ten thousand a year livelihood? and can you afford the one you want? It is a matter of taste; it is not in the least degree a question of duty, though commonly supposed so. But there is no authority for that view anywhere. It is nowhere in the Bible. It is true that we might do a vast amount of good if we were wealthy, but it is also highly improbable; not many do; and the art of growing rich is not only quite distinct from that of doing good, but the practice of the one does not at all train a man for practising the other. 'Money might be of great service to me,' writes Thoreau; 'but the difficulty now is that I do not improve my opportunities, and therefore I am not prepared to have my opportunities increased.' It is a mere illusion that, above a certain income, the personal desires will be satisfied and leave a wider margin for the generous impulse. It is as difficult to be generous, or anything else, except perhaps a member of Parliament, on thirty thousand as on two hundred a year.

ROBERT LOUIS STEVENSON, 'Henry David Thoreau', *Familiar Studies of Men and Books*, 1882

## BRIDE PRICE

You must pay the price
Of wanting to marry
A university graduate,
A Ph.D. at that!
She's worth every bit
Of six thousand naira;
We must uphold tradition.

Agreed, but then
Can you give a guarantee
She's not shop-soiled—
All those years on the campus,
Swotting and sweating,
Sucking up to lecturers
For all those degrees?

Shop-soiled, you ask?
What do you mean 'shop-soiled'?
Our daughter's not old clothes,
She's not old books
That get soiled in the shop;
She's old wine, matured over the years
For the discerning taste.

Shop-soiled she may not be,
Matured no doubt she is;
But then is she untouched?
Has nobody removed the cork,
All those years in the varsity?

That we cannot tell you,
That's your business to find out
On your nuptial night
In the privacy of your bedroom.

In that case, in-laws, dear,
Can I return her then
And obtain a refund
According to tradition
If I should discover
Someone has sipped the wine
Before I got there?

MABEL SEGUN, in *Voices from Twentieth-Century Africa*, ed. Chinweizu, 1988

The real price of every thing, what every thing really costs to the man who
wants to acquire it, is the toil and trouble of acquiring it.

ADAM SMITH, *The Wealth of Nations*, 1776

In Germany the want of worldly goods is very amiably excused, and with
us genius may suffer and hunger without being despised. In England men
are less tolerant; a man's merit is there measured by his income, and 'How
much is he worth?' means literally, either, 'How much money has he?' or
'What are his merits?' I myself once heard a burly Englishman seriously ask
a Franciscan monk how much he made annually by going about barefoot
with a rope round his body?

HEINRICH HEINE, *Lutetia*, 1854, tr. Charles Godfrey Leland, 1906

Ernest was terribly shocked when he heard of the loss of his money, but his
ignorance of the world prevented him from seeing the full extent of the
mischief. He had never been in serious want of money yet, and did not

know what it meant. In reality, money losses are the hardest to bear of any by those who are old enough to comprehend them.

A man can stand being told that he must submit to a severe surgical operation, or that he has some disease which will shortly kill him, or that he will be a cripple or blind for the rest of his life; dreadful as such tidings must be, we do not find that they unnerve the greater number of mankind; most men, indeed, go coolly enough even to be hanged, but the strongest quail before financial ruin, and the better men they are, the more complete, as a general rule, is their prostration. Suicide is a common consequence of money losses; it is rarely sought as a means of escape from bodily suffering. If we feel that we have a competence at our backs, so that we can die warm and quietly in our beds, with no need to worry about expense, we live our lives out to the dregs, no matter how excruciating our torments. Job probably felt the loss of his flocks and herds more than that of his wife and family, for he could enjoy his flocks and herds without his family, but not his family—not for long—if he had lost all his money. Loss of money indeed is not only the worst pain in itself, but it is the parent of all others. Let a man have been brought up to a moderate competence, and have no specialty; then let his money be suddenly taken from him, and how long is his health likely to survive the change in all his little ways which loss of money will entail? How long again is the esteem and sympathy of friends likely to survive ruin? People may be very sorry for us, but their attitude towards us hitherto has been based upon the supposition that we were situated thus or thus in money matters; when this breaks down there must be a restatement of the social problem so far as we are concerned; we have been obtaining esteem under false pretences. Granted, then, that the three most serious losses which a man can suffer are those affecting money, health and reputation. Loss of money is far the worst, then comes ill-health, and then loss of reputation; loss of reputation is a bad third, for, if a man keeps health and money unimpaired, it will be generally found that his loss of reputation is due to breaches of parvenu conventions only, and not to violations of those older, better established canons whose authority is unquestionable. In this case a man may grow a new reputation as easily as a lobster grows a new claw, or, if he have health and money, may thrive in great peace of mind without any reputation at all. The only chance for a man who has lost his money is that he shall still be young enough to stand uprooting and transplanting without more than temporary derangement, and this I believed my godson still to be.

SAMUEL BUTLER, *The Way of All Flesh*, 1903

The *Value*, or WORTH of a man, is as of all other things, his Price; that is to say, so much as would be given for the use of his Power: and therefore is not absolute; but a thing dependant on the need and judgement of another. An able conductor of Souldiers, is of great Price in time of War present, or imminent; but in Peace not so. A learned and uncorrupt Judge, is much Worth in time of Peace; but not so much in War. And as in other things, so in men, not the seller, but the buyer determines the Price. For let a man (as most men do,) rate themselves at the highest Value they can; yet their true Value is no more than it is esteemed by others.

THOMAS HOBBES, *Leviathan*, 1651

Mr and Mrs Milvey had found their search a difficult one. Either an eligible orphan was of the wrong sex (which almost always happened) or was too old, or too young, or too sickly, or too dirty, or too much accustomed to the streets, or too likely to run away; or, it was found impossible to complete the philanthropic transaction without buying the orphan. For, the instant it became known that anybody wanted the orphan, up started some affectionate relative of the orphan who put a price upon the orphan's head. The suddenness of an orphan's rise in the market was not to be paralleled by the maddest records of the Stock Exchange. He would be at five thousand per cent. discount out at nurse making a mud pie at nine in the morning, and (being inquired for) would go up to five thousand per cent. premium before noon. The market was 'rigged,' in various artful ways. Counterfeit stock got into circulation. Parents boldly represented themselves as dead, and brought their orphans with them. Genuine orphan-stock was surreptitiously withdrawn from the market. It being announced, by emissaries posted for the purpose, that Mr and Mrs Milvey were coming down the court, orphan script would be instantly concealed, and production refused, save on a condition usually stated by the brokers as a 'gallon of beer.' Likewise, fluctuations of a wild and South-Sea nature were occasioned by orphan-holders keeping back, and then rushing into the market a dozen together. But, the uniform principle at the root of all these various operations was bargain and sale; and that principle could not be recognised by Mr and Mrs Milvey.

CHARLES DICKENS, *Our Mutual Friend*, 1864–5

LADY BRACKNELL. Gwendolen! the time approaches for our departure. We have not a moment to lose. As a matter of form, Mr Worthing, I had better ask you if Miss Cardew has any little fortune?

JACK. Oh! about a hundred and thirty thousand pounds in the Funds. That is all. Good-bye, Lady Bracknell. So pleased to have seen you.

LADY BRACKNELL [*sitting down again*]. A moment, Mr Worthing. A hundred and thirty thousand pounds! And in the Funds! Miss Cardew seems to me a most attractive young lady, now that I look at her. Few girls of the present day have any really solid qualities, any of the qualities that last, and improve with time. We live, I regret to say, in an age of surfaces.

OSCAR WILDE, *The Importance of Being Earnest*, 1895, Act III

> What makes all doctrines plain and clear?—
> About two hundred pounds a year.
> And that which was prov'd true before,
> Prove false again?—Two hundred more.

SAMUEL BUTLER, *Hudibras*, 1678, part iii

LADY FIDGET. But are you sure he loves play, and has money?

SIR JASPER FIDGET. He loves play as much as you, and has money as much as I.

LADY FIDGET. Then I am contented to make him pay for his scurrility. Money makes up in a measure all other wants in men.

WILLIAM WYCHERLEY, *The Country Wife*, 1671–2, II. i

The day was bright, the trees of the Park in the full beauty of mid-June foliage; the brothers did not seem to notice phenomena, which contributed, nevertheless, to the jauntiness of promenade and conversation.

'Yes,' said Roger, 'she's a good-lookin' woman, that wife of Soames'. I'm told they don't get on.'

This brother had a high forehead, and the freshest colour of any of the Forsytes; his light gray eyes measured the street frontage of the houses by the way, and now and then he would level his umbrella and take a 'lunar,' as he expressed it, of the varying heights.

'She'd no money,' replied Nicholas.

He himself had married a good deal of money, of which, it being then the golden age before the Married Women's Property Act, he had mercifully been enabled to make a successful use.

'What was her father?'

'Heron was his name, a Professor, so they tell me.'

Roger shook his head.

'There's no money in that,' he said.

'They say her mother's father was cement.'

Roger's face brightened.

'But he went bankrupt,' went on Nicholas.

'Ah!' exclaimed Roger, 'Soames will have trouble with her; you mark my words, he'll have trouble—she's got a foreign look.'

Nicholas licked his lips.

'She's a pretty woman,' and he waved aside a crossing-sweeper.

'How did he get hold of her?' asked Roger presently. 'She must cost him a pretty penny in dress!'

'Ann tells me,' replied Nicholas, 'he was half-cracked about her. She refused him five times. James, he's nervous about it, I can see.'

'Ah!' said Roger again; 'I'm sorry for James; he had trouble with Dartie.' His pleasant colour was heightened by exercise, he swung his umbrella to the level of his eye more frequently than ever. Nicholas's face also wore a pleasant look.

'Too pale for me,' he said, 'but her figure's capital!'

Roger made no reply.

'I call her distinguished-looking,' he said at last—it was the highest praise in the Forsyte vocabulary. 'That young Bosinney will never do any good for himself. They say at Burkitt's he's one of these artistic chaps—got an idea of improving English architecture; there's no money in that! I should like to hear what Timothy would say to it.'

They entered the station.

'What class are you going? I go second.'

'No second for me,' said Nicholas; 'you never know what you may catch.'

He took a first-class ticket to Notting Hill Gate; Roger a second to South Kensington. The train coming in a minute later, the two brothers parted and entered their respective compartments. Each felt aggrieved that the other had not modified his habits to secure his society a little longer; but as Roger voiced it in his thoughts:

'Always a stubborn beggar, Nick!'

And as Nicholas expressed it to himself:

'Cantankerous chap Roger always was!'

There was little sentimentality about the Forsytes. In that great London, which they had conquered and become merged in, what time had they to be sentimental?

JOHN GALSWORTHY, *The Man of Property*, 1906

That which exists for me through the medium of *money*, that which I can pay for (i.e. which money can buy), that *I am*, the possessor of the money. My own power is as great as the power of money. The properties of money are my own (the possessor's) properties and faculties. What I *am* and *can do* is, therefore, not at all determined by my individuality. I *am* ugly, but I can buy the most beautiful woman for myself. Consequently, I am not *ugly*, for the effect of ugliness, its power to repel, is annulled by money. As an individual I am *lame*, but money provides me with twenty-four legs. Therefore, I am not lame. I am a detestable, dishonourable, unscrupulous and stupid man, but money is honoured and so also is its possessor. Money is the highest good, and so its possessor is good. Besides, money saves me the trouble of being dishonest; therefore, I am presumed honest. I am *stupid*, but since money is *the real mind* of all things, how should its possessor be stupid? Moreover, he can buy talented people for himself, and is not he who has power over the talented more talented than they? I who can have, through the power of money, *everything* for which the human heart longs, do I not possess all human abilities? Does not my money, therefore, transform all my incapacities into their opposites.

> KARL MARX, *Economical and Philosophical Manuscripts*, 1844, tr. T. B. Bottomore, 1963

TIMON. Destruction fang mankind!—Earth, yield me roots!      [*Digging*
   Who seeks for better of thee, sauce his palate
   With thy most operant poison! What is here?
   Gold? yellow, glittering, precious gold? No, gods,
   I am no idle votarist. Roots, you clear heavens!
   Thus much of this, will make black, white; foul, fair;
   Wrong, right; base, noble; old, young; coward, valiant.
   Ha, you gods! why this? What this, you gods? Why this
   Will lug your priests and servants from your sides;
   Pluck stout men's pillows from below their heads:
   This yellow slave
   Will knit and break religions; bless the accurs'd;
   Make the hoar leprosy ador'd; place thieves,
   And give them title, knee, and approbation,
   With senators on the bench: this is it,
   That makes the wappen'd widow wed again;
   She, whom the spital-house, and ulcerous sores

Would cast the gorge at, this embalms and spices
To the April day again. Come, damned earth,
Thou common whore of mankind, that put'st odds
Among the rout of nations, I will make thee
Do thy right nature.—[*March afar off* ]—Ha! a drum? —Thou'rt quick,
But yet I'll bury thee: Thou'lt go, strong thief,
When gouty keepers of thee cannot stand:—
Nay, stay thou out for earnest.                          [*Keeping some gold*

WILLIAM SHAKESPEARE, *Timon of Athens,* 1606


LEAR. The usurer hangs the cozener.
   Through tatter'd clothes small vices do appear;
   Robes, and furr'd gowns, hide all. Plate sin with gold,
   And the strong lance of justice hurtless breaks:
   Arm it in rags, a pigmy's straw doth pierce it.

WILLIAM SHAKESPEARE, *King Lear,* 1605


The two waiters inside the café knew that the old man was a little drunk,
and while he was a good client they knew that if he became too drunk he
would leave without paying, so they kept watch on him.
   'Last week he tried to commit suicide,' one waiter said.
   'Why?'
   'He was in despair.'
   'What about?'
   'Nothing.'
   'How do you know it was nothing?'
   'He has plenty of money.'

ERNEST HEMINGWAY, 'A Clean, Well-Lighted Place', 1933


The value of a dollar is social, as it is created by society. Every man who
removes into this city with any purchasable talent or skill in him, gives to
every man's labor in the city a new worth. If a talent is anywhere born into
the world, the community of nations is enriched; and much more with a
new degree of probity. The expense of crime, one of the principal charges
of every nation, is so far stopped. In Europe, crime is observed to increase
or abate with the price of bread. If the Rothschilds at Paris do not accept

bills, the people at Manchester, at Paisley, at Birmingham are forced into the highway, and landlords are shot down in Ireland. The police-records attest it. The vibrations are presently felt in New York, New Orleans, and Chicago. Not much otherwise the economical power touches the masses through the political lords. Rothschild refuses the Russian loan, and there is peace and the harvests are saved. He takes it, and there is war and an agitation through a large portion of mankind, with every hideous result, ending in revolution and a new order.

RALPH WALDO EMERSON, 'Wealth', 1860

I had been now thirteen days on shore, and had been eleven times on board the ship; in which time I had brought away all that one pair of hands could well be supposed capable to bring, though I believe verily, had the calm weather held, I should have brought away the whole ship piece by piece. But preparing the twelfth time to go on board, I found the wind begin to rise. However, at low water I went on board, and though I thought I had rummaged the cabin so effectually as that nothing more could be found, yet I discovered a locker with drawers in it, in one of which I found two or three razors, and one pair of large scissors, with some ten or a dozen of good knives and forks; in another, I found about thirty-six pounds value in money, some European coin, some Brazil, some pieces of eight, some gold, some silver.

I smiled to myself at the sight of this money. 'O drug!' said I aloud, 'what art thou good for? Thou art not worth to me, no, not the taking off of the ground; one of those knives is worth all this heap. I have no manner of use for thee; even remain where thou art, and go to the bottom as a creature whose life is not worth saving.' However, upon seeond thoughts, I took it away.

DANIEL DEFOE, *Robinson Crusoe*, 1719

'American City isn't, by the way, his native town, for, though he's not old, it's a young thing compared with him—a younger one. He started there, he has a feeling about it, and the place has grown, as he says, like the programme of a charity performance. You're at any rate a part of his collection,' she had explained—'one of the things that can only be got over here. You're a rarity, an object of beauty, an object of price. You're not perhaps absolutely unique, but you're so curious and eminent that there are very few others like you—you belong to a class about which everything is known. You're what they call a *morceau de musée.*'

'I see. I have the great sign of it,' he had risked—'that I cost a lot of money.'

'I haven't the least idea,' she had gravely answered, 'what you cost'—and he had quite adored for the moment her way of saying it. He had felt even for the moment vulgar. But he had made the best of that.

'Wouldn't you find out if it were a question of parting with me? My value would in that case be estimated.'

She had covered him with her charming eyes, as if his value were well before her. 'Yes, if you mean that I'd pay rather than lose you.'

HENRY JAMES, *The Golden Bowl*, 1904

What has been said of the influence of the law of conspicuous waste upon the canons of taste will hold true, with but a slight change of terms, of its influence upon our notions of the serviceability of goods for other ends than the æsthetic one. Goods are produced and consumed as a means to the fuller unfolding of human life; and their utility consists, in the first instance, in their efficiency as means to this end. The end is, in the first instance, the fulness of life of the individual, taken in absolute terms. But the human proclivity to emulation has seized upon the consumption of goods as a means to an invidious comparison, and has thereby invested consumable goods with a secondary utility as evidence of relative ability to pay. This indirect or secondary use of consumable goods lends an honorific character to consumption, and presently also to the goods which best serve this emulative end of consumption. The consumption of expensive goods is meritorious, and the goods which contain an appreciable element of cost in excess of what goes to give them serviceability for their ostensible mechanical purpose are honorific. The marks of superfluous costliness in the goods are therefore marks of worth—of high efficiency for the indirect, invidious end to be served by their consumption; and conversely, goods are humilific, and therefore unattractive, if they show too thrifty an adaptation to the mechanical end sought and do not include a margin of expensiveness on which to rest a complacent invidious comparison. This indirect utility gives much of their value to the 'better' grades of goods. In order to appeal to the cultivated sense of utility, an article must contain a modicum of this indirect utility.

While men may have set out with disapproving an inexpensive manner of living because it indicated inability to spend much, and so indicated a lack of pecuniary success, they end by falling into the habit of disapproving cheap things as being intrinsically dishonourable or unworthy because they are cheap. As time has gone on, each succeeding generation has received this tradition of meritorious expenditure from the generation before it, and has in its turn further elaborated and fortified the traditional canon of pecuniary reputability in goods consumed; until we have finally reached such a degree of conviction as to the unworthiness of all inexpensive things, that we have no longer any misgivings in formulating the maxim, 'Cheap and nasty.' So thoroughly has this habit of approving the expensive and disapproving the inexpensive been ingrained into our thinking that we instinctively insist upon at least some measure of wasteful expensiveness in all our consumption, even in the case of goods which are consumed in strict privacy and without the slightest thought of display.

THORSTEIN VEBLEN, The Theory of the Leisure Class, 1899

*Bringing in money*—that is the magic phrase determining everything in Verrières; by itself alone it represents the usual subject for thought of more than three-quarters of its population. *Bringing in money* is the decisive reason for everything in this little town you thought so pretty. A stranger to it, on his first arrival there, enchanted by the cool, deep valleys that surround it, imagines its inhabitants are sensitive to beauty. They speak all too frequently of the beauty of the town and its environment; nobody can deny that they set a high value on it; but that is only because this beauty attracts visitors, whose money makes the innkeepers rich, while they, in their turn, by paying tax on commodities from outside, increase the revenue of the town.

STENDHAL, Scarlet and Black, 1831, tr. Margaret R. B. Shaw, 1953

Not only the economic, but also the personal relations between men have this character of alienation; instead of relations between human beings, they assume the character of relations between things. But perhaps the most important and the most devastating instance of this spirit of instrumentality and alienation is the individual's relationship to his own self. Man does not only sell commodities, he sells himself and feels himself to be a commodity. The manual labourer sells his physical energy; the business man, the physician, the clerical employee, sell their 'personality'. They have to have a 'personality' if they are to sell their products or services. This personality should be pleasing, but besides that its possessor should meet a number of other requirements: he should have energy, initiative, this, that, or the other, as his particular position may require. As with any other commodity it is the market which decides the value of these human qualities, yes, even their very existence. If there is no use for the qualities a person offers, he *has* none; just as an unsaleable commodity is valueless though it might have its use value.

ERICH FROMM, The Fear of Freedom, 1942

That is the way of things in Slaka; but then, where is life not like that? The world is full of money-talk; economists are our new wise men. The linguists, whom one meets everywhere these days, explain that every transaction in our culture—our money and mathematics, our games and gardens, our diet and our sexual activity—is a language; this, of course, is why one meets so many linguists these days. And languages, too, are simply invented systems of exchange, attempts to turn the word into the world, sign into value, script into currency, code into reality. Of course, everywhere, even in Slaka, there are the politicians and the priests, the ayatollahs and the economists, who will try to explain that reality is what they say it is. Never trust them; trust only the novelists, those deeper bankers who spend their time trying to turn pieces of printed paper into value, but never pretend that the result is anything more than a useful fiction. Of course we need them: for what, after all, is our life but a great dance in which we are all trying to fix the best going rate of exchange, using our minds and our sex, our taste and our clothes, according to Valdopian principles? So you, *cher lecteur*, with your customized Volvo and your Seiko quartz digital, your remote control telephone and your high opinion, so loudly expressed over the Campari soda, of Woody Allen up to but not including *Interiors*; or you, *chère ms*, with your Gucci shoes, the tales of ego your analyst told you, and the buttons of your designer dress left strategically undone, to display the Seychelles tan and that tempting mammary interface, so raising the interest without lowering the price; or even you, *cher enfant*, with your Kids-In-Gear boilersuit and your endless new scram on Emerson, Lake and Palmer— what are you doing but putting what you like to think of as your self in the pan, bartering your mind and body, your youth and opinions, on the economic frontier, in an attempt to find a meaning, invent a value, find your highest price, trade at the best possible rate of exchange?

MALCOLM BRADBURY, Rates of Exchange, 1983

The value of a thing, is what it will exchange for: the value of money, is what money will exchange for; the purchasing power of money. If prices are low, money will buy much of other things, and is of high value; if prices are high, it will buy little of other things, and is of low value.

J. S. MILL, *Principles of Political Economy*, 1848

Value is, so to speak, the epigone of price, and the statement that they must be identical is a tautology. I base this view upon the earlier statement that in any individual case no contracting party pays a price that seems to be too high under the given circumstances. If—as in the poem by Chamisso—the robber forces someone at pistol point to sell his watch and rings for three pennies, what he receives under these conditions is worth the price, since it is the only way to save his life. Nobody would work for starvation wages if he were not in a situation in which he preferred such wages to not working at all. The apparent paradox of the assertion that value and price are equivalent in every individual case results from the fact that certain ideas concerning other equivalents of value and price are introduced into it.

GEORG SIMMEL, *The Philosophy of Money*, 1907, tr. Tom Bottomore and David Frisby, 1978

No one can discuss the economic situation (and how I wish that were the end of a sentence) without deciding whether he is an inflationist or a deflationist. I can see the good points of both systems and I have worked out a scheme for a planned society which takes into consideration the merits of everything. Everybody knows that there is a paradox involved here: that, for the first time in the history of the world, we are dealing with the Economics of Abundance. The Economics of Abundance means that there is an abundance of economists. In other words, the harder times get, the harder the reading gets. It's a vicious circle. People who should be out purchasing something are sitting indoors reading an interpretative article in a magazine. (That goes for you, reader!) The more they read, the less they buy; and the less they buy, the sooner it's next month. Each new month brings a new issue of the magazine, so where is this thing going to end? Or don't you care any more?

E. B. WHITE, 'Swing Low, Sweet Upswing', *Quo Vadimus?*, 1939

Exchange and Equity.—In an exchange, the only just and honest course would be for either party to demand only so much as he considers his commodity to be worth, allowance being made for trouble in acquisition, scarcity, time spent and so forth, besides the subjective value. As soon as you make your price bear a relation to the other's need, you become a refined sort of robber and extortioner.—If money is the sole medium of exchange, we must remember that a shilling is by no means the same thing in the hands of a rich heir, a farm labourer, a merchant, and a university student. It would be equitable for every one to receive much or little for his money, according as he has done much or little to earn it. In practice, as we all know, the reverse is the case. In the world of high finance the shilling of the idle rich man can buy more than that of the poor, industrious man.

FRIEDRICH NIETZSCHE, The Wanderer and his Shadow, 1880, tr. Cohn, 1911

Sir,

I have so little concern in paying or receiving of 'interest,' that were I in no more danger to be misled by inability and ignorance, than I am to be biassed by interest and inclination, I might hope to give you a very perfect and clear account of the consequences of a law to reduce interest to 4 per cent. But since you are pleased to ask my opinion, I shall endeavour fairly to state this matter of use, with the best of my skill.

The first thing to be considered is, 'Whether the price of the hire of money can be regulated by law?' And to that I think, generally speaking, one may say, it is manifest it cannot. For since it is impossible to make a law that shall hinder a man from giving away his money or estate to whom he pleases, it will be impossible, by any contrivance of law, to hinder men, skilled in the power they have over their own goods, and the ways of conveying them to others, to purchase money to be lent them, at what rate soever their occasions shall make it necessary for them to have it; for it is to be remembered, that no man borrows money, or pays use, out of mere pleasure: it is the want of money drives men to that trouble and charge of borrowing; and proportionably to this want, so will every one have it, whatever price it cost him. Wherein the skilful, I say, will always so manage it, as to avoid the prohibition of your law, and keep out of its penalty, do what you can.

JOHN LOCKE, 'Some Considerations of the Consequences of the Lowering of<br>Interest, and Raising the Value of Money', 1691

Much money makes a country poor, for it sets a dearer price on every thing.

GEORGE HERBERT, Jacula prudentum, 1640

The circumstances under which our early emissions were made, could not but strongly concur with the futurity of their redemption, to debase their value. The situation of the United States resembled that of an individual engaged in an expensive undertaking, carried on, for want of cash, with bonds and notes secured on an estate to which his title was disputed; and who had besides, a combination of enemies employing every artifice to disparage that security. A train of sinister events, during the early stages of the war likewise contributed to increase the distrust of the *public ability* to fulfill their engagements. Before the depreciation arising from this cause was removed by success of our arms, and our alliance with France, it had drawn so large a quantity into circulation, that the quantity soon after begat a distrust of the *public disposition* to fulfill their engagements; as well as new doubts, in timid minds, concerning the issue of the contest. From that period, this cause of depreciation has been incessantly operating. It has first conduced to swell the amount of necessary emissions, and from that very amount has derived new force and efficacy to itself. Thus, a further discredit of our money has necessarily followed the augmentation of its quantity; but every one must perceive, that it has not been the effect of the quantity, considered in itself, but considered as an omen of public bankruptcy.

JAMES MADISON, *National Gazette*, 1791

MISS PRISM. Cecily, you will read your Political Economy in my absence. The chapter on the Fall of the Rupee you may omit. It is somewhat too sensational. Even these metallic problems have their melodramatic side.

OSCAR WILDE, *The Importance of Being Earnest*, 1895, Act II

### THE FALL OF THE FRANC

Franc little franc what have you done with your bones
What can they have become but the poker dice
which throws these words on to the paper
as a pansy vicar you used to minister in the corridors of brothels
distributing the host to starved whores
in whose eyes your double image was reflected

And before that your bloated chaps
insulted the skeleton goats

who gave off an old French and Christian smell
as they followed you round like the shadow of a sun

Sun more like a lamp
for you never lit up any but barricaded streets
where the paving-stones were replaced by broken bottles

But to-day like a worm cut up by dozens of shovels
you are vainly attempting to escape back among the fish
how you would like to become a jesuit leader once again
but the jesuits have died off like rats
and their guts oozing with soft francs
and their eucharistic decay fills all their chalices
as the last survivors appeal to god
Alas god poor worn out franc
lies among the excrements of his priests
Here lies the franc a beet without sugar

> BENJAMIN PERET, *Remove your Hat*, tr. David Gascoyne and Humphrey
> Jennings, 1937

Although the price of provisions is at present very high, they cannot with
propriety be said to be dear. Nothing is properly dear, except some commodity, which, either from real or fictitious scarcity, bears a higher price
than other things in the same country, at the same time. In the reign of
Henry II the value of money was about fifteen times greater than in the
present age: a fowl then was sold for a penny, which cannot now be bought
under fifteen pence; but fowls are not for that reason dearer now, than they
were at that time; because one penny was then earned with as much
labour, and when earned would fetch as much of everything at market, as
fifteen will in these days.

> SOAME JENYNS, *Thoughts on the Causes and Consequences of the Recent High
> Price of Provisions*, 1767

Boethius, as president of the university, enjoyed a revenue of forty Scottish
marks, about two pounds four shillings and sixpence of sterling money. In
the present age of trade and taxes, it is difficult even for the imagination so
to raise the value of money, or so to diminish the demands of life, as to
suppose four-and-forty shillings a year an honourable stipend; yet it was,
probably, equal, not only to the needs, but to the rank of Boethius. The
wealth of England was, undoubtedly, to that of Scotland more than five to

one, and it is known that Henry the eighth, among whose faults avarice was never reckoned, granted to Roger Ascham, as a reward of his learning, a pension of ten pounds a year.

SAMUEL JOHNSON, *A Journey to the Western Islands of Scotland*, 1775

The past to me is the period before the Second World War; everything after is the present. To a later generation the past is the period before the new currency was imposed and inflation began, when a £20 fee for a magazine article was good money and it was possible to buy a leasehold house for a couple of thousand, with a ground rent of £10 per annum. I remember the author Arthur Calder-Marshall saying to me, as late as 1967, that if a writer could earn a steady £40 each week he was doing well enough; whatever he earned over that was champagne and a little caviar. It was true. In 1964 I woke cautiously to find myself well off, with a solidity of bobs and tosheroons and oncers in my pockets. It did not seem right that an ill-selling novelist like myself should have money in the bank. But the money came from journalism and the great new dangerous boon of television appearances. The novels were the topping up, the spume or spindrift. They had been meant to be the means of basic subsistence.

ANTHONY BURGESS, *You've Had your Time*, 1990

It is impossible to conclude, of any given mass of acquired wealth, merely by the fact of its existence, whether it signifies good or evil to the nation in the midst of which it exists. Its real value depends on the moral sign attached to it, just as sternly as that of a mathematical quantity depends on the algebraical sign attached to it. Any given accumulation of commercial wealth may be indicative, on the one hand, of faithful industries, progressive energies, and productive ingenuities: or, on the other, it may be indicative of mortal luxury, merciless tyranny, ruinous chicane. Some treasures are heavy with human tears, as an ill-stored harvest with untimely rain; and some gold is brighter in sunshine than it is in substance.

And these are not, observe, merely moral or pathetic attributes of riches, which the seeker of riches may, if he chooses, despise; they are, literally and sternly, material attributes of riches, depreciating or exalting, incalculably, the monetary signification of the sum in question. One mass of money is the outcome of action which has created,—another, of action which has annihilated,—ten times as much in the gathering of it; such and such strong hands have been paralyzed, as if they had been numbed by nightshade: so many strong men's courage broken, so many productive operations hindered; this and the other false direction given to labour, and lying image of prosperity set up, on Dura plains dug into seven-times-heated furnaces. That which seems to be wealth may in verity be only the gilded index of far-reaching ruin; a wrecker's handful of coin gleaned from the beach to which he has beguiled an argosy; a camp-follower's bundle of rags unwrapped from the breasts of goodly soldiers dead; the purchase-pieces of potter's fields, wherein shall be buried together the citizen and the stranger.

JOHN RUSKIN, *Unto This Last*, 1860

But, as this way of reasoning may seem to bear a more favourable eye to the clergy, than perhaps will suit with the present disposition, or fashion of the age; I shall, therefore, dwell more largely upon the second reason for the rise of land, which is the perpetual decrease of the value of gold and silver.

This may be observed from the course of the Roman history, above two thousand years before those inexhaustible silver mines of Potosi were known. The value of an obolus, and of every other coin between the time of Romulus and that of Augustus, gradually sunk about five parts in six, as appears by several passages out of the best authors. And yet, the prodigious wealth of that state did not arise from the increase of bullion in the world, by the discovery of new mines, but from a much more accidental cause, which was, the spreading of their conquests, and thereby importing into Rome and Italy, the riches of the east and west.

When the seat of empire was removed to Constantinople, the tide of money flowed that way, without ever returning; and was scattered in Asia. But when that mighty empire was overthrown by the northern people, such a stop was put to all trade and commerce, that vast sums of money were buried, to escape the plundering of the conquerors; and what remained was carried off by those ravagers. . . .

I do not rely on the account given by some historians, that Harry the Seventh left behind him eighteen hundred thousand pounds; for although the West Indies were discovered before his death, and although he had the best talents and instruments for exacting of money, ever possessed by any prince since the time of Vespasian, (whom he resembled in many particulars); yet I conceive, that in his days the whole coin of England could hardly amount to such a sum. For in the reign of Philip and Mary, Sir Thomas Cokayne of Derbyshire, the best housekeeper of his quality in the county, allowed his lady fifty pounds a year for maintaining the family, one pound a year wages to each servant, and two pounds to the steward; as I was told by a person of quality who had seen the original account of his economy. Now this sum of fifty pound, added to the advantages of a large domain, might be equal to about five hundred pounds a year at present, or somewhat more than four-fifths.

The great plenty of silver in England began in Queen Elizabeth's reign, when Drake, and others, took vast quantities of coin and bullion from the Spaniards, either upon their own American coasts, or in their return to Spain. However, so much hath been imported annually from that time to this, that the value of money in England, and most parts of Europe, is sunk above one half within the space of an hundred years, notwithstanding the great export of silver for about eighty years past, to the East Indies, from whence it never returns. But gold being not liable to the same accident, and by new discoveries growing every day more plentiful, seems in danger of becoming a drug.

This hath been the progress of the value of money in former ages, and must of necessity continue so for the future, without some new invasion of Goths and Vandals to destroy law, property and religion, alter the very face of nature; and turn the world upside down.

> JONATHAN SWIFT, 'Some Arguments against Enlarging the Power of Bishops in Letting of Leases', 21 October 1723

It may be said, That there are great Quantities of Silver in Plate, and if the Plate were coined, there would be no Want of Silver Money: But I reckon that Silver is safer from Exportation in the Form of Plate than in the Form of Money, because of the greater Value of the Silver and Fashion together; and therefore I am not for coining the Plate till the Temptation to export the Silver Money (which is a Profit of 2*d*. or 3*d*. an Ounce) be diminished: For as often as Men are necessitated to send away Money for answering Debts Abroad, there will be a Temptation to send away Silver rather than Gold, because of the Profit, which is almost 4 *per Cent*. And for the same Reason Foreigners will choose to send hither their Gold rather than their Silver.

> *All which is most humbly submitted to Your*
> *Lordships great Wisdom.*
> *Isaac Newton.*

*Mint-Office, Sept.*
21, 1717.

> SIR ISAAC NEWTON, 'Representation to the Right Honourable the Lords Commissioners of His Majesty's Revenue', 1717

Some Men have so great an Esteem for Gold and Silver, that they believe they have an intrinsick Value in themselves, and cast up the value of every thing by them: The Reason of the Mistake, is, Because Mony being made of Gold and Silver, they do not distinguish betwixt Mony, and Gold and Silver. Mony hath a certain Value, because of the Law; but the Value of Gold and Silver are uncertain, & varies their Price, as much as Copper, Lead, or other Metals: And in the Places where they are dug, considering the smalness of their Veins, with the Charges of getting them, they do not yield much more Profit than other Minerals, nor pay the Miners better Wages for digging them.

And were it not for the Waste, made of Gold and Silver, by Plate, Lace, Silks, and Guilding, and the Custom of the *Eastern* Princes, to lay them up and bury them, that Half which is dug in the *West*, is buried in the *East*. The great Quantities dug out of the Earth, since the Discovery of the *West-Indies*, would have so much lessened the Value, that by this time, they would not have much exceeded the Value of Tin, or Copper: Therefore, How greatly would those Gentlemen be disappointed, that are searching after the *Philosopher's Stone*, if they should at last happen to find it? For, if they should make but so great a Quantity of Gold and Silver, as they, and their Predecessors have spent in search after it, it would so alter, and bring down the Price of those Metals, that it might be a Question, whether they would get so much *Over-plus* by it, as would pay for the Metal they change into Gold and Silver. It is only the Scarcity that keeps up the Value, and not any Intrinsick Vertue or Quality in the Metals; For if the Vertue were to be considered, the *Affrican* that gives Gold for Knives, and Things made of Iron, would have the Odds in the Exchange; Iron being a much more Useful Metal, than either Gold or Silver. To Conclude this Objection, Nothing in it self hath a certain Value; One thing is as much worth as another: And it is time, and place, that give a difference to the Value of all things.

NICHOLAS BARBON, A Discourse of Trade, 1690

Many persons believe that the Bank of England has some peculiar power of fixing the value of money. They see that the Bank of England varies its minimum rate of discount from time to time, and that, more or less, all other banks follow its lead, and charge much as it charges; and they are puzzled why this should be. 'Money,' as economists teach, 'is a commodity, and only a commodity;' why then, it is asked, is its value fixed in so odd a way, and not the way in which the value of all other commodities is fixed?

There is at bottom, however, no difficulty in the matter. The value of money is settled, like that of all other commodities, by supply and demand, and only the form is essentially different. In other commodities all the large dealers fix their own price; they try to underbid one another, and that keeps down the price; they try to get as much as they can out of the buyer, and that keeps up the price. Between the two what Adam Smith calls the higgling of the market settles it. And this is the most simple and natural mode of doing business, but it is not the only mode. If circumstances make it convenient, another may be adopted. A single large holder—especially if he be by far the greatest holder—may fix his price, and other dealers may say whether or not they will undersell him, or whether or not they will ask more than he does. A very considerable holder of an article may, for a time, vitally affect its value if he lay down the minimum price which he will take, and obstinately adhere to it. This is the way in which the value of money in Lombard Street is settled.

WALTER BAGEHOT, *Lombard Street: A Description of the Money Market*, 1873

But money should always be money. A foot is always twelve inches, but when is a dollar a dollar? If ton weights changed in the coal yard, and peck measures changed in the grocery, and yard sticks were to-day 42 inches and to-morrow 33 inches (by some occult process called 'exchange') the people would mighty soon remedy that. When a dollar is not always a dollar, when the 100-cent dollar becomes the 65-cent dollar, and then the 50-cent dollar, and then the 47-cent dollar, as the good old American gold and silver dollars did, what is the use of yelling about 'cheap money,' 'depreciated money'? A dollar that stays 100 cents is as necessary as a pound that stays 16 ounces and a yard that stays 36 inches.

HENRY FORD, *My Life and Work*, 1922

The two greatest events that have occurred in the history of mankind have been directly brought about by a contraction and, on the other hand, an expansion of the circulating medium of society. The fall of the Roman Empire, so long ascribed, in ignorance, to slavery, heathenism, and moral corruption, was in reality brought about by a decline in the silver and gold mines of Spain and Greece. And, as if Providence had intended to reveal in the clearest manner the influence of this mighty agent on human affairs, the resurrection of mankind from the ruin which those causes had produced was owing to a directly opposite set of agencies being put in operation. Columbus led the way in the career of renovation; when he spread his sails across the Atlantic, he bore mankind and its fortunes in his barque. The annual supply of the precious metals for the use of the globe was tripled; before a century had expired the prices of every species of produce were quadrupled. The weight of debt and taxes insensibly wore off under the influence of that prodigious increase. In the renovation of industry the relations of society were changed, the weight of feudalism cast off, the rights of man established. Among the many concurring causes which conspired to bring about this mighty consummation, the most important, though hitherto the least observed, was the discovery of Mexico and Peru. If the circulating medium of the globe had remained stationary, or declining, as it was from 1815 to 1849, from the effects of the South American revolution and from English legislation, the necessary result must have been that it would have become altogether inadequate to the wants of man: and not only would industry have been everywhere cramped, but the price of produce would have universally and constantly fallen. Money would have everyday become more valuable: all other articles measured in money less so; debt and taxes would have been constantly increasing in weight and oppression. The fate which crushed Rome in ancient, and has all but crushed Great Britain in modern times, would have been that of the whole family of mankind. All these evils have been entirely obviated, and the opposite set of blessings introduced, by the opening of the great treasures of Nature in California and Australia.

Sir Archibald Alison, *History of Europe*, 1849

It has been long known that the first markets were sacred markets, the first banks were temples, the first to issue money were priests or priest-kings. But these economic institutions have been interpreted as in themselves secular-rational, though originally sponsored by sacred auspices. The crucial point in Laum's argument is that the institutions are in themselves sacred. Laum derives the very idea of equivalence (equal value) from ritual tariffs of atonement, the very idea of a symbol of value from rituals of symbolic substitution, and the very idea of price from ritual distribution of the sacred food. In other words, the money complex, archaic or modern, is inseparable from symbolism; and symbolism is not, as Simmel thought, the mark of rationality but the mark of the sacred.

If we recognize the essentially sacred character of archaic money, we shall be in a position to recognize the essentially sacred character of certain specific features of modern money—certainly the gold standard, and almost certainly also the rate of interest. As far as gold and silver are concerned it is obvious to the eye of common sense that their salient characteristic is their absolute uselessness for all practical purposes.

NORMAN O. BROWN, 'Filthy Lucre', *Life against Death*, 1959

The choice of gold as a standard of value is chiefly based on tradition. In the days before the evolution of Representative Money, it was natural, for reasons which have been many times told, to choose one or more of the metals as the most suitable commodity for holding a store of value or a command of purchasing power.

Some four or five thousand years ago the civilised world settled down to the use of gold, silver, and copper for pounds, shillings, and pence, but with silver in the first place of importance and copper in the second. The Mycenaeans put gold in the first place. Next, under Celtic or Dorian influences, came a brief invasion of iron in place of copper over Europe and the northern shores of the Mediterranean. With the Achaemenid Persian Empire, which maintained a bimetallic standard of gold and silver at a fixed ratio (until Alexander overturned them), the world settled down again to gold, silver, and copper, with silver once more of predominant importance; and there followed silver's long hegemony (except for a certain revival of the influence of gold in Roman Constantinople), chequered by imperfectly successful attempts at gold-and-silver bimetallism, especially in the eighteenth century and the first half of the nineteenth, and only concluded by the final victory of gold during the fifty years before the war.

Dr Freud relates that there are peculiar reasons deep in our subconsciousness why gold in particular should satisfy strong instincts and serve as a symbol. The magical properties, with which Egyptian priestcraft anciently imbued the yellow metal, it has never altogether lost. Yet, whilst gold as a store of value has always had devoted patrons, it is, as the sole standard of purchasing power, almost a parvenu. In 1914 gold had held this position in Great Britain *de jure* over less than a hundred years (though *de facto* for more than two hundred), and in most other countries over less than sixty. For except during rather brief intervals gold has been too scarce to serve the needs of the world's principal medium of currency. Gold is, and always has been, an extraordinarily scarce commodity. A modern liner could convey across the Atlantic in a single voyage all the gold which has been dredged or mined in seven thousand years. At intervals of five hundred or a thousand years a new source of supply has been discovered—the latter half of the nineteenth century was one of these epochs—and a temporary abundance has ensued. But as a rule, generally speaking, there has been not enough.

Of late years the *auri sacra fames* has sought to envelop itself in a garment of respectability as densely respectable as was ever met with, even in the realms of sex or religion. Whether this was first put on as a necessary armour to win the hard-won fight against bimetallism and is still worn, as the gold-advocates allege, because gold is the sole prophylactic against the plague of fiat moneys, or whether it is a furtive Freudian cloak, we need not be curious to inquire. But we may remind the reader of what he well knows—namely, that gold has become part of the apparatus of conservatism and is one of the matters which we cannot expect to see handled without prejudice.

One great change, nevertheless—probably, in the end, a fatal change—has been effected by our generation. During the war individuals threw their little stocks into the national melting-pots. Wars have sometimes served to disperse gold, as when Alexander scattered the temple hoards of Persia or Pizarro those of the Incas. But on this occasion war concentrated gold in the vaults of the Central Banks; and these Banks have not released it. Thus, almost throughout the world, gold has been withdrawn from circulation. It no longer passes from hand to hand, and the touch of the metal has been taken away from men's greedy palms. The little household gods, who dwelt in purses and stockings and tin boxes, have been swallowed by a single golden image in each country, which lives underground and is not seen. Gold is out of sight—gone back again into the soil. But when gods are no longer seen in a yellow panoply walking the earth, we begin to rationalise them; and it is not long before there is nothing left.

Thus the long age of Commodity Money has at last passed finally away before the age of Representative Money. Gold has ceased to be a coin, a hoard, a tangible claim to wealth, of which the value cannot slip away so long as the hand of the individual clutches the material stuff. It has become a much more abstract thing—just a standard of value; and it only keeps this nominal status by being handed round from time to time in quite small quantities amongst a group of Central Banks, on the occasions when one of them has been inflating or deflating its managed representative money in a different degree from what is appropriate to the behaviour of its neighbours. Even the handing round is becoming a little old-fashioned, being the occasion of unnecessary travelling expenses, and the most modern way, called 'ear-marking,' is to change the ownership without shifting the location. It is not a far step from this to the beginning of arrangements between Central Banks by which, without ever formally renouncing the rule of gold, the quantity of metal actually buried in their vaults may come to stand, by a modern alchemy, for what they please, and its value for what they choose. Thus gold, originally stationed in heaven with his consort silver, as Sun and Moon, having first doffed his sacred attributes and come to earth as an autocrat, may next descend to the sober status of a constitutional king with a cabinet of Banks; and it may never be necessary to proclaim a Republic. But this is not yet—the evolution may be quite otherwise. The friends of gold will have to be extremely wise and moderate if they are to avoid a Revolution.

J. M. KEYNES, 'Auri sacra fames', 1930

In the Pentateuch a curse is pronounced against the man who changes the weights and measures. In the present day, the laws of exchange are based upon a constant alteration of weights and measures.

The value of gold is to be measured by itself; how can any substance be the measure of its own worth—in other things? the worth of gold is to be established by its own *weight*, under a false denomination of that weight—and an *ounce* is to be worth so many '*pounds*' and fractions of pounds. This is—falsifying a *measure*, not establishing a *standard*!

The gold money that circulates in England amounts to but a tenth part of the paper money that circulates with it, and both constitute but a small portion of the aggregate wealth and obligations of the community and of individuals. This mass is subjected to change by every change in this fictitious standard.

The worth of gold, like that of any other commodity, depends on the quantity on hand—make it depend on the amount of paper in circulation, which paper is to be regulated by it!

If I give a man a piece of coin in lieu of something else, it is barter. If I give him a note of hand, or if he trusts me without it, it is credit. All the reasoning in the world will make nothing more of commerce. All that philosophers ever talked or wrote, could not disturb a single transaction of the value of a groat between the humblest artizans, it is another thing when idle speech is transformed into legislation. 'A standard of value' as a proposition is an absurdity, but when parliament decides that you shall not measure this commodity by that commodity, according to your wants, or those of others, but by a curious plan of its own 'for regulating the Bank issues,' 'preventing fluctuations,' and 'protecting the nation against the drain of Foreign Exchange,'—then is it colossal robbery.

DAVID URQUHART, 'Standard of Value', *Familiar Words as Affecting England and the English*, 1856

'But, if we had free silver, you'd charge thirty cents for the drink,' said Mr McKenna.

'I wud not,' said Mr Dooley, hotly. 'I niver overcharged a man in my life, except durin' a campaign.'

'No one accuses you of overcharging,' explained Mr McKenna. 'Every-body would charge the same. It'd be the regular price.'

'If it was,' said Mr Dooley, 'they'd be a rivolution. But I don't believe it, Jawn. Let me tell ye wan thing. Whisky is th' standard iv value. It niver fluctuates; an' that's funny, too, seein' that so much iv it goes down. It was th' same price—fifteen cints a slug, two f'r a quarther—durin' the war; an' it was th' same price afther the war. The day befure th' crime iv sivinty-three it was worth fifteen cints: it was worth th' same th' day afther. Goold and silver fluctuates, up wan day, down another; but whisky stands firm an' strong, unchangeable as th' skies, immovable as a rock at fifteen or two f'r a quarther. If they want something solid as a standard iv value, something that niver is rajjooced in price, something ye can exchange f'r food an' other luxuries annywhere in th' civilized wurruld where man has a thirst, they'd move th' Mint over to th' internal rivinue office, an' lave it stay there.'

Both Mr Larkin and Mr McKenna were diverted by this fancy.

F. P. DUNNE, *Mr Dooley in Peace and War*, 1899

Cameron made a deep impression on Adams, and in nothing so much as on the great subject of discussion that year—the question of silver.

Adams had taken no interest in the matter, and knew nothing about it, except as a very tedious hobby of his friend Dana Horton; but inevitably, from the moment he was forced to choose sides, he was sure to choose silver. Every political idea and personal prejudice he ever dallied with held him to the silver standard, and made a barrier between him and gold. He knew well enough all that was to be said for the gold standard as economy, but he had never in his life taken politics for a pursuit of economy. One might have a political or an economical policy; one could not have both at the same time. This was heresy in the English school, but it had always been law in the American. Equally he knew all that was to be said on the moral side of the question, and he admitted that his interests were, as Boston maintained, wholly on the side of gold; but, had they been ten times as great as they were, he could not have helped his bankers or croupiers to load the dice and pack the cards to make sure his winning the stakes. At least he was bound to profess disapproval—or thought he was. From early childhood his moral principles had struggled blindly with his interests, but he was certain of one law that ruled all others—masses of men invariably follow interests in deciding morals. Morality is a private and costly luxury. The morality of the silver or gold standards was to be decided by popular vote, and the popular vote would be decided by interests; but on which side lay the larger interest? To him the interest was political; he thought it probably his last chance of standing up for his eighteenth-century principles, strict construction, limited powers, George Washington, John Adams, and the rest. He had, in a half-hearted way, struggled all his life against State Street, banks, capitalism altogether, as he knew it in old England or new England, and he was fated to make his last resistance behind the silver standard.

HENRY ADAMS, *The Education of Henry Adams*, 1907


Every man is rich or poor according to the degree in which he can afford to enjoy the necessaries, conveniencies, and amusements of human life. But after the division of labour has once thoroughly taken place, it is but a very small part of these with which a man's own labour can supply him. The far greater part of them he must derive from the labour of other people, and he must be rich or poor according to the quantity of that labour which he can command, or which he can afford to purchase. The value of any commodity, therefore, to the person who possesses it, and who means not to use or consume it himself, but to exchange it for other commodities, is equal to the quantity of labour which it enables him to purchase or command. Labour, therefore, is the real measure of the exchangeable value of all commodities.

ADAM SMITH, *The Wealth of Nations*, 1776


The moon people do not eat by swallowing food but by smelling it. Their money is poetry—actual poems, written out on pieces of paper whose value is determined by the worth of the poem itself.

PAUL AUSTER, *Moon Palace*, 1989

My father's generation grew up with certain beliefs. One of those beliefs is that the amount of money one earns is a rough guide to one's contribution to the welfare and prosperity of our society. I grew up unusually close to my father. Each evening I would plop into a chair near him, sweaty from a game of baseball in the front yard, and listen to him explain why such and such was true and such and such was not. One thing that was almost always true was that people who made a lot of money were neat. Horatio Alger and all that. It took watching his son being paid 225 grand at the age of twenty-seven, after two years on the job, to shake his faith in money. He has only recently recovered from the shock.

I haven't. When you sit, as I did, at the center of what has been possibly the most absurd money game ever and benefit out of all proportion to your value to society (as much as I'd like to think I got only what I deserved, I don't), when hundreds of equally undeserving people around you are all raking it in faster than they can count it, what happens to the money belief? Well, that depends. For some, good fortune simply reinforces the belief. They take the funny money seriously, as evidence that they are worthy citizens of the Republic. It becomes their guiding assumption—for it couldn't possibly be clearly thought out—that a talent for making money come out of a telephone is a reflection of merit on a grander scale. It is tempting to believe that people who think this way eventually suffer their comeuppance. They don't. They just get richer. I'm sure most of them die fat and happy.

For me, however, the belief in the meaning of making dollars crumbled; the proposition that the more money you earn, the better the life you are leading was refuted by too much hard evidence to the contrary. And without that belief, I lost the need to make huge sums of money. The funny thing is that I was largely unaware how heavily influenced I was by the money belief until it had vanished.

MICHAEL LEWIS, *Liar's Poker*, 1989

# Coda: Hells and Heavens

Finally, a brief visit to some monetary infernos and paradises, both figurative and real. Among the authentic hells are a few of the major bubbles, panics, crashes, and depressions of the last couple of centuries; and then the German hyperinflation; and then the obscene acts which followed it. Auschwitz, as Kitty Hart and Primo Levi suggest, can be seen as a hideous monument to the profit motive as well as to barbarism. The atrocities which took place there grew both from modern nightmares about financial conspiracies and from ancient fantasies about usury, so that this subsection ought to be read as a stinging rebuke to some of the implicitly anti-Semitic texts in 'Borrowing and Lending'.

After the horrors, a concluding review of the Utopias which are either founded on the wise use of money, or, more commonly—it is almost a sine qua non of Utopian fiction—in which the need for a medium of exchange has finally been outgrown and money has been put away as a childish thing.

❧

## CHARON

The conductor's hands were black with money:
Hold on to your ticket, he said, the inspector's
Mind is black with suspicion, and hold on to
That dissolving map. We moved through London,
We could see the pigeons through the glass but failed
To hear their rumours of wars, we could see
The lost dog barking but never knew

That his bark was as shrill as a cock crowing,
We just jogged on, at each request
Stop there was a crowd of aggressively vacant
Faces, we just jogged on, eternity
Gave itself airs in revolving lights
And then we came to the Thames and all
The bridges were down, the further shore
Was lost in fog, so we asked the conductor
What we should do. He said: Take the ferry
Faute de mieux. We flicked the flashlight
And there was the ferryman just as Virgil
And Dante had seen him. He looked at us coldly
And his eyes were dead and his hands on the oar
Were black with obols and varicose veins
Marbled his calves and he said to us coldly:
If you want to die you will have to pay for it.

LOUIS MACNEICE, 1962

## ON THE MONEY MONOPOLIST BEING LIKE HELL

### (Adapted from Gower's *Confessio Amantis*.)

There was no competition for riches
When God made the world and men were still few,
All was in common, with no thought of fortune
In good times or bad, until avarice grew.

The world had grown greatly in men and cattle,
When men started to use the curst trick of money,
Peace departed then. War developed on every side,
Thrusting out all love, making common goods private property.

Given the world the miser would find it too small.
He never lets go again of anything he can grasp,
But seeks more and more, as if life had no end
Or Death itself might fail to loosen his clasp.

In this he's like Hell, for as the old books say,
What comes in there, be it great or small,

Never wins out again. Thus the wealthy are poor,
And most lack that of which they have most withal.

For anyone with a decent understanding
It is impertinent to say such criminals and fools
Possess wealth. Wealth possesses *them*,—
Dehumanised and made its senseless tools!

Hugh MacDiarmid, Second Hymn to Lenin and Other Poems, 1935

## THE LADY PECUNIA'S JOURNEY UNTO HELL, WITH HER SPEECH TO *PLUTO*, MAINTAINING THAT SHE SENDS MORE SOULES TO HELL THEN ALL HIS FIENDS

Great Pluto, Prince of hell, I come to thee,
To give account what hath been done by mee:
When all your Fiends (great Pluto) did small good
In bringing soules to Hell, I understood,
I sent you thousands, who my wayes then trod,
That honour'd me, as I had been their God;
Forgot their prayers, neglected their owne soules,
And all for love of me, poore simple fooles!
And many of them too (such is their case)
They cannot rest untill they see my face;
Nay, when they are in bed, so kinde they bee,
They cannot sleep for thinking then of me.
The Clergy mourns, my absence oft doth grieve 'em,
Till I come double handed to relieve 'em.
Which of your Fiends can do more feats than I?
I can foole Conscience, make the guiltless die,
Pull Justice from her seat, and free the guilty,
Make the impure seem pure, though ne're so filthy.

  ·  ·  ·  ·  ·  ·  ·

I ruine Towns, and make the slave rebell,
And after send the Rebels souls to hell.
Some think the Poet for applause doth sing,
When for my sake he undertakes this thing;
A Cup of Sack doth make his spirits glad,
But without me there's no Sack to be had:

Of all men living he cares least for mee,
For a rich Poet who did ever see?
My silver hooke can never bring him in,
Though many years about it I have bin:
I have lookt here about me pritty well.
Yet I can see no Poets here in hell.
And so great Lord I have no more to say,
All living men but Poets me obey.

.    .    .    .    .    .    .    .

With that the Fiends on Lady PECUNIA fell,
And cast her in great fury out of Hell:
And since she's come againe, thus stands the case,
She makes division still in every place.

> *O love not Money then so well,*
> *That sends so many souls to Hell.*

                              HUMPHREY CROUCH, 1654


Here saw I people, more than elsewhere, many,
   On one side and the other, with great howls,
   Rolling weights forward by main force of chest.
They clashed together, and then at that point
   Each one turned backward, rolling retrograde,
   Crying, 'Why keepest?' and, 'Why squanderest thou?'
Thus they returned along the lurid circle
   On either hand unto the opposite point,
   Shouting their shameful metre evermore.
Then each, when he arrived there, wheeled about
   Through his half-circle to another joust;
   And I, who had my heart pierced as it were,
Exclaimed: 'My Master, now declare to me
   What people these are, and if all were clerks,
   These shaven crowns upon the left of us.'
And he to me: 'All of them were asquint
   In intellect in the first life, so much
   That there with measure they no spending made.
Clearly enough their voices bark it forth,
   Whene'er they reach the two points of the circle,
   Where sunders them the opposite defect.

Clerks those were who no hairy covering
   Have on the head, and Popes and Cardinals,
   In whom doth Avarice practise its excess.'
And I: 'My Master, among such as these
   I ought forsooth to recognise some few,
   Who were infected with these maladies.'
And he to me: 'Vain thought thou entertainest;
   The undiscerning life which made them sordid
   Now makes them unto all discernment dim.
Forever shall they come to these two buttings;
   These from the sepulchre shall rise again
   With the fist closed, and these with tresses shorn.
Ill giving and ill keeping the fair world
   Have ta'en from them, and placed them in this scuffle;
   Whate'er it be, no words adorn I for it.
Now canst thou, Son, behold the transient farce
   Of goods that are committed unto Fortune,
   For which the human race each other buffet;
For all the gold that is beneath the moon,
   Or ever has been, of these weary souls
   Could never make a single one repose.'

DANTE (1265–1321), *Inferno*, canto vii, tr. Longfellow, 1867

A general confusion now took place in the financial world. Families who had lived in opulence, found themselves suddenly reduced to indigence. Schemers, who had been revelling in the delusion of princely fortune, found their estates vanishing into thin air. Those who had any property remaining, sought to secure it against reverses. Cautious persons found there was no safety for property in a country where the coin was continually shifting in value, and where a despotism was exercised over public securities, and even over the private purses of individuals. They began to send their effects into other countries—when lo! on the 20th of June, a royal edict commanded them to bring back their effects, under penalty of forfeiting twice their value; and forbade them, under like penalty, from investing their money in foreign stocks. This was soon followed by another decree, forbidding any one to retain precious stones in his possession, or to sell them to foreigners: all must be deposited in the bank, in exchange for depreciating paper! . . .

The calamitous effects of the system had reached the humblest concerns of human life. Provisions had risen to an enormous price; paper money was refused at all the shops; the people had not wherewithal to buy bread. It had been found absolutely indispensable to relax a little from the suspension of specie payments, and to allow small sums to be scantily exchanged for paper. The doors of the bank and the neighbouring street were immediately thronged with a famishing multitude, seeking cash for bank-notes of ten livres. So great was the press and struggle, that several persons were stifled and crushed to death. The mob carried three of the bodies to the court-yard of the Palais Royal. Some cried for the Regent to come forth and behold the effect of his system; others demanded the death of Law, the impostor, who had brought this misery and ruin upon the nation.

. . . A universal panic succeeded. '*Sauve qui peut!*' was the watchword. Every one was anxious to exchange falling paper for something of intrinsic and permanent value. Since money was not to be had, jewels, precious stones, plate, porcelain, trinkets of gold and silver—all commanded any price, in paper. Land was bought at fifty years' purchase, and he esteemed himself happy who could get it even at this price. Monopolies now became the rage among the noble holders of paper. The Duke de la Force bought up nearly all the tallow, grease, and soap; others, the coffee and spices; others, hay and oats. Foreign exchanges were almost impracticable. The debts of Dutch and English merchants were paid in this fictitious money, all the coin of the realm having disappeared. All the relations of debtor and creditor were confounded. With one thousand crowns one might pay a debt of eighteen thousand livres.

The Regent's mother, who once exulted in the affluence of bank paper, now wrote in a very different tone: 'I have often wished,' said she in her letters, 'that these bank-notes were in the depths of the infernal regions.'

WASHINGTON IRVING (1783–1859), 'The Great Mississippi Bubble'

Oh! may some western tempest sweep
   These locusts whom our fruits have fed,
That plague, directors, to the deep,
   Driven from the South Sea to the Red!

May he, whom Nature's laws obey,
   Who lifts the poor, and sinks the proud,
'Quiet the raging of the sea,
   And still the madness of the crowd!'

But never shall our isle have rest,
   Till those devouring swine run down,

(The devils leaving the possest)
 And headlong in the waters drown.

The nation then too late will find,
 Computing all their cost and trouble,
Directors' promises but wind,
 South Sea, at best, a mighty bubble.

Jonathan Swift, 'The Bubble', 1721

## PAPER MONEY LYRICS

FALSTAFF.—Master Shallow, I owe you a thousand pound.

SHALLOW.—Ay, marry, Sir John, which I beseech you to let me have home
with me.

SHAKSPEARE.

PEREZ.—Who's that is cheated? Speak again, thou vision.

CACAFOGO.—I'll let thee know I am cheated, cheated damnably.

BEAUMONT AND FLETCHER.

## PREFACE

These 'Lyrics' were written in the winter of 1825–26, during the prevalence
of an influenza to which the beautiful fabric of paper-credit is periodically
subject; which is called commercial panic by citizens, financial crisis by
politicians, and day of reckoning by the profane; and which affected all
promisers to pay in town and country with one of its most violent epidemic
visitations in December, 1825. The 'Lyrics' shadow out, in their order, the
symptoms of the epidemic in its several stages; the infallible nostrums,
remedial and preventive, proposed by every variety of that arch class of
quacks, who call themselves political economists; the orders, counter-
orders, and disorders, at the head of affairs, with respect to joint-stock
banks, and the extinction of one-pound notes, inclusive of Scotland, and
exclusive of Scotland; till the final patching up of the uncured malady by a
series of false palliatives, which only nourished for another eruption the
seeds of the original disease. The *tabes tacitis concepta medullis* has again
blazed forth in new varieties of its primitive types—broken promises and

---

*tabes tacitis concepta medullis*] the corruption engendered in her silent marrow

bursting bubbles. Persons and things are changed, but the substance is the
same; and these little ballads are as applicable now as they were twelve
years ago. They will be applicable to every time and place, in which public
credulity shall have given temporary support to the safe and economical
currency, which consists of a series of paper promises, made with the
deliberate purpose, that the promise shall always be a payment, and the
payment shall always be a promise.

   20 July, 1837.


## PAN IN TOWN

### (*Metrum Ithyphallicum cum anacrusi.*)

FALSTAFF.—If any man will caper with me for a thousand marks, let him
   lend me the money, and have at him.


#### PAN AND CHORUS CITIZENS


##### PAN

            The Country banks are breaking:
            The London banks are shaking:
            Suspicion is awaking:
            E'en quakers now are quaking:
            Experience seems to settle,
            That paper is not metal,
            And promises of payment
            Are neither food nor raiment;
            Then, since that, one and all, you
            Are fellows of no value
            For genius, learning, spirit,
            Or any kind of merit
            That mortals call substantial,
            Excepting the financial,
            (Which means the art of robbing
            By huckstering and jobbing,
            And sharing gulls and gudgeons
            Among muckworms and curmudgeons)
            Being each a flimsy funny
            On the stream of paper money,

---

*metrum Ithyphallicum cum anacrusi*] Ithyphallic metre with anacrusis

All riding by sheet anchors,
Of balances at Bankers;
Look out! for squalls are coming,
That if you stand hum-drumming,
Will burst with vengeance speedy,
And leave you like the needy
Who have felt your clutches greedy,
All beggarly and seedy
And not worth a maravedi.

CHORUS

Our balances, our balances,
Our balances, our balances:
Our balances we crave for:
Our balances we rave for:
Our balances we rush for:
Our balances we crush for:
Our balances we call for:
Our balances we bawl for:
Our balances we run for:
Our balances we dun for:
Our balances we pour for:
Our balances we roar for:
Our balances we shout for:
Our balances we rout for:
Our balances, our balances,
We bellow all about for.

THOMAS LOVE PEACOCK, 1825

As a starting-point for a new education at fifty-five years old, the shock of finding one's self suspended, for several months, over the edge of bankruptcy, without knowing how one got there, or how to get away, is to be strongly recommended. By slow degrees the situation dawned on him that the banks had lent him, among others, some money—thousands of millions were—as bankruptcy—the same—for which he, among others, was responsible and of which he knew no more than they. The humor of this situation seemed to him so much more pointed than the terror, as to make him laugh at himself with a sincerity he had been long strange to. As far as he could comprehend, he had nothing to lose that he cared about, but the banks stood to lose their existence. Money mattered as little to him as to anybody, but money was their life. For the first time he had the banks in his power; he could afford to laugh; and the whole community was in the same position, though few laughed. All sat down on the banks and asked what the banks were going to do about it. To Adams the situation seemed farcical, but the more he saw of it, the less he understood it. He was quite sure that nobody understood it much better. Blindly some very powerful energy was at work, doing something that nobody wanted done. When Adams went to his bank to draw a hundred dollars of his own money on deposit, the cashier refused to let him have more than fifty, and Adams accepted the fifty without complaint because he was himself refusing to let the banks have some hundreds or thousands that belonged to them. Each wanted to help the other, yet both refused to pay their debts, and he could find no answer to the question which was responsible for getting the other into the situation, since lenders and borrowers were the same interest and socially the same person. Evidently the force was one; its operation was mechanical; its effect must be proportional to its power; but no one knew what it meant, and most people dismissed it as an emotion—a panic—that meant nothing.

Men died like flies under the strain, and Boston grew suddenly old, haggard, and thin.

HENRY ADAMS, *The Education of Henry Adams*, 1907

## NEWSREEL LXVIII

### WALL STREET STUNNED

*This is not Thirty-eight but it's old Ninety-seven
You must put her in Centre on time*

### MARKET SURE TO RECOVER FROM SLUMP
Decline in Contracts

### POLICE TURN MACHINE-GUNS ON COLORADO MINE
### STRIKERS KILL 5 WOUND 40

sympathizers appeared on the scene just as thousands of office workers were pouring out of the buildings at the lunch hour. As they raised their placard high and started an indefinite march from one side to the other, they were jeered and hooted not only by the office workers but also by workmen on a building under construction

### NEW METHODS OF SELLING SEEN
Rescue Crews Try To Upend Ill-fated Craft While Waiting
For Pontoons

*He looked 'round an' said to his black greasy fireman*
*Jus' shovel in a little more coal*
*And when we cross that White Oak Mountain*
*You can watch your Ninety-seven roll*

I find your column interesting and need advice. I have saved four thousand dollars which I want to invest for a better income. Do you think I might buy stocks?

JOHN DOS PASSOS, *The Big Money*, 1936

But Black Thursday was only the overture. The ticker, unable to keep up with the rapidity of transactions, ran until after seven o'clock that evening before completing the recording of trades that had stopped at three. A bankers' syndicate was formed to support the market, and the next day President Hoover said, 'The fundamental business of the country . . . is on a sound and prosperous basis'; there was a two-day rally on Friday and Saturday, but on Monday the decline resumed, and on Tuesday the twenty-ninth, the worst day in the history of the Stock Exchange, the holocaust went far beyond the possibility of control and the national depression was on. The next day, John D. Rockefeller, Sr. came forward with *his* famous try at restoring confidence ('My son and I have for some days been purchasing sound common stocks'); after another brief rally the decline was resumed again and went on day after day with such intensity that the machinery of Wall Street was all but paralyzed. By November 13, when bottom for the year was reached at last, of the eighty billion dollars that stocks listed on the Exchange had been worth in September, thirty billion was gone. Jesse Livermore said, 'To my mind this situation should go no further.' He was right, as far as 1929 was concerned. But 1929 was only the first act of the tragedy.

By December a mood of permanent crisis and settled gloom had descended on the Street. Workers there who opened their office windows on mild days heard a steady, low murmur coming from the crowd that gathered daily outside the Stock Exchange. One of those workers would recall a generation later, 'The sound went on all through trading hours, and reached its peak around noon. It wasn't an angry or hysterical sound. That was the most ominous thing about it. It was a kind of hopeless drone, a Greek dirge kind of thing. It was damned distracting, I must say.' The search for scapegoats had begun in earnest; new charges and indictments of stock swindles during the past summer and fall cropped up almost every day, and one Wall Street element after another—bucket shops, bear raiders, pool operations, put-and-call brokers, even the slowness of the Exchange ticker—was pointed to in turn as the cause of the crash. Meanwhile, the first tidal waves from the earthquake were already spreading across the city, the nation, and the world. The Russians were crowing that the crash proved their point—capitalism was decadent and doomed. Subway cars plunged under the New York sidewalks carrying carfuls of weirdly keening women. Coast to coast, there were no bread lines yet, but lifelong businesses and long-held insurance policies that had been pledged against loans to buy stock were being lost. College plans for young people were being canceled. Life styles were being changed—some thought for the better; Edwin Lefèvre quoted an intelligent traveling salesman as saying, 'I firmly believe that there isn't a town of ten thousand inhabitants or over in the United States that hasn't at least one night club. In the past year and a half I have been in a hundred or more of them, and I'll swear that nine-tenths of the people I saw were having the time of their lives spending their uncashed stock-market profits. It struck me that these people had acquired the worst habits of the idle rich, without the riches.'

Yet the real rich, especially the conservative rich, were the least hurt of anyone involved in the stock market—so far.

JOHN BROOKS, *Once in Golconda: A True Drama of Wall Street 1920–1938*, 1970

## BEHAVIOUR OF MONEY

Money was once well known, like a townhall or the sky
or a river East and West, and you lived one side or the other;
Love and Death dealt shocks,
but for all the money that passed, the wise man knew his brother.

But money changed. Money came jerking roughly alive;
went battering round the town with a boozy, zigzag tread.
A clear case for arrest;
and the crowds milled and killed for the pound notes that he shed.

And the town changed, and the mean and the little lovers of gain
inflated like a dropsy, and gone were the courtesies
that eased the market day;
saying, 'buyer' and 'seller' was saying, 'enemies.'

The poor were shunted nearer to beasts. The cops recruited.
The rich became a foreign community. Up there leaped
quiet folk gone nasty,
quite strangely distorted, like a photograph that has slipped.

Hearing the drunken roars of Money from down the street,
'What's to become of us?' the people in bed would cry:
'And oh, the thought strikes chill;
what's to become of the world if Money should suddenly die?

Should suddenly take a toss and go down crack on his head?
If the dance suddenly finished, if they stopped the runaway bus,
if the trees stopped racing away?
If our hopes come true and he dies, what's to become of us?

Shall we recognise each other, crowding around the body?
And as we go stealing off in search of the town we have known
—what a job for the Sanitary Officials;
the sprawled body of Money, dead, stinking, alone!'

Will X contrive to lose the weasel look in his eyes?
Will the metal go out of the voice of Y? Shall we all turn back
to men, like Circe's beasts?
Or die? Or dance in the street the day that the world goes crack?

BERNARD SPENCER, 1943

In England the ending of the war had come like waking from a bad dream: in defeated Germany, as the signal for deeper levels of nightmare. The symbols and the occasion had changed but in Germany it was still that same kind of compulsive dreaming. The ex-soldier, expelled from the crumbled Gemeinschaft of army life, had stepped out into a void. The old order had shattered: even money was rapidly ebbing away from between men, leaving them desperately incommunicado like men rendered voiceless by an intervening vacuum: millions, still heaped on top of each other in human cities yet forced to live separate, each like some solitary predatory beast.

Now in 1923 prices were already a billion times the pre-war figure and still rocketing. These were the days spoken of by Haggai the prophet, when 'he that earneth wages, earneth wages to put it into a bag with holes': by

Monday a workman's whole last-week's wages might not pay his tramfare back to work. The smallest sum in any foreign currency was hoarded for it would buy almost anything; but nobody held German money five minutes. Even beer was an investment for presently you got more for the empty bottle than you had paid for it full.

The salaried and rentier classes were becoming submerged below the proletariat. Wages could rise (even if always too little and too late); but interest and pensions and the like, and even salaries, were fixed. Retired senior officials swept the streets. The government official still in office had to learn to temper his integrity to his necessities: had he tried to stay strictly honest a little too long, he would have died.

When the solid ground drops utterly away from under a man's feet like that he is left in a state of free fall: he is in a bottomless pit—a hell. Moreover this was a hell where all were not equitably falling equally together. Some fell slower than others: even peasants could resort to barter (you went marketing with your poultry, not your purse); and many rich men had found means of hardly falling at all. There they were still, those Walther von Kessens and the like, tramping about solidly up there like Dantes in full view of all the anguished others who were falling. People who could buy things for marks and sell them for pounds or dollars even rose.

A hell where justice was not being done, and seen not being done.

RICHARD HUGHES, *The Fox in the Attic*, 1962

Why did the German government not act to halt the inflation? It was a shaky, fragile government, especially after the assassination. The vengeful French sent their army into the Ruhr to enforce their demands for reparations, and the Germans were powerless to resist. More than inflation, the Germans feared unemployment. In 1919 Communists had tried to take over, and severe unemployment might give the Communists another chance. The great German industrial combines—Krupp, Thyssen, Farben, Stinnes—condoned the inflation and survived it well. A cheaper mark, they reasoned, would make German goods cheap and easy to export, and they needed the export earnings to buy raw materials abroad. Inflation kept everyone working.

So the printing presses ran, and once they began to run, they were hard to stop. The price increases began to be dizzying. Menus in cafés could not be revised quickly enough. A student at Freiburg University ordered a cup of coffee at a café. The price on the menu was 5,000 marks. He had two cups. When the bill came, it was for 14,000 marks.

'If you want to save money,' he was told, 'and you want two cups of coffee, you should order them both at the same time.'

The presses of the Reichsbank could not keep up, though they ran through the night. Individual cities and states began to issue their own money. Dr Havenstein, the president of the Reichsbank, did not get his new suit. A factory worker described payday, which was every day at 11:00 A.M.: 'At eleven o'clock in the morning a siren sounded and everybody gathered in the factory forecourt where a five-ton lorry was drawn up loaded brimful with paper money. The chief cashier and his assistants climbed up on top. They read out names and just threw out bundles of notes. As soon as you had caught one you made a dash for the nearest shop and bought just anything that was going.' Teachers, paid at 10:00 A.M., brought their money to the playground, where relatives took the bundles and hurried off with them. Banks closed at 11:00 A.M.; the harried clerks went on strike.

Dentists and doctors stopped charging in currency and demanded butter or eggs, but the farmers were holding back their produce. 'We don't want any Jew-confetti from Berlin,' a chronicler quotes a Bavarian farmer. The flight from currency that had begun with the buying of diamonds, gold, country houses, and antiques now extended to minor and almost useless items—bric-a-brac, soap, hairpins. The law-abiding country crumbled into petty thievery. Copper pipes and brass armatures weren't safe. Gasoline was siphoned from cars. People bought things they didn't need and used them to barter—a pair of shoes for a shirt, some crockery for coffee. Berlin had a 'witches' Sabbath' atmosphere. Prostitutes of both sexes roamed the streets. Cocaine was the fashionable drug. In the cabarets the newly rich and their foreign friends could dance and spend money. Other reports noted that not all the young people had a bad time. Their parents had taught them to work and save, and that was clearly wrong, so they could spend money, enjoy themselves, and flout the old.

The publisher Leopold Ullstein wrote: 'People just didn't understand what was happening. All the economic theory they had been taught didn't provide for the phenomenon. There was a feeling of utter dependence on anonymous powers—almost as a primitive people believed in magic—that somebody must be in the know, and that this small group of "somebodies" must be a conspiracy.'

When the one-thousand-billion-mark note came out, few bothered to collect the change when they spent it. By November 1923, with one dollar equal to one trillion marks, the breakdown was complete. The currency had lost meaning.

'ADAM SMITH' (George J. W. Goodman), *Paper Money*, 1981

What is it that happens in an inflation? The unit of money suddenly loses its identity. The crowd it is part of starts growing and, the larger it becomes, the smaller becomes the worth of each unit. The millions one always wanted are suddenly there in one's hand, but they are no longer millions in fact, but only in name. It is as though the process of sudden increase had deprived the thing which increases of all value. The movement has the character of a flight and, once it has started within a currency, there is no foreseeable end to it. Just as one can go on counting upwards to any figure, so money can be devalued downwards to any depth.

This process contains that urge to rapid and unlimited growth which I have characterized as one of the most important and striking psychological attributes of the crowd. But here the growth negates itself; as the crowd grows, its units become weaker and weaker. What used to be one Mark is first called 10,000, then 100,000, then a million. The identification of the individual with his mark is thus broken, for the latter is no longer fixed and stable, but changes from one moment to the next. It is no longer like a person; it has no continuity and it has less and less value. A man who has been accustomed to rely on it cannot help feeling its degradation as his own. He has identified himself with it for too long and his confidence in it has been like his confidence in himself. Not only is everything visibly shaken during an inflation, nothing remaining certain or unchanged even for an hour, but also each man, as a person, becomes less. Whatever he is or was, like the million he always wanted he becomes nothing. Everyone has a million and everyone is nothing. The process of the formation of treasure has become its opposite, and all the reliability of money is blown away by the wind. No treasure can be added to; each, on the contrary, grows less and less; every accumulation of treasure disappears. An inflation can be called a witches' sabbath of devaluation where men and the units of their money have the strangest effects on each other. The one stands for the other, men feeling themselves as 'bad' as their money; and this becomes worse and worse. Together they are all at its mercy and all feel equally worthless.

Thus in an inflation something happens which was certainly never intended and which is so dangerous that anyone with any measure of public responsibility who is capable of foreseeing it must fear it. It is a double devaluation originating in a double identification. The *individual* feels depreciated because the unit on which he relied, and with which he had equated himself, starts sliding; and the *crowd* feels depreciated because the *million* is. It has been shown that the word million is ambiguous, standing for both a large sum of money and a large number of people, particularly the people inhabiting a modern city; and that one meaning passes into the other and feeds on it. All the crowds which form in times of inflation—and they form very frequently—are subject to the pressure of the depreciated million. Together people are worth as little as each is worth alone. As the millions mount up, a whole people, numbered in millions, becomes nothing.

The process throws together people whose material interests normally lie far apart. The wage-earner is hit equally with the rentier. Overnight a man can lose a large part, or all, of what he thought safe in his bank. An inflation cancels out distinctions between men which had seemed eternal and brings together in the same inflation crowd people who before would scarcely have nodded to each other in the street.

No one ever forgets a sudden depreciation of himself, for it is too painful. Unless he can thrust it on to someone else, he carries it with him for the rest of his life. And the crowd as such never forgets its depreciation. The natural tendency afterwards is to find something which is worth even less than oneself, which one can despise as one was despised oneself. It is not enough to take over an old contempt and to maintain it at the same level. What is wanted is a dynamic process of humiliation. Something must be treated in such a way that it becomes worth less and less, as the unit of money did during the inflation. And this process must be continued until its object is reduced to a state of utter worthlessness. Then one can throw it away like paper, or repulp it.

The object Hitler found for this process during the German inflation was the Jews. They seemed made for it: their long-standing connection with money, their traditional understanding of its movements and fluctuations, their skill in speculation, the way they flocked together in money markets, where their behaviour contrasted strikingly with the soldierly conduct which was the German ideal—all this, in a time of doubt, instability and hostility to money, could not but make them appear dubious and hostile. The individual Jew seemed 'bad' because he was on good terms with money when others did not know how to manage it and would have preferred to have nothing more to do with it. If the inflation had led only to the depreciation of Germans as individuals, the incitement of hatred against individual Jews would have sufficed. But this was not so, for, when their millions tumbled, the Germans also felt humiliated as a crowd. Hitler saw this clearly and therefore turned his activities against the Jews as a whole.

In its treatment of the Jews National Socialism repeated the process of inflation with great precision. First they were attacked as wicked and dangerous, as enemies; then they were more and more depreciated; then, there not being enough in Germany itself, those in the conquered territories were gathered in; and finally they were treated literally as vermin, to be destroyed with impunity by the million. The world is still horrified and shaken by the fact that the Germans could go so far; that they either participated in a crime of such magnitude, or connived at it, or ignored it. It might not have been possible to get them to do so if, a few years before, they had not been through an inflation during which the Mark fell to a billionth of its former value. It was this inflation, as a crowd experience, which they shifted on to the Jews.

ELIAS CANETTI, *Crowds and Power*, 1960, tr. Carol Stewart, 1962

Auschwitz nevertheless continued to be a profit-making enterprise almost until the end. The accumulation of possessions brought in by hundreds of thousands of prisoners made it the biggest black market in Europe. No matter how much their senior executives might complain, the factories achieved an output which might have been higher with healthy employees but still could hardly lose money when paying only a pittance to the half-dead. The S.S. got the biggest rake-off. They estimated the cost of keeping one prisoner in the camp at less than one-tenth of the average rate they charged the firms. And when the remains of human beings were despatched to the gas chambers and the crematoria, soap was made of fats drained from the bodies, fertilizer from bones, and cloth and felt from human hair. . . .

At one stage I was sorting male jackets. All the pockets had to be emptied—it would never do for some innocent German civilian to find uncomfortable reminders of the previous owner—and often there were photographs among the contents. I never dared look at these. How could I, when a few yards away that very person might at this moment be burning? During another spell, sorting through ladies' underwear, I often found jewellery sewn into seams and corsets. Slit them open, and jewels and gold pieces would pour out. By the end of the session I often had a whole bucketful. Determined to hand in as little as possible, I buried some in the ground near the hut. Banknotes we never handed in: we used them as toilet paper.

. . . Bribery was the only valid currency in Auschwitz. Even our *Kapo* had to be given regular handouts to keep her sweet. Inducements like this were possible because although the *Kapo* was in charge of a squad of sorters, she herself was officially allowed no access to the material we sorted. So we filched a bit here, a bit there, and bribed her; she in turn bribed the minor S.S., who were also not allowed near all that loot. We had to be wary during such transactions. The S.S. you could bribe were rarely the true

Germans. The best targets were those uniformed but non-Reich collabora-
tors who took part in selections, did guard duty, and supervised gas-
chamber procedures because this meant extra rations of food and vodka.
Even then their rations were small, and they could easily be corrupted by
offers of extras from the wealth of that huge black market, perhaps the
biggest in occupied Europe. These toadies accepted more and more bribes
as they grew less optimistic about the Nazis' chances of winning. There was
even an instance, I discovered much later, of some Ukrainians whose
disillusion was such that after a fairly short period as Auschwitz guards they
ran off with their arms and ammunition. But they didn't get far.

KITTY HART, *Return to Auschwitz*, 1981

When I returned from Auschwitz, I found in my pocket a strange coin of
a lightweight metal alloy. . . . It is scratched and corroded, and on one face
has the Jewish star (the 'Shield of David'), the date 1943, and the word
'*getto*,' which in German is pronounced 'ghetto.' On the other face are the
inscriptions '*Quittung über 10 Mark*' and '*Der Aelteste der Juden in Litzmannstadt*,'
that is, respectively, 'Receipt against 10 marks' and 'The Elder of the Jews
in Litzmannstadt.' For many years I didn't pay any attention to it; for some
time I carried it in my change purse, perhaps inadvertently attributing to it
the value of a good luck charm, then left it in the bottom of a drawer.
Recently, information which I gathered from various sources has made it
possible for me to reconstruct, at least in part, its history, and it is unusual,
fascinating, and sinister. . . .

His name was Chaim Rumkowski, formerly co-owner of a velvet factory
in Lodz. He had gone bankrupt and made several trips to England, perhaps
to negotiate with his creditors; he had then settled in Russia, where somehow he had again become wealthy; ruined by the revolution in 1917 he had
returned to Lodz. By 1940 he was almost sixty, was twice widowed, and
had no children. He was known as the director of Jewish charitable institutions, and as an energetic, uneducated, and authoritarian man. The office
of president (or elder) of a ghetto was intrinsically dreadful, but it was an
office; it represented recognition, a step up on the social ladder, and it
conferred authority. Now Rumkowski loved authority. How he managed
to obtain the investiture is not known: perhaps thanks to a joke or hoax in
the sinister Nazi style (Rumkowski was or appeared to be a fool with a very
respectable air; in short, an ideal puppet), perhaps he himself intrigued in
order to obtain it, so strong in him must have been the will to power.

It has been proved that the four years of his presidency, or better, his dictatorship, were an amazing tangled megalomaniacal dream of barbaric vitality and real diplomatic and organizational ability. He soon came to see himself in the role of absolute but enlightened monarch, and certainly he was encouraged on this path by his German bosses, who, true enough, played with him but appreciated his talents as a good administrator and man of order. From them he obtained the authorization to mint money, both metal (that coin of mine) and paper—on watermarked paper which was officially issued to him: this was the money used to pay the enfeebled ghetto workers, and they could spend it in the commissaries to buy their food rations, which on the average amounted to 800 calories per day.

PRIMO LEVI, 'Story of a Coin', *Moments of Reprieve*, tr. Ruth Feldman, 1986

Values have shrunken to fantastic levels; taxes have risen; our ability to pay has fallen; government of all kinds is faced by serious curtailment of income; the means of exchange are frozen in the currents of trade; the withered leaves of industrial enterprise lie on every side; farmers find no markets for their produce; the savings of many years in thousands of families are gone.

More important, a host of unemployed citizens face the grim problem of existence, and an equally great number toil with little return. Only a foolish optimist can deny the dark realities of the moment.

Yet our distress comes from no failure of substance. We are stricken by no plague of locusts. Compared with the perils which our forefathers conquered because they believed and were not afraid, we have still much to be thankful for. Nature still offers her bounty and human efforts have multiplied it. Plenty is at our doorstep, but a generous use of it languishes in the very sight of the supply. Primarily this is because rulers of the exchange of mankind's goods have failed through their own stubbornness and their own incompetence, have admitted their failure, and have abdicated. Practices of the unscrupulous money changers stand indicted in the court of public opinion, rejected by the hearts and minds of men.

True they have tried, but their efforts have been cast in the pattern of an outworn tradition. Faced by failure of credit they have proposed only the lending of more money. Stripped of the lure of profit by which to induce our people to follow their false leadership, they have resorted to exhortations, pleading tearfully for restored confidence. They know only the rules of a generation of self-seekers. They have no vision, and when there is no vision the people perish.

The money changers have fled from their high seats in the temple of our civilization. We may now restore that temple to the ancient truths. The measure of the restoration lies in the extent to which we apply social values more noble than mere monetary profit.

F. D. ROOSEVELT, Inaugural Address, 4 March 1933

Therefore, when I consider and weigh in my mind all these common-wealths which now a-days any where do flourish, so GOD help me, I can perceive nothing but a certain conspiracy of rich men procuring their own commodities, under the name and title of the common-wealth! They invent and devise all means and crafts; first, how to keep safely without fear of loosing, what they have unjustly gathered together: and next, how to hire and abuse the work and labour of the poor for as little money as may be. These devices, when the rich men have decreed to be kept and observed under colour of the commonalty, that is to say, also of the poor people, then they be made laws. But these most vicious and wicked men, when they have by their unsatiable covetousness divided among themselves all those things which would have sufficed all men, yet how far be they from the wealth and felicity of the TOPIAN common-wealth? Out of the which, in that all the desire of money with the use thereof is utterly secluded and banished, how great a heap of cares is cut away? How great an occasion of wickedness and mischief is pulled up by the root? For who knoweth not that fraud, theft, ravine, brawling, quarrelling, brabbling, strife, chiding, contention, murder, treason, poisoning, which by daily punishments are rather revenged than refrained, do die when money dieth? And also that fear, grief, care, labours, and watching, do perish even the very same moment that money perisheth? Yet poverty itself, which only seemed to lack money, if money were gone, it also would decrease and vanish away. And that you may perceive this more plainly, consider with yourselves some barren and unfruitful year, wherein many thousands of people have starved for hunger—I dare be bold to say, that in the end of that penury, so much corn or grain might have been found in rich men's barns, if they had been searched, as, being divided among them whom famine and pestilence then consumed, no man at all should have felt that plague and penury! So easily men might get their living if that same worthy *Princess*, *Lady* MONEY, did not alone stop up the way between us and our living, which a God's name was very excellently devised and invented, that by her the way thereto should be opened! I am sure the rich men perceive this; nor be they ignorant how much better it were to lack no necessary thing, than to abound with overmuch superfluity: to be rid out of innumerable cares and troubles, than to be besieged and encumbered with great riches.

Sɪʀ Tʜᴏᴍᴀs Mᴏʀᴇ, Utopia, 1516, tr. Raphe Robinson, 1551

Commerce is of little use to them, but nevertheless they do know the value of money and they mint coins for their ambassadors so that they can purchase with money the provisions which they are unable to take with them, and they get merchants to come to them from all parts of the world in order to sell them their surplus wares, and they do not want money, but goods of all kinds which they do not possess. And the children laugh when they see those merchants giving so much merchandise for so little silver, but the older people do not laugh. They do not want to have slaves or foreigners corrupting the city with bad customs.

Tᴏᴍᴍᴀsᴏ Cᴀᴍᴘᴀɴᴇʟʟᴀ, The City of the Sun, 1623, tr. A. M. Elliott and R. Millner, 1981

Gradually, assaulted from beneath and from above, the Stygian mud-deluge of Laissez-faire, Supply-and-demand, Cash-payment the one Duty, will abate on all hands; and the everlasting mountain-tops, and secure rock-foundations that reach to the centre of the world, and rest on Nature's self, will again emerge, to found on, and to build on. When Mammon-worshippers here and there begin to be God-worshippers, and bipeds-of-prey become men, and there is a Soul felt once more in the huge-pulsing elephantine mechanic Animalism of this Earth, it will be again a blessed Earth.

Tʜᴏᴍᴀs Cᴀʀʟʏʟᴇ, Past and Present, 1843

Money, which has hitherto been the root, if not of *all evil*, of great injustice, oppression, and misery to the human race, making some slavish producers of wealth, and others its wasteful consumers or destroyers, will be no longer required to carry on the business of life: for as wealth of all kinds will be so delightfully created in greater abundance than will ever be required, no money price will be known, for happiness will not be purchaseable, except by a reciprocity of good actions and kind feelings.

Rᴏʙᴇʀᴛ Oᴡᴇɴ, The Book of the New Moral World, 1842–4

He resolved to make a division of their movables too, that there might be no odious distinction or inequality left amongst them; but finding that it would be very dangerous to go about it openly, he took another course, and defeated their avarice by the following stratagem: he commanded that all gold and silver coin should be called in, and that only a sort of money made of iron should be current, a great weight and quantity of which was but very little worth; so that to lay up twenty or thirty pounds there was required a pretty large closet, and, to remove it, nothing less than a yoke of oxen. With the diffusion of this money, at once a number of vices were banished from Lacedæmon; for who would rob another of such a coin? Who would unjustly detain or take by force, or accept as a bribe, a thing which it was not easy to hide, nor a credit to have, nor indeed of any use to cut in pieces? For when it was just red hot, they quenched it in vinegar, and by that means spoilt it, and made it almost incapable of being worked.

> PLUTARCH (1st century AD), 'Lycurgus', *Lives*, the translation called Dryden's, ed. A. H. Clough, 1891

JACK CADE. Be brave then; for your captain is brave, and vows reformation. There shall be, in England, seven half-penny loaves sold for a penny: the three-hooped pot shall have ten hoops; and I will make it felony, to drink small beer: all the realm shall be in common, and in Cheapside shall my palfry go to grass. And, when I am king, (as king I will be)—
ALL. God save your majesty!
JACK CADE. I thank you, good people:—there shall be no money; all shall eat and drink on my score; and I will apparel them all in one livery, that they may agree like brothers, and worship me their lord.
BUTCHER. The first thing we do, let's kill all the lawyers.

> WILLIAM SHAKESPEARE, *2 Henry VI*, *c.*1590–2

To mend the world by banishing money is an old contrivance of those who did not consider that the quarrels and mischiefs which arise from money, as the sign, or ticket, of riches, must, if money were to cease, arise immediately from riches themselves; and could never be at an end till every man was contented with his own share of the goods of life.

> SAMUEL JOHNSON, note to Shakespeare, *2 Henry VI*, IV. ii. 69, 1765

Whereas the pecuniary economy expanded the rôle of the machine, the biotechnic economy enlarges the rôle of the professional services: a greater proportion of the income and free energy go into the support of the artist, the scientist, the architect and technician, the teacher and physician, the singer, the musician, the actor. This shift has been going on steadily during the last generation: the tendency is statistically demonstrable. But its significance has not been generally grasped: for its result must be the transfer of interest from the subordinate mechanical arts to the direct arts of life. And it brings with it another possibility, indeed another necessity: the universal rebuilding of cities for the sake not merely of better conditions of living, but of a more purposive creation and utilization of the social heritage—such a life as men have occasionally had a glimpse of in Jerusalem, Athens, Florence, or Concord.

LEWIS MUMFORD, 'From a Money-Economy to a Life-Economy', 1938

In a trice we were at the landing-stage again. He jumped out and I followed him; and of course I was not surprised to see him wait, as if for the inevitable after-piece that follows the doing of a service to a fellow-citizen. So I put my hand into my waistcoat-pocket, and said, 'How much?' though still with the uncomfortable feeling that perhaps I was offering money to a gentleman.

He looked puzzled, and said, 'How much? I don't quite understand what you are asking about. Do you mean the tide? If so, it is close on the turn now.'

I blushed, and said, stammering, 'Please don't take it amiss if I ask you; I mean no offence: but what ought I to pay you? You see I am a stranger, and don't know your customs—or your coins.'

And therewith I took a handful of money out of my pocket, as one does in a foreign country. And by the way, I saw that the silver had oxydised, and was like a blackleaded stove in colour.

He still seemed puzzled, but not at all offended; and he looked at the coins with some curiosity. I thought, Well after all, he *is* a waterman, and is considering what he may venture to take. He seems such a nice fellow that I'm sure I don't grudge him a little over-payment. I wonder, by the way, whether I couldn't hire him as a guide for a day or two, since he is so intelligent.

Therewith my new friend said thoughtfully:

'I think I know what you mean. You think that I have done you a service; so you feel yourself bound to give me something which I am not to give to a neighbour, unless he has done something special for me. I have heard of this kind of thing; but pardon me for saying, that it seems to us a troublesome and roundabout custom; and we don't know how to manage it. And you see this ferrying and giving people casts about the water is my *business*, which I would do for anybody; so to take gifts in connection with it would look very queer. Besides, if one person gave me something, then another might, and another, and so on; and I hope you won't think me rude if I say that I shouldn't know where to stow away so many mementos of friendship.' And he laughed loud and merrily, as if the idea of being paid for his work was a very funny joke.

WILLIAM MORRIS, *News from Nowhere*, 1891

As soon as dinner was over, both Candide and Cacambo thought they should pay very handsomely for their entertainment by laying down two of those large gold pieces which they had picked off the ground; but the landlord and landlady burst into a fit of laughing, and held their sides for some time. When the fit was over: 'Gentlemen,' said the landlord, 'I plainly perceive you are strangers, and such we are not accustomed to see; pardon us therefore for laughing when you offered us the common pebbles of our highways for payment of your reckoning. To be sure, you have none of the coin of this kingdom; but there is no necessity for having any money at all to dine in this house. All the inns, which are established for the convenience of those who carry on the trade of this nation, are maintained by the government. You have found but very indifferent entertainment here, because this is only a poor village; but in almost every other of these public-houses you will meet with a reception worthy of persons of your merit.' Cacambo explained the whole of this speech of the landlord to Candide, who listened to it with the same astonishment with which his friend communicated it.

VOLTAIRE, *Candide*, 1759

The old-regime version of benevolent capitalism never expressed its evolutionary cheerfulness so eccentrically as in the extraordinary *Testament of M. Fortuné Ricard*. Published as a supplement to the universally popular French edition of Franklin's *Poor Richard's Almanack*, the *Testament* was written by Charles Mathon de La Cour, a Lyonnais man of letters and art critic. In the text, the fictitious M. Ricard remembers his own grandfather, who had taught him reading, arithmetic and the principles of compound interest whilst Ricard was still a lad. ' "My child," he had said drawing 24 livres from his pocket, "remember that with economy and careful calculation, nothing is impossible for a man. Invested and left untouched, at your death you will have enough to do good works for the repose of your soul and mine."'

At the age of seventy-one Ricard had accumulated 500 livres from this original sum. Though this was no great fortune, he had great plans for it. Dividing it into five sums of 100 livres each, he proposed leaving the first for one hundred years, the second for two hundred and so on. Each would thus generate sums from which a progressively ambitious program could be funded. The first sum, after a century, would yield a mere 13,100 livres, from which a prize would be awarded for the best theological essay proving the compatibility of commerce and religion. A hundred years later the second sum (1.7 million) would expand this prize program into eighty annual awards for the best work in science, mathematics, literature, agriculture ('proven through the best harvests') and a special category for 'virtuous deeds.' The third sum (three hundred years on) would amount to more than 226 million, enough to establish throughout France five hundred 'patriotic funds' for the relief of poverty and for investment in industry and agriculture, administered by 'the most honest and zealous citizens.' A remaining sum would endow twelve *musées* in Paris and the major towns of France, each to house forty superior intellectuals in all fields. Lodged in comfort but not opulence, they would have a concert hall, theater, laboratories of chemistry and physics, natural history shops, libraries and experimental parks and menageries. The libraries and art collections would be open every day free to the public and members of the *musées* would give public lectures in their respective fields. Members would be admitted 'only after having submitted proof, not of nobility, but of morals' and would take an oath 'to prefer virtue, truth, and justice over everything.'

This is heady stuff but it is nothing compared with what was to follow in the fourth and fifth centuries of the Ricard will. The fourth sum (30 billion livres) would suffice, he thought, to build 'in the most pleasant sites one could find in France' a hundred new towns each of forty thousand people, planned on ideal lines of beauty, salubriousness and community. With the final sum (3.9 trillion livres) it would be possible to solve pretty much all that remained of the world's problems. Six billion would be enough to pay off the French national debt (even at the rate the Bourbons were spending); 12 billion as a gesture of magnanimity and the opening of *entente cordiale* would do the same for the British. The remainder would go into a general fund to be distributed among all the powers of the world *on condition they never went to war with each other.*

SIMON SCHAMA, *Citizens*, 1989

## INVEST IN DADA!

dada is the only savings bank that pays interest in eternity. The Chinese has his tao and the Indian his brahma. dada is more than tao and brahma. dada doubles their income. dada is the secret black market and protects against inflation and malnutrition. dada is the war bond of eternal life; dada is comfort in dying. dada should be in every citizen's testament. Why should I unveil dada? dada works in the cerebellum and in the cerebrum of apes as well as in the hindquarters of statesmen. Whoever puts his money in the dada savings bank need not fear confiscation, for whoever touches dada is dada-tabu.

Every hundred-mark bill multiplies according to the law of cellular division. 1327-fold a minute. dada is the only salvation from the slavery of the entente. Every dada savings-bank check is valid all over the world. When you are dead, dada will be your only nourishment; even the ancient Egyptians fed their dead with dada.

RICHARD HÜLSENBECK and others, *Der Dada*, 1919, tr. Gabrielle Bennett, 1971

They leave the hospitable mansion, and we next see them passing down State Street. The clock on the old State House points to high noon, when the Exchange should be in its glory and present the liveliest emblem of what was the sole business of life, as regarded a multitude of the foregone worldlings. It is over now. The Sabbath of eternity has shed its stillness along the street. Not even a newsboy assails the two solitary passers-by with an extra penny-paper from the office of the 'Times' or 'Mail,' containing a full account of yesterday's terrible catastrophe. Of all the dull times that merchants and speculators have known, this is the very worst; for, so far as they were concerned, creation itself has taken the benefit of the Bankrupt Act. After all, it is a pity. Those mighty capitalists who had just attained the wished-for wealth! Those shrewd men of traffic who had devoted so many years to the most intricate and artificial of sciences, and had barely mastered it when the universal bankruptcy was announced by peal of trumpet! Can they have been so incautious as to provide no currency of the country whither they have gone, nor any bills of exchange, or letters of credit from the needy on earth to the cash-keepers of heaven?

Adam and Eve enter a Bank. Start not, ye whose funds are treasured there! you will never need them now. Call not for the police. The stones of the street and the coin of the vaults are of equal value to this simple pair. Strange sight! They take up the bright gold in handfuls and throw it sportively into the air for the sake of seeing the glittering worthlessness descend again in a shower. They know not that each of those small yellow circles was once a magic spell, potent to sway men's hearts and mystify their moral sense. Here let them pause in the investigation of the past. They have discovered the mainspring, the life, the very essence of the system that had wrought itself into the vitals of mankind, and choked their original nature in its deadly gripe. Yet how powerless over these young inheritors of earth's hoarded wealth! And here, too, are huge packages of bank-notes, those talismanic slips of paper which once had the efficacy to build up enchanted palaces like exhalations, and work all kinds of perilous wonders, yet were themselves but the ghosts of money, the shadows of a shade. How like is this vault to a magician's cave when the all-powerful wand is broken, and the visionary splendour vanished, and the floor strewn with fragments of shattered spells, and lifeless shapes, once animated by demons!

'Everywhere, my dear Eve,' observes Adam, 'we find heaps of rubbish of one kind or another. Somebody, I am convinced, has taken pains to collect them, but for what purpose? Perhaps, hereafter, we shall be moved to do the like. Can that be our business in the world?'

'O no, no, Adam!' answers Eve. 'It would be better to sit down quietly and look upward to the sky.'

They leave the Bank, and in good time; for had they tarried later they would probably have encountered some gouty old goblin of a capitalist, whose soul could not long be anywhere save in the vault with his treasure.

NATHANIEL HAWTHORNE, 'The New Adam and Eve', *Mosses from an Old Manse*, 1846

In the Land of the Dead quantitative coinage is worthless, and anyone proffering such tender would reveal himself as totally unchic. But at the bottom of the stairway, which leads to a stone promenade by a river, I spot a coin about the size of a silver dollar. The coin is of silver or some bright metal. Two shoulder blades in bas-relief almost meet in the middle of the coin, just as the shoulder blades of a Russian Blue cat almost meet if the cat is a star. This is a Cat Coin, more specifically a Russian Blue Coin, for in the Land of the Dead coinage is qualitative, reflecting the qualities the pilgrim has displayed during his lifetime. A Cat Coin will only be found by a cat lover.

There are Kindness Coins: the bearer has helped someone without consideration of payment, like the hotel clerk who warned me the fuzz is on the way, or the cop who laid a joint on me to smoke in the wagon. There are Child Coins. I remember a dream child with eyes on stalks like a snail, who said, 'Don't you want me?'—'*Yes!*'

There are Tear Coins, Courage Coins, Johnson Coins, Integrity Coins.

Are there things you would not do for any amount of money? For any consideration? For a young body? The Integrity Coin attests to the bearer's inaccessibility to any quantitative bribe. The coin certifies that the bearer has definitely refused the Devil's Bargain.

WILLIAM S. BURROUGHS, *The Western Lands*, 1987

'You were surprised,' he said, 'at my saying that we got along without money or trade, but a moment's reflection will show that trade existed and money was needed in your day simply because the business of production was left in private hands, and that, consequently, they are superfluous now.'

'I do not at once see how that follows,' I replied.

'It is very simple,' said Dr Leete. 'When innumerable, unrelated, and independent persons produced the various things needful to life and comfort, endless exchanges between individuals were requisite in order that they might supply themselves with what they desired. These exchanges constituted trade, and money was essential as their medium. But as soon as the nation became the sole producer of all sorts of commodities, there was no need of exchanges between individuals that they might get what they required. Everything was procurable from one source, and nothing could be procured anywhere else. A system of direct distribution from the national storehouses took the place of trade, and for this money was unnecessary.'

'How is this distribution managed?' I asked.

'On the simplest possible plan,' replied Dr Leete. 'A credit corresponding to his share of the annual product of the nation is given to every citizen on the public books at the beginning of each year, and a credit card issued him with which he procures at the public storehouses, found in every community, whatever he desires whenever he desires it. This arrangement, you will see, totally obviates the necessity for business transactions of any sort between individuals and consumers. Perhaps you would like to see what our credit cards are like?

'You observe,' he pursued, as I was curiously examining the piece of pasteboard he gave me, 'that this card is issued for a certain number of dollars. We have kept the old word but not the substance. The term, as we use it, answers to no real thing, but merely serves as an algebraical symbol for comparing the values of products with one another. For this purpose they are all priced in dollars and cents, just as in your day. The value of what I procure on this card is checked off by the clerk, who pricks out of these tiers of squares the price of what I order.'

'If you wanted to buy something of your neighbour could you transfer part of your credit to him as consideration?' I inquired.

'In the first place,' replied Dr Leete, 'our neighbours have nothing to sell us, but in any event our credit would not be transferable, being strictly personal. Before the nation could even think of honouring any such transfer as you speak of, it would be bound to inquire into all the circumstances of the transaction, so as to be able to guarantee its absolute equity. It would have been reason enough, had there been no other, for abolishing money, that its possession was no indication of rightful title to it. In the hands of the man who had stolen it, or murdered for it, it was as good as in those which had earned it by industry. People nowadays interchange gifts and favours out of friendship, but buying and selling is considered absolutely inconsistent with the mutual benevolence and disinterestedness which should prevail between citizens and the sense of community of interests which supports our social system. According to our ideas, buying and selling is essentially anti-social in all its tendencies. It is an education in self-seeking at the expense of others, and no society whose citizens are trained in such a school can possibly rise above a very low grade of civilization.'

'What if you have to spend more than your card in any one year?' I asked.

'The provision is so ample that we are more likely not to spend it all,' replied Dr Leete. 'But if extraordinary expenses should exhaust it, we can obtain a limited advance on the next year's credit, though this practice is not encouraged, and a heavy discount is charged to check it.'

'If you don't spend your allowance, I suppose it accumulates?'

'That is also permitted to a certain extent, when a special outlay is anticipated. But unless notice to the contrary is given, it is presumed that the citizen who does not fully expend his credit did not have occasion to do so, and the balance is turned into the general surplus.'

'Such a system does not encourage saving habits on the part of citizens,' I said.

'It is not intended to,' was the reply. 'The nation is rich, and does not wish the people to deprive themselves of any good thing. In your day, men were bound to lay up goods and money against coming failure of the means of support and for their children. This necessity made parsimony a virtue. But now it would have no such laudable object, and, having lost its utility, it has ceased to be regarded as a virtue. No man any more has any care for the morrow, either for himself or his children, for the nation guarantees the nurture, education, and comfortable maintenance of every citizen, from the cradle to the grave.'

EDWARD BELLAMY, *Looking Backward*, 1888

When the accumulation of wealth is no longer of high social importance, there will be great changes in the code of morals. We shall be able to rid ourselves of many of the pseudo-moral principles which have hag-ridden us for two hundred years, by which we have exalted some of the most distasteful of human qualities into the position of the highest virtues. We shall be able to afford to dare to assess the money-motive at its true value. The love of money as a possession—as distinguished from the love of money as a means to the enjoyments and realities of life—will be recognised for what it is, a somewhat disgusting morbidity, one of those semi-criminal, semi-pathological propensities which one hands over with a shudder to the specialists in mental disease.

J. M. KEYNES, 'Economic Possibilities for our Grandchildren', 1930

There I stood in a dreamy mood, and rubbed my eyes as if I were not wholly awake, and half expected to see the gay-clad company of beautiful men and women change to two or three spindle-legged back-bowed men and haggard, hollow-eyed, ill-favoured women, who once wore down the soil of this land with their heavy hopeless feet, from day to day, and season to season, and year to year. But no change came as yet, and my heart swelled with joy as I thought of all the beautiful grey villages, from the river to the plain and the plain to the uplands, which I could picture to myself so well, all peopled now with this happy and lovely folk, who had cast away riches and attained to wealth.

WILLIAM MORRIS, *News from Nowhere*, 1891

# ACKNOWLEDGEMENTS

The editor and publishers are grateful for permission to include the following copyright material:

Gilbert Adair, extract from 'The Last Detail' first published in *The Independent*, 21 Aug. 1992. Reprinted with permission.

Theodor Adorno, from *Minima Moralia* (Verso, 1974).

James Agee, 'Money' from *Let us Now Praise Famous Men* (Peter Owen, 1965). Reprinted by permission.

Brian Aldiss and David Wingrove, from *Trillion Year Spree* (Gollancz, 1986). Reprinted by permission of Victor Gollancz Ltd.

Nelson W. Aldrich Jr., from *Old Money* (Random House Inc., 1989).

Woody Allen, from *Without Feathers*, © Woody Allen 1976.

Martin Amis, from *Money, a Suicide Note*. Reprinted by permission of Random House UK Ltd., and the Peters Fraser & Dunlop Group Ltd.

Ivo Andrić, from *The Days of the Consuls*, trans. © Celia Hawkesworth 1992 (Forest Books, 1992).

Sir Norman Angell, from *The Story of Money* (Cassell, 1930).

W. H. Auden, from *The Dyer's Hand*. Reprinted by permission of Faber & Faber Ltd. and Random House Inc.

Paul Auster, extracts from *Moon Palace* (Viking, 1989).

James Baldwin, 'The Black Boy Looks at the White Boy', originally published in *Esquire*, from *Nobody Knows my Name*, © 1960 James Baldwin. Copyright renewed. Reprinted by permission of Michael Joseph Ltd. and the Estate of James Baldwin. Published in the US by Vintage-Books.

Roland Barthes, from *Roland Barthes par Roland Barthes*, trans. Richard Howard (Macmillan, 1977).

Charles Baudelaire, extracts from *Intimate Journals*, trans. Christopher Isherwood © the Estate of Christopher Isherwood.

Samuel Beckett, from *Murphy* (1938).

Max Beerbohm, extracts. Reprinted by permission of Mrs Eva Reichmann.

Hilaire Belloc, extracts from *Complete Verse* (Pimlico), and *The Aftermath* (Duckworth, 1920). Reprinted by permission of the Peters Fraser & Dunlop Group Ltd.; and from 'A Few Kind Words to Mammon' in *On* (Methuen, 1923).

Saul Bellow, from *Humboldt's Gift*. Reprinted by permission of Secker & Warburg Ltd.

Walter Benjamin, from *One-Way Street* (Verso, 1979).

Bruno Bettelheim, from *The Informed Heart* (Thames & Hudson, 1960). Reprinted by permission.

Morris Bishop, 'I Hear America Singing, Credit Lines' from *A Nest of Bishop* (Dial Press Inc.).

Kyril Bonfiglioli, from *After You with the Pistol* (Secker & Warburg, 1979), © Kyril Bonfiglioli, 1979.

John Boorman, from *Money into Light* (Faber & Faber, 1985). Reprinted by permission of Faber & Faber Ltd.

Jorge Luis Borges, 'The Zahir', trans. Dudley Fitts, in *Partisan Review*, Feb. 1950, reprinted in *Labyrinths, Selected Stories and Other Writings*, © 1962 by New Directions.

Malcolm Bradbury, from *Rates of Exchange*. Reprinted by permission of Secker & Warburg Ltd., and Alfred A. Knopf, Inc.

Fernard Braudel, from *Capitalism and Material Life 1400–1800*, trans. Miriam Kochan (Weidenfeld & Nicolson, 1973).

Hugh Brody, from *Inishkillane* (Faber & Faber, 1973). Reprinted by permission of Faber & Faber Ltd., and Sheil Land Associates Ltd.

John Brooks, from *Once in Golconda, a True Drama of War Street 1920–1938* (Gollancz, 1970). Reprinted by permission of Aicken, Stone & Wylie.

Norman O. Brown, from 'Filthy Lucre' in *Life Against Death* (1959).

Anthony Burgess, extracts from *You've Had Your Time*. Reprinted by permission of William Heinemann Ltd. and the estate of Anthony Burgess c/o Atellus Ltd.

William S. Burroughs, from *The Western Lands* (Penguin, 1987).

Albert Camus, from *Carnets 1935–1942*, trans. Philip Thody (Hamish Hamilton, 1963), © Librairie Gallimard, 1962, trans. © Hamish Hamilton Ltd., and Alfred A. Knopf, Inc., 1963. Reproduced with permission.

Elias Canetti, extracts from *Crowds and Power*, trans. Carol Stewart (Gollancz, 1962). Reprinted by permission of Victor Gollancz Ltd. and Seabury Press.

Raymond Carver, 'Money' from *In a Marine Light: Selected Poems* (1987). Reprinted by permission of HarperCollins Publishers, and Rogers Coleridge & White Ltd.

Chamfort, from *Products of the Perfected Civilization*, trans. W. S. Merwin (North Point Press, 1984), © 1968, 1969 by W. S. Merwin. Used by permission of Georges Borchardt, Inc.

Raymond Chandler, from *Selected Letters*. Reprinted by permission of A. M. Heath.

Bruce Chatwin, from *The Songlines* and *The Viceroy of Ouidah*. Reprinted by permission of Random House UK Ltd., USA Rogers, Coleridge & White Ltd.

G. K. Chesterton, 'The Paradise of Thieves' from *The Wisdom of Father Brown*. Reprinted by permission of A. P. Watt Ltd. on behalf of the Royal Literary Fund.

Caryl Churchill, from *Serious Money* (Methuen, 1987). Reprinted by permission of the publisher.

Alexander Cockburn, from *Corruptions of Empire* (Verso/New left Books, 1987). Reprinted with permission.

G. D. H. Cole, from *Principles of Economic Planning* (1935) © the Estate of G. D. H. Cole.

Jim Crace, from *Arcadia* (Jonathan Cape, 1992). Reprinted by permission.

Guy Davenport, 'Making it Uglier to the Airport' from *Every Force Evolves a Form* (North Point Press, 1987). Reprinted by permission of the author.

Dick Davis, 'Byzantine Coin' from *In the Distance* (Anvil Press Poetry, 1975). Used with permission.

Mary Douglas, from *Purity and Danger* (Routledge, 1966). Reprinted by permission.

Umberto Eco, from *Misreadings* (Arnoldo Mondadori and Random House UK Ltd.).

William Empson, from *Milton's God* (Chatto & Windus, 1965). Reprinted by permission of Random House UK Ltd. and published in the US by New Directions.

Hans Magnus Enzensberger, from *Selected Poems* (Penguin, 1968).

Sandor Ferenczi, 'The Ontogenesis of the Interest in Money' from *First Contributions to Psycho-Analysis*, trans. Ernest Jones (Hogarth Press, 1952). Reprinted by permission of Random House UK Ltd.

F. Scott Fitzgerald, extracts from *The Great Gatsby* (New Directions, 1925); and *The Crack Up*, ed. Edmund Wilson (New Directions, 1945).

Gustave Flaubert, 'Dictionary of Received Ideas' from *Bouvard and Pecuchet*, trans. A. J. Krailsheimer (Penguin, 1976).

Henry Ford, from *My Life and Work*, © the Estate of Henry Ford.

E. M. Forster, extract from *Howard's End*. Reprinted by permission of King's College, Cambridge and The Society of Authors as literary representatives of the E. M. Forster Estate.

Erich Fromm, from *The Fear of Freedom*. Reprinted by permission of Routledge and Curtis Brown Ltd.

Robert Frost, 'The Hardship of Accounting' ('Money'), first published in *Poetry*, Apr. 1936; and 'Provide, Provide' from *A Further Range* (1936), © The Estate of Robert Frost.

J. K. Galbraith, from *The Affluent Society* (Houghton Mifflin, 1958).

M. K. Gandhi, from *Non-Violence in Peace and War*, vol. ii (Navajivan Publishing House, 1949).

John Paul Getty, from *How to be Rich* (W. H. Allen, 1966).

André Gide, from *Les Faux-monnayeurs*, trans. (as *The Coiners*) Dorothy Bussy (Cassell, 1950).

Françoise Gilot and Carlton Lake, from *Life with Picasso* (Virago, 1990). Reprinted by permission.

Allen Ginsberg, from *Collected Poems 1947–1980* (Viking, 1985), © Allen Ginsberg, 1963. Reprinted by permission of Penguin Books Ltd.

Dana Gioia, 'Money' from *The Lions of Winter* (Peterloo Poets, 1991), © Dana Gioia 1991.

Jean-Luc Godard, in Colin MacCabe, *Godard: Images, Sounds, Politics*. Reprinted by permission of British Film Institute Publishing.

Harry Graham, 'The Millionaire' from *The World's Workers* (Methuen, 1928).

Albert Hackett, Frances Goodrich and Frank Capra, from *It's a Wonderful Life* (Pavillion Books).

Tony Harrison, from *Palladas: Poems* (Penguin, 1984).

Kitty Hart, from *Return to Auschwitz*, © Kitty Hart, 1981.

G. W. F. Hegel, from *Philosophy of Right*, trans T. M. Knox (Oxford University Press, 1952).

Joseph Heller, from *Catch-22*. Reprinted by permission of A. M. Heath on behalf of the author and Jonathan Cape Ltd.

Ernest Hemingway, first published in *Scribner's Magazine*, vol. 93, Mar. 1933, re-printed in *Winner Take Nothing* (Cape, 1934), © the Estate of Ernest Hemingway.

Geoffrey Hill, from *Mercian Hymns*, xi, reprinted in *Collected Poems* (Andre Deutsch, 1986).

Richard Hughes, from *The Fox in the Attic* (Chatto, 1962). Reprinted by permission of David Higham Associates Ltd.

Robert Hughes, extracts from *Nothing If Not Critical* (Collins, 1990). Reprinted by permission of Harnill, an imprint of HarperCollins Publ. Ltd., and Jacklow & Nesbit.

Julian Huxley, from *Essays of a Biologist*. Reprinted by permission of the Peters Fraser & Dunlop Group Ltd.

Lewis Hyde, from *The Gift: Imagination and the Erotic Life of Property* (Random House Inc., 1979).

Randall Jarrell, 'Money' from *Selected Poems*. Reprinted by permission of Faber & Faber Ltd. and Farrar, Straus and Giroux.

B. S. Johnson, from *Christie Malry's Own Double-Entry* (Collins, 1973). Reprinted permission of HarperCollins Publ. Ltd., and Max Bakewell Associates.

LeRoi Jones, 'Expressive Language' from *Home: Social Essays* (1963).

James Joyce, from *Ulysses*, © the Estate of James Joyce, reprinted by permission of Random House Inc.; from *A Portrait of the Artist as a Young Man*, copyright 1916 by B. W. Huebsch, copyright 1944 by Nora Joyce, © 1964 by the Estate of James Joyce. 'Grace' from *Dubliners*, copyright 1916 by B. W. Huebsch. Definitive text © 1967 by the Estate of James Joyce. Used by permission of Viking Penguin, a division of Penguin Books USA Inc.

George S. Kaufman, and Moss Hart, from *You Can't Take it with You* (Methuen, 1981).

John Maynard Keynes, extracts from 'Economic Possibilities for our Grand-children', first published in *Essays in Persuasion* (1931), and extract from 'Auri Sacra Fames', first published in *A Treatise on Money* (1930), reprinted in *Collected Writings of J. M. Keynes* (Macmillan: London, 1971–89), Vols. V–VI and IX. Re-printed by permission of the publisher.

Ibn Khaldun, from *The Muqaddimah*, trans. Rosenthal (Random House Inc.)

Eric Korn, from *Remainders*. Reprinted by permission of Carcanet Press Ltd.

Lewis H. Lapham, extracts from *Money and Class in America* (Random House Inc., 1988).

Philip Larkin, 'Homage to a Government' and 'Money' from *High Windows* (1974), © 1974 by Philip Larkin. Reprinted by permission of Faber & Faber Ltd., and Farrar, Straus & Giroux, Inc.

D. H. Lawrence, 'Strike-Pay', from *Complete Short Stories of D. H. Lawrence*, copyright 1922 by Thomas Seltzer, Inc., renewal copyright 1950 by Frieda Lawrence. 'Money Madness' from *The Complete Poems of D. H. Lawrence*, ed. V. de Sola Pinto & F. W. Roberts, © 1964, 1971 by Angelo Ravagli and C. M. Weekley, Executors of the Estate of Frieda Lawrence Ravagli. Used by permission of Viking Penguin, a division of Penguin Books USA Inc.

Primo Levi, 'Story of a Coin' from *Moments of Reprieve*, trans. Ruth Feldman (Simon & Schuster Inc.).

Michael Lewis, from *Liar's Poker: Rising through the Wreckage on Wall Street*, © Michael Lewis 1989. Reprinted by permission of Hodder & Stoughton Ltd. and W. W. Norton & Company, Inc.

David Lodge, from *Nice Work*, © David Lodge 1988.

Anita Loos, from *Gentlemen Prefer Blondes* © 1925 by Anita Loos. © 1925 by the International Magazine Co., Inc. Copyright renewed 1953 by Anita Loos Emerson. © 1963 by Anita Loos © renewed 1991 by Jay S. Harris. Reprinted by permission of Liveright Publishing Corporation.

Robert Lynd, from *The Pleasure of Ignorance* (Methuen, 1930).

Georg Christoph Lichtenberg, from *Aphorisms*, trans. R. J. Hollingdale (Penguin, 1990), © R. J. Hollingdale.

Mary McCarthy, from *The Group* (Weidenfeld & Nicolson, 1954).

Hugh MacDiarmid, 'Another Epitaph on an Army of Mercenaries' and 'On The Money Monopolist being like Hell' from *Second Hymn to Lenin and other poems* (Oliver & Boyd, 1962).

Alan MacFarlane, from *The Culture of Capitalism*. Reprinted by permission of Blackwell Publishers.

William McGuire, from *Bollingen: An Adventure in Collecting the Past*. Published by Princeton University Press.

Malcolm McLeod, 'Paolozzi and Identity' in Eduardo Paolozzi, *Lost Magic Kingdoms* (British Museum Publications, 1985).

Marshall McLuhan, from *Understanding Media*. Reprinted by permission of Routledge and McGraw Hill Inc.

Louis MacNeice, 'Charon' from *Collected Poems*. Reprinted by permission of Faber & Faber Ltd.

Geoffrey Madan, from *Notebooks*, ed. J. A. Gere and John Sparrow (Oxford University Press, 1981).

Rene Magritte, from *Anecdotes of Modern Art* (Oxford University Press).

Somerset Maugham, from *Of Human Bondage*. Reprinted by permission of William Heinemann Ltd. and A. P. Watt Ltd., on behalf of the Royal Literary Fund.

Marcel Mauss, from *The Gift*, trans. Ian Cunnison. Reprinted by permission of Routledge.

Lewis Mumford, 'From a Money-economy to a Life-economy' from *Culture of Cities* (1938).

Les Murray, 'Letters to the Winner' from *The Daylight Moon*, © Les Murray, 1987. Reprinted by permission of Carcanet Press Ltd., and Farrar, Straus & Giroux Inc.

Ogden Nash, from *The Face is Familiar* (Dent & Son, 1954). 'The Terrible People' from *Verses from 1929 On*, © 1933 by Ogden Nash, renewed. Reprinted by permission of Curtis Brown Ltd.

Howard Nemerov, 'Money' from *The Blue Swallows*.

Flann O'Brien (Myles na Gopaleen/Brian O'Nolan), from *The Best of Myles* (MacGibbon & Kee, 1968). Reprinted by permission of A. M. Heath on behalf of the Estate of the late Flann O'Brien, and of McGibbon & Kee, an imprint of HarperCollins Publishers Ltd.

Juan Carlos Onetti, 'Presence' from *Index on Censorship*, reprinted in *The Faber Book of Contemporary Latin American Short Stories* (1989).

P. J. O'Rourke, 'Moving to New Hampshire' from *Republican Party Reptile* (Atlantic Monthly Press, 1987).

George Orwell, from *Keep the Aspidistra Flying*. Reprinted by permission of the Estate of the late Sonia Brownell Orwell and Martin Secker and Warburg, and Harcourt Brace Jovanovich, Inc.

Palinurus (Cyril Connolly), from *The Unquiet Grave* (Penguin, 1967). By permission of Rogers, Coleridge & White Ltd.

Dorothy Parker, from *Writers at Work: The Paris Review Interviews, First Series*. Reprinted by permission of Secker & Warburg. US rights: Penguin USA.

C. Northcote Parkinson, from *Parkinson's Law*. Reprinted by permission of John Murray (Publishers) Ltd.

John Dos Passos, from *The Big Money* (Constable, 1936). Used with permission.

Octavio Paz, from *The Labyrinth of Solitude: Life and Thought in Mexico*, trans. Sander Kemp (Viking, 1967), © Grove Press Inc. 1961. Reprinted with permission.

Max Plowman, 'Money and the Merchant' from *The Adelphi* (Penguin, 1931).

Ezra Pound, from *The Cantos*. Reprinted by permission of Faber & Faber Ltd., and New Directions Publ. Corp.

J. B. Priestley, from *Delight*. Reprinted by permission of William Heinemann Ltd. and the Peters Fraser & Dunlop Group Ltd.

Propertius, from *Elegies*, trans. Seymour G. Tremenheere (Simpkin & Marshall, 1931).

Marcel Proust, 'To Leon Neuburger' from *Selected Letters*, vol. 2, 1904–1909, trans. Terence Kilmartin (Collins, 1989). Reprinted by permission of HarperCollins Publishers Ltd.

Kathleen Raine, 'Worry about Money' from *The Pythoness and Other Poems*. Reprinted by permission of Allen & Unwin Ltd., a Division of HarperCollins Publishers.

Peter Robinson, 'Plain Money' from *This Other Life* (1988). Reprinted by permission of Carcanet Press Ltd.

F. D. Roosevelt, from *Inaugural Address March 4 1933* (Random House Inc., 1938), © F. D. Roosevelt.

Damon Runyon, 'A Very Honourable Guy' from *Furthermore* (1938), © the Estate of Damon Runyon.

Carl Sandburg, from *The People, Yes*, copyright Carl Sandburg, 1936. Reprinted by permission of Harcourt Brace Jovanovich, Inc.

Simon Schama, from *Citizens* (Penguin, 1989).

Roger Scruton, from *Untimely Tracts* (Macmillan, 1987).

Mabel Segun, 'Bride Price', reprinted in *Voices from Twentieth-Century Africa* (Faber & Faber, 1988).

Will Self, from *My Idea of Fun* (Bloomsbury, 1993). Reprinted by permission of Bloomsbury plc.

W. C. Sellar and R. J. Yeatman, from *1066 and All That* (Methuen). Reprinted by permission of the publisher.

Hjalmar Schact, from *The Magic of Money*, trans. Paul Erskine (Oldbourne, 1967), © Paul Erskine 1967.

George Bernard Shaw, extracts from Preface to *Major Barbara*, *Pygmalion* and Preface to *The Irrational Knot*. Reprinted by permission of the Society of Authors on behalf of the Bernard Shaw Estate.

Georg Simmel, from *The Philosophy of Money*, trans. Tom Bottomore and David Frisby (Routledge, 1992).

Mark Singer, from *Funny Money* (Picador, 1985) © Mark Singer 1985.

C. H. Sisson, 'Money' from *The London Zoo*, reprinted in *Collected Poems*. Used by permission of Carcanet Press Ltd.

Barbara Skelton, from *Tears before Bedtime* (Hamish Hamilton, 1987), © Barbara Skelton, 1987. Reproduced by permission of Hamish Hamilton Ltd. and Aitken, Stone & Wylie Ltd.

Adam Smith, from *Paper Money* (Macdonald & Co., 1981), © Adam Smith 1981.

Logan Pearsall Smith, from *Trivia* (Constable, 1918). Used with permission.

Bernard Spencer, 'Behaviour of Money' from *Collected Poems* (Oxford University Press, 1981).

Gertrude Stein, first published in *Saturday Evening Post*, 22 Aug. 1936; this text from *How Writing is Written*, ed. R. B. Hass (Black Sparrow Press, 1974). Used with permission.

Adrian Stokes, 'Weathering' from *With all the Views: Collected Poems*. Reprinted by permission of Carcanet Press Ltd.

R. H. Tawney, from *Religion and the Rise of Capitalism*. Reprinted by permission of John Murray (Publishers) Ltd.

George Thomson, from *Island Home* (Brandon Books, Dingle, 1987).

Charles Tomlinson, 'The Rich' from *The Way In* (Oxford University Press, 1974).

John Kennedy Toole, from *A Confederacy of Dunces* (Allen Lane, 1981), © Thelma D. Toole, 1980. Reprinted by permission.

Lionel Trilling, 'Art and Fortune' from *The Liberal Imagination*. Reprinted by permission of Secker & Warburg Ltd., and Charles Scribner's Sons.

Amos Tutuola, from *Ajaiyi and His Inherited Poverty* (Faber & Faber, 1967), © 1967 Amos Tutuola. Reprinted by permission of the author and Faber & Faber Ltd.

John Updike, from *Rabbit is Rich* (Andre Deutsch & Random House Inc.).

Paul Valéry, from *Bad Thoughts and Not so Bad*, trans. Stuart Gilbert (Routledge, 1970).

Dai Vaughan, from *Portrait of an Invisible Man*. Reprinted by permission of the British Film Institute Publishing.

Kurt Vonnegut, from *God Bless You, Mr Rosewater*. Reprinted by permission of Random House UK Ltd., USA: Bantam Doubleday Dell.

Andy Warhol, extracts from *From A to B and Back Again* (Cassell, 1975), © Andy Warhol, 1975.

Max Weber, from *The Protestant Ethic and the Spirit of Capitalism*. Reprinted by permission of ITPS Ltd.

H. G. Wells, from *The Outline of History*, reprinted by permission of A. P. Watt Ltd. on behalf of the Executors of the Estate of H. G. Wells; and from *Kipps*, reprinted by permission of A. P. Watt Ltd. and the Literary Executors of the Estate of H. G. Wells.

Robert Wells, 'A Coin' from *Selected Poems* (1986). Reprinted by permission of Carcanet Press Ltd.

Lawrence Weschler, 'Money Changes Everything' in *New Yorker*, 18 Jan. 1993, © Lawrence Weschler 1993.

Edmund Wilson, from *The Cold War and the Income Tax: A Protest* (1964). By permission of Farrar, Straus & Giroux Inc.; from *Europe Without-Baedeker*, reprinted by permission of Secker & Warburg Ltd.

P. G. Wodehouse, from *Big Money*. Reprinted by permission of A. P. Watt Ltd. on behalf of the Trustees of the Wodehouse Estate and Random House UK Ltd.

E. B. White, from *Quo Vadimus? or The Case for the Bicycle*. Copyright 1933 by E. B. White, © renewed 1960 by E. B. White. Used by permission of HarperCollins Publishers Inc.

Tom Wolfe, from *Mauve Gloves and Madmen, Clutter and Vine*, © 1967, 1968, 1969, 1973, 1974, 1975, 1976 by Tom Wolfe, reprinted by permission of Farrar, Straus and Giroux; and *The Bonfire of the Vanities*, reprinted by permission of Random House UK Ltd. and Farrar, Straus and Giroux.

Virginia Woolf, from *Three Guineas* and *A Room of One's Own*. Reprinted by permission of Harcourt Brace Jovanovich, Inc.

Benjamin Zephaniah, from *City Psalms* (1992). Reprinted by permission of Bloodaxe Books Ltd.

Any errors or omissions in the above list are entirely unintentional. If notified the publisher will be pleased to make any necessary corrections at the earliest opportunity.

# INDEX OF AUTHORS